THE LIFE OF THE SOUL

THE LIFE *of* THE SOUL

Jewish Perspectives on Reincarnation from the Middle Ages to the Modern Period

EDITED BY ANDREA GONDOS
AND LEORE SACHS-SHMUELI

SUNY
PRESS

Cover art: painting by William Blake (circa 1800)
entitled *The Witch of Endor* (from Wikipedia).

Published by State University of New York Press, Albany

Printed in the United States of America

For information, contact State University of New York Press, Albany, NY
www.sunypress.edu

Library of Congress Cataloging-in-Publication Data

Names: Gondos, Andrea, editor. | Sachs-Shmueli, Leore, editor.
Title: The life of the soul : Jewish perspectives on reincarnation from the middle ages to the modern period / edited by Andrea Gondos and Leore Sachs-Shmueli.
Description: Albany, NY : State University of New York Press, [2024] | Includes bibliographical references and index. | Summary: "Offers a comprehensive and nuanced treatment on the topic of reincarnation in Judaism, covering a wide range of kabbalistic and philosophical sources"—Provided by publisher.
Identifiers: LCCN 2024012432 | ISBN 9798855800050 (hardcover) | ISBN 9798855800074 (ebook)
Subjects: LCSH: Future life—Judaism. | Eschatology, Jewish. | Immortality—Judaism. | Transmigration—Judaism.
Classification: LCC BM635 .L53 2024 | DDC 296.3/3—dc23/eng/20240805
LC record available at https://lccn.loc.gov/2024012432

To Csaba –
may we always merit to fly side-by-side

In memory of my cousin Árpád Matusovits z"l (1971–2020)
May your soul soar through the firmament of the heavens
to find yourself a Palace of Light

To my mother, Batya Sachs
Who taught me to believe in the hidden

CONTENTS

Acknowledgments xi

Introduction 1
Andrea Gondos and Leore Sachs-Shmueli

SECTION I. MEDIEVAL APPROACHES TO REINCARNATION

1. The Secrets of Soul Impregnation (*Ibbur*) in Early Kabbalah and the Doctrine of Reincarnation 27
Moshe Idel

2. The Effaced Eagle-Man and Other Problems: Reincarnated Embodiment in *Guf ha-Zohar* 49
Ellen D. Haskell

3. The Emergence of the Concept *Gilgul*: The *Sefer ha-Bahir* and the *Ba'al ha-Tikkunim* 73
Pinchas Giller

4. "And the Next Day Her Belly Is Between Her Teeth": Feminine Symbolization in R. Joseph Angelet's Doctrine of *Gilgul* and *Ibbur* 98
Ruth Kara-Ivanov Kaniel

SECTION II. THE COSMIC, PHILOSOPHICAL, AND TEMPORAL DIMENSIONS OF REINCARNATION

125 5. Lives and Afterlives: Reincarnation, Cosmic Cycles, and the Medieval Jewish Present
Hartley Lachter

151 6. R. Joseph ben Shalom Ashkenazi's Cosmic Theory of Reincarnation, *Din Bnei Halof*
Jonnie Schnytzer

177 7. The Soul's Point of No Return: Jewish Philosophical Perspectives on Reincarnation
James A. Diamond

SECTION III. REINCARNATION, PSYCHOLOGY, AND LURIANIC KABBALAH: FROM SAFED TO EASTERN EUROPE TO BAGHDAD

203 8. Personal Identity and the Ontology of the Soul: Aspects of Reincarnation in Ḥayyim Vital's *Shaʿar ha-Gilgulim*
Eitan P. Fishbane

225 9. A Seething Cauldron of Infinite Soul-Sparks: Lurianizing Introjection/Psychoanalyzing *Gilgul*
Nathaniel Berman

249 10. Reincarnation (*Gilgul*) as Traversing Boundaries of Identity from Lurianic Kabbalah to Joel Teitelbaum of Satmar
Shaul Magid

273 11. The Dead Who Yearn to Die: Spirit-Possession and Soul-Healing in the Accounts of R. Hillel Ba'al Shem of Eastern Europe and R. Yehudah Fetaya of Baghdad
Andrea Gondos

SECTION IV. HASIDIC TEACHINGS ON REINCARNATION: BETWEEN THE INDIVIDUAL AND THE COMMUNITY

12. Devotion Reborn: *Gilgul* and the Life of Praxis in Hasidism 303
Ariel Evan Mayse

13. Reincarnation in Hasidic Literature: Hagiography, Social Justice, and Halakhah 327
Roee Y. Goldschmidt

14. The Bratslav Hasidic Approach to Reincarnation into Animals: Morality, Society, and Financial Concerns 347
Leore Sachs-Shmueli

Contributor Biographies 373
Index 377

ACKNOWLEDGMENTS

THIS BOOK IS THE PROJECT of two female scholars who have relentlessly pursued the study of kabbalah — a discipline that for centuries was restricted to men. We are humbled to be part of a large cohort of female scholars who teach and study kabbalah not only in Israel, but also in North America and in other parts of the world. Meeting in university classrooms, synagogues, libraries, and informal "study salons," women scholars and educators have eagerly mined kabbalistic texts and speculative thought, writing dissertations, books, and creative pieces while at the same time, teaching the secrets of the divinity to scores of students. Through discussions, debates, and *havruta*-style groups, women have followed the time-honored rabbinic way of learning — in pairs and assemblies — while adding their own voices, perspectives, and insights. In this way, women scholars have managed to galvanize and add their own bright sparks to the traditional male study of the Torah and its mysteries.

We first conceived of this project at the National Library of Israel in Jerusalem during an informal coffee meeting about insufficiently explored topics in the academic study of kabbalah. While acknowledging several important works written on the concept of reincarnation in Jewish thought, we realized the desideratum for a comprehensive volume that would address geographical, temporal, and thematic diversity regarding this topic. We would like to thank the book's contributors for joining us on this stimulating and creative journey, and we hope that this volume will inspire further comparative studies between Jewish concepts of reincarnation and those espoused in Eastern traditions and other religious systems.

We also would like to thank Ẓvi Leshem, the director of the Scholem Library at the NLI in Jerusalem, for always providing us the space for learning and scholarly exchange. We gratefully acknowledge the financial assistance of a number of institutions and grants. The German Research

Council (DFG) has generously supported the work of Andrea Gondos within the Emmy Noether Research Group, "Patterns of Knowledge Circulation: The Transmission and Reception of Jewish Esoteric Knowledge in Manuscript and Print in Early Modern East-Central Europe," led by Dr. Agata Paluch at Freie Universität in Berlin (Project number 401023278).

Finally, Andrea would like to thank her parents, Drs. Csilla Barta and George Gondos, for their enduring love and support — you walk before me in true greatness. A special acknowledgment to the Department of Religion and Classics at the University of Rochester, where this volume receives its final shape and completion. Extraordinary women have shaped my life in more than one way during my stay in Jerusalem as a post-doctoral fellow. Special thanks to Barbara Diamond and Bernard z"l, Dinah Stillman, Biti Roi, Shoshanah Shtern, Suzie Frankel, Valerie Adler, Noomi Lifshitz, Lesley Prais, and Gloria Kramer for inspiring me with your zeal, commitment, and passion for building a just and better world.

Leore expresses deep gratitude to her teachers, colleagues, and students at the Jewish Philosophy Department of Bar-Ilan University, which has been her academic home for more than a decade, nurturing and supporting all of her research, including this volume. Special thanks to the souls who share with me life, light, and space: Gideon-Osher, Hallel A., Tohar, Avigail, Naomi, and Yarden; and to my parents, Jeffrey and Batya who always kindled the sparks in me.

A special gratitude to James Peltz, editor-in-chief at SUNY Press, who believed in our project and offered us his unwavering support through all stages of the editorial process. Lastly, thank you to Marian Pinsky for helping us improve the final version of the manuscript.

ANDREA GONDOS AND LEORE SACHS-SHMUELI

Introduction

On the mystery of metempsychosis and its details: Know that God will not subject the soul of the wicked to more than three reincarnation; for it is written, *Behold, all these things does God work twice, yeah three times, with a person* (Job 33:29). Which means, He makes him appear twice and thrice in a human incarnation; but the fourth time he is incarnated as a clean animal. And when a man offers a sacrifice, God will, by miraculous intervention, make him select an animal that is an incarnation of a human being. Then will the sacrifice be doubly profitable: to the one that offers it and to the soul imprisoned in the brute. For with the smoke of the sacrifice the soul ascends heavenward and attains its original purity. Thus, the mystery involved in the words, *O Lord, you preserve the human being and the beast* (Psalm 36:7) is explained.
— **AVRAHAM AZULAY, *Hesed le-Avraham*** *

REINCARNATION, commonly referred to in Hebrew as *gilgul* — denoting the transmigration of the soul into a new body — is neither overtly discussed in the Hebrew Bible nor systematically expounded in rabbinic sources. Yet this concept has generated explosive interest and elicited fierce polemics in various parts of the Jewish world beginning with the Middle Ages. Until recently, scholarship on reincarnation was mainly concerned with discrete works and ideas without undertaking a more comprehensive treatment of this subject. Brian Ogren's important study, *Renaissance and Rebirth: Reincarnation in Early Modern Italian Kabbalah* (2009), offers one of the most comprehensive treatments to date but focuses only on one geographical and temporal setting without a broader discussion of parallel developments

* Avraham Azulay, *Hesed le-Avraham* (Amsterdam: Meshullam Zalman ben Avraham Berak of Gorice, 1685), 57d.

in earlier and later sources beyond the Italian milieu. This volume aims to redress this major lacuna by engaging a variety of important themes connected to metempsychosis examined over an extended historical period that spans from the Middle Ages to modernity.

For the first time, studies devoted to the teachings of Hasidic masters on the transmigration of the soul will be presented alongside medieval kabbalistic theories regarding the psychological dimensions of the soul and its afterlife, the changing notions of the self, and its theurgic role to affect restoration and attain redemption. By examining the above themes, the studies in this volume will expose the multifarious views and articulations concerning metempsychosis as they pertain to six distinct fields within the Jewish tradition: dimensions that relate to historiography and the conceptualization of temporality; its emergence in the Middle Ages followed by its internal development within kabbalah and relationship to Jewish philosophy; implications for the proper understanding of the commandments and halakhic precepts prescribed in the Bible; Christian theories focused on the afterlife of the soul; the psychological dimensions of this concept and its deployment as a vehicle for blurring binary categories (pure/impure, good/evil, Jew/gentile); and its social impact expressed particularly in Hasidism through concepts such as the Ẓaddik and his social-spiritual responsibility for his followers. Collectively, these studies aim to stimulate future comparative investigations of the conceptualizations of the soul and its afterlife in other religious traditions that engage the concept of reincarnation, such as Buddhism and Hinduism.

Reincarnation Inflected through Time, History, and Justice

Theories concerning the afterlife of the soul began to appear in classical works of medieval Kabbalah, the Bahir, and textual fragments that came to comprise the printed editions of the Zohar, offering novel, psychologically nuanced theories of the individual, the family, and human history. Beginning with the sixteenth century, the soul as the locus not only of the individual but also of the cosmos, received renewed significance in the writings of the Safed kabbalists and a few centuries later in the teachings of Hasidic masters. These mystics placed paramount importance on the notion of interiority, encompassing intentionality, status, and past experiences of the human soul. That death constituted but one station in the travails of the soul on its path toward completeness abetted new theological conceptualizations of the vicissitudes of Jewish history and refocused attention not only on Jewish ritual and ethical conduct but also on the spiritual ramifications of legal precepts in the field of halakha (Jewish law) while promoting a general reorientation toward religious piety and the cultivation of self-perfection.

Geographic and the attendant semantic shifts in the Jewish intellectual and religious landscape from the Middle Ages onward — such as recurrent persecutions of Jews in different corners of Christian Europe — foregrounded certain religious doctrines, such as reincarnation, that offered theological answers to the precariousness of Jewish existential continuity. On the basis of historiographical inquiry, Gershom Scholem argued that the sudden eruption of interest in metempsychosis in the aftermath of the large-scale expulsion of Jews from the Iberian Peninsula in the sixteenth century was consistent with emerging questions of theodicy and the ostensible injustices in the face of Jewish belief in an ethically calibrated universe.[1] A number of medieval kabbalistic sources reveal an acute investment in the task of theologically accounting for the challenges of Jewish historical experience. Reincarnation is one strategy that some kabbalists employed to explain tragic events on both the individual and the collective levels. By situating the "Jewish present" in a much longer continuum of successive lives and worlds, these texts suggest that the meaning, and justice, of Jewish individual and collective experience can be better understood. Questions of theodicy are decentered from the experience of a single historical moment or event and recast on a much broader temporal canvas. The life of the individual takes on meaning according to this view by playing a role in a much grander narrative of lives and afterlives. Reincarnation, and the question of the developmental arc of the soul over a vast temporal duration, is a fruitful domain of discourse for gaining better insight into how a group of Jews — who studied, inscribed, and promulgated the principles of Kabbalah — understood themselves and their present moment, and how they made theological sense of the conditions of Jewish history.

In the wake of the large-scale expulsion of Jews from the Iberian Peninsula, the continuing stream of immigrants who settled in Italy, the Ottoman Empire, and on various smaller islands in the Mediterranean bolstered the trading of books and manuscripts, which ensured the steady flow of new ideas and sparked fresh intellectual debates and exchanges. Manuscripts and books disseminated across the Mediterranean contributed to the circulation of kabbalistic texts and teachings that brought to the fore — at times through heated communal debates — esoteric religious precepts, such as the issue of the soul and metempsychosis, that required some degree of harmonization with the normative framework of Jewish religious life. The idea that the soul did not perish with the demise of the body, but was renewed by entering a new form of material existence, offered kabbalists a framework to recast not only history but also a variety of other perplexing issues, including theodicy, the meaning of Biblical narratives and commandments, the complex identity of biblical figures, and the issues of sin, punishment, and redemption, in a new frame.

Medieval Origins of the Doctrine of Reincarnation: Kabbalah and Philosophy

Generally, those thinkers who could be classified as belonging to the philosophical school in the history of Jewish thought did not find belief in reincarnation very appealing. The medieval philosopher Saadya Gaon (882–942) summarily dismissed it as "popular nonsense," while others like Maimonides, the leading twelfth-century Jewish philosophical theologian, remained silent on the topic. Consistent with Maimonides's emphasis throughout his oeuvre on intellectual perfection as the means of actualizing all aspects of human life — religious and secular — he categorically identifies cumulative knowledge, acquired during one's lifetime, as the only posthumous remnant of the human being. Maimonides thus forms an absolute identity between the soul and intellect, which he consistently upholds in his other works as well, both philosophical and rabbinic, including his *Commentary on the Mishnah* and his *Guide of the Perplexed*. Another seminal philosopher of the fourteenth century, Hasdai Crescas (1340–1410), begrudgingly endorsed the reincarnation "as if tradition demanded it." Crescas's stance, one that neither overtly rejects nor wholeheartedly embraces reincarnation, presents a new hybridic attitude toward it as an essential dogma of the Jewish faith. Still other major philosophers, such as Joseph Albo (1380–1444), despite rejecting it as theologically unwarranted, considered it philosophically palatable. Their diverse positions, surveyed in this volume, are intimately connected to their overall attitude toward Kabbalah as well as to their notions of the soul, identity, and the vicissitudes of the soul after death.

Although there already is evidence for Jewish belief in transmigration in the tenth century,[2] the first systematic treatment of this idea can be traced to the medieval pseudepigraphic treatise, the *Book Bahir* (*Book of Illumination*). In his discussion of metempsychosis, Gershom Scholem, the preeminent scholar of Kabbalah in the twentieth century, highlighted select passages in the Bahir that expose a preoccupation with the afterlife of the soul.[3] Correlating these passages with earlier Gnostic tenets on the soul, Scholem highlighted the possibility of a shared intellectual context transmitted either from the Near East via the eleventh-century German Jewish pietistic communities, the Hasidei Ashkenaz, or, alternatively, from the Bahir's immediate intellectual environment of twelfth-century Languedoc and its religious dissidents, the Cathars.[4] Further expanding the theoretical discourse on reincarnation, Scholem made an important distinction between the semantically related terms[5] reincarnation (*gilgul*), which denoted the entrance of the soul into the body at the time of birth, representing a vertical pathway; and soul impregnation (*ibbur*), which signified a horizontal movement of a soul that enters a host person at an undefined moment in one's lifetime.[6]

The leading medieval rabbi, scholar, and kabbalist Moses ben Nahman (1194–1270) was one of the first authorities to offer an early conceptualization of reincarnation focusing on the doctrine of *ibbur* as "one of the great secrets of the Torah," which he relates to the nature and dimensions of the human soul. His followers from the thirteenth and fourteenth centuries Shem Tov ibn Gaon, David ben Judah ha-Hasid, and Shem Tov ibn Shem Tov expanded his teachings and developed complex systems of rules that governed the order and occurrence of reincarnation, including how many times a soul would be permitted to return.[7] Other kabbalists, such as the thirteenth-century Spanish kabbalist Rabbi Joseph ben Shalom Ashkenazi, added further stratification to the theoretical dimensions of reincarnation, adding two new concepts: metensomatosis — the transmigration of physical matter from one body to another; and metamorphosis — a radical process of transformation by which both the spiritual and the physical aspects of the human being transmigrate from one body to another. Rabbi Ashkenazi's teachings therefore aim to nuance the essential quality of matter and spirit, discussing them in a holistic framework of the natural world where substances are in a perpetual cycle of transmutation and transformation, fomenting regeneration and perfection. By expanding the theoretical discourse on reincarnation by way of reference to metensomatosis and metamorphosis, Rabbi Ashkenazi's works help to refine the myopic tendency to define reincarnation singularly as the transmigration of a soul into a body.

Further problematizing questions of the soul, its recycle, and afterlife, Moshe Idel has called for applying a more granular approach to the treatment of metempsychosis in the development of Kabbalah. Using the exegesis of the medieval kabbalist Azriel of Gerona as his point of departure, Idel argued that reincarnation interpreted as soul impregnation (*sod ha-ibbur*) encompassed not merely inter-human but also intra-divine processes.[8] Accordingly, Azriel projects the cycle of reincarnation away from the material world and into the divine realm of the ten sefirot of divine potencies, asserting that soul impregnation as a generative process applies both in the material world as well as within the divine organism. Impregnation in this context therefore denotes not only the cohabitation of a supernal soul with the spirit of a living person, but also the continuous ascent, descent, and conjunction of the male and female influx within the divinity contributing to the generation of souls in the supernal realms, leading to the perpetual renewal of the divinity itself. Conceived in this way, reincarnation serves as a conduit that can connect horizontally between one generation and another while at the same time reinvigorating the emanatory potencies of the divine structure.

Reincarnation and Jewish Law: Revealing the Secret of the Commandments

By framing reincarnation within the Jewish legal discourse, a number of kabbalistic authors posit an innovative conceptualization between the commandments mandated by the Torah and their mystical rationale. The kabbalistic understanding of metempsychosis as pivotal in the development of Jewish religious thought precipitated its influence not only on the theoretical and exegetical but also on the halakhic, the legal and ritual, dimensions of Jewish life. Beginning with the Toderus Abulafia (1247–1306), Castilian kabbalists accorded special literary treatment to the halakhic implications of reincarnation.[9] Levirate marriage (*yibbum*), the commandment that stipulates the betrothal of a childless widow to the brother of her deceased husband to engender a progeny for the departed soul (Genesis 38:8 and Deuteronomy 25:5–19), emerged as one of the most conspicuous precepts of the Torah informed by metaphysical considerations. The boldest expression of exegetical creativity concerning reincarnation can be found in the main section of the Zohar in the composition *Sabba de-Mishpatim*. This distinct textual unit constitutes the main source for the Zohar's teaching about transmigration, offering a carefully nuanced psychological understanding of the relational anxieties that *yibbum* can engender at multiple levels: within the Jewish family on earth as well as within the divine structure itself.

The protagonist of this literary unit is the Old Man or *Sabba*, whose central discourse is devoted to esoteric speculations on reincarnation and the law of levirate marriage.[10] The tragedy of a Jewish man who dies without an offspring is underscored by the decree of *yibbum*, which stirs up its own psychological tensions and anxieties as the recycled soul of the first husband wages a battle against the soul of the brother, or second husband, inside the woman's womb. At the same time, *yibbum* was commonly regarded as offering theological and existential repair to brokenness that threatened to leave a family and an individual without hope of continuity and redemption. As Pinchas Giller underscores, thirteenth-century kabbalists attributed the Torah law of *yibbum* to the doctrine of reincarnation, establishing a direct impact between the legal and metaphysical areas of Jewish religious life and thought.[11]

The transmigration of human souls into animal bodies is another topic that generated debate in the history of Jewish mysticism and thought, beginning with the works of the thirteenth-century kabbalist Joseph of Hamadan. Through a series of systematic articulation of reincarnation unprecedented in Jewish tradition before him, Hamadan developed an innovative doctrine of reincarnation that involved the transfer of human souls into animal bodies as a punishment for specific types of transgression.[12] His theory added an interesting gendered conceptualization of reincarnation suggesting that Jewish men could find themselves reincarnated not just as men in new lives, but also as Jewish women, prostitutes, gentile women, and animals — an idea that exerted a decisive influence on the development of the belief in reincarnation in the Jewish tradition.

Traditions expressing a belief of reincarnation of human souls into animals invoked a philosophical dilemma concerning the relationship between animal and human souls. From thirteenth-century Spanish Kabbalah to Hasidic masters such as Nachman of Bratslav, kabbalists offered elaborate theories that, while refraining from positing an ontological parity, nevertheless ostensibly blurred the boundaries separating the soul of a human being from that of an animal. More importantly, by investigating the nature of the soul in animals, the kabbalists refocused Jewish religious life in regard to both law (halakhah) and ritual, away from a strictly human-centered point of view to a more integrated and holistic understanding of the relationship between the natural and supernatural worlds. The suffering of animals alongside the role of ritual slaughter in Jewish ritual practice became integrated into a broader metaphysical discourse on redemption and human perfection.

Transmigration in the Early Modern Mediterranean: Dissemination, Disputation, and the Christian Perspective

The island of Crete, under the political authority and cultural influence of Venice,[13] was an important station on the trading route that connected Europe, the East, and North Africa.[14] In the fifteenth and sixteenth centuries, Crete emerged as a vibrant center of Jewish scholarship and a repository of important libraries and book collections.[15] Fomented by the gradual proliferation of Jewish mystical collections on the island, Kabbalah emerged as a defining discipline that at times complemented, but more often competed with, philosophy for "intellectual hegemony and in the shaping of Renaissance modes of consciousness."[16] It is indicative of the elevated status of Kabbalah that when Umberto Cassuto discovered a trove of mid-sixteenth-century manuscripts at the Vatican that originated from the Island of Crete, out of a hundred and seventy five manuscripts twenty-seven works belonged to the genre of Kabbalah, twenty-six to philosophy and Bible respectively, four to medicine, eleven to mathematics, and nineteen each to the areas of Talmud, Codes, and Halakhah.[17]

In 1466, Crete was the locus of a fierce debate concerning the theological veracity of the doctrine of metempsychosis and its relevance to the commandment of levirate marriage.[18] The disputation between the respected communal leaders Rabbi Michael Balbo and Rabbi Moses ha-Cohen Ashkenazi threw into sharp relief a broader question regarding the absolute position of philosophy versus Kabbalah as authoritative interpretive modalities.[19] To advance their positions in the debate, the opponents had to be erudite in both philosophical and kabbalistic discourse. The public nature of the discussion meant that certain esoteric teachings, especially those regarding the nature of the soul and the mystical implications of the levirate marriage, would be made, even with some limitation and self-censorship, exoteric.[20] Thus the debate itself, regardless of its outcome, conveyed a sense of accessibility, signaled exposure, and legitimized to an extent the overt use of kabbalistic concepts and teachings in a controlled but open forum.

Bolstered by the humanist fascination with esoteric tenets and metaphysical speculations set against the backdrop of early modern Italy, a second debate erupted on the issue of transmigration in the last decades of the sixteenth century between two prominent members of the Italian Jewish community. In delineating the consequences of human sin in one of his sermons, the rabbi of Modena, Barukh Abraham da Spoleto, contended that souls that transgress during their lifetime would be reincarnated into animals and will depart again upon the animal's demise. Taking issue with the principle that human souls can enter into the bodies of beasts for the duration of a lifetime, R. Abraham Yagel, the prominent Italian physician and scholar, articulated his commitment to uphold the veracity of the notion of metempsychosis while concomitantly endorsing a different set of teachings on this subject than his colleague and coreligionist, Rabbi Barukh.[21] As David Ruderman has incisively demonstrated, the exchange concerning the transmigration of the human soul that ensued between these equally learned and respected rabbinic figures in early modern Italy reaches beyond their immediate temporal and cultural environments and illuminates broader intellectual trajectories.

For Italian Jews, teachings concerning the soul and its relation to the body probed the boundaries of divine knowledge, throwing into sharp relief the relationship among diverse epistemic fields: received esoteric knowledge, the kabbalah, contemporary science, and philosophy. At the same time, Christian theologians, while unequivocally disavowing the doctrine of metempsychosis, became entangled in a protracted internecine debate concerning the afterlife of the soul and the belief in purgatory. As an intermediate station of the soul between death and final judgment, purgatory became inscribed into Catholic dogma by the second half of the twelfth century and gradually gained popular dimensions through discrete devotional rites offering salvation to the dead. While the Protestant Church rejected belief in purgatory and the associated levity that the Catholic Church demanded in exchange for salvation, the afterlife of the soul continued to occupy a prominent place in early modern religious discourse and to reshape contemporary intellectual debates.[22]

Speculations concerning the doctrine of reincarnation were not limited to Jewish thinkers alone, and although metempsychosis was not sanctioned by the Church as part of official doctrine, Christian humanists nevertheless engaged extensively kabbalistic teachings concerning reincarnation in their theories about the soul, its origins, and its relation to cosmic forces and processes.[23] Marcilio Ficino (1433–1499) and his student Giovanni Pico della Mirandola (1463–1494), one of the preeminent exponents of Christian Kabbalah, synthesized vast sources of ancient knowledge of the Chaldeans,

Indians, and Egyptians to the Greek philosophies of Plato and Aristotle aimed at the erasure of the boundary separating religion and philosophy, and they further presented these disciplines as sharing a common spiritual core, whether it was centered on belief in the Trinity, an Aristotelian maxim, an Orphic hymn, or a kabbalistic text. To locate the original wellspring of truth, these humanist thinkers sifted through layers of historical epochs and their idiosyncratic religious and cultural manifestations and arrived at the Mosaic tradition, equating the ultimate source of ancient wisdom with the revelation of the Hebrew Bible encoded in the doctrines of Kabbalah.[24]

The kabbalistic teachings concerning metempsychosis provided an important epistemological language for both Ficino and Pico to articulate their respective theories regarding the human soul and its relation to the cosmos. Ficino deploys the Neo-Platonic concept of circularity, a movement common to the universe and the soul, which operates as a conduit that moves between the upper and lower worlds in a perpetual act of connectivity. As a microcosm, the human soul constitutes a chariot or seat for the divine and exhibits perfect circular motion reflective of the celestial forces that move the astral bodies in the cosmic structure of the universe.[25] The process of transmigration enables the soul to ascend and descend through consecutive cycles of birth and death in a perpetual motion, notes Ficino, although he rejects the idea that human souls can transmigrate into beastly animals.

Pico della Mirandola inherited and availed himself of philosophical and textual sources that his teacher Ficino deployed in his discussions on metempsychosis, and he shared Ficino's inclination to use allegory and symbolic language to navigate carefully between Jewish or other extraneous tenets that might be deemed controversial if not heretic and Christian theology. In addition to accepting the idea that the soul's primary nature was circular, he also advocated the idea that likened the soul to a seed planted by God in living beings that grows according to its own proclivity, inclining either toward the spiritual or the more physical aspects of existence. In his encyclopedic *Conculsiones nongentae* (*900 Conclusions*), composed in 1486, he mentions the concept of reincarnation at least on four separate occasions, and his overall theory of the soul was strongly shaped by the thirteenth-century Kabbalist Joseph ben Shalom Ashkenazi's cosmic model that linked reincarnation to divine judgment.

Inversion and the Traversal of Boundaries: Soul-Repair, Redemption, and Biblical Characters

In the anonymous composition *Galya Raza*, composed between the years 1543 and 1553, probably in Greece or Turkey,[26] we find a twofold interpretation of metempsychosis as punishment of the soul for various transgressions, on the one hand, and as an opportunity for redemption and repair, on the other hand. The dynamic of this drama involves ruse, cunning, and deception on the part of demonic ruler Samael to entice the Jewish people to sin. The transgression committed by Jews sets into motion a cycle of reincarnations that can involve the passing of the soul into lower life-forms, such as animals, whose flesh are served up as feasts for Samael. To counter the evil machinations of the demon king, the Divine deploys "holy subterfuge" to mitigate the power of Samael by arranging marriages with foreign women, who derive from the power of Samael, and the righteous in Israel. The ultimate weapon against evil stems from the secret of reincarnation — known to God but not to Samael — that enables the substitution of righteous and pure souls in exchange for spirits of pollution to enter into the bodies of these impure women. The marriages between the biblical characters Rebecca and Isaac, Jacob with Rachel and Leah, Judah and Tamar, Moses and Zipporah, Boaz and Ruth the Moabite, and Joshua and the harlot Rahab provide evidence that reincarnation and the exchange of souls are potent weapons in the divine arsenal for the neutralization and defeat of the *Sitra Ahra*.[27]

The belief in reincarnation can offer human beings a sense of relief in the face of death, while at the same time can pose new theological and emotional challenges for the soul. The psychological dimensions of reincarnation can be fruitfully traced through a close examination of the figure of the biblical monarch, King David, whose personal greatness and dramatic persona served as a paradigm for the eminent kabbalist Rabbi Hayyim Vital (1542–1620). The prodigious disciple of Rabbi Isaac Luria, Vital saw himself as the reincarnation of King David, and in a number of his writings, such as *The Gate of the Reincarnations*, and in his autobiography, *The Book of Visions* (*Sefer ha-Hezyonot*), he describes his deep attachment to David as a key to understanding his own psychological disabilities that plagued him for most of his life including bouts of anguish, depression, and emotional suffering.

In Lurianic Kabbalah as transmitted through the writings of Hayyim Vital, reincarnation is used as a catalyst to traverse the boundary separating Jew and gentile to redeem lost sparks embedded in the husks of evil (*kelipot*). By evoking the notion of reincarnation, Vital depicts a web of complex interrelationships among biblical characters, including Abraham and his idolatrous father, Teraḥ; followed by Moses, Balaam, and Job and their respective wives, to problematize the concept of "otherness" and the porous boundaries between ostensibly opposite identities of Jew and gentile. In Lurianic theories, as well as in the later traditions of the Hungarian Hasidic group of Satmar, reincarnation is closely related to, and constitutes an integral part of, religious conversion. Both Lurianic kabbalists and Hasidic thinkers contend conversion is a necessary, even crucial, part of the redemptive process without which remnants of the holy would remain embedded in the dross of creation, preventing the descent of "new souls" into the world, tasked to impel it toward an intended eschatological fulfillment.[28]

Drawing on certain Lurianic traditions, R. Naftali Hertz Bacharach, in his work *The Valley of the King* (*Emeq ha-Melekh*), printed in 1648, developed his unique theory of messianic reincarnation of Adam's soul. In Bacharach's teachings, Adam's reincarnation is split into the souls of Cain and Abel. The world's salvation is dependent on the purification of Adam's soul from the filth of the Serpent (Sama'el) and reincarnated in Cain and various other biblical figures, ending with the Christian savior, Jesus. The Messiah, who is Abel's reincarnation in Enoch, Metatron, Jacob, Moses, and Isaac Luria, comprises the filth of Jesus as an immanent part of himself and therefore needs to be purified. The integration of Christian and Jewish religious motifs and personalities in Bacharach's exegetical enterprise underlines the potential of reincarnation to serve as a potent literary and religious trope that could transcend religious boundaries and provide a unified mythical construct for dialogue between these historically acrimonious religious traditions. Through inversion, however, Bacharach emphasized that Christianity ultimately required redemption, which can only be attained when all the incarnations of Adam's soul are fulfilled and the filth of the serpent is purified, which will result in the ultimate redemption of the soul of Jesus.

Social Dimensions of Reincarnation: The *Ẓaddik* and the Community

Beyond the historiographic and halakhic dimensions, at the locus of metempsychosis is a fundamental preoccupation with the nature of the soul: from its affinity to, and likeness of, the divine being and its quiddity to transcend both physical and metaphysical boundaries. While reincarnation relates primarily to the tribulations of individual souls because of its polysomatic predisposition, it encapsulates broader communal and intergenerational aspects as well. Accordingly, kabbalists like Rabbi Moses Cordovero (1522–1570) boldly claimed that all Jewish sages possesses a part of the soul of Moses in such a way that their souls become impregnated by a spark of his soul. He further illustrated this process by reference to how fire gets passed from a candle to ignite another one without diminishing the strength or essence of the original spark.[29] Furthermore, the diffusion of soul-sparks in all forms of existence provides the theological justification for the law of cohabiting with a non-Jewish woman captured in war, delineated in Deuteronomy 21:10–14. According to Rabbi Avraham Azulay's kabbalistic interpretation of this biblical law, the Jewish captor's arousal for this alien woman stems not from his base materialistic inclination, but rather from the realization that "there is a holy spark mixed in that nation, found in that alien woman, a spark that belongs to the soul of that man."[30] The retrieval of that lost spark and its reunification with its source, the righteous person (*Ẓaddik*), is depicted as a war that requires the extraordinary measure to temporarily exit the domain of holiness and enter the realm of impurity and the demonic — represented by the alien woman — to subsequently redeem the lost vestiges of his soul.[31]

In Lurianic Kabbalah, the idea of reincarnation reached a new phase of precision and extensive systemization. Concerns with the issue of soul roots and soul families impelled the sixteenth-century sage Rabbi Isaac Luria and his students, including his main proponent, Rabbi Hayyim Vital, to devise specific theurgic practices aimed at facilitating the impregnation of one's soul by progressively higher levels of souls. Attention to the psychological dimensions of the human being — a preoccupation with the self, its emotional upheavals, and its moral responsibilities — informs significant parts of the Lurianic theory on transmigration that contribute to modern discourse on the construction of the self and processes of individuation.[32] Embedded in Luria's concept of transmigration, we find concerns not only for the perfection of an individual soul — as a part and extension of the self — but also for expediting collective redemption. Thus, the kabbalistic theory of soul-sparks (*niẓoẓot*) — the shattering of the divine light concentrated in the Primordial Adam (Adam Kadmon), which were subsequently scattered into various forms of material existence — contributed to the development of the kabbalistic teaching that each righteous man (*ẓaddik*) is responsible for the redemption of the soul-sparks that live in close proximity to him, facilitating communal cooperation and ethical responsibility.[33]

The study of reincarnation in Hasidism and modern Jewish thought remains an important desideratum in Jewish studies, and this volume aims to offer a preliminary examination of major Hasidic schools, texts, and authors who illuminate the significance of reincarnation for Hasidic life and thought. Hasidic thinkers followed medieval and early modern kabbalistic sources, drawing on Zoharic and Lurianic textual traditions in articulating their teachings about the role of reincarnation in Jewish life yet managed to move beyond the narrow questions of theodicy and mythic redemption. Hasidic sages offered a vastly different understanding of this classical kabbalistic concept, displaying fundamental shifts in Jewish communal organizations and concerns reflective of new social, political, and religious realities. Arising from a preoccupation with the suffering of animals, the role of slaughter in Jewish ritual practice became integrated by Hasidic writers, such as R. Nahman of Bratslav, into a broader metaphysical discourse on redemption and human perfection. These ideas had a direct influence on the practical dimensions of Jewish life, stimulating greater concern for the proper observance of kosher slaughter that would minimize animal suffering. The belief in reincarnation of the soul into animals combined with social and economic interests encouraged Hasidic leaders to appoint their own ritual slaughterers, a tendency that aroused intracommunal tension and strife in a number of Jewish communities.

Hasidic hagiographic and homiletic literature accord a special status to the role of the *Ẓaddik*, the righteous of the generation, who is able to comprehend God's hidden ways and the secrets of reincarnation as a component of "divine justice." As in Buddhism, where certain kinds of religious specialists are often responsible for breaking the cycle of rebirth, the Ẓaddik's role is to assist in the repair of others.[34] Indeed, there is sometimes a distinction made in the Buddhist literature between rebirth — the uncontrolled continuity through states of existence in *saṃsāra* characterized by suffering — and reincarnation — the willful and controlled rebirth by dint of spiritual mastery, as in the Tibetan reincarnate lama system.[35] Likewise, the *ẓaddik*, a figure of tremendous spirit and power, is delivered back to this world to be reborn to help other people[36] — even one's enemies, since they are rooted in the *ẓaddik* himself.[37] One must come back for the good of the community, for the good of the generation. While the use of this motif in hagiographic literature has received a certain amount of scholarly attention, its appearances in homiletic, ethical, and Hasidic literature, which vary greatly, have been largely overlooked. Hasidic homiletic literature written by the students of the Baal Shem Tov (the Besht), the followers of the Maggid of Meziritsh and the Hasidic Masters of the mid-nineteenth century, narrate an important yet unexplored chapter in the history of Hasidism that highlight intense preoccupation with the concept of reincarnation and pinpoint the different kabbalistic traditions that influenced their approaches to this concept.

The present volume seeks to highlight the multivalent approaches that kabbalists from different geographical regions and historical periods adopted for the articulation of their unique teachings on the afterlife and the nature of the human soul. Just as the concept of metempsychosis is inherently about boundary crossing, so does its investigation engage and operate at the intersection of several different epistemic fields and disciplines, including philosophy, psychology, science, history, and cultural studies. These fields serve as useful methodological pivots for illuminating diverse diachronic conceptualizations of reincarnation within Judaism while, at the same time, offering some preliminary points of comparison and contact with other religious cultures, such as Hinduism and Buddhism. The chapters of the book illuminate how Jewish thinkers reconceptualized multifaceted theoretical approaches to understanding reincarnation as embedded in a broader discourse of entanglement that traverse porous boundaries between the corporeal and the spiritual; the transient and the eternal; Jew and non-Jew; and gendered binaries of male and female. These detailed studies demonstrate that the question of reincarnation served as a central concern for engaging broader issues that fundamentally impact our understanding not only of Kabbalah — the esoteric kernel of Judaism — but also the more general profile of the Jewish tradition itself.

Chapter Summaries

The opening section of this volume presents analyses of canonical kabbalistic texts, such as the Zohar, alongside other medieval works of kabbalah of the thirteenth and early fourteenth centuries, laying the groundwork for the articulation of the core concepts of reincarnation. These chapters serve as foundations for later developments concerning reincarnation in relation to other esoteric speculations, such as the theosophical structure of the sefirot, the feminine aspects of divinity, and the kabbalistic ethos of the family and sexuality. Moshe Idel's chapter on Moses ben Nahman (Nahmanides, 1194–1270) highlights the groundbreaking contributions of this Geronese kabbalist, physician, and communal leader in shaping the traditions related to reincarnation in the Middle Ages.

Ellen D. Haskell, in her chapter, "The Effaced Eagle-Man and Other Problems: Reincarnated Embodiment in Guf ha-Zohar," foregrounds the central role of the body in the process of reincarnation as delineated by the late thirteenth-century Castilian work the Zohar. She analyzes the tension between the reincarnation of the soul and the "embodied" reincarnation of physical parts of the human being and between the concepts of reincarnation and resurrection. Furthermore, she explores the cultural significance of these beliefs for the ethos of procreation in the context of Jewish-Christian polemics concerning reproduction, marriage, and the family. Finally, she discusses the status and normativity of reincarnated souls.

Pinchas Giller's chapter, devoted to the early circulation of the doctrine of reincarnation, explores this idea in two classic sources of kabbalah, first in the *Book Bahir* and then in Zoharic literature, with a special focus on the sections *Tikkunei Zohar* and *Ra'aya Meheimna*. These writings portray reincarnation in ways that would become normative in sixteenth-century Kabbalah. The idea that a person is required to "fix" a certain aspect of his soul in each reincarnation — delineated in the *Tikkunei Zohar* — a process that ultimately culminates in the soul's final liberation, became central in the Lurianic idea of repair or *tikkun*, which has had an enduring influence on modern Jewish spirituality and kabbalistic speculation. This chapter engages with questions such as how many opportunities the soul receives, and what precisely the role of the *Shekhinah* — the feminine aspect of the divinity — is in this process.

In her chapter, Ruth Kara Ivanov-Kaniel presents the innovative ideas of the fourteenth-century Catalonian kabbalist Rabbi Joseph Angelet, who reworked earlier kabbalistic views of reincarnation, theodicy, and theosophy articulated by a number of medieval kabbalistic sources, including the works of R. Moses ben Nahman (Nahmanides), R. Jacob ben Sheshet, R. Joseph Ashkenazi, and the Zohar. She argues that reincarnation in Angelet's theosophic system served the primary goal of promoting the repair and perfection of the generation, which in turn aimed to hasten messianic redemption. She highlights that the feminine aspect of the Divine plays a pivotal role in the transformation of souls and bodies, as well as in the process of reparation and atonement caused by sin. With specific focus on the gendered aspects of reincarnation, she discusses how Angelet's doctrine of *gilgul* deploys the biblical female figures Rachel and Leah, the wives of the Patriarch Jacob, who symbolize central figures in the divine schema and distinct stations in the process of repentance and in the soul's journey back to its source.

In his chapter, "Lives and Afterlives: Reincarnation and the Medieval Jewish Present," Hartley Lachter traces the kabbalistic deployment of reincarnation as a strategy for coping with historical tragedies. With a special focus on the anonymous treatise *Book of Cosmic Cycles (Sefer ha-Temunah)*, written in the Iberian Peninsula in the fourteenth and fifteenth centuries, he convincingly demonstrates that through the doctrine of cosmic cycles (*shemitot*), this work decenters the calamities of the present and reframes these events in a larger theological-historical narrative. Offering a unique understanding of reincarnation, *Sefer ha-Temunah* presents the aspirations of Jewish mystics, who regarded the individual soul and its suffering over multiple lifetimes as arising from the divine attribute that governs that particular historical epoch. Lachter frames his analysis of the soul and its afterlife within broader questions of exile and messianic visions of redemption.

The cosmic theory concerning the life of the soul is at the center of Jonnie Schnitzer's chapter, which presents a profound conceptualization of reincarnation offered by the medieval kabbalist Rabbi Joseph ben Shalom Ashkenazi, who was active during the thirteenth century in Catalonia. Reflecting possible influences from Islamic mystical sources, such as the *Epistles of the Brethren of Purity* (*Rasāʾil Ikhwān al-ṣafāʾ*), Ashkenazi posited a theory in which all aspects and parts of creation — the inanimate vegetative, animal, and human — participate in cycles of renewal and transmigration that involve both divine justice as well as divine compassion in the sustenance of all life-forms in the sublunar and higher worlds. Ashkenazi's doctrine, unparalleled in its meticulous and systematic presentation, provides a prolegomenon on how ideas relating to the soul and its counterparts, including its associations within the physical world, were transmitted and adapted into the theoretical apparatus of later kabbalists, such as the influential system of the sixteenth-century kabbalist Rabbi Isaac Luria Ashkenazi (Ari).

James Diamond's chapter complements this volume by presenting a survey of Jewish philosophical attitudes toward the idea of reincarnation. Diamond demonstrates that while most rationalist philosophers of the Middle Ages found this belief unappealing, and in many cases irrational and unreasonable, a small group endorsed this idea, albeit begrudgingly. New conceptions of the soul, the self, death, and the afterlife, as well as the broader circulation of kabbalistic ideas and texts in the fourteenth and fifteenth centuries, impelled philosophers, such as Hasdai Crescas and Joseph Albo, to regard reincarnation as philosophically palatable.

Rabbi Hayyim Vital's systematic and exhaustive formulations of the principles of reincarnation in *Sha'ar ha-Gilgulim* became a major force in modern kabbalistic understanding of the topic. Modern Kabbalah presented, on the one hand, a continuation of core concepts and terms, and, on the other hand, a move toward systematization and a deeper engagement with the questions of self. Thus, the second section of the book presents different angles of the Lurianic doctrine of reincarnation and its contribution to the understanding of the "self" and other. Eitan Fishbane's chapter locates reincarnation within the broader system of Lurianic "anthropology," with its ontological roots deep within the divinity. Through a close reading of Vital's works, he argues that reincarnation facilitates the perfection of the individual soul and abets the soul's attainment of its ultimate purpose in life through Torah study and the performance of the commandments. Furthermore, he discusses how reincarnation changes one's understanding not only of the self, but also of relationships with significant others in familial bonds of parents, children, and spouses; and between a teacher and his students.

Shaul Magid further explores the topic of identity and the "other," starting with the writings of Hayyim Vital through Eastern European Hasidic texts of the Satmar dynasty. His main argument is anchored in the idea that reincarnation, in these texts, contributes to the mechanism of boundary crossing, where differences between Jew and gentile, pure and impure, sacred and the demonic, become erased as a prelude to the redemption of the soul. Nathaniel Berman, in his chapter, "'A Seething Cauldron' of 'Infinite Soul-Sparks:' Lurianizing Introjection/Psychoanalyzing *Gilgul*," adds to the former discussions by highlighting the notion of the multiplicity of the self as expounded in Vital's *Sha'ar ha-Gilgulim*. By offering an existential and psychoanalytical reading of reincarnation, Berman shows that a clear distinction between the defined multiplicity of the soul-levels and the infinitude of the soul-sparks becomes attenuated and the achievement of complete *tikkun* becomes an ever-receding utopian goal in the Lurianic framework. By comparing Freudian metapsychology with Vital's theory of metempsychosis, he highlights the significance of the fraught — at times even sinister — power dynamics inherent in Lurianic concepts of *gilgul*.

In the last chapter of this section, "The Dead Who Yearn to Die: Spirit-Possession and Soul-Healing in the Accounts of Hillel Ba'al Shem and Yehudah Fetaya of Baghdad," Andrea Gondos examines various healing techniques and rituals to treat possessions by malevolent spirits in two distinct sources. These accounts are methodologically framed within a broader discourse on shamanism and shamanic operations within early modern and modern Judaism in geographically disparate places. Drawing on Jonathan Garb's focused study on the shamanic dimensions of Hasidism, she argues that adopting this terminology is an important step in deconstructing the phenomenological aspects of Jewish mystics and healers, including *Ba'alei Shem* (Masters of the Name). She further posits that this semantic adjustment will shed new light on the social, cultural, and religious impact of a group of Jewish men — shamanic healers — who served as important cultural agents in Jewish communities both in Europe and the Middle East. The first account is set in eighteenth-century Poland and offers a detailed and lengthy possession account recorded in the *Book of Longing* (*Sefer ha-Heshekh*), written by R. Hillel Ba'al Shem (c. 1690–c. 1741). By comparing this work to *Talking Souls* (*Ruhot Mesaprot*), written by the Baghdadi Rabbi Yehudah Fetaya (1859–1942), allows her to draw points of contact in the modus operandi of shamanic healers who shared a common worldview centered on the psychological preoccupation with the soul, yet who operated in temporal, cultural, and geographical distance from one another. Focusing on the religious imperative of apotropaic human action, Hillel Ba'al Shem and Rabbi Fetayya articulate a theory of reincarnation and soul impregnation that is both psychological and medicalized. In their conceptualization, healing the "wandering soul" that seeks to possess the living also contributes to healing the universe, affecting all levels of existence in the great chain of being including the ontological source of life, the Creator.

The final section of this volume explores the adaptation and reworking of the belief in reincarnation in Hasidic texts. These chapters underscore how this concept is used to address modern challenges of the self, along with social and cultural transformations. Within the Hasidic context, these chapters demonstrate that, contrary to common scholarly assumptions that viewed reincarnation as a marginalized phenomenon in Hasidic thought, it in fact assumed a pivotal role not only in Hasidic narratology, but also in its core theology. As the chapters of this section demonstrate, Hasidic texts, ranging from eighteenth-century Eastern Europe to twentieth-century America, inherited and reconfigured basic kabbalistic principles of reincarnation and rituals as responses to contemporary challenges they faced.

Ariel Evan Mayse argues that Hasidic teachings invoke the concept of *gilgul* to underscore the absolute meaning of this-worldly religious action. In his analysis, Mayse proposes a number of comparative insights concerning the similarities between Hasidic and Buddhist teachings. According to his reading, these traditions evince a similar tension between the ubiquity of rebirth and the specific focus on this-worldly "action" (karma) and the domains of the self as composed of "body" (*kāya*), "speech" (*vāk*), and "mind" (*citta*). As well as exploring how various Hasidic texts view rebirth as enhancing religious practice with a new spectrum of meaning and intention, Mayse also discusses how claims to authority by Hasidic leaders were often justified through appeal to their status in previous incarnations. Finally, he posits that in twentieth-century Hasidic teachings, reincarnation served as a tool in addressing broader discourse on gender, socioreligious continuity, and cohesion in a new cultural and historical context.

In his chapter, "Reincarnation in Hasidic Literature: Hagiography, Social Justice, and Halakhah," Roee Y. Goldschmidt demonstrates that reincarnation constituted a central motif in diverse Hasidic literary genres — hagiography, homiletical works, and books focused on rationalizing the commandments — throughout eighteenth- and nineteenth-century Europe. Building on Lurianic concepts and engaging with halakhic discourse, reincarnation served to enhance major elements of Hasidic life and religious praxis, such as prayer and external thoughts, devotion or *devekut*, the authority of the *ẓaddik*, repairing souls, and social responsibility. Through his study of works composed by Yaakov Yosef of Polonoy, R. Moshe Shoham of Dolina, and Ẓvi Elimelekh of Dynov, his chapter reconceptualizes the transition of the idea of reincarnation from the early modern to the modern period, stressing how it received existential and practical dimensions and was used to justify community organization and hierarchy and the commitment to meticulous performance of the commandments.

Finally, Leore Sachs-Shmueli, in her chapter, "The Bratslav Hasidic Approach to Reincarnation into Animals: Morality, Society, and Financial Concerns," focuses on the social impact and didactic ramifications of reincarnation in Bratslav Hasidism. Her analysis reveals the ways in which kabbalistic traditions were used to enhance the communal authority of Hasidic slaughterers. Comparing R. Nachman of Bratslav's innovative metaphoric interpretation of the idea with his student R. Nathan of Nemerov's more simplified interpretation of it, returning to the classical belief emphasizes the powerful moral power of reincarnation when viewed as punishment, not only in the medieval and early modern period, but also in the nineteenth century.

Notes

1. Gershom Scholem, *Major Trends in Jewish Mysticism* (New York: Schocken Books, 1974), 280–84.

2. On theories of reincarnation articulated in the tenth century, see Haggai Ben-Shammai, "Transmigration of Souls in Tenth-Century Jewish Thought in the Orient," *Sefunot: Studies and Sources on the History of the Jewish Communities in the East* 5 (1991): 117–36 [Hebrew]. In this article, Ben-Shammai provided evidence that supported the belief in transmigration espoused by Middle Eastern Jews from the tenth century on while at the same time discussing emphatic opposition expressed against metempsychosis by Saadia Gaon.

3. Gershom Scholem, "*Gilgul*: The Transmigration of Souls," in *The Mystical Shape of the Godhead: Basic Concepts in the Kabbalah* (New York: Schocken Books, 1991), 197–250.

4. Joseph Dan, *Gershom Scholem and the Mystical Dimensions of Jewish History* (New York: New York University Press, 1987), 127–461; and Gershom Scholem, *The Origins of Kabbalah and Sefer ha-Bahir*, ed. Rivka Schatz (Jerusalem, 1962) [Hebrew]. On the composite nature of the Bahir as a literary artifact, see Elliot R. Wolfson, "Hebraic and Hellenic Conceptions of Wisdom in *Sefer ha-Bahir*," *Poetics Today* 19 (1998): 147–76. On the connection between the Cathars and Kabbalah, see S. Shahar, "Catharism and the Beginning of Kabbalah in Languedoc," *Tarbiẓ* 40 (1971): 483–507 [Hebrew].

5. Scholem, *On the Mystical Shape of the Godhead* (New York: Schocken, 1991), 197–251.

6. See Menachem Kallus, "Pneumatic Mystical Possession and the Eschatology of the Soul in Lurianic Kabbalah," in *Spirit Possession in Judaism: Cases and Contexts from the Middle Ages to the Present*, ed. Matt Goldish (Detroit: Wayne State University Press, 2003), 160.

7. Rami Shkalim, in his book *The Beginning of the Doctrine of Reincarnation in Kabbalah in the 12-15th Centuries* (Tel Aviv: Private press, 1994), presented a detailed survey of different aspects of the concept of reincarnation through the works of these kabbalists.

8. Moshe Idel, "The Secret of Impregnation as Metempsychosis in Kabbalah," in *Verwandlungen: Archäologie der Literarischen Kommunikation IX*, ed. Aleida and Jan Assmann (Munich: Wilhelm Fink Verlag, 2006), 375.

9. Michal Oron discussed the thirteenth-century Castilian short comments about transmigration in Toderus Abulafia's *Sha'ar ha-Razim.* See Michal Oron, "The Doctrine of the Soul and Reincarnation in 13th Century Kabbalah," in *Studies in Jewish Thought*, ed. Sara O. Heller Willensky and Moshe Idel (Jerusalem: Magnes Press, 1989), 277–89 [Hebrew].

10. Pinchas Giller, "Love and Upheaval in the Zohar's Sabba de-Mishpatim," *Journal of Jewish Thought and Philosophy* 7 (1997–1998): 44–48; Oded Yisraeli, *The Interpretation of Secrets and the Secrets of Interpretation: Midrashic and Hermeneutic Strategies in Sabba de-Mishpatim of the Zohar* (Los Angeles: Cherub Press, 2005)

[Hebrew]; and Ruth Kara Ivanov Kaniel, "Between Kabbalah, Gender and Law: Sexual Ethics in the Zohar," *AJS Review* 39, no. 1 (2015): נא -יד [Hebrew].

11. Pinchas Giller, "Love and Upheaval in the Zohar," 45.

12. Leore Sachs-Shmueli, "The Rationale of the Negative Commandments by R. Joseph Hamadan: A Critical Edition and Study of Taboo at the Time of the Composition of the Zohar" (PhD diss., Bar-Ilan University, 2018).

13. Isaac Barzilay, *Yoseph Shlomo Delmedigo (Yashar of Candia): His Life, Works, and Times* (Leiden: Brill, 1974), 7. Venice ruled Crete for 450 years, 1204 to 1669.

14. Moshe Idel, *Kabbalah in Italy*, 1280–1510 (New Haven: Yale University Press, 2011), 288; and Barzilay, *Yoseph Shlomo Delmedigo*, 8.

15. Barzilay mentions Elijah Capsali as a defining Rabbinic leader of the Jewish community in Crete in the first half of the sixteenth century (*Yoseph Shlomo Delmedigo*, 9). He further notes that while the Jewish community on the island was small, it produced numerous outstanding scholars including Elijah Delmedigo, Elijah Capsali, Shaul ha-Cohen, and Yoseph Delmedigo; and a number of lesser-known but equally respected rabbinic teachers and leaders (*Yoseph Shlomo Delmedigo*, 20).

16. Barzilay, *Yoseph Shlomo Delmedigo*, 3.

17. Barzilay, *Yoseph Shlomo Delmedigo*, 22, based on the research of Umberto Cassuto at the Vatican Library (Cassuto, "I Manoscritti Palatini," 1935).

18. See Andrea Gondos, "Kabbalah in Print: Literary Strategies of Popular Mysticism in Early Modernity" (PhD diss., Concordia University, 2013), 50–51.

19. See the article of Boaz Huss, "Mysticism versus Philosophy in Kabbalistic Literature," *Micrologus* 11 (2001): 125–35, in which he identifies three models that typify the relationship between philosophy and Kabbalah: 1) At the core, Kabbalah and philosophy "represent the same body of knowledge"; 2) While philosophy is a valid source of wisdom, it is ultimately inferior to Kabbalah; 3) Philosophy is the very antithesis of Kabbalah and therefore it is entirely negative, misleading, devoid of truth, and extraneous to Judaism (124–25). Brian Ogren adds yet a fourth category of scholars, such as Elijah Delmedigo and Rabbi Ashkenazi (above), who explicitly criticized the Kabbalah and regarded it as inferior to philosophy. See Brian Ogren, *Renaissance and Rebirth: Reincarnation in Early Modern Italian Kabbalah* (Leiden: Brill, 2009), 53 n. 46.

20. See Brian Ogren, who emphatically states: "Never before in the recorded history of Jewish literature had two contemporary scholars at the forefront of two antithetical societal camps candidly gone head-to-head over this doctrine, which was previously considered to be arcane by its very nature" (Ogren, *Renaissance and Rebirth*, 48).

21. David Ruderman, "On Divine Justice, Metempsychosis, and Purgatory: Rumination of a Sixteenth Century Italian Jew," *Jewish History* 1 (1986): 9–30.

22. Ruderman, "On Divine Justice," 22.

23. Ogren, *Renaissance and Rebirth*, 1–2.

24. David Ruderman, *Kabbalah, Magic, and Science: The Cultural Universe of a Sixteenth-Century Jewish Physician* (Cambridge, MA: Harvard University Press, 1988), 140–41.

25. Ogren, *Renaissance and Rebirth*, 238–39.

26. Rachel Elior, "The Doctrine of Metempsychosis in '*Galya Raza*,'" *Jerusalem Studies in Jewish Thought* 3, no. 1–2 (1984): 208 [Hebrew].

27. Elior, "The Doctine of Transmigration," 254–58.

28. For a comprehensive treatment of this topic, see Shaul Magid, "The Politics of (Un) Conversion: The 'Mixed Multitude' ('Erev Rav') as Conversos in Rabbi Hayyim Vital's "Ets Ha-Da'at Tov,'" *Jewish Quarterly Review* 95, no. 4 (2005): 625–66, esp. 631–32, 659–60.

29. Moshe Idel, "The Secret of Impregnation," 367.

30. Avraham Azulay, *Ba'alei Berit Avram* (Jerusalem: Ahavat Shalom, 1982), fol. 87b [Hebrew], cited in Moshe Idel, "The Secret of Impregnation," 370.

31. On Safed Kabbalah, see Eitan Fishbane, "Chariot for the *Shekhinah*: Identity and Ideal Life in Sixteenth-Century Kabbalah" *Journal of Religious Ethics* 37, no. 3 (2009): 385–418. Ron Margolin's book *The Human Temple: Religious Interiorization and the Structuring of Inner Life in Early Hasidism* (Jerusalem: Magnes Press, 2005) [Hebrew] provides a comprehensive overview of the spiritual and interior dimensions of Jewish religious life by exploring Hasidic texts.

32. Assaf Tamari, "Human Sparks: Readings in the Lurianic Theory of Transmigration and Its Concepts of the Human Subject" (MA thesis, Tel Aviv University, 2009). Daphna Levin, in her book based on her dissertation, presented a comparative study between kabbalistic traditions (especially Lurianic) of reincarnation and modern techniques of transpersonal psychology. See Daphna Levin, *Mystery of Reincarnation in Kabbalah and Transpersonal Psychology: The Doctrines of the Soul, of Reincarnation, of Karma and of Healing the Soul* [Hebrew] (Tel Aviv: Gvanim, 2016). In an additional volume, she presented an introduction of the main principles of reincarnation in Kabbalah and an anthology of tales about reincarnation; see Daphna Levin, *Lord of Karma: Reincarnation and Karma in Kabbalah: An Anthology* (Tel Aviv: Idra, 2016).

33. Moshe Idel, 370. The important Lurianic discussions on the topic were collected and arranged in two different editorial projects, one by Meir Poppers, *Sefer ha-Gilgulim*, popular in Europe; the other by Hayyim Vital's son, Shmuel, *Sha'ar ha-Gilgulim*, printed only in the twentieth century. *Sha'ar ha-Gilgulim* was printed in Jerusalem in 1912. An autographed copy written by Samuel Vital is available in a private manuscript collection in Petah Tikvah. See Yosef Avivi, *Kabbala Luriana, II: The Lurianic Writings after 1620* (Jerusalem: Ben Ẓvi Institute, Jerusalem: 2008), 697–98 [Hebrew].

34. See Geoffrey Samuel, *Introducing Tibetan Buddhism* (Abingdon: Routledge: 2012), 129–64.

35. See Samuel, *Introducing Tibetan Buddhism*, 145.

36. See Ẓvi Elimelekh of Dinov, *Igra de-Kalla* (Jerusalem: Machon Benei Shileshim), *Ḥayyei Sarah* [Hebrew].

37. R. Jacob Joseph of Pollnoye, *Ben Porat Yosef* (Jerusalem: 2011), vol. 1, *Noah*, 121 [Hebrew].

SECTION I

MEDIEVAL APPROACHES TO REINCARNATION

MOSHE IDEL

The Secrets of Soul Impregnation (*Ibbur*) in Early Kabbalah and the Doctrine of Reincarnation

1

BIBLICAL AND RABBINIC LITERATURE traditionally showed limited interest in psychological matters, emphasizing action and external events over inner life. Individuals were primarily judged by their deeds rather than their intentions, with a focus on obedience and compliance to divine behavior. The absorption of Torah content and its performance was considered sufficient to shape one's personality. While some rabbinic literature explored tensions between inclinations or instincts (*yeẓarim*), the emphasis remained on shaping the evil instinct rather than annihilating it. Mystical systems, particularly in ancient Jewish mysticism, delved into corporeal transformations and changes in the human body. However, these transformations were connected to the physical realm, as seen for instance in Enoch's transmutation and transformation in Heikhalot literature.

During the Middle Ages, religious transformations turned inward as Jewish philosophers and mystics engaged with Greek psychology. This shift coincided with a spiritualization of the concept of the divinity, with a growing emphasis on the human intellect. Theosophical Kabbalah, emerging during this period, introduced a more inclusive vision of divinity and a complex theory of poly-psychism. In the theosophical kabbalistic framework, various psychological systems were explored, addressing concepts such as *nefesh*, *ruaḥ*, *neshamah*. Nefesh was considered the lowest faculty, emerging with birth, while higher powers like *ruaḥ* and *neshama* were received later as part of spiritual development. These concepts stemmed from different theosophical powers and contributed to the intricate system of poly-psychism.[1]

Changes in personality, according to theosophical Kabbalah, were gradual, with the reception of higher spiritual faculties linked to spiritual development, Torah study, and the performance of biblically ordained commandments. Neoplatonic theories and the concept of the cosmic soul influenced many Jewish mystics, emphasizing transformation as a return to a higher source. Under an umbrella of terms — metempsychosis, reincarnation, soul-impregnation — different concepts of the soul and its reincarnation were discussed. Various views included transmigration between human forms into nonhuman entities, and even into animals, with the goal of either exercising punishment for sins committed in previous lives or offering opportunities for self-improvement. The survival of the soul after a cycle of existence, unrelated to concepts of Heaven and Hell, represented a spiritual assumption transcending present personalities and the accounting for deeds. The higher soul, according to this perspective, retains a core identity throughout various incarnations, making choices and undergoing transformations in a continuous spiritual journey.

Judaism, and particularly Jewish mysticism, underwent a profound transformation within a relatively short period of time between the tenth and the thirteenth centuries. Absorbing certain psychological elements found in Platonic and Aristotelian philosophical texts combined with Arabic sources, medieval Jewish philosophers including Moses Maimonides, Abraham Ibn Ezra, and Bahya Ibn Pakuda turned toward the spiritualization of Jewish religious life in their interpretation of Scripture, the commandments, and Jewish theology. Neoplatonic speculations on the cosmic soul as an agent that connects between the upper and the lower created world brought the hidden but powerful interior world of the psyche into sharp relief. [2]

Academic studies concerning reincarnation (*gilgul*) in the early Kabbalah largely focus on tracing the appearance of this term as referring to a post-mortem transfer of the soul from one body to another — a process that is regulated by a certain system of laws relating to sin and the commandments of the Hebrew Bible.[3] However, the early layers of kabbalistic literature do not use the term in this sense. We do not find this meaning in the various sections of *Sefer ha-Bahir*[4] or in the writings of the kabbalists who were active in Gerona and Catalonia, continuing the path of Rabbi Isaac the Blind.[5] Based on Scholem's assumption that *Sefer ha-Temunah*, a work that employs the term on a number of occasions, was written in Catalonia or Provence in the mid-thirteenth century,[6] many determined that this work constituted the source for later usage of this term. However, it is now clear that *Sefer ha-Temunah* was in fact penned much later, once again confounding our understanding concerning the precise kabbalistic source that influenced the use of this term. Before doing so, I explore a term that was connected to the concept of reincarnation in the thought of the Geronese kabbalists. According to one of the common assumptions vis-à-vis thirteenth-century Kabbalah, references to the secret of impregnation (*sod ha'ibbur*) by the Gerona kabbalists often concern reincarnation of the soul, although some scholars, in particular Gershom Scholem, believed that this term had other meanings.[7] However, detailed investigations of kabbalistic texts that were written by or can be attributed to the Gerona kabbalists, in which scholars interpreted references to the secret of impregnation as alluding to reincarnation, cast doubt on this general statement.[8]

To improve our understanding of how these concepts developed, it is necessary first and foremost to focus on interpretations of the secret of *ibbur* (impregnation) rather than on *gilgul* (reincarnation), a term that was less important in the thirteenth century. If we do not do so, we run the risk of drawing anachronistic conclusions. Likewise, to further our knowledge about the two schools of kabbalistic thought in Catalonia, we must separate Nahmanides's discussions regarding this topic as well as his discourse on other issues from those of his contemporaries. Discussions of the secret of impregnation by Nahmanides's contemporaries rely only minimally on the discourse regarding reincarnation in *Sefer ha-Bahir*, thus, we should avoid suggesting that kabbalistic thought on this matter and others developed in a linear fashion and that the appearance of *Sefer ha-Bahir* constituted a definitive step in this process. However, even if we minimize the role of *Sefer ha-Bahir* in the development of the kabbalah, as a balanced assessment of the Gerona kabbalah and the prophetic kabbalah appears to suggest, we must set aside the harmonistic approach, which interprets the words of one kabbalistic school according to the terms used by another, based on the unproven assumption that in its early stages kabbalistic thought was relatively homogeneous. This is especially prominent vis-à-vis approximations of Nahmanides's discussions of the secret of impregnation with those of Rabbi Azriel of Gerona.[9]

Indeed, a close look at recent studies, such as those by Haviva Pedaya, Moshe Halbertal, Yair Lorberbaum, and Adam Afterman,[10] which touch on the figures mentioned above, have moved away from the harmonistic approach that previously ruled scholarship on early kabbalah. Yet traces of the harmonistic approach, which minimizes the phenomenological differences between the various schools, are clearly evident in recent scholarship concerning the kabbalah in general.

Reincarnation in Nahmanides and His School

According to Nahmanides and his circle, souls are reincarnated only three times after their first birth. This perspective differs from that of *Sefer ha-Bahir*, which maintains that one thousand reincarnations are possible. Almost certainly, Nahmanides's opinion on reincarnation pertains to the entire soul and not certain parts of it, unlike later kabbalistic traditions, which speak of the transfer of parts of the soul, or soul-sparks. Reincarnations are likewise not sequential, as certain beliefs posit, for example, the Druze tradition; rather, there is an interlude between one reincarnation and the next, during which the soul remains in the upper world. This temporal hiatus can sometimes last for hundreds of years. Furthermore, a human soul is reincarnated only in a human body and not in animals or lower beings — a theory embraced by kabbalists who lived in the generation following Nahmanides, particularly among the kabbalists of Castille. Similarly, these mystics maintained that male souls can only reincarnate into male bodies and Jewish souls could not be reincarnated into non-Jews, or vice versa.

In general, this kabbalistic school regarded reincarnation as an expression of divine grace, enabling the repair of sins caused by human transgressions, and therefore held that a perfect saint will not be reincarnated. In my opinion, this approach draws on assumptions concerning the importance of the commandments, which are a central tool in achieving repair (*tikkun*). Therefore, it is possible to perceive reincarnation as a certain type of rationale for the commandments. Nahmanides's approach to reincarnation is closely connected to the interpretation of biblical verses. Indeed, it posits a basis for understanding a lengthy series of biblical events. Only in the case of the ten martyrs is this approach associated with non-biblical figures, although their fate is connected to the sin of Joseph's brothers. Thus, the secret of impregnation constituted an integral part of the Torah's secrets. At the same time, texts by Nahmanides's students do not refer to members of their generation as certain reincarnations — first, second, or third — or as reincarnations of biblical figures, as we find in many other cases, particularly among the kabbalists of Safed.

For Nahmanides, reincarnation was explicitly connected to what he regarded as an ancient ritual — the institution of levirate marriage (*yibbum*) and its corollary ritual, which exempted the man from this ritual through the shoe-removal ceremony, or *haliẓah*.[11] He further highlighted the close connection between the levirate marriage and another foundational biblical commandment: *be fruitful and multiply* (Gen. 1:28). Both, he underscores, have been instituted as processes through which souls could continuously and without disruption return to the material world and repair those parts that became darkened and blemished because of transgressions committed in a previous life. Indeed, according to the school of Nahmanides, a person who has no children can never enter the divine presence.

The Secret of Impregnation (*Ibbur*) as the Impregnation of the Divine Presence

According to the kabbalists of Gerona and their sources in the Provencal Kabbalah, the secret of impregnation was not connected to the reincarnation of human souls in the lower material world, but rather alludes to the transfer of divine flow (*shefah*) from the upper *sefirot* to the lower rungs of the heavenly world. These writers posit that the cosmic stream stems from the sefirah *Ḥokhmah* and flows downward into the last sefirah *Malkut* identified with the *Shekhinah*, which was understood as the impregnated entity, the lower mother, who brings all of existence into being. The dynamic between the male and female aspects of the divinity was depicted as *hieros gamos*, a sacred act of coupling, according to which the female and male aspects of the Divine "unite" and procreate (*ḥibbur hakodesh*). At times, the meaning of this secret was further extended to encompass the descent of the heavenly affluence even unto select individuals who, through their extraordinary piety and devotion to God, were able to draw this flow down into the material world.

As Rabbi Ezra of Gerona wrote in the introduction to his commentary on the Song of Songs: "The *true* knowledge of God was transmitted to the forefathers who fulfilled the *Torah*, the *miẓvot* and the *'avodah* (divine service) from their knowledge of their Creator, their *'avodah* lacking nothing, as it is written,[12] *And Judah said unto Onan: 'Go in unto thy brother's wife, and perform the duty of a husband's brother unto her, and raise up seed to thy brother.'*"[13] Yehudah

Aryeh (George) Vida, who discussed the Gerona Kabbalah in a number of his studies, understood this short passage as dealing with reincarnation of the soul; indeed, he argued that the majority of kabbalistic interpretations of levirate marriage alluded to this.[14] However, it seems to me that these words constitute a general statement regarding the special qualities of the patriarchs; it is difficult to prove based on these brief sentences that this is an example of understanding the commandment to perform levirate marriage as connected to the secret of impregnation as a kind of reincarnation, as we will indeed see in the next section concerning Nahmanides's circle, and therefore as a commandment that extends to the secret of reincarnation. In my opinion, in his discussion of the meaning of the commandment to perform levirate marriage, Rabbi Ezra determines that

> to contract a levirate marriage with his brother's wife is to act benevolently toward the dead — that he will not be cut off nor will his image diminish[15] from the picture that contains all pictures,[16] and to give him an eternal name that will never be cut off (*karet*) — or to the ceremony via which a woman is exempted from it (*ḥalitzah*), and these are alluded to in the verse, "and to them that keep my commandments."[17] This alludes to upholding the levirate marriage or the *haliẓah*.[18]

Here levirate marriage is described as promising that the soul of the dead will remain intact, both in the upper world — in the sefirah *Malkhut*, which is the picture mentioned in the text — and in this world by means of offspring. At any rate, here there is no allusion whatsoever to reincarnation or impregnation.

Likewise, in other discussions, Rabbi Ya'akov bar Sheshet, a kabbalist from Gerona, demonstrates that reincarnation does not provide sufficient theoretical foundation to explain the meaning of the secret of impregnation. In his book *Faith and Trust* (*ha-Emunah ve'ha-Bitaḥon*), Rabbi Ya'akov draws attention to the unclear place of the "eagle" mentioned in Ezekiel's chariot vision (Ezekiel 1:4–28) in explaining the structure of the world of the heavenly chariot (*merkabah*). However, afterward he claims that "to everyone who is enlightened and wise he warned to reveal the matters of this attribute, and we do not impart the secret of impregnation to anyone apart from one who is in possession of the tradition of wisdom. I explicated this according to the true matter in the manner of the correct tradition that I received concerning the verse,[19] 'the patriarchs, they are the chariot.'"[20] Rabbi Ya'akov bar Sheshet's claim that he received traditions concerning the secret of impregnation in the context of the midrash about the three fathers of the nation rests on firm ground: in the quote from the words of Rabbi Ezra, we indeed find a connection of this kind, and it is very reasonable to presume that a link exists between these two discussions and that Rabbi Ezra's discussion preceded that of Rabbi Ya'akov.[21]

It seems to me that the words of Rabbi Ya'akov offer further clarity on the matter. Thus, the "eagle" here represents the last sefirah *Malkhut*, which alludes to David, who is the fourth leg of the chariot and the figure added to the three patriarchs, who are connected to the sefirot of *Hesed*, *Gevurah*, and *Tiferet*. Thus, the secret of impregnation has a certain connection with the final sefirah *Malkhut*, which is the divine presence (*Shekhinah*). If so, then the connection between levirate marriage and "the general picture of all pictures," which is mentioned in the second quote from Rabbi Ezra, appears to hint at the link between levirate marriage and the impregnation of the divine presence. I argue that, according to these Gerona kabbalists, the main focus of the secret of impregnation concerns the last sefirah. This assumption is likely, in my opinion, to help us decode a further discussion, which appears completely indecipherable, found in another place in *The Book of Belief and Security* (*Sefer ha-Emunah ve'ha-Bitaḥon*): "And even though I wrote all this, I am forced to say that the meaning was according to the [letter] *yud* and according to the [letter] *he* alone, which is close to the *yud* in His name, blessed be He ... And one will not understand the equal side between them, by the distance alone that is between them, but rather the secret of impregnation will reveal this principle."[22]

The two traditions available to Rabbi Ya'akov Ben Sheshet present different perceptions regarding the connection between the creation of the world and the letters of God's name: according to one, the upper world was created with the Hebrew letter *yud*, while the lower world was created with the letter *he*; another tradition determines that the upper world was created with *yud*, while the lower world was created using the letter *vav*.[23] In my opinion, the secret of impregnation (*sod ha'ibbur*) is connected to understanding the creation of the lower world, the letter *he*, and the *Shekhinah*, which is signified by this letter. Indeed, a contemporary of Rabbi Ya'akov, Rabbi Azriel of Gerona, also suggested, as we saw above, that "the secret of the divine presence" is the letter "*he*" identified further with impregnation. If so, the creation of the lower world by means of the letter *he* can be interpreted as the creation of the world by means of the divine presence or the last sefirah within the divine structure.

In addition, as we found in this tradition, apparently from Gerona, the descent of the flow, via "lines," is connected to the divine union (*hireos gamos*, in Hebrew *ḥibbur hakodesh*), which is connected to the secret of impregnation. It is reasonable to presume that this kabbalistic term hints, as I suggested, at the connection between a male sefirah — *Tiferet* or *Yesod* — and the last sefirah, the female, meaning *Malkhut* or the divine presence. Thus, understanding the theosophical process means the entry of the divine flow into the last sefirah and its impregnation. It is likely that this process is the source for the subsequent descent of the flow to the lower world, a process that can be interpreted as a kind of revelation. This explanation may account for the words of Rabbi Azriel in *Perush ha-Tefilot*, where we find a prayer for the return of the judges in connection with impregnation in a context that can be interpreted as a prayer for the impregnation of the divine presence, giving birth to the souls that will descend into our world. Indeed, an interpretation of the kind suggested here is found in connection with a discussion attributed, apparently correctly, to Rabbi Isaac the Blind himself, reported by Rabbi Bahya ben Asher:

> A tradition of the sage Rabbi Isaac the Blind, of blessed memory, regarding a woman impregnated with the letter *bet*.[24] And that which is called the secret of impregnation in the name of the force of the generations, which is "He that called the generations from the beginning,"[25] which is impregnated from the internal force,[26] and in the name that everything that reincarnates will do so from the force of the generations, therefore the secret of impregnation is called the force of the generations.[27]

In an additional passage, apparently stemming from the Gerona tradition and found in a collection of kabbalistic writings from the circle of the thirteenth-century rabbinic leader and kabbalist Shlomo ben Avraham ibn Aderet (Rashba), we read a commentary on one of the morning blessings:

> Another matter regarding the blessing, "Who did not make me a woman." I received [the tradition] that the female soul comes from the left side, all its *atzilut* is from *teshuva* to *paḥad Yitzḥak*, and from *paḥad Yitzḥak* to *hod*, and from *hod* to *rafe*,[28] it does not pass through the middle line at all.[29] And therefore all man's blood and all melancholy originate from the side of the mother. And the matter of the eunuch and women with masculine traits and persons of indeterminate sex and androgynous, they have a secret (*sod*)[30] in the secret of impregnation.[31]

This passage appears to discuss the ways in which various souls descend from the world of the sefirot, beginning with the third sefirah *Teshuvah* or *Binah* — identified as the supernal Mother in the kabbalistic system — to the human body. The "distortions" referred to in this passage, are explained as a result of the soul passing through the left line of the system of sefirot rather than through the middle. I believe that this reflects a perspective hinted at already in *Sefer ha-Bahir*, which determines that "the soul of the female is from the female."[32] Indeed this connection appears to indicate a justification for the "distortions," which imply a disruption in the way that souls descend in different lines from the world of the sefirot. Presumably the three categories mentioned in this text concern people whose gender is unclear and therefore cannot bear children.

A similar idea is expressed in *Commentary on the Aggadah* (*Perush ha-Aggadot*) by Rabbi Azariah of Gerona: "And the soul of the female suckles from the female, and therefore they instituted in the prayer: 'Who did not make me a woman,' because sometimes the souls change places and consequently barrenness occurs."[33] The assumption is that the souls are liable to change places, meaning that the soul of a male enters the body of a female and vice versa, thus explaining a woman's infertility: "she" has a man's soul. Thus, the explanation for barrenness introduced by the sixteenth-century legal authority and mystic Rabbi Yosef Karo — who learned it from his *maggid*, the divine voice that revealed itself to him intermittently — attributed the inability of one of his wives to bear children to the fact that she had a male soul. As we see based on the sources cited above, this was not an original idea at all. Rather, it continued a principle that was phrased quite clearly in the early stages of Kabbalah.[34]

If our analysis is accurate, we can conclude that the kabbalists of Gerona and their sources in the Provencal Kabbalah did not connect the secret of impregnation to the reincarnation of souls in this world; rather, it alluded to the transfer of the flow from the upper sefirot, apparently the sefirah *Ḥokhmah* in particular, to the last sefirah *Malkuth*, the divine presence, which was understood as the entity that gets impregnated in the context of sacred union between the male and female parts of the divine being. Sometimes the meaning of this secret was expanded to include the flow descending to select individuals in this world.

Ma'arekhet ha-Elohut: A Synthesis between Impregnation and Reincarnation

The most comprehensive theosophical kabbalistic discourse that integrates Nahmanides's teachings on both the impregnation of the *Shekhinah* and the reincarnation of the human soul is offered in the anonymously written fourteenth-century work *Ma'arekhet ha-Elohut*. Indeed, this work, which is generally based on the teachings of Nahmanides and his followers, albeit not on them alone, was apparently composed in Catalonia in the early decades of the fourteenth century.[35] Through a carefully constructed narrative that integrates biblical passages, midrash, and esoteric teachings concerning the sacrifices, the *Ma'arekhet* offers an interesting reading on reincarnation:

> What this matter alludes to in [the context of] the sacrifice of the new month with the term "to the Lord," when we explained regarding impregnation, because this is the time when the moon unites with the middle line of the sun to receive power and light from it and to rule the world with mercy, and to hint also at the secret of the sacrifice, because through it, "*ha'ishe*" [fire offering] comes close "to the Lord"[36] and there will be a ransom to protect against damages/injuries. And this is the matter of impregnation that descends downwards to the lower moon, in the secret of the pious ones of Israel, who know the time when [the *sefirot*] "*atarat Tiferet* is renewed, as in the recitation of the blessings of the new Moon, 'and to the Moon He said ...'" For when the bride and groom enter under one marriage canopy, then the month is sanctified and impregnated [*me'ubar*] by *Tiferet* and gives birth to the offspring (*'ubar*). And they have compared this matter to a pregnant woman, who gave birth in the presence of witnesses, who said that they saw the moon and the light of its impregnation, and they did not see [it], and they said of them that they are false witnesses. How do they testify about the woman that gave birth and the next day she is in an advanced stage of pregnancy?[37]

For the first time, we learn clearly about the connection between the secret of reincarnation and the impregnation of the *Shekhinah* embedded within a broader theological discourse centered on the sanctification of the new moon and the sacrificial offering connected with the new month. Although we already explored the notion of sacred marriage above, in the discussion attributed to Rabbi A., apparently Rabbi Abraham son of Isaac of the school of Rabbi Isaac the Blind, here the writer extends the discussion to include multiple levels of existence. Here the anonymous kabbalist suggests that impregnation unfolds simultaneously and in parallel fashion from the highest to the lower levels of the cosmos: first, in the divine world, in which the *Shekhinah* becomes impregnated; second, in the planetary world, in which the moon is impregnated; and in the lower, physical, world, through the impregnation of human souls.

The idea that impregnation can occur concurrently in three worlds is also articulated in a text composed by Rabbi Todros Halevi Abulafia a few decades before the *Ma'arekhet*: "For based on the case of impregnation, they will explicate all the ways and all the things that unfold and regenerate in the upper, middle, and lower worlds — both for good and for bad — and even in the highest of heights and in the worlds below them ... and he did not give me permission to reveal more until I will find a suitable place in which to speak."[38] Indeed, what is missing from the earlier discussion, which attributes to the secret of impregnation a more extensive meaning, similarly to Rabbi Todros Abulafia, is the motif of the impregnated moon, which returns again in another discussion, parallel in a number of aspects to the previous quote from *Ma'arekhet ha-Elohut*, and underlines that a number of other religious issues depend on the secret of impregnation:

> And we have already expanded upon the secret of creation and the reason for *'atarah* being a cornerstone, and the matter of the diminution of the moon according to the principle that we mentioned concerning it. Because many have failed in this matter and speak insolently about God, we will provide an explication, and the secret of the matter of creation will be revealed. And if we have already mentioned it, it is sufficient for the enlightened, and also the secret of the sanctification of the month, called the secret of impregnation, which descends downwards in the moon, will be revealed. And furthermore, the matter of the sacrifice of the new moon will be revealed, why we say in it, "to the Lord," and many more mysteries in the words spoken by them [the kabbalists], of blessed memory, will be explained, with great and diverse principles.[39]

At the center of this passage is the impregnation of the last sefirah, *Malkuth/Atarah/Shekhinah*, commonly associated in kabbalistic nomenclature with the moon, which, because of its position as the lowest and therefore the closest from among the ten sefirot to the physical world, endures constant attacks from the unholy, polluting, and demonic elements (*kelipot*) that populate the created world. The *Shekhinah*, therefore, always stands at the crossroads between the sacred and its antithesis, the demonic, expressed often in the idiom "cutting the shoots" (*kiẓuẓ be-netiyyot*). This expression hints at the danger of esoteric contemplation that is focused so singularly on the *Shekhinah* that it results in her disassociation from the rest of the divine structure, thereby causing her to be cut off and *inter alia* contributing to the separation between the lower and upper worlds.[40] And indeed, the *Ma'arekhet* devotes an entire chapter to enumerating various examples based on the kabbalistic notion of "cutting the shoots."[41] In a passage, the author of *Ma'arekhet ha-Elohut* connects the secret of impregnation to the secret of levirate marriage and to the last sefirah, highlighting the feminine symbol of the moon and its cycles: "Concerning the matter of cutting the shoots, it will become clear that it is heresy and sacrilege, the matter of the menorah and the citron (etrog) will be revealed . . . And based on this we will understand the reason for the secret of impregnation by means of the rule (*klal*) accepted regarding it together with the secret of levirate marriage and its matters."[42]

At the same time, the anonymous kabbalist of the *Ma'arekhet* adds a further layer to our understanding of reincarnation by distinguishing between an internal and external aspect of the process: "The second [sefirah] is *Ḥokhmah*, and concerning it, [Scripture] states, *But wisdom, where shall it be found?*[43] *Whence then comes [wisdom]?*[44] Awe (*yir'ah*) is *Ḥokhmah*, it is called awe, this [second sefirah combined] with the third [sefirah], and this is the internal aspect of the secret of reincarnation, which will be explained in the [later section of the work dealing with the] 'Gate of Destruction.'"[45] The word "third" refers to the third sefirah, *Binah*, which Nahmanides considered the ontological source of all souls, and the anonymous kabbalist refers to it here as the place from which the souls descend. This kabbalist also uses the term reincarnation as emanation (*hitpashtut*),[46] which accords with the use of the term here. The assumption that the secret of reincarnation of the souls in our world has a meaning or a parallel in the upper world, which is its "internal aspect,"[47] is very interesting, because it can explain the connection between impregnation and the world of the souls.

The author of *Ma'arekhet ha-Elohut* accepts on a number of occasions the theosophical conclusions of Nahmanides on reincarnation. For instance, he strongly advocates for delimiting the number of times a soul can return to the body and sets this at a maximum of three or four.[48] Another passage that evinces the influence of Nahmanides presents a discourse on the progenitors of humanity and the secret of reincarnation while also alluding to levirate marriage:

> Adam and Eve were the roots for [future] progeny, like the tree is a root for [its] branches. And since it is known that the roots do not give fruit, but rather the branches [perform this function], he [Cain] thought that his father will not engender more children, because he and his wife are like the root of the tree that produces branches, meaning him and his brothers and their twins, and the existence of the world is worthy

> because of them, in the form of the upper model.[49] And when God was not pleased with his offering, he decided to kill his brother, Abel. Thus, once one was lacking from the esteemed group, either the world would return to chaos, or it would exist because of him [Cain]. And he arose and killed him [Abel]. Yet another seed was raised up for Adam in Abel's place, and the world was founded on this, contradicting the thought of Cain, the fool who did not know and did not understand that even though the trunk does not bear fruit, at any rate when the branch dries up there is wetness in the root to bring forth another branch in its stead, which will bear fruit, and this is the matter of reincarnation of the soul, known as *sod ha'ibbur*, about which I will speak in the future. In the end, Abel's soul transmigrated into Seth and the world derived from him, because Cain was not worthy of the existence of the world, even though he repented because he had murdered.[50]

In this passage, Cain is portrayed as misunderstanding and therefore misrepresenting the secret mechanism of generation and creation, which is at the heart of reincarnation. His ignorance of the "inner" as opposed to the "external" aspects of this process led him to erroneous conclusions and heretical beliefs, which resulted in destruction and death. The reincarnation of Abel into Seth represents the secret of impregnation as a vertical process originating in the divine realm, from the influx of the life-spirit of Abel into the soul of Seth. In this radical interpretation of Scripture, control over life, conception, and continuity stand at the epicenter of the family drama that plagued the first family. Cain's lack of understanding of the subtleties and hidden modus operandi of the divine processes contained in the secret of impregnation, and alluded to by "the sap that remains in the roots," caused his transgression and downfall.

Last, it is important to emphasize a distinction that became blurred at the end of the thirteenth century and later in scholarly research regarding the basic difference between the perception of reincarnation in *Sefer ha-Bahir* and between Nahmanides's understanding of the secret of impregnation. While this idea is not mentioned at all in *Sefer ha-Bahir*, and in the sense that Nahmanides uses this term it does not derive from the teachings of the Gerona kabbalists, it once again gains a place of great prominence in Lurianic Kabbalah of the sixteenth century. Indeed, in this respect it seems that Nahmanides pioneered a singular kabbalistic attitude toward reincarnation that was subsequently adopted by those who continued his path. As a halakhist, he was less concerned with metaphysical problems, focusing more on the kabbalistic traditions that he received for interpreting the Bible and, in particular, the meaning of the commandments, with a special focus on levirate marriage.[51] This analysis, as we saw in *Ma'arekhet ha-Elohut*, also included the sacrifice for, and sanctification of, the new moon. The distinction between the internal and the external, the vertical or the horizontal, aspects of reincarnation almost completely disappeared in the generation after Nahmanides, in the writings of Rabbi Baḥya ben Asher and other kabbalists, such as Rabbi Menachem Recanati, and later still in the writings of Rabbi Meir Ibn Gabbai.[52]

Conclusion

In my opinion, there were three different trends in understanding reincarnation derived from separate theoretical sources, even if they became integrated, and the later tendencies built on the earlier ones. As early as the tenth century, various Jewish circles were aware that Jews in the East held beliefs about reincarnation, as we learn from the article by H. Ben Shamai.[53] Thus, presumably, a number of the ideas discussed above were not created ex nihilo at the end of the twelfth century and beginning of the thirteenth century in Western Europe. Rather, traditions that previously circulated in limited Jewish circles — perhaps outside the area in which the literary works were formulated — were set down in this period. The use of the term *gilgul* by members of Nahmanides's circle — Rabbi Sheshet; Nahmanides's student Rabbi Baḥya ben Asher; Rabbi Shem Tov Ibn Gaon; Rabbi Meir Abi Sahula; Rabbi Isaac of Akko; and in Italy, Rabbi Menachem Recanati — led to its spread and acceptance in later Kabbalah, including in *Sefer ha-Temunah*. In other words, the opinion of *Sefer ha-Bahir* regarding reincarnation of the soul influenced kabbalists who related only minimally to Nahmanides's distinction between the two topics, and over time the secret of impregnation was pushed into a secondary status, yet it rose to the fore again forcefully among the Safed kabbalists and their generation, albeit in a reductive meaning. Indeed, the especially secretive nature of this topic is evident also in much later discussions, even in the Safed Kabbalah.[54]

Notes

1. For my earlier discussions on reincarnation that informs the current analysis, see Moshe Idel, "The Secret of Impregnation as Metempsychosis in Kabbalah," in *Verwandlungen: Archäologie der Literarischen Kommunikation IX*, ed. Aleida and Jan Assmann (Munich: Wilhelm Fink Verlag, 2006), 341–80.

2. Idel, "The Secret of Impregnation," 341–43.

3. See Gershom Scholem, "A Study of the Theory of Transmigration in Kabbalah during the XIII. Century," *Tarbiẓ* 16, no. 2–3 (1945): 135–50 [Hebrew]; Scholem, "*Gilgul*," in *Pirkei yesod behavanat hakabala usemalaeha* (Jerusalem: Mosad Bialik, 1977), 308–57; Michal Oron, "Different Approaches to Teachings on the Soul and Reincarnation in Thirteenth-Century Kabbalah/*Kavim* le-Torat hanefesh veha*gilgul* bekabalat hame'a ha-13," in *Studies in Jewish Thought*, ed. Sh. A. Heller Vilensky and Moshe Idel (Jerusalem: Magnes, 1989), 277–89 [Hebrew]; Oron, "Musagei yesod bekabala vehitavutam," *Te'uda: Meḥkarim bemada'ei hayahadut* 4 (1986): 212; Rami Shekalim, *Doctrine of the Soul and Reincarnation According to Several Kabbalistic Writers in the 14th and 15th Centuries* (Tel Aviv: R. Shekalim, 1994).

4. See Scholem's analysis in *Pirkei Yesod*, 310–16, and Scholem, *Origins of the Kabbalah*, trans. A. Arkush, ed. R. J. Zwi Werblowsky (Princeton, NJ: Princeton University Press, Princeton, 1987), 188–98. I do not reiterate the matters discussed therein. Notably, I have yet to find the use of these passages among the students of Rabbi Isaac the Blind. See Gershom Scholem, *Das Buch Bahir* (Leipzig, 1923), 93, 111–12, 135–39. On the topic of reincarnation in *Sefer ha-Bahir* more generally, see Dina Ripsman Eylon, *Reincarnation in Jewish Mysticism and Gnosticism* (Lewiston, NY: Edwin Mellen Press, 2003); Mark Verman, "Reincarnation and Theodicy: Traversing Philosophy, Psychology, and Mysticism," in *Be'erot Yitzhak; Studies in Memory of Isadore Twersky*, ed. Jay M. Harris (Cambridge, MA: Harvard University Press, 2005), 399–426, particularly 420–26. I find it surprising that the passages from *Sefer ha-Bahir* discussing reincarnation are mentioned so rarely in studies of early Kabbalah. Verman presumes that *Sefer ha-Bahir* was written in the 1230s in Catalonia. This assumption is furtively connected to the assumption that Rabbi Azriel accepted the concept of reincarnation. However, if the following analysis is correct, and these kabbalists did not accept the outlook concerning the reincarnation of the soul, it is impossible that they were involved in one way or another in editing *Sefer ha-Bahir*, at least in its current form (Verman, "Reincarnation and Theodicy, 423–24). For an alternative position, which maintains that Rabbi Azriel wrote *Sefer ha-Bahir*, see Israel Weinstock, *In the Circles of Revelation and Concealment: Studies in the History of Philosophy and Esoterism* (Jerusalem: Mossad ha-Rav Kook, 1969), 35–76 [Hebrew]. Regarding the possibility of a Provencal editing of *Sefer ha-Bahir*, see Haviva Pedaya, "The Provencal Layer in the Editing of the *Book Bahir*," in *Shlomo Pines Jubilee Volume*, ed. M. Idel, Z. Harvey, and E. Schweid (Jerusalem: n.p., 1990), 139–63 [Hebrew].

5. Regarding this kabbalist see in particular the studies by Gershom Scholem, *The Kabbalah in Provence*, ed. R. Shatz Uffenheimer (Jerusalem: Akademon, 1963), and Scholem, *Origins of the Kabbalah*, 252ff; Haviva Pedaya, *The Divine Name and the Temple in the Teaching of R. Yizhak Sagi Nahor* (Jerusalem: Magnes, 2001); Mark Sendor, "The Emergence of Provencal Kabbalah, R. Isaak the Blind's Commentary on Sefer Ye" (PhD diss., Harvard University, 1994), two parts; Martel Gavrin, "The Concept of Evil in the Thought of R. Yitsḥak Sagi Nahor and His Students in Gerona," *Da'at* 20 (1988): 29–50 [Hebrew].

6. Scholem, "A Study of the Theory of Transmigration," 136–37.

7. Scholem, *Hakabalah*, 348; Scholem, *Origins of the Kabbalah*, 457; and indeed, in his study "A Study of the Theory of Transmigration," 138 n. 15, which is parallel to the chapter in Esther Liebes, ed., *Devils, Demons and Souls: Essays in Demonology by Gershom Scholem.*(Jerusalem: Ben-Ẓvi Institute, 2004), 192 n. 20. Scholem correctly noted that the secret of impregnation also incorporates other topics apart from reincarnation of the soul. See also Haviva Pedaya, *Haramban: Hit'alut — Zeman maḥzori vetekst kadosh* (Tel Aviv: Am Oved, 2003), 366, 376 n. 53, and Oron, "Kavim letorat hanefesh."

8. Scholem, "A Study of the Theory of Transmigration," 138. Scholem relates mainly to possible attribution of the material to Rabbi Yosef ben Shmuel, a less well-known kabbalist from Catalonia. This attribution is by no means certain, as delineated in the Hebrew version.

9. See mainly Scholem, *Origins of the Kabbalah*, 457–60, and Gabrielle Sed-Rajna, *Commentaire sur la Liturgie Quotidienne* (Leiden: Brill, 1997), 111 n. 1; and Oron, "Kavim letorat hanefesh," 284–86. On this harmonistic approach, which mixes the approaches of Nahmanides with those of the kabbalists of Gerona who belonged to a different camp, see also Isaiah Tishby, *Mishnat ha-Zohar*, vol. 2 (Jerusalem: Bialik Institute, 1961), 293 [Hebrew]. From this perspective, the scholars followed in the footsteps of some kabbalists from the end of the 13th century and beginning of the fourteenth century. Sometimes, as in the case of the words of Rabbi Ya'akov Bar Sheshet in *The Gate of Heaven* (*Sefer Sha'ar ha-Shamayim*) printed in *Otzar Nehmad* (1960): 153–65, understanding the verses that he employs from a perspective of reincarnation is an anachronistic reading by scholars who assume that certain passages were interpreted in the same way by different kabbalists who lived in the same period.

10. Haviva Pedaya, "The Provencal Editing of *Sefer ha-Bahir*," in *Shlomo Pines Jubilee Volume*, ed. M. Idel, Z. Harvey, E. Schweid (Jerusalem: Jerusalem Studies of Jewish Thought, The Hebrew University, 1990), 139–63 [Hebrew]; Haviva Pedaya, The Divine Name and the Temple in Teaching of R. Yizhak Segi Nahor (*Hashem vehamikdash bemishnat R. Yitsḥak Segi Nahor*) (Jerusalem: Magnes, 2001) [Hebrew]; Haviva Pedaya, *Nahmanides: Cyclical Time and Holy Text* (Tel Aviv: Am Oved, 2003), especially 209–73 [Hebrew]; Moshe Halbertal, *Nahmanides: Law and Mysticism* (New Haven: Yale University Press, 2020); Yair Lorberbaum, "The Kabbalah of Nahmanides on the Creation of Man in the

Divine Image," *Kabbalah: Journal for the Study of Jewish Mystical Texts* 5 (2000): 326 [Hebrew]; Yair Lorberbaum, *In God's Image: Myth, Theology, and Law in Classical Judaism* (Cambridge: Cambridge University Press, 2015; Adam Afterman, "The Mystical Dynamics of the Holy Spirit in Moses Nahmanides' Writings," *Jewish Quarterly Review* 113, no. 4 (2023): 639–68; A. Afterman, *And They Shall Be One Flesh: On the Language of Mystical Union in Judaism* (Leiden: Brill, 2016).

11. Deuteronomy 25:5–10.

12. Genesis 38:8.

13. Translation from Yakov M. Travis, "Kabbalistic Foundations of Jewish Spiritual Practice: Rabbi Ezra of Gerona — On the Kabbalistic Meaning of the Miẓvot" (PhD diss., Brandeis University, 2002). For the original Hebrew, see Nahmanides's *Perush 'al Shir hashirim*, in *Kitvei Rabeinu Moshe ben Nahman*, ed. Hayyim Chavel (Jerusalem: Mosad Harav Kook, 1973), vol. 2, 476–77.

14. Vida, R. Ezra, *Perush shir hashim*, 334.

15. Apparently influenced by the words of the sages in b. Yevamot 63b.

16. Apparently meaning the sefirah *Malkhut*. This expression recurs in many interpretations of the secret of levirate marriage. On the appearances of the expression in general, see Moshe Halamish's comment in his monograph *Kabbalistic Commentary of Rabbi Joseph ben Shalom Ashkenazi on Genesis Rabbah* (*Perush leparshat bereshit shel R. Yosef Ashkenazi*) (Jerusalem: Magnes, 1985), 148 n. 201 [Hebrew].

17. Exodus 20:6.

18. *Perush Shir ha-Shirim* in *Kitvei Rabeinu Moshe ben Nahman*, ed. Chayim D. Chavel (Jerusalem: Mossad ha-Rav Kook, 1967), vol. 2, 537. This quote is cited in the name of Rabbi Azriel in Rabbi Menachem Recanati, *Commentary on the Commandments* (*Perush leta'amei hamiẓvot*), Sh. B. Liberman edition (London: n.p., 1963), 72b.

19. See the midrash in *Bereshit Rabba*, 47:6.

20. Chapter 15 in *Kitvei Rabeinu Moshe ben Nahman*, vol. 2, 386.

21. For the discussions of the early kabbalists concerning this topic, see Micheline Chaze, "De l'identification des Patriarches au char divin: recherches du sens d'un enseignement rabbinique dans le Midrash et dans la Kabbale prézoharique et ses sources," *Revue des Ètudes Juives* 149, no. 1–3 (1990): 5–75.

22. Chapter 4, *Kitvei Rabeinu Moshe ben Nahman*, vol. 2, 363–64. See Scholem, "A Study of the Theory of Transmigration," 138, note 15, who notes correctly that here impregnation is not hinted at "specifically by the teaching of reincarnation." Compare with the discussion of Rabbi Todros Halevi Abulafia, *'Otsar hakavod* (Warsaw, 1879), fol. 29a, who suggests the following explanation for the midrash: "If man and woman merit [reward], the divine presence is between them; if they do not merit it, fire consumes them."

23. See Tzachi Weiss, "Shalosh masorot 'al bri'at ha'olam ha'otiyot," *Kabbalah* 17 (2008): 169–200 [Hebrew].

24. On the midrashic source of the discussion, see Shaul Lieberman, *Midrashei Teman*, 2nd ed. (Jerusalem: Sifre Ṿahrman, 1970), 34, quoted in Efraim

Gottlieb, in the name of Gershom Scholem, in his book *The Kabbalah in the Writings of R. Bahya Ben Asher ibn Khaliava* (Jerusalem: Kiryat Sefer, 1963), 31 n. 3 [Hebrew]. Concerning an impregnated woman and the *'ibbur*, see also *Tikkunei ha-Zohar, Tikkuna Shetita*, ed. Reuven Margaliot (Jerusalem: Mosad Harav Kook: 1978), 145b and also *Sefer Tsofnat P'aneaḥ* by Rabbi Yehuda Halliawah, Ms. Dublin, University, Trinity College 27, 5, B, 85a.

25. Isaiah 41:4. It is reasonable that the verse is interpreted thus: "The force known by the name *dorot* (generations) is impregnated from the force known as *rosh* (head)."

26. On this expression, which recurs in the writings of Rabbi Asher, see Daniel Abrams's ed., *R. Asher ben David: His Complete Works and Studies in His Kabbalistic Thought* (Los Angeles: Cherub, 1996), 105, 106 [Hebrew], and also Rabbi Ezra in *Perush Shir ha-Shirim, Kitvei Rabeinu Moshe ben Nahman*, vol. 2, 477.

27. See Rabbi Bahya ben Asher, in his commentary on the Torah, Deuteronomy 3:26, in Chavel, ed., vol. 3, 247. See Scholem's important comments in *Origins of the Kabbalah*, 459, n. 225; he mentions this passage as the words of Bahya. Notably, the mention of Rabbi Isaac the Blind as Rabbi Isaac, son of the Rabbi appears in other places among the students of Rabbi Shlomo ibn Aderet.

28. Meaning the attribute of justice is sefirah *Malkhut*.

29. Meaning that the soul does not go through the sefirot of *Tiferet* and *Yesod*, which are the middle line.

30. In several manuscripts the word *'inyan* (matter) is written rather than *sod* (secret). In the commentary of Rabbi Isaac the Blind on *Sefer Yeẓira*, printed in Gershom Scholem, the Kabbalah in Provence/*Hakabala beProvens (ḥug haRabad uveno R. Itsḥak segi nahor). Hartsa'otav shel Prof. Gershom Scholem*, ed. Rivka Shatz (Jerusalem: Akademon, 1970), 14, the birth of a person of indeterminate sex is explained as being due the "juxtaposition of the letters."

31. Ms. Oxford-Bodleian 1610, 99a; Ms. Cambridge Add. 671.[8], 125b; Ms. Harvard-Houton 58, 105b; Ms. Vatican 202, 63a; Ms. Parma, Di Rossi 1221, 112a; Ms. Berlin OR 942, 61a. A section from this discussion was printed already by Scholem in *Tarbiẓ* (1934): 318, and in note 3 he debates between attributing the saying to Rabbi Moshe of Burgos or Nahmanides.

32. *Sefer ha-Bahir*, ed. Daniel Abrams (Los Angeles: Cherub, 1994), section 140, 223.

33. Ms. Vatican 441, 53a, printed in *Likutei Shikhaḥa vepe'a* (Ferrara: n.p., 1658), fol. 14b and Scholem, *Origins of the Kabbalah*, 458, Rabbi Yosef of Shushan, *Perush leta'amei hamiẓvot*, negative commandment 17; Recanati, *Perush 'al ha-Torah*, 90d and compare also ibid., 98c, and *Sefer migdol yeshu'ot* by Rabbi Yehoshua ben Shmuel Ibn Naḥmias, who was active apparently in the fourteenth century, Ms. Mussaief 122, 40a, R. Cohen ed., 79. See also the words of Rabbi Moshe of Kiev, *Sefer Shushan Sodot* (Korets, 1884), 62a. Here the

juxtaposition is not a matter of the soul returning in a *gilgul* as it seems to be in the school of Nahmanides. And see also Scholem, *Pirkei Yesod*, 331, n. 55.

34. See Charles Mopsik's comments in *Le sexe des ames, Aléas de la difference sexuelle dans la Cabale* (Paris-Tel Aviv: Éclat, 2003), 90–91, n. 57. It is likely that the version printed in Ferrara predated Yosef Karo, who was raised with this perception. At any rate, the assumption that it is possible for a male soul to be reincarnated in a female body appears also in the Lurianic kabbalah.

35. On the kabbalistic background of this work, see Scholem, "Lebe'ayot sefer ma'arekhet ha'elohut umefarshav," *Kiryat sefer* (1945): 284–95; Gottlieb, *Meḥkarim besifrut hakabala*, ed. Joseph Hacker (Tel Aviv: University of Tel Aviv, 1976), 289–343; and Gottlieb, *The Kabbalah in the Writings of R. Bahya Ben Asher*, 18, 249–63; and Avraham Elkayam, "Between Referentialism and lebitsu'a: Shtei gishot behavanat hasemel hakabali besefer *'Ma'arekhet ha'elohut'*," *Da'at* 24 (1990): 5–40 [Hebrew]; Elqayam, "The Architectonic Structure of *Ma'arekhet ha-Elohut*," *Kiryat Sefer* 64 (1993): 289–304 [Hebrew]. For more recent engagement with the *Ma'arekhet*, see Levana Meira Chajes, "On the Discourse of Unity and the Discursive Unity of *Ma'arekhet ha-Elohut*" (MA thesis, Hebrew University, 2021); Ruth Kara Ivanov-Kaniel, "Gender and Power in *Ma'arekhet ha-Elohut* and the Zohar," *Da'at* 89 (2021): 193–217 [Hebrew]; Andrea Gondos, "Biblical Narratives in a Kabbalistic Key: Sin, Heresy, and the Destruction of Divine Unity in *Ma'arekhet ha-Elohut*," in *"Philosophy in Scripture": Jewish Philosophical Interpretation of the Hebrew Bible in the Late Medieval Period*, ed. Paul Fenton and Raphael Dascalu (Leiden: Brill, 2024), forthcoming.

36. See Exodus 28:11, etc. The theosophical explanation is *'ishe* = the female force, to the Lord = the male force.

37. *Ma'arekhet ha-Elohut*, 109a. An interesting parallel to this discussion is found in the words of the commentator on the book, Rabbi Reuven Tsarfati of the fourteenth century, in Ms. Paris in the National Library of Israel, 824, 159b. There is no doubt that the anonymous commentator was well acquainted with Nahmanides's discussion on the connection of the last female sefirah *Malkuth/Shekhinah* and the moon, the sanctification of the month, and the concept of reincarnation. See for example the text that I printed in Moshe Idel, "Perush lo yadu'a lesodot ha-Ramban," *Da'at* 2–3 (1977): 124 [Hebrew].

38. *Otsar ha-Kavod*, 6d. Of course this tradition does return to the claim that is hidden in the words of Rabbi Todros Halevi concerning *Sefer Ma'arekhet ha-Elohut*. See Michal Oron, "Ha'im ḥiber R. Todros Halevi Abulafia et sefer *ma'arekhet ha'elohut*," *Kiryat sefer* 51 (1976): 697–704. It should be noted that in the circle of kabbalists from whom Rabbi Todros received his kabbalistic traditions there is perhaps an allusion connecting the reincarnation of souls in this world to the *sefira Malkhut* in a rather explicit manner. See the words of Rabbi Yitsḥak ben Ya'akov Hacohen, quoted by Rabbi Isaac of Akko, and mainly in the commentaries of Rabbi Isaac of Akko quoted by Gershom Scholem, "An Inquiry in the Kabbala of R. Isaac ben Jacob Hacohen:

III. R. Moses of Burgos, the disciple of R. Isaac," *Tarbiẓ* 13, no. 3 (1932): 285–86 [Hebrew]. On the link between the secret of impregnation and the third sefira, see the words of Rabbi Yitsḥak Hacohen in *Sod ha'atsilut hasm'olit*, ibid., 261.

39. *Ma'arekhet ha-Elohut*, 106 a–b. The opinions about the secret of impregnation in this book, as well as those of Rabbi Isaac of Akko, greatly influenced Rabbi Menachem Tsioni in his commentary on the Torah.

40. On a comprehensive treatment of the concept of "cutting the shoots," see Tzahi Weiss, *Cutting the Shoots The Worship of the Shekhinah in the World of Early Kabbalistic Literature* (Jerusalem: Magnes, 2015) [Hebrew].

41. As Yehudah Liebes has shown that the symbolism of the moon in similar contexts existed a few decades earlier among the German pietists, see Yehudah Liebes, "*De Natura Dei* — 'al mitos hayehudi ve*gilgulo*," *Mesu'ot: Meḥkarim besifrut hakabala ubemaḥshevet Yisra'el mukdashim lezikhro shel Prof Efraim Gottllieb z"l* (Jerusalem: Mosad Bialik, 1994), 282–87.

42. *Ma'arekhet ha-Elohut*, 103a. Note the use of the term *klal*, which appears, as we noted above, in connection with the secret of impregnation three times in the writings of Nahmanides.

43. Job 28:12.

44. Job 28:20.

45. *Ma'arekhet ha-Elohut*, 50b–51a. See also the response of Rabbi Yosef Elkastiel, printed in *Gershom Scholem*, *Lurianic Kabbalah: Collected Studies*, ed. Daniel Abrams (Los Angeles: Cherub Press, 2008), 49–50.

46. *Ma'arekhet ha'elohut*, 91a–b, and see there also 149b.

47. On Nahmanides's use of this term, see the *Kitvei Rabeinu Moshe ben Nahman*, vol. 1, 15–17. In *Perush lesefer yestira*, printed in Scholem, *Meḥkarei ha-Kabbalah*, ed. Y. Ben Shlomo and M. Idel (Tel Aviv: Am Oved, 1998), vol. 1, 91, and also on the opening page of Rabbi Meir Abi Sahula, *Bi'ur 'al Perush ha-Torah*, a number of times, and also in *Sefer Ma'arekhet ha-Elohut*, 90b.

48. *Ma'arekhet ha-Elohut*, 149b.

49. Compare also the words of *Ma'arekhet ha-Elohut*, 91a and see also above, the text noted in note 200.

50. *Ma'arekhet ha-Elohut*, 127a.

51. See Idel, "R. Moshe ben Naḥman," 553–54; Yair Lorberbaum, "Kabalat haRamban 'al bri'at ha'adam betselem Elohim," *Kabbalah* 5 (2000): 326.

52. See in particular *Perush leta'mei hamiẓvot*, 72b–73d. Indeed, this distinction returns in the writings of a number of kabbalists of Safed, and it also made an important contribution to molding the teachings of the soul and eschatology in the thought of Rabbi Moses Cordovero and Rabbi Isaac Luria. See Scholem, *Pirkei yesod*, 337–49; Bracha Sack, "Some Remarks on Rabbi Moses Cordovero's "Shemu'ah be-'Inyan ha-*Gilgul*," in *Perspectives on Jewish Thought and Mysticism: Dedicated to the Memory of Alexander Altmann*, ed. A. Ivri, E. R. Wolfson, and A. Arkush (Amsterdam: Harwood Academic Publishers, 1998), 277–87; concerning Cordovero, in particular, see *Sefer 'Or Yakar*, vol. 13 (Jeru-

salem: Achuzat Israel, 1985), 4; and Boaz Huss, *'Ednei paz*, 164–66; Idel, "The T*Ẓaddik* and His Soul's Sparks: From Kabbalah to Hasidism," *Jewish Quarterly Review* 103, no. 2 (2013): 196–240. See also the kabbalistic works of Rabbi Judah Haliwa at the end of the first half of the fifteenth century and Rabbi Ovadia Hamon, who was active in the second half of that century in Safed, some of which remain in manuscript form. See in the meantime Moshe Idel, "R. Judah Haliwa and His Composition *Sefer Ẓafnat Pa'aneaḥ*" *Shalem* 4 (1984): 119–48 [Hebrew]. For more on the *gilgul* in the fifteenth century, see Rachel Elior, "Torat ha*gilgul* besefer *Gli'a raza*," *Meḥkarim bekabala ubefilosofiya yehudit ubesifrut hamusar vehahagut hamugashim leY Tishbi*, ed. Y. Dan and Y. Hacker (Jerusalem: Hebrew University of Jerusalem, 1986), 207–39; Rachel Elior, "The Conflict over the Status of Kabbalah in the Sixteenth Century," *Jerusalem Studies in Jewish Thought* 1 (1981): 177–90 [Hebrew], and the now-outdated article by Shalom Pushinsky, "Ha*gilgul*," *Yavne* 2 (1939): 137–53, which also briefly discusses the secret of impregnation, 150–51.

53. Haggai Ben Shammai, "The Transmigration of Souls in Tenth Century Jewish Thought in the Orient," *Sefunot* 5, no. 2 (1991): 117–36 [Hebrew].

54. See further discussion in Idel, "The T*Ẓaddik* and His Soul's Sparks: From Kabbalah to Hasidism," *Jewish Quarterly Review* 103, no. 2 (2013): 196–240.

ELLEN D. HASKELL

The Effaced Eagle-Man and Other Problems

2

REINCARNATED EMBODIMENT IN *GUF HA-ZOHAR*

Reincarnation as an Embodied System in the Zohar: Historical Observations

Reincarnation, though commonly understood as the transmigration of souls, is also a carnal phenomenon concerned with re-embodiment. While the journeys of souls and their parts through life, death, and transmigration have been much explored by scholars of classical Kabbalah, reflections on reincarnated bodies have been less common.[1] Yet the main sections of the multiauthored, late thirteenth-century Castilian work *Sefer ha-Zohar*, known collectively as *Guf ha-Zohar*, highlight the physical dimensions of reincarnation by interrogating reincarnated embodiment; that is, the conditions under which previously embodied human souls return to earthly existence through rebirth in newly embodied forms, and that return's effects on such bodies and the communities in which they find themselves.[2]

Scholarly interest in embodiment has grown in recent decades. Underlying this movement is the understanding that, while the human body is a uniquely apt symbol for complex social structures, these same complex social structures — which include religion, gender, and politics — reciprocally construct and interpret human bodies.[3] Attention to embodiment has reshaped the study of Kabbalah as well, extending it beyond the history of theology into investigations of kabbalistic anthropology, myth, and ritual. Far from an imposition of modern scholarship, this concern with the body's integration into social and religious structures is a central concern of Kabbalah itself.[4] Joel Hecker writes, "Embodiment acts as a primary element comprising the kabbalist's horizon as he envisions the world."[5] Such a view is consistent with Judaism's inherent character, which encompasses both theological teachings and the embodied performance of miẓvot. Furthermore, investigating the body in relation to kabbalistic tradition offers an important corrective to earlier scholarship that privileged the interpretations of medieval rationalists.[6] Reflections on the relationship between Kabbalah and embodiment can be found in the works of Moshe Idel, Joel Hecker, Marla Segol, Robert Jutte, Maria Diemling and Giuseppe Veltri, Roni Weinstein, and others.[7]

Guf ha-Zohar offers a unique opportunity to reflect on kabbalistic embodiment teachings through the lens of reincarnation, since it collects multiple views from the thirteenth century while presenting a system distinct from ideas expressed in kabbalistic writings that frame it chronologically, such as the earlier *Sefer ha-Bahir* and the slightly later *Tikkunei ha-Zohar*.[8] Bearing a strong resemblance to Eastern "karmic" reincarnation systems focused on individual action, whether ritual or ethical, these earlier and later works view reincarnation as a universal process governed by cosmic circumstance or regard it as a consequence of human sin.[9] *Guf ha-Zohar*, in contrast, presents a limited, non-universal version of reincarnation that marks a shift from viewing reincarnation as a redemptive aspect of divine grace toward understanding it as a form of divine punishment.[10] Its limited vision of reincarnation focuses extensively on reincarnated bodies, investigating what prompts such bodies' creation, their social consequences before and after death, and their presumed differences from non-reincarnated bodies.

In their treatment of reincarnation, the authors of *Guf ha-Zohar* (hereafter simply the Zohar) both construct and problematize reincarnated bodies in ways that can be read for insight into their own social concerns. These social concerns are centered largely on anxieties about the continuity of Jewish lineage and community. Reproductive success and the status of bodies in general also appear as formative tensions in the work's reincarnation teachings. By looking to the Zohar's cultural context, it is possible to suggest some motivations for these preoccupations. Topics surrounding the body, its procreative status, and Jewish communal continuity were indeed under stress during the Zohar's composition in late thirteenth-century Castile. These stresses engage all four types of danger from social pollution that Mary Douglas identifies, each of which prompts reflection on bodies as symbols of society: danger from external boundaries, danger from transgressing internal lines, danger at social margins, and danger from internal contradictions.[11]

Danger at the medieval Jewish community's external boundaries has been well documented. Interactions between European Jews and Christians became more tense and dangerous during the thirteenth century as Christians forced interreligious debates and engaged in aggressive proselytizing campaigns.[12] These debates and proselytizing attempts were particularly assertive in the regions where Kabbalah developed and where the Zohar was composed. Steven Kruger writes, "Body and embodiment were especially crucial terms in medieval Jewish-Christian interactions . . . Jewish thinkers and writers had both to respond to the accusation that Judaism was an excessively corporeal religion and to attempt to make Jews visible in their actual embodiment, without visibility becoming simply a spur to renewed violence and erasure."[13] Similarly, David Shyovitz notes, "In medieval Europe explorations of the workings of embodiment and the natural world were inseparable from interreligious polemic," identifying motifs in Jewish texts that respond to Christians' incarnational worldview.[14] This worldview involved distinctive ideas about Jesus's body, Christian bodies, and Jewish bodies, which were viewed as other to and deficient from Christian bodies — ideas that prompted Jewish self-reflection and defense.[15]

Debate between Jews and Christians also specifically engaged the topic of procreation, as Christians embraced clerical celibacy and came to view married life as a distraction from a life lived wholly in the service of God; scholars have demonstrated that medieval Jewish polemic works, kabbalistic writings, and the Zohar itself consider and react to such teachings.[16] This rethinking regarding the value of sexuality and procreation also threatened medieval Spanish Jews' internal social lines, as Jewish acceptance of Aristotelian philosophy, with its negative views of women, sensuality, and eroticism, called the virtue of engendering children into question from within the tradition.[17] Avraham Grossman and Tova Rosen identify an internal Jewish debate on marriage during this period.[18] Other thirteenth-century kabbalistic works reflect debate on married life and reproduction as well.[19] The most famous of these, the anonymous *Iggeret ha-Kodesh*, focuses almost exclusively on marital sexuality's relationship to procreation.[20]

Spanish kabbalists also experienced disruption at the margins of their communities regarding levirate marriage — a topic closely connected to reincarnation in the Zohar.[21] Divisions over whether to favor levirate marriage (*yibbum*) or the *halitzah* ritual that negated its necessity split European Jews.[22] Rabbinic authorities in Germany and northern France favored *halitzah*, while the Provençal community embraced both practices situationally. Spain — the outlier among European Jews — strongly preferred levirate marriage.[23] The kabbalist and community leader Nahmanides advocated for it, while Solomon ibn Adret suggested forcing unwilling women into such relationships.[24] The Zohar's reincarnation teachings argue in favor of *yibbum* and bolster the Spanish community's position against that of other European Jews. Indeed, the ritual of levirate marriage can be understood as one that enables people "to know their own society" by engaging the sociopolitical body through the medium of the physical body and its cultural duties.[25]

Finally, the Zohar's reincarnation narratives document its authors grappling with danger from internal contradictions, as new ideas about reincarnation and procreation came into conflict with more traditional beliefs regarding resurrection. None of these cultural motivations fully explains Zoharic reincarnation and its focus on family and communal continuity, but collectively they contextualize the work's teachings within a pattern of cultural debates that affected the kabbalists of late thirteenth-century Castile, where the work's main sections were composed. The boundaries of bodies, including those of men, women, the living, and the re-embodied dead all figure into the Zohar's sociocultural negotiations, as the work's authors strive to understand and construct their place within a society that includes the greater cosmos of the unseen world.

Procreation, Reincarnation, and Disruption: Tensions in the System

The Zohar's main interest in the doctrine of reincarnation is procreation: rebirth happens for the sake of birth, emphasizing the commandment to reproduce and its role in communal vitality.[26] This is not unusual for the Jewish tradition, in which the divine exhortation to *be fruitful and multiply* (Genesis 1:28) has long been considered the first commandment and therefore of preeminent concern.[27] Zohar 1:228b extends this commandment beyond death, linking it to the disposition of souls in the afterlife: "All who do not strive to produce children are not established in the world that is coming and will not have a portion in that world. And his soul ... does not find rest in a place in the world."[28] Likening a man without progeny to a barren tree that must be replanted in order to flourish, Zohar 1:48a declares: "A man who is blemished by not leaving behind a son in this world, when he goes out from it, he does not cleave to the holy name and does not enter into the curtain (*pargod*) . . . And a tree that is barren must be planted another time."[29]

Both the commandment to procreate and the act of reincarnation, as necessary theosophical consequence for violating that commandment, hinge on embodiment. The sin of not producing another embodied person in the world requires returning as an embodied person, until the deficit is erased by engendering a newly embodied person. The Zohar imagines this system as a disjunctive parallelism in which an old soul in a new body stands in place of a new soul in a new body. Solving the *miẓvah*-related problem of childlessness in this manner is reminiscent of medieval Jewish folktales, where punishment for bodily sins is expressed through the body in a "measure-for-measure" manner that emphasizes concrete connection between specific sins and their punishments.[30] As folklorist Eli Yassif explains, "The punishment . . . was not sending the sinner to hell or depriving him of heaven, but the imposition of concrete bodily suffering."[31] The Zohar's stance on reincarnation, too, takes a measure-for-measure approach in which the bodily sin of one's failure to reproduce is rectified through the punishment of bodily reincarnation. A person contributes to embodiment within the community by reproducing or by being reproduced, and reincarnation therefore represents a balanced punishment by providing the individual a redemptive opportunity to pursue and fulfill this key biblical injunction. Reincarnation associated with levirate marriage, which involves rebirth into the same family for the purpose of further birth within that family, is part of this pattern and contributes to Jewish continuity by extending a specific lineage.[32] In this sense, the Zohar's teachings on reincarnation share less with Eastern karmic systems than they do with West African and Indigenous American traditions, where rebirth happens along family lines, reinforcing communal connections with the past.[33] As Moshe Idel explains, the kabbalists' perceptions of individual bodies are reliant on those bodies' integration into larger social contexts.[34]

Yet the Zohar's focus on reincarnation for the sake of procreation creates tensions in the social institutions it seeks to uphold, inspiring paradoxical disjunctions in individual, familial, and communal continuity. These disruptions take two main forms. First, a reincarnated person has more than one body, and therefore has more than one family, creating conflict between an individual's multiple lineages and his roles within them.[35] He contributes to communal continuity while disrupting familial bonds. A man reincarnated through levirate marriage inspires disruption within a single lineage, since he is reborn as the child of his own former wife and brother.

His continuation as an individual contributes to his family's continuity at the expense of that same family's internal relationships, which he complicates in emotionally confounding ways. As Zohar 2:100b explains, "His mate has been lost from him. The mate that was his has become his mother, and his brother his father."[36] Second, because Zoharic reincarnation affects only the limited group of people who have not fulfilled the procreation miẓvah, reincarnated people and their bodies are considered different from those who do not reincarnate. Their status as better, worse, or merely distinct from the non-reincarnated drives further kabbalistic reflections on what qualities individuals carry between lives and how repeated embodiment might affect a human life in the world. While the complex permutations of the soul-parts *nefesh*, *ruah*, and *neshamah* described in the Zohar might be expected to help reconcile such issues, this is not generally the case; individual identity of both souls and bodies remains important to the work.[37] The collective result of these varying tensions is that, for the Zohar, reincarnated persons and their bodies occupy a paradoxical status, simultaneously maintaining and confusing social networks.

These contradictions arise in part because the Zohar embraces two distinct reincarnation systems, with neither resting comfortably alongside the other. *Gilgul* (rolling) reincarnation, a term used reservedly in the Zohar but more freely in later sources, refers to reincarnation during normative worldly time.[38] In the Zohar, *gilgul* usually is inspired by one specific sin — failure to reproduce — and affords opportunity for that sin's rectification.[39] On the other hand, the Zohar follows previous Jewish tradition by embracing resurrection (*tehiyyat ha-metim*), a final re-embodiment at the end of normative time.[40] Although resurrection is not usually thought of as reincarnation, it too is understood as a re-enfleshment that leads to further embodied experience.[41] The Zohar's authors are compelled to reflect on the relationship between these two different systems — a concern they share with other classical kabbalists.[42] Such attempts commonly understand *gilgul*-reincarnation to operate in the service of resurrection-reincarnation, though harmonizing the two creates conceptual problems. It is from these conceptual problems that the Zohar's main conflicts regarding reincarnated embodiment emerge. Without resurrection-reincarnation, *gilgul*-reincarnation's multiple family connections would remain unproblematic. And without *gilgul*-reincarnation's non-universality, differences between reincarnated and non-reincarnated bodies would not arise pre- or postmortem.

The Zohar's reflections on these types of disruptions may emerge not only from its sociocultural environment, but also from shifting notions in the history of Jewish thought regarding how individuals versus communities achieve lasting continuity. According to Jon Levenson, biblical literature subordinates individual continuity to that of the extended lineal group, so that "the hope for survival centers on the family, including (eventually) the extended family that is the nation, the whole House of Israel."[43] This concept remains active in the Zohar. Indeed, Levenson notes that levirate marriage is a legal fiction by which a family brings a dead kinsman back to life — an understanding that the Zohar adapts and spiritualizes in its teachings on levirate marriage and reincarnation.[44] This scriptural emphasis on descendants as the main means to triumph over death precedes and forms the backdrop to classical rabbinic notions of individualized afterlife in "the world that is coming" (*olam ha-ba*), and both views in turn underlie medieval ideas about *gilgul*, helping to explain the Zohar's ambivalent positions on Jewish continuity at individual, familial, and communal levels.[45]

The following passage from the Zohar's *Saba de-Mishpatim* (The Old Man of the Torah Portion *Mishpatim*), a textual unit containing many of the work's best-known teachings on reincarnation, summarizes the concerns that arise both from the disrupted family connections produced by the reincarnation process, and from the conflict between reincarnation and resurrection.[46] Problematizing the clash between these different types of re-embodiment, the passage anticipates the social confusion suffered by reincarnated individuals and their multiple families after the final resurrection, which involves the re-embodiment of the Jewish people as a whole. Its two main concerns are 1) given a sequence of multiple reincarnations, which body will a person occupy at the final resurrection?, and 2) how that final re-embodiment will affect a person's family connections, since their multiple families can be assumed to have resurrected as well? The passage also hints at the idea that reincarnated persons are different from non-reincarnated persons, since they are the only group to whom these questions apply and as such are the only ones to negotiate and theologically resolve these future problems. The text offers no constructive answers. Yet the passage ends on a positive note, emphatically underlining that no element of God's creation will be lost. The Zohar's willingness to hold such problems of bodies and embodiment in tension to press its case for procreation-based reincarnation highlights its authors' social anxieties regarding family and communal continuity: "At the hour that the Blessed Holy One arises to resurrect the dead, these that returned in reincarnation — two bodies with one spirit, two fathers, two mothers — how many reincarnations do they reincarnate through for this? ... And He will repair all, and nothing will be lost, and all will arise." [Zohar 2:105b]

In the next passage, the Zohar further problematizes the question of embodiment at the time of resurrection by asking what ultimately will happen to a reincarnated person's multiple bodies. The topic is staged as a conversation among three rabbis, with Rabbi Yosi and Rabbi Yitzhak responding to Rabbi Hizkiyah. Rabbi Yosi claims that only an individual's child-producing body will be resurrected; other bodies will not be. Rabbi Yitzhak argues that only a procreative reincarnated body will be resurrected with its original spirit, while non-reproducing bodies will be resurrected with spirits other than their original inhabitants. He does not speculate regarding the origin of these spirits.[47] His view reaffirms the Zoharic position articulated above (Zohar 2:105b, which similarly posits that God will not allow elements of creation to be lost). However, Rabbi Yitzhak suggests a further trial post-resurrection, in which the newly embodied souls either prove themselves worthy to continue existing or fail and become ashes.[48] Both views are conceptually problematic. Rabbi Yosi's dismissal of non-reproducing bodies contradicts the view that God would not allow any form of creation to be lost. Rabbi Yitzhak temporarily manages to avoid the loss of non-procreative bodies, but only by suggesting a further embodied trial that in turn may result in loss. Both rabbis separate reincarnated individuals from their families post-resurrection. Rabbi Yosi leaves some families with missing persons, while Rabbi Yitzhak offers a body-horror scenario in which a resurrected person or their loved ones might encounter a familiar body occupied by a stranger of unspecified origins, only to see that body traumatically destroyed:[49]

> Rabbi Hizkiyah said: If you will say that all the bodies of the world will rise and will be aroused from the dust, those bodies that were implanted with a single soul — what will become of them? Rabbi Yosi said: Those bodies that were not worthy and did not prosper, they will be as though they did not exist. As they were a withered tree in this world, so they will be in that time. And the last body that was implanted and prospered and took root as is fitting — it will rise. And of this one it is written, *And he will be like a tree planted next to water* ... [it shall not cease from making fruit] (Jeremiah 17:8). For it made fruits and planted roots and prospered as is fitting. And of that first body that did not make fruits and plant roots it

is written, *He will be like a bush in the desert and will not see when good comes* (Jeremiah 17:6). *When good comes* — this is the resurrection of the dead ... And then those former bodies will be as though they had not been.

Rabbi Yitzhak said: The Blessed Holy One will prepare to pour upon those bodies other spirits. And if they are worthy of them, they will arise in the world as is fitting. And if not, they will be ashes under the feet of the righteous. As it is written, *And many of those who sleep in the ground of dust will awake* (Daniel 12:2).[50] And all will arise and will be designated before the Blessed Holy One, and all of them will be counted. As it is said, *Who brings out their host by number* [calls all by name; because of His great might and strong power, no one is missing] (Isaiah 40:26). [Zohar 1:131a]

In the passage from *Saba de-Mishpatim* below, the venerable Old Man (Saba) addresses the problem of levirate marriage by highlighting the ambiguities reincarnated bodies create not only within their earthly families but also in the cosmic cycles of life and death. By becoming the child of his former wife and brother (the text's "redeemer") — now his new mother and father — the reincarnated man restructures his family. His lineage is repaired, but his past relationships are broken. Yet the Saba offers a partial solution. Rebutting the assumption that a non-procreative body must be lost to its original inhabitant, he explains that the original body itself attained merit. Lacking one critical commandment does not render it worthless; the body's other strivings in Torah continue to earn merit. Additionally, this body has already suffered punishment in service of rectification. The Saba seems to claim that the body itself can accrue virtue separate from the spirit/soul that inhabits it. Having erred and after receiving its punishment, that body will be rewarded at the resurrection with a portion of its original spirit if the reincarnated man successfully reproduces in his next life. This teaching offers a variation on resurrection in which the spirit is the restored body's reward, or the reward is mutually beneficial to both.

The Saba further suggests that levirate marriage inspires soul-sharing, a teaching that addresses the multiple-body problem of reincarnation and resurrection together, while introducing further personal disjunction. At resurrection, the miẓvah-possessing but non-procreative body of a man subject to levirate marriage gets a portion of that man's soul reserved by God specifically for that purpose. The reincarnated body receives a portion of the same man's soul drawn to it by his rebirth from his former wife and brother. It is unclear which soul inhabits the reincarnated body at resurrection, but since "nothing is lost," the reincarnated body may be understood to resurrect with the soul portion that inhabited it. Such a man is divided from himself before resurrection, and possibly after as well. This man becomes "the one that is two," occupying two bodies that are both in some sense the same person, divided between life and between death.[51] No part of him is truly lost, yet portions of him appear lost to themselves, distributed among multiple bodies that are still technically his own. Further, at least one body loses its wife. Procreation and duty to family lineage take precedence over romantic love.[52] Despite the Saba's restorations, his solution remains disruptive, creating tensions and ambiguities, pre- and post- resurrection.

> That first body that he left, what happens to it? Either this one or that one is in vain. According to our human understanding, it is inferred that the first one that did not complete itself at first is lost, since it was not worthy. If so, it was for nothing that he strove in the commandments of Torah — even just one of them! . . . And this body, even though it was not completed by increasing and being worthy and multiplying, observed other commandments of Torah that were not lost from it. And was it for nothing? Companions, companions, open your eyes! . . . That first body that he left is not lost, and it will have existence in the time that is coming. For it has endured many kinds of punishment, and the Blessed Holy One does not withhold the reward of any creatures that He created, except for those who have departed from faith in Him and never had any good in them . . . But these not so . . . If that spirit merits to be repaired in this world in that other body, what does the Blessed Holy One do? That redeemer who redeems him, that spirit of his that was inserted there and combined and mingled with that spirit that was in that vessel, surely it is not lost. And what does He do? For three spirits are there![53] One that was in that vessel and remained there, and one that was drawn there that was naked, and one that that redeemer inserted there and mingled with them.[54] To have three spirits is impossible . . . But rather, thus are the exalted mighty acts that the Blessed Holy One does. That spirit that that redeemer inserted there — that soul is clothed in it . . . and that naked spirit that returned there to be built will be a garment for the upper soul. And that spirit that formerly remained in that vessel flies from there. And the Blessed Holy One prepares a place for it amid the secret hollows of the rock that are behind the back of the Garden of Eden, and it is hidden there and raised to that former body that was at first. And with that spirit will rise that body. And this is the one that is two . . . [2:100b]

Yet if that naked spirit that returned from before merits to be repaired, worthy is he. For that spirit of whom it was said that it was hidden away in the rock will be restored to that first body . . . And these are the mighty exalted acts of the supernal Holy King, and nothing is lost. Even a breath of the mouth has a place and a placement, and the Blessed Holy One does with it what he does. And even a human word and even a voice are not in vain, and there is a place and a placement for everything. This [body] that is now built and goes forth into the world is a new creature. He has no mate. And for this one there is no announcement.[55] Because his mate has been lost from him. The mate that was his has become his mother, and his brother his father. [Zohar 2:100a–b]

Despite its strong emphasis on lack of procreation inspiring reincarnation, the Zohar offers reassurance that righteous individuals, who have sincerely tried to produce children but failed, need not be reincarnated. Their learning of the Torah and performance of the commandments (*miẓvot*) earn them reward. The following passage addresses these childless righteous ones while acknowledging that earthly assessment of perfect virtue is uncertain. In this teaching, levirate marriage offers the virtuous deceased spiritual insurance, and if unnecessary for him it becomes a community service for wandering spirits who lack their own brother-and-widow redeemer pairs. Underlying the teaching, however, is a threat to the childless man's widow. She is not released from her ritual duty even after a righteous husband's death and must do *yibbum* for a stranger, bearing and raising that man's reincarnation rather than her husband's.[56] Another teaching in Zohar 2:106a features a related set of concerns, distinguishing between one who tried but failed to procreate and one who willfully refused this essential commandment. The first reincarnates with his own mate, raising further questions about a woman's role in Zohar's discourse on reincarnation, while the second suffers travails whose cessation requires the non-familial levirate service described in Zohar 1:187b below. In both teachings, familial continuity is subordinated to communal need.

Rabbi Hiyya asked: One who is completely meritorious and strives in Torah, day and night, and all of his deeds are for the name of the Blessed Holy One, yet he does not merit children in this world — such as one who has striven for them and not merited or who had them and they died — what of him in the world that is coming?

Rabbi Yosi said to him: His deeds and that Torah shield him for that world.

Rabbi Yitzhak said: For them and for those who are truly meritorious . . . of them it is written, *Thus says the LORD to the eunuchs who keep my Sabbaths, and choose things that I desire, and hold on to My covenant . . . I will give to them in My house and in My walls a memorial and a name better than sons and daughters, an eternal name that will not be cut off* (Isaiah 56:4–5).[57] For these have a portion in the world that is coming.

Rabbi Yosi said to him: . . . A perfectly virtuous man, who includes all these, and is complete as is fitting, but dies without children and thus he inherits his place in that world, must his wife do *yibbum* or not? . . . She truly must do *yibbum*. Because we do not know if he was perfect in his works or not. And if she does do *yibbum* it is not in vain, because the Blessed Holy One has a place for that soul. Behold a man who was in the world and died without children and who did not have a redeemer in the world — when this perfectly virtuous man dies and his wife does *yibbum* and he has inherited his place, that one can come and be perfected here . . . The Blessed Holy One plants trees in this world. If they prosper, it is as is fitting. If they do not prosper, He uproots them and plants them, even many times. And therefore, all the ways of the Blessed Holy One are all for the good and in order to repair the world. [Zohar 1:187b]

Embodiment and Normativity: The Status of Reincarnated Persons

The passages examined thus far regard *gilgul*-reincarnation as non-normative since those who produce offspring in the normal course of their lives need not be reborn. This implies that the bodies and souls of persons who do undergo rebirth are non-normative as well. When *Saba de-Mishpatim* suggests that those who reincarnate through levirate marriage have a fragmented spiritual status caused by soul-sharing, it indicates that the spirits of individuals reborn through a levirate marriage are structured differently from the spirits of those who never reincarnate. Persons who have reincarnated with or without levirate marriage are different in other ways as well. Zohar 2:139a features a miracle child informing Rabbi Yitzhak and Rabbi Yehudah that they should avoid arguing with evildoers (referencing Psalm 37:1) since a person's reincarnation status is unknown. The child warns, "Perhaps he is a tree that has never been uprooted and you will be thrust down by him."[58] The text does not explain why a virtuous reincarnated person is weaker than a wicked non-reincarnated one, but it does connect reincarnation to weakness of spirit, body, or will.

The following text highlights the physical and theological ambiguities surrounding reincarnated persons by focusing on the questions of their sin, atonement, and spiritual status in relation to others in the Jewish community. Rabbi Hiyya's argument — that the reincarnated are more praiseworthy than remove non-reincarnated persons — hinges on the concept that spiritual merit accrues to the individual who has already experienced the punishment of death, which acts as absolution for sins committed in a previous earthly life. Such an individual's worthiness and portion in the world to come are established, unlike the uncertain futures of those born for the first time. However, the status of these returnees is different and deceptive. Though they appear living, "they are called dead," deemed as deceased even while occupying new bodies. Paradoxically, their physical demise in a previous life and the attendant suffering they endured already purified them, yet their rebirth indicates that their punishment and spiritual rectification are ongoing. Still, the text ultimately anticipates a positive outcome as their travails prepare them to be worthy for the world to come. Reincarnation here is portrayed as an act of divine grace bestowed on the individual that helps to raise his status by granting further opportunities for improvement:

> Rabbi Hiyya opened: *And I praise the dead who have already died [more than the living who are yet alive]* (Ecclesiastes 4:2) ... Another time, they departed from the world and were repaired in the dust, and it was appointed to them to return to this world in order to be repaired.[59] After that person's time is completed, he dies. Truly he is more praiseworthy than the rest of the dead of the world. If you will say, is he not judged another time in that world, as it is written, *Trouble does not arise twice* (Nahum 1:9). All the more so because he receives punishment once and twice. And therefore, truly his place is established with more excellence than that of the living who have not yet received punishment ... These are the living that are called dead. Why are they called dead? Because they have tasted the taste of death, and even though they exist in this world they are dead and have returned from among the dead. And furthermore, they are existing to repair their former deeds, and they are called dead. "More than the living, who are yet alive," since they have not tasted the taste of death and not received their punishment, and do not know if they are worthy of that world or not. [Zohar 3:182a–b]

Defining reincarnated persons as the "dead who have already died" indicates that such individuals are different and distinct from "the living who are yet alive." The next passage introduces a diagnostic practice for identifying these *gilgul*-reincarnated persons drawn from the Zohar's physiognomic material. The next passage introduces a diagnostic practice for identifying *gilgul*-reincarnated persons drawn from the Zohar's physiognomic material.[60] The Zohar contains two substantial physiognomic sections: the non-narrative *Mystery of Mysteries* (*Raza de-Razin*) and Zohar 2:70a–2:76a, which appears as a long descriptive discourse following a brief opening narrative. While these sections mainly provide instructions for reading physical features — that is, they describe an exoteric physiognomic practice that reads signs of the body's surface for insight into an individual's character — Zohar 2:73b–75b offers a glimpse into an esoteric physiognomy performed by kabbalistic masters intended to read "the mark of the features of the concealed face of the spirit that dwells within" (Zohar 2:73b). This practice of esoteric gazing renders an individual's status visible in his face, which reveals one of four spiritual countenances aligned symbolically with Ezekiel's throne vision of four-faced heavenly creatures, the *hayyot* (Ezekiel 1:5).[61] Three of these spiritual-facial types — the human, the ox, and the lion — represent qualities related to perfection, sin, and the potential for redemption, and do not indicate incarnational status. Their lack of specific connection to reincarnation indicates that these individuals are living their primary lives. A reincarnated person's spiritual countenance, however, appears as an eagle. This eagle-faced man exemplifies the problems associated with the religious and spiritual status of reincarnated embodiment in the Zohar.

Echoing Rabbi Hiyya's teaching above, the reincarnated person is both deceptive and non-normative. He defies esoteric interpretation, receding from the gaze even as he appears to it and suffering from an effacement that rebuffs physiognomy: "He is unable to be observed by observing the face." Instead, he is identifiable mainly through the lack of spiritual letters that would normally become visible to a kabbalistic master adept at such diagnosis. Occupying this paradoxical status of visibility and invisibility, he is alive, while numbering among "the dead who have already died." He is present and absent at once, to his beholder and to himself. This absence affects his experience: he lacks a "sparkle" that renders his joy less joyous and diminishes his happiness — a status reminiscent of *Sefer ha-Bahir*'s description of reincarnated persons as worn garments.[62] His physical and spiritual existence have been eroded through the process of reincarnation, though again the Zohar implies that his ultimate fate will be a redemptive reparation effected through this non-normative embodiment.[63] The text declines to tell its readers whether he is the product of levirate marriage or not, or what his status will be at the time of the final resurrection. Instead, it is concerned with the tensions of presence and absence that he holds in an uneasy truce. The effaced eagle-man is not what he seems to the casual observer. He embodies a ripple of cosmic contradiction that can be smoothed only through spiritual rectification. His status is secretive and ambiguous, and his renewed embodiment disrupts the normal state of humanity as paradoxically as the Zohar's reincarnation teachings disrupt the lineages that they seek to uphold.

> Fourth figure: This is the figure of a man who is always existing to be repaired for the mystery of the past. This one appears to the wise of heart in the image of an eagle. That spirit of his is a weak spirit. This one does not show letters on his face that project, because they were lost from him and receded at another time in the past and were removed from him, and therefore they do not project from him. His secret: His eyes do not shine with sparkle when he is joyous, nor at the time when he cuts the hair of his head and his beard, because his spirit does not shine with letters and his sparkle from before has receded. He is unable to be observed by observing the face. And the secret of this one: *And I praise the dead who have already died more than the living who are yet alive* (Ecclesiastes 4:2) [Zohar 2:75a].

Concluding Thoughts: Diversity and Determination

As is often the case with esoteric writings, the Zohar does not contain straightforward answers to the questions that it raises. Its reincarnation teachings offer no definitive resolutions to the tensions that they generate in the areas of *gilgul* versus resurrection, disrupted interpersonal relationships, or the status of reincarnated versus non-reincarnated individuals. Instead, the work tends toward self-reflection, narrativizing authorial uncertainties as unresolved internal discussions among its characters, or as mysteries alluded to but never fully explained.[64]

Still, some tentative conclusions may be drawn. Overall, the Zohar's teachings on reincarnation present rebirth as a redemptive opportunity to fulfill the divine commandment of procreation through the measure-for-measure punishment of re-embodiment, which leads to a second chance at reproductive success. The Zohar tends to characterize this second chance as a beneficial opportunity with an ultimately positive outcome. The passages above repeatedly reassure readers that "nothing will be lost," "even a human word and even a voice are not in vain," and "all the ways of the Blessed Holy One are all for the good and to repair the world." Although reincarnation is construed as a type of punishment, it is a redemptive punishment that points toward its own rectification. Non-procreative embodiment begets reincarnated embodiment that in turn begets a newly embodied member of the Jewish community. This encouraging attitude may arise from the Zohar's acknowledgment that while many commandments' fulfillment is under human control, fertility is not — a theme well-known from many Torah narratives and reflected in Zohar 1:187b's discussion of the worthy but childless man.

The Zohar leaves in place the most significant conceptual problems about individual, familial, and communal continuity that its ideas about reincarnated embodiment generate, even as its reflections on these topics indicate its authors' awareness of internal doctrinal conflicts. Such lack of resolution is characteristic of the Zohar, but also testifies to the intense, unresolved cultural pressures surrounding procreation and Jewish continuity during the work's main period of composition. These pressures came from Christians interrogating embodied religious identity at Jewish external social boundaries, from new philosophical trends that raised questions about marriage and procreation within Jewish communities, from conflict surrounding levirate marriage at the borders of European Jewish groups, and from Kabbalah's own theological contradictions as new ideas about reincarnation came into conflict with older beliefs about resurrection and afterlife.[65] Reincarnation, constructed as a problematized individual re-embodiment for the sake of continued communal embodiment, highlights these tensions without fully illuminating them. Ultimately, the Zohar remains more concerned with using reincarnation to assert reproduction's importance than with systematically resolving the questions about embodiment and continuity that reincarnation raises. This lack of determination is consistent with the scholarly observation that theories of embodiment are notoriously diverse. As Howard Eilberg-Schwartz writes, "There is often no coherent theory of the body, but a multiplicity of competing assumptions."[66] Perhaps more than any other topic of Zoharic speculation, reincarnation encapsulates the work's multivocal, nested writing strategy. Here, a group of men with multiple minds, bodies, and opinions — the authors — address the question of being men with multiple minds, bodies, and opinions — reincarnated and resurrected persons — through the lens of a group of men with multiple minds, bodies and opinions — the Zoharic companions.[67] This strategy's beauty lies in its diversity, rather than in its ability to offer firm solutions.

Notes

1. See Gershom Scholem, *On the Mystical Shape of the Godhead: Basic Concepts in the Kabbalah* (New York: Schocken, 1991), 197–212; Gershom Scholem, "Research on the Concept of Reincarnation in Thirteenth-Century Kabbalah" (Le-Heqer torat ha-*gilgul* ba-qabbalah be-me'ah ha-yud gimel), *Tarbiz* 16 (1945): 135–50 [Hebrew]; Gershom Scholem, *Kabbalah* (New York: Meridian, 1974), 344–47; Isaiah Tishby and Fischel Lachower, eds., *The Wisdom of the Zohar: An Anthology of Texts*, trans. David Goldstein (Washington, DC: Littman Library of Jewish Civilization, 1989), 2: 677–722, 2:749–776; Pinchas Giller, *Reading the Zohar: The Sacred Text of Kabbalah* (New York: Oxford University Press, 2001), 35–68; Michal Oron, "Lines of Influence in the Doctrine of the Soul and Reincarnation in the Thirteenth Century and in the Writings of R. Todros ha-Levi Abulafia," in *Studies in Jewish Thought* (Jerusalem: Magnes, 1989), 277–90 [Hebrew]. These sources also offer insight into the Zohar's teachings on the tripartite human soul, composed of *nefesh*, *ruah*, and *neshamah*. While the various soul-parts do figure into Zoharic reincarnation teachings, they do not substantially affect the material presented below.

2. This chapter agrees with the understanding held by many but not all scholars of Kabbalah that the Zohar's main body is the product of a group of mystics from late thirteenth-century Castile. Dating the Zohar's composition with precision is a topic of scholarly debate, as are the work's authorship and writing process. See Gershom Scholem, *Major Trends in Jewish Mysticism*, fwd. Robert Alter (Jerusalem: Schocken Publishing House, Ltd., 1941; rpt., New York: Schocken Books Inc., 1995), 163–68, 188; Yehuda Liebes, *Studies in the Zohar*, trans. Arnold Schwartz, Stephanie Nakache, and Penina Peli, SUNY Series in Judaica: Hermeneutics, Mysticism, and Religion, ed. Michael Fishbane, Robert Goldenberg, and Arthur Green (Albany: State University of New York Press, 1993), 11–12, 85–138; Eitan P. Fishbane, *The Art of Mystical Narrative: A Poetics of the Zohar* (New York: Oxford University Press, 2018), 38–50, 54, 184, 336–37, 415; Nathan Wolski, "Moses de Leon and Midrash ha-Ne'elam: On the Beginnings of the Zohar," *Kabbalah* 34 (2016): 27–116; Ronit Meroz, "And I Was Not There?: The Complaints of Rabbi Simeon bar Yohai According to an Unknown Zoharic Story," *Tarbiẓ* 71 (2002): 163–93 [Hebrew]; Ronit Meroz, "On the Time and Place of Some of *Sefer ha-Bahir*," *Da'at* 49 (2002): 137–80 [Hebrew]; Boaz Huss, *Like the Radiance of the Sky: Chapters in the Reception History of the Zohar and the Construction of Its Symbolic Value* (Jerusalem: Mosad Bialik, 2008), 43–44 [Hebrew]; Elliot R. Wolfson, "The Anonymous Chapters of the Elderly Master of Secrets — New Evidence for the Early Activity of the Zoharic Circle," *Kabbalah: Journal for the Study of Jewish Mystical Texts* 19 (2009): 144–45, 173–75; Daniel Abrams, "The Invention of the *Zohar* as a Book: On the Assumptions and Expectations of the Kabbalists and Modern Scholars," *Kabbalah: Journal for the Study of Jewish Mystical Texts* 19 (2009): 89, 111–13, 139.

3. See Mary Douglas, *Purity and Danger* (New York: Routledge Classics, 2002; Routledge & Kegan Paul, 1966), 142. See also Howard Eilberg-Schwartz,

"The Problem of the Body for the People of the Book," in *People of the Body: Jews and Judaism from an Embodied Perspective*, ed. Howard Eilberg-Schwartz (Albany: State University of New York Press, 1992), 21–22; David. I. Shyovitz, *A Remembrance of His Wonders: Nature and the Supernatural in Medieval Ashkenaz* (Philadelphia: University of Pennsylvania Press, 2017), 74; Maria Diemling and Giuseppe Veltri, "Introduction," in *The Jewish Body: Corporeality, Society, and Identity in the Renaissance and Early Modern Period*, ed. Maria Diemling and Giuseppe Veltri (Leiden, Netherlands: Brill, 2009), 2.

4. See Moshe Idel, "On the Performing Body in the Theosophical-Theurgical Kabbalah: Some Preliminary Remarks," in *The Jewish Body: Corporeality, Society, and Identity in the Renaissance and Early Modern Period*, ed. Maria Diemling and Giuseppe Veltri (Leiden, Netherlands: Brill, 2009), 251–53.

5. Joel Hecker, *Mystical Bodies, Mystical Meals: Eating and Embodiment in Medieval Kabbalah* (Detroit, MI: Wayne State University Press, 2005), 11.

6. Marla Segol, *Kabbalah and Sex Magic: A Mythical Ritual Genealogy* (University Park: Pennsylvania State University Press, 2021), 10–14; Robert Jütte, *The Jewish Body: A History* (Philadelphia: University of Pennsylvania Press, 2021), 9.

7. See Idel, "On the Performing Body in the Theosophical-Theurgical Kabbalah," 251–71; Hecker, *Mystical Bodies, Mystical Meals*, 1–18; Segol, *Kabbalah and Sex Magic*, 10–14; Robert Jutte, *The Jewish Body*, 3–5; Diemling and Veltri, "Introduction," 1–12; Roni Weinstein, "The Rise of the Body in Early Modern Jewish Society: The Italian Case Study," in Diemling and Veltri, *The Jewish Body: Corporeality, Society, and Identity*, 15–55.

8. Giller, *Reading the Zohar*, 38; Scholem, *Kabbalah*, 345–47; Scholem, *On the Mystical Shape of the Godhead*, 207, 209, 212; Tishby, *The Wisdom of the Zohar*, 2:692–93.

9. See *Sefer ha-Bahir* 155, 184, 185, 195. The edition consulted is Margaliot, Reuven Moshe, ed. *Sefer ha-Bahir* (Jerusalem: Mosad ha-Rav Kook, 1994). See also Giller, *Reading the Zohar*, 37–38; Scholem, *On the Mystical Shape of the Godhead*, 207–29, 212. See also Scholem, *Kabbalah*, 345; Gananath Obeyesekere, *Imagining Karma: Ethical Transformation in Amerindian, Buddhist, and Greek Rebirth* (Berkeley: University of California Press, 2002), 1–2.

10. Scholem, "*Le-Heqer torat ha-gilgul ba-qabbalah be-me'ah ha-yud gimel*," 139, 142; Oron, "Lines of Influence," 289; J. H. Chajes, *Between Worlds: Dybbuks, Exorcists, and Early Modern Judaism* (Philadelphia: University of Pennsylvania Press, 2003), 15.

11. Douglas, *Purity and Danger*, 151–52.

12. For a selection of sources on these developments, see Ellen D. Haskell, *Mystical Resistance: Uncovering the Zohar's Conversations with Christianity* (New York: Oxford University Press, 2016), 1–11; Jeremy Cohen, *The Friars and the Jews: The Evolution of Medieval Anti-Judaism* (Ithaca, NY: Cornell University Press, 1982), 62–63, 81–3, 105, 109–10, 125, 134, 157–58, 244–45, 249; Jeremy Cohen, "The Christian Adversary of Solomon ibn Adret," *The Jewish Quarterly Review* 71, no. 1 (1980): 52–53; Jeremy Cohen, *Living Letters of the Law: Ideas of*

the Jew in Medieval Christianity (Berkeley: University of California Press, 1999), 330; Robin Vose, *Dominicans, Muslims and Jews in the Medieval Crown of Aragon* (Cambridge: Cambridge University Press, 2009), 171–73; Yitzhak Baer, *A History of the Jews in Christian Spain*, vol. 1, *From the Age of Reconquest to the Fourteenth Century*, trans. Louis Schoffman, intro. Benjamin R. Gampel (Philadelphia, PA: Jewish Publication Society of America, 1961), 155; Ram Ben-Shalom, "Between Official and Private Dispute: The Case of Christian Spain and Provence in the Late Middle Ages," *AJS Review* 27, no. 1 (2003); Norman Roth, "Forgery and Abrogation of the Torah: A Theme in Muslim and Christian Polemic in Spain," *Proceedings of the American Academy for Jewish Research* 54 (1987): 227–28; Lucy Pick, *Conflict and Coexistence: Archbishop Rodrigo and the Muslims and Jews of Medieval Spain* (Ann Arbor: University of Michigan Press, 2004), 170; Mark Cohen, *Under Crescent and Cross: The Jews in the Middle Ages* (Princeton, NJ: Princeton University Press, 1994), 142–43; Robert Chazan, "Undermining the Jewish Sense of Future: Alfonso of Valladolid and the New Christian Missionizing," in *Christians, Muslims, and Jews in Medieval and Early Modern Spain: Interaction and Cultural Exchange*, ed. Mark D. Meyerson and Edward D. English (Notre Dame, IN: University of Notre Dame Press, 1999), 181–83; Miri Rubin, *Mother of God: A History of the Virgin Mary* (New Haven, CT: Yale University Press, 2009), 167; Hartley Lachter, *Kabbalistic Revolution: Reimagining Judaism in Medieval Spain* (New Brunswick, NJ: Rutgers University Press, 2014). Lachter's book argues that Kabbalah developed in part as a response to Christian pressure.

13. Steven F. Kruger, *The Spectral Jew: Conversion and Embodiment in Medieval Europe* (Minneapolis: University of Minnesota Press, 2006), xxiv–xxv.

14. Shyovitz, *A Remembrance of His Wonders*, 4

15. For examples of Christian thought about Jewish bodies and Jewish responses, see Ellen Haskell, "Countenancing God: Facial Revelation and Physiognomy in Sefer ha-Zohar," *Journal of Religion* 101, no. 2 (2021): 151–82, esp. 166–68; Irven Resnick, *Marks of Distinction: Christian Perceptions of Jews in the High Middle Ages* (Washington, DC: Catholic University of America Press, 2012), 12–18, 29–52; 291–93; David Berger, *The Jewish-Christian Debate in the High Middle Ages: A Critical Edition of the Nizzahon Vetus with an Introduction, translation, and commentary by David Berger*, Judaica Texts and Translations Number Four (Philadelphia, PA: Jewish Publication Society of America, 1979), 224; Ivan Marcus, "A Jewish-Christian Symbiosis: The Culture of Early Ashkenaz," in *Cultures of the Jews: A New History* (New York: Schocken Books, 2002), 500; Moses Gaster, *Studies and Texts in Folklore, Magic, Medieval Romance, Hebrew Apocrypha and Samaritan Archaeology*, vol. 2 (New York: Ktav Publishing House, Inc., 1971), 799; Marc Michael Epstein, "Dialogue and Disputation: Cultural Negotiation," in *Skies of Parchment, Seas of Ink: Jewish Illuminated Manuscripts*, ed. Marc Michael Epstein,(Princeton, NJ: Princeton University Press, 2015), 145; Lucy Pick, *Conflict and Coexistence*, 140; Norman Roth, "Forgery and Abrogation of the Torah," 227–28; Anna Sapir Abulafia, *Christians and Jews in the Twelfth-Century Renaissance* (New York: Routledge, 1995), 77; Daniel Lasker and Sarah Stroumsa, eds., *The Polemic of Nestor the Priest:*

Qissat Mujadalat al-Usquf and Sefer Nestor Ha-Komer, vols. 1–2 (Jerusalem: Ben-Ẓvi Institute for the Study of Jewish Communities in the East, 1996), 1:103 (section 28), 1:108 (section 50), 1:104–5 (sections 29–31).

16. I discuss the Zohar's critique of Christian celibacy in Haskell, *Mystical Resistance*, 49–55. See also Daniel Matt, trans. and ed., *The Zohar: Pritzker Edition*, vol. 5 (Stanford, CA: Stanford University Press for Zohar Education Project, 2009), 61 n. 176; Avishai bar Asher, "Penance and Fasting in the Writings of Rabbi Moshe de Leon and the Zoharic Polemic with Contemporary Christian Monasticism," *Kabbalah* 25 (2011): 293–319 [Hebrew]; David Biale, *Eros and the Jews: From Biblical Israel to Contemporary America* (Berkeley: University of California Press, 1997), 97–98; Yehudah Liebes, *Studies in the Zohar*, 144–56; Daniel Abrams, "The Virgin Mary as the Moon That Lacks the Sun: A Zoharic Polemic Against the Veneration of Mary," *Kabbalah: Journal for the Study of Jewish Mystical Texts* 21 (2010): 13, 18; Hartley Lachter, *Kabbalistic Revolution*, 97–98. For more on the Zohar's defense of Jewish marriage and marital sexuality, see Ellen Haskell, *Suckling at My Mother's Breasts: The Image of a Nursing God in Jewish Mysticism* (Albany: State University of New York Press, 2012), 92–95, 106–8; 151–54; Biale, *Eros and the Jews*, 97–98; Tova Rosen, *Unveiling Eve: Reading Gender in Medieval Hebrew Literature* (Philadelphia: University of Pennsylvania Press, 2003), 119; Elliot R. Wolfson, "Re/membering the Covenant: Memory, Forgetfulness, and the Construction of History in the Zohar," in *Jewish History and Jewish Memory: Essays in Honor of Yosef Hayyim Yerushalmi*, ed. Elisheva Carlebach, John M. Efron, and David N. Myers, Tauber Institute for the Study of European Jewry Series, ed. Jehuda Reinharz and Michael Brenner (Hanover, NH: Brandeis University Press, 1998): 217–18, 222–24, 240–41 n. 75, 242 n. 84; Elliot R. Wolfson, *Venturing Beyond: Law and Morality in Kabbalistic Mysticism* (London: Oxford University Press, 2006), 151–54.

17. See Haskell, *Suckling at My Mother's Breasts*, 92–94, 107–8; Biale, *Eros and the Jews*, 100; Collette Sirat, *A History of Jewish Philosophy in the Middle Ages* (Paris: Cambridge University Press, 1985), 163; Elliot R. Wolfson, *Language, Eros, Being: Kabbalistic Hermeneutics and Poetic Imagination* (New York: Fordham University Press, 2005), 265–66.

18. Avraham Grossman, *Pious and Rebellious: Jewish Women in Medieval Europe* (Waltham, MA: Brandeis University Press, 2004), 14; Rosen, *Unveiling* Eve, 122–23,

19. Rosen, *Unveiling* Eve, 122; Moshe Idel, *Kabbalah and Eros* (New Haven, CT: Yale University Press, 2005), 61–62; Biale, *Eros and the Jews*, 97–103.

20. Charles Chavel, ed., "*Iggeret ha-Qodesh*," in *Kitve Rabenu Moshe ben Nahman*, vol. 2 (Jerusalem: Mosad ha-Rav Kook, 2002), 321–37. Moshe Idel sees *Iggeret ha-Qodesh*'s defense of marriage and sexuality as a reaction against Aristotelian ideas about sexuality, especially as they appear in Maimonides's *Guide of the Perplexed*. See Moshe Idel, "Maimonides and Kabbalah," in *Studies in Maimonides*, ed. Isadore Twersky (Cambridge, MA: Harvard University Press, 1990), 43–44.

21. For reflections on *Saba de-Mishpatim* and levirate marriage, see Giller, *Reading the Zohar*, 36, 41, 54–60. Michal Oron connects the Zohar's reincarnation beliefs to rationalizing the seemingly irrational commandment of levirate marriage. Oron, "Lines of Influence," 286.

22. Grossman, *Pious and Rebellious*, 92. *Halitzah* signified the ritualized release of the brother-in-law to marry the widow of his brother by the woman untying/unsandaling the shoe on his feet as specified in Deut. 25: 7–10.

23. Grossman, *Pious and Rebellious*, 97–100.

24. Grossman, *Pious and Rebellious*, 97–98. Grossman connects these Spanish ideas to the Zohar's views on levirate marriage. See Grossman, *Pious and Rebellious*, 100–1.

25. Douglas, *Purity and Danger*, 159.

26. See also Elliot R. Wolfson, *Circle in the Square: Studies in the Use of Gender in Kabbalistic Symbolism* (Albany: State University of New York Press, 1995), 93, 209 n. 69; Scholem, *On the Mystical Shape of the Godhead*, 209; Giller, *Reading the Zohar*, 37–38, 55; Lawrence Fine, *Physician of the Soul, Healer of the Cosmos: Isaac Luria and His Kabbalistic Fellowship* (Stanford, CA: Stanford University Press, 2003), 305; Chajes, *Between Worlds*, 16.

27. Zohar 1:115a states, "A man, who merits children in this world merits through them to enter the curtain of the world that is coming. Because that son that he leaves behind . . . makes him worthy to enter into the inheritance of the LORD." Translations of the Zohar are my own and are based on Reuven Moshe Margaliot, ed., *Sefer ha-Zohar al Hamishah Humshei Torah*, 3 vols. (Jerusalem: Mosad ha-Rav Kook, 1999), with reference to Daniel Matt. In places where Matt and Margaliot differ, I note the difference and prefer Matt.

28. It is unclear whether "son" and "children" in these passages mean male children only or children in general.

29. The curtain, or *pargod*, refers to the curtain screening the divine throne in the utmost height of heaven. Known from *hekhalot* literature such as *3 Enoch* 45 and adapted by later Jewish esotericists — including the Spanish kabbalists and German pietists — the curtain was understood to record the history and destiny of human souls. See James H. Charlesworth, ed., *The Old Testament Pseudepigrapha*, vol. 1 (Garden City, NY: Doubleday & Company, 1983), 296–99; Scholem, *Kabbalah*, 121–22. Additional passages on reincarnation not addressed below include Zohar 1:13a, 2:91b, 2:106a, 3:7a, 3:217a, 3:308a–b.

30. Eli Yassif, "The Body Never Lies: The Body in Medieval Jewish Folk Narratives," in *People of the Body: Jews and Judaism from an Embodied Perspective*, ed. Howard Eilberg-Schwartz (Albany: State University of New York Press, 1992), 209.

31. See Yassif, "The Body Never Lies," 208–9.

32. Reincarnation associated with levirate marriage is a special concern of the Zohar's *Saba de-Mishpatim* section. See Giller, *Reading the Zohar*, 36, 41, 54–60.

33. Obeyesekere explains that among the Benin of Nigeria, babies are examined to identify which deceased relative has reentered the family, while among

some northwestern American coastal groups, new babies often are understood as close kinfolk who have been reborn. The Alaskan Tlingit have a practice by which women actively seek reincarnation of beloved relatives as the outcome of their own pregnancies — a practice similar to the Zohar's understanding of levirate marriage. See Obeyesekere, *Imagining Karma*, 19–20, 38–41, 53.

34. Idel, "On the Performing Body in Theosophical-Theurgical Kabbalah," 252, 271. See also Jutte, *The Jewish Body*, 52.

35. I use the language of "he/his" because most Zoharic reincarnation teachings focus on men, by and for whom the work was composed. However, Zohar 2:106a does mention women reincarnating along with their husbands (see Zohar 2:105b–106a). Gender in Zoharic reincarnation teachings is a complex topic beyond this study's scope. Some of the many studies on gender, sexuality, and kabbalah include Daniel Abrams, *The Female Body of God in Kabbalah: Embodied Forms of Love and Sexuality in the Divine Feminine* (Jerusalem: Hebrew University Magnes Press, 2004) [Hebrew]; Haskell, *Suckling at My Mother's Breasts*; Moshe Idel, *The Privileged Divine Feminine in Kabbalah* (Berlin: Walter De Gruyter, 2018); Segol, *Kabbalah and Sex Magic*; Wolfson, *Circle in the Square*.

36. This text is explained further below in the section on *Saba de-Mishpatim*.

37. For sources on tripartite souls in Kabbalah, see footnote 1.

38. Classical Kabbalah appears to be the first system of Jewish thought broadly to accept this belief, which eventually thrives in Lurianic Kabbalah and Hasidism. See Scholem, *Kabbalah*, 344–55; Fine, *Physician of the Soul*, 300–58; Giller, *Reading the Zohar*, 35–68; Chajes, *Between Worlds*, 17–31; Ronit Meroz, "The ARI's Homily in Jerusalem and the Kavvanot of Eating, from the Likkutim of Ephraim Panzieri," in *The Kabbalah of the Ar"I*, ed. R. Elior and J. Dan, *Jerusalem Studies in Jewish Thought* 10 (Jerusalem: Magnes Press, 1989), 211–57 [Hebrew]; Gedalyah Nigal, *The Hasidic Tale*, trans. Edward Levin (Liverpool University Press: Littman Library of Jewish Civilization, 2008), 195–211.

39. Scholem, *Kabbalah*, 345; Scholem, *The Mystical Shape of the Godhead*, 201, 209; Giller, *Reading the Zohar*, 36–37; Chajes, *Between Worlds*, 16.

40. For some examples of resurrection discourse in classical rabbinic literature, see b. Berakhot 33a; Pesahim 68; Sanhedrin 90b, 91b–92b. For a study of Hebrew terms for resurrection and related words, see John F. A, Sawyer, "Hebrew Words for the Resurrection of the Dead," *Vetus Testamentum* 23, no. 2 (1973): 218–34.

41. Pinchas Giller provides helpful summaries of these systems, as well as a third set of beliefs involving reward and punishment pre-resurrection. See Giller, *Reading the Zohar*, 35–36.

42. See Scholem, "Research on the Concept of Reincarnation in Thirteenth-Century Kabbalah" (Le-Heqer torat ha-*gilgul* ba-qabbalah be-me'ah ha-yud gimel), *Tarbiz* 16 (1945): 135–50 [Hebrew], see 142.

43. Jon D. Levenson, *Resurrection and the Restoration of Israel: The Ultimate Victory of the God of Life* (New Haven, CT: Yale University Press, 2006), 113, 118.

44. Levenson, *Resurrection and the Restoration of Israel*, 121.

45. The Babylonian Talmud frequently discusses the world that is coming. For a few examples, see b. Berakhot 4a–5a, 57b; b. Sanhedrin 88b, 90a–91b, 109a–b; b. Avodah Zarah 4a–5a.

46. For more analysis of this important Zoharic section, see Giller, *Reading the Zohar*, 35–68; Oded Yisraeli, *The Interpretation of Secrets and the Secret of Interpretation: Midrashic and Hermeneutic Strategies in Saba de-Mishpatim of the Zohar* (Los Angeles: Cherub Press, 2005) [Hebrew].

47. The teaching is similar to one of Jacob ben Sheshet's, in which bodiless souls remaining from the Creation are given these leftover bodies. Scholem, "Research on the Concept of Reincarnation," 142.

48. For further reflection on Rabbi Yitzhak's proposed system, see Daniel Matt, *The Zohar: Pritzker Edition*, vol. 2 (Stanford, CA: Stanford University Press, 2004), 233–34 and 234–36.

49. The passage's continuation indicates that the kabbalists expected a physical resurrection with rules similar to life on earth in a physical land of Israel.

50. For "ground of dust" (*admat afar*), see Zohar 2:100b and Matt, *The Zohar*, 5:43 n. 119; 5:79–80 n. 226.

51. For the sake of space, I decline to further explore the nested soul of the man who at first is occupied by "three spirits" but eventually becomes "the one that is two." For further reflection on this topic, see Matt, *The Zohar*, 5:42n17. For another rumination on *gilgul*-reincarnated bodies and their role at the resurrection, see Zohar 3:308a–b.

52. This is consistent with Giller's reading of love in *Saba de-Mishpatim*. See Giller, *Reading the Zohar*, 66–68.

53. Here I exclude Margaliot's alternative in favor of Matt's choice.

54. "Redeemer" signifies the *levir* (Latin for brother-on-law) — the dead man's brother, who inserts a portion of his spirit into the child. Delineated in the biblical portion Deut. 25:5–10, a sonless widow is married to her brother-in-law to generate an offspring for the deceased. The naked spirit is that of the dead childless man. The third spirit is evidently a portion of the dead man's that remained with his wife postmortem. See Matt, *The Zohar*, 5:41n116.

55. The announcement would be of his eventual mate.

56. The threat becomes more explicit when read in the context of Spanish Jewish ideas about levirate marriage as discussed above. The problematic treatment of women in the Zohar, particularly related to the question of reincarnation, affords material for a follow-up study. Questions of whether women reincarnate independently of their husbands and whether fathering only daughters negates the need to reincarnate are not clearly addressed in the text.

57. The redacted section of the text acknowledges the problem of male infertility.

58. This passage appears to be a less complete version of the *Yanuka* narrative of Zohar 3:186a–192a. See Daniel Matt, trans. and ed., *The Zohar: Pritzker*

Edition, vol. 3 (Stanford, CA: Stanford University Press for Zohar Education Project, Inc., 2006), 455n719. For the *Yanuka* (young child) and *Saba* (old man) narratives, see Yonatan Benarroch, *Sava and Yanuqa: God, the Son, and the Messiah in Zoharic Narratives* (Jerusalem: Magnes Press, 2018) [Hebrew].

59. Here I follow Matt, who prefers Margaliot's alternative.

60. This material is separate from the better-known *Raza de-Razin*'s physiognomy. In printed editions, *Raza de-Razin* (*Secret of Secrets*) occupies Zohar 2:70a–75a and appears alongside *Guf ha-Zohar*'s physiognomic section in separated columns. A section on reading the hands begins in Zohar 2:76a. Zoharic physiognomy inspires Isaac Luria's later esoteric metoposcopy. See Lawrence Fine, "The Art of Metoposcopy: A Study in Isaac Luria's 'Charismatic Knowledge'" *AJS Review* 11, no. 1 (1986): 82, 85 n. 11, 85–86 n. 12; Fine, *Physician of the Soul*, 153–54, 402 n. 18.

61. For a look at Zoharic physiognomy with references to studies by other authors, see Haskell, "Countenancing God."

62. See *Sefer ha-Bahir*, 122; Margaliot, *Sefer ha-Bahir*, 54. The permutations of inner and outer person are especially fascinating in this Bahir passage, where the garment, normally the outermost layer, seems to represent the spirit, which is normally the innermost layer.

63. It is possible that the absence of letters from his face indicates that the eagle-man has been repaired through reincarnation to the extent that the spiritual burden normally revealed through the letters has been wiped away, along with much of the rest of his personal affect. On the other hand, his visible/invisible status and lack of sparkle may reflect his occupying the world as one who is at once both living and dead. The text is intriguing but obscure.

64. For examples, see Haskell "Countenancing God," 151–82; Joel Hecker, "The Face of Shame: The Site and Sight of Rebuke (*Tazri'a* 45b–47a)," *Kabbalah: Journal for the Study of Jewish Mystical Texts* 23 (2010): 29–67; Fishbane, *The Art of Mystical Narrative*, 84–113.

65. See the introductory section of this chapter for further detail and Douglas, *Purity and Danger*, 151–52.

66. Howard Eilberg-Schwartz, "Introduction: People of the Body," in *People of the Body: Jews and Judaism from an Embodied Perspective*, ed. Howard Eilberg-Schwartz (Albany: State University of New York Press, 1992), 12.

67. For the idea that the Zohar's authors wrote themselves into the Zohar as the kabbalistic companions, see Liebes, *Studies in the Zohar*, 85–138.

PINCHAS GILLER

The Emergence of the Concept *Gilgul* 3

THE *SEFER HA-BAHIR* AND THE *BA'AL HA-TIKKUNIM*

R. Shimon opened and said *These are the statutes that you should put before them* (Exodus 21:1) and the *Targum* states "these are the laws that you should order before them." These are the orders of *gilgul*, the laws of the souls (*nishmatin*), for each one of them is judged to receive its punishment . . . Comrades, this is the time to reveal some hidden secrets of *gilgul*!
— *ZOHAR* II 94A

Kabbalistic Origins of *Gilgul*: The Case of *Sefer ha-Bahir*

Although the main sections of the Zohar are famously reticent about *gilgul*, reincarnation traditions had been circulating among kabbalists from the moment that the Kabbalah emerged in medieval Spain, France, and the Rhineland. The first "kabbalistic" book, the *Sefer ha-Bahir*, ascribed by tradition to the sage Rabbi Nehuniah ben Ha-Kanah, based itself on two general principles: one, that the soul was ontologically derived from the Divine, and two, that the soul on its path to perfection underwent a series of reincarnations.[1] These ideas were further developed by the Gerona and Provencal kabbalists as underlined by Gershom Scholem in his programmatic essays on the *Bahir* and other kabbalistic teachings on the soul.[2] My main goal in this chapter is to trace the beginning of the doctrine of reincarnation in the

Bahir and then to follow the evolution of this concept in Zoharic literature, with a particular focus on *Tikkunei Zohar* and *Ra'aya Meheimna*.

The *Bahir* accepts the phenomenon of *gilgul* without explicitly using this terminology. Introducing the cyclical nature of existence, the author of the text develops the theme of reincarnations using biblical allusions and the recurrent topos of generations that are replaced by earlier generations through the reincarnation of souls that lived previously. The author cites a biblical reference to link the cyclical nature of time with that of human fate: "What is the meaning of the verse, *The Lord shall reign forever, your God, O Zion, from generation to generation*? (Psalm 146:10). *From generation to generation*? R. Papias said: It is written, *A generation goes, and a generation comes* (Ecc. 1:4). And R. Akiva said: [that generation] has already come."[3] In other passages, the Bahir invokes the image of a garment. This image is built, as is common in the *Bahir*, on the midrashic parable of the king, representing the actions of God. The parable of the garment also distinguishes the transience and impermanence of the body from the eternality of the soul. "This is like a king who owned slaves. He dressed them in fine garments, which they neglected. He expelled them from his presence, exiled them and took the garments. The king washed the garments and erased the stains and prepared them again. He bought other slaves and dressed them with these garments ... so they benefited from the used garments."[4] Building on this image of the cleansing and purification of the soul, *gilgul* is further deployed in the text to resolve theological problems, such as the sufferings of the innocent or the righteous: "'Why is there a righteous person who has good, and [another] righteous person who has evil?' ... The righteous person (who is suffering) was wicked before and is now being punished. For the sins of his youth? ... No, [not for those committed] in this life, but [for the ones transgressed] in a previous one ..."[5] Another theological issue the author of the *Bahir* repeatedly grappled with was the number of reincarnations the soul was bound to undergo, a topic that would also come to preoccupy the theosophical kabbalists of Safed in the fifteenth century. Replacing the metaphor of a "garment" with that of a "field" allows the *Bahir* to introduce a theory in which reincarnation serves the purpose of the purification of the soul. Accordingly, each new return to the material world allows the soul to be weighed, balanced, and "cleared," so it would ultimately acquire greater perfection:

> A person planted a vineyard in his garden and hoped to grow grapes, but instead, sour grapes grew. He saw that his planting and harvest were not

successful, so he tore it out. He cleaned out the sour grapes and planted again. When he saw that his planting was not successful, he tore it up and planted again. How many times? He said to them: For a thousand generations. It is thus written, *The words that He commanded for a thousand generations* (Psalm 105:8).[6]

Here, the word "field" denotes the soul, while "planting" represents the deeds and life events that occur in the life of the embodied soul, which after having accumulated too much sin requires "clearing" in the form of death and a new life, just as a farmer clears his field. Finally, the function of *gilgul* is placed in an eschatological framework, where the soul's refinement and purification serve the function of creating a generation of perfected souls that is worthy of the coming of the Messiah. Alluding to a messianic prophecy cited in the Talmud, the *Bahir* demonstrates the esoteric properties of *gilgul*:

> He is All, and in His hand is the Treasury of Souls. And when Israel is good, souls are worthy to come and go. If they are unworthy for this world, and if they are unworthy, they do not go out. So, we say, "the Son of David will not come until all souls in the body have been consumed."[7] Then the new ones will come and the Son of David will be worthy to be born, they will be worthy that new ones go out. And then Son of David succeeds in being born, for his soul will go anew with all the others.[8]

Through these passages the *Bahir* was one of the earliest texts of Kabbalah to present a sustained discourse on the doctrine of *gilgul*, which would find full expression in Zoharic literature and be further expanded by the Safedian kabbalists of the sixteenth century. As a central mystery and object of speculation, reincarnation served as the lynchpin of the entire speculative system developed by Isaac Luria and his student Hayyim Vital, yet its origins seem to lie in a largely forgotten and obscure text that has nonetheless fascinated the scholarly study of Kabbalah. Thus, the *Bahir* has served as something of a muse or object of fascination for subsequent scholars of Kabbalah, and its few enigmatic passages on reincarnation set a modest template for what was to come.

Variant Doctrines of Reincarnation Cycles in the *Tikkunim*

If one reads the Zohar as a book,[9] one will find in the later sections of the text, such as the *Tikkunei ha-Zohar* ("Aspects of the Zohar") and *Ra'aya Meheimna* ("The Faithful Shepherd"), a bold theory of the transmigration of the soul that goes far beyond the reticent positions expressed in the main sections of the Zohar. These writings portray reincarnation in ways that would become normative in sixteenth-century Kabbalah.[10] The mysterious author, whom we call the "*Ba'al ha-Tikkunim*" or "Master of the *Tikkunim*," has been the object of scholarly interest for as long as scholars have addressed Kabbalah.[11] Among the kabbalists who predated the *Ba'al ha-Tikkunim*, the teachings regarding the soul contradicted one another. The doctrine of resurrection at the end of time conflicts with the concurrent afterlife of the *nefesh*, *ruaḥ*, and *neshamah* found in the early sections of the Zohar. If the *nefesh*, *ruaḥ*, and *ruaḥ* had set roles and gone — upon an individual's death — to finite places, at what point did the process of reincarnation take place?[12] The initial reason for *gilgul*, as posited in the virtuosic composition *Sabba de-Mishpatim*, was to resolve the problem of suffering, particularly the anguish of oppressed children.[13]

In his self-conscious use of the term *gilgul*, and in connecting it to prior *Zoharic* themes, the *Ba'al ha-Tikkunim* certainly set the stage for the flourishing of the concept in later Kabbalah. The implication of this teaching, which would be fleshed out in the teachings of the Galilean kabbalists, is that in every reincarnation a person has to "fix" a certain aspect of his soul. This idea resembles the work of reincarnation in Eastern religions, which is to expunge the particular karma that has attached to one's soul in a past life.[14] When this process is completed, the soul undergoes a final liberation, as it has a reincarnation in the realm of the *Shekhinah*, the sefirah *Malkhut*. In fact, the *Ba'al ha-Tikkunim* "had before him all the sections of the Zohar, and since he found that they differed from, and even contradicted, one another, he tried to reconcile them and produce one unified system."[15] He took the Zohar's earlier implications regarding *gilgul* and moved those ideas toward the doctrines that would become normative as Kabbalah became a more popular, national enterprise in the late Middle Ages and early Renaissance. His ideas underlay the systematic presentations of *gilgul* in later speculative thought. The two main kabbalists of Safed, Moshe Cordovero (1522–1570) and Isaac Luria (1534–1572), based their understandings of reincarnation on this idea.

The enigmatic persona of the *Ba'al ha-Tikkunim*, his dark preoccupations and romantic conceits, have been the subject of a number of recent studies that underscore his style of writing as wildly associative and possibly the result of a mystical practice of automatic writing.[16] He is portrayed as a lonely outsider, perhaps the last of the original circle of kabbalists who compiled the Zohar, and the last who was in on the literary conceit of its composition, the pseudepigraphal record of a circle of medieval Castillean kabbalists who chose to cloak their activities in an imagined Galilee in late antiquity. Otherwise, his theology was sound, besting that of the Zohar's main sections. His understanding of divine immanence, the separation of the divine emanation into God's essence (*aẓmut*) and vessels (*kelim*), his absorption of the four worlds of creation and his adaptation of the Zohar's latter doctrine of the divine countenance, make him the more sophisticated kabbalist and, arguably, the more consistent theologian of Judaism, notwithstanding his full embrace of reincarnation as a pillar of his mysticism.

In the compositions, which are scattered across the *Zoharic* canon, two doctrines of *gilgul* exist uneasily under the aegis of a single author. The most common doctrine articulates that there are six reincarnations or *gilgulim*, which, according to the basic doctrine of theosophical Kabbalah, correspond to the six intermediate sefirot of the sefirotic tree. Each of these reincarnations is devoted to resolving outstanding issues of the soul according to the defining nature of each of the six intermediate sefirot, which frequently have been interpreted in a psychological key. These sefirot exemplify six aspects of the human psyche: lovingkindness, judgment, mercy, existence, prestige, and sexuality. In linking *gilgul* to emotional qualities, the author implies that the soul is reincarnated because there is something to fix, correct, or cleanse in its ethical character. Hence there would be a reincarnation to address sexual issues, for instance, corresponding to the sefirah *Yesod*, a reincarnation to resolve issues of judgment for the sefirah *Gevurah*, lovingkindness for the sefirah *Ḥesed*, and so forth. The soul's empowerment comes from the psychic energies of the middle six sefirot when they are gathered under the control of the sefirah *Tiferet*.

Metatron is the demiurgic angel, who, according to the *Tikkunim*, governs the successive cycles of *gilgul* and is therefore called "the higher servant."[17] From the *Tikkunim* to the teachings of the Vilna Gaon, "Metatron" is identified with both the demiurgic angel derived from the ancient mystical tradition of the Heikhalot or Palace texts as well as the embodiment of the intermediate sefirot that are subsumed under the sefirah *Tiferet*.[18] In his central statement on *gilgul*, the *Ba'al ha-Tikkunim* associates *gilgul* with slavery and identifies it with the domain of Metatron, who as a servant is in charge of judging and meting out the sentence of a soul in need of purification: "When a soul (*neshamah*) is sentenced to *gilgul*, if it is from the realm of the servant Metatron, which encompasses six aspects; it is written of him, *six years shall he labor* (Exodus 21:2) his sentence of *gilgul* will only be for six years, until he completes the six levels."[19] Life in the present reality is depicted as a form of slavery for the "enslaved," feminized highest level of the soul (*neshamah*), or divine soul. In this tradition and at this point, Metatron has been reduced from his personal, mythic identity — the demiurge of early Jewish esotericism — to a mere confluence of energies, a certain configuration of sefirot, rather than a mythic personality.

In his conception of Metatron, the *Ba'al ha-Tikkunim* speaks of six "aspects," thus implying that Metatron is the confluence of the middle six sefirot, not merely the penultimate sefirah *Yesod* or the final level of the *Shekhinah*, both of which had been invoked as spiritual "locations" for Metatron by other kabbalistic traditions.[20] Another passage speaks of six "drops" of *gilgul*, with the implication that they are seminal emissions, a secretion of the divine mind:[21] "In you is contingent the redemption of the *Shekhinah* and her children, in order to fix what was destroyed before. And because of your love, six drops of *gilgul* return to you, which are implied in your highest branches, these are *shin shin* (ש ש), doubled as in *Moses Moses*" (Exodus 3:4). The six reincarnations are comparable to the six days of the week, and the final reincarnation acts as a release similar to the Sabbath, which is free of "labor," namely the "enslavement of being reincarnated."[22] The penultimate *gilgul* is in the persona of the *Ẓaddik*, "righteous saint," who in kabbalistic parlance has mastered his sexual desires and is therefore poised for union with the *Shekhinah*, the feminine divine presence.[23] The *gilgul* of the *Ẓaddik* commits the soul to an incarnation that benefits the entire generation into which it is born. [24] This is, as well, the *gilgul* of *Yesod*, the sefirah that governs sexuality. Many overlapping images are employed to invoke the *Ẓaddik*'s incarnation. Images of the last reincarnation include the letter *vav*, whose numerical coefficient is six, the pointillistic *yud* and the *vav*, the *Ẓaddik*, and, implicitly, his union with the *Shekhinah*.[25] All of these images are presented in the *Ba'al ha-Tikkunim*'s characteristic narrative reinforcing the idea of six incarnations, corresponding to the middle six sefirot, with redemption coming at the onset of the seventh incarnation:

> Moses is reincarnated in the complete *Ẓaddik*, and when the *Ẓaddik* is incomplete, he returns in *gilgul* until he finds his place . . . and if their *gilgul* causes them to have the experience of the wicked, they will have the sufferings of the wicked, for their *neshamot* are from the realm of Adam and Abel, who sinned in thought and action . . . When the evil are successful, it is similarly because of their earlier *gilgulim* as *Ẓaddikim* . . . How many *gilgulim* they will have from the Holy Blessed One to give them their reward in this world.[26]

At the same time, the author avers that[27] in the final incarnation, the soul has attained the status of the *Shekhinah* herself. This incarnation at the level of the *Shekhinah* releases the soul from the cycle of *gilgul*, so that the enslaved soul can go "utterly free."[28] The process of working toward the seventh *gilgul*, with its release from the cycle of birth and death, is the ultimate goal of the *gilgul* cycle. This release, with its sense of redemptive liberation from the bondage of life, is the goal in the *Ba'al ha-Tikkunim*'s worldview.

Alongside traditions that emphasize six reincarnations, there are alternative teachings that posit three incarnations.[29] Reflecting the earlier school of Geronese Kabbalah, the *Ba'al ha-Tikkunim* evokes the biblical passage *God does all these things to a person — twice, even three times* (Job 33:29) to set the limit of the reincarnation at three.[30] In light of this latter doctrine, there is a recurrent image of "three drops" secreted from the divine mind, or, as Gershom Scholem understood them, three sparks of existence.[31] "Three drops flow from the hidden consciousness, these are the three *gilgulim*, three drops ... like three forefathers, from which a man descends in three *gilgulim*, like the three pieces of unleavened bread (*matzot*) on Passover."[32] The three *gilgulim* and the three drops are symbolized by the Hebrew vowel *segol* (ֶ).[33] At the same time, it is unclear whether the drops are secretions of the cosmic phallus or synapses of the divine mind. "There are three *gilgulim* which are the three forefathers, of whom it says, *all these things God will do, twice or three times with man*, they are his salvation and his redemption because the Holy Blessed One has no right to bring him out of exile, and they are his prophecy, which has six levels."[34] Hence the three drops, secreted by the divine mind, are also three *gilgulim*, symbolized by three forefathers, who are at the same time the three pillars of truth. The drops assimilate into a turbulent damaged world, with the subliminal goal of *tikkun*, or rectification, nascent in the doctrine. These associations reinforce a theme in the *Tikkunim* that I have elsewhere termed the *Ba'al ha-Tikkunim*'s "myth of original chaos."[35]

The Wheel of *Gilgul* and the Circles of Life-Death

The legal and legendary traditions of Judaism provided many metaphors for *gilgul* through the *Ba'al ha-Tikkunim*'s rich deployment of halakhic or legal language.[36] *Gilgul* is implied in the dowering of the bride,[37] the vicissitudes of exile,[38] the pathos of the Hebrew slave,[39] and the laws regarding the grafting of trees.[40] The commandment of sending away the mother bird upon taking her eggs is combined with images of the biblical flood and the redemptive process of rebirth, with the recurrent image of the bird or dove and redolent of the Shekinah herself.[41] Even the vowels of the Torah text are considered the *ruaḥ*, or inner soul, of the text, "like the ones that roll over into *gilgul*."[42]

The *Ba'al ha-Tikkunim* also portrayed the rhythm of *gilgul* as the relentless turning of a wheel, an image that occurs throughout the *Tikkunim* and *Ra'aya Meheimna*. As the wheel rises and falls, so goes the endless cycle of birth and death, an essential image in Eastern cultures but novel in medieval Judaism, perhaps similar to the Bhavachakra tradition of classical Buddhism or the wheel of Samsara in the Vedic religious system. The wheel could also denote the sefirot themselves, which are often portrayed as interlocking spheres. The concentric circles of the firmament are also described as a kind of wheel.[43] The swinging double-edged sword wielded by the two cherubs in Genesis 3:24 is yet another metaphor for *gilgul*, "for all the *gilgulim* rise and fall similarly."[44] Sometimes the three parts of the soul — the *nefesh*, *ruaḥ*, and *neshamah* — are similarly described as circular.

> All the *gilgulim* are like wheels that go up and down, and one wheel is set in the middle of all of them ... so the *nefesh* is set in the body, and the *ruaḥ* rises and falls and it circulates to all the veins of the beating heart ... so the central column goes up and down but the *Shekhinah* remains in her place ... [45] The wheel moans and turns in *gilgul*, up and down and raising its voice in a pleasant sound, with three sparks coming from the rising of every voice. The wheel goes up and down, as a swirling spark comes to the wheel, with a flashing fire in its axle.[46]

Complementing the notion of the wheel, two additional images of *gilgul* are presented in the *Ra'aya Meheimna* deploying primarily language mysticism. The letter *vav* (ו), implying six essential *gilgulim*, is depicted as the axle of the wheel of *gilgul*. At the same time, *vav* is also portrayed as a water channel or aqueduct (*amat ha-mayim*), where flowing water moves the wheel of *gilgul*, reminiscent of the structural dynamic of waterwheels that take moving water to run a mill: "This is the secret of *gilgul*, *gilgul* has no movement, it is like the aqueduct (*amat ha-mayim*) for the aqueduct is made of a rolling *vav*, the secret of *gilgul*, meaning that the *vav* has no movement without the aqueduct, so there is no *gilgul* without the *vav*, the wheel is *yud* and it has no movement without the aqueduct which is *vav*."[47] The image of the *amat ha-mayim*, or aqueduct, is unique to this passage, and is without counterparts elsewhere in the *Zohar*. In another image drawn from the *Ba'al ha-Tikkunim*'s Hebrew writings, the pointillistic letter *yud*, elsewhere portrayed as the hub of the letter *vav*, is another symbol to depict the process of *gilgul*. Here, the verb *gal* simultaneously means to roll and to reveal, after the earliest images of rolling in the Genesis portion of the Torah referring to the rolling away of the stone over a water source. "Jacob called it Gilead, from the word *galgal*. What is a *galgal*? A rounded *yud*. And that is the secret of *gilgul*, and of it, it says *Reveal my eyes (gal einai) and I will see the wonders of your Torah* (Psalms 119:18)."[48] From these latter examples, it seems that the wheel described is a millwheel, driven by the force of the flow of water from an aqueduct. Hence, the "moaning" of the wheel, as it sits in place points to this understanding. This wheel is not a conveyance, moving from place to place, but is fixed in its place, groaning, and flashing from the friction of the process. In this way, the wheel of death and rebirth assumes a paradigmatic relationship to other traditions of karma and rebirth.

The Maidservant and the Redemption of the *Shekhinah*

The boldest reincarnation tradition to be found in the main sections of the Zohar is in the composition *Sabba de-Mishpatim*, "The old man of the (Torah reading) *Mishpatim*."[49] The Zoharic discussion is based, partially, on a passage in the Torah (Exodus 21:7–10) that conveys the laws of the Hebrew bondswoman. This text details the minimalist approach to reincarnation characteristic of the main circle of the Zohar's composers. The editors of the Mantua Zohar presented a parallel text by the author of the *Tikkun*im and possibly embellished it to serve as an introduction to *Sabba de-Mishpatim*.[50] As with the main text of the Zohar, the Ba'al ha-*Tikkun*im couched his presentation of *gilgul* in the context of the laws of the maidservant sold into bondage by her family. For the Zohar, the laws of the maidservant are but a metaphor for the experience of reincarnation, for the soul, like the maidservant, is enslaved in a physical incarnation in the phenomenal world. In this fragment, the "maidservant," or "slave girl," is a metaphor for the soul that, as a result of its transgressions, may be reincarnated in lower forms. This lower incarnation, according to the *Ba'al ha-Tikkunim*, "... is truly *Havdalah*,[51] the profaning of Shabbat. It is the 'other one' that is not the profaning of Shabbat, but rather the profaning of the unclean maidservant ... the slave-girl, which is the body of the only daughter, of whom it says (Ex. 21:10) *if he takes another one*." This possibility of negative incarnations is echoed in the composition *Ra'aya Meheimna*. That text similarly depicts negative incarnations — defined as lives lived at lower rungs of society — as forms of enslavement: "There is a person who is slave or a maidservant regarding his *neshamah*. Sometimes the *neshamah* goes out in the secret of *gilgul*, as it says, *the dove found not place to perch* (Gen. 8:9), and the evil inclination pursues it, and it goes into a body which is like the maidservant."[52] The author portrays the process of reincarnation as the vicissitudes of the *Shekhinah*.[53] The human soul is based on incarnations of the *Shekhinah* that can derive from various parts of the sefirotic tree. Therefore, there may be an incarnation of the *Shekhinah* that is influenced by sources as high as the sefirah *Tiferet*, here representing the midpoint of the sefirotic emanation, and there might be a negative dimension to the *Shekhinah* that comes from lower rungs on the sefirotic hierarchy, even from the realm of the demonic, the "negative elementary" aspects of the *Shekhinah* that originate lower on the divine structure. The introduction to *Sabba de-Mishpatim* may be a reworking of a passage in the *Tikkunim* that is printed in the work *Zohar Ḥadash*,[54] in which the fluid identification of the soul with the *Shekhinah* is particularly pronounced:

> Come and see, there is a *neshamah* (*Shekhinah*) that is called the slave-girl, and there is a *Shekhinah* that is called the maidservant and there is a *Shekhinah* that is called the daughter of the king, so there is a man and a man of which it says, *YHVH is a man of war* (Exodus 15:3), and there is a man of whom it says, *the man Gavriel* (Daniel 9:21). Therefore, the *neshamah* that is sentenced to *gilgul*, if she is a daughter of the Blessed Holy One, of whom it says that she has been acquired by a foreign body, wherein there is the reign of the evil inclination, and that body, suffused by the princess, you might say that it has been acquired by the lower crowns of impurity, God forbid! Of her it says, *you shall not sell the land permanently for the land is mine* (Lev. 25:23). What is the body of the princess? This is Metatron. This is the body that is the slave-girl of the *Shekhinah*, even though she is the *neshamah* that is the daughter of the king, taken hostage there, and *gilgul* comes . . . for she is brought there.[55]

The author's central exegetical task, in this case, is to link the biblical passages dealing with the laws of slave girls, maidservants, and slaves to the processes of the soul and its reincarnations. To that end, the *Ba'al ha-Tikkunim* sets up a number of interpretive typologies. The various images of slavery are identified according to the experience of the *Shekhinah*. At the same time, the text emphasizes the use of the term "man," particularly the "man who sells his daughter into bondage" in Exodus 21:7–11. The soul's essential identity derives from its placement along the sefirotic tree. To be a soul that is "the daughter of the Blessed Holy One" implies that the soul originates from the level of the sefirah *Tiferet*, the central cluster of sefirot that make up the torso of the primordial Adam. The *Ba'al ha-Tikkunim*'s framing of *gilgul* as "incarnations of the soul/*Shekhinah*" supports the contemporary view regarding the author's preoccupation with the *Shekhinah*.[56] In all his discourses, the author obsessively oscillates from the subject of his discussion to the condition of the *Shekhinah*, which, increasingly, is his ongoing metaphor for the nature of existence.

At the same time, the *Ba'al ha-Tikkunim* also frames the experience of reincarnation in terms of the doctrine of the "four worlds," present in contemporary kabbalistic works but largely absent in the earlier parts of the Zohar.[57] Over the course of maturation, an individual becomes endowed with a series of souls. This process evolves not only along the "sefirotic Tree," but also across a continuum called the "path of emanation," taking place along the continuum of the four worlds.[58] The soul's path along the four worlds is combined with the "countenance" tradition of the penultimate sections of the Zohar, with its motif of a divine family: a patriarch, father, mother, child, and consort. The graduated presentation of new aspects of the soul is defined in terms of "countenances" or *parẓufim*, such as Abba and Imma, the Father and Mother in a divine family. Finally, as is often his wont, the *Ba'al ha-Tikkunim* includes the characteristic sacred names that, for him, define this process as well, in this case the *milui*, or consonantal vocalization of the name YHVH. In the incarnation that is at the level of the *Shekhinah*, souls may move into a state in which it is possessed by the demonic, for the *Shekhinah* has a dark aspect, a reversed quality. This negative elementary character is called the "slave girl" or "maidservant." If this happens, the apparent conclusion of the text is that the body in which the soul is imprisoned assumes the aspect of the "slave-girl of the *Shekhinah* . . . taken hostage there." In this way, the process of release from the endless cycle of "birth and death" can always be frustrated in one's lifetime.

According to Scholem, the larger part of the Zohar's view was that only the earthly *nefesh* reincarnates.[59] Hence, it is striking that throughout the writings of the *Ba'al ha-Tikkunim*, the three levels of the soul — *nefesh*, *ruaḥ*, and *neshamah* — all reincarnate. The goal of the practitioner is to get all the parts of the soul to align in an even, final departure from present existence. Another remark appropriates the Zohar's earlier doctrine of "naked souls" who are trapped in the present world and cannot transmigrate, joining this to the mythos of the birds:

> This is the realm of the naked souls, as it says, *even the sparrow has found a home* (Psalms 84:4). This is the *nefesh* that is reincarnated the first time,

> *and a swallow a nest for herself*, this is the *ruaḥ* that comes in the second reincarnation, where she placed her chicks. The third time [*in which to set her young*], this is the *neshamah* and from her come the chicks that are children. In the secret of Levirate marriage, all three descend at once, as it says *if he puts to his heart, his spirit and his soul.* (Job 34:14)[60]

The goal of the process of *gilgul* is the "fixing" (*tikkun*) of the soul.[61] To purify and rectify itself, the pure soul is exiled to an alienated, impure body. "Exile, wearing down their feet from state to state, is a kind of *gilgul*."[62] This exile leads to incarnations in the society of the ignorant, unlettered *amei ha-aretz*, a particular *bête noire* of the *Ba'al ha-Tikkunim*:[63] "There are the ignorant (*amei ha-aretz*), whose houses are filled with demonic angels, which are the serpents and scorpions that bite and cause harm before they even come to the world, because they reincarnate ('come in *gilgul*') in those bodies and those abodes."[64] The various incarnations could affect gender and fertility. In one instance, the *Ba'al ha-Tikkunim* interpreted the suffering of the righteous (*Ẓaddik ve ra' lo*) as being in an unfortunate marriage, "for a bad body and a bad spouse are his punishment which his *gilgul* decrees on him."[65] *Gilgul* can rectify this situation and others, as stated in *Ra'aya Meheimna*, "One who dies without progeny comes back in *gilgul* and is renewed."[66] *Gilgul* could also have certain effects on the gender identity of the soul in question, given the essential androgyny of the tripartite soul. In all these respects, the kabbalists viewed the *neshamah* as androgynous and able to alternate between male and female bodies. The *Ba'al ha-Tikkunim* points out that if a soul changes gender in the course of *gilgul*, gender dysphoria could result in the soul's next incarnation.[67] The androgyne (*tumtum*) "will come back in *gilgul* until he is made whole."[68] Infertility is another result of gender confusion in the processes of reincarnation.[69]

Based on this androgenous nature of the soul, later authorities, such as Moshe Cordovero, Yosef ben Shalom Ashkenazi, and David Ibn Zimra, posited that the *neshamot* of humans could reincarnate into animals and even plants.[70] Sin, of course, and the general influence of the demonic could cause a *neshamah* to be reincarnated into an animal.[71] There are also reincarnations that are associated with the "beasts," which here refers to the creatures that pull the chariot in Ezekiel 1. In the *Ba'al ha-Tikkunim*'s dark pantheon, these are euphemisms for the forces of evil. The individual begins with an "animal soul," *nafsha de-beira*, to which higher gradations of the soul that derive from higher entities in the sefirotic hierarchy are symbolized by people of higher social status in biblical society.[72]

At the same time, the emphasis on "fixing" the soul is directly linked to the isomorphic understanding of the miẓvot themselves, the body of the adherent and the divine body, so that the neglect of a commandment linked to a certain limb would result in a whole *gilgul* to rectify that omission.[73] The possibilities of *gilgul* are nourished or damaged by the performance or transgression, respectively, of the 613 commandments. Hence, an individual's moral history, the observance of the commandments and the avoidance of sin, are the greatest determinants of the soul's fate in the afterlife. One undergoes reincarnation to redeem those physical limbs of the body that have been tainted by transgression. There is a *gilgul* for every limb not rectified, so as to make the body "a throne for the *Shekhinah*."[74] To expunge the burden of sin for which there has been no repentance, the three parts of the soul might even transmigrate separately.[75]

Biblical Personalities and Reincarnation

Another innovation of the *Ba'al ha-Tikkunim*, which would be influential on the later strata of Lurianic writing, was to anthropomorphize the process of *gilgul* and locate it in the inner structure of *Adam Kadmon*, the Primordial Man, a dynamic that would reassert itself throughout the development of Lurianic Kabbalah.[76] Since the divine body is mirrored in the human body, the reincarnation of souls in this world corresponds to the processes of reincarnation occurring in the divine world, so that the whole cosmos is renewing itself all the time and human *gilgul* is just an aspect of this ongoing renewal. The same is true for the primordial Adam, the Anthropos that is the incarnate form of the Divine. The reconstruction of the primordial Adam proceeds from the reincarnation of a spark of divine thought, the "World Soul."[77]

At the same time, this process is historical, with the first *gilgulim* originating from the first generations of humankind as recorded by the book of Genesis. As has been noted, the *Ba'al ha-Tikkunim* had a well-developed concept of the Fall of Adam, which he saw as underlying the existential state of humankind. In this, the *Ba'al ha-Tikkunim* was perhaps more concerned with the primordial Fall than were other primary Jewish sources.[78] The events of the Fall and the lineages of Genesis initiated a series of *gilgulim*, lineages that would come to be considered normative in Lurianic Kabbalah. These ideas characteristically are presented in a tangle of disparate images that must be separated and reorganized by the reader to be made coherent:

> *The man knew Eve his wife* (Gen. 4:1) ... he knew the corruption (of the serpent) that was in her, up to Keni the father-in-law of Moses. (Adam) saw his *gilgul* and his repentance ... R. Shimon asked, why did the Holy Blessed One trouble himself to bring him back in *gilgul?* ... for the honor of the righteous, to remove sin from his children ... *And she continued to bear his brother, Abel (Gen. 4:2) You hide Your face, they are troubled: you take away their breath, they die, and return to their dust.* (Psalms 104:29) This implies the *gilgul* of the righteous, for the Holy Blessed One foresees their *gilgul* in every generation, how it goes from Ẓaddiq to Ẓaddiq in every generation, up to 600,000.[79]

The first, pivotal fork in the road of the *gilgul* lineages is the issue of whether one is descended from Cain or Abel. Clearly, the line of Cain is destined to be bad seed. Cain's soul has its origins in the forbidden Tree of Knowledge of Good and Evil, and his soul reincarnates until it is cleansed, by his reincarnation as Keni, the father-in-law of Moses (Judges 1:16; a rearrangement of the same letters that make up the name "Cain").[80] His curse, that he wander through the world, is his fate of being reincarnated[81]; the "labor" to which he is cursed (Genesis 4:2) is the labor of *gilgul*[82]; and his children are his *gilgulim* of evil.[83] *Gilgul* is offered to him as a way to rectify his state.[84] For Cain, being sentenced to *gilgul* is positive, because he can work to improve his spiritual position; he has nowhere to go but up.[85] In that respect, his remonstration with God (Genesis 4:14), *you exiled me*, refers to his first *gilgul*, while (Ibid 4:12) *to and fro* refers to his subsequent *gilgulim*.[86]

Seth, Adam's third son, is created from the three *gilgulim* of Adam, Enosh, and Abel, with the three *gilgulim* of Abel, Noah, Shem, and Yafet[87] His very name means "six" in Aramaic, so that he is therefore the product of these three upper *gilgulim* and the three lower *gilgulim*.[88] The line of Abel is refined, though a series of tests, into the reincarnated line of the forefathers, Abraham, Isaac, and Jacob.[89] Noah's son Ham, in turn, is reincarnated in Abraham's slave Eliezer.[90] As Cain produced a demonic line of incarnations, so the line of Enosh is righteous and redemptive, the source of the *gilgulim* of the righteous.[91] Enoch (*Ḥanokh*) was similarly a direct incarnation of Adam, hence his transfiguration as the angel Metatron.[92] Eventually Adam himself is employed as symbolic of all of his subsequent reincarnations.[93] Eventually Abraham would emerge as the direct reincarnation of Adam, but the intervening generations saw many complications in that soul lineage.[94] In fact, in a confusion of kabbalistic systems, the sefirah *Ḥokhmah*, in the form of the countenance Abba, is present in the incarnations of Abraham,

Isaac, and Jacob.[95] They are all, respectively, bridegrooms of the *Shekhinah*, to cite the recurring theme of the *Tikkunim* and *Ra'aya Meheimna*. [96]

For all the forefathers, the specter of Moses looms over them as the final end of the *gilgul* process. In fact, in terms of sefirotic paradigms, Moses, in this treatment, seem more paradigmatic of the *Ẓaddik*, emblematized in the sefirah *Yesod*, than its usual exemplar, Joseph, who seems absent from the *Ba'al ha-Tikkunim*'s *gilgul* lineage. In one instance, Moses is described as the "Great Fish," an appellation usually applied to the mysterious, departed Rav Hamnuna Sabba of the Zohar's main sections.[97] This obsession with Moses, is, of course, characteristic of the *Ba'al ha-Tikkunim*. Many scholars have opined that his name was Moses and that this was part of his troubled self-image.[98] In any case, Moses is the final *gilgul*, the *gilgul* of the *Ẓaddik*.[99] So it is that the tensions and rivalries of those previous generations continue into contemporary history. The Edenic generations[100] and the lineages around Moses[101] confront one another again, renewed through *gilgul*. The seasonal ruminations of Ecclesiastes, and the interpretation of them as indicating a cyclical nature to existence, are employed to this end throughout the *Tikkunim*.

> Happy is he who was present at the six days of creation, for every *neshamah* has a season and time in *gilgul*, as Ecclesiastes declared (Eccles. 3: 1) *to everything there is a season and a time for every purpose under heaven*, this is the lower *Shekhinah*, which is a time and season for every sefirah, for every *gilgul*, there is a season and part-season, a season for all seasons truly.[102] As the sun is revealed in the day and covered in the night and shines in 20,000 stars, so the Faithful Shepherd, after he enters the world, shines in 600,000 souls of Israel. If the generation is worthy, this is the secret of *gilgul*, of which it says (Ecc. 1:4) *a generation comes and a generation goes*, and there is no generation less than 600,000, *and the land remains forever*, this the community of Israel.[103]

Similarly, the *Ba'al ha-Tikkunim* toys with the idea of pre-destination, reading hints of the same in certain other verses of the Bible. "As you say, *there is nothing new under the sun* (Ecclesiastes 1:9), he is already required to be in this *gilgul*, as it says, *before you were formed in the womb, I knew you* (Jeremiah 1:5) *that which will be already has been*, that is to be in this world, is already required to be before he comes to this world in *gilgul*."[104]

Conclusion

The bundle of traditions surveyed above have constituted a watershed in the development of Kabbalah, yet the characteristic teachings of the *Ba'al ha-Tikkunim* have been subsumed into the general development of the Zohar, its bundling as a series of writings, and its creation as a "book." The initial statement, placed strategically as an introduction to Sabba de-Mishpatim, directed the reader to see the Sabba's teachings in the light of a more developed theology of reincarnation. The doctrine was addressed already in earlier kabbalistic works, the *Sefer ha-Bahir* and *Sefer ha-Temuna*, along with polemics against *gilgul* in the philosophical community that predate the Zohar by centuries. At the same time, in his self-conscious use of the term *gilgul*, and in wedding it to prior Zoharic themes, the *Ba'al ha-Tikkunim* set the stage for the flourishing of the concept in later Kabbalah.

A core concept of this teaching, which reappears in the speculations of the Galilean kabbalists, is that in every reincarnation a person has to "fix" a certain aspect of his soul. When this process is completed, the soul undergoes a final liberation associated with the realm of the *Shekhinah*, the sefirah *Malkhut*. Or, as Yonatan Benarroch and Oded Yisraeli have pointed out, the reason for *gilgul*, according to the original text of Sabba de-Mishpatim, is to resolve the problem of suffering, particularly the suffering of oppressed children.[105] These theological interpretations display certain commonalities with Eastern religions — Buddhism and Hinduism — where reincarnation serves to expunge the particular karma that has attached to one's soul in a past life.[106]

The moody persona of the *Ba'al ha-Tikkunim* has been the subject of a number of studies, focusing on his dark preoccupations and romantic conceits. The wildly associative style of writing adopted in the work might be attributed, as has been claimed, to the mystical practice of automatic writing.[107] He was a lonely outsider, possibly the last of the original circle of kabbalists who compiled the Zohar, and the last who was in on the literary conceit of its composition, the pseudepigraphal record of a circle of medieval Castilian kabbalists who chose to cloak their activities in the imagined Galilean landscape of late antiquity. Otherwise, his theology was sound, besting that of the Zohar's main sections. His understanding of divine immanence, the separation of the divine emanation into God's essence (*aẓmut*) and vessels, (*kelim*), his absorption of the four worlds of creation, and his adaptation of the Zohar's latter doctrine of the divine countenance make him a sophisticated theoretician of Kabbalah.

Perhaps, as some scholars have argued, his poignant tone in the writing may reflect an inner psychological state of regret and remorse and as such may denote elegy for the decline of the movement. Be that as it may, his world was a broken one, a post-catastrophe dystopia, and his Torah is haunted. The topic of reincarnation — a cosmic system of birth and death — was by all accounts a fitting preoccupation for him. Was he a fallen angel, the disgraced wunderkind of the early sections of the Zohar, as suggested by Ronit Meroz? Was he simply besotted by the mythos of the *Shekhinah*, constantly toggling back to his muse and primary metaphor — her last great knight errant — as demonstrated by Biti Roi?[108] How did his art interact with his life? These are not our concerns in this study, but they hover in the background of the *Ba'al ha-Tikkunim*, as he was, perhaps, the original tormented master, so that for all his peregrinations, his life ended as he was still in the process of becoming.[109]

Notes

1. Daniel Abrams, *The Book Bahir* (Los Angeles: Cherub, 1994), 170–73 (henceforth *Bahir*) #86 (#122–23), Margoliot ed., henceforth "M"). For a recent treatment of the Bahir, see Marla Segol, *Kabbalah and Sex* Magic (University Park: Pennsylvania State University Press, 2021), 102–6.

2. Gershom Scholem, *On the Mystical Shape of the Godhead: Basic Concepts in the Kabbalah* (New York: Schocken), 200–3, 207–9, 219–21; *Origins of the Kabbalah*, 188–98. Avishai Bar Asher contradicts Scholem's understanding of the origins of the Bahir's notion of *gilgul*, "Lab Grown Historiography: The Imaginary Origins of *Sefer ha-Bahir* and the Reconstruction of the 'Origins' of the Kabbalah," *Zion* 84 (2019): 512–13. For a detailed treatment of the term *gilgul* in the Zohar, see Yehudah Liebes, *Sections of the Zohar Lexicon* (PhD diss., Hebrew University, 1976), 295.

3. *Sefer Ha-Bahir*, S #86, M #121.

4. *Sefer Ha-Bahir*, S #86, M #122.

5. *Sefer Ha-Bahir*, S #135, M #194.

6. *Sefer Ha-Bahir*, S #135, M #194.

7. b. Yevamot 62a.

8. *Sefer ha-Bahir*, S #126, M #184.

9. For scholarship on the problematic nature of the Zohar as a book, see Daniel Abrams, "The Invention of the Zohar as a Book—On the Assumptions and Expectations of the Kabbalists and Modern Scholars," *Kabbalah: Journal for the Study of Jewish Mystical Texts* 19 (2009): 7–142; Daniel Abrams, *Kabbalistic Manuscripts and Textual Theory: Methodologies of Textual Scholarship and Editorial Practice in the Study of Jewish Mysticism* (Los Angeles: Cherub and Magnes Press, 2011).

10. Amos Goldreich lists a number of possible dates for the composition of the *Tikkunim*, citing Scholem, *Major Trends in Jewish Mysticism* (New York: Schocken, 1995), 188; and Scholem, *Kabbalah* (New York: Meridian, 1978), 59. He places the text in the late thirteenth or early fourteenth century; see Goldreich, "Iberian Dialect in an Unknown Fragment from the Author of *Tikkunei* ha-Zohar," in *The Zohar and Its Generation: Jerusalem Studies in Jewish Thought* 8, ed. Joseph Dan [Hebrew] (Jerusalem: Magnes, 1989), 89–122, n. 91, n. 96. Scholem, *Kabbalah*, 232, dated the works prior to 1312 according to eschatological predictions made therein. Ronit Meroz has tentatively placed its composition at 1312; R. Meroz, *The Spiritual Biography of R. Simeon Bar Yochay: An Analysis of the Zohar's Textual Components* [Hebrew] (Jerusalem: Mossad Bialik 2018), 119–44, esp. 125. Amiel Vick, qualifying in many ways the absolute identity of many parts of the literature, considers the *Ba'al ha-Tikkunim* to have been active from 1313 to as late as 1338; see "A Textual History of *Tikkunei ha-Zohar:* The Career of a Kabbalistic Classic from the Earliest Known Manuscripts to the 1740 Printing in Constantinople" (PhD diss., Bar Ilan University, 2019), 61–65. Intriguingly, a passage in *Ra'aya Meheimna* lists a messianic prediction for the year 1324; see R. Meroz, *The Spiritual Biography*, 139.

11. The *Ba'al ha-Tikkunim* has, of late, been the subject of a number of complex and compelling studies: see Biti Roi, *Love of the Shekhinah* (Ramat Gan: Bar Ilan University Press, 2017), 16–17, note 8; Moshe Idel, "Introduction" to E. Gottlieb, *The Hebrew Writings of the Author of Tikkunei Zohar and Ra'aya Mehemna* (Jerusalem: Israel Academy of Sciences and Humanities, 2003), 29–30; Yehudah Liebes, "Zohar and *Tikkunim*: From Renaissance to Revolution," in *Teudah XXI–XXII: New Developments in Zohar Studies*, ed. Ronit Meroz (Tel Aviv: Tel Aviv University Press, 2007), 251–301; Ronit Meroz, "An Old Man, a Child and a Princess in the Floating Tower: *Tikkunei Zohar* as an Encoded Ego-Document," *Zemanim* 123 (2013): 94–107 [Hebrew].

12. *Tikkunei Zohar Hadash* 109b–110b. See Pinchas Giller, *The Enlightened Will Shine: Symbolization and Theurgy in the Later Strata of the Zohar* (New York: State University of New York Press, 1993), 93–96.

13. Yonatan Benarroch, *Sava and Yanuka: God, the Son and the Messiah in Zoharic Narrative* [Hebrew] (Jerusalem: Magnes 2018), 196–97; Oded Yisraeli, *The Interpretation of Secrets and the Secret of Interpretation: Midrashic and Hermeneutic Strategies in Sabba de-Mishpatim of the Zohar* [Hebrew] (Los Angeles: Los Angeles Cherub Press, 2005), 139–49.

14. See Wendy O'Flaherty, ed. *Karma and Rebirth in Classical Indian Traditions* (Berkeley: University of California 1980); Joseph Campbell, *The Mythic Image* (Princeton, NJ: Bollingen, 1974), 330–91; C. G. Jung, *Mandala Symbolism, Collected Works of C. G. Jung*, trans. R. C. H. Hull (Princeton, NJ: Princeton Bollingen, 1972), IX.1, para. 647–49.

15. Isaiah Tishby, *The Wisdom of the Zohar* II, 714.

16. See Giller, *The Enlightened*, 7–20; Goldreich, *Automatic Writing in Zoharic Literature and Modernism* [Hebrew] (Los Angeles: Cherub Press 2010), 65; A.

Goldreich. "Clarifying the Self-Image of the Author of *Tikkunei ha-Zohar*," in *Massuot: Studies in Kabbalistic Literature and Jewish Thought Presented in Memory of Professor Ephraim Gottlieb* [Hebrew] (Jerusalem: Mossad Bialik 1994), 459–95, especially, 488; Meroz, *The Spiritual Biography*, 128; Biti Roi, *Love of the Shekhinah*, 39, n. 105, 106, and 291.

17. *Tikkunei Zohar* (henceforth TZ) 131a; Benarroch, *Sava and Yanuka*, 186; Benarroch, "Metatron 'the Youth' and the Bride: A Zoharic Hieros Gamos," in *The Zoharic Story*, ed. Y. Liebes, J. Benarroch, and M. Hellner-Eshed [Hebrew] (Jerusalem: Ben TẒvi: 2017), 619, 630–34 (on the identification of Metatron with the Tzaddiq), 642.

18. Elijah, Gaon of Vilna, *Sifra de-Tzeniuta 'Im Biur h,a-Gr"A.*, ed. Bezalel Naor (Jerusalem: self-published, 1998), 142, Aaron Meyer Altshuler, *Kelalei Hatchalat ha-Ḥokhmah* (Warsaw: Schuldberg Brothers, 1893), 82. The Gaon was enamored by the origin story for Metatron in *Zohar Ḥadash* 42d, wherein the origin story for Metatron eschews the classical Heikhalot narrative. See J. C. Reeves and A. Yoshiko Reed, eds., *Enoch from Antiquity to the Middle Ages: Sources from Judaism, Christianity, and Islam* (Oxford: Oxford University Press, 2018), 264–65; 296–300; Andrei A. Orlov, *The Enoch-Metatron Tradition* (Tübingen: Mohr Siebeck, 2005), 103, 122–25, 249 n. 178; Agata Paluch, *Megalleh 'Amuqot:* The Enoch-Meṭaṭron Tradition in the Kabbalah of Nathan Neṭa Shapira of Kraków (1585–1633) (Los Angeles: Cherub, 2015), 34–36, 180–86; Elliot R. Wolfson, *Along the Path: Studies in Kabbalistic Myth, Symbolism, and Hermeneutics* (Albany: State University of New York Press, 1995), 16, 128–30 n. 1.

19. Zohar II 94a.

20. Cordovero, *Sefer Pardes Rimmonim, Sha'ar Erkhei Kinnuyim* 27b; Yellish, *Kehillat Ya'akov.* 54b.

21. *Tikkunei Zohar Ḥadash* (henceforth TZḤ) 98a.

22. TZ 96a, *Ra'aya Mehemna* (henceforth RM), III 216a, Z II 94a.

23. See Arthur Green, "The Ẓaddik as *Axis Mundi* in Later Judaism," *Journal of the American Academy of Religion* 45 (1977): 327–47.

24. RM III 216a.

25. TZ 100a.

26. TZ 111a, also TZ 113a; Biti Roi, *Love of the Shekhinah*, 263 n. 65.

27. TZ 100a.

28. TZ 100a.

29. TZ 76b, TZ115a , 126a RM II 114a–b, III 111a.

30. G. Scholem, *On the Mystical Shape of the Godhead: Basic Concepts in the Kabbalah* (New York: Schocken, 1991), 219; G. Scholem, "The Doctrine of *Gilgul* in the Thirteenth Century" [Hebrew], *Tarbiẓ* 16 (1945): 135–50, especially 143. See also TZ 72a, TZ 116b–117a; TZḤ 106c, cf. bT *Kiddushin* 30a, "Let (a man) divide his years into thirds."

31. Scholem, *On the Mystical Shape*, 221.

32. TZ 109b.

33. TZ 110a, 139a.

34. TZ 56a.

35. TZ 110a; Giller, *The Enlightened Will Shine,* 33–69.

36. Giller, *The Enlightened Will Shine*, 13–20.

37. TZ 23b, 100b.

38. TZ 101a, TZḤ 117d.

39. RM II 114b.

40. TZ 23b.

41. TZ 23b, RM III 216a, 254a–b; Giller; *The Enlightened Will Shine*, 143–44 n58; cf. Avishay Bar Asher, "The Soul Bird: Ornithomancy and the Theory of the Soul in the Zohar Pericope Balak," in *The Zoharic Story*, ed. Y. Liebes, M. Hellner-Eshed, and Y. Benarroch, (Jerusalem: Makhon Ben TẒvi, 2017), 354–406 [Hebrew].

42. TZḤ 107d.

43. TZ 126a.

44. TZ 133a.

45. TZ 110b.

46. TZḤ 105b.

47. RM III 215b, TZ 100a; Abrams, *The Book Bahir* #53–54, 149 (Margoliot ed. #79–80), Abrams, #135, 219 (Margoliot ed. #184), Abrams, #135, 219 (Margoliot ed. #195), Abrams, #126, 209 (Margoliot ed. #184), *Zohar* III 280.

48. Ephraim Gottlieb, *The Hebrew Writings*, 162.

49. Yonatan Benarroch, *Sava and* Yanuka, 56–70, 211, 213, 217; Giller, *Reading the Zohar*, 54–57.

50. Few passages in the Zohar have been so thoroughly analyzed as *Saba de-Mishpatim*, see, for instance, D. Abrams, "Knowing the Maiden Without Eyes: Reading the Sexual Reconstruction of the Jewish Mystic in a Zoharic Parable," *Da'at* 50/51 (2003): 487–511 [Hebrew]; P. Giller, *Reading the Zohar: The Classic Text of the Kabbalah* (New York: Oxford University Press 2000), 35–68; Michal Oron. "Place Me for a Sign upon Your Heart: Studies in the Poetics of the Zohar's Author in Saba de-Mishpatim," in *Massuot: Studies in Kabbalistic Literature and Jewish Thought Presented in Memory of Professor Ephraim Gottlieb* [Hebrew] (Jerusalem: Mossad Bialik 1994), 459–95; Oded Porat, *'Who Is a Beautiful Maiden without Eyes' and the Riddle of the Ta'ya: A Chapter in the History of Kabbalah in the Second Half of the Thirteenth Century* [Hebrew] (Los Angeles: Cherub, 2019); Tzahi Weiss, "Who Is a Beautiful Maiden without Eyes? The Metamorphosis of a Zohar Midrashic Image from a Christian Allegory to a Kabbalistic Metaphor," *Journal of Religion* 93, no. 1 (2017): 60–76.

Elliot R. Wolfson, "Beautiful Maiden without Eyes: *Peshat* and *Sod* in Zoharic Hermeneutics," in *The Midrashic Imagination*, ed. Michael Fishbane (Albany: State University of New York Press, 1993), 155–203. See also Y. Benarroch, *Sava and Yanuka*, 3.

51. Separation between sacred and profane time. It also alludes to the Jewish ritual associated with the end of the Sabbath, a holy day, and the beginning of the six days of the week linked with worldly affairs.

52. RM III 277a.

53. This has been emphasized by Biti Roi; see *Love of the Shekhinah*, 139–68.

54. A. Vick, "A Textual History," 141–44.

55. Zohar II. 94b, ZH 117a.

56. B. Roi, *Love of the Shekhinah*, 181, n. 44.

57. See Gershom Scholem, "The Development of the Tradition of the Worlds," *Tarbiẓ* 2:415–42, 3:33–66, 46, 59, 67, 82 [Hebrew]; Giller, *The Enlightened Will Shine*, 54–57.

58. Giller, *The Enlightened Will Shine*, 54–57; Giller, *Reading the Zohar*, 52–53.

59. Scholem, *On the Mystical Shape of the Godhead*, 219.

60. TZ 72a, cf. *Zohar* III 178b; Giller, *The Enlightened Will Shine*, 55–56, Giller, *Reading the Zohar*, 46–48; Benarroch, *Sava and Yenuka*, 226–34; TZ 72a–b; Roi, *Love of the Shekhinah*, 32.

61. TZ 100a.

62. TZḤ 107a, also TZ 23a, 119a, TZḤ106a, RM II 114b; Roi, *Love of the Shekhinah*, 262, n. 63, and n. 65; Liebes, *Some Chapters in a Zohar Lexicon*, see under *Gilgula*, notes 15, 32, 81.

63. Giller, *The Enlightened Will Shine*, 49–53.

64. TZ 96a.

65. TZ 134a, c.f. TZ 124b.

66. RM III 245a.

67. TZ 133a.

68. TZ 137b.

69. Scholem, *On the Mystical Shape of the Godhead*, 221

70. Scholem, *On the Mystical Shape of the Godhead*, 226; Giller, *Reading the Zohar*, 37–43.

71. TZ 133a.

72. Z II 94a.

73. TZ 131a, 132a. See Giller, *The Enlightened Will Shine*, 93–96.

74. TZ 132a, Scholem, *On the Mystical Shape*, 220.

75. Scholem, *On the Mystical Shape*, 219–21; Giller, *The Enlightened Will Shine*, 95–96, c.f. *TZ* 132a; RM III 178b.

76. Scholem, *On the Mystical Shape of the Godhead*, 220, Benarroch, "Metatron 'the Youth'" and Benarroch, "The Bride," 650.

77. TZḤ 109b–110b, Giller, *The Enlightened Will Shine*, 93–96.

78. Giller, *The Enlightened Will Shine*, 33–40; Scholem, *On the Mystical Shape of the Godhead*, 220.

79. TZ 99b.

80. From Cain to Keni is a play on the letters of each name, which need merely be rearranged; TZ 113a.

81. TZḤ 116b.

82. TZḤ 114d.

83. TZ 119b.

84. TZḤ 114c.

85. TZ 112b.
86. TZ 113a.
87. TZ 110, 112a–b, 119b.
88. TZ 23b, 110a–b, 113a.
89. TZ 102a, c.f. *Genesis Rabbah* 1:4.
90. RM III 111a.
91. TZ 119b, TZḤ 116b.
92. TZ 119b.
93. TZ 91b.
94. TZ 139a.
95. TZ 102a, 100b.
96. TZḤ 114a; TZ 101a.
97. TZ 53b. On Rav Hamnuna Sabba, see Benarroch, *Sava and Yanuka*, 376–78; Jonatan Bennaroch, "Metatron 'the Youth' and the Bride: A Zoharic Hieros Gamos," in *The Zoharic Story*, ed. Y. Liebes, J. Benarroch, and M. Hellner-Eshed [Hebrew] (Jerusalem: Ben TẒvi: 2017), 643–52; Liebes, "The Zohar and the *Tikkunim*," 279; Liebes, "Myth vs, Symbol in the Zohar and Lurianic Kabbalah," in *Essential Papers in Kabbalah* ed. Lawrence Fine (New York: New York University Press, 1995), 212–44 especially 221–23; Y. Liebes, "Two Roes of the Doe *The Kabbalah of the AR"I: Jerusalem Studies in Jewish Thought 10* [Hebrew] (Jerusalem: Magnes 1992), 117–18 and 152–57; Ya'akov Ẓvi Mayer, "Rashbi and Rav Hamnuna: Between Sepharad and Ashkenaz," in *The Zoharic Story* [Hebrew] (Jerusalem: Ben Ẓvi: 2017), 445–62 [Hebrew]; Meroz, *The Spiritual Biography*, 407–55.
98. Goldreich, "The Self Image of the Author," 488; Roi, *Love of the Shekhinah*, 18. Yehudah Liebes has argued that the figure of Moses represents the author himself (Liebes, "Zohar and *Tikkun*im-From Renaissance to Revolution," 254; "The Zohar and the *Tikkunim*," 279). The relationship between Moses and Shimon Bar Yochai throughout the Zohar literature is treated in Boaz Huss, "A Sage is Better than a Prophet," *Kabbalah 4* (1989): 103–39 [Hebrew]; Roi, "The Myth of the *Shekhinah*," 226–27; Meroz, *The Spiritual* Biography, 123.
99. Roi, *Love of the Shekhinah*, 411; Boaz Huss, *Sockets of Fine Gold* [Hebrew] (Jerusalem: Magnes, 2000), 165; Meroz, *The Spiritual Biography*, 135.
100. Z I (TZ) 25a; TZ 40a, 99b, 100a, 102b, 112a, 114a. See *Kohelet Rabbah* 1:4.
101. TZ 99b, 119a.
102. TZ 101a; Roi, *Love of the Shekhinah*, 201, n. 102.
103. RM III 216b.
104. TZ 101b.
105. J. Benarroch, *Sava and Yanuka*, 196–97; Yisraeli, *The Interpretation of Secrets*, 139–49.
106. See Wendy O'Flaherty, ed., *Karma and Rebirth in Classical Indian Traditions* (Berkeley: University of California Press, 1980); Joseph Campbell, *The Mythic Image* (Princeton, NJ: Bollingen, 1974), 330–91; C. G. Jung, *Mandala Sym-*

bolism, Collected Works of C. G. Jung, trans. R. C. H. Hull (Princeton: Princeton Bollingen, 1972), Book IX.1, para. 647–49.

107. P. Giller, *The Enlightened Will Shine*, 7–20. See also Goldreich, "Automatic Writing," 65; Goldreich, "The Self Image of the Author," 488; R. Meroz, *The Spiritual Biography*, 128; Roi, *Love of the Shekhinah*, 39, notes 105, 106, and 291.

108. Roi, *Love of the Shekhinah*, 25.

109. Zohar II 94a–b; see also the work of Shimon ben Zemach Duran (1361–1444) titled *Zohar ha-Raki'a* (Constantinople: Yoseph ben Ayid Qabiẓi, 1515), 63a. Other contemporary theorists posited a set number of reincarnations to resolve residual problems of the soul. According to R. Joseph of Hamadan, the person has three reincarnations, which comprise chances for the individual to repent his sins; see R. Meroz, "Selections from Ephraim Penzieri: Luria's Sermon in Jerusalem and the *Kavvanah* in Taking Food," in R. Elior and J. Dan, eds., *Jerusalem Studies in Jewish Thought* 10 (1992), 211–58 [Hebrew], see especially on 227; R. Yosef of Hamadan *Ta'amei Miẓvot,* Negative Miẓvah #57 in Leore Sachs-Shmueli, "The Rationale of the Negative Commandments by R. Joseph Hamadan: A Critical Edition and Study of Taboo in the Time of the Composition of the Zohar," vols. 1, 2 (PhD diss., Bar-Ilan University, 2019), 220– 21 [Hebrew].

RUTH KARA-IVANOV KANIEL[1]

"And the Next Day Her Belly Is Between Her Teeth"

4

FEMININE SYMBOLIZATION IN R. JOSEPH ANGELET'S DOCTRINE OF *GILGUL* AND *IBBUR*

IN A REMARKABLE ANONYMOUSLY WRITTEN TREATISE titled *Twenty-Four Secrets*, there are three separate discussions devoted to the subject of the transmigration of souls. The work was most likely composed between 1311 and 1327 and is commonly ascribed to Joseph Angelet, a prolific kabbalist active in Saragossa in the early decades of the fourteenth century.[2] Using technical kabbalistic terminology *gilgul* and soul impregnation (*ibbur*) interchangeably,[3] the treatise is composed of three sections of secrets, "The Secret of the Reason for *Gilgul*," "The Secret of *ibbur* [Spiritual Impregnation]," and "The Secret of the Calendrical *ibbur* [the Leap Year]." Through an extensive discussion of motifs and symbols that relate the *Shekhinah* — the feminine aspect of the Divine in Kabbalah — to the concept of reincarnation, this chapter argues that Angelet regarded reincarnation less as a divinely sanctioned punishment for human transgression and more as a "positive process" of *tikkun* (reparation) of both the individual, and the collective, soul. Indeed, the author himself declares, "A person is created *for good*, and he is given time, through reincarnation, *to return to the fullness of that good*."[4] In addition, Angelet intentionally sows confusion between different kabbalistic meanings of the terms *gilgul* and *ibbur*, and he suggests that *gilgul* promoted intergenerational repair — a responsibility borne by the leader —to hasten redemption.[5] This motif was adopted and intensified later in sixteenth-century Safedian Kabbalah, which focused on *gilgul* as a means of personal and cosmic repair.[6]

Angelet's understanding of *gilgul* as the reformation and ultimate return of the soul stands in marked contrast to Gershom Scholem's conceptualization of this concept. Accordingly, Scholem posited that transmigration (*gilgul*) was a form of existential exile: "Just as bodies are in *galut*, so also there is inward *galut* for souls. And the '*galut* of souls' is transmigration."[7] Angelet's multivalent use of the terms *gilgul* and *ibbur* integrates otherwise separate concepts: premortem and postmortem activities of the soul; the *ibbur* of the *Shekhinah* within the other sefirot as well as within the souls of the righteous; individual reincarnation and collective or generational reincarnation in parallel to the exile of both the soul and the nation; the recycling of bodies and souls within multiple generations; and earthly figures who reincarnate within the *Shekhinah* and later are elevated to the sefirah *Binah* to merit eternal life (through the cycles of Repentance, *Teshuva*, and the World-to-Come, *Olam ha-Ba*).[8]

The three sections of the Angelet's "Twenty-Four Secrets" cover a wide range of topics and move from concerns about the fate of the individual, through the vicissitudes of Israel as a nation, to arrive finally at the question of the cosmic changes associated with the moon and heavenly constellations that represent the cycles of the *Shekhinah*. Thus, in the chapter "Secret of *Ibbur*," he turns to illustrating the fate of the individual soul by embedding this discourse into a broader theological framework in which life and death stand for cosmic activities by which a person's soul is purified and refined in order to return to the Divine. Moving away from the individual, the second text, "The Secret of the Reason for *Gilgul*," presents the notion of Israel as a nation that undergoes cycles of life and death, expiation, and repentance. The author provides a birds-eye view of the concepts of the Jewish nation and peoplehood and their relation to the movement of the *sefirot*, individual souls, supernal worlds, and the chain of generations, all according to the principle of "the secret of the generation that turns like a sphere (*sod ha-dor ha-mitgalgel ke-kadur*)."[9]

Angelet's intentional shift from the individual to the collective, and his integration of human attributes with sefirotic ones, is evident from the opening lines of each of these secrets, in which the orthographic root of the Hebrew verb, *g.l.g.l* גלגל, also carries additional layers of meaning: the moon *mitgalgelet* (passes through cyclical phases), a person is allowed *lehitgalgel* (to reincarnate), and the generation *mitgalgel* (turns like a sphere).[10] The same terms, concepts, and biblical prooftexts appear throughout the three secrets, joining the journey of the individual soul to that of the unified souls of the entirety of the Israelite nation. The result is a multigenerational view of the cyclical cosmic motion anchored in the *Shekhinah*, the supernal axis that joins heaven and earth. Finally, moving toward cosmic history, "The Secret of Regular *Ibbur*" treats the cycle (*gilgul*) of the *Shekhinah* through the monthly and yearly phases of the moon and her impregnation by, and interaction (*ibbur*) with, the other *sefirot*, as well as Her relationship to the forces of evil.[11] Furthermore, this text, which focuses on the idea of repentance occurring at the start of each lunar cycle, invokes strikingly mythic language. It is based on the rabbinic legend of the diminishing of the moon as well as on the relationships between the patriarch Isaac's sons, the biblical twins Jacob and Esau, and the sisters Rachel and Leah, through which the dynamic interaction of the sefirot are expressed.

Angelet's Sources and Teachers in His Chapters on the Secrets of *Ibbur* and *Gilgul*

THE BOOK BAHIR (SEFER HA-BAHIR)

Angelet draws on eclectic sources, including the *Book Bahir*, along with the kabbalists of Gerona and Castile, to present his theories on reincarnation. His approach marks a sharp contrast with Nahmanides, who regarded these topics as esoteric in the extreme and limited written speculation on them. Angelet's three secrets are based primarily on sources from the early Kabbalah. The "Secret of *Ibbur*" cites several traditions drawn from the *Bahir* on *gilgul* and understands the concept of soul impregnation or *ibbur* as referring to wrath (*evrah*, with which it shares its lexical root), an idea that first appears in R. Azriel of Gerona's commentary on the New Year (*Rosh Hashanah*) liturgy.[12] Castilian Kabbalah posits a variety of eclectic approaches to the mysteries of *gilgul* and *ibbur* that integrate horizontal models of *gilgul*, denoting the reappearance of individual souls in new bodies, with vertical models of the *ibbur* of the *Shekhinah* in the divine realm.[13] Furthermore, among the contemporaries and successors of the Zohar, the shroud of secrecy that had previously dominated these topics — as exemplified by Shem Tov ibn Gaon (1283–1330) — was lifted. Ibn Gaon, following the school of Nahmanides, articulates a starkly conservative attitude to openly discussing reincarnation in *Keter Shem Tov*:

> I cannot hint at the ancient tradition we have received on this matter, for it would require lengthy discussion. For there is a great and profound secret, on which depends the essence of Faith and Truth, and one who has received this tradition can answer any question about the matter and lead those who have gone astray back to a correct understanding. Then he will understand the death of the ten martyrs and their judgment, and the matter of Er and Onan, Pinhas, Nadav and Avihu, as well as Abel. And I have already hinted at every one of these matters and I have provided an answer to the one who asked about it, praise be to God. I can only explain it orally, according to the question and the understanding of the one who asks it.[14]

His approach is consistent with Nahmanides's position, according to which it is permissible to reveal these secrets only to a faithful student, and so, as Idel notes, in the tradition of R. Solomon ibn Aderet and Ibn Gaon, these secrets are discussed only in whispers: "Since the master has concealed the matter, we have no authority to reveal it except orally. But I will offer a hint based on what has been written in truth regarding the matter of Abel."[15]

I would argue that Angelet reinforces the tradition of his teacher, Ibn Gaon, to challenge the two fundamental conceptions propagated by *Sefer ha-Bahir*. First, he rejects the assertion of the *Bahir*, which states that a soul is reincarnated only three times and firmly maintains that it can undergo even a thousand reincarnations. Second, he attributes no superiority to a new soul that has never undergone reincarnation and becomes lodged in a physical body for the first time in contrast to what he calls an "admixed soul," which has already experienced several cycles of transmigration. While other kabbalists also contested the *Book Bahir*'s stance, Ibn Gaon's unique emphasis on the superiority of the third reincarnation reinforces Angelet's messianic self-understanding, alluded to by his remark, "I have another hidden secret, understood from the verse, *But the Lord was angry with me ["vayit'abar bi"] on your account* (Deut. 3: 26).[16] The idea that the soul of Moses reincarnates in the righteous members of all future generations is a common theme also shared by the author of *Tikkunei Zohar*, who was writing at the same time as Angelet.[17]

According to the *Bahir*, seed is considered "old" when it passes through the womb of the *Shekhinah*, which is called "the aspect that inclines toward the west" (*ha-midda she-nota le-ma'arav*) and is identified with the process of mixing of the seed ("for there all seeds are mixed," *she-sham mit'arev kol ha-zera*). By contrast, a "new" seed is transferred directly and exclusively through the male figure (the sefirot of *Tife'eret* and *Yesod*), without any intervention of the female building on the gendered hierarchy espoused by kabbalistic theosophy that assigns a more elevated religious status to the male in contrast to the female. These absolute categories of gender are further associated with the right and left dimensions of the ten sefirot — the hypostases of the Divine — and the qualities of mercy and judgment, respectively.[18] From the text it becomes clear that the "old" seed is of lesser value, since it is already used and soiled. Thus, we may say that the new souls are unconnected to the *Shekhinah*, while the old ones undergo a transformation with her help:

> It is written, *I will bring you seed from the East* (Isa. 43:5). This implies, when Israel is righteous [before God], I will bring your seed from this place [the East] and will generate new seed for you; but when Israel is wicked, I will take of the seed that is already in the world, as it is written, *One generation passes away, and another generation comes* (Eccles. 1:4), this teaches that it has already come. But what is meant by the verse, *and gather thee from the West* (Isa. 43:5)? From that attribute that always leans toward the West. Why is [the West] called *ma'arav* ["mixture"]? Because all the seeds are mixed there. To what is this comparable? To a prince, who had a comely and modest bride in his chambers and took riches from his father's house and always brought them to her; and she took everything, putting it aside and mixing it all together. After many days, he wished to see what she had gathered and collected. Of this it is written, *I gather you from the West [mixture]* (Isa. 43:5). And what is her father's house? As is written, *I will bring your seed from the East* — this teaches that He brings [the seed] from the East, which he sows in the West, and afterward he gathers what he has sown.[19]

Gershom Scholem notes that this passage of the *Bahir* reveals a messianic and eschatological view.[20] I would add that the image of the king's daughter, as the one who "would take all of it, conceal it, and mix it all together,"[21] bears a paradoxical sexual meaning, juxtaposing concealment and modesty with mixing and joining together. Moreover, the metaphor of the bride hides an incestuous element, which reinforces the connection between the king's daughter and her brother, the king's son (as the Bahir follows, "A parable of a king who married his daughter to his son"), as well as the connection between the daughter and her father ("whenever the daughter needed her father or the father needed his daughter, they would embrace through the window").[22]

By contrast, Angelet, following Ibn Gaon, the Zohar, and other sources, pursues a dramatically different approach to the *Bahir* by emphasizing the necessity of the *Shekhinah*'s involvement in the process of *gilgul*, not only ex post facto but ex ante. As mentioned above, the *Bahir* states that if Israel is righteous, there is no need to pass the seed through the daughter's room (or womb), while the *Shekhinah* is repeatedly associated with pejorative characteristics emphasizing sin, fault, and impurity invoking the Hebrew root (ערב), denoting the West (*ma'arav*) and the mixing of the seed (*zera mit'arev*). Turning to creative exegesis, Angelet views precisely these seemingly impure or negative aspects of the *Shekhinah* as the most suitable tools for reparation or *tikkun*. He emphatically states, "You will understand this from the secret of the wheel (*galgal*), which continuously returns to its place until it has completed its motion, and if it has not achieved its goal in one cycle it returns a second time and a third . . . and whoever did not merit to ascend to the world of eternity (the sefirah *Netzah*) returns to the West (the sefirah *Malkhut*) until the night will come (*erev*)."[23] Angelet challenges the *Bahir*'s formulation, *im lo zahu* ("whoever did not merit") and suggests a reinterpretation of the subject by comparing the rotation of the cosmic spheres and the cycle of human generations with the reincarnation (*gilgul*) of the individual's soul. According to him, just as the wheel turns "naturally" until the completion of the cyclic process ("*if it has not achieved its goal*"), so, too, the soul has an opportunity to return and purify itself through the aspect of the night (*erev*) and the West (*ma'arav*).

A similar technique, which moves from a position of ethical judgment to a positive and natural rotation, appears in the section "The Secret of *Ibbur*," where the author claims that the soul gets a second and a third opportunity to purge and brighten (*le-marek*) its sins through the western entrance (*sha'ar ha-ma'aravi*), a process that eventually will aid the coming of the Messiah and the return to the Divine, defined as the upper source (*ad she-itaknu ka-raui*):

> If you understand the secret of the soul that returns *to the God who has given it* (Eccl. 12: 7), you will understand this: when she (the soul) needs purification, and if her purification is efficacious, she will return by dint of the secret of *ibbur* from the West. As it is said, *I will gather you from the West* (Isa. 43:5). Those who did not merit the first time and stayed at the opening of the Western entrance (*sha'ar ha-ma'aravi*) and cannot ascend until they are properly rectified, [God] will remove from them any impurities. As it is said, "the Messiah, son of David, will not come until all the

> souls in the *body* [treasure-house] have been completed"[24] ... this is the mystery of the verse, and *you will return to the Lord your God.* (Deut. 30:2)[25]

Since both *gilgul* and *ibbur* intend to return the soul "to the fullness of its good,"[26] Angelet insists on the inclusion of the *Shekhinah* in these processes. As we have noted above, the *Shekhinah* always symbolizes a mixture of good and evil, transgression and repair. Her essence, in her depiction as both a daughter and a bride, hints at the idea that the sefirotic structure is built on illicit intercourse between the father (sefirah *Ḥokhmah*), the mother (sefirah *Binah*), the son (sefirah *Tife'eret*), and the daughter (sefirah *Malkhut*).

REINCARNATION AS A SECRET TRANSMITTED BY "MY TEACHER" — IBN GAON

Throughout his work, Angelet seems to allude to the discussion of R. Shem Tov ben Abraham Ibn Gaon (1283–c. 1330) concerning the secret of Abel's reincarnations in "The Secret of *Ibbur*," in which he refers to the words of his teacher, "And it is for this purpose, for when will he merit such a great and pure sanctity as this, that he is fitting to enjoy the good delight, that he may be sanctified by this Crown (*Atarah*) in the World to Come. These are the words of my teacher, may the memory of the righteous be a blessing."[27] He presents *gilgul* here as a secret divine ploy emerging from God's grace to provide sinners with an opportunity to rectify their transgression: "A person is born for good, and he is given time to reincarnate and to return to the fullness of that good, three times."[28] Significantly, according to Ibn Gaon's understanding, the third reincarnation constitutes the ultimate and final stage of atonement as it denotes the completion and final phase of processes that began in previous lives:

> A very great secret is known to be found in the story of Abel, for the secret of *ibbur* in the third [reincarnation] is the greatest, for one may return up to three times, as it is written, *Unto the third and fourth [generations]* (Ex. 20: 4) and *Truly, God will do all these things two or three times to a man* (Job 33: 29) ... and God (spiritually) incarnated in Moses, too, as alluded to by the verse, *And God incarnated in me* (Deut. 3:26) and so Moses received the Torah, for he was fit and suitable for it.[29]

This passage explains that after his murder, Abel was reincarnated first in Seth, then in Moses, and finally as the Messiah, a sequence alluded to in Moses's own name, the three Hebrew letters of which are interpreted as the initials of Messiah, Seth, and Abel.[30] It is noteworthy that he applies a more radical exegesis offering an innovative reading of the verb ויתעב in Deuteronomy 3:26, which he associated with the root *ibbur* or impregnation, and not its more traditional interpretation as becoming angry or incensed. A parallel position is expressed in the Zohar's interpretation of the verse "*Then I accounted those who have died more fortunate than those who are still living* (Eccl. 4:2), for the former are on a higher level than the latter. Who are these? Those who have died and received their punishment three times, who are called refined silver, for they have passed through the fire three times, and the dross has been purged from them, and they have been purified and cleansed."[31]

THE INFLUENCE OF R. JOSEPH SHALOM ASHKENAZI (THE RY"SH)

In forging his own theory of reincarnation, Angelet integrated teachings received from Ibn Gaon with speculations articulated by another medieval kabbalist, R. Joseph ben Shalom Ashkenazi (the RY"Sh), an influential Spanish kabbalist of the fourteenth century, who is mentioned by name in Angelet's work, *A Peddler's Basket* (*Sefer Qupat ha-Rokhelin*).[32] In an enigmatic passage on the afterlife of the soul, he delineates two different destinations where the souls are sequestered and bases his teaching on his teacher, the RY"SH. Those that are meritorious "ascend to the world of eternity," while those that are still blemished return to a place called West (*ma'arav*), a word that hints at admixture (mixed or, in Hebrew, *meurav*). "Whoever did not merit to ascend to the world of eternity returns to the West (*ma'arav*) until the night will come (*erev*). Understand this. And according to RY"SH, [this means] *until he is refined as one smelts silver* (Zecheriah 13:9) *so that no one may be kept banished* (2 Samuel 14:14) and in mystical visions, *for die, we will die* (2 Samuel 14:14) — die in this world, and we will die in the World to Come."[33] The metaphor of smelting and refining metal is repeatedly deployed by R. Joseph Shalom Ashkenazi in his commentary on *Sefer Yeẓirah* (misattributed to R. Avraham ben David), where he mentions the concepts of *gilgul* and *ibbur* in his overall treatment of all transient beings.[34] He continues to apply the language of metal working to characterize the process by which the soul becomes divested of the superfluous dross (sin, transgression) with each reincarnation it is subjected to. He further links this process to the world of the sefirot, the "ten sefirot of nothingness (*bli mah*)," as discussed in *Sefer Yeẓirah*:

> Regarding [the sefirot] *Ḥokhmah* and *Binah*, the instruction is to "discern" them, that is, you must discern and purify and contemplate the end and the root of [the sefirot] *Gedulah* and *Gevurah*, how their roots originate from *Ḥokhmah* and *Binah*, for discernment and smelting have one meaning, and that is to purify and clarify, as it is stated, *I will smelt them as one smelts silver and discern them as one discerns gold* (Zecheriah 13:9). So [*Sefer Yeẓirah*] says "discern them," meaning in the emanation that is drawn down into *Ḥokhmah* and *Binah*, and likewise *Gedulah* and *Gevurah*, as their roots were in *Ḥokhmah* and *Binah*.[35]

To understand Angelet's use of Ashkenazi's words, it should be underlined that fundamentally Angelet challenges Nahmanides's interpretation of the verse *for die, we will die* (2 Samuel 14:14) as implying absolute spiritual excision. Rather, he interprets the phrase metaphorically as as a reference to poverty and blindness, meted out to soften the punishment of sin, so that one would not lose one's portion in the World to Come. For Angelet, death is a metaphor for transient states of punishment — such as poverty, blindness, and suffering — connected with "tarrying in the West,"[36] and further identified with periods of darkness within the *Shekhinah*. By contrast, R. Joseph Shalom Ashkenazi, if our presumption concerning his identity in Angelet's Secrets is correct, speaks of ascent in the sefirotic realm to *Ḥokhmah* and *Binah*, the sources of *Ḥesed* and *Gevurah*, as a model for the ascent of the human soul. Even if Ashkenazi does not directly refer to *gilgul* in this passage, he describes a process of refining the soul through ascent to the upper sefirot as based on the expression of *Sefer Yeẓirah*: "discern them and investigate them and clarify the matter fully and seat the Maker on His foundation."[37]

Although Angelet frequently challenges Ashkenazi's conclusions in *Twenty-Four Secrets*, it is evident that he nonetheless respects his opinions, citing him on eight different occasions, by the acronym "the RY"Sh." It is a yet-unsolved question why he never chooses to cite Ashkenazi's full name, as he does with other kabbalists. In "Twenty-Four Secrets," Angelet consistently calls his deceased teacher R. Shem Tov ben Abraham ibn Gaon, *mori z"l* ("my teacher of blessed memory"). In all his references, the RY"Sh receives the special blessing *ha-RY"Sh N"R* (*natrei raḥmana*, "God will protect him"), an appellation intended for living kabbalists and indicating that unlike the teacher who already died, the RY"Sh was Angelet's living contemporary.

In consolidating his own position vis-à-vis his teachers, Angelet polemicizes on two fronts: by insisting on the centrality of the *Shekhinah* as a refining fire through which a person achieves rectification even before his final death, he rejects the school of Nahmanides pursued by Ibn Gaon. At the same time, by proposing that the Israelite nation and each human being can achieve rectification or *tikkun* without ascending to the upper sefirot, he marshals an argument against R. Joseph Ashkenazi. Thus, the section closes with the words, "And Israel has found nothing better than poverty, which takes the place of death, from which they escape, repenting and returning and meriting the world to come."[38] I would suggest that Angelet uses the term "poverty" (*ve-lo matza le-israel middah tovah ke-'aniut*) to refer to the *Shekhinah*, placing her at the center of the salvific process and the ascent to the sefirah *Binah*, which symbolizes freedom and the World to Come.[39] In the examples cited above, Angelet consistently stresses the primary and positive role of the *Shekhinah* in the process of *gilgul*. In both secrets, Angelet claims that the soul can be renewed by ascending to the heights of the sefirotic schema only after passing through the sefirah *Malkhut* or by descending to the lower world that is admixed with the *Shekhinah*, where the soul can live through multiple reincarnations of poverty, blindness, and suffering. The source of these ideas seems to be the introduction of the commentary to *Sefer Yeẓirah*, where R. Yosef Ashkenazi focuses on the inherently cyclical nature of human existence, in keeping with the general and positive the "law of all transient things" (*din benei ḥalof*), which emphasized divine providence in this world.[40]

> When every one of you understands and returns to his homeward path, then you will know that you will be born in the mystery of *ibbur* and renewed as a new creation, and your days will be many. The Sun (*Tiferet*) and the Moon (*Ateret*), from whom comes the light of darkness and every event and loss, that is to say, the "law of all transient things" (*din benei ḥalof*), will both pass through the sphere of the Name of YHVH in the Name of Adonai. Thus, when the soul has reached the limit of its adventures, which is the semicircle above the earth, the movement having reached its end in the one-hundred and eighty degrees [of a semicircle], from *there he will descend to death or poverty or some other suffering*. But in the "law of transient things" (*din benei ḥalof*), and from there onward, you will see and understand it is bound *to complete the circle and return to its homeward path*. And so, it will be made clear to you that in his return

> to this world in the form of vegetative life you will be born in the law of transient things and your days will be many according to the power of vegetative life.[41]

Based on the examples cited above, I suggest that Joseph Angelet was clearly influenced by Joseph Ashkenazi's teachings on the doctrine of the soul's ascent, with its emphasis on the *Shekhinah* and its role as the metaphorical lynchpin, as signaled by the references to "his homeward path" and the image of the *Shekhinah* as the center line of a circle or sphere. The image of a 180-degree arc lies at the heart of his analysis in "The Secret Meaning of *Gilgul*" and its discussion of the "generation that turns like a sphere," a theme I elaborate in the following section. Finally, I would suggest that even though Angelet at times disagrees with Ashkenazi's theory, he nevertheless follows his definition of the secret of *ibbur* and *gilgul* as pertaining not necessarily to *literal* death or transmigration from one body to another, but to the totality of movement from one level to another and from one state to another in the *sefirotic* system.

Gilgul and *Ibbur* as Processes of Birthing

In shedding light on the various articulations of *gilgul* in the thought of R. Joseph Angelet, I suggest that the feminine aspect of divinity plays a pivotal role in the transformation of souls and bodies and in the erasure of sin and its atonement through reincarnation. This is due to the erotic nature of the *Shekhinah* and the heroines who represent Her. Building on Zoharic literature and the writings of Castilian kabbalists, Angelet emphasizes the importance of the maternal *sefirah* Binah, referred to as "return" or "repentance," since only through her unique filial relationship to the *Shekhinah* can the worlds and souls ascend on the theosophic ladder.[42] As I suggested in my book *Human Throes*, whether *gilgul* is defined as a situation in which multiple souls find a home in one body, or in which soul sparks accrue over multiple reincarnations, the totality of these phenomena relate to the desire to blur the boundary between the "I" and the "not-I."[43] Kabbalistic exegeses (*derashot*) frequently posit a unifying experience (*unio mystica*), implying the absorption of the soul within the Divine and within the Other, which echoes the symbiotic dyad of a mother and her infant. Furthermore, the ontological unity between the mother and her child in the womb is further reinforced in the Zohar's language, as *gilgul* is sometimes referred to as "enclothing" (*hitlabshut*), especially when describing divine reproduction and generation.[44]

The concept of *gilgul* is closely associated with the notion of birth, which unfolds simultaneously on multiple levels of being. *Gilgul* blurs the sharp distinction between "nothingness" and "being," and instead implies a fluidity between the past and the future, which gradually reveals the addition of one garment to another in the great chain of being. This process unfolds in the womb of the *Shekhinah*, as primordial mother, and aids the transformation of the self to hasten the redemption and atonement of the supernal worlds. Likewise, *gilgul* is understood as an intermediary to a "second birth," as an expression of the desire to be born anew, not only as an individual but also as a family and a collective through the purification of the divine world affected by human acts.

A soul is impregnated within another body just as a baby is enwombed within its mother, as the various expressions of "the mystery of *ibbur*" (a recurring phrase in kabbalistic works to signify the journey of the soul and its passage from potentiality to actuality) allude.[45] Indeed, in a series of articles, Moshe Idel discussed the differences in the development of the doctrine of *gilgul* and *ibbur* in early Kabbalah and deduced important distinctions in a vertical versus a horizontal model of *ibbur*. The former, Idel posited, characterized the movement of the *Shekhinah* in relation to the sefirot above Her, while the biblical commandment of levirate marriage alludes to the horizontal activity of the human soul as it transmigrates from one body into another. However, I would contend that in the literature of the Zohar it is difficult to distinguish between the two models.[46]

In the writings of Angelet, the mystery of *ibbur* is connected primarily to the intra-divine dynamic among the sefirot, more particularly to the relationship between the last sefirah *Shekhinah/Malkuth* and the upper sefirah *Binah*. He further alludes to the symbiosis between the souls of the righteous below and the womb of the *Shekhinah* above. The result is a more complex paradigm conjoining heavenly and earthly processes concerning which he frequently uses the terms *ibbur* and *gilgul* interchangeably. Furthermore, Angelet's unique conception draws on the idea that human action governs the family relations among the ten sefirot, particularly those connected to *Shekhinah/Malkhut*, from whose womb people are born and to which they will return. As such, we may say that every reincarnation reenacts and adds to the primordial narrative or, in Freud's terms, creates a new "family romance."[47] Every reincarnation returns to the original couple and to the "primal scene," which serves as the basis of human existence for all future generations. If, as I suggest, each human being indeed constitutes a part of the "divine family," then variations of the doctrine of metempsychosis reveal an additional aspect of theogony [Θεογονία] — that is, the formation of the upper worlds, and therefore the births, within the divinity. Moreover, the combination of doctrines of *gilgul* and *ibbur* hints at the possibility that the primordial womb and "prenatal" states of the divine being can be depicted as pregnant with a kind of secret knowledge concerning all future souls that would emanate from therein.

Understood this way, a single body can encompass "multiple selves" that exist in dialogue with all previous generations. As such, it expresses the human narrative voice, for without the life story of the individual, there is no meaning to the ways in which a person reincarnates and lives again through other beings, both human and divine. The parts of the soul unique to a person combined with the account of another human being allow for a thick narrative in which the lives of the sefirot and the histories of individuals are intertwined.

Gilgul and the Cyclical Nature of the *Shekhinah*

In his explanation of "The Secret of *Ibbur*," Angelet makes use of a well-known Talmudic trope about the moon, in which the term *ibbur* refers to the sanctification of the new month and appears most frequently in the context of legislating against false witnesses. The Mishnah compares the moon to a pregnant woman, and in response to the two witnesses who said, "'We saw it in its [anticipated] time, and on the night of its fullness [*ibbur*] we did not see it,' R. Dosa ben Hurkynus replies caustically, 'They are false witnesses. How can they testify that a woman gave birth and the next day her belly is (again) between her teeth?'"[48] The use of the phrase "her belly is between her teeth" to describe a fetus on the verge of being born is perplexing, yet one cannot help but note the vulgarity of his language, which is presumably intended to drive away the false witnesses.[49] The expression is meant to accentuate the impossibility that a woman could give birth and then immediately return to the state of pregnancy.

In kabbalistic symbolism, *ibbur* and cycles of the moon are connected to the figure of the *Shekhinah,* pregnant with the souls of the righteous, who share in her suffering caused by the damage and the defects (*pegam*) of the world.[50] Angelet applies the legalistic and logical thinking of the rabbis to the mystical and metaphysical realms, declaring that although such a feat is impossible for a flesh-and-blood woman, it is not for the *Shekhinah*: "They said in the last chapter of b. Ketubot that a person is born for good, and he is given time to reincarnate and to return to the fullness of that good three times, and this is the *ibbur* of the moon, of which they said, 'her belly is between her teeth.' For it is fitting that 'no one be kept banished,' but rather everyone should merit the hidden good."[51] In fact, Angelet subverts the charge of false testimony by claiming that, since the *Shekhinah* can always return to its state of fullness, pregnancy or *ibbur*, the souls that pass through her also merit such an atonement over the course of their lives, as well as after their deaths. Thus, the author describes a process of ascent and rectification. While, for the rabbis, "her belly is between her teeth" is an expression of derision or a declaration of false testimony, for Angelet it is given new meaning, becoming an affirmation of truth: an individual does indeed reincarnate three times, that is, he is born and returns to his divine mother's (*Shekhinah*) womb, and is born yet again. While Angelet's treatment of the *mythos* of the sanctification of the month relies on rabbinic conceptions, he reverses their original meaning and adds a distinctively mystical overtone to it.

Throughout *Twenty-Four Secrets*, Angelet describes humanity as the offspring of the *Shekhinah*, especially when engaged in the process of elimination, purge, and expiation through the mercy of the sefirat *Malkhut*. At the same time, the connection between the upper mother (*Binah*) and daughter (*Shekhinah*) — a theme on which I expand below — enables human souls to derive from a higher level the quality of the uppermost source of souls and as well as Bina's "treasure-house" (*oẓar ha-neshamot*).[52] Indeed, one of the main symbols of Bina as *Teshuvah* (repentance/return) stands at the center of two of the texts discussing human deeds, "The Secret Meaning of *Gilgul*" and "The Secret of *Ibbur*." The former concludes with the words "They said that the Holy One, blessed be He, searched through all the attributes and did not find any so beneficial for Israel as poverty, for it takes the place of death, from which they escape, repenting and returning and meriting the World to Come."[53] This notion is further reinforced in another secret, when Esau is sacrificed by the supernal High Priest: "And the Prince of Hesed, the High Priest, brings the image of the Goat, the great Prince who had been called Samael, who defends the wicked Esau, and sacrifices him on the altar that stands *before Repentance*."[54] Angelet portrays wicked rulers and false prophets in the harshest of terms. As they prevented people from repenting, they are punished most severely: "The false prophets who led many to sin are not allowed to repent . . . and since [Menashe] caused many to stumble, he was not granted repentance to merit the World to Come."[55] According to this reading, repentance is the path by which one merits eternal life and enters the World to Come, from which we can derive that *gilgul*, which allows for repentance, is an ascent to the World of Life.

Rachel and Leah as *Malkuth* and *Binah*: The Feminine Aspects of the Soul's Ascent

R. Joseph Angelet deploys the biblical female figures Rachel and Leah, whom he identifies with the sefirot *Malkhut* and *Binah*, respectively, to depict distinct stations in the soul's path of penitence and its return journey.[56] For him, these two heroines symbolize central figures in the divine schema.[57] In another passage following similar conceptualization in the Zohar, Angelet posits that a repentant individual who has suffered for the expiation of sins during one's lifetime becomes the sibling and the son of the sefirot, *Shekhinah/Malkhut* and *Binah*, after death.[58] This dual position allows a mortal (unlike an angel) to merit eternal life by ascending the sefirotic structure. Reincarnation and thus the process of *gilgul* takes place in the world of repentance, one of the primary names for the sefirah *Binah* associated here with Leah, from where it flows into the lower entity of the sefirah *Malkhut* corresponding to Rachel.[59] The connection of the two sisters is summarized in the role of the altar "that stands before repentance" in light of the well-known rabbinic statement that nothing can stand before it,[60] as Angelet says in "The Secret of the Calendrical *Ibbur* (the Leap Year)":

> There are times decreed upon the attribute of mercy, seven days before the sighting of the moon, to wage war with Samael and his forces for having diminished the Moon. And the hairy Goat[61] challenges the *Smooth Man* ["*ish chalak*," Jacob][62] in a competition over the love of She who is *beautiful as the Moon* (Song of Songs 6:10, referring to the *Shekhinah*). Michael, the Prince of Mercy (*Ḥesed*), and Gavriel, the Prince of Judgment (*Gevurah*), both serve Him in the war against the sect of the evil prosecutors [*mekatregim*]. And the Prince of *Ḥesed*, the High Priest, brings the image of the Goat, the great Prince who is called *Shemasael* [Samael], who defends the wicked Esau, and sacrifices him on the altar that stands before *Repentance* on the day of the new moon, and then the [divine] will is appeased and made content. And the emanation that is lacking from the glory, which appears as a punishment for the diminishing of

the Moon, multiplies and grows full, and this is the image of atonement through the sacrifice of the Goat.[63]

While noting the stridently mythic treatment of atonement and the battle between good and evil as symbolized by the twins Jacob and Esau, who complement the two sisters Rachel and Leah, I would like to focus on Angelet's efforts to connect the new moon sacrifice to the secret of *gilgul* and the concepts of repentance and return (*teshuvah*).[64] As we saw, Angelet's conception of *gilgul*, influenced by Ibn Gaon and R. Joseph Ashkenazi, focuses on the possibility of the final rectification in the third reincarnation and in the ascent from one sefirah to the next. Death is not a precondition for *gilgul* and suffering is not the goal, but rather represents the means for ascending in repentance. The process of repentance and return, as it plays out within the relationship between Rachel and Leah, reveals that the primary intention is to unite the daughter and mother, the younger sister to the elder.

The rupture between the two sisters haunts Angelet, and the biblical rivalry between them is represented here as a reflection of a larger mythical drama of a battle that ensues on a cosmic level between God, and the archetype of the demonic "other side" (*sitra aḥra*), Samael.[65] Rachel and Leah, Jacob and Esau, are all involved in the divine and cosmic processes of purification that unfold concurrently in heavenly and earthly realms. The male figures fight a duel over the *Shekhinah*, who is described as *beautiful as the Moon* (Song of Songs 6:10), and identified with the biblical Rachel. In the passage cited above from the secret of calendrical *ibbur*, Angelet depicts the sacrifice of the goat on the Day of Atonement by the High Priest as a theosophical drama. The goat represents the demonic power Samael, and the altar signifies Leah, the sefirah *Binah*, and the aspect of repentance. The sacrifice of the goat enables the triumph of the Divine over evil and its powers. This process happens on the "day of the new moon," a symbolic cipher denoting the union of the lower sisters, Rachel and Leah, and also of the upper forces and the sefirot, *Shekhinah/Malkuth* and *Binah*.

A Jungian reading of the complicated narrative recounted by Angelet portrays an individual coming face-to-face with his own shadow, with whom he must reconcile, as Rachel and Leah ("the symbolic twins") represent the shadow of the Other and await reconciliation.[66] In Angelet's thought, *gilgul* becomes a spiritual tool affecting repentance as well as a means of joining the maternal figures of the two mothers of the Jewish nation, who embody the birth of the twelve tribes. While the Book of Genesis presents the relationship between Jacob's two wives as acrimonious (Gen. 30–31), the Book of Ruth offers a more positive reading, as Rachel and Leah are united in the blessings the elders extend to Boaz at the gates of the city: "Then all the people who were at the gate along with the elders said, We are witnesses, may the Lord make the woman who is coming into your house like Rachel and Leah, *who together built up the house of Israel.* May you produce children in Ephrathah and bestow a name in Bethlehem (Ruth 4:11)." The tendency to unite the sisters and to mend the rift between them can be observed later in Lamentations Rabba (Proem 24) in which the Midrash describes how Rachel revealed her secret sign with Jacob in order to avoid Leah's public humiliation. According to this midrash, when the Temples was destroyed, all the patriarchs asked God for mercy for the Jewish nation, which went into exile. But only Rachel succeeded in arousing God's mercy because of her selflessness in relation to Leah by giving her the secret signs. Moreover, Rachel speaks to Jacob on Leah's behalf from under the marital bed to ensure the consummation of their marriage. Unlike Moses and the Patriarchs, Rachel is rewarded by God for her selflessness by gathering her sons, the Jewish nation, from their Exile:

> At that moment, Rachel, our mother, jumped up before the Divine (Hashem), and said: "Master of the Universe, you know that Yaakov, your servant, loved me with a great love and worked for me for my father for seven years. And when the seven years were up, and the time came for me to be married to my husband, my father devised a plan to have my sister switch places with me for my husband. And this was very difficult for me as I heard about the plan, but *I swallowed my suffering and had mercy on my sister so that she should not be shamed in public.* And that evening [of my marriage], my sister took my place with my husband, and I gave her all the signs that I gave my husband so that he would think that she was Rachel. And not only that, but I lay under the bed where he lay with my sister and when he spoke with her, she was silent, and I answered each time so that he would not recognize her voice and I acted with loving-kindness toward her, and I was not jealous of her, and I did not put her to shame.[67]

Beginning with the writings of the medieval kabbalists Moses de Leon and Joseph Gikatilla, who were first to identify Leah with the sefirah *Binah*,[68] the bond between Rachel and Leah is transformed in the Zohar into a symbol for the attachment of the feminine sefirot, *Malkuth/Shekhinah*, with the upper sefirah *Binah*. Following the Castilian kabbalistic readings articulated toward the end of thirteenth century, Angelet portrays the love between the sisters as a mythical reflection of the way the sefirot continue to support each other in the battle against the powers of evil. The role of human beings in this cyclical theurgical process is to continue this struggle and refine their souls through reincarnation.

In "The Secret of the Calendrical *Ibbur*," Angelet attempts to show that the rite of the New Moon is a repetitive, ongoing means to their reconciliation, to the joining of above and below, heaven and earth. According to the radical legend told in the Babylonian Talmud, every new Moon, God requests, "Bring an atoning sacrifice for Me for having diminished the moon."[69] The day of the New Moon is a day of divine repentance. According to this legend, God requires the aid of the female forces or the human representations of the female aspect of the *Shekhinah* to atone for His sin. Angelet seems to hint that the *gilgul* of the individual aids the *gilgul* of the *sefirot* and raises one to the next level until their ascent and rectification in the unified schema become complete.

Conclusion

In this chapter, I have analyzed the feminine elements in R. Joseph Angelet's doctrine of *gilgul* in light of the roles played by the sefirot *Binah* and *Malkuth/Shekhinah*. At the same time, following the earliest traditions of *gilgul*, as well as the kabbalistic identification of the feminine with "dark sides," this doctrine connotes not only birth but also aspects of death, sin, and punishment. Angelet's dual use of the term *ibbur* reflects his attempts in these three secrets to integrate various doctrines and teachings, including the metaphysical conceptualization of pregnancy and the mystery of procreation; an emphasis on the need to return to the womb of the *Shekhinah* or the "West," linking *ibbur* with sin and anger (as an alliteration with the words *evrah ve'za'am*); and the motif of annihilation in "The Secret of the Calendrical *Ibbur*.[70] He further hinted at the secret that God "is conceived or impregnated" (*mit'aber*) within the leaders and the righteous of the generation (the "Secret of *Ibbur*"). As an important community leader in the town of Saragossa, this statement may have resonated with the author on an autobiographic level as he identified with Moses, "I have another hidden secret, understood from the verse, 'But the Lord was angry with me on your account' (Deut. 3:26)."[71] Finally, Angelet's use of the term *ibbur* alludes to punishment that can extend over multiple generations by way of transmigration through the *Shekhinah*, the supernal Mother, who not only loves but also chastises her children in her role as the "earthly court."

On the psychological level, belief in the transmigration of souls responds to the fear of death and provides a certain level of calm to a person facing his or her own end. If we have an opportunity to return once again to this world — even if in a different form — then we can presumably complete that which we left unfinished or amend any damage we have caused in our current lives. Unlike the belief that death means the extinction of the self, belief in return allows for the possibility of repair and change. As my analysis of Angelet's works on *gilgul* and *ibbur* show, one's life does not begin with our physical birth and does not end with our death, but persists through a continued existence in both the physical and metaphysical realms. In the personal dimension, *gilgul* is expressed in its relationships with future generations and the way in which internalized and projected aspects of the father and mother are rooted and reenacted within the psyche of their child. Similarly, on the mythical level, the images of Adam and Eve reincarnate within every person.

In the divine dimension, however, *gilgul* finds expression in the human images woven into the divine schema and identified with the sefirot. Within the dynamic of the interrelationships of the sefirot, one's individual story is reborn again and again, for while one's life does indeed end, the sefirah — as the archetype of individuality — represents eternity.[72] In our case, although the struggle between the biblical figures of the matriarchs, Rachel and Leah, is part of the past, through the kabbalistic identification between them and the sefirot of *Malkuth/Shekhinah* and *Binah*, they exist forever. Read through mythical, ritual, and psychological lenses, their story constitutes an ongoing repair of the traumatic past. Angelet, in using feminine and maternal images in his interpretation of the secrets of *gilgul* and *ibbur*, delineates a new path for reconciliation between human beings, and between the lower and the upper worlds.

Notes

1. I'm grateful to my colleagues and teachers: Yehuda Liebes, Bracha Sack, Moshe Idel, Iris Felix, Leore Sachs Shmueli, Andrea Gondos, and Biti Roi. This chapter is dedicated to my mother-in-law, Malka Kaniel, who taught me much about generosity and charity (tzedakah), as it says, "One should always request mercy regarding this condition [of poverty], for if he does not come to it, his son will, and if his son does not, his grandson will, *for due to this thing (ki biglal)*" (Deut. 15:10). A tanna from the school of R. Ishmael taught, "It is a wheel (galgal) that turns in the world" (b. Shabbat 151b).

I would like to acknowledge the financial assistance received from the Azrieli Institute of Israel Studies at Concordia University (Montreal, Canada), for generously supporting the translation of this chapter from Hebrew to English. In addition, This research was supported by the Israeli Science Foundation (grant No. 2749/21) dedicated to the Writings of R. Joseph Angelet and the Zohar. The grant managed by Ronit Meroz and me and assisted by a wonderful team, who contributed helpful comments to this article: Iris Felix, Noam Lefler, Hadas Sabato, Ayellet Walfish, Hod Zaguri.

2. These works were written between the completion of his earlier tractate, *Qupat ha-Rokhelin* (1311), MS Oxford Bodleian Opp. 288; his later work, *Livnat ha-Sapir*: *Peirush midrah ha-Ne'elam ve-Tosefta le-Sefer ha-Zohar,* attributed [mistakenly] to Rabbi David, son of Judah the Pious (Jerusalem: Unknown Publisher, 1988); and his commentary on R. Joseph Gikatilla's work, *Peirush le-Sha'arei Orah* (1325–1327). It is beyond the scope of this chapter to address connections between Angelet's vast library, but for a more extensive treatment of Angelet, his works, and mystical system, see Leore Sachs-Shmueli, Iris Felix, and Ruth Kara-Ivanov Kaniel, "R. Joseph Angelet's Twenty-Four Secrets (Introduction, Study and Edition)," *Kabbalah* 50 (2021): 193–320 [Hebrew]. Henceforth, I refer to this critical edition throughout this chapter as "Twenty-Four Secrets."

3. Henceforth I refer to these two concepts in their Hebrew original, *gilgul* and *ibbur*. This chapter is an expansion of the discussion presented in the critical edition prepared by Leore Sachs Shmueli, Iris Felix, and me, see note 2 above. I wish to extend my deep gratitude to Iris and Leore for our shared conversations, out of which this chapter developed.

4. Secret of *Ibbur*, "Twenty-Four Secrets," 306 (emphasis mine). This declaration reflects the author's optimistic attitude, which stands in contrast for example to the tragic description of reincarnation in the Zohar, *Saba de-Mishpatim*, and in the works of other contemporary kabbalists such as R. Joseph Hamadan and the anonymous work *Tikkunei ha-Zohar*.

5. This sentiment is echoed throughout the Zohar's discussions of the mystery of levirate marriage and *gilgul* in the lineage of the Messiah. For reference, see R. Kara-Kaniel *Holiness and Transgression: Mothers of the Messiah in the Jewish Myth* (New York: Academic Studies Press, 2017).

6. See, for example, Gershom Scholem, *On the Mystical Shape of the Godhead* (New York: Pantheon Books, 1991), 228–41; Ronit Meroz, "Teachings about Exile in Lurianic Kabbalah [Hebrew] (PhD diss., Jerusalem: Hebrew University, 1988); Lawrence Fine, *Physician of the Soul, Healer of the Cosmos: Isaac Luria and His Kabbalistic Fellowship* (Stanford: Stanford University Press, 2003).

7. Gershom Scholem, *The Messianic Idea in Judaism* (New York: Schocken, 1971), 47. In his profound discussion on the notion of *ẓelem* (image/likeness), Scholem claims that the doctrine of transmigration challenges the notion of the uniqueness of the individual distinguished from its fellow: "What in fact constituted the special, individual essence of each human being? This problem arises in connection with the theory of transmigration, which seemed to

throw into question the *unique and irretrievable nature of human existence*. What then is the *principium individuationis* of a person, that element that constitutes his unique existence and sustains his identity throughout its various transmigrations?" (Scholem, *On the Mystical Shape*, 251–52). In his research, Scholem has demonstrated various kabbalistic perspectives on the subject of *gilgul*, among which we can find negative and positive attitudes. See, for example, G. Scholem, "Levush ha-Neshamot ve-Haluka deRabbanan," *Tarbiẓ* 24 (1955): 290–306 [Hebrew]; Scholem, "Studies in the Doctrine of Transmigration in 13th-Century Kabbalah," *Tarbiẓ* 16 (1945): 135–50 [Hebrew]; Scholem, *On the Mystical Shape*, 197–250.

8. Indeed, the *sefirah* Binah, which represents the ascent of the soul affected by *gilgul*, is referred to in *Zoharic* literature as "repentance/return" and "source of life," terms that were later applied to the *Shekhinah* as well. See Isaiah Tishby, ed., *The Wisdom of the Zohar, vol. 3* (Oxford: Littman Library of Jewish Civilization, 1989), 1499–1510.

9. "Twenty-Four Secrets," 296.

10. "Twenty-Four Secrets," 298–99; 306–7.

11. The *Shekhinah* is perceived as the "earthly court" and a punishing judge, yet she is also identified with the destructive aspects of humanity and existence. On Her relationship to the "other side," see, for example, Scholem, *Mystical Shape of the Godhead*, 140–96; Tishby, *Wisdom*, 219–31, 285–307; Idel, *Kabbalah and Eros* (New Haven: Yale University Press, 2005); Liebes, "Zohar and Eros." *Alpayyim* 9 (1994): 67–119 [Hebrew]; Elliot R. Wolfson, *Circle in the Square* (Albany: State University of New York Press, 1995); Melila Hellner-Eshed, *A River Flows: The Language of Mystical Experience in the Zohar* (Stanford: Stanford University Press, 2009); Daniel Abrams, *The Female Body of God in Kabbalistic Literature* (Jerusalem: Magnes Press, 2004) [Hebrew]; Ronit Meroz, "The Weaving of a Myth: An Analysis of Two Stories in the Zohar," in *Study and Knowledge in Jewish Thought*, vol. 2, ed. Howard Kreisel (Beer-Sheva: Ben-Gurion University Press, 2006): 167–205; Nathaniel Berman, *Divine and Demonic in the Zohar and Kabbalistic Tradition* (Leiden: Brill, 2018), among others. For the connections of the *Shekhinah* to the dark side in Angelet's secrets, and her description as the "destroying angel," see the section *Sod ha-Miqreh veha-Pegiah*, where the *Shekhinah* is called an "evil woman" and identified with the sword, the plague, and the avenging scourge, in "Twenty-Four Secrets," 239–42; 300–2.

12. Oded Porat, *Kabbalistic Works by R. Azriel of Girona* (Los Angeles: Cherub Press, 2020) 83, and the notes on 85 [Hebrew].

13. Moshe Idel, "The Secret of Impregnation as Metempsychosis in Kabbalah," in *Verwandlungen. Archäologie der literarischen Kommunikation IX*, ed. A. and J. Assmann (Munich: Wilhelm Fink, 2006), 341–79; M. Idel, "Commentaries on the Secret of *Ibbur*," *Da'at* 72 (2012): 5–49 [Hebrew]; and M. Idel, "Commentaries on the Secret of *Ibbur*," *Da'at* 73 (2013): 4–44 [Hebrew].

14. Shem Tov ibn Gaon, MS Paris 774, 112b, cited by Moshe Idel, "Commentaries on the 'Secret of *Ibbur*,'" 40.

15. Ibn Gaon, Ms. Paris 774, 82a; Idel, "*Peirushim le-Sod ha-Ibbur*," 36–37. See also R. Sheqalim, *Doctrine of the Soul and Reincarnation in the 14th and 15th centuries* (self-published, 1994), 151–72.

16. The Hebrew expression *vayit'abar bi* hints at the meaning, *the Lord conceived in me*. Compare to R. Joseph Angelet, Livnat Ha-sapir Vaikra, London -British Library Add. 27000, fols. 240a-b. Ronit Meroz alludes that while dealing with the messianic importance of the biblical Joseph, Angelet may be actually alluding to himself as a messianic figure: Meroz R. "R. Joseph Angelet and His Zoharic Writings." *Te'uda* 21–22 (2007): 303–404, esp. p. 339).

17. On the relations between Angelet and *Tikkunei Zohar: Meroz*, idem, 334-340. On Moses in the *Tikkunim* literature see: A. Goldreich, "The Mystical Self-Image of the Author of *Tikkunei* ha-Zohar," in *Massu'ot*, ed. M. Oron and A. Goldreich (Jerusalem: Bialik Institute, 1994), 459–96; Y. Liebes, "The Zohar and the *Tikkunim*: From Renaissance to Revolution," in *New Developments in Zohar Studies*, ed. Ronit Meroz (Tel Aviv: Chaim Rosenberg School, 2007), 251–302; Biti Roi, *Love of the Shekhinah: Mysticism and Poetics in Tikkunei ha-Zohar* (Ramat Gan: Bar Ilan University, 2017), 408–10 [Hebrew].

18. See Elliot R. Wolfson, "Left Contained in the Right: A Study in Zoharic Hermeneutics," *AJS Review* 11, no. 1 (1986): 27–52.

19. *Sefer ha-Bahir*, §104–5; Daniel Abrams, ed., *Sefer ha-Bahir al pi Kitvei ha-Yad ha-Qedumim* (Los Angeles: Cherub Press, 1994), 187–89 [Hebrew]. For a preliminary discussion of the affinity between this text and Angelet, see "The Secret of the Reason for *Gilgul*," in "Twenty-Four Secrets," notes 163, 234. The translation follows Scholem, *Mystical Shape of the Godhead*, 204.

20. Scholem, *Mystical Shape*, 204, n. 14; Scholem, *Origins of the Kabbalah* (Princeton, NJ: Princeton University Press, 1991), 154.

21. *Sefer ha-Bahir*, §104–5.

22. *Sefer ha-Bahir*, §3; Abrams, ed., *Sefer ha-Bahir*, 119; §43–45, Abrams, ed., *Sefer ha-Bahir*, 141–43.

23. "The Secret of the Reason for *Gilgul*," in "Twenty-Four Secrets," 298–99.

24. See Rashi's comment on b. Yevamot 62a regarding the heavenly "body/treasury" (*otsar*) containing all souls.

25. "Twenty-Four Secrets," 306.

26. The section "The Secret of *Ibbur*," in "Twenty-Four Secrets," 306–7.

27. The section "The Secret of *Ibbur*," in "Twenty-Four Secrets," 306–7 (emphasis mine).

28. The section "The Secret of *Ibbur*," in "Twenty-Four Secrets," 306–7.

29. Shem Tov ben Abraham Ibn Gaon is explicit in his work *Keter Shem Tov* as he comments on the words of Nahmanides. See *Keter Shem Tov*, in *Sefer Amudei ha-Qabbalah* (Jerusalem: n.p., 2001), 13, citing Ex. 20:5, Job 33:29, and Deut. 3:26.

30. In similar fashion, the name ADaM can be read as an acronym signifying Adam, David, and Messiah.

31. Zohar III, 182b (*Huqat*), citing Ecclesiastes 4:2. On this passage, R. Haim Joseph David Azulai comments, "This means that those who are reincarnated are more beloved than those new souls that have never been in the world before." See Haim J. D. Azulai, *Nitzutzei Orot* (Jerusalem: Maoz Meir, 1970), §2 [Hebrew] on Zohar III, 182b (*Huqat*).

32. Iris Felix, "Chapters in the Kabbalistic Thought of R. Joseph Angelet" (MA thesis, Hebrew University of Jerusalem, 1991), 32. See further, "I heard from R. J. ha-Ashkenazi," in his *Quppat ha-Reukhlin*, 44a. I hope to elaborate on the possibility of identifying Ri"sh with R. Joseph Ashkenazi elsewhere. For a background on this influential kabbalist, see Gershom Scholem, *Studies in Kabbalah*, ed. J. ben Shlomo and M. Idel (Tel Aviv: Am Oved, 1998), 112–36 [Hebrew]; Georges Vajda, "Un chapitre de l'histoire du conflit entre la Kabbale et la philosophie," *AHDLMA* 23 (1956): 45–143; Moshe Idel, "The Meaning of '*Ta'amei Ha-'Ofot Ha-Teme'im*' of R. David ben Yehuda He-Hasid,'" *Alei Shefer*, ed. M. Hallamish (1990): 11–27; Moshe Hallamish, preface to *Ashkenazi's Commentary on Genesis Rabbah* (Jerusalem: Magnes, 1984), 11–27; Haviva Pedaya, "Sabbath, Sabbatai, and the Diminution of Moon," in *Myth in Judaism*, ed. H. Pedaya (Beer-Sheva: Ben-Gurion University Press, 1996), 150–53 [Hebrew].

33. Angelet, "Twenty-Four Secrets," 299, in the chapter "The Secret of the Reason for *Gilgul*."

34. For discussions of Ashkenazi's terminology on *gilgul* and *ibbur*, such as the unique term *din benie ḥalof*, see recently Moshe Idel, "Multiple Forms of Redemption in Kabbalah and Hasidism," *Jewish Quarterly Review* 101 (2011), 53 n. 101; Jonnie Schnytzer, "Metempsychosis, Metensomatosis and Metamorphosis: On Rabbi Joseph ben Shalom Ashkenazi's Systematic Theory of Reincarnation," *Kabbalah* 45 (2019): 221–44. According to Schnytzer, the author defines three different phases of transformations: 1) metempsychosis, which is linked to Ashkenazi's term "*shiluah ha-nefesh*" after the person's death; 2) metensomatosis (*gilgul* in Ashkenazi's thought), which means transmigration of physical elements from one body to another for their purification; and 3) metamorphosis, indicating the union of body and soul during one's lifetime (as a combination of *gilgul* and *shiluah* for R. Joseph). Schnytzer claims that the research literature focused only on the first model while ignoring the other two models, although they appear widely in Ashkenazi's theory and have influenced many later major texts and kabbalists, such as R. Isaac of Acre, the anonymous fourteenth-century work *Ma'arekhet ha-Elohut*, and others. Unlike Idel, Schnytzer suggests that the mystery of *ibbur* is not linked in Ashkenazi's writing to the mystery of *gilgul*; rather, it reflects the process of *shiluah hanefesh* into the person's body, as a parallel process to transportation of the soul (*shiluah ha-neshama*) to the upper realm. See recently Judith Weiss, "'dehiya, halifa, ibbur'- Tfisot Sfiratiot al Gilgul Neshamot bein Gufim be-Sifrut ha-Kabala ha-Mukdemet," *Jewish Studies* 57 (2022), pp. 65-104.

35. *Pseudo-Ra'avad le-Sefer Yeẓirah* (Jerusalem 1962, following Warsaw 1884), 24a on *Sefer Yeẓirah* 1:4, citing Zech. 13:9. The text of *Sefer Yeẓirah* reads, "ten sefirot of nothingness, ten and not nine, ten and not eleven, understand with wisdom and be wise in understanding, discern them and investigate them and clarify the matter fully, and seat the Maker on His foundation."

36. The Secret of the Reason for *Gilgul*, "Twenty-Four Secrets," 299.

37. *Pseudo-Ra'avad le-Sefer Yeẓirah* (Jerusalem: n.p., 1962, following Warsaw: n.p., 1884), 24a.

38. "Twenty-Four Secrets," 299.

39. In the Zohar the *Shekhinah* is wandering with her children, the nation of Israel. She is identified with poverty (*middah tovah*) and with exile, as she is bereft of all property. On the subject see, H. Pedaya, *Walking through Trauma* (Tel Aviv: Resling, 2011) [Hebrew]; on the sefirah *Binah* as the World to Come, as well as *Teshuvah* ("Return" and "Repentance") and "the World of Freedom," see Joseph Gikatilla, *Sha'arei Orah*, ed. J. Ben Shlomo (Jerusalem: n.p., 1970), Gate 8, 61, 64–65 [Hebrew].

40. On this term here and in Ashkenazi's commentary to Genesis Rabbah, see Schnytzer, "Metempsychosis"; Sheqalim, *Doctrine of the Soul*, 79–80. R. Asher ben David refers to the process of *gilgul* as *hitḥalfut*, which we might translate as "replacement" but which shares its lexical root with *ḥiluf*, meaning both "replacement" and "transience." See Yehudah Liebes, *Sections of the Zohar Lexicon* (PhD diss., Hebrew University, 1976), 291–27, esp. section 7.

41. *Pseudo-Ra'avad le-Sefer Yeẓirah* (Jerusalem 1962, following Warsaw 1884), Introduction (the emphasis is mine).

42. For additional feminine aspects of his thought, see the discussion by Iris Felix on the commandment of building a *sukkah* in a halakhic context: I. Felix, "Chapters in the Kabbalistic Thought," 95–99. See also the case of the "blasphemer," who uses improperly the Ineffable Name and thus profanes God, "to increase the female force," in Jonathan Benarroch, "Son of an Israelite Woman and an Egyptian Man: Jesus as the Blasphemer," *Harvard Theological Review* 110, no. 1 (2017): 100–24.

43. Ruth Kara-Ivanov Kaniel, *Human Throes — Birth in Kabbalah and Psychoanalysis* (Jerusalem: Carmel Press, 2018), 358–64.

44. See Kara-Ivanov Kaniel, *Human Throes*, ch. 3.

45. The Hebrew term *ibbur* means impregnation and applies both to the metaphorical mother and fetus alike.

46. Yehuda Liebes noted this in his 1989 article, and other scholars have expanded on the topic over the years; see Liebes, "How Was the Zohar Written," *Jerusalem Studies in Jewish Thought* 8 (1989): 71–72 [Hebrew].

47. Sigmund Freud, The *Standard Edition* of the Complete Psychological Works of Sigmund Freud, Volume *IX* (1906–1908), chapter, "Family Romances" (New York: W.W. Norton, 1976), 235–42.

48. M. *Rosh Hashanah*, 2:10.

49. This expression might echo the Latin term *vagina dentate,* in keeping with Rashi's comment on b. Niddah 41b, "there are curls of flesh inside the

womb that are like teeth," and likewise the phrase "chamber of teeth" (y. Yevamot 35:1). Liebes suggests that the source is the root *shin-nun-nun*, meaning the place of urination, a root that appears in Isa 36:12 (where the text is written as *shineihem* but is read as the euphemistic *mei raglayim*).

50. "Twenty-Four Secrets"; see for example discussion and comments on 248. Compare to Zohar I: 181a–b. On the defect of the moon, see Y. Liebes, "Long Live the King," *Religion and Politics in Jewish Thought*, ed. M. Lorberbaum, A. Rosenak et al. (Jerusalem: IDI, 2012), 459–89, esp. near fn. 24–41.

51. Citing 2 Sam 34:7.

52. Angelet's positive attitude toward the process of repentance might stand in contrast to Nahmanides's description of the upper mother as attached to aspects of destruction and annihilation. For more on the subject, see H. Pedaya, *Nahmanides: Cyclical Time and Holy Text* (Tel Aviv: Am Oved, 2003), as well as her paper: H. Pedaya, "The Great Mother: The Struggle between Nahmanides and the Zohar Circle," *Temps i espais de la Girona jueva* (Girona: Patronat del Call de Girona, 2011), 311–28.

53. "Twenty-Four Secrets," 299.

54. "Twenty Four Secrets" (introduction), 212–13, and "The Secret of the Calendrical *Ibbur*," 307. This quote is taken from the Epistle of R. Yehushiel Gaon (spurious attribution) and appears in other works of Angelet, for instance, *Livnat ha-Sapir*, Vayikra, portion Ahrei Mot, fols. 332b–333a.

55. "Twenty Four Secrets," (introduction), 212–13, and "The Secret of the Calendrical *Ibbur*," 307.

56. See the section "The Secret of the Calendrical *Ibbur* (the Leap Year)."

57. Compare also the mythical description of the figures of Rachel and Leah in "The Secret of the Divine Name of Prayer (*shem-hatefila*)" and "The Secret of the Firmament (*ha-rakiya*)," in our discussion "Twenty-Four Secrets," 256–60, 263–66.

58. See for example our discussion in "The Secret of the Exile of the *Shekhinah*," in "Twenty-Four Secrets," 231.

59. As mentioned earlier, the sefirah *Binah* is referred to in Zoharic literature as "repentance/return" and "source of life," terms that were later applied to the *Shekhinah* as well. See Isaiah Tishby, ed., *The Wisdom of the Zohar, vol. 3* (Oxford: Littman Library of Jewish Civilization, 1989), 1499–1510. See also Jeremy Brown, "Forgiveness and Repentance in Medieval Iberian Jewish Mysticism 12th–13th Centuries" (PhD diss., New York University, 2015); R. Kara-Kaniel, *The Feminine Messiah* (Leiden: Brill, 2021), 65–74.

60. M Peah 1:5; Maimonides, *Mishneh Torah*, "Laws of Repentance," 3:14.

61. A reference to Esau based on Genesis 27:11; see the verse in the next footnote.

62. Jacob refers to himself as *ish chalak* in Gen. 27:11: "Look, my brother Esau is a hairy man, and I am a man of smooth skin."

63. See "Twenty-Four Secrets," 307.

64. Along with Iris Felix and Leore Sachs-Shmueli, I elaborate on this theme in our edition of "Twenty-Four Secrets," 251–53.

65. Joseph Dan, "Samael, Lilith, and the Concept of Evil in Early Kabbalah," *AJS Review* 5 (1980): 17–40; on a comprehensive conception of evil in Kabbalah, see G. Scholem, "The Kabbalah of R. Yaakov and R. Yitzhak the sons of R. Yaakov ha-Cohen," *Maddaei ha-Yahadut* 2 (1927): 244–64 [Hebrew].

66. Tamar Kron, *We, Adam and Eve*, 97. I hope to expand on the symbolization of Rachel and Leah in the Zohar elsewhere. See Yehudah Liebes, "Myth vs. Symbol in the Zohar and Lurianic Kabbalah," in *Essential Papers on Kabbalah*, ed. Lawrence Fine (New York: New York University Press, 1995), 212–42. On Rachel the "queen of heaven" as a counterpart to Christ but also like the *Shekhinah*, see E. D. Haskell, *Mystical Resistance: Uncovering the Zohar's Conversations with Christianity* (Oxford: Oxford University Press 2016), 15–38.

67. *Lamentations Rabba*, ed. Solomon Buber (Vilna, 1899), Proem 24, 28 (the emphasis is mine). More on this homily and the figure of Rachel in the Zohar, Sharon Koren, "Rachel and Mary Weep for Their Children in the Age of the Zohar," in *Mothers in the Jewish Cultural Imagination*, ed. M. Lehman and S. J. Bronner (Liverpool: Littman, 2017), 225–54.

68. As Oded Israeli has shown recently, Moses de Leon, Joseph Gikatilla, and the Zohar are the first to identify Leah with the sefirah *Binah*. See O. Yisraeli, "The Lord Saw That Leah Was Hated," in *Reading the Bible in the Pre-Modern World: Interpretation, Performance, and Image*, ed. Chanita Goodblatt and Howard Kreisel (Beer Sheva: Ben-Gurion University Press, 2021), 333–58, on the hidden anti-Christian polemic that is reflected in the Zoharic affirmation of the superiority of the "despised" Leah.

69. b. Hullin 60b.

70. "The power of the supernal Goat is entirely spiritual extinction in the fire of the sefirah *Gevurah*, and it returns and is renewed within the power of the Will until the time of extinction" ("*koah ha-seir shel ma'ala kale kulo kilion ruhani . . . umithadesh bekoah haRaTzon ad bo zeman ha-kila'ion*") in "Twenty-Four Secrets," 307. See also *Livnat ha-Sapir*, Vayikra, Portion Aharei-Mot, 333a.

71. "Twenty-Four Secrets," 306. This reading also reveals Angelet's understanding of the biblical punishment of *karet* (spiritual excision), which is similar to that found in R. Bahaye ben Asher's comment on this verse (Deuteronomy 3:26): "According to the *peshat* meaning: I am filled with wrath because of your complaints . . . And that which is called "the secret of *ibbur*" because of the power of the generations, for it calls the generations from the beginning, for it is pregnant (*me'ubar*) with the inner power, and because everyone who reincarnates will do so from the power of the generations, and so "the secret of *ibbur*" is called the power of the generations, and also because *ibbur* comes from the word *ribua* (square) . . . and also because he will not pass (over) from his family." See Bahaye ben Asher, *Commentary on the Torah*, vol. 3, ed. Dov Chavel (Jerusalem: Mossad Rav Kook, 1974) [Hebrew].

72. As I suggested in my article "Matriarchs and Patriarchs as *Sefirot* — Multiple Self in Kabbalistic Literature," *Peamim* 157 (2019): 135–75 [Hebrew].

SECTION II

THE COSMIC, PHILOSOPHICAL, AND TEMPORAL DIMENSIONS OF REINCARNATION

HARTLEY LACHTER

5 Lives and Afterlives

REINCARNATION, COSMIC CYCLES, AND THE MEDIEVAL JEWISH PRESENT

SALO BARON FAMOUSLY ARGUED that medieval Jewish life, and Jewish history in general, should not be regarded as merely a succession of moments of oppression.[1] Despite the expulsions, outbreaks of violence, legal and social restrictions, and Church-backed anti-Jewish polemicizing, Jewish life found a way to flourish in many places throughout the Christian West in the Middle Ages. A "lachrymose" history of pre-modern Jewish life, he argued, creates an incomplete picture of Jewish history. Nonetheless, medieval Jewish thinkers could not avoid the significant theological dilemma posed by the conditions of Jewish life. The basic tenant of the covenant — that Jewish acceptance of divine law and performance of the commandments will be reciprocated by divine protection and messianic redemption — was difficult to reconcile with the realities of Jewish historical experience in the medieval Christian West. Even for those Jews who lived in moments of relative security, they did so with the constant awareness that their fate was contingent. Moreover, they were acutely aware of the misfortunes of Jews in other regions, past and present. While Baron's caution against an overly "lachrymose" history of pre-modern Jewish life is sound, we must also be open to the fact that many medieval Jews themselves often embraced a narrative of decline in Jewish historical fortune. As Adam Teller has observed, "[w]hen pre-modern Jews thought about themselves and their place in the world, they did so not in liberal, but in lachrymose terms."[2]

A number of medieval kabbalistic texts reveal an acute investment in the task of theologically accounting for the challenges of Jewish historical experience.[3] Reincarnation is one strategy that some kabbalists employed to explain tragic events on both the individual and collective levels. This chapter explores select kabbalistic texts from the fourteenth and fifteenth centuries to consider how the concept of reincarnation is combined with the doctrine of *shemittot* or cosmic cycles to advance a discursive strategy to account for the negative events of Jewish history. By situating the "Jewish present" in a much longer continuum of successive lives and worlds, these texts suggest that the meaning, and justice, of Jewish individual and collective experience can be better understood. Questions of theodicy are decentered from the experience of the single moment or event and recast on a much broader temporal canvas. The life of the individual takes on meaning according to this view by playing a role in a much grander narrative of lives and afterlives. Reincarnation, and the question of the developmental arc of the soul over a vast temporal duration, is a fruitful domain of discourse for gaining better insight into how medieval Jews understood themselves and their present moment and how they made theological sense of the conditions of Jewish history.

Reincarnation and the Doctrine of *Shemittot*

For the kabbalists under consideration, reincarnation is closely related to the doctrine of the *shemittot* or cosmic cycles.[4] This was not a universal phenomenon in medieval Kabbalah. Important Castilian kabbalists, including the authorship of the Zohar, Moses de Leon, and Joseph Gikatilla, either ignored or rejected the idea of cosmic cycles. Starting in the latter half of the sixteenth century, Moses Cordovero and Isaac Luria polemicized vehemently against the most common formulations of this doctrine.[5] Kabbalists who embraced this idea included Nahmanides[6] and the subsequent school of his interpreters,[7] as well as the texts associated with the *Sefer ha-Temunah*, the *Sefer ha-Peli'ah* and the *Sefer ha-Kanah*,[8] and other kabbalists from the fourteenth through the early sixteenth centuries. The intersection of the ideas of reincarnation and cosmic cycles thus provides a window into an important facet of kabbalistic discourse from the period between the completion of the main body of the Zoharic texts and the rise of the school of Isaac Luria.

The kabbalistic idea of cosmic cycles is based on an interpretation of the biblical laws regarding the sabbatical year, or *shemittah*, requiring Israelites to allow their fields to lie fallow and to forgive debts every seven years,[9] as well as the commandment to count seven cycles of *shemittot*, culminating in the *Yovel* or Jubilee every fiftieth year.[10] The kabbalistic interpretation understood the biblical doctrine of the *shemittot* to allude to the idea that the world exists in seven cycles of seven thousand years, with each cycle governed by one of the seven lower sefirot. The 50,000th year entails the final redemption in the form of a return to *Binah* and the reassimilation of the souls of the Jewish people, along with the world, into the Godhead. In some versions, the cycle of seven cycles then begins again. Reincarnation and the doctrine of the *shemittot* both entail an analogous form of recycling that extends the temporal frame of the individual and the cosmos. Bahya ben Asher notes this symmetry at one point in his commentary on the Torah where he observes, "just as the *shemittot* of the world return and remanifest (*mitgalgalot*), so too the soul, after it has received its recompense in the Garden of Eden or its punishment in *Gehennom* (hell), returns after a time to the body to receive that which is its due, measure of measure."[11]

Each cycle of seven thousand years constitutes its own world, governed by one of the seven lower sefirot. In a relatively early formulation of this idea, David ben Yehudah he-Hasid describes the progression of worlds/*shemittot* as follows:

> You must understand that the secret of the *shemittah* is a wondrous and concealed matter . . . The secret of the *shemittah* is, *A generation goes, and a generation comes, and the earth lasts forever* (Eccl. 1:4) . . . Thus, each *shemittah* departs and another arrives, and each *sefirah* [of the seven lower sefirot] rules over one *shemittah*. In keeping with the character of the sefirah, so too the nature of the *shemittah*. If the sefirah inclines toward judgment, the *shemittah* is judgment. If the *sefirah* is compassion, the *shemittah* is compassion. If it is justice, so too is the *shemittah*. The true Kabbalah that we have received, one from the mouth of another, back to Moses our teacher, peace be upon him, is that the previous *shemittah* was of *Hesed* (lovingkindness), while the *shemittah* we are in now belongs to *Gevurah* (harsh judgment). That is why so many harsh decrees have been aroused in this *shemittah*, as well as severe judgments, numerous persecutions, due to our many sins, and the harshness of exile. On account of this, the present overpowering exile is an indication of *Gevurah*, [the sefirah] that is now ruling. When six thousand years pass, which is [the duration] of the world, then twilight will immediately commence, when the righteous will sit with their crowns upon their heads, basking in the

> splendor of the *Shekhinah*. They will adorn themselves to enter the Great Sabbath, mother of the children. When the sabbath begins, all worlds, gradations, and chariots will be drawn up to *Binah*, as it is written, "dust you are, and to dust you shall return" (Gen. 3:19). Nothing will remain but He and his name, as before the world was created.[12]

Each *shemittah* cycle of seven thousand years, according to this view, is governed by one of the seven lower sefirot, taking on the character of that particular divine attribute. Redemption begins to dawn at some point the sixth millennium, which in the Hebrew calendar begins in the Gregorian year 1240 and culminates in the assimilation of all being in the "Great Sabbath," or the sefirah *Binah* the seventh millennium. Some early fourteenth-century kabbalists, such as the anonymous author of the *Ma'arekhet ha-Elohut*, state that they do not know the current *shemittah* in which human life takes place.[13] Joseph Angelet adopts the unique position that the present cycle is the final one, governed by the sefirah *Malkhut*.[14] David ben Yehudah he-Hasid maintains the position that becomes most common among kabbalists who embrace the doctrine of the *shemittot* and argues that the current world takes place in the *shemittah* governed by the sefirah *Din*, or harsh judgment.[15] He points out that this explains the historical misfortunes of the Jewish people, including in particular the phenomenon of exile. He goes on to connect this to the permutations of the soul,[16] arguing that future worlds in subsequent *shemittot* will be generated by means of the souls of the righteous. As he states the matter: "When the Holy One, blessed be He, renews the *shemittah*, then he will reign through the souls of the righteous ... The secret meaning of this is that their very souls are the sacred beings that will be refined and reincarnated in their reincarnations (*yitgalgalu be-gilguleihen*) and their relocations (*tenu'oteihem*), for they are the souls that enter the world. Through those souls the Holy One, blessed be He, creates all these worlds and chariots and hosts."[17] In this formulation, the time frame of the world extends beyond the present iteration from creation to messianic redemption. A series of worlds exist, and the souls of the righteous play a vital role in all of them. The current world is of a severe nature that entails suffering, but this experience "refines" righteous souls and enables them to go on to future life in worlds that will be different and better than the present.

The texts associated with the *Sefer ha-Temunah*,[18] composed in mid-fourteenth-century Byzantium, provide a particularly detailed engagement with the idea of *gilgul* and the doctrine of the *shemittot*.[19] Like David ben

Yehuda he-Hasid, the *Sefer ha-Temunah* literature unambiguously embraces the idea that the present world takes place within the *shemittah* cycle of the sefirah *Din*, or strict divine judgment. All the other cosmic cycles are spiritual paradises in comparison to the present world. In a very real sense for this author, the present *shemittah* is the worst of all possible worlds.[20] The negative character of the current cycle is described in stark terms: "In the current *shemittah* one finds every intense and overpowering thing, such as demons and impure powers and evil spirits, the evil inclination and many bastards and rebels, and peoples of diverse languages, forms of idol worship, and powers confined to the territory of their lands and peoples, harsh decrees, sins, transgressions, sexual immorality, lengthy exiles, defiled powers, defiled forms of intercourse, impure animals and beasts, fiery serpents, plagues, and all kinds of impurity."[21] Exile is included in the list of evils manifest in the present world as a result of the power of the attribute of harsh judgment that controls the current reality. The category of exile is used in a double sense, referring both to the exile of the body, in the form of the collective displacement of the Jewish people from their ancestral land, as well as the exile of the soul through the experience of reincarnation.[22] As the anonymous author of the commentary on the *Sefer ha-Temunah* puts it in a discussion of the above-cited passage: "Due to the excessive harshness of the attribute [of Judgment], he would 'build worlds and destroy them' (*Bereishit Rabbah*, 3:7), such that God had to stipulate for all of the work of creation that it would be [performed through the attribute of] Judgment, and upon this condition everything was created. It was due to this stipulation that all souls must undergo reincarnation, and all bodies must experience exile."[23] The wandering of the soul through reincarnation, and the wandering of the body in diaspora, are cast here as the inevitable consequences of the state of cosmos in its current temporal incarnation.[24] Collective historical misfortune and individual suffering over the course of multiple lifetimes is accounted for as a result of the divine attribute governing the span of time in which Jewish life currently takes place.[25] As the author of the commentary puts it elsewhere, the nature of this *shemittah* accounts for "the difficulty of this *shemittah*, causing the Israelite soul to undergo reincarnation and exile."[26]

The highly negative characterization of the present *shemittah* is contrasted with the previous cycle, governed by the *sefirah Hesed*, or divine loving kindness. The commentary on the *Sefer ha-Temunah* describes that *shemittah* as follows: "All creatures in the *shemittah* that has just passed were sacred and pure, without any evil inclination or transgression or idolatry or jealousy or hatred. Their eating and drinking were like the delectation of the angels of this *shemittah* . . . The beasts of that *shemittah* were like the supernal angels now in this *shemittah*."[27] In the previous world, as with future worlds, reincarnation is not necessary, because there will be no sin. Only the present world, with its negative characteristics, presents a need for the kind of *gilgul* of the soul that constitutes a form of punishment to rectify transgressive behavior from a previous incarnation. According to this school of thought, the course of the events of individual Jewish lives, and Jewish history itself, is directed by a series of factors that accrue over the course of multiple lifetimes, shaped by the character of the particular world in which Jews find themselves. This world, like the present life, is merely one iteration in a series.

Reincarnation and the Crucible of History

Collective and individual suffering in the current *shemittah* serves an important purpose according to these texts. By enduring the trauma of national displacement and the attendant disempowerment and oppression over the course of multiple lifetimes, Jewish souls are able to refine themselves.[28] This process, in which the "dross" that the soul has accrued as a result of the nature of the present *shemittah* is eliminated, is painful but necessary. According to this view, both collective and individual Jewish misfortune helps to move history forward toward redemption and enable the return of the soul to its source in the divine.

This process is often associated with the cryptic comment in the Babylonian Talmud that "the son of David will not arrive until all of the souls of the *guf* have been consumed."[29] The *guf* or body referred to in this passage is interpreted by Rashi to be a kind of supernal storehouse of souls that must be depleted before the messiah can arrive.[30] However, according to *Sefer ha-Bahir*, § 184, this comment is taken to mean that the messiah will not arrive until "all of the souls in the human body [have been consumed], and then the new ones will merit to go forth, and then, 'the son of David will arrive,' will merit to be born, for his soul will come forth new with the others."[31] In his commentary on the Torah, Nahmanides briefly notes in his exegesis of Deut. 30:2 that this passage from the Talmud entails a "great secret,"[32] which is interpreted by some of his expositors as a reference to reincarnation. For instance, the text known as the *Kabbalat Saporta*[33] explains Nahmanides's allusion as referring to those souls "that will reincarnate in the future, [until] they are purified and no further souls any longer reincarnate in a body, as it is said, *and you shall return to the Lord your God* (Deut. 30:2), which is to say, when they will be purified and will return to God, then, *the Lord God will restore your former state and have mercy upon you* (Deut. 30:3)."[34] Reincarnation in this view purifies souls. When the existing souls have been sufficiently refined, they cease to reincarnate into a human body or *guf*, enabling them to return to their source in the divine and to usher in the messianic era. Reincarnation is thus connected to the progression of the individual soul toward perfection over the course of multiple lifetimes and the progression of the Jewish collective toward national redemption.[35] Isaac of Acre makes a comment to that effect on the meaning of this obscure Talmudic passage, noting that "the messiah son of Joseph arrives close to the end of the period of reincarnation, so that all those souls that remain from sinners and who are still subject to reincarnation will, through their deaths, obtain absolution and be redeemed from reincarnation. Then, truly, the Messiah son of David will arrive."[36]

The opportunity to refine one's soul and correct past transgressions through reincarnation is regarded by many kabbalists as an act of divine grace that enables the soul to attain perfection. As the *Sefer ha-Temunah* describes it, "[God] establishes a covenant with the righteous as well as the wicked, for He does not desire the death of the wicked,[37] but rather that he should return by means of reincarnation (*gilgul*) ... this attribute refines silver sevenfold (based on Ps. 12:7)."[38] The anonymous commentary on this passage notes: "They shall return, and their souls will be reincarnated from generation to generation, for the Holy One, blessed be He, "reaches out His hand to transgressors,"[39] so that their souls will be reincarnated and thus cleansed of their sins, *and they shall return to God* (Ps. 22:8)."[40]

The cleansing effect of reincarnation takes place, as we have seen, in the context of exile. The pain of the current exile of the Jewish people is particularly severe for a reason, in that it enables the final stage of the necessary spiritual refinement. The tribulations of Jewish history, according to this view, are not to be viewed as setbacks in the progression of sacred time, nor as a problem for covenantal theology; they are part of a necessary cosmic unfolding that Jewish souls must endure over the course of multiple lives to be refined of their impurities. According to the *Sefer ha-Temunah*, of the four main historical Jewish exiles — Babylonia, Persia, Greece, and Edom — the current exile of Edom, associated with Christianity, is the longest and most severe. However, such suffering serves a purpose according to the anonymous author. Exile, both physical and spiritual, serves to purify the soul and prepare the world for redemption. The present exile is exceptionally harsh and lengthy to accomplish this purpose.

> Great is the final exile; longest of all of them. By means of its prolongation, sins and evildoers are neutralized, as well as everything that is harsh and difficult, *and they shall return to the Lord* (Ps. 22:8). Our exiles and redemption are delayed to purify and distill all souls in order to appear before our God, and rectify form and soul . . . Thus, souls are reincarnated for purity and cleansing so that all will return to their point of origin as in the beginning, cleansed of the filth that derives from the [current] attribute with its harsh nature.[41]

The delayed arrival of the Messiah during the current extended exile, according to our anonymous author, enables Jewish souls to undergo the necessary reincarnations to purify their souls. This process requires multiple lives that occur in the context of national exile. The severity and duration of the current exile is designed to enable the necessary spiritual refinement to take place to bring about the spiritual and physical "return to the Lord." How long this will take is unknown, though there is an "appointed season" for the end of the current exile. On this passage the commentary notes, "even though each of the exiles has appointed durations, they have not been revealed to us."[42] However, the anonymous commentator also notes that at the end of the process of suffering that plays out over the course of Jewish history, "both the body and the soul will be purified, for punishment and reincarnation are expiatory for them."[43] According to the author of the anonymous *Sod Ilan ha-Aẓilut*, souls that have intermixed with impure spirits or other entities over the course of their permutations in the current *shemittah* "must undergo an exceedingly lengthy and grievous exile in the fourth generation, at the end of which *he will perform mercies for thousands* (Ex. 20:6). Therefore, the soul needs to be purified of all of the contaminants."[44]

The events of Jewish history are rendered meaningful through the combined lenses of *shemittot* and *gilgul*. The misfortunes that occur to individuals over the course of a single lifetime, as well as those that accrue over time for the Jewish collective, cannot be understood in their plain historical sense. The nature of the *shemittah* requires that souls reincarnate into exiled Jewish bodies to be refined of their impurities. The precise details and timeline of this process are nonetheless inscrutable,[45] as the author of the commentary to the *Sefer ha-Temunah* observes: "We are unable to grasp a single one of the thousands of myriads of wonders of the Holy One, blessed be He, that are alluded to in the harshness of this *shemittah*, and [how] all of the difficulties that the people of Israel have experienced have occurred because of the power of this *shemittah*, even concerning Pharaoh, Sennacherib, and Sisera."[46]

Collective national suffering, together with the individual trials and tribulations associated with reincarnation, are all part of a necessary process to refine Jewish souls and eventually to overcome all forms of adversity in the physical world, according to our author. In the meantime, however, the text asserts that historical tragedies, in the form of wars and violence, are to be expected. The commentary on the *Sefer ha-Temunah* notes, "It is necessary that the exile of the body and exile of the soul be very long, in order that every harsh and evil thing, sins and transgressions, shall be brought to an end, and they will all then return to God, for they shall all be righteous. Therefore, he sealed this, our exile, and lengthened it in order that the souls shall be purified, and they shall return pure before God . . . For both the body and the soul shall be purified, since punishment and reincarnation are a purification for them."[47] While the anonymous authorship of *Sefer ha-Temunah* accepts that the current *shemittah* is filled with misfortune, they also reassure the reader that they are living in the waning years of the dominance of the power of this eon. Soon, they claim, the process of messianic redemption will begin. Before that, however, they believe that the negative forces of the attribute of *Din* will become only more manifest in the world in the form of wars and tragedies. As the commentary on the text understands it, "We are already at the end of the harsh attribute, and the exiles are already ending, and the harshness of the attribute is departing, and since it is departing, it functions with greater force."[48]

Building upon the notion of the divine "*sarim*," or supernal archons that oversee the seventy nations of the world,[49] the authorship of the *Sefer ha-Temunah* and its commentary maintain that the current *shemittah* causes conflict between them and gives them the temporary capacity to overpower the divine forces sustaining the people of Israel. This, they claim, results in catastrophic world wars, with tragic consequences for the people of Israel.[50] The anonymous commentary predicts the onset of the process of redemption to begin in either 1531 or 1409. In the meantime, they anticipate that

> all kingdoms, Greece and Edom, will battle one another, these against those, and thus the words of the prophet shall come to pass, *[On that day] the Lord will punish the hosts of heaven in heaven, and the kings of the earth*

upon earth (Isa. 24:21). From this God will begin to arouse the advent of the Messiah to redeem Israel. One need not be dismayed and say, "what sign is this, for haven't there always been numerous wars between kingdoms and cities? . . . The answer is that thus is the truth: at the time of redemption, all of them will be cast into disarray . . . and it shall be a time of suffering for the people of Israel as has never been seen before, and only a few shall remain from among the many . . . and God in His great mercy, through his providence, shall be gracious and have mercy upon them."[51]

These dark predictions of the calamitous suffering brought about by the final pangs of the influence of the attribute of *Din* in the current *shemittah* are instrumental in bringing about the arrival of the days of the messiah over the course of the sixth millennium. The text goes on to state that the onset of redemption will occur in stages, the first with the end of the exile of "bodies," or the physical exile of the Jewish people, followed by the end of the exile of "souls," or the process of reincarnation.[52] In other words, when the pangs of history have completed their purpose of purifying the souls of Israel, the exile of body and soul comes to an end, along with human history as we know it.

Writing at the end of the fourteenth century in Castile in the wake of the wave of violence that spread throughout that region killing as many as 100,000 Jews, Shem Tov ibn Shem Tov[53] suggested a particularly pointed explanation of Jewish history through the idea that Jewish souls require refinement.

All our exiles, and all who have been slain, and who groan and are oppressed, it is in keeping with perfect justice. This is as they have said, "The son of David will not arrive until all of the souls of the *guf* have been consumed" (b. Yevamot 62a.), to reincarnate. And verily the verse says, *for I will not be angry forever, and I will not be wroth eternally; for spirit is enshrouded before me, in the body, and souls I have created* (Isa. 57:16). When reincarnation ends, the divine light will arrive by means of the new, pure forms, and there is no doubt that since the day of the destruction of the first temple, there have been no new souls, rather all of them reincarnated . . . And the generations became increasingly degraded. The more they progressed, the more the shells gained power, and the ten sefirot of impurity were active . . . All of the children of the exiles were designated to reincarnate in exile and to fall under the exile of the *sarim* . . . for the longer the exile persists, the divine light is more concealed, and the

> handmaid reigns and dominates increasingly . . . and the rebels and heretics of the prior generations reincarnate . . . and the Sages have said, "The Son of David will not arrive until all of the kingdom has turned to heresy" (b. Sanhedrin 97a) . . . The generations closest to redemption are the *bad figs* (Jer. 24:8; b. Eruvin 21b), and they themselves are the ones prepared to bear their sins and to enter into the refiner's crucible . . . The one who bears the afflictions *and makes of himself a guilt-offering* (Isa. 53:10), that is to say, a sacrifice, he shall live eternally in the world that is entirely good . . . When all of the souls have ceased and have been refined and tested in the crucible of deprivation at the hands of the archons of the gentile nations (*sarei ha-umot*) . . . then, the supernal God will arouse the supernal glory to wage his wars, and the time of the great judgment will arrive, and the rebels and the sinners will be judged for all generations.[54]

Ibn Shem Tov draws upon a combination of some of the ideas that we have seen to sketch a comprehensive view of Jewish history, and in particular Jewish suffering at the hands of foreign entities, in a way that demonstrates the "perfect justice" of the divine plan. Like other kabbalists before him, he asserts that reincarnation refines Jewish souls and prepares the way for messianic redemption. The refining process entails suffering at the hands of the gentile nations overseen by the archons or "*sarim*" that draw their negative powers from the external regions of the divine realm. As history progresses, according to ibn Shem Tov, conditions deteriorate, and the evil forces gain in strength to perform the increasingly difficult task of purifying the remaining Jewish souls. This is because, over time, the souls that remain that require reincarnation are particularly problematic. Therefore, historical suffering must increase to rise to the task. The obligation of Jews in his moment, in ibn Shem Tov's view, is to accept their fate and "bear their sins" in the "refiner's crucible" of history. Their suffering renders them equivalent to a guilt-offering sacrifice, which will then purify their souls and hasten messianic redemption. In the portrait ibn Shem Tov seeks to depict, the increasing intensity of Jewish suffering is the sign of the impending redemption that is to come. Reincarnated souls must accept and endure their suffering in the "crucible of depravation" inflicted on them by gentiles as a vital contribution they make in the final pangs at the culmination of history. The end result, he argues, will be an inversion of the conditions of his present moment — the enemies of Israel will be defeated, sinners will be judged, and the righteous will be vindicated.

This begs the question as to why the present cosmic cycle must be so problematic in the first place. Would it not be possible for God to assemble creation differently? A partial answer to this question offered by some kabbalists is provided by attributing the deeply negative character of this *shemittah* to the sin of Adam and Eve in Eden.[55] Had they not eaten from the tree of knowledge of good and evil, they would have enjoyed eternal life, and there would have been neither human history as we know it nor a process of expiatory reincarnation. The anonymous authorship of the *Sefer ha-Peliah* and *Sefer ha-Kanah* texts, composed in the late fourteenth or early fifteenth century in Byzantium and influenced by the *Sefer ha-Temunah* literature,[56] regards the sin of Adam and Eve as the key event that pushed history off course during the current *shemittah* and created the need for reincarnation. According to the *Sefer ha-Kanah*, "there is not a single soul in existence until the end of this *shemittah* that does not undergo judgment deriving from Adam."[57] In an intriguing passage from the *Sefer ha-Peli'ah*, Adam and Eve's eating from the Tree of Knowledge in the Garden of Eden caused

> three deaths; one above,[58] second, the corporeal present death — two deaths — and then also the death of the reincarnation that will be reincarnated. When Adam came and was led astray by the woman and took hold of the attribute that he was warned against, divine mercy immediately departed, and it was decreed that everything should be conducted according to this principle until the end of the *shemittah*; sometimes life, sometimes death, above as below. The Holy One, blessed be He, knew all of this [in advance]. Adam did not heed the command because the *shemittah* required this, so that everything would undergo trial, for if it were not so, then Adam would live forever and never die, since the soul that God breathed into him would grant eternal life, and God did not intend this, except in the *shemittah* of *Tiferet*, since the righteous at that time live forever and ever. Do not say, "if this is so, why did he command him?" For trial is only for those who have been commanded.[59]

In response to the question as to why God would arrange things in the Garden of Eden such that death, misfortune, and reincarnation — in short, history itself — would be possible through the transgression of eating from the Tree of Knowledge, the anonymous author offers a bold reading of Genesis. God knew, the author claims, that Adam would not obey the admonition not to eat from the tree, and this was part of a broader plan to ensure that the current *shemittah* would involve human death rather than eternal life, and the attendant woes of history. By introducing death into the human and divine realms, as well as in future lives through reincarnation, the author suggests that Adam was in fact creating the outcome God intended. An eternal life of bliss is appropriate for the next *shemittah*, governed by the sefirah *Tiferet*. For the present world, however, it seems that our author regards death and suffering over the course of multiple lives as a necessary feature: so much so that God felt compelled to contrive a situation in which that would be the inevitable result. The text reflects a degree of anxiety regarding the possible implications of this idea, since this passage concludes with the exhortation to the reader that "this secret must not depart from your mouth, and even though it is written in a book, hide it away and conceal it."

Jewish Souls in Foreign Territory

Starting in the late thirteenth century, some kabbalists came to embrace the idea that Jewish souls can reincarnate into the bodies of non-Jews and animals.[60] As Leore Sachs-Shmueli has demonstrated, "Joseph of Hamadan was the first kabbalist to develop this doctrine in an explicit and systematic manner," and his work, via other kabbalists such as Menahem Recanati, came to have an important influence on later authors, including the *Temunah* texts, as well as the *Peliah* and *Kanah*.[61] This wandering of Jewish souls beyond the confines of Jewish bodies constituted an extra layer of exile. For some kabbalists, that predicament of the Jewish soul will persist until the world returns to its source in *Binah* at the end of the current *shemittah*. As the main text of the *Sefer ha-Temunah* describes it, the final redemption of the Jubilee will entail the return of

> the wandering and exiled [souls] from all those worlds, due to their many wrongdoings; some in the bodies of human beings in keeping with the cause of the *shemittah*; some in beasts, some in animals, either pure or impure, or in creeping things — all in keeping with a supernal or lower cause. Some are in lifeless vessels, such as the wood of trees or other such things, or in fire or water — everything in keeping with the cause of the supernal or lower gradations of the soul summoned forth since the day of its emergence from its source until its return to the gate of its point of origin; some at times that are near, and some at times that are distant, some confined to bodies, and some in the supernal entities, and some suspended among the spirits, some to receive punishment,

> and some at rest. All these paths are sealed and are known, according to the scriptures, only by the ones who comprehend — the kabbalists. All of this occurs to bring about the purification of the soul by means of the path upon which it proceeds.[62]

Souls, according to the anonymous author, can end up via *gilgul* manifesting in the bodies of animals, insects, and even inanimate substances and elements.[63] They can also find themselves suspended in the spiritual realm. The duration of such wanderings and the degree of suffering it entails vary from soul to soul. However, all souls undergo such experiences "to bring about the purification of the soul." The anonymous author of the *Sefer ha-Kanah* argues that the reincarnation of a human soul into an animal is generally a final step in the soul's process of purification. Individuals who require only a limited degree of additional refinement, rather than those who are particularly blameworthy, are among those who reincarnate in animal form: "Even though [the souls of] people can be found in some animals and birds, know that they are completely righteous when they depart from there. They required a small measure of purification, and then they are as the supernal angels."[64]

The reincarnation of Jewish souls into gentile bodies[65] is understood in some cases as a mechanism not simply for purifying Jewish souls, but also as a form of divine intervention to move history forward during the course of the present *shemittah* and to provide covert protection for the Jewish people as they suffer at the hands of gentile nations. According to the commentary on the *Sefer ha-Temunhah*, for example, "Ruth's soul was originally from among the holy souls of the people of Israel, and because of the fact that she transgressed earlier and was obligated to undergo reincarnation and exile, and she was reincarnated among gentile nations. But then Boaz returned to the world, and Ruth's soul was his soulmate, and she had already received all of her punishment and her time had arrived to be reincarnated into this world together with Boaz, her soulmate."[66] This claim reflects more than the prehistory of the biblical character of Ruth. The implication is that Ruth underwent reincarnation into a gentile body to prepare her soul to be ready at the same time as Boaz, so that at the proper time she would be able to "return" to the Jewish people and serve her unique and essential historical role as the great-grandmother of King David. Ruth's experience of *gilgul* into a gentile body was, the anonymous author suggests, a divine stratagem for keeping Jewish history on track.

The same text also suggests that the reincarnation of Jewish souls into gentile bodies is a method whereby God blunts the force of gentile oppression of Jews in exile. This is not done to punish or refine Jewish souls, since it is *righteous* individuals in such cases who are reincarnated into gentiles: "Sometimes the souls of righteous individuals are reincarnated into gentiles, and this is for the benefit of Israel, so that they will have mercy upon Israel . . . It is for this reason that they have mercy and protect those of the people of Israel who speak and act contrary to the gentile nations — not from their own nature that derives from being a gentile and [deriving from] the power of Esau, but rather from the power of those souls that were reincarnated into their physical matter from the seed of Israel."[67] Instances of Jewish flourishing under gentile authority, or moments of comity with non-Jewish powers, this text suggests, are in fact the result of *Jewish* souls reincarnated among gentile peoples to grant protection to their fellow Jews. Intercommunal dynamics in which Jews encounter sympathetic non-Jewish partners are not, the author asserts, a reflection of a quality that those who draw from the "power of Esau," an amplified force of the attribute of harsh judgment that governs the current *shemittah*. Such moments of calm in the Jewish journey through the course of history are secretly engineered by divine providence by means of the strategic reincarnation of Jewish souls.

Shem Tov ibn Shem Tov understood the reincarnation of Jewish souls into gentiles to be a particularly elevated kabbalistic secret. In his *Sefer ha-Emunot*, he observes:

> Sometimes reincarnation does not occur only among close relatives, and sometimes the inner [souls] are brought outside, according to one's deeds . . . regarding these matters I have discovered wonderous insights recorded by the wise ones, and "they are the concealed matters of the world" (b. Hagigah, 13a), and I have not presumed to record it, however I will convey one matter to you; that Ovadia, who was an Edomite proselyte, was a prophet who prophesied regarding the fall of Edom, and he was reincarnated according to a supernal plan for his body to be in the state of a gentile until the arrival of the proper time for him to convert, and therefore it would be more fitting for him to prophesy regarding the fall of his people. The truth is that his inner form was holy, of *the council of holy beings* (Ps. 89:8). Thus, the wise ones have said that the souls of converts were also present at the giving of the Torah (b. Shevuot, 39a), to indicate that their origin is the house of God, and there they return.[68]

The kabbalistic idea related here, which ibn Shem Tov claims to have received from an unnamed source, plays on the tradition related in the name of Rabbi Meir in tractate *Sanhedrin* 39b that "the prophet Ovadia was an Edomite convert, in keeping with the expression, 'from the forest derives the axe [that cuts it down].'" In the Talmudic context, the claim is merely that Ovadia's birth among the people of Edom lent a degree of ironic divine justice to his service as the prophet relaying the divine predictions of that people's destruction at the hand of God. In the kabbalistic rendering of Ovadia's origin among the Edomites, there is more than irony at play.[69] The implication is that Ovadia's soul was in fact of Israelite extraction, and it was placed into an Edomite body via reincarnation as part of a "supernal plan" that would enable him, over the course of multiple lives, to have the proper impact on the course of human events in this world. The divine choice of the timing of the multiple lives of this particular prophet, according to this tradition, is an example of how God uses the multigenerational process of reincarnation to intervene into Jewish history. Ovadia's soul was selected to experience this particular fate through reincarnation to affect the course of human affairs in a manner that helps to steer the fate of the Jewish people. For kabbalists like ibn Shem Tov, the divine use of reincarnation in this fashion provides a discursive strategy for suggesting that God has not abandoned the people of Israel to their fate. The extended duration of pre-planning implied in this idea coveys the notion that God has an arrangement in place for ensuring that Jewish historical experience moves forward according to a predetermined course, even if that often does not appear to be the case. An important tool, according to the above-cited passage, for accomplishing this divine oversight of the historical process is the selective placement of Jewish souls into gentile bodies.

Imagining the Present Through Past and Future Lives

According to the *Sefer ha-Temunah*, the weakening of the aspect of *Din* in this *shemittah* during the sixth millennium will entail a significant slowing of time.[70] After the wars and human conflicts have passed, the souls of the Jewish people will be purified and transformed, the harshness of this *Shemittah* will be ameliorated, and the reincarnation of souls will cease. The onset of the messianic period will emerge progressively. The spheres of the heavens will slow as the influence of the attribute of *Din* becomes less and less present, leading to very significant extensions of the duration of time,[71] during which the Jewish people will enjoy the delights of a world devoid of the evil manifestations of unbalanced divine forces. The radical extension of time as the end of the *shemittah* approaches, according to this view, guarantees that the duration of reward after the end of exile will be far longer than the periods of suffering that have occurred over the course of Jewish history up to that point.[72] The progression of Jewish lineage then begins to move in reverse, and the souls of Israel consolidate in a kind of backward reincarnation until eventually humanity regains its prelapsarian perfection, and only Adam and the *Shekhinah* remain.[73] They too eventually return to their divine source through the full reassimilation of the world and the sefirot into *Binah* and *ein sof* in an all-encompassing supernal Sabbath.[74] The author of the commentary concludes by noting that all of these events are brought about "through the power of the second *shemittah* in which we currently find ourselves, with all of its powers regarding the matter of exiles [of the people of Israel] in their proper times, and from now until their redemption, demonstrating the secret of their task in their exiles and redemptions, until their proper time arrives."[75]

The doctrine of cosmic cycles and reincarnation presents an extended meditation on the nature of historical time and the place Jews have in the interaction of cosmic and divine forces that result in world events. As Scholem has noted, kabbalists who embraced the doctrine of the *shemittot* "wrestled no less than Yehudah Halevi in his *Kuzari* with the problem of the history of Israel,"[76] and for those like the authorship of the *Sefer ha-Temunah*, "[t]he history of the world unfolds according to an inner law that is the hidden law of the divine nature itself."[77] This discourse involves the claim that both Jewish and world history holds a secret, and that Kabbalah provides Jews with exclusive access to that concealed truth. The experiences of the Jewish people in history, and their struggle with exile and subjugation to foreign powers, are recast not as setbacks or divine abandonment, but rather the opposite — such experiences are necessary steps in a carefully designed divine process that cannot be avoided, a process that reflects the structure of the inner life of God. The travails of the present moment of history, according to these texts, should not be regarded as a challenge to the validity of covenantal theology, but instead as confirmation of what the secrets of the kabbalistic tradition have anticipated all along. Wars among nations of the world and suffering inflicted on the disempowered people of Israel, according to these texts, is exactly what one should expect. Such experiences for Jewish souls on the stage of world history and over the course of multiple lives is a consequence of the nature of the present stage of cosmic time. Negative events in Jewish history reflect the *presence* of the divine attribute of *Din* in the current *shemittah*, not the *absence* of divine providence or the abrogation of the covenant. The authors of these texts also offered the reassurance that, after a final cataclysm that will soon come to an end, an inversion will take place, and the imbalances in the world that have persisted since the sin of Adam and Eve in the Garden of Eden will be corrected. The bodies and souls of the Jewish people will finally be cleansed of their dross and returned to their proper, sanctified state. The enemies of Israel will be defeated, and history as we know it will come to an end.

Serving as both map and calendar, these texts advance the notion that time and space are nothing like they appear. Their vast complexity can only be understood through the kabbalistic tradition, which advances the ironically comforting truth that exiles of the body and soul, as well as global war and extermination campaigns against Jews, are all part of the final process that will initiate the messianic age. Then the world will reverse itself, evil will cease, Jews will assume their proper place as the single ruling nation on earth, regain their luminous bodies, and settle their transmigrating souls as time marches forth in the succession of ages and worlds. Moreover, the present life of any individual Jew in the current *shemittah* is only one short moment when considered in the context of the broad sweep of cosmic history. The medieval Jewish consumer of such discourses is encouraged to regard the present in which they live as merely one painful episode in the longer life of their soul. Past and future worlds, they are assured, offer a much better and more sacred existence. For the moment, their task of adhering to the strictures of Judaism while enduring the difficulties of Jewish history is filled with secret meaning. The doctrine of the *shemittot* and the idea of *gilgul* allows for a macro-historical time frame in which to situate Jewish experience.[78] Such a discourse offered medieval Jews a privileged glimpse into the broader dimensions of a concealed divine plan in which Jews play a vital role in sustaining the multifaceted structure of being and time through the traumas suffered over the course of their exile.

By claiming such a bird-eye view of the placement of the present eon of history and the unfolding of the multiple lives of the soul, this doctrine provided a tool for medieval Jews to understand the present. The concern, it seems to me, that these texts are seeking to address is cultural despair. How are Jews to understand their own history? And what are they to make of Jewish experiences of violence, displacement, and political disempowerment over time? Are these to be understood as signs of the impending end of Judaism and validation of Christian or Muslim claims? The texts examined above suggest that Jews alone understand the real forces at work in history, and in fact those forces, both in terms of the extension of time and the dimensions of space, depart so sharply from the simple appearance of the world that only those who have received the divinely revealed secrets of the Kabbalah are able to understand the true nature of the world. By embracing that tradition, Jews could reimagine their own present and orient themselves to a radically altered future. These texts suggest that the present conditions of medieval Jewish life enable Jewish souls, over the course of their reincarnations, to serve as agents of a divine plan for the unfolding of both human and cosmic history.

Notes

1. See, for example, Baron, "Newer Emphases in Jewish History," *Jewish Social Studies* 25, no. 4 (1963): 245–58.

2. "Revisiting Baron's 'Lachrymose Conception': The Meanings of Violence in Jewish History," *AJS Review* 38, no. 2 (2014): 439.

3. For a discussion of this idea in medieval Kabbalah, see Rachel Elior, "Exile and Redemption in Jewish Mystical Thought," *Studies in Spirituality* 14 (2004): 1–15.

4. On this doctrine in medieval kabbalah, see Gershom Scholem, *The Kabbalah of Sefer ha-Temunah and Abraham Abulafia*, ed. Joseph Ben-Shlomo (Jerusalem: Academon, 1965), 5–84 [Hebrew]; Scholem, *Kabbalah*, 120–22; Scholem, *Origins of the Kabbalah*, 461–75; Ehud Krinis, "Cyclical Time in the Isma'ili Circle of the Ikhwan al-Safa (Tenth Century) and in Early Jewish Kabbalistic Circles (Thirteenth and Fourteenth Centuries)," *Studia Islamica* 111 (2016): 20–108; Israel Weinstock, *Studies in Jewish Philosophy and Mysticism* (Jerusalem: Mossad ha-Rav Kook, 1969), 153–229 [Hebrew]; Shifra Asulin, "R. Joseph Angelet and the Doctrine of Seven Cosmic Cycles: Between the Zohar and Nahmanides's Kabbalah," *AJS Review* 43, no. 2 (2019): 1–25 [Hebrew]; Roee Goldschmidt, "Two Historical Conceptions in Kabbalah: Between Safed and Byzantine Kabbalah," *Judaica Petropolitana* 11 (2019): 73–86 [Hebrew]; Moshe Idel, "Sabbath: On Concepts of Time and History in Kabbalah," in *Jewish History and Jewish Memory: Essays in Honor of Yosef Hayim Yerushalmi*, ed. Carlbach, Efron, and Myers (Hanover: Brandeis University Press, 1998), 167–70; M. Idel, "'Higher than Time': Observations on Some Concepts of Time in Kabbalah and Hasidism," in *Time and Eternity in Jewish Mysticism*, ed. Brian Ogren (Leiden: Brill, 2015), 179–210, see especially 179–210; Haviva Pedaya, "The Divinity as Place, Time, and Holy Place in Jewish Mysticism," in *Sacred Space: Shrine, City, Land*, ed. B. Z. Kedar and R. J. Zwi-Werblowski (New York: New York University Press, 1988), 91–94; Nicholas Sed, "Le Sefer ha-Temunah et la Doctrine des Cycles Cosmiques," *Revue des Etudes Juives* 126, no. 4 (1967): 399–415.

5. See Bracha Sack, *The Kabbalah of Rabbi Moshe Cordovero* (Beer Sheva: Ben Gurion University, 1995), 267–90 [Hebrew]; Scholem, *The Kabbalah of Sefer*

ha-Temunah, 84; Scholem, *Kabbalah*, 122; Goldschmidt, "Two Historical Conceptions," 80–84. Goldschmidt also points out that a number of post-Lurianic Eastern European kabbalists embraced the doctrine of the *shemittot* and the *Sefer ha-Temunah*, despite Cordovero and Luria's strong reservations regarding the implications of this idea for theodicy and free will.

6. See Haviva Pedaya, *Nahmanides: Cyclical Time and Holy Text* (Tel Aviv: Am Oved, 2003), especially 209–73 [Hebrew]; Moshe Halbertal, *Nahmanides: Law and Mysticism* (New Haven: Yale University Press, 2020), 201–8.

7. See Ephraim Gottleib, *The Kabbalah in the Writings of R. Bahya ben Asher ibn Halawa* (Jerusalem: Kiryath Sepher, 1970), 233–37 [Hebrew]; Gottleib, *Studies in Kabbalah Literature*, ed. Joseph Hacker (Tel Aviv: Tel Aviv University Press, 1976), 332–39 [Hebrew]. On texts stemming from this group, see Daniel Abrams, "Orality in the School of Nahmanides: Preserving and Interpreting Esoteric Traditions and Texts," *Jewish Studies Quarterly* 3, no. 1 (1996): 90–93.

8. See Kushnir-Oron, *The* Sefer *ha-Peli'ah and the Sefer ha-Kanah*, 294–300.

9. Ex. 23:10–11; Lev. 25:1–7; Deut. 15:2.

10. Lev. 25:8–13. On the medieval kabbalistic interpretations of the Jubilee and *Binah*, see Idel, "The Jubilee in Jewish Mysticism," in *Fins de Siecle — End of Ages*, ed. J. Kaplan (Jerusalem: Shazar, 2005), 209–32; Pedaya, *Nahmanides: Cyclical Time*, 380–89.

11. *Rabbenu Bahya on the Torah*, vol. 3, ed. C. Chavel (Jerusalem: Mossad Harav Kook, 1968), 480 [Hebrew]. On this passage, see the discussion in Moshe Idel, "Peirushim le-Sod ha-Ibbur be-Kabbalot Catalonia be-meah ha-13 u-mashma'utam le-havanatah shel ha-Kabbalah be-reishitah u-lehitpathutah," *Da'at* 72 (2012): 11–12 [Hebrew].

12. David ben Yehudah he-Hasid, *Mara'ot ha-Tzova'ot*, ed. Matt, 102. Also cited and translated in Matt, ibid., 32. See also *Ma'arekhet ha-Elohut*, 179b–180a, 187a–190b; Weinstock, *Studies in Jewish Philosophy*, 162–64. On the indebtedness of this kabbalists to Joseph ben Shalom Ashkenazi on this doctrine, see Idel, "Some Concepts of Time," 168; Idel, "An Additional Commentary to the Alphabet by R. David ben Yehudah he-Hasid and *Sefer ha-Temunah*," *Alei Sefer* 26/27 (2017): 242–45.

13. *Ma'arekhet ha-Elohut*, 189b. See Pedaya, *Nahmanides: Cyclical Time*, 255.

14. See *Livnat ha-Sappir* (Jerusalem: n.p., 1913), 1a–b, and the discussion in Asulin, "R. Joseph Angelet and the Doctrine," 6–9. See also Angelet's comments in his "Twenty-Four Secrets," MS Columbia X 893 G 363, 91b.

15. See Scholem, *The Kabbalah of Sefer ha-Temunah*, 52; Scholem, *Origins of the Kabbalah*, 468–69; Idem, *Kabbalah*, 121; Idel, "On Concepts of Time," 168; Gottleib, *Studies in Kabbalah*, 338.

16. See Rami Shekalim, *Torat ha-Nefesh ve-haGilgul be-Reishit ha-Kabbalah* (Tel Aviv: n.p., 1998), 203–7 [Hebrew].

17. *Mara'ot ha-ẓovaot*, 103.

18. While Gershom Scholem, following other early scholars of Kabbalah, surmised that the *Sefer ha-Temunah* was composed in mid-thirteenth-century

Spain, Moshe Idel has argued that the text was composed in Byzantium in the fourteenth century. See "The Kabbalah in Byzantium: Preliminary Remarks," in *The Jews in Byzantium: Dialectics of Minority and Majority Cultures*, ed. R. Bonfil, O. Irshai, G. Stroumsa, and R. Talgam (Leiden: Brill, 2012), 679–88. This text seems to have circulated in multiple versions simultaneously, along with a commentary by a kabbalist also likely from the mid-fourteenth century that is included in many of the manuscripts as well as the printed editions. See the important recent study by Roee Goldschmidt, "From Byzantium to Eastern Europe: The Textual Versions of *Sefer ha-Temunah* and their Circulation in Manuscript and in Print," *Kabbalah* 46 (2020): 287–316 [Hebrew]. Goldschmidt demonstrates the presence of the *Temunah* literature in Spain already before the end of the fourteenth century and suggests the possibility that the lengthy anonymous commentary may in fact have been written in Spain. See ibid., especially 300–6. Numerous other texts emanated from this circle, including commentaries on the alphabet, three commentaries on the "divine name of seventy-two" (subsequently published in *Sefer Raziel*, 1701); a commentary on the Song of Songs mistakenly attributed to Joseph Gikatilla in MS Paris 790; a commentary on the Passover Haggadah mistakenly attributed Moses de Leon, printed in *Hagadah Shelemah: The Complete Passover Haggadah*, ed. M. Kasher (Jerusalem: Torah Shelema Institute, 1967), 121–32; another commentary on the Passover Haggadah preserved in Parma 3511 and several other manuscripts; a text titled *Sod Ilan ha-Atzilut* published by Gershom Scholem, *Qovetz al Yad*, New Series 5 (1951): 67–102 [Hebrew]. Another version of which is known as *Sod ha-Shem*, published at the end of the Constantinople edition of *Zohar Hadash*; and a shorter text, *Seder ha-Atzilut*, preserved in MS Vatican 194 and recently published by Na'ama ben Shachar and Tzahi Weiss, "The Order of Emanation Regarding 'The Unity of Our God and Our Torah for Our People' — A Commentary on the Ten Sefirot from the 'Circle of the *Sefer ha-Temunah*,'" *Kabbalah* 41 (2018): 279–304 [Hebrew].

19. See Brian Ogren, *Renaissance and Rebirth: Reincarnation in Early Modern Italian Kabbalah* (Leiden: Brill, 2009), 20–21.

20. See Scholem, *The Kabbalah of Sefer ha-Temunah*, 62–64, 68.

21. *Sefer ha-Temunah*, 29a. See also Scholem, *The Kabbalah of Sefer ha-Temunah*, 60–61; Goldschmidt, "Two Historical Conceptions," 77–78. See also the anonymous *Seder ha-Atzilut*, MS Vatican 194, 100b, ed. Shachar and Weiss, 296.

22. See Idel, "The Meaning of 'Ta'amei Ha-'Ofot Ha-Teme'im' of Rabbi David ben Yehuda He-Hasid," in *'Alei Shefer: Studies in the Literature of Jewish Thought Presented to Rabbi Dr. Alexandre Safran*, ed. Moshe Hallamish (Ramat Gan: Bar-Ilan University Press, 1990), 18 [Hebrew].

23. *Sefer ha-Temunah*, 29a.

24. See Scholem, *The Kabbalah of Sefer ha-Temunah*, 53, 57; Scholem, "The Study of the Theory of Transmigration During the XIII Century," *Tarbiẓ* (1945): 136; Goldschmidt, "From Byzantium to Eastern Europe," 307–9.

25. Menahem Recanati also notes in his commentary on the Torah that reincarnation is an element of the current *shemittah*. See *Perush ha-Recanati*, 1:295.

26. *Sefer ha-Temunah*, 36a.

27. *Sod Ilan ha-Aẓilut* published by Gershom Scholem, *Qovetz al Yad*, New Series 5 (1951): 67–102, on 95 [Hebrew].

28. See Leore Sachs-Shmueli, "The Rationale of the Negative Commandments by Rabbi Joseph Hamadan: A Critical Edition and Study of Taboo in the Time of the Composition of the Zohar," vol. 1 (PhD diss., Bar-Ilan University, 2018), 191–98 [Hebrew]. On the influence of Hamadan on the *Temunah* texts with regard to this issue, see Sachs-Shmueli, "The Rationale," 192. On the relation of this idea to the Christian notion of purgatory, see Sachs-Shmueli, "The Rationale," 193–96.

29. b. Yevamot 62a.

30. See Mark Verman, "Reincarnation and Theodicy: Traversing Philosophy, Psychology, and Mysticism," in *Be'erot Yitzhak: Studies in Memory of Isadore Twersky* (Cambridge: Harvard University Press, 2005), 414–15.

31. See Scholem, *On the Mystical Shape*, 205; Oron, "The Doctrine of the Soul and Reincarnation in 13th Century Kabbalah," *Studies in Jewish Thought*, ed. S. Wilensky and M. Idel (Jerusalem: 1989), 287–89 [Hebrew].

32. *Peirush ha-Torah*, vol. 2, 479. On kabbalistic interpretations of this secret, see Pedaya, *Nahmanides: Cyclical Time*, 444–52.

33. On this text and its relationship to Isaac of Acre, see Amos Goldreich, *Sefer Me'irat Einayim by Rabbi Isaac of Acre: A Critical Edition*, ed. Amos Goldreich (PhD diss., Hebrew University, 1981), 76–89.

34. Bodleian Opp. Q. 43 (Neubauer 1945), 96a. Isaac of Acre also cites this passage from *Kabbalat Saporta*. See *Sefer Me'irat Einayim by Rabbi Isaac of Acre*, ed. A. Goldreich, 239. See also the interpretation of Nahmanides's allusion in the anonymous supercommentary on Nahmanides, mistakenly attributed to Meir ibn Sahula, *Bi'ur le-Feirush ha-Ramban* (Warsaw: n.p., 1875), 34a [Hebrew].

35. See Zwi Werblowsky, *Joseph Karo: Lawyer and Mystic* (Philadelphia: Jewish Publication Society, 1977), 237; Krinis, "Cyclical Time," 74; Kushnir-Oron, *The* Sefer *ha-Peli'ah and* the Sefer ha-Kanah, 207.

36. *Sefer Oẓar Hayyim*, 165.

37. based on Ezek. 33:11.

38. *Sefer ha-Temunah*, 17a.

39. Yom Kippur Mahzor, Ashkenaz, Neila.

40. *Sefer ha-Temunah*, 17a.

41. *Sefer ha-Temunah*, 56b–57a.

42. *Sefer ha-Temunah*, 56b.

43. *Sefer ha-Temunah*, 56b.

44. *Sod Ilan ha-Aẓilut*, ed. Scholem, 90.

45. On esotericism and ineffability in the *Sefer ha-Temunah* and related texts, see Wolfson, "Murmuring Secrets: Eroticism and Esotericism in Medi-

eval Kabbalah," in *Hidden Intercourse: Eros and Sexuality in the History of Western Esotericism*, ed. J. Kripal and W. Hanegraff (Leiden: Brill, 2008), 77–84.

46. *Sefer ha-Temunah*, 39b.

47. *Sefer ha-Temunah*, 56b. See Idel, "The Meaning of 'Ta'amei Ha-'Ofot Ha-Teme'im', 19; Rachel Elior, "The Doctrine of Transmigration in *Galya Raza*," in *Essential Papers on Kabbalah*, ed. Lawrence Fine (New York: New York University Press, 1995), 269 n. 82.

48. *Sefer ha-Temunah*, 57a.

49. Joseph Gikatilla is an important source for this idea; *Sha'arei Orah*, 2 vols., ed ben Shlomo (Jerusalem: Mosad Bialik, 1996), 1:203–4; 2:17–20. On this idea in Gikatilla's corpus, see Joseph ben Shlomo, ibid., 1:36–39; Roland Goetschel, "Le Motif de Sarim dans les Ecrits de Joseph Giqatilla," in *Michael: On the History of the Jews in the Diaspora*, ed. S. Simonsohn (Tel Aviv: Diaspora Research Institute, 1989), 9–31. See also *Ma'arekhet ha-Elohut*, 151a–152b; Kushnir-Oron, *The Sefer ha-Peli'ah and the Sefer ha-Kanah*, 287–89.

50. The author of the introduction to the *Sefer ha-Kanah* argues that the subjugation of the Jewish people by Christian and Muslim nations is a consequence of divine punishment. They identify the specific *sarim* of those peoples with Jesus and Muhammad. See the discussion in Kushnir-Oron, *The Sefer ha-Peli'ah and the Sefer ha-Kanah*, 311.

51. *Sefer ha-Temunah*, 58a.

52. *Sefer ha-Temunah*, 58a.

53. On reincarnation in this author, see Shekalim, *Torat ha-Nefesh ve-haGilgul*, 247–345.

54. *Sefer ha-Emunot*, 157–58. See also the discussion in Roland Goetschel, "Providence et Destinees de l'Ame dan le *Sefer ha-Emunot* de Shem Tob ibn Shem Tob (1380–1441), *Misgav Yerushalayim* (1987): LIII–LXXI.

55. On this topic in relation to rabbinic and medieval Jewish notions of original sin, see Alan Cooper, "A Medieval Jewish Version of Original Sin: Ephraim of Luntshits on Leviticus 12," *Harvard Theological Review* 97, no. 4 (2004): 445–59. On interpretations of the sin of Adam and Even in medieval Kabbalistic texts, see Oded Yisraeli, *Temple Portals: Studies in Aggadah and Midrash in the Zohar*, trans. Liat Karen (Berlin: De Gruyter and Magnes, 2018), 50–66. On this idea in Nahmanides's works, see Moshe Halbertal, *Nahmanides: Law and Mysticism* (New Haven: Yale University Press, 2020), 107–12, 129–30. See also *Ma'arekhet ha-Elohut*, 104.

56. On the *Sefer ha-Peliah* and *Sefer ha-Kanah*, see Michal Kushnir-Oron, *The Sefer ha-Peli'ah and the Sefer ha-Kanah: Their Kabbalistic Principles, Social and Religious Criticism, and Literary Composition* (PhD diss., Hebrew University, 1980). On the doctrine of reincarnation in these texts, see Kushnir-Oron, *The Sefer ha-Peli'ah*, 301–8. See also Idel, "The Kabbalah in Byzantium," 693–95.

57. *Sefer ha-Kanah*, 114b. See discussion of this passage in Kushnir-Oron, *The Sefer ha-Peli'ah and the Sefer ha-Kanah*, 304.

58. The author treats the separation caused between the sefirot *Tiferet* and *Malkhut* as a kind of supernal manifestation of death.

59. *Sefer ha-Peliah*, 241–42.

60. See Sachs-Shmueli, "The Rationale of the Negative Commandments," vol. 1, 187–208, 215–16; Scholem, *On the Mystical Shape*, 225–28; Scholem, *Kabbalah*, 346–47; Idel, "The Meaning of 'Ta'amei Ha-'Ofot Ha-Teme'im,' 11–27; Moshe Hallamish, *An Introduction to Kabbalah*, trans. R. Bar-Ilan and O. Wiskind-Elper (Albany: State University of New York Press, 1999), 300–2; Goldschmidt, "Two Historical Conceptions," 79; Elior, "The Doctrine of Transmigration," 259, 269n79. See also Recanati, *Commentary on the Torah*, 2:34, 2:47–48, 2:104. On his qualified doubts regarding this matter, see Recanati, *Commentary on the Torah* 2:108–9.

61. Sachs-Shmueli, *The Rationale of the Negative Commandments*, 188, 211–12. See also Koren, "Kabbalistic Physiology: Isaac the Blind, Nahmanides, and Moses de Leon on Menstruation," *AJS Review* 28, no. 2 (2004): 334–36.

62. *Sefer ha-Temunah*, 66b. See discussion in Scholem, *The Kabbalah of Sefer ha-Temunah*, 57–58; Hellner-Eshed, "Torat ha-*Gilgul* be-Sifrei ha-Kabbalah shel R. David ibn Zimra," *Pe'amim* 43 (1990): 25 [Hebrew]. Idel notes that this passage, and the approach to reincarnation into animals more generally in the *Sefer ha-Temunah*, also reflects the influence of Joseph ben Shalom Ashkenazi and David ben Yehudah he-Hasid. See "The Meaning of 'Ta'amei Ha-'Ofot Ha-Teme'im,'" 18–20.

63. Here the text reflects a view first articulated in the works of Joseph ben Shalom Ashkenazi. See the study by Jonnie Schnytzer, "Metempsychosis, Metensomatosis, and Metamorphosis: On Rabbi Joseph ben Shalom Ashkenazi's Systematic Theory of Reincarnation," *Kahhalah* 45 (2019): 221–44 [Hebrew].

64. *Sefer ha-Kanah*, 230. See also the discussion in Oron, *The Sefer ha-Peli'ah and the Sefer ha-Kanah*, 303–4. On the influence of Joseph ben Shalom Ashkenazi and David ben Yehudah he-Hasid on the *Sefer ha-Temunah* in relation to this idea, and this passage in particular, see Idel, "The Meaning of '*Ta'amei ha-Ofot ha-Teme'im*' of Rabbi David ben Yehuda he-Hasid," in *Alei Shefer: Studies in the Literature of Jewish Thought Presented to Dr. Alexander Shafran* (Ramat Gan: Bar-Ilan University Press), 1990, 18–20 [Hebrew].

65. In addition to the writings of Joseph of Hamadam, this idea is found in other texts. On idea in the *Sabba de-Mishpatim* stratum of the Zohar, see Pinchas Giller, *Reading the Zohar: The Sacred Text of the Kabbalah* (New York: Oxford University Press, 2001), 44–48. See also Hallamish, *An Introduction to Kabbalah*, 304–5. On this idea in Alcastiel and ibn Gabbai, see Scholem, "The Kabbalistic Responsa of R. Joseph Alcastiel to R. Judah Hayyat," *Tarbiẓ* 24 (1955): 194–95.

66. *Sefer ha-Temunah*, 39b.

67. *Sefer ha-Temunah*, 39b.

68. *Sefer ha-Emunot*, 154. See also Goetschel, "Providence et Destinees de le'Ame," LXVI.

69. Isaac of Acre also mentions Ovadia among other famous converts whose souls, he claimed, were originally Israelite in origin. See *Sefer Otzar Hayyim*, ed. Amnon Gross (Tel Aviv: n.p., 2020), 80.

70. See Krinis, "Cyclical Time," 61, 67.

71. See Scholem, *The Kabbalah of Sefer ha-Temunah*, 69–73; *Kabbalah*, 121. Isaac of Acre argues that the 49,000-year time frame of the seven *shemittot* refers to divine years, which constitutes a duration of 17,896,270,000 human years. See Isaac of Acre, *Sefer Or Hayyim*, ed. Amnon Gross (Tel Aviv: n.p., 2020), 88 [Hebrew].

72. See Scholem, *The Kabbalah of Sefer ha-Temunah*, 72.

73. *Sefer ha-Temunah*, 58b–59a. See M. Idel, "Multiple Forms of Redemption in Kabbalah and Hasidism," *Jewish Quarterly Review* 101, no. 1 (2011): 47–51; Scholem, *The Kabbalah of Sefer ha-Temunah*, 69. A version of this idea also appears in the anonymous commentary on the Haggadah mistakenly attributed to Moses de Leon, "Peirush ha-Haggadah le-R. Moshe bar R. Shem Tov me-'Ir Leon," in *Hagadah Shelemah: The Complete Passover Haggadah* (Jerusalem: Torah Shelema Institute, 1967), 130–31. See also Pedaya, *Nahmanides: Cyclical Time*, 444–45.

74. *Sefer ha-Temunah*, 68b. See Elliot Ginsburg, *The Sabbath in the Classical Kabbalah*, (Albany: State University of New York Press, 1989), 99.

75. *Sefer ha-Temunah*, 59a.

76. Scholem, *Origins of the Kabbalah*, 471.

77. Scholem, *Origins of the Kabbalah*, 474.

78. See Idel, "The Secret of Impregnation as Metempsychosis in Kabbalah," in *Verwandlungen: Archaologie der Literarischen Kommunikation IX* (Munich: Wilhelm Fink Verlag, 2006,) 378, and comments in n. 179.

JONNIE SCHNYTZER

R. Joseph ben Shalom Ashkenazi's Cosmic Theory of Reincarnation, *Din Bnei Ḥalof*

6

All beings go through din bnei ḥalof in ascent or in descent and everything is according to true justice.[1]

And the Raven, never flitting, still is/ sitting, still is sitting/ On the pallid bust of Pallas/ just above my chamber door;/ And his eyes have all the seeming of/ a demon's that is dreaming.
— EDGAR ALLAN POE, "THE RAVEN"

THE QUESTION OF THE SOUL and its relationship to the natural world and the afterlife have raised debate among philosophers, Neoplatonist mystics, poets, and scholars across a variety of disciplines.[2] On the Jewish bookshelf, thirteenth-century kabbalists, while grappling with what was considered an esoteric secret, were the first to voice a variety of views and contexts on reincarnation in both Hebrew and Aramaic. While the earlier kabbalistic texts of the period cryptically allude to the doctrine, toward the end of the thirteenth century the matter is discussed more explicitly. It is in this period that the doctrine's scope and essence fork off in various directions.

Offering a radical conceptualization of reincarnation, the medieval kabbalist Rabbi Joseph ben Shalom Ashkenazi,[3] active during the thirteenth century in Catalonia, delineated a systematic theory of cosmic reincarnation, which he coined *din bnei ḥalof* (the judgment of those who transmigrate).[4] *Din bnei ḥalof* was unique in medieval Jewish speculation, singular in its attempt to describe a complete system coupled with specific terminology. Ashkenazi's theory can be seen as the first comprehensive attempt to place transmigration at the core of the divine cosmic plan, along with a meticulous attention to its manifestation in all aspects of being. While other kabbalists around his time wrote on reincarnation, some even extensively,[5] Ashkenazi's grand project is unparalleled in its scope, let alone the centrality the doctrine holds in his writings. In contrast to other kabbalists, and the conventional understanding of reincarnation as metempsychosis, or the movement of a spiritual entity from, usually one human body to another, Ashkenazi proposed a cosmic system whereby all parts of creation — from the spiritual to the corporeal — participate in cycles of renewal that involve both divine justice as well as divine compassion in the sustenance of all aspects of creation. *Din bnei ḥalof* emphasized the interconnectedness of all aspects of existence from the loftiest heights of the heavens — the divine pleroma, the sefirot, and the angels as well as the forces of impurity — to the smallest creatures of the universe — the flora, fauna, inanimate rocks, and even the dew. At its core, therefore, Ashkenazi's theory functions as a prism through which the totality of existence unfolds while the activities of the forces of purity and impurity are revealed from creation to redemption.

The kabbalist's systematic theory also includes an in-depth, albeit scattered, description of the nature of the process of reincarnation. Ashkenazi provides an almost Darwinist theory of the evolution that reincarnated spirits are subjected to as they ascend and/or descend the cosmic chain of being. The kabbalist's all-encompassing theory includes enigmatic and complex depictions concerning the forces of impurity *temurot* (contraries) that not only execute the divine judgment in the world, but also attempt to disrupt the divine plan by harming spirits and snatching human souls.

According to Ashkenazi's idiosyncratic theory, reincarnation was not limited to the soul's transfer into a new body (metempsychosis), but also included the transmigration of physical matter into new corporeal forms (metensomatosis) in addition to simultaneous corporeal and spiritual transformations (metamorphosis). To carefully distinguish these processes, Ashkenazi introduced the Hebrew terms *shelaḥ* (lit. sending off, implying metempsychosis), *gilgul* (lit. circulation, implying metensomatosis), and *ibbur* (lit. impregnation, implying the stage in which a spiritual entity becomes ontologically connected to a physical body) to designate different aspects of material and spiritual transformation of beings.

Ashkenazi's works follow a systematic organizational structure in much the same way that the kabbalist was systematic in the way he concealed his ideas. Influenced by the rationalist system of the medieval Jewish philosopher Moses Maimonides (1138–1204), Ashkenazi contends with offering only "chapter headings" (ראשי פרקים) – a technique that deliberately veils part of the content.[6] Another esoteric technique deployed by Ashkenazi is known as "dispersion of knowledge," a term discussed by Daniel De Smet regarding various Isma'ili texts to which Ashkenazi may well have had access. The technique is one of scattering secrets in diverse sections of the text. Thus, in several cases, the kabbalist mentions a term only to explain its meaning several folios later.[7]

Similar hermeneutic techniques of concealment were used by other esoteric groups active in the Middle Ages, such as the Muslim fraternity called Brethren of Purity or Ikhwân al-Safâ, who were active in the cities of Basra and Baghdad in the ninth and tenth centuries. Their encyclopedic compendium, *Epistles of the Pure Brethren and the Sincere Friends or in Arabic, Rasâ'il Ikhwân al-Safâ' wa Khullân al-Wafâ'* contains ideas concerning reincarnation that were closely aligned with kabbalistic formulations of transmigration.[8] This corpus enjoyed wide circulation throughout several regions of the Mediterranean and even reached Al-Andalus, from where it was transmitted and translated into various languages.[9] Furthermore, the broadness of Ashkenazi's theory on reincarnation is reminiscent of the doctrine's scope among the Nusayiri-Alawis.[10]

Ashkenazi's speculative system became widely influential not only for later kabbalists, but also for medieval thinkers and Renaissance philosophers, such as renowned Italian humanist Count Giovanni Pico Della Mirandola (1463–1494),[11] the seventeenth-century Sabbatians, and even Hasidic masters of the eighteenth and nineteenth centuries.[12] Spanning many centuries and widespread across a number of geographical regions, his doctrine of *din bnei ḥalof* had its deepest influence on the kabbalistic thought of the Rabbi Isaac Luria (1534–1572) and Rabbi Hayyim Vital (1542–1620), two of the most prominent sixteenth-century Safedian kabbalists.[13] The doctrine of *din bnei ḥalof*, the focus of the present chapter, became a core concept in Lurianic kabbalah[14] and the subject of a select number of scholarly studies in the field of kabbalah and Jewish thought.[15]

The Cosmic System of Reincarnation: *Din Bnei Ḥalof*

An analysis of *din bnei ḥalof* reveals three distinct dimensions of Ashkenazi's unique theory of reincarnation. The first, *metempsychosis*, is designated by the kabbalist as *shelaḥ* — the transmigration of spiritual entities from one physical body to another. The second, *metensomatosis*, is defined by the kabbalist as *gilgul* — the transmigration of physical matter from one body to another. The use of this term may seem, and indeed has become, confusing for scholars given that in other kabbalistic texts, *gilgul* refers to metempsychosis. The third, *metamorphosis*, refers to rare cases when both the spiritual (*shelaḥ*) and the physical (*gilgul*) transmigrate simultaneously from one body into another. A close examination of textual sources shows that while Ashkenazi scattered his explanations of the various technical terms of which he avails himself, the concept of *din bnei ḥalof* serves as the general term for his cosmic theory of reincarnation, while *shelaḥ* and *gilgul* constitute vital stages in the overall process. As I demonstrate, these two aspects are not only complementary — in that *shelaḥ* pertains to spiritual matter (metempsychosis) while *gilgul* relates to physical matter (metensomatosis) — but also constitute a vertical and a horizontal process, respectively. Together, they act as a circumference and diameter to the cosmic circle of life as described by Ashkenazi.[16]

A survey of Ashkenazi's surviving works — a commentary on *Genesis Rabbah* and a commentary on *Sefer Yeẓira* — indicates that the concept of *din bnei ḥalof* functions as a broad term encompassing the hidden secrets of *gilgul* of physical matter (inanimate beings, plants, animals, and mankind) and *shelaḥ* of spiritual matter, designated in kabbalistic literature as spirits (*nefashot*) and souls (*neshamot*). The term *din bnei ḥalof* refers to the overall process — God's system of divine providence and justice — as it is deployed in the sustenance and governance of the created world. Thus, for instance, in his commentary on Genesis Rabbah, Ashkenazi mentions a Talmudic *midrash* of the division of shifts in a single day of God's conduct of creation:

> "The first three [hours of the day], the Holy One, Blessed is He, sits and involves himself with Torah ... the second [three hours] He sits and judges the entire world ... the third [three hours] He sits and provides [nourishment] for the entire world, from the horns of the reindeer to the eggs of lice. . . ."[17]

Upon citing this *midrash*, Ashkenazi states that "This *Aggadah* doubtless is about [God] dealing with all beings, *din bnei ḥalof*, and the order of things."[18]

A more radical statement appears on the first page of his commentary on *Sefer Yeẓira*, where the law of *din bnei ḥalof* is applied to all levels of existence, including the Godhead and its structural pillar of the sefirotic system with the exclusion of the highest sefirot.[19] Here reincarnation is presented as the central pivot supporting creation in its entirety. Indeed, this view, that various forms of transmigration apply to the Godhead itself is unparalleled in its radicality and is expanded on in the section of this chapter focused on metensomatosis.

Reincarnation of Spirits — Metempsychosis (*Shelaḥ*)

Since the late thirteenth century, the most common term used for reincarnation in kabbalistic literature has been *gilgul neshamot* (the recycling/recirculation of souls).[20] Yet, interestingly, this term does not appear in the works of Ashkenazi, and in fact, as it will become apparent, *gilgul neshamot* is a contradiction in terms for this kabbalist. Instead, Ashkenazi proposes the term *shelaḥ* (sending off).[21] It is of note that the word is also a rare biblical noun, implying a kind of sword or dagger (Nehemiah 4:11; Job 33:18). In Ashkenazi's works, the word *shelaḥ* is consistently applied to the activities of the spirit (*nefesh*), as in the example "when the time comes for the spirit to be launched (*shelaḥ*)."[22] This is of interest, as it could imply a form of vertical movement, whereby spiritual beings ascend and descend (for judgment between the time spent within physical bodies). Thus, whether the kabbalist's intention was to borrow a rare biblical word or to use a known verb, the word becomes the term he uses for metempsychosis.[23]

Studies relating to Ashkenazi's thought have already pointed out that the purpose of the transmigration of the spirit (*nefesh*) constitutes one of the laws of nature and an integral part of a cosmic process, whereby the *nefesh* is judged for its actions between dwellings in one body or another, and rises or is sent into the spiritual world to receive its judgment: "the angel of God stands to receive that *nefesh* and oversees its judgment, decreeing whether it shall ascend or descend, going higher up in rank, or whether it is to be degraded."[24] Relating to the various possibilities of judgment, that is into what body the *nefesh* can next enter, the kabbalist states, "And the supreme forces sent to this world are called *nefashot* ... [they] can become an animal or a beast, bird or insect, an inanimate being or a plant."[25] In other words, the *nefesh* can move and enter multiple embodied forms during its wanderings. Thus far, it is evident that for Ashkenazi, the *nefesh* can ascend and descend. What is unique in Ashkenazi's speculative system is the all-encompassing application of transmigration not only to human beings but to all levels of existence. This idea, I would posit, appears perhaps for the first time across the Jewish religious corpus in Ashkenazi's oeuvre.

Distinguishing between Spirit (*Nefesh*) and Soul (*Neshamah*)

To fully understand the role of spiritual substance in the process of reincarnation and its unique deployment in Ashkenazi's systematic theory, it is helpful to elucidate the concept of the soul and its counterparts, specifically the spirit (*nefesh*) and the soul (*neshama*) as they are extensively discussed in his works. While the soul is considered to have five parts or facets,[26] namely *nefesh*, *ruaḥ*, *neshama*, *yeḥidah*, and *ḥaya*, this chapter focuses only on two of them, the *nefesh* and the *neshama*. In general, the *yeḥidah* and *ḥaya* are considered the concealed aspects of the spiritual structure and therefore are rarely discussed in Ashkenazi's texts or, for that matter, in other kabbalistic literature produced at the time. The *ruaḥ* is closely connected to the body and is defined as the source of vitality for the physical body and consequently appears marginal to kabbalist's discussion of reincarnation.

According to Ashkenazi, one of the key differences between the *nefesh* and the *neshamah* is their ontological source and location. As it will be shown in this section, a person's *nefesh* is localized within their physical body, while their *neshamah* is situated in the divine world. The precise location of the *neshamah* will be illustrated through the following examples — one connected to birth (as part of his discussion of *sod ha-ibbur*, the secret of impregnation), and another related to death (the rationale for the law of ritual slaughter of cattle): "And you should know that at the precise moment when a woman gives birth below, the *neshamah* above is being refined and is then sent from [the realm of the *sefirah*] *Malkhut* toward *pnei adam*, human face (mankind), corresponding to the newborn."[27] This passage problematizes the precise meaning of the phrase "toward *pnei adam* corresponding to the newborn."[28] What precisely is the trajectory of the *neshamah*, and what is the meaning of the phrase "human face" (*pnei adam*)? To explain why the *neshamah* during its transmigration does not descend into the body, Ashkenazi refers to issues related to the meaning of death and the secret of hell (*Gehinnom*), which appear a few folios before this passage: "You, who understand these matters, should know that the force which is called death is not the absence of life. Rather, there are instances when the *neshamah* resides with the vital force, *ruaḥ*, and spirit, *nefesh*, and then, they are part of life which is the Lord's [*sefirah*] *Tiferet* and the secret is, *But you who cling to Hashem, your God — you are all alive today* (Deut. 4:4)."[29] The sequence of words "there are instances when the *neshamah* resides with the *ruaḥ* and *nefesh*" hints at the possibility that the *neshamah* generally does not reside with these two parts of the soul, both of which are generally identified as residing within the physical body. If so, what is the precise location and role of the *neshamah*? The term *pnei adam* is drawn from the biblical book of Ezekiel (1:5–28), where the prophet describes God's throne as a heavenly chariot composed of four spiritual entities or facets: the face of a human being (*pnei adam*), the face of a lion (*pnei arye*), the face of an ox (*pnei shor*), and the face of an eagle (*pnei nesher*). It may be argued that in the case of Ashkenazi's speculation, these entities represent spiritual manifestations of parallel realms on earth. Thus, the "human face" represents mankind, the "eagle face" denotes the bird kingdom, while the ox and the lion signify the kingdom of pure and impure animals, respectively, based on biblical dietary laws. Consequently, the *neshamah* does not dwell together with the *nefesh* and the *ruaḥ*, which are located within physical bodies, but is sequestered instead in a parallel spiritual realm ontologically connected to the body. The relationship between spirit and soul, *nefesh* and *neshamah*, is poignantly illustrated in Ashkenazi's commentary on Genesis Rabbah concerning the ritual slaughter of animals:

> It is necessary to cut the pipe that has been replaced from *pnei adam*, human face (mankind) to *pnei ha-ḥai*, animal face (the animal kingdom). This action enables bringing it back to the first person that preceded this animal ... When he [the ritual slaughterer] does what is commanded of him and slaughters the animal and cuts open the area where the *nefesh* should depart from, like the barrel of the esophagus, the Angel of God comes to dwell upon this *nefesh*. Then the Angel of God stands to receive that *nefesh* and oversees its judgment, decreeing whether it shall ascend or descend, going higher up in rank or lower down ... The area being cut on the neck must be exposed. That is, the place where the *neshamah* departs [above], so that the slaughterer not be likened to one who steals *nefashot* in disguise.[30] Also, it is not acceptable to divert from above the pipes next to the head, Upper Crown (*Keter Elyon*), for *who can send forth his hand against God's anointed one and be absolved?* (1 Samuel 26:9). If he slaughters below the marked location, he does not let the *neshamah* depart from the pipes.[31]

Based on this passage, the slaughterer is executing two actions simultaneously. The slaughterer cuts the barrel and the esophagus in this physical world so that the *nefesh* could depart from the body (to be judged in the divine realm). The correct manner of slaughtering also enables the *neshamah* to depart from its parallel pipes in the upper world, a process which enables the *neshamah*, in this case, to transmigrate from a spiritual realm representing the animal kingdom (*pnei ha-ḥai*) to the realm representing mankind (*pnei adam*) in preparation for its next reincarnation, which, it is assumed, will be an elevation to the rank of mankind. In other words, the process enables the *neshamah* to ascend in rank in the circle of life.[32]

To strengthen the case that the passage alludes to two simultaneous processes, the word *ẓinor* (pipe) appears in the writings of Ashkenazi not only as a signifier of a part of the body, but also as an apparatus within the sefirotic Godhead.[33] Hence, using Ashkenazi's terminology and being mindful of his esoteric style of writing, the cutting of the animal's pipe and the subsequent release of spirit from the esophagus alludes to a parallel process in the divine realm, where the soul is released from its pipe. Further evidence in favor of this argument is signified in the passage by the direct association between the head of the animal and the *sefirotic* designator, *Keter Elyon* (Supernal Crown), implying that the word not only refers to the release of the *nefesh* from the esophagus next to the animal's head, but simultaneously also alludes to the release of the *neshamah* in the sefirotic realm.

Ashkenazi's teaching affirms that every person is born with both a *nefesh* and a *neshamah*. The difference between the two is that while the *nefesh* is within the physical body, the *neshamah* remains in the upper divine realm, albeit ontologically connected to the person. Both the *nefesh* and *neshamah* transmigrate (in the form of *shelaḥ*) — the *nefesh* into a physical body, whereas the *neshamah* remains to transmigrate in the divine realm. It should be noted that this idea is in contrast to Gershom Scholem's conclusion, based on his extensive analysis and study of kabbalistic texts, that the bestowal of the higher levels of the soul, the *ruah* and the *neshamah*, is conditioned by human action and can be removed from or alternatively never granted to a human being, "Everyone is born with a *nefesh*, but whether or not he will succeed in bringing down his own *ruah* and *neshamah* from the treasure house of souls ... depends upon his own choice or spiritual development."[34]

The spiritual hierarchy mentioned by Scholem, doubtless influenced by the idea found throughout Zoharic literature, does not seem to depict Ashkenazi's theory. While the *neshamah* is at a higher spiritual level, this indicated by its position in the divine realm, it appears to be associated with each person from birth regardless of their actions. Furthermore, the earthly position of the *nefesh* alongside the loftier position of the *neshamah* highlights the parallelism between micro- and macrocosm and reinforces the idea of an all-encompassing cosmic system:[35] "And the proper analogy for this would be the human being. For a person has an intellect from the upper worlds . . . which is the beginning of all beings under the moon's orbit in the secret of *gilgul* and *shelaḥ* for it is through an individual that intellects descend and through the human being that all other beings, that are within a person's domain and surrounding, can ascend."[36] Fundamentally, Ashkenazi understands the purpose of transmigration as aimed at the purification of the soul and in this sense shares the view of his contemporaries as expressed by the authors of the Zohar in the section, *Saba de-Mishpatim*,[37] or in the writings of Rabbi Joseph Hamadan.[38] At the same time, he offers a radical reading in that while other kabbalists stress the purification of the soul as the ultimate goal of reincarnation, Ashkenazi underlines that *din bnei ḥalof* is set in motion to purify all forms of impurity reaching beyond the spiritual parts of the world to include all dimensions of physical matter.

In this sense, Ashkenazi's elaborate discussion of reincarnation in his commentary on *Genesis Rabbah* can also be read as a philosophical debate regarding divine judgment and providence. Ashkenazi offers a critique on the Maimonidean concept of divine providence, which is delimited in scope to the human species alone and is dependent on the person's intellectual achievement.[39] By contrast, *din bnei ḥalof*'s extension to inanimate objects, such as rocks, may be viewed as an ecocritique of the Maimonidean model, which stems from the Greek philosophical concept of the soul,[40] namely as differentiating between animate and inanimate things.[41] According to this implicit critique, spiritual forms, which animate all beings, receive their judgment and are refined through the process of *shelaḥ*, while *gilgul*, the topic of the next section, focuses on purifying the physical aspects of creation through embodied reincarnation, or metensomatosis.

Metensomatosis (*Gilgul*)—The Recycling of Physical Matter

The doctrine of metensomatosis, the transmigration of physical matter into another corporeal form, complements the process of metempsychosis and was discussed in thirteenth-century kabbalistic literature, albeit far less than its spiritual counterpart. Similarly, the topic still awaits comprehensive scholarly treatment. When medieval kabbalists discussed metempsychosis, they generally applied the specific terminology, *gilgul*, while kabbalistic discourse on metensomatosis typically was not associated with a fixed designator. Ashkenazi's speculative system is unique in positing metensomatosis as a distinct element in the reincarnation process designated by a specific term, *gilgul*.[42]

A short passage from *Iggeret ha-Kodesh* (The Holy Letter),[43] a work arguably contemporaneous with Ashkenazi and attributed to R. Joseph Gikatilla, provides an apt point of departure for framing Ashkenazi's theory of metensomatosis. Here eating and corporeal consumption serve as central images of transformation from one physical entity into another:

> It follows that when an animal is slaughtered for human consumption, it is for the animal's good, for it rises from the level of the body of an animal to the level of the body of a human being, and these are the ways of the four chariots of the lower world. They are elements; minerals; plants; living things that do not speak; and living things that speak. The minerals are composed of and sustained by the four elements, the plants are nourished by the elements and minerals, the non-rational animals are nourished by plants, minerals, and the four elements, and the rational animals use the non-rational animals, plants, and minerals. This process proceeds hierarchically until the cycle of the sphere is completed. About this is said: "God is good to all" . . . and so we find that all of them become food for other species in order that they attain a level higher than their own.[44]

From the above passage we see that lower beings go through a form of metensomatosis and are thus elevated in rank, and that this process is related to God's divine providence. Other kabbalistic works, such as R. Joseph Gikatilla's *Sha'arei Orah* (*The Gates of Illumination*)[45] and R. Joseph Hamadan's *Ta'amei ha-Mitzwot Lo-Ta'ase* (*The Rationale of the Negative Commandments*),[46] while expressing similar views, expand the doctrine by including the phenomenon of apotheosis through which a human being is elevated to the rank of angels. As we will see shortly, Ashkenazi builds both on the image of eating as well on apotheosis, but introduces the radical idea that human beings can be transformed into aspects of the Godhead.

While the process of *shelaḥ* purifies the spiritual matter, such as the spirit and the soul, as we have seen in Ashkenazi's commentary on Genesis Rabbah, *gilgul* purifies physical matter. Metensomatosis, often expressed by evoking the image of eating, completes the spiritual process of metempsychosis and unfolds through the act of consumption that pervades the universe, from inanimate objects to the lofty heights of angels:

It is known that everything transmigrates (*mitgalgel*) according to whatever eats it. For example, from the food eaten by an animal, that which is worthy of generation will become part of the animal and that which is worthy to become an insect will become feces and from the feces an insect. In much the same way, that which is worthy to become human, will become human upon a person's eating it, and what is worthy of corruption will become feces. So too is the case with wild animals, birds, cattle, fish, detestable things (שקץ), and every insect which swarms the land. And from here you learn that every inanimate being, plant, living and speaking being, all undergo the judgment of transmigration (דין בני חלוף) to ascend or descend and it is all in accordance with true justice that "at the commandment of the Lord, they shall journey, and at the commandment of the Lord, they shall encamp."[47] So, how is it possible for an [impure] insect to become a pure bird? If the bird feeds off the insect, in turn, the insect becomes an egg and that very egg will return to become another pure bird, or it shall be eaten by a human being.[48]

To illustrate the limitless potential of human beings in the universal process of reincarnation, Ashkenazi proposed a radical reading regarding the transformation of physical matter.[49] He therefore maintained that the human body shared certain likeness with the essence (עצם) of the divine potencies, the *sefirot*, which enabled the transfusion of one substance into the other:[50] "And therefore he [the human being] has the potential to transmigrate and be transmigrated into any inanimate, plant, animal, intelligent being [human], [or into one of the] the celestial orbs, planets, zodiacal signs, [separate] intellects, angels, and [into] the essence (עצם) of [and into] any of the ten sefirot, blessed be His name and remembrance." This passage raises obvious philosophical and theological problems, which deal at the core with the question of the ontological relationship between created substance and divinity. In other words, can the ontological divide between the creator and the created being be overcome so that a person could attain and be elevated to the status of the sefirot, and thus become part of the Godhead? Understanding the verb להתגלגל (to transmigrate into) as metensomatosis leads to the following corollary — the word "core" (עצם) in the passage "the core of the ten *sefirot*" is not incidental.[51]

While Ashkenazi makes no explicit reference to the limits of possibility regarding the transmigration of spiritual matter (spirits and souls through *shelaḥ*), in the case of the transmigration of physical bodies (*gilgul*), the above passage seems quite explicit. According to the kabbalist, the transmigration of physical matter has no limits. In both his commentary on *Genesis Rabbah* and on *Sefer Yeẓira*, Ashkenazi describes the process by which human beings can transmigrate into the Godhead based on ontological parallelism between the human and the divine structures: "You should know that in a person's unshaped form, God, blessed be Thy name, embedded all kinds of creations, forms and actions, including those found in the ten *sefirot*."[52] Elsewhere he articulates a similar notion: "And this is the secret of formation, that all creations are embedded in the human being man and the human being is embedded in them."[53] For Ashkenazi, as it becomes clear, all beings are interconnected and dependent on the other, while the role of human beings constitutes the center and driving force of existence. Just as spiritual entities participate in the cosmic cycle of purification and in the process receive their judgment by means of metempsychosis, so too physical matter joins the universal path to renewal through metensomatosis or physical transmigration.

Once the distinction has been made between *gilgul* and *shelaḥ* and their respective processes, metensomatosis, and metempsychosis, one can posit a radical case whereby both body and spirit transmigrate simultaneously by way of metamorphosis. An analysis of the following cryptic passage sheds light on the matter:

> And he first mentioned the transmigration (*gilgul*) of aquatic species, for they are finer beings than the species of the land. If he did not return [as an aquatic species] but rather as *a fool who repeated his folly*[54] [he would become] a bird, that is, a species which comes from the seabed, and if not [as a bird], into an animal, and if not as such, then into an insect, and if not as such, then into any animal that swarms the land. A testament to this secret of transmigration (*gilgul*) can be found in connection with Nebuchadnezzar II, regarding descent, and Enoch and Elijah, in regard to ascent.[55]

The first part of the passage, which suggests a process of spiritual evolution, discusses metempsychosis and the hierarchical order of transmigration based on a person's actions.[56] In the continuation of the passage, the kabbalist likely alludes to a form of transmigration whereby the physical body and spirit are transformed simultaneously, undergoing metamorphosis. The biblical characters Elijah and Enoch, on the one hand, and Nebuchadnezzar, on the other hand, cited in the passage represent extreme and opposite typologies of the phenomenon of metamorphosis. Thus, while all three depart from the realm of humanity during their lifetime — body and soul — the two former personalities are rewarded with ascent to the heavenly realm, while the king of Babylonia is punished for his wicked actions against Israel by descending to the animal kingdom and joining the realm of beasts.

Nebuchadnezzar II, the great king of the Chaldean dynasty of Babylonia, discussed in the Book of Daniel, is likened to Pharoah, the ruler of Egypt, as both are depicted as having dreamt a disturbing dream. Medieval commentators posited that Nebuchadnezzar's dream can be interpreted to suggest the loss of not only his kingdom but also his humanity in a literal sense, implying that the Chaldean king ultimately metamorphosed into an animal.[57] Thus, it may be assumed that Ashkenazi fits squarely into this hermeneutic tradition. This assumption is further supported by Ashkenazi's discussion of Enoch and Elijah, both of whom are described in the Bible as having ascended from the physical world to the heavenly realm, as their "flesh transformed into torches of fire."[58] Thus, it may be established that Ashkenazi's systematic theory not only discusses metensomatosis and metempsychosis but also refers to metamorphosis, a simultaneous transformation involving both the corporeal and the spiritual aspects of the human being.[59]

It should be noted that Ashkenazi's interpretation concerning the transmigration of Nebuchadnezzar II echoes the literary discourse of Jewish thinkers from tenth-century Babylonia on this question. In his book *Moslem Schisms and Sects* (al-Fark bain al Firak), Islamic scholar and heresiologist Abu Mansur el-Baghdadi (died 1037) provides a comprehensive review of the subject of reincarnation, including a Jewish position based on the case of Nebuchadnezzar II.[60] With the addition of interpretative parallels between Ashkenazi's formulation of reincarnation and views on the matter brought forth by tenth-century Babylonian Karaite scholar Jacob Qirqisani (c. 890–c. 960),[61] a case can be made for the possibility that earlier Eastern influences left their mark on Spanish kabbalists concerning theories of reincarnation.[62]

Reincarnation and the Forces of Impurity

Kabbalists, unlike philosophers, perceived evil as having a separate existence and an ontological realty. While the root of evil was debated in various kabbalistic texts, it is commonly derived from the process of creation and linked to the emanation of the Godhead.[63] Moreover, its primary manifestation seems to derive from the sefirah of judgment, *Gevurah*. As such, and as it will be shown in the case of Ashkenazi, the initial purpose of the forces of evil is to execute divine justice. However, by some manner, these forces have a tendency to become seemingly independent of the Godhead, and in this state, they seek to interfere with the divine plan.

The divine mechanisms that sustain all forms of existence in the universe and oversee the process of transmigration in Ashkenazi's theory are the sefirot of the Godhead and their contraries, the *temurot* (lit. contraries), forces of impurity. Both play complementary, albeit at times contradictory, roles.[64] This world, according to Ashkenazi's conceptualization, is moved by the perpetual and dynamic interplay between spiritual contraries, where he sees the primary function of the temurot as executing the divine decree issued to spirits and souls. However, they also disrupt and obstruct divine decrees: "Know that *ḥerpah* [disgrace] is the contrary of hakavod [literally 'respect', however here referred to as a term for the sefirot], and she (*ḥerpah*) tries to convert the respect into disgrace."[65]

Similarly, Ashkenazi describes hell as a double-edged sword, a characterization he also uses for his depiction of the forces of impurity. In Ashkenazi's great cosmic system, life and death, the sefirot and the *temurot*, share a certain degree of commonality, which is expressed by the idea that hell is formed by the fire of the sefirah *Gevurah*,[66] as well as being composed of the wicked: "The wicked one, who often frequented hell, cleaving to it, until he transmigrated himself into hell."[67] Thus, it seems that while the root of hell is the sefirotic Godhead, it is in constant metamorphosis, fueled by the wicked. In line with the kabbalist's use of esoteric techniques of scattering the pieces of an idea, Ashkenazi's discussion of these forces is dispersed throughout his oeuvre. These scattered fragments reveal the darker side of his cosmic theory. They are drawn primarily from two places — the introduction to his commentary on *Sefer Yeẓira*,[68] focused on death, combined with his discussion on the rationale behind the biblical laws of ritually pure or impure birds,[69] examined in his commentary on *Genesis Rabbah*.[70] While the kabbalist embeds these secrets in various texts, it is apparent that each sheds light and clarifies certain ideas in the other. The discussion in the commentary on *Sefer Yeẓira* is focused on the essence of death, a reality associated with hell, and in his commentary on *Genesis Rabbah*, the role and nature of various forces of impurity, which are ontologically connected to and represented in the physical world by impure birds.

As contraries, the *temurot* represent death, while sefirot exemplify life. Death for this kabbalist, does not simply mean lack of life. Rather, like hell or the act of cutting off a spirit from the bond of life (*karet*), it is a form of infernal punishment with various hierarchies corresponding to the sin a person committed while being alive. In the state of purgatory, spirits are at the disposal of the *temurot* until they return to life. Ashkenazi further asserts that when a spirit is sentenced to death, its connection to the Tetragrammaton (the divine name of four letters) that embodies its spiritual sustenance also gets eliminated, and the spirit is handed over "to the *temurot*, and that which is sentenced to death shall die and that which is sentenced to transmigrate shall transmigrate."[71] Thus, there is a degree of differentiation between aspects of being, which at death is among the forces of impurity, and other parts of being, which reenter the circle of life, albeit in new forms. However, whether the spirit, *nefesh*, is doomed to descend in transmigration or death, while the spirit hovers from place to place, *Duma*, the Minister of the dead, shepherds the souls, *neshamot*, "until they [the spirits] have served their judgment."[72]

This period, in which the spirit departs from the physical body, is described by the kabbalist as an extremely fragile and liminal period fraught with danger for the soul. Until the human body is ritually buried, the spirit cannot ascend to receive its judgment, which has ramifications for the soul above. To a certain extent, this scenario is somewhat similar to the one illustrated in the passage relating to ritual slaughter — the performance of rituals in the physical world has ramifications for the *neshamah* above. In this perilous state, on the one hand, the *temurot* emerge to demand the soul that awaits in limbo, while, on the other hand, various kinds of demons seek to penetrate the physical body.[73]

Upon the departure of the spirit from the physical body, there are several kinds of forces of impurity, *temurot*, lurking in wait for spirits and souls in the process of *shelaḥ*, metempsychosis. Ashkenazi further explains that these forces are represented by impure birds, and the primary function of each is concealed in the bird's name.[74] There are the forces of impurity that kill spirits associated with the כוס (Athene), a genus of owls, and the תחמס, a type of owlet.[75] There are other forces that want to proscribe and destroy spirits and even demand possession of souls while the spirit awaits its judgment. The kabbalist associates these with the תנשמת, another type of owl.[76] There are forces that seek to obtain the rejected spirits, torment, and torture them, at times handing them over to other forces according to the spirit's judgment. These are associated with the בת יענה, or ostrich.[77] There is yet another group of impure forces, whose main task is to cut spirits off from the bond of life and send them on a new course of transmigration into flora. These forces are associated with the נץ, birds of the Accipiter genus, such as hawks.[78] Like the sefirah *Binah*, which is frequently depicted as the mother or womb to the other sefirot, its equivalent in the world of *temurot* is a force called רחם, alluding both to a genus of vultures as well as to the womb, which conceives these demonic spirits and empowers them to multiply.[79] While these forces act upon divine judgment, Ashkenazi surprisingly depicts them as possessing additional yearning to overthrow, discard, and destroy the spirits in their possession. Finally, there are forces tasked with sending spirits to the gates of hell and "the land of darkness, where there are no firmaments, constellations of signs of the zodiac — a land in the shadow of death."[80]

Dwelling in darkness for the spirits sentenced to hell is not equivalent to a complete absence of light — rather, darkness assumes both a demarcated place and a distinct and separate form of being:

> And just as the darkness separates and mixes forms to the point where one cannot tell a difference between them, so too in this darkness, which is the *temura* of light, nothing can be distinguished. And this darkness is not simply the absence of light but has an actual existence. As it is written, *For, behold, darkness may cover the earth and a thick cloud may cover the kingdoms* (Isaiah 60:2) and it says *the wicked are stilled in darkness* (1 Samuel 2:9), thus these souls have eyes, but they cannot see.[81]

The darkness described is almost schizophrenic, confusing, and terrifying. Without the ability to differentiate between forms, the spiritual entities are in a state of utter chaos. This idea is further alluded to in what Ashkenazi calls "the secret of the disintegration of the organs (סוד פירוק האברים), both of the sefirot, and of the physical body."[82] Without attempting to make complete sense of these secrets scattered by the kabbalist, the descriptions, much like Edgar Allan Poe's raven, or Hitchcock's birds, for that matter, are chilling. Moreover, Ashkenazi's meticulous depiction of the role of the demonic attests to the centrality of this doctrine in his theosophical system, while at the same time allowing him to offer a deft and systematic presentation of transmigration as a cosmic process involving existence in its totality.

Conclusion

Joseph ben Shalom Ashkenazi's cosmic theory of reincarnation reaches beyond a kabbalistic description of the doctrine and has implications for the existence of all life-forms as the very essence and purpose of creation that is perpetually moving toward redemption. At the center of this process, the actions of human beings — the performance of biblical commandments and rituals — determine the outcome of the cosmic battle between the sefirotic Godhead and the forces of impurity, which, while having a part in the divine plan, nevertheless aim to disrupt and sabotage the process.

Ashkenazi's *din bnei ḥalof* is unparalleled in its meticulous and systematic presentation of the cosmic process of transmigration. Uncovering his unique understanding of the interrelated nature of all forms of existence — from the lofty sphere of angels and the Godhead to the realm of dew and dust — allows us to offer a more nuanced picture of the relationship between the natural world and the divine realm. This depiction enriches our understanding of the development of the doctrine of transmigration in medieval Jewish thought, nuancing Gershom Scholem's scholarly contribution on the topic, which was based primarily on his reading of Zoharic literature. Furthermore, the arguments presented in this chapter provide a prolegomenon to how ideas relating to the soul and its counterparts, including its associations within the physical world, were transmitted and adapted into the theoretical apparatus of later kabbalists, such as the influential system of the sixteenth-century mystic Rabbi Isaac Luria Ashkenazi (Ari). It is for this reason that Ashkenazi's carefully crafted system can assist in gaining a more refined appreciation for these complexities as well as shed light on important points of contact and difference with other esoteric formulations during a period in which kabbalistic thought was being crystallized.

Unlike the teachings of his contemporaries, Ashkenazi's doctrine was predicated on conceptualizing existence as all-encompassing — moving from the *sefirotic* Godhead through the natural hierarchy of humans, animals, flora, fauna, inanimate objects, and even the lowest point of being, Hell. Metempsychosis provided the intellectual framework for discussing the reincarnation of a living organism into any other natural form, while the concept of metensomatosis radically reformulated the transmigration of the body even into the Godhead.

This essentially limitless process of dissolution and reconstitution sets Ashkenazi apart not only from the fundamental teachings of the Zohar, but also from contemporary kabbalists such as R. Joseph Hamadan. Thus, the Zohar and Hamadan present a doctrinally more limited understanding of reincarnation as a form of punishment for transgressing specific biblical commandments and embed their discussion of transmigration within a broader ethical discourse. Interestingly, in both Hamadan and Zoharic literature the discourse on reincarnation is embedded within an ethical-exhortative framework to arouse fear of sin in the reader. By contrast, Ashkenazi's treatment of reincarnation, with its specific terminology and careful detail, even in its chilling descriptions of the forces of impurity, seems to stem from a scientific modus operandi, albeit inspired by the construction of a mystical zeitgeist. It is through this confluence of the scientific and mystical that the kabbalist portrays God's providence, which imbues all levels of existence and creates a great chain of being of interconnections between its higher and lower realms.

Notes

1. Ms. Oxford, Bodleian, Opp. 464, fol. 57a. All citations from Ashkenazi's commentary on *Sefer Yeira* are from this manuscript, on which the edition I prepared is based. For the edition, see Jonnie Schnytzer, "Scientific Kabbalah: The System of Thought of Rabbi Joseph ben Shalom Ashkenazi: A Study of His Works & Critical Edition of *The Commentary on Sefer Yesira*," vol. 2 (PhD diss., Bar-Ilan University, 2023).

2. See for example John Michael Corrigan's study on American poets Ralph Waldo Emerson and Walt Whitman, in which the metempsychosis of the classic age transmigrates into new realms of meaning. See John Michael Corrigan, *American Metempsychosis: Emerson, Whitman and the New Poetry* (New York: Fordham University Press, 2012).

3. Ashkenazi's oeuvre includes a commentary on *Genesis Rabbah*, a commentary on *Sefer Yesira*, as well as a commentary on several *Psalms*. In addition, in these works, the kabbalist refers to a commentary on *Heichalot* and *Ma'ase Merkavah* literature; however, these have yet to be found in the manuscript. Further literature on Ashkenazi: Gershom Scholem, "The Real Author of the *Commentary on Sefer Yesira* Attributed to the R. Abraham ben David and His Works," *Kiryat Sefer* 4 (1927): 286–302 [Hebrew]; Georges Vajda, 'Un chaptire de l'histoire du conflit entre la Kabbale et la philosophie. La polémique anti-intellectualiste de Joseph b. Shalom Ashkenazi de Catalogne," *Archives d'histiore doctrinale et Littéraire du moyen âge* (1956): 45–144 [French]; Moshe Hallamish, ed. *A Kabbalistic Commentary of Rabbi Yoseph Ben Shalom Ashkenazi on Genesis Rabbah* (Jerusalem: Magness Press, 1984) [Hebrew]; M. Hallamish, "Remnants from the Commentary on Psalms by R. Joseph ben Shalom Ashkenazi," *Da'at* 10 (1983): 57–50 [Hebrew]; Elliot. R. Wolfson, *Language, Eros, Being: Kabbalistic Hermeneutics and Poetic Imagination* (New York: Fordham University Press, 2005), 64, 178–79; Haviva Pedaya, "Sabbath, Sabbatai, and the Diminution of Moon — The Holy Conjunction, Sign and Image," *Eshel Beer Sheva* 4 (1996): 91–143 [Hebrew]; Yehuda Liebes, "Sabbatianism and the Bounds of Religion," in *The Sabbatian Movement and Its Aftermath: Messianism, Sabbatianism and Frankism*, ed. R. Elior (Jerusalem: Institute of Jewish Studies, Hebrew University of Jerusalem, 2001), 1–21; Moshe Idel, *Enchanted Chains: Techniques and Rituals in Jewish Mysticism* (Los Angeles: Cherub Press, 2005), 228–32; Idel, *Sat-*

urn's Jews: On Witches' Sabbat and Sabbateanism (New York: Bloomsbury, 2001), 16–22; Idel, "Ashkenazi Esotericism and Kabbalah in Barcelona," *Hispania Judaica Bulletin* 5 (2007): 100–4; Idel, "Visualization of Colors in David ben Yehuda he-Hasid's Kabbalistic Diagram," *Ars Judaica* (2015): 31–54; ;Brian Ogren, *Renaissance and Rebirth: Reincarnation in Early Modern Italian Kabbalah* (Leiden: Brill, 2009), 18–20; Jonnie Schnytzer, "Metempsychosis, Metensomatosis, and Metamorphosis: On Rabbi Joseph ben Shalom Ashkenazi's Systematic Theory of Reincarnation," *Kabbalah* 45 (2019): 221–44; Jonnie Schnytzer, "Creation Ex Nihilo and the Primordial Union of the First and Tenth Sefirot: Philosophy and Kabbalah in the Thought of Rabbi Joseph ben Shalom Ashkenazi," *Kabbalah* 48 (2021): 131–66; Jonnie Schnytzer, "Scientific Kabbalah."

4. While several scholars have acknowledged Ashkenazi's important contribution to developing a unique formulation of the doctrine of transmigration, the present chapter offers a comprehensive scholarly treatment of the topic in English and is based on my previous research conducted in Hebrew. See Schnytzer, "Metempsychosis" and "Scientific Kabbalah."

5. Rabbi Joseph Hamadan's work on the rationales for the biblical commandments makes a significant contribution to the theoretical formulation of the doctrine. Both Hamadan's work and Zoharic literature place emphasis on instilling fear in an attempt to deter readers from transgressing certain commandments lest they be punished through transmigration. In contrast, Ashkenazi's theory is practically boundless in its scope both in terms of beings participating in the act of constant cosmic transmigration and in terms of the kabbalist's attention to detail. For an elaborate discussion on reincarnation in the writings of Hamadan, see Leore Sachs-Shmueli, *The Rationale of the Negative Commandments by R. Joseph Hamadan* (PhD diss., Bar Ilan University, 2018), 184–216. Regarding reincarnation in Zoharic literature, see Pinchas Giller, *Reading the Zohar: The Sacred Text of the Kabbalah* (Oxford: Oxford University Press, 2001), 35–68; Jonathan M. Benarroch, *Sava and Yanuka: God, Son, and the Messiah in Zoharic Narratives* (Jerusalem: Magness Press, 2018), especially 211–34 [Hebrew]; Oded Israeli, *The Interpretation of Secrets and the Secrets of Interpretation: Midrashic and Hermeneutic Strategies in Sabba de-Mishpatim of the Zohar* (Los Angeles: Cherub Press, 2005).

6. On the deployment of this technique of using terse allusions (chapter headings), see Jonathan V. Dauber, *Secrecy and Esoteric Writing in Kabbalistic Literature* (Philadelphia: University of Pennsylvania Press, 2022), 35, 38, 48, 50, 53, 117.

7. In Arabic, this esoteric style of writing is called *Tabdid al-Alm*. For a discussion on the use of this method in the East, see Daniel de Smet, "Isma'ili-Shi'i Visions of Hell From the 'Spiritual' Torment of the Fatimids to the Tayyibi Rock of Sijjin," *Locating Hell in Islamic Traditions*, ed. C. Lange (Leiden: Brill, 2006), 242. See also Ehud Krinis, "The Philosophical and Theosophical Interpretations of the Microcosm-Macrocosm Analogy in *Ikhwan al-Safa* and Jewish Medieval Writings," *L'esoterisme Shi'ite Shi'I Esotericism*, ed. M. Amir-

Moezzi, M. De Cillis, D. De Smet, and O. Mir-Kasimov (Turnhout: Brepols, 2016), 403.

8. Haggai Ben-Shammai, "Transmigration of Souls in Tenth Century Jewish Thought in the Orient," *Sefunot* (1990): 123 [Hebrew]. Regarding potential links between this group and kabbalistic literature in general and Ashkenazi in particular, see note 14. See also Ehud Krinis, "Cyclical Time in the Ismaili Circle of Ikhwan al-Safa (Tenth Century) and in Early Jewish Kabbalists Circles (Thirteenth and Fourteenth Centuries)," *Studia Islamica* 111 (2016): 20–108.

9. For more on the conceptual ties between the Brethren of Purity and kabbalistic literature, see the pioneering study of Shlomo Pines, "Shi'te Terms and Conceptions in Judah Halevi's Kuzari," in *Jerusalem Studies in Arabic and Islam II*, ed. S. Pines, M. Kister, and S. Shaked (Jerusalem: Magnes Press, 1980), 165–251. See also Moshe Idel's studies, which built upon Pines and mention a number of similarities between the Brethren and Ashkenazi; see M. Idel, "Harut and Marut: Jewish Sources for the Interpretation of the Two Angels in Islam," in *L'esotericism Shi'ite Shi'I Esotericism*, ed. M. Amir-Moezzi, M. De Cillis, D. Smet, and O. Mir-Kasimov (Turnhout: Brepols, 2016), 127–37; M. Idel, "An Additional Commentary to the Alphabet by R. David ben Yehuda he-Hasid and Sefer ha-Temunah," *Alei Sefer: Studies in Bibliography and in the History of the Printed and the Digital Hebrew Book* 26/27 (2017): 45 [Hebrew].

10. See note 18. See also Paul Walker, "Metempsychosis in Islam," in *Islamic Studies Presented to Charles J. Adams*, ed. W. Hallaq and D. Little (Leiden: Brill, 1991), 219–38.

11. Brian Ogren, "The Law and Change and the Nature of the Chameleon: Yosef ben Salom Askenazi and Picco Della Mirandola," in *Giovanni Pico e la Cabbala*, ed. Fabrizio Lelli (Florence: Centro Internazionale Di Cultura, 2014); and Fabrizio Lelli, "Giovanni Pico Della Mirandola," *Studi Pichiani* 16 (1996): 121–33.

12. For a partial list, see *Kabbalistic Commentary*, 15 [Hebrew]; Schnytzer, "Creation Ex Nihilo," 135–36, fn. 18; 145–56, fn. 49; 155–56, fn. 81, fn. 82.

13. Yehuda Liebes underscored the centrality of the doctrine of reincarnation in the writings and system of thought attributed to these kabbalists, see Liebes, "New Directions in the Study of Kabbalah," *Pe'amim: Studies in Oriental Jewry* 50 (1991): 150–70 [Hebrew]; Ronit Meroz traced the concept in Ashkenazi's influence on Safedian kabbalists, see Meroz, "Selections from Ephraim Penzieri: Luria's Sermon in Jerusalem and Kavvanah in Taking Food," *Jerusalem Studies in Jewish Thought: Proceedings of the Fourth International Conference on the History of Jewish Mysticism: Lurianic Kabbalah* (1991–1992): 211–57 [Hebrew].

14. As did scholar Yehuda Liebes, see Liebes, "New Directions in the Research of Kabbalah," *Pe'amim* 50 (1991): 161–66 [Hebrew].

15. In describing Ashkenazi's theory of reincarnation, two preeminent scholars of Kabbalah, Gershom Scholem and Moshe Idel, have highlighted a number of ostensible inconsistencies and contradictions, see G. Scholem, *On the Mystical Shape of the Godhead: Basic Concepts in the Kabbalah* (New York: Schocken, 1991), 227; Moshe Idel, 'The Meaning of "Ta'amei Ha-'Ofot' Ha-Teme'im of Rabbi David ben Yehuda He-Hasid," in *'Alei Shefer: Studies in the*

Literature of Jewish Thought: Presented to Rabbi Dr. Alexandre Safran, ed. M. Hallamish (Ramat Gan: Bar-Ilan University Press, 1990), 18, fn. 48 [Hebrew].

16. While Idel makes a distinction between horizontal and vertical aspects regarding various schools of kabbalistic thought in late thirteenth-century Spain, Ashkenazi's system incorporates both, see Idel, "The Meaning of 'Ta'amei Ha-'Ofot.'"

17. See b. Avodah Zara, 3b.

18. Hallamish, *Kabbalistic Commentary*, 73.

19. Ms. Oxford, Bodleian, Opp. 464, fol. 44b.

20. The term appears throughout *Sefer ha-Temuna* and in the works of the thirteenth-century kabbalist R. Joseph Hamadan. Regarding the term *gilgul neshamot*, see Schnytzer, "Metempsychosis, Metensomatosis and Metamorphosis." For an example of the term in *Sefer ha-Temuna*, see *Sefer ha-Temuna* (Lemberg: Hayyim Rohatyn, 1891), 29a. Regarding the dating of *Sefer ha-Temuna*, see Roee Goldschmidt, "From Byzantium to Eastern Europe: The Textual Versions of *Sefer ha-Temuna* and Their Circulation in Manuscript and Print," *Kabbalah* 46 (2020): 287–316 [Hebrew]. For an example in the works of Hamadan, see Leore Sachs-Shmueli, *The Rationale of the Negative Commandments*, vol. 2, 57.

21. According to my research, *shelaḥ* (being sent) and *gilgul neshamot* (circulation of souls), along with *ibbur* (impregnation), seem to be the first terms to appear describing the doctrine of reincarnation in Hebrew. However, various forms have previously circulated in Judeo-Arabic, particularly in the writings of Rabbi Saadia Gaon (died 1942) — Tanasukh (تناسخ) or several forms of the root Karr (قرر), literally meaning copying or cloning. Another verb used in Arabic, albeit not found in Judeo-Arabic texts to the best of my knowledge, is Nakal (نقل), literally transferring. The latter appears for instance at the end of Epistle 41 of the Brethren of Purity. For an elaboration on the biography of reincarnation in Jewish literature, specifically in kabbalistic literature, see G. Scholem, *On the Mystical Shape of the Godhead*, 197–250. See also Moshe Idel's discussion on the term *ibbur*, Moshe Idel, "The Secret of Impregnation as Metempsychosis in Kabbalah," in *Verwandlungen: Archäologie der literarischen Kommunikation IX*, ed. Aleida and Jan Assmann (Munich: Fink, 2006), 341–79. Regarding the doctrine in Saadia, see Leon Nemoy, "Biblical Quasi-Evidence for the Transmigration of Souls: (From the Kitab al-Anwar of Ya'qub al-Qirqisani)," *Journal of Biblical Literature* 59 (1940): 159, n. 3. Regarding the Brethren of Purity, see *Epistles of the Brethren of Purity: An Arabic Critical Edition and English translation of Epistles 39–41, Part III*, "Science of the Soul and Intellect," ed. and trans. Carmela Baffioni and Ismail Poonawala (Oxford: Oxford University Press, 2017), 237. For an elaboration on the various possible terms in Arabic, see Daniel De Smet, "La Transmigration Des Âmes Une Notion Problematique Dans L'Ismaelisme D'Époque Fatimide," in *Unity and Diversity: Mysticism, Messianism and the Construction of Religious Authority in Islam*, ed. O. Mir-Kasimov (Leiden: Brill, 2014), 77–110. For a discussion of terms for specific kinds of transmigration, as, for instance, transmigration into a sick person

or gold (specifically among the Nusayiri-Alawis), see Yaron Friedman, *The Nusayri-Alawis: An Introduction to the Religion, History, and Identity of the Leading Minority in Syria* (Leiden: Brill 2009), 102–10. See also Mushegh Asatryan, *Heresy and Rationalism in Early Islam: The Origins and Evolution of the Mufaddal-Tradition* (PhD diss., Yale University, 2012), 101–18.

22. Hallamish, *Kabbalistic Commentary*, 183.

23. Interestingly, the phrase *sod ha-shelaḥ* (the secret of metempsychosis) appears often in the kabbalist's commentary on Genesis Rabbah, while it is absent in his later work, his commentary on *Sefer Yesira*. In the latter, the term appears as *shelaḥ* (transmigration) alone. See for example Hallamish, *Kabbalistic Commentary*, 66, 73, 89 and Ms. Oxford, Bodleian, Opp. 464, fol. 48b and 57b.

24. Hallamish, *Kabbalistic Commentary*, 89.

25. Hallamish, *Kabbalistic Commentary*, 102.

26. For an account of the soul and its counterparts, albeit using Zoharic literature as the primary source material, see Isaiah Tishby, *The Wisdom of the Zohar: Texts from The Book of Splendor: Systematically Arranged and Translated into Hebrew with Introductions, Explanations and Variants*, vol. 2 (Jerusalem: Mossad Bialik, 1961), 16–42 (Hebrew); Avishai Bar-Asher, *Journeys of the Soul: Concepts and Images of Paradise in Medieval Kabbalah* (Jerusalem: Magness Press, 2019), 192–240 [Hebrew].

27. Ms. Oxford, Bodleian, Opp. 464, fol. 57b.

28. In Hebrew אל פני אדם אשר ביחס לנולד.

29. Ms. Bodleian, Opp. 464, fol. 50a.

30. Ashkenazi alludes to Numbers 21:37-22-3

31. Hallamish, *Kabbalistic Commentary*, 89–90.

32. It is worthwhile comparing this to an interpretation of reincarnation and the reasons for sacrificial slaughter in certain Ismaili circles; see Lisa Alexandrin, "Razi and His Medieval Opponents: Discussions Concerning Tanasukh and the Afterlife," *Cahiers de Studia Iranica* 26 (2002): 397–409.

33. Alexandrin, "Razi and His Medieval Opponents," 61, 71. It should be noted that the word implies divine pipes in this context in other kabbalistic works as well. Reference should be made to Jonathan Garb's discussion on the hydraulic theurgic force; see Johnathan Garb, *Manifestation of Power in Jewish Mysticism* (Jerusalem: Magnes Press, 2004), 73 [Hebrew]. For an example of the term in other kabbalistic texts, see Castilian kabbalist R. Joseph Gikatilla's Gates of Light/*Sha'arei Ora* (Warsaw: S. Ergelbrand 1882), 35.

34. Scholem, *On the Mystical Shape of the Godhead*, 218.

35. While it is outside of the scope of this chapter, it is of note that when a spirit (*nefesh*) transmigrates into a planet or an inanimate object, the soul (*neshamah*) remains waiting elsewhere until the spirit is reincarnated back into a higher form of being.

36. Ms. Oxford, Bodleian, Opp. 464, fol. 85b.

37. From the picture painted by Oded Israeli regarding the intention and style of *Saba de-Mishpatim*, the Zoharic author deploys lyric poetic tropes and rhetoric to depict reincarnation as the hovering of the soul as from one place to the next. Ashkenazi's style, by contrast, is more scientific describing the details of the process. Yet the soul's wanderings delineated in the Zohar and the process of reincarnation itself display important commonalities with Ashkenazi's conceptualization of soul impregnation (*ibbur*), which in his theoretical system leads to the soul being sent forward, *shelaḥ*. See Oded Israeli, *The Interpretation of Secrets and the Secrets of Interpretation: Midrashic and Hermeneutic Strategies in Sabba de-Mishpatim of the Zohar* (Los Angeles: Cherub Press), 2005.

38. Sachs-Shmueli, *The Rationale of the Negative Commandments*, 191.

39. As succinctly put by Dov Schwartz. See Dov Schwartz, "The Debate over the Maimonidean Theory of Providence in Thirteenth-Century Jewish Philosophy," *Jewish Studies Quarterly* 2 (1995): 185.

40. See especially *A Kabbalistic Commentary*, 109–10; Schnytzer, "Scientific Kabbalah," 47–48.

41. For a biography of the soul's development in philosophy, see https://plato.stanford.edu/entries/ancient-soul/.

42. However, there are exceptions to the rule. In general, the term comes to describe the horizontal axis of existence (as opposed to *shelaḥ*, which can be described as relating to the vertical axis). As such, much like the act of eating enables physical matter to transmigrate horizontally, so too the process of the reincarnated soul of messiah is described as such. See further Schnytzer, "Scientific Kabbalah."

43. On the ambiguity regarding the author of the text, see Gershom Scholem, "Did Nachmanides Write Iggeret ha-Kodesh?," *Kiryat Sefer* 21 (1944): 179–86 and especially 183.

44. Seymour J. Cohen, *The Holy Letter: A study in Medieval Jewish Sexual Morality* (New York: Ktav Publishing House, 1976), 89–93.

45. Gikatilla, *Sha'arei Orah* (Warsaw: S. Ergelbrand 1882), 70b–71a.

46. Joseph Hamadan, *The Rationale of the Negative Commandments*, 225.

47. Numbers 9:18.

48. Ms. Bodleian, Opp. 464, fol. 57a.

49. On the topic of consumption within the medieval mystical context, see Joel Hecker, *Mystical Bodies, Mystical Meals: Eating and Embodiment in Medieval Kabbalah* (Detroit: Wayne State University Press, 2005). Regarding Ashkenazi, see 179.

50. Hecker, *Mystical Bodies, Mystical Meals*, 137.

51. This interpretation differs from that of Hallamish, whose interpretation takes into consideration Maimonides's influence on Ashkenazi. For Hallamish's interpretation, see *Kabbalistic Commentary*, 24–27.

52. Hallamish, *Kabbalistic Commentary*, 24–27.

53. Ms. Bodleian, Opp. 464, fol. 69b.

54. Proverbs 26:11.

55. Hallamish, *Kabbalistic Commentary*, 145.

56. While the term in the passage is *gilgul*, which is understood in this chapter to mean metensomatosis, here it seems to connote metempsychosis. The assumption being, as the literal description seems to imply, a series of transmigrations of the spirit from one form to another. While these may each be seen individually as occurring vertically, over historic time they may be depicted as circulating horizontally.

57. For an analysis of the commentaries given to this ambiguous episode in Nebuchadnezzar's life, see Eliezer Schlossberg, "Did Nebuchadnezzar Transform into an Animal?," *Beit Mikra* 4 (1992): 343–53.

58. Hallamish, *A Kabbalistic Commentary*, 240.

59. Although it should be noted that while this extreme case clearly denotes that physical matter underwent metensomatosis, it is less clear if the transmigration of the spirits constitutes a clear case of metempsychosis. However, this is a matter beyond the scope of this study.

60. See *Moslem Schisms and Sects = al-Fark bain ak-firak: Being the History of the Various Philosophical Systems Developed in Islam: Part II, by Abu-Mansur 'Abd-al-Kahir ibn Tahir al-Baghdadi*, translated from Arabic with introduction and note by Abraham S. Halkin (Tel Aviv: Palestine Publishing, 1935), 92.

61. To be sure, Qirqisani opposed these views. In his *Book of Lights* (*Kitab El-Anwar*), Qirqisani evokes the verse *Whoever sheds the blood of man, by man shall his blood be shed* (Genesis 9:6) as proof among those who believe in the doctrine of reincarnation into animal bodies. Ashkenazi also applies the same verse with regard to reincarnation. For an analysis of Qirqisani, see Samuel Posnanski's article "Aus Qirqisani's Kitab al-anwar," *Semitic Studies in Memory of Rev. Dr. Alexander-Kohut*, ed. George A. Kohut (Berlin: S. Calvary, 1897), 35–453 and especially 449. For the passage in two of Ashkenazi's works, see Ms. Oxford, Bodleian, Opp. 464, fol. 69b. See also *A Kabbalistic Commentary*, 151–52. In the former, the implication follows Qirqisani in stating the possibility of reincarnation into other forms of being.

62. This, despite Gershom Scholem's view that "it is difficult to assume a direct link" between these oriental Jewish beliefs in reincarnation and those of the Spanish kabbalists. While Scholem was inclined to see a possible connection between the doctrine among the Catharist movement in southern France, it should be noted that regarding reincarnation, only some accepted the possibility of reincarnation into animals. For Scholem's view, see Scholem, *On the Mystical Shape of the Godhead*, 199. For the varying views regarding the Cathars, see Alexander Alexakis, "Was There Life Beyond the Life Beyond? Byzantine Ideas on Reincarnation and Final Restoration," *Dumbarton Oaks Papers* 55 (2001): 171.

63. For an overview of the idea of evil among kabbalists, see Scholem, *On the Mystical Shape of the Godhead*, 72–77.

64. As Elliot R. Wolfson has already noted, Ashkenazi's theory distinguishes between "contraries" (*temurot*), and "opposites" (*hafakhim*); see Elliot R. Wolfson, *Language, Eros, Being: Kabbalistic Hermeneutics and Poetic Imagination* (New York: New York University Press, 2005), 64.

65. See Hallamish, *A Kabbalistic Commentary*, 113.

66. Hallamish, *A Kabbalistic Commentary*, 36.

67. Hallamish, *A Kabbalistic Commentary*, 79. For a somewhat similar view among the Manicheans, see Jackson, "The Doctrine of Metempsychosis," *Journal of the American Oriental Society* 45 (1925): 246–68, especially on 254.

68. Ms. Bodleian, Opp. 464, fol. 50b–51b.

69. For a previous discussion on the rationale of impure birds, see Idel, "The Meaning of 'Ta'amei Ha-'Ofot,'" 12–16.

70. Hallamish, *A Kabbalistic Commentary*, 106–15.

71. Ms. Bodleian, Opp. 464, fol. 48b.

72. Ms. Bodleian, Opp. 464, fol. 50b.

73. See Hallamish, *A Kabbalistic Commentary*, 258–59.

74. Hallamish, *A Kabbalistic Commentary*, 217 as well as 142. For an elaboration on this, see Schnytzer, "Scientific Kabbalah," 44–47.

75. Hallamish, *A Kabbalistic Commentary*, 109–10.

76. Hallamish, *A Kabbalistic Commentary*, 111.

77. Hallamish, *A Kabbalistic Commentary*, 109.

78. Hallamish, *A Kabbalistic Commentary*, 110.

79. Hallamish, *A Kabbalistic Commentary*, 112. There, it is interesting to note that the kabbalist describes a positive association of this bird with redemption.

80. Hallamish, *A Kabbalistic Commentary*, 111.

81. Ms. Bodleian, Opp. 464, fol. 49a.

82. Ms. Bodleian, Opp. 464, fol. 48b.

JAMES A. DIAMOND

The Soul's Point of No Return 7

JEWISH PHILOSOPHICAL PERSPECTIVES ON REINCARNATION

That pile of papers on his left was still alive like watches
ticking on the wrists of dead soldiers.
— JEAN COCTEAU at Marcel Proust's deathbed
looking at the manuscript of *In Search of Lost Time*

Jewish Philosophy's Disenchantment with the Concept of Reincarnation

The overwhelming attitude of Jewish philosophers toward reincarnation discloses resistance that, at times, was tempered by measured openness. However, reincarnation never attained the widespread affirmation and broad appeal that characterized the general posture of kabbalistic thinkers to this concept. Indeed, the failure of philosophical opposition to restrain the indefatigable trend to embrace reincarnation highlights the power of its theological attraction, which often prevailed over cogently reasoned objections. This chapter examines some of the prominent Jewish philosophical positions toward reincarnation during the medieval period — the golden age of Jewish philosophy — exposing ruptures in fundamental theological notions concerning the soul, immortality, reward and punishment, divine justice, personal identity, and religious conduct.[1]

The story of Jewish philosophy's engagement with reincarnation extends well beyond the narrow parameter of the possibility of a transmigrating soul. The question of reincarnation is also integrally connected to differing conceptions of the soul, personal identity, and whether it was Platonism or Aristotelianism that better determined one's philosophical inclinations. Within Judaism, the issue was also impacted by the extent of the affinity or disdain a particular philosopher in question might have generally held toward kabbalistic notions and beliefs. Conceptions of the soul are crucial to the viability of reincarnation since it requires some posthumous remnant of a person's identity capable of migrating elsewhere. Whatever survives the body must be equipped with migration qualities necessary for transmigration to another body. Within Judaism, as well as other religious and philosophical traditions, that component is generally identified with a soul, thus necessitating an examination of a particular thinker's stance on the nature of the soul. Since philosophy primarily involves an exercise of the mind, philosophers tend to place a premium on thought as a lasting value. Thus, one of the major obstacles to a migrating soul for the protagonists in the history of Jewish philosophical theology is a general identification of aspects of the soul with the mind, especially its immortal dimensions.[2]

Those thinkers who could be classified as belonging to the philosophical school in the history of Jewish thought did not generally find the idea of reincarnation particularly appealing. Despite being less attracted to the belief than their kabbalistically inclined counterparts, Jewish philosophers articulated dynamic and complex differences on whether that which survives the demise of the physical body is capable of transmigrating into another animate or inanimate body. Some, like the early medieval philosopher Sa'adyah Gaon (882–942), summarily dismissed the concept of reincarnation as popular nonsense. Others, like Moses Maimonides, the leading twelfth-century Jewish philosophical theologian, remained silent on it, though, as I argue, it is a loudly antagonistic silence. Hasdai Crescas (1349–1410), the seminal philosopher of the late medieval period, begrudgingly endorsed it if "tradition demanded it." Still other major philosophers, like Joseph Albo (1380–1444), active in Christian Spain, despite rejecting it as theologically unwarranted, considered it philosophically palatable.

Though there may be philosophical objections to the soundness of reincarnation, reason has never proven an impenetrable barrier to the popular imagination and to beliefs that flow from "the inner life of the people themselves" rather than "the cultural and religious creations of the intellectual elite."[3] So ingrained did this belief become that Manasseh ben Israel, a major rabbinic figure in the seventeenth century who dedicated an entire treatise to the subject, claimed that a majority of the great sages affirmed it as a "true belief (*emunah*) and a principle (*iqar*) among the principles of the Torah that resolves the problem of the righteous who experience suffering and we are all obliged to accept their words and believe in it without any hesitation or doubt whatsoever."[4] The belief in reincarnation became so firmly established as to be practically enshrined in law when a relatively recent nineteenth-century classic halakhic compendium took it for granted that if God wills a soul be perfected, it necessarily will "even if it requires repeated returns to this world to do so."[5]

Philo and the Ladder of Eternal Recurrence

There were serious divisions among Jewish philosophers on the nature of the soul, often distinguished by commitment to various philosophical traditions such as Platonism, Neo-Platonism, Aristotelianism, or anti-Aristotelianism. The particular school of philosophy one subscribed to also informed what activity primarily constituted and actualized the soul in whole or in part, whether pure reason or actions, such as the fulfillment of commandments. However, the common thread that weaves through all of them is the soul's potential to disembody and gain some form of immortality.[6] Since the Jewish medieval philosophical tradition traces its ancient roots to the first century, I begin with Philo of Alexandria (c. 20 BCE–50 CE),[7] whose notions of the soul offer evidence of an early philosophical endorsement of reincarnation.[8] First, setting the stage for the notion of the soul's ability to attain some form of self-subsistence, Philo's adoption of a Platonic duality between soul and body allows for the soul's potential severability from the body. Second, he alludes often to the soul's immortality, thereby enabling a post-corporeal continuum from which it could return to corporeal existence.

As with others in the Jewish philosophical school, philosophy was practiced as exegesis of scripture.[9] Thus, the locus classicus cited in support of Philo's belief in reincarnation is his allegorical exegesis of the Jacob's ladder dream in Genesis (28:10–12) that eventually became a crux in both the kabbalistic and philosophical exegetical traditions.[10] He represents the angels ascending and descending the ladder as souls, stating, "Of these [souls separated from the body at death] some, longing for the familiar and accustomed ways of mortal life, hurry back again."[11] Once the soul is disembodied, signified by its ascent on the ladder, it becomes in a sense conflicted, nostalgic for its previously embodied state to which it is drawn, and thus follows its descent. The ascent and descent of the angels figuratively chart the soul's recurring loop, departing one body and entering another. At this early ancient stage of Jewish philosophy, however, Philo generally remains vague in his endorsement of reincarnation, anticipating an esoteric strategy that was to become emblematic of the later medieval rationalist Moses Maimonides. As David Winston observes, "Philo's sparse references to reincarnation reveal a reluctance on his part to give undue prominence to a Platonic conception that was essentially alien to Jewish tradition."[12] That reluctance also might reflect a common ambivalence often expressed by the philosophical mind thereafter toward the idea.

Sa'adyah Gaon: No Turning Back for the Soul

The first rabbinic philosopher who explicitly addressed reincarnation within the specific context of the soul was Sa'adyah Gaon (882–942) in his groundbreaking *Book of Beliefs and Opinions,* whose purpose was "to demonstrate the absolute consonance between the truths that were divinely revealed to the children of Israel and the ineluctable conclusions of rational enquiry."[13] Where Philo is ambiguous, Sa'adyah is outspokenly belligerent, dismissing it as the very antithesis of what he deems "rational":

> Yet, I must say that I have found certain people, who call themselves Jews, professing the doctrine of metempsychosis (reincarnation) which is designated by them as the theory of "transmigration" of souls. What they mean thereby is that the spirit of Ruben is transferred to Simon and afterward to Levi and after that to Judah. Many of them would go so far as to assert that the spirit of a human being might enter into the body of a beast, or that of a beast into the body of a human being, and other such nonsense and stupidities.[14]

Here Sa'adyah's ire is most likely directed at Karaites, "certain people,"; however, regardless of whom precisely Sa'adyah attacks, it can be unambiguously stated that he found the belief in transmigration so grievously offensive that he regarded it as a badge of inauthentic Jewishness.[15] He further denigrates the concept of metempsychosis by attributing its origin to what a philosopher, firmly ensconced in the rabbinic tradition, would have considered the cardinal theological crime of idolatry, and accuses such Jewish pretenders of "being unaware of the fact that the advocates of the doctrine of transmigration have derived it from the theory of the dualists and the spiritualists."[16] Regardless of whether he associates reincarnation with Manichaean dualism, this sentence deftly highlights that reincarnation as a concept was anathema to a rabbinic thinker such as Sa'adyah.[17]

Sa'adyah's harsh categorical rejection of reincarnation is a logical consequence of, first, his position on the soul and, second, of his theodicy delineated in his treatise prior to this juncture.[18] The reasoning that leads from his initial stance to his all-embracing rejection of reincarnation presents an instructive model for probing philosophical attitudes toward reincarnation. The soul, according to Sa'adyah, is the faculty responsible for cognition, whose essence, when cultivated, resembles the heavenly spheres as borne out by the verse *The enlightened shall shine like the radiance of the sky* (Daniel 12:3). Sa'adyah's philosophical exegesis already anticipates what will become a core distinction in the exegetical struggle between philosophers and kabbalists concerning the meaning of the words "enlightened" (*maskilim*) and "radiance"*(zohar)* appearing in this verse. For Sa'adyah, the light expressed by these terms signifies the accumulation of knowledge that illuminates the soul.[19] In stark contrast, it is no coincidence that the Zohar, composed a few centuries after Sa'adyah in the thirteenth century and gradually becoming the foundational canon of the kabbalistic tradition, derived its title from this verse and replaced Sa'adya's light of rational wisdom with the light of divine emanations (the sefirot): "a hidden radiance issuing forth from the highest sefirotic realms, a showering of sparks lighting up all that comes in its path."[20] Kabbalistic exegesis transformed Sa'adyah's abstract luminescence into a divine hypostatic radiance more capable of the itinerancy a soul might need to effect transmigration.[21]

At the theological level, reincarnation ostensibly offers a positive solution to sin, transgression, and human imperfection by offering a second chance to resolve the deeds of an incomplete life. It conveniently affords the opportunity either to fulfill a previously violated commandment or to engage in atonement for earlier transgressions.[22] Sa'adyah's trajectory of the soul, however, clearly excludes this possibility, stating that once the soul leaves the body, the opportunity for the soul's rehabilitation is forfeited:

> even the soiled souls are capable, so long as they are within the body, of being purified and cleansed again. That is why repentance is accepted so long as the human being is alive. Once, however, the soul has departed from him, it is incapable of being cleansed any longer of the corruption

> that has accumulated in it. In fact, nothing of the kind is to be expected for it anymore, as Scripture says: *When a wicked man dies, his hopes shall perish.* (Prov. 11:7)[23]

As we see above, upon the demise of the body, the soul cannot be expatriated into another physical entity, but is stored in abeyance until its ultimate recompense at the "time of retribution" (*et hagemul*).[24] In other words, Sa'adiah's theory of the soul restricts its domicile to the individual who embodied it in first place and to a singular span of individual existence, rejecting the idea of any sense of temporal continuity.

More importantly, however, at the center of Sa'adyah's systematic evisceration of four arguments in favor of reincarnation[25] is his explicit dismissal of theodicy, popular among the proponents of reincarnation both during Sa'adya's lifetime and in subsequent centuries. Theodicy as a religious tenet concerns God's benevolent governance of the created world as it offers justification for human torment, particularly that of the righteous and children, who suffer or die prematurely and without a discernible cause. Belief in reincarnation, popular among kabbalistic thinkers, provided an expedient justification for divine governance and justice, arguing that "Inasmuch as the Creator is just, it is inconceivable that He should occasion suffering to little children, unless it be for sins committed by their souls during the time that they were lodged in their former bodies."[26] Importantly, Sa'adyah describes the claim of the pro-reincarnation school as a "logical argument," thus provoking his own challenge and reflecting a much more profound disagreement than previously articulated since it addresses the mode of divine justice.[27] Sa'adyah, in typical logical-philosophical style, exposes the incoherence of the theodicy claim propagated by the pro-reincarnation thinkers by compelling them to reexamine their fundamental assumptions about the nature of the soul and its relationship with its Creator:

> We should like to ask them what they conceive the original status of the soul to be — we mean its status when it is first created. Is it charged by its Master with any obligation to obey Him or not? If they allege that it is not so charged, then there can be no punishments for it either, since it was not charged with any obligations to begin with. If, on the other hand, they acknowledge the imposition of such a charge, in which case obedience or disobedience did not apply to the soul theretofore, they thereby admit that God charges His servants with obligations on account of the future and not at all on account of the past. But then they return

> to our theory of compensation and are forced to give up their insistence on the view that man's suffering in this world is due solely to his conduct in a previous existence.[28]

Sa'adyah presses his opponents to test their theory's coherence against the very first incarnation of an individual soul that has not previously experienced physical life. Since it did not initially materialize in its embodied state burdened with obligations that a reincarnated soul would have imported from a prior life, it would enter its first existence as a blank slate. That would leave any suffering — endured before a person reaches the age of majority, the time when one assumes responsibility for fulfilling the biblical commandments — inexplicable in terms of reward and punishment for past actions. Therefore, Sa'adyah proposes an alternative theory concerning the suffering of children and the righteous, which he deems compensatory suffering (*'iwad*), and frames it within the discourse of increased future reward.[29] His first argument against the proponents of the theory that reincarnation rationalizes the innocent suffering of children as atonement for sins committed in a previous incarnation is "that they have forgotten what we have mentioned on the subject of compensation in the hereafter for misfortunes experienced in this world."[30] Regardless of the merits of Sa'adyah's theory and whether it offers a superior theodicy to those who advocate reincarnation, he does introduce a profound theoretical element into any discussion of theodicy and the operative principles underlying God's governance.[31] More importantly, by problematizing the causal relationship between human action and divine justice, he is able to sever the link between the vicissitudes of material existence and religious/moral behavior, thereby challenging the theory that suffering constitutes a punishment for transgressive behavior — a presumption that lies at the theological core of kabbalistic proponents of reincarnation, as well as other theories of theodicy.

Maimonides: Why Spoil the Joy of the Disembodied Soul?

Even though Maimonides has nothing explicit to say directly about the subject of reincarnation, any discussion of this topic would be remiss without a customary examination of the ideas espoused by the doyen of the rationalist movement in Judaism. On the issue of compensation, he unambiguously rejects Sa'adyah's position claiming that innocent suffering — regardless of its ultimate consequences — is not only patently unjust and irreconcilable with a perfect and just God, but also offends the teachings of both the written Torah and the rabbinic tradition. As Maimonides states:

> The principle of the Law that runs counter to this opinion, is that contained in His dictum, may He be exalted: *A God of faithfulness and without iniquity* (Deut. 32: 4). Nor do all the Sages profess this opinion of the multitude, for they say sometimes: There is no death without sin and no sufferings without transgression. And this [the quoted view of the Sages] is the opinion that ought to be believed by every adherent of the Law who is endowed with intellect, for he should not ascribe injustice to God.[32]

For Maimonides, as it was for Sa'adyah, reincarnation as a belief is bound up with conceptualizations of the soul. One of his clearest statements on the nature of the soul and its potential immortality appears in his halakhic work, the *Mishneh Torah*. Consistent with his emphasis throughout his oeuvre on intellectual perfection as the means for accomplishing and fulfilling all dimensions of human life — what in modern parlance we would consider both religious and secular aspects of life — he categorically identifies what remains of a person posthumously with the cumulative knowledge acquired during physical existence:

> Thus did the ancient sages say, "In the World to Come there is no eating, no drinking, and no family life, save that the righteous are sitting, graced with crowns upon their heads, and enjoying the radiance of the Shekinah" ... the crown spoken of by the sages refers to knowledge and for the sake of which they have attained life in the world to come ... The term soul employed on this subject refers not to the breath of life necessary for the body, but the form of the soul which is the intelligence by which it attained knowledge of the Creator's Being according to its intellectual power, and apprehends other abstract concepts and other things.[33]

Maimonides thus establishes an absolute identity between the soul and the intellect in his legal code, a position that he maintains consistently throughout his other works as well, both philosophical and rabbinic, including his *Commentary on the Mishnah* and his *Guide of the Perplexed*.[34]

He firmly maintains that the disembodied state of the soul, composed of intellection and knowledge acquired during a lifetime, is the ultimate goal of a human being and amounts to all that remains of an individual after death. Consequently, any return to corporeal existence entailed by transmigration would be a punishment rather than a reward. Not only would reincarnation not perfect a previously embodied deficient soul, it would in fact impede its utopian posthumous existence predicated on the idealized form of incorporeal existence, "it would not enjoy bodily pleasures nor desire them any more than a king would abdicate his throne to return to play ball in the streets, for there would have been a time when he would have preferred ball sports to kingship, when he was an infant ignorant of either pursuit, just as we prioritize the pleasures of the body over the soul."[35]

Though the implications are far-reaching, perhaps the one most inimical to the possibility of reincarnation is that it likely rules out any individuated immortality. Arguably, Maimonides subscribed to monopsychism, the doctrine that all knowledge accumulated during an embodied lifetime survives the body only as an indistinguishable part of universal truth, thereby surrendering its individuality.[36] Maimonides appears to explicitly endorse this doctrine in his *Guide of the Perplexed*, where he states that for intellects, which is all the soul comprises and which survives posthumously, "there can be no thought of multiplicity of any mode whatever ... consequently all are one in number."[37] Accordingly, the soul, after having amassed different types of knowledge during a lifetime, would become absorbed into a universal intellect, erasing any individual identity it may have possessed and nullifying merits and punishment associated with the cycle of reincarnation. Maimonides's inconspicuous silence on reincarnation prompts further examination of his attitude concerning resurrection, a belief considered foundational to rabbinic Judaism. Suspicion that he secretly harbored a heterodox rejection of resurrection raged already in his own time. Yet the same reasons that militate against reincarnation would also challenge the concept of resurrection, which, for Maimonides, would entail an illogical regression from a perfected incorporeal state to an imperfect corporeal one.[38]

A striking incongruence between Maimonides's notion of an individual soul's afterlife and the possibility of its reincarnation is aptly illustrated by his interpretation of death by God's kiss, historically reserved for the biblical siblings Moses, Aaron, and Miriam.[39] In the *Guide*, he highlights the unparalleled degree of intellection inherent in soul's detachment from the material dimensions of existence and its subsequent cleaving to a perfect immaterial life, metaphorically expressed by the "kiss:" "when a perfect man is stricken with years and approaches death, this apprehension increases very powerfully, joy over this apprehension becomes stronger, until the soul is separated from the body at that moment in this state of pleasure ... the three of them died in the pleasure of this apprehension due to the intensity of passionate love."[40] Maimonides's description of the joy experienced by the strengthening of the intellect to the point where it can finally liberate itself from the body militates against any return to physicality, which would entail a demotion of the soul from its pristine incorporeality to debilitated embodiment.[41] Consequently, transmigration would surely turn the soul's bliss into severe depression.

Maimonides concludes his discussion of this utopian state of the soul with what I believe is an implicit coup de grace against reincarnation: "After having reached this condition of enduring permanence, the intellect remains in one and the same state, the impediment that sometimes screened him off having been removed. And he will remain permanently in that state of intense pleasure, which does not belong to the genus of bodily pleasures."[42] Maimonides adds the quality of "enduring permanence" to the pleasure enjoyed by this de-corporealized soul. Since reincarnation entails a re-corporealized soul, it would rudely interrupt that enduring "pleasure" whereby the soul enjoys the permanent bliss of incorporeal existence. For Maimonides, while the unperfected soul simply disappears, God's "kiss" signifies the perfected soul's final act as it departs the body, reunited with its beloved, never to be dragged back to its repressed state in the body, which impedes its ability to consummate its love.[43]

The issue of commandments and their rationale was one of the major points of contention between kabbalistic theology and Maimonides. Kabbalistic theosophy correlated commandments to the supernal structures of the Godhead, opposing Maimonides's philosophical abstractions of God's Being and, consequently, His practical, historical, and intellectual reasons for the miẓvot that kabbalists considered a "devaluation of the secret significance of the commandments."[44] Maimonides's supremely intellectualized version of the soul brings into sharp focus a command-oriented theology exemplified by the kabbalistic tradition that is far more welcoming to reincarnation. In kabbalistic theosophy, imperfect souls emerge from defects in religious adherence rather than Maimonides's inadequately realized contemplative life. Those "kabbalistic" souls consolidate themselves incrementally, building their way toward completion with each additional commandment (*miẓvah*), only ending the cycle of rebirth once the soul has exhausted the full complement of commandments. As Michael Fishbane, in his study of the "kiss of God" trope, characterizes it, "each completed commandment adds a piece to the supernal garment that a person weaves upon his astral body. Failure to fully clothe one's heavenly alter ego results in a deficit that returns the earth-bound soul to the travails of rebirth."[45] Alternatively, for Maimonides, instead of a "heavenly alter ego," the true reality of a human being consists of intellectual apprehension, which is the sole means of cultivating the image (*ẓelem*) of God.[46] What is left of Moses, for example is the inimitable amount of knowledge he accumulated during a lifetime of contemplation rather than a cosmic reification available for recycling as a composite soul in the future.[47] Maimonides's overall treatment of the soul, therefore, precludes the possibility of postmortem development affirming the conclusions articulated earlier by Sa'adyah, "after death there is no perfection or addition . . . and there is no compensating for what is lacking here."[48]

Yedayah Bedersi: The Religious Meaninglessness of Experience

The Provençal philosopher Yedayah Bedersi (c. 1270–c. 1340), renowned for championing the study of philosophy during the raging Maimonidean controversy, reframed the intellectual discourse on reincarnation in novel ways.[49] Embedded in his formal rebuttal of a religious ban on philosophy is an assault on the belief in reincarnation, which, among others, introduced a new objection. Beyond proving that the study of philosophy was not detrimental to Judaism, he vigorously argued that philosophy was theologically indispensable to affirming the Jewish religion and the teachings of the Torah: "[it] is unimpeachably valuable both for reinforcing demonstrable knowledge about the Creator and for refuting beliefs that are an affront to the Torah."[50] He holds up philosophy as an indispensable tool for refuting popular beliefs, such as reincarnation, that could potentially undermine the basic tenets of Jewish belief. He offers proof by first citing how the concept of reincarnation grievously offends the logic of two of Maimonides's thirteen principles — belief in just reward and punishment, and resurrection. He further points to the inherent injustice produced by one individual enjoying the rewards or alternatively suffering the consequences of another person's conduct. Finally, he underscores the absurdities a transmigrating soul poses for the practicalities of future resurrection when, as logic would demand, multiple bodies would need to be reconstituted with one soul.

At its core, Bedersi's refutation of reincarnation aims to offer an apologia for philosophy as a bulwark of, rather than a threat to, Judaism, as the "abrogation of it [reincarnation] serves to buttress faith because it leads to frustrating assiduousness in worshipping God."[51] Not only is the belief in reincarnation absurd from a theoretical point of view, but its practical impact on religious conduct is corrosive since living with the predetermined baggage of another's life would provoke an unnecessarily harsh psychological burden of one's own existence. Bedersi further argues that individuals whose religious life is motivated primarily by reward and punishment would have to endure immense anxiety due to the thought of suffering for someone else's misconduct in anticipation of undeserved punishment, while enjoying the rewards of another's righteous behavior would disincentivize self-perfection. In general, those who endorse reincarnation would eventually be overcome by a sense of absolute futility caused by an ostensible lack of causality between their own behavior and its anticipated consequences.

Bedersi continues his tirade against the concept of reincarnation by positing that it ultimately undermines confidence in God's goodness. Suffering, he argues, generally provokes profound self-reflection in a righteous person inspiring "profuse confessions and repentance and increasing one's love of God."[52] However, belief in reincarnation will stunt one's relationship with God, since "he will attribute his suffering to the evil of another individual, leading him to question God's providence while certainty of his own innocence, will deter him from repentance."[53] Perhaps even more threatening to Jewish faith than the theoretical notions of the soul and immortality previously articulated by Sa'adyah and Maimonides, metempsychosis would erode the very foundations of a life built on Torah and the fulfilment of Jewish religious precepts.[54]

Hasdai Crescas and Religious Ambivalence: Tradition over Philosophy

The Spanish philosopher Hasdai Crescas (1340–1410) mounted the most philosophically sophisticated and systematic medieval assault on Maimonides and his scrupulous rationalist form of Judaism. It comes as no surprise therefore that he sharply diverges from Maimonides's position on reincarnation, although not as assertively as he does on other fundamental beliefs, such as miracles, prophecy, or providence. It is important to preface Crescas's attitude to reincarnation with a concise summary of his general opposition to Maimonides in his magnum opus, *Light of the Lord,* to fully unpack its implication for the development of Jewish thought.[55] Crescas aims primarily to undermine the Aristotelian-based philosophical framework, within which Maimonides conducts his exegesis, to liberate Jewish scriptural sources from the strictly rationalist constraints with which Maimonides shackled them. As a result, Crescas realigns the classical texts of the Jewish canon to gain greater conformity with traditional rabbinic interpretations on such fundamental issues as the nature of God, providence, prophecy, and Israel's chosenness. The paradoxical contrast that distinguishes the fundamental stance of Crescas from that of Maimonides is aptly encapsulated by Eliezer Schweid inversely pitting Crescas's "innovative and revolutionary stance in philosophy stemm[ing] from his extreme conservativism in religious thought" against Maimonides's "conservativism in philosophy and extraordinary radicalism in religious thought."[56]

It is not surprising therefore that Crescas neither overtly rejects reincarnation nor wholeheartedly embraces it, but instead articulates a new hybrid attitude toward it as fundamental and dogmatic to Judaism:

> [because] the soul of man is a substance disposed to intellection, it would appear that transmigration is impossible for anyone who has acquired some of the intelligibles in actuality. For otherwise, the second being will be born intellecting in actuality without having learned, which contradicts what sense experience attests through the entire span of time past whose events have been transmitted to us — unless, by God, the intelligibles he acquired were rendered non-existent in him by the will of God, for some end known to Him. Yet, since the sect that affirms transmigration has a foundation in the tradition, the doors of investigation are locked in this matter. If it is a received tradition, we shall receive it favorably.[57]

In contradistinction to the philosophers previously discussed, Crescas's ambivalence emerges from an internal struggle between the dedicated man of faith and the rigorous philosopher. Though troubled by an ostensible conflict between the two, he refused to bow to the dictates of rationalist philosophy, as is evinced by his vigorous opposition to Maimonides's conceptualization of the soul as composed purely of intellection. Thus, while he maintained that love of God, as distinct from pure intellection, is an essential component of the soul, he accedes to Maimonides's claim that the acquisition of knowledge does partially contribute to the attachment to God, which is necessary for the soul's immortality.[58] In other words, intellection plays a role in the soul's endurance, but insufficiently so, and is only supplemental to adhering to the Torah's commandments. As he states, the "end sought by the Torah is to hearken to God with extraordinary zeal to fulfill His prescriptions, and to exercise great caution, lest one transgress His proscriptions [which] . . . guarantees happiness and eternal life according to the Torah and tradition."[59] Reason demands intellection, while the patent meaning of Scripture and Jewish tradition dictates the obeisance to the word of God, for it is "an idea accepted in the nation, and one in which we were raised. The Torah illumined it for us, even as the notion is in agreement with speculation and does not contradict it."[60]

Crescas's dual commitment to reason and revelation extends to his rumination on reincarnation, inspiring first the philosopher's objection that it defies both reason and experience. If even just one constituent of the soul is indeed intellection, then how is it that the posthumous soul does not carry with it the memory of those intellectual achievements from its previous identity into its new physical incarnation? Yet empirical evidence establishes the indisputable fact that this has never occurred and therefore "contradicts what sense experience attests through the entire span of time past whose events have been transmitted to us."[61] Crescas posits that only a miraculous divine intervention that defies irrefutable scientific evidence could account for the erasure of a soul's indelible memories of its intellections. At the same time, as a discriminating philosopher, Crescas resists admitting such an inscrutable "miracle" that flouts any rational purpose — "unless, by God, the intelligibles he acquired were rendered non-existent in him by the will of God, for some end known to Him."[62] Even though miracles interrupt nature, Crescas contends that they must demonstrate some definite purpose and end, particularly regarding divine governance.[63]

Nowhere does this emerge more clearly than in his discussion of the miracle of resurrection, a subject closely related to reincarnation and one that perplexed Crescas because of its philosophical incoherence. First, the miracle of resurrection does pass the test of having a defined purpose and end because, "were it not for this miracle, there would indeed be a flaw, God forbid, in divine justice. Therefore, divine wisdom decreed this great miracle, through which divine justice and righteousness will be perfected in every respect."[64] Crescas finds such purpose or end absent for the "miracle" he says would be required of erasing the transmigrated soul's memory of its intellectual achievements from its previous identity into its new physical incarnation. Second, when addressing the question of how the identity of the person can continue in its resurrected form, Crescas locates such perpetuity in precisely that which reincarnation cannot rationally accommodate. It is the soul's accumulated memories and imagination that constitute the unchanging form of the body; "Since among its faculties as a whole are memory and imagination, the soul in this [resurrected] body will remember how it was at first."[65] In light of Crescas's exposition of the soul's journey through the various stages of the resurrection process, his position on the philosophical incoherence of reincarnation is far more trenchant than it first appears.

Crescas's excuse for his acceptance of reincarnation when reason would dictate its rejection is simply an exasperated surrender of reason to the superiority of the Jewish tradition, most likely combined with the broader circulation of sections of the Zohar during his lifetime and acceptance of its theologies. When faced with an irreconcilable conflict between reason and revelation, Maimonides's unassailable fealty to reason is expressed in his creative deployment of interpretive tools, such as textual exegesis, that assist in mitigating the potentially heterodox implications inherent in ideas borrowed from rationalist philosophical discourse; "the gates of figurative interpretation are [never] shut in our faces."[66] By contrast, Crescas arrests the impulse to reconcile esoteric tenets of the Jewish tradition, such as transmigration, with the logic demanded by philosophical argumentation. He thereby sharply delineates a separate sphere for each discipline that should not be forced to intersect: "the doors of investigation are locked in this matter. If it is a received tradition, we shall receive it favorably."[67]

Joseph Albo: The Soul Condemned to Freedom

It is fitting to end this interlocking chain of medieval philosophers with Joseph Albo (c. 1380–1444), a disciple of Crescas, depicted as the last of the medieval Jewish philosophers.[68] However, beyond constituting a chronological closure in a line of medieval philosophers, Albo contributes in significant ways to perennial philosophical debates on the nature of the soul, its relationship to the body, and its potential for a posthumous existence. Following his teacher's philosophical objection to reincarnation, Albo articulates an entirely new objection to reincarnation as follows:

> The divine Wisdom did indeed decree that the spiritual substance, which by its nature is not a free agent, should dwell in the human body in order that it may become a free agent in the body, because this is no doubt a valuable quality in it. So much so that, as we are told by the Rabbis, the angels made a mistake and when God created man, they wanted to worship him ... This was because he was a free agent, and they were not. Nevertheless, why should a soul which has already functioned in a human body and has become a free agent, return to the body again? And why should the seminal drop have the capacity to receive a soul which has already functioned in a body rather than to receive a soul which has

> not functioned in a body and is not a free agent? A still less likely view is that of those who say that human souls are transmigrated into bodies of animals. God knows.[69]

Albo mounts his assault on reincarnation on two fronts. The first is conceptual, based on his view of the human ability to exercise free will as a cornerstone of reward and punishment, an issue on which he diverges from his mentor, Crescas.[70] A soul in its pristine, disembodied state does not have that capacity, only assuming it when it becomes embodied. Immediately prior to his rejection of reincarnation, he explains the resolution of a Talmudic debate as to whether it is better for a human being to be created or not in favor of the latter. Since the soul is a viably independent incorporeal spiritual substance, "Now as a result of creation the soul may be destroyed or severely punished. Hence, he said, It would have been better if man had not been created, meaning that the soul had not been put into the human body."[71] Inserting the soul, which is a pure spiritual substance that on its own only aspires to the good, into a combined spiritual/ material form capable of choosing evil would be a demotion from a state of perfection to another inferior state of existence vulnerable to imperfection and degradation. Albo attacks the logic of re-embodying the soul once it has been liberated and repatriated to its original "spiritual substance" having already tasted whatever "valuable quality" free will affords. Reincarnation then would belie "divine wisdom."

Albo's second challenge is informed by natural-scientific reasons based on the ancient rabbinic view that the soul enters the sperm at the moment of conception.[72] Assuming there are pristine souls along with previously embodied ones available for entry into semen, Albo raises the question concerning aspects of the sperm that would enable it to discriminate between or attract one or the other. More importantly, however, Albo is reticent about reincarnation because of its implication for the concept of free will, a fundamental aspect of human existence — which even angels envy — and what uniquely distinguishes the human from a purely incorporeal existence. Ultimately for Albo, the idea of reincarnation is incompatible with both the scientific origins of the soul at the embryonic beginning of a new life and with the conduct of life informed by free choice. I suggest regarding Albo's reticence to resolve the questions he posed as reflective of his repudiation of the reincarnation doctrine. His conclusion with the phrase "God knows" alludes to a place of ambiguity, where the Jewish philosopher is caught between received tenets of the Jewish tradition and the demands of philosophical exactitude and logic.[73]

Postmortem

This chapter aimed to present the views of seminal medieval thinkers in the continuing debate over belief in reincarnation.[74] The issue of reincarnation exercised these figures because of the deeper stakes involved that touched on core theological principles impacting both belief and conduct.[75] The debate did not end with the close of the Middle Ages, and, as noted at the beginning of this chapter, reincarnation as a tenet of Jewish belief is widely accepted in contemporary orthodox theology. What Sa'adyah explicitly rejected as a theodicy of suffering children in the tenth century persists and is explicitly endorsed in the twenty-first to account for the millions killed during the Shoah.[76] Arguments advanced by philosophers like Sa'adyah, Bedersi, Albo, and perhaps even Crescas, considering his lukewarm endorsement, expose serious problems with reincarnation as a coherent theodicy. It would not be stretching the limits of speculation to conclude that they would consider it a hollow theological consolation, if not an obscenity, in the shadow of a million murdered children.

Last, I return to the epigraph of my chapter and Cocteau's suggestive metaphor of watches still ticking on the wrists of the dead. What remained alive of Proust after his physical demise, what remained "ticking," was his vast literary masterpiece of some 1.5 million words — the most valuable thing that he soldiered to completion — that consumed his life and continues to consume readers to this day.[77] Philosophers are much more attracted to the idea that an individual's afterlife consists of the sum total of his or her inimitable accomplishments, and his or hers alone. Those discussed in this chapter favored, either categorically or by implication, an ethereal soul constituted by what they respectively deemed human perfection accumulated during life in one form or the other. The watches on their wrists timed their accomplishments during their lifetime, while posthumously their achievements, the "ticking," endure as the measure of their distinctive time on earth.

Notes

1. See for example Isaac Husik's provocative assessment at the end of his *A History of Medieval Jewish Philosophy* (Philadelphia: Jewish Publication Society, 1958), 431–32, which claims the death of Jewish philosophy at the end of the medieval period after which Jews either "philosophized without regard to Judaism" or "sought to dissociate Judaism from theoretical speculation on the ground that the Jewish religion is not a philosophy but a rule of conduct."

2. For a concise survey of the link between soul and intellect during the golden age of Jewish philosophical theology from the tenth to the fifteenth centuries, see James T. Robinson, "Soul and Intellect," in *The Cambridge History of Jewish Philosophy: From Antiquity Through the Seventeenth Century*, ed. S. Nadler and T. Rudavsky (New York: Cambridge University Press, 2009), 524–58.

3. See Joshua Trachtenberg, *Jewish Magic and Superstition: A Study in Folk Religion* (Philadelphia: University of Pennsylvania Press, 2004), xxviii.

4. Manasseh ben Israel, *Sefer Nishmat Hayyim* (Leipzig: H. L. Shnoys, 1861), 98.

5. *Mishnah Berurah, Sha'ar Ha-Ẓiyyun*, 622:6, https://www.sefaria.org/Mishnah_Berurah.622?lang=bi. See also *Mishnah Berurah, Orakh Ḥayyim* 23:5, where a halakha forbidding insulting behavior in a cemetery is considered applicable even at the grave of a minor because the grave might "contain the soul of a great man." Another example of reincarnation (*gilgul*) as a factor seeping into halakhic reasoning is the responsum by Ezekiel Landau, one of the most renowned eighteenth-century halakhic decisors, concerning whether to disinter an infant who died before his eighth day to be circumcised. See Sharon Flatto, *The Kabbalistic Culture of Eighteenth Century Prague: Ezekiel Landau (the Noda Biyehudah) and His Contemporaries* (Oxford: Littman Library of Jewish Civilization, 2010), 125–26; 199–201.

6. See James T. Robinson, "Soul and Intellect."

7. See Harry Austyn Wolfson, *From Philo to Spinoza: Two Studies in Religious Philosophy* (New York: Behrman House, 1977).

8. See for example Colette Sirat, *A History of Jewish Philosophy in the Middle Ages* (Cambridge: Cambridge University Press, 1990), which begins with Philo since "one cannot begin to discuss medieval Jewish philosophy without recalling that the first contact between Greek philosophy and biblical thought took place at Alexandria," 6.

9. See Pierre Hadot, *Philosophy as a Way of Life: Spiritual Exercises from Socrates to Foucault* (Oxford: Blackwell Publishers, 1999), who states, "Both Judaism and Christianity sought to present themselves to the Greek world as philosophies; they thus developed, in the persons of Philo and Origen respectively, a biblical exegesis analogous to the traditional pagan exegesis of Plato," see on 72.

10. See for example chap. 5, "The Seven Units of Jacob's Ladder and Their Message," in my *Maimonides and the Hermeneutics of Concealment: Deciphering Scripture and Midrash in the Guide of the Perplexed* (Albany: State University of New York Press, 2002), 85–130.

11. *De Somniis* 1:139. For a full-length detailed treatment of this issue, see Sami Yli-Karjanmaa, *Reincarnation in Philo of Alexandria*, Studia Philonica Monographs 7 (Atlanta: Society of Biblical Literature, 2015).

12. *Logos and Mystical Theology in Philo of Alexandria* (Cincinnati: Hebrew Union College Press, 1985), 42. There is some debate as to whether Plato himself took reincarnation seriously or understood it as myth. See Erland Ehnmark, "Transmigration in Plato," *Harvard Theological Review* 50 (1957): 1–20.

13. Robert Brody, *Sa'adiah Gaon* (Oxford: Littman Library of Jewish Civilization, 2013), 50.

14. *The Book of Beliefs and Opinions*, trans. Samuel Rosenblatt (New Haven: Yale University Press, 1948), hereinafter cited as *Beliefs*, 259 and *Sefer ha-Nivhar ba-Emunot uva-De 'ot*, ed., Joseph Kafih (Jerusalem: Emunim Press, 1970) (Arabic text in Hebrew characters, with Hebrew translation), hereinafter cited as *Sefer Ha-Nivhar*, 214.

15. See L. Nemoy, "Al-Qirqisani's Account of the Jewish Sects and Christianity," *Hebrew Union College Annual* 7 (1930): 386 for locating the metempsychosis reference to earlier Karaite writers.

16. Rosenblatt, *Book of Beliefs*, 259.

17. R. J. Werblowsky, in his entry on Manichaeism in *Encyclopedia Judaica* (Jerusalem: Keter, 1972) 11:875, notes that Sa'adyah's polemic against dualism targeted Manichaeism as well as Zoroastrianism. See also A. V. Williams Jackson, "The Doctrine of Metempsychosis in Manichaeism," *Journal of the American Oriental Society* 45 (1925): 246–68.

18. It is always crucial to read philosophers such as Sa'adyah within the context of their overarching positions to appreciate fully their statements on a particular narrow issue such as reincarnation. In what follows I do so in contrast to those who fail to see Sa'adyah's rationale because they only examine it in isolation. For an example of the latter, see Yitzchak Blau, "Body and Soul: *Teḥiyyat ha-Metim* and *Gilgulim* in Medieval and Modern Philosophy," *Torah U-Madda Journal* 10 (2001): 1–19, who states "R. Sa'adyah explicitly rejects belief in *gilgul*im. Unfortunately, Rasag fails to clarify the basis of his objection," on 10.

19. See Rosenblatt, *Book of Beliefs*, supra, 242–43.

20. See Arthur Green's Introduction to Daniel Matt's English edition of the *Zohar: Pritzker Edition* (Stanford, CA: Stanford University Press, 2004), vol. 1, LXXII, and 109 of the text (*Bereshit* 1:15a). Green considers this the "strongest expression" of the Zohar's mystical reality. See also Elliot R. Wolfson, who sees this verse as instrumental for mystical hermeneutics being the "main vehicle for achieving revelatory experience of a primary visual sort." in *Through a Speculum that Shines: Vision and Imagination in Medieval Jewish Mysticism* (Princeton, NJ: Princeton University Press, 1994), 383.

21. See for example Moshe Idel, "The *Ẓaddik* and His Soul's Sparks: From Kabbalah to Hasidism," *Jewish Quarterly Review* 103, no. 2 (2013): 196–240, esp. 204–6, where he states, "the soul of the righteous ... is conceived of as emanating sparks, which belong to him personally but, most probably, enter the body and soul of other persons," on 205–6.

22. For a summary of the various reasons for reincarnation, see Moshe Hallamish, *Introduction to Kabbalah* (Jerusalem: HaKibbutz HaMe'uchad, 1991), chap. 6 [Hebrew]; English trans., Ruth Bar Ilan and Ora Wiskind, *An Introduction to the Kabbalah* (Albany: State University of New York Press, 1999), 284–90.

23. *Book of Beliefs*, 247. *Sefer Ha-Nivhar*, 204.

24. *Book of Beliefs*, 257; *Sefer Ha-Nivhar*, 212.

25. See Beliefs, 259–63; *Sefer HaNivhar*, 214–17.

26. *Beliefs*, 260 (Hebrew, 215). For a concise summary of those philosophical schools that subscribed to this tenet, see Yitzchak Blau, "Body and Soul," specifically 6–7.

27. On this position and Sa'adyah's rebuttal, see Haggai Ben-Shammai, "Transmigration of Souls in Tenth Century Jewish Thought in the Orient," *Sefunot* 20, 5 (1991): 117–36 [Hebrew]. Ben-Shammai identifies this position with a Manichaean-leaning Mutazilite school, who "attempted to resolve certain theological problems with reincarnation"; see on 130.

28. *Beliefs*, 261; *Sefer Ha-Nivhar*, 215.

29. For Sa'adyah's theory of compensation, see *Sefer Ha-Nivhar*, 166–67; and *Saadia Ben Joseph Al-Fayyu¯mı, The Book of Theodicy. Translation and Commentary on the Book of Job*, trans. Lenn E. Goodman (New Haven: Yale University Press, 1988), 125–26. I thank Danny Lasker for his elucidation of this passage to me in a private communication. See also Daniel Lasker, "The Theory of Compensation (*'Iwad*) in Rabbanite and Karaite Thought: Animal Sacrifices, Ritual Slaughter and Circumcision," *Jewish Studies Quarterly* 11 (2004): 59–72.

30. *Book of Beliefs*, 260.

31. For a debate over the philosophical cogency of Sa'adyah's compensation theodicy, see Eleonore Stump, "Saadia Gaon on the Problem of Evil," *Faith and Philosophy: Journal of the Society of Christian Philosophers* 14, no. 4 (1997): 523–49 and her responses to Oliver Leaman's negative assessment of Sa'adyah's compensation theory in chap. 3 of O. Leaman, *Evil and Suffering in Jewish Philosophy* (Cambridge: Cambridge University Press, 1995), 48–63.

32. *Guide of the Perplexed*, trans., S. Pines (Chicago: University of Chicago Press, 1963) hereinafter GP, III:24, 497–98.

33. *Mishneh Torah*, ed. Shabse Frankel (Bnei Beraq: Shabse Frankel, 1985–2006), 15 vols., hereinafter MT, Laws of Repentance, 8:2–3.

34. See GP, I:68 and *Introduction to Heleq* in I. Shilat, *Maimonides' Introductions to the Mishnah* (Jerusalem: Hotza'at Shilat, 1992), 136.

35. *Introduction to Heleq* in I. Shilat, *Maimonides's Introductions to the Mishnah*, 135–36. For al-Ghazali's influence on Maimonides's choice of metaphors here, see Amira Eran, "Al-Ghazali and Maimonides on the World to Come and Spiritual Pleasures," *Jewish Studies Quarterly* 8, no. 2 (2001): 137–16, especially 146–53. If, as Eran concludes, "Maimonides' choice to follow Al-Ghazali by making a 'little boy' the center of his main parables implies that the failure to identify the true end of man's life and the true reward of the service of God can be remedied through devoted education and in the attainment of maturity" (150) then, by implication, belief in reincarnation would be childish and immature.

36. See Philip Merlan, *Monopsychism Mysticism Metaconsciousness: Problems of the Soul in the Neoaristotelian and Neoplatonic Tradition* (The Hague: Martinus Nijhoff, 1963), who characterizes the Neo-Aristotelian union with a universal intellect as "the counterpart of the [Neoplatonic] *Unio Mystica* usually

so called. In this union the individual is absorbed into the universal, i.e. the supra-personal"; see on 19–20.

37. See GP, I:74, 221; also I:70, 173. For a long list of other primary and secondary references, see the Hebrew edition of the *Guide* compiled by Michael Schwartz, *The Guide to the Perplexed* (Jerusalem: Gefen Publishing House, 2003), vol. 1, 183, note 26 [Hebrew]; and for a concise overview, see Alfred Ivry, "Moses Maimonides: An Averroist Avant La Lettre?," *Maimonidean Studies* 5 (2008), 121–39, and on 124–26.

38. The literature is vast, but for two detailed examinations of Maimonides's position on resurrection with whose conclusions, as evidenced by the title, I agree, see Robert Kirschner, "Maimonides' Fiction of Resurrection," *Hebrew Union College Annual* 52 (1981): 163–93, who argues persuasively, "Maimonides declares his belief in corporeal resurrection while simultaneously denying it any discernible purpose. By this fiction he virtually eviscerates the doctrine he claims to profess. The enlightened will perceive the ruse; the masses, for whom the promised reward of resurrection serves a useful purpose, will remain serene in their belief," on 190. See also Albert D. Friedberg, "Maimonides' Reinterpretation of the Thirteenth Article of Faith: Another Look at the Essay on Resurrection," *Jewish Studies Quarterly* 10, no. 3 (2003): 244–57, who, assessing Maimonides's allowance for a fleeting instant of bodily resurrection followed by an immediate relapse, concludes, "the ephemeral existence of the resurrected, however, cannot be an ultimate reward since it can bring no lasting joy. Rather, as he affirms all along, the soul of the righteous attains immortality in *olam ha-ba*, the purely spiritual world-to-come," 257.

39. See b. Baba Bathra, 17a.

40. GP, III:51, 627–28.

41. See Josef Stern's chapter "The Embodied Life of an Intellect," in his *Matter and Form of Maimonides' Guide* (Cambridge, MA: Harvard University Press, 2013), 306–49, where he concludes that Maimonides's conception of intellectual perfection is "a condition that requires the de-corporealization of the human to the greatest extent possible," 348–49.

42. GP, III:51, 628.

43. See Peter Eli Gordon, "The Erotics of Negative Theology: Maimonides on Apprehension," *Jewish Studies Quarterly* 2, no. 1 (1995): 1–38, who states, "One can now see that the route leading from corporeal indulgence to textual misinterpretation — from the body of the philosopher to God's body is not entirely a metaphorical relationship, affirming that where bodily obstructions have been removed philosophical perfection can be achieved" (35–36).

44. See Moshe Idel, "Maimonides and Kabbalah," in *Studies in Maimonides*, ed. I. Twersky (Cambridge, MA: n.p., 1992): 31–82, on 42; On this see also Elliot R. Wolfson, "By Way of Truth: Aspects of Nahmanides' Kabbalistic Hermeneutic," *AJS Review* 14, no. 2 (1989): 103–78, particularly on 119–20.

45. See Michael Fishbane, *The Kiss of God: Spiritual and Mystical Death in Judaism* (Seattle: University of Washington Press, 1994), 78. For recent articles

on the concept of the "kiss" in kabbalistic texts, see Adam Afterman, "As in Water Face Reflects Face: Mystical Union in *Sefer Reshit Chochman*," *Daat* 84 (2017): 155–82; and Andrea Gondos, "Seekers of Love: The Phenomenology of Emotion in Jewish, Christian, and Sufi Mystical Sources," in *Esoteric Transfers and Constructions: Judaism, Christianity and Islam*, ed. Mark Sedgwick and Francesco Piraino (London: Palgrave, 2021), 21–42.

46. GP, I:1, 22–23.

47. See Shaul Magid, "Lurianic Kabbalah and Its Literary Form: Myth, Fiction, History," *Prooftexts* 29, no. 3 (2009): 362–97, where he states that in Lurianic exegesis, "the biblical characters, reified in the cosmos, are recast as rabbinic heroes and then reincarnated as the composite souls of his disciples" (369).

48. *Mishnah im Perush Rabbenu Mosher ben Maimon*, ed. and trans. Joseph Kafih (Jerusalem: Mossad ha-Rav Kook, 1984), vol. 2 of 3, Avot, 4:17, 293.

49. *Ketav Hitnazzelut, She'elot u-Teshuvot ha-Rashba* (Bnei Braq: Sifriyati, 1958), 1:418, 154–74. See Halkin, "Yedaiah Bedershi's Apology," *Jewish Medieval and Renaissance Studies*, ed. Alexander Altmann (Cambridge, MA: Harvard University Press, 1967), 165–84. See also Daniel Jeremy Silver, *Maimonidean Criticism and the Maimonidean Controversy, 1180-1240* (Leiden: Brill, 1965), 41–48.

50. *Ketav Hitnazzelut*, 165, my translation.

51. *Ketav Hitnazzelut*, 165.

52. *Ketav Hitnazzelut*, 165.

53. *Ketav Hitnazzelut*, 165.

54. On the problem of innocent suffering, especially according to the main philosophers mentioned in this chapter (Maimonides, Crescas, and Sa'adyah), see H. T. Kreisel, "The Suffering of the Righteous in Mediaeval Jewish Philosophy," *Da'at* 19 (1987): 17–29 [Hebrew].

55. *Light of the Lord*, trans. Roslyn Weiss (Oxford: Oxford University Press, 2018), hereinafter LL, 24 and the Hebrew edition *Or Hashem*, ed. Rabbi Shlomo Fisher (Jerusalem, Ramot, 1990) hereinafter OH.

56. See his chapter on Crescas in *Our Great Philosophers: Jewish Philosophy in the Middle-Ages* (Tel Aviv: Yedioth Ahronoth, 1999), 362 [Hebrew]; English trans., Leonard Levin, *The Classic Jewish Philosophers: From Saadia Through the Renaissance* (Leiden: Brill, 2007).

57. Book IV, Issue VII, LL, 347: OH, 405.

58. See LL, 214–20, 220; OH, 238–44.

59. LL, 215; OH, 239.

60. LL, 220; OH, 244. For another excellent study of a fifteenth-century debate in Candia on the issue of reincarnation between R. Moses Ashkenazi who repudiated it, and R. Michael Balbo (1411–c. 1484), who, like Crescas, combined both philosophical rigor with kabbalistic leanings and accommodated it, see Aviezer Ravitzky, "A Kabbalist Confutation of Philosophy — The Fifteenth-Century Debate in Candia," *Tarbiẓ* 58, no. 3/4 (1989): 453–82 [Hebrew], English trans. in Ravitzky, *History and Faith: Studies in Jewish*

Philosophy (Amsterdam: J. C. Gieben, 1996), 115–53. See also Brian Ogren's first chapter, "Metempsychosis, Philosophy, and Kabbalah: The Debate in Candia, in his *Renaissance and Rebirth: Reincarnation in Early Modern Italian Kabbalah* (Leiden: Brill, 2009), 41–70.

61. LL, 347, OH, 405.

62. LL, 347, OH, 405.

63. See Howard Kreisel, "Miracles in Medieval Jewish Philosophy," *Jewish Quarterly Review*, 75, no. 2 (1984): 99–133, who states, "For Crescas, miracles are purposeful acts performed directly by God out of knowledge of each of the recipients. They are the product of His infinite eternal power, not bound in any way by the operations of nature," 131.

64. LL, 298; OH, 343.

65. LL, 301; OH, 347. For an extended discussion of the question of what preserves personal identity in a resurrected person see J. David Bleich, "Resurrection and Personal Identity," *Tradition: A Journal of Orthodox Jewish Thought* 45, no. 3 (2012): 73–88, esp. 82–84, who states with respect to Crescas, "the soul is constant and undergoes no change in leaving the body for a transcendental existence or in its restoration to a corporeal body. Accordingly, it is the unchanging soul that accounts for constancy of personal identity" (83). Crescas here anticipates Locke's groundbreaking philosophical discussion of personal identity in the context of resurrection, which consists of consciousness where "The great and reliable sign of being the same consciousness, and so the same person or self that existed at an earlier time is memory of experiences had and deeds done, at that earlier time"; see Mark Johnston, *Surviving Death*, (Princeton, NJ: Princeton University Press, 2010), 25–26.

66. GP, II:25, 327.

67. Crescas refers to kabbalistic traditions. For this, see W. Z. Harvey, "Kabbalistic Elements in Crescas' *Light of the Lord*," *Jerusalem Studies in Jewish Thought* (1982): 75–109, and in particular for the use of the phrase, "If it is a received tradition, we shall receive it," see 101–3.

68. See Isaac Husik, "Joseph Albo the Last of the Mediaeval Jewish Philosophers," *PAAJR* 1 (1928–1930): 61–72.

69. Joseph Albo, *Sefer haIkkarim*, ed. J. Gutman (Israel: *Hotza'at Mahbarot leSifrut*, 1964) (Heb.), 2 vols., vol. 1, 763; *Sefer ha-'Ikkarim* [Book of Principles], Eng. trans., ed. I. Husik (Philadelphia: Jewish Publication Society of America, 1929), 4:29.

70. See *Sefer ha-'Ikkarim* 4:5 and Seymour Feldman, "A Debate concerning Determinism in Late Medieval Jewish Philosophy *Proceedings of the American Academy for Jewish Research* 51 (1984): 15–54, at 38–41. See also Shira Weiss, *Joseph Albo on Free Choice: Exegetical Innovation in Medieval Jewish Philosophy* (New York: Oxford University Press, 2017) and Shalom Sadik, "Free Will in the Thought of Rabbi Joseph Albo," *Jewish Studies Internet Journal* 11 (2012): 139–51 [Hebrew], who states, "Free will is not the outcome of a psychological process known from the outset, but rather a process which initiates in the human

soul the ability to examine circumstances and shape them in different directions," on 146.

71. *Sefer haIkkarim*, 762

72. See b. Sanhedrin 91b; see also Samuel S. Kottek, "Embryology in Talmudic and Midrashic Literature," *Journal of the History of Biology* 14, no. 2 (1981): 299–315, and 308–10.

73. I take this expression to indicate his repudiation of reincarnation rather than leaving it as a viable option. Here I am supported by the way Menachem Kellner interprets the same locution used by Maimonides in GP, III:4, 424. See his *Maimonides on the "Decline of the Generations" and the Nature of Rabbinic Authority* (Albany: State University of New York Press, 1996), 64–65. However, Dror Ehrlich argues that the expression allows for either alternative in *The Thought of R. Joseph Albo: Esoteric Writing in the Late Middle Ages* (Ramat Gan: Bar-Ilan University Press, 2009), 270–71 [Hebrew]. There is also the possibility that, though he may have begrudgingly accepted reincarnation, he was particularly uncomfortable with the prospect of reincarnation into animals.

74. There are a number of other positions that space limitations prevent me from exploring but one, Don Isaac Abravanel, who qualifies somewhat as a philosopher/exegete, deserves mentioning briefly for those deciding to pursue this further. Though he attempted to prove reincarnation by way of rational demonstration, he ultimately followed Crescas's approach, but with a far stronger embrace, stating, "it is a received tradition from our holy ancestors which should be received with a happy countenance." See his lengthy exposition in his commentary to Deut. 25:5 in I. Abarbanel, *Commentary on the Torah/ Perush al ha-Torah* (Jerusalem: Bene Arbe'el, 1964), vol. 3, 228–33, at 231. See also chap. 3 in Brian Ogren, *Renaissance and Rebirth*, 102–38, and the remarks by Eric Lawee, "Abravanel in Italy: The Critique of the Kabbalist Elijah Hayyim Genazzano," *Jewish History* 23, no. 3 (2009): 223–53, on 241–42.

75. Differences on reincarnation even impact on halakhic positions as evidenced by debates regarding levirate marriage (*yibbum*), where it figured prominently as a rationale. See the detailed study of Shaul Regev, "The Reasons for Yibum — Philosophy and Kabbalah," *Daat: A Journal of Jewish Philosophy & Kabbalah* 28 (1992): 65–86 [Hebrew].

76. See for example Aharon Roth, *Kunteras hatsava'ah* (Jerusalem: Horeb Printing, 1947), 23b [Hebrew], who presents reincarnation as the justification for murdered children during the Shoah. Their martyrdom forms a "*tikkun*" for the sins of the transmigrated souls they embodied. See Gershon Greenberg, "R. Arele Roth's Pristine Faith: Through Holocaust to Redemption," *Journal of Modern Jewish Studies* 14, no. 1 (2015): 72–88, on 80–81. R. Ovadya Yosef, Sephardic Chief Rabbi of Israel at the time, is reported to have made the same claim in an oral sermon delivered July 5, 2009. See https://www.makorrishon.co.il/nrg/online/1/ART1/912/007.html.

77. Cited by Frances Steegmuller, *Cocteau: A Biography* (Boston: Little, Brown, 1970), 296.

SECTION III

REINCARNATION, PSYCHOLOGY, AND LURIANIC KABBALAH

FROM SAFED TO EASTERN EUROPE TO BAGHDAD

EITAN P. FISHBANE

Personal Identity and the Ontology of the Soul

8

ASPECTS OF REINCARNATION IN ḤAYYIM VITAL'S *SHAʿAR HA-GILGULIM*

IN THIS CHAPTER I seek to probe the ontology of personal identity (the being and essence of a human self) and the correlated theory of reincarnation primarily as it was conceptualized by R. Yiẓḥaq Luria (the ARI) and R. Ḥayyim Vital. I seek to clarify the degree to which these thinkers understood the defining elements of human selfhood and individuality to be ontologically distinct or inseparable from Divinity, and what such distinctions or commonalities ultimately reveal about both kabbalistic anthropology and theology. I then reflect on the manner in which this view of ontology relates dynamically to the variations and thematics of Vital's elaborations on the theory of reincarnation (*gilgul*) in his classic work *Sefer Shaʿar ha-Gilgulim*. Because of the limitations of this chapter, I have selected several prominent and representative ideas and themes for analysis; it perhaps goes without saying that this inquiry is in no way exhaustive, and instead sets out to formulate a phenomenology of several key types and aspects of the Lurianic theory of rebirth and reincarnation. I consider the following subtopics in the Lurianic theory of soul and reincarnation as further developed and written by Vital: (I) defining the core ontology of the human soul in direct relation to its rootedness in the divine source; (II) the metaphysical status of the Torah (both in its origins and its continued unfolding) and the role of directed exegesis and Torah study in the maintenance and rectification of the individual human soul and its heavenly roots; (III) the practice of the *miẓvot* as formative and instrumental in the repair of the soul and its ongoing quest for wholeness; (IV) the intertwined and often generative relationship between a person's soul and that of others — specifically those of romantic soulmates, parents and children, as well as teachers and students.[1]

Divine Source and the Ontology of the Soul

As one of the primary transmitters of R. Isaac Luria's mystical thought, R. Ḥayyim Vital presents an intricate theory of the soul and humanness, especially through the prism of reincarnation and rebirth, in his *Sha'ar ha-Gilgulim*. Several other claims about mystical anthropology are distilled, however, Vital's *Sha'arei Kedusha* — a brief classic of kabbalistic theology, piety, and ethics — and it is here that we begin. Reflecting on what he characterizes as "the essence of the human being" (מהות האדם) in his *Sha'arei Kedusha*, Vital formulates a strong vision of the human self as composed of divine substance, as ontologically inextricable from Divinity:[2] "The essence of a person is that he includes all the worlds (מהות האדם כי הוא כולל כל העול־מות כולן) in their generality and their particularity — something that is not the case with regard to all other upper and lower creatures."[3] Having made this far-reaching metaphysical claim, Vital then proceeds to assert that this state of human composition includes elements from all planes of cosmic and mundane reality — from the coarsest particulars of physicality (יש לו גוף מהעפר הנקרא עולם השפל) to elements of the *kelipot*,[4] the angelic realm, and the higher reaches of divine sefirotic emanation. In this Great Chain of Being model, the human self is viewed as an atomistic, microcosmic entity that contains — on a concentrated, miniature scale — all the vast elements of cosmic reality. All these cosmic pieces of the human self, Vital avers, are united and infused with an exalted and luminous energy from the transcendent realms of the sefirot, reflecting an interconnectedness, indeed an ultimate unity, between the ten sefirot and the human being:

> All these become a chariot for the light that is drawn forth from the lights of the ten sefirot that are within [the world of] *Asiyah*, which are in turn [contained] within four foundational elements in order to give them life (וכל אלו נעשין מרכבה אל אור הנמשך מן אורות העשר ספירות שבעשיה אשר בתוך ארבעה היסודות כדי להחיותן). And they are within everything (or: "the most interior of all" — והם לפנים מן הכל). So too is this the way it is [in regard to] what is [contained] within the person from the spheres of *Asiyah*, and from the three [other] worlds — *Yeẓirah, Beri'ah,* [and] *Aẓilut* ...

The light of the quarry of souls is inward and higher than the light of the quarry of angels (אור מחצב הנשמות פנימי ועליון מאור מחצב המלאכים), and thus they are its servants. For it is through that [light of the quarry of souls] that their light and life-force is drawn forth from the ten sefirot unto them (כי על ידו נמשך הארתם וחיותם מאור העשר ספירות אליהם) . . .

The greatness of the soul is further clarified insofar as it is a light that is born and drawn from the light of the ten sefirot themselves (אור מתילד ונמשך מאור העשר ספירות עצמן), which is not through an intermediary. For this [reason] are they calle *children of the Lord your God* (בנים אתם לה' אלהיכם) [Deut. 14:1], for they are like a son who grasps hold of his father and is drawn forth from him (ונמשך ממנו). And this is the secret of "The Fathers are the Chariot" (וזהו סוד האבות הן הן המרכבה) — [a chariot] for the light of the ten sefirot that rides upon them (אל אור העשר ספירות הרוכב עליהם), not through the intermediary of another light (שלא על ידי אמצעות אור אחר).

This is the secret of *Israel, you in whom I become glorified* (ישראל אשר בך אתפאר) [Is. 49:3]. For the human garment is His glorification (כי לבוש האדם הוא תפארתו) . . . The light of the souls is a garment for the light of the ten sefirot (אור הנשמות לבוש לאור העשר ספירות), and this is the secret of *My beloved has descended to his garden* (דודי ירד לגנו) [Song. 6:2], which is this world (העולם הזה) . . .

This is the secret of *You who cleave to YHVH* (ואתם הדבקים בה') [Deut. 4:4], a complete conjoining with the light of the ten sefirot (דבוק גמור עם אור העשר ספירות) — that which is not the case with all [other] creatures.[5]

In this ontological vision, the Chain of Being is depicted as a nested series of infusions and enclosures — the emanational substance of divine reality, characterized as a flowing luminosity, reaches forth from its most transcendent dimensions into the core of the human self, an essence of personhood that is a soul composed of all cosmic particles. Indeed, as Vital emphasizes elsewhere in *Shaʿarei Kedushah* and *Shaʿar ha-Gilgulim*, it is this interior core that constitutes the true defining element of humanness — האדם הוא הפנימיות ("a person is the interiority"),[6] האדם הוא הרוחניות ("a person is the spirituality"),[7] and is decidedly not defined in identity by his embodiment (הגוף איננו האדם עצמו).[8] So understood, true human nature is the overflow emanation of divine light from the sefirot — thus greatly blurring the lines between human and divine, conceiving of essential human identity as divine being terrestrially manifest, a modality of mundane divine incarnation. In the same manner in which the child is born and emerges organically from the body of the parent, the human soul is born directly from the divine Self (כי הוא אור מתילד ונמשך מאור העשר ספירות עצמן) without any intermediary. So constructed, the essential truth of human nature is its status as a *divine child* — an entity that ontologically continues the divine substance in the same way that a baby physically grows out of the substance and cells of its mother and father's bodies.[9]

That contiguity of cells and DNA between human parent and child is expressed here as the outflow of emanational light from the ten sefirot to the human soul. To be sure, this construction of the human being as a child born of God's very Self, an ontological outgrowth of the divine Being, gestures toward a merger of theology and anthropology more commonly associated with Christology. The essence of human identity retains a metaphysical contiguity with the divine identity, blurring the lines between person and Divinity. It is notable that Vital does not make an assertion about simple identity between Divinity and humanity; instead, the essence of a person is characterized as a container for the supernal divine energy force, a chariot for the light of the ten sefirot. This is Vital's adaptation of the enigmatic remark found in *Bereishit Rabba*, "The Fathers are the Chariot" (וזהו סוד האבות הן הן המרכבה).[10]

In Vital's construction, the human self receives the emanational indwelling of the divine light, serving as its garment and chariot, though not indistinctly blended into the divine Self. Vital explicitly depicts the human soul as the site of divine Presence in this world; the garden of the divine beloved, the realm into which Divinity descends in order to dwell, is the earthly domain (העולם הזה). It is through the human self that God-as-Beloved descends into that lower world; for Vital, the will of God is expressed in this desire to become present in *ʿolam ha-zeh*, a desire that is articulated in the language of the Song of Songs, in its rhetoric of eros and passionate love. As such, the act of divine descent — of emanating into the human soul — might be read as a gesture of love, an entrance of divine lover into the human beloved. The image here, however, appears to manifest as the love of parent garbed in the new reality of its offspring — the descent to the garden of this world (*ʿolam ha-zeh*) is an act of divine procreation, of becoming present in the mundane realm through the clothing of the human being, the divine child. Notably, this moment of indwelling does suggest the blurring of boundaries, an assertion by Vital that a complete state of *devekut* (cleaving) between human and deity is achieved. Born of the metaphysical substance of Divinity, the human soul is characterized as a conjoined extension of divine emanation, one with the light of the *sefirot*.

Torah, Interpretation, and Soul Roots

The substance of the soul, the essence of personhood, is, according to Vital, hewn from the quarry of divine light, explicitly asserting that humanness is carved out of the larger divine totality. A related image of hewnness is offered by Vital in *Shaʿar ha-Gilgulim* — one that further integrates the idea of a metaphysical Torah from which all Jewish soul roots derive. As I discuss, this model is particularly revealing insofar as kabbalists understood the celestial Torah also to be ontologically contiguous with Divinity:

> A person is obligated to study Torah according to the four rungs that it contains (האדם מחוייב לעסוק בתורה בארבעה מדרגות שבה). Know that the total of all the souls is 600,000 and not more. The Torah is the root of the souls of Israel (התורה היא שרש נשמות ישראל), for from her were they hewn (כי ממנה חוצבו), and in her they are rooted. And thus, there are 600,000 meanings in the Torah (יש בתורה ס׳ רבוא פירושים), all of which are according to the *peshat*. And 600,000 [meanings according] to *remez*, 600,000 [according] to *derash*, and 600,000 [according] to *sod*. From each of the 600,000 meanings one soul from Israel came into being (ממנו נתהווה נשמה אחת של ישראל), and in the time to come each and every Jew will know the entire Torah according to the meaning that is aligned with the root of his soul (ולעתיד לבא כל אחד ואחד מישראל ישיג לדעת כל התורה כפי אותו הפירוש המכוון עם שרש נשתמו), for through that meaning he was created and brought into being (אשר ע״י הפירוש ההוא נברא ונתהווה).[11]

The rhetoric of a primordial hewnness (חוצבו) clearly recalls an important motif in kabbalistic metaphysics, one that is most prominently found in *Sefer Yeẓirah* and the twelfth- and thirteenth-century kabbalistic commentaries on *Sefer Yeẓirah*.[12] To speak of human reality as carved from the primordial rock of Torah, the paradigmatic source of the holy language, is to invoke the imagination of *Sefer Yeẓirah* in which the letters of the holy language are hewn from the fundamental ether of cosmic beginnings.[13] As such, the metaphysical origins of the human being are textual — the soul is hewn from the ultimate celestial textuality. For our purposes, it is particularly important to note that this primordial and metaphysical Torah appears to be an ontological extension of the dynamically emanating divine Self, a continuous reality that is asserted throughout early and late kabbalistic literature[14] and then in the theology and anthropology of early Ḥasidism.[15] If Torah is an emanational extension of the upper divine dimensions and if souls come into being through, and are rooted in, different layers of the Torah, then Torah serves as a metaphysical bridge of continuity in the ontological unity between human being and Divinity. Framed as such, rootedness in the heavenly Torah is a grounding in the divine Self; the meanings of Torah that give birth to Jewish souls *are nothing less than portions of divine Being*.

Here manifold meaning is not merely that which emerges through human cognitive engagement with the sacred text and tradition; it is an organic component of divine metaphysics. The Jewish soul is a dynamic hermeneutics come alive — a person's soul traces its origins to, and is grounded in, a pathway of interpretation and meaning, a *peirush*.[16] The core of the Jew's identity originates from and is metaphysically bound to the celestial Torah and its meanings, an ontological and inseparable offshoot of the divine Self. Meaning itself carries a metaphysical status, a reality of substance in the heavenly realm. It is not purely a dimension of knowledge realized in the human mind; it is woven into the fabric of reality, so much so that it brings souls into being. The core terms of ontological derivation in this passage — חוצבו (they were hewn), שרש (root), and נתהווה (brought into being) — vividly underscore the claim that the coming-into-being of the person is not merely an act of divine creation of an extra-divine entity, but rather an assertion that the identity of the individual is ontically grounded in the supernal realm, in the divine Self.

The belief in the ontological connection between a specific Jewish soul and a thread of meaning in the celestial Torah-as-divine-emanation seems to have played a special role in the clairvoyant and diagnostic practice of R. Isaac Luria vis-à-vis his students.[17] Sleep was understood to be a time when the Torah-roots of one's soul were disclosed upon the nocturnal ascent of the soul to the heavenly Garden of Eden while the body remained asleep in the world below.[18] Thus the disciples of Luria would visit with their master each evening for his reading of their soul and of the manifestation of particular scriptural verses and meanings upon their physical visage:

> Thus, every night while a person sleeps, and he deposits his soul, and it departs and ascends above — [if indeed he] merits to ascend above — they teach him there that meaning upon which the root of his soul is based [or "depends"] (מלמדים לו שם אותו הפירוש שבו תלוי שרש נשמתו). And indeed, all is according to [the manner of] his actions on that day (ואמנם הכל כפי מעשיו ביום ההוא): on that night, they teach him an individual verse or a particular section — for at that time that verse shines in him more than on other days (כי אז מאיר בו יותר פסוק ההוא משאר הימים). And on another

> night, a different verse will shine in his soul, according to his deeds on that day — and all of them according to meaning upon which the root of his soul is based, as mentioned [above]. My teacher of blessed memory, each and every night, would gaze upon his disciples standing before him, and he would see in them which verse was shining more on the forehead of that [particular] man, based on the indwelling of his soul that was shining there (ומורי ז״ל בכל ערב וערב היה מסתכל בתלמידיו העומדים לפניו ורואה בהם איזה פסוק מאיר יותר באיש ההוא מצחו מצד השרת נשמתו המאירה שם).[19]

In this anecdote by Vital we see the vividly embodied side of identity and practice in the circle of Luria — for while it is the soul that is correlated ontologically with the heavenly *peirushim*, it is through the physical face of the person, and specifically their forehead, that the master is able to discern an individual disciple's status along the path of spiritual development, the connection between their soul and the Torah above. The illuminated scriptural verse is visible to the diagnostic master in the corporeal visage of the person; as such, the body becomes the site of the soul's manifestation, a lens through which the clairvoyant teacher can see the metaphysical condition of the student, an ultimate instance of embodied spiritual practice and the bridging of the physical manifestation and the metaphysical spiritual correlation. Vital goes on to explain that upon gazing at the forehead of the disciple, Luria would then proceed to clarify some of that underlying *peirush* to which the individual's soul was bound. What is more, the disciple would then integrate the master's explanation into a pre-sleep recitative and contemplative exercise that was meant to prepare his soul for the heavenly learning that would take place during the imminent sleep: "And before that individual would go to sleep, he would contemplate that meaning that [the ARI] partially explained to him, and he would recite that verse with his mouth (וקודם שהיה ישן האיש ההוא, היה מכוין את הפירוש ההוא שבאר לו קצתו, והיה קורא בפיו הפסוק ההוא), so that when his soul would ascend above in deposit during his sleep, they would teach it to him more completely."[20] The progress of the soul, which occurs while the body is asleep, is stimulated and facilitated by embodied practices during the evening in preparation for the soul-ascent of unconsciousness. First the disciple comes before the master in a session of soul-reading through the illuminated textuality visible on the forehead; then the consultation offered by the teacher is enacted as a recitative technique combined with focused contemplation. The learning performed in wakefulness, as an evening practice in anticipation of sleep, creates a dynamic continuity between different states of consciousness in the unbroken quest for meaning and the study of Torah. Remarkably similar to contemporary research on the neurobiology of sleep and learning,[21] and also parallel to medieval notions of sleep as a time when difficulties in thought and theological revelations take place,[22] it is in the sleep state that the person is able to delve into the deepest roots of mind and knowledge — here framed as the reconnection of the soul with its metaphysical Torah-roots. Learning of Torah becomes a constant cycle, with waking and sleep serving different functions — integrating knowledge and understanding from the mundane and celestial realms respectively. What is more, this learning in divergent modes of consciousness aligns the mind of a person with the divinely originated nature of his soul.

Gilgul and the Practice of the Commandments (*Miẓvot*)

The relationship between the learning of Torah, sleep, and transformed practice upon waking flows naturally into a further understanding of the role of the practice of the *miẓvot* (and their correlated intentions) in the Lurianic conception of cosmic brokenness and repair in general and individual psychic brokenness and repair at the particular level. In the grand scheme of the Lurianic mythos, the primordial cosmos shattered and fragmented in its cataclysmic origins as a consequence of the First Man's (*Adam ha-Rishon*) Edenic sin, which in turn caused a fragmentation and deconstruction of the originally unified totality into sparks of divine light that are the roots of human souls. The primary mechanism by which this fragmentation and brokenness are repaired, and the cosmos ultimately redeemed, is through the gradual enactment of a panoply of *miẓvot* by the individual Jew.[23]

In this sense, as with the sources we examined in the first parts of this chapter, the ontology of the individual soul and the journey toward its gradual repair through an often long series of sacred actions and behaviors is bound up with the larger metaphysical realm, the fabric of divine Being. The expositions on this topic in *Shaʿar ha-Gilgulim* and elsewhere are too immense for full discussion here, but we must recall that the *miẓvah* of Torah study, culminating in the ultimate requirement discussed above to learn and clarify the entirety of the fourfold method of interpretation (the PaRDeS), is part of a more comprehensive schema in which the wholeness of the multi-part soul is tautly bound to the performance of the plenitude of the *miẓvot* by the person. Let us consider the following key and paradigmatic passage on this subject from *Shaʿar ha-Gilgulim*:

Know that a person needs to fulfill all the 613 *miẓvot*. And if he lacks one of them, [then] his soul is still lacking (ואם חסר אחת מהם, עדיין נפשו חסירה),[24] in accordance with the number [lit. "measure"] of *miẓvot* that are lacking from him. Indeed, the 248 positive commandments divide into five parts. First: the *miẓvot* that a person is prevented from fulfilling, such as the commandments that are dependent upon the time that the Temple was standing, such as the sacrifices and the like. [For] these a person does not return in reincarnation (*ḥozer be-gilgul*) to fulfill them, for what purpose [would there] be in [such a] reincarnation? When the Temple will be rebuilt, [then] he will fulfill them. The second: the commandments that a person can fulfill, such as *ẓiẓit* and *tefilin* and the like. [With regard to] these, if one did not fulfill them, then he certainly needs to return in reincarnation, [perhaps even] many times, until he completes them all (צריך בהכרח שיחזור להתגלגל פעמים רבות, עד שישלים את כלם). [This will be] in a manner in which one, who has previously reincarnated (*she-kevar nitgalgeil*) and [already] fulfilled some [lit. "a few"] commandments, it will be sufficient for him, in this reincarnation, that he fulfill the commandments that are lacking from him (כשקיים המצות החסירות ממנו), those that he never fulfilled before. Know that when he reincarnates for this [reason] it is possible that he will sin and commit many transgressions.[25]

Vital proceeds to explicate the various categories and contingencies in which the improper performance of an individual *miẓvah* requires the person (who, we may recall from earlier, *is the soul, is the spirit*) to reincarnate again — that is, for the physical body, which is understood to be but a passing garment for the true essence of personal identity, to die, and for the necessary part of the soul to undergo (another) transmigration. These include *miẓvot* that a person does not have an obligation to fulfill unless they come before him (lit. "come to his hand," *ela ʾim kein baʾah le-yado*), such as *terumot, maʿaserot* (gifts and tithes), and *shiluaḥ ha-qein* (the sending away of the mother bird before taking her chicks or her eggs), as well as those *miẓvot* that a person cannot perform unless God brings them before him — such as *pidyon ha-ben* (redeeming a firstborn son), *yibbum* (levirate marriage), *ḥaliẓah* (the ritual of severing the connection of the widowed woman from her brothers-in-law/freeing the woman from the need of levirate marriage), or *get* (a divorce decree).

This categorization culminates, as mentioned above, in the stipulation of the imperative to study Torah according to the fourfold method of *Peshat*, *Derash*, *Remez*, and *Sod* — the so-called PaRDeS methodology. Though Vital's discussion of the impact of Torah study on the rectification of the soul is intricate and discussed in other writings of his and of the broader Lurianic corpus, it is relevant to mention that in this same section of *Shaʿar ha-Gilgulim*, Vital details some of the distinctions involved in this intricacy, as different parts of the soul correspond to and are rectified in accord with different worlds of the divine realm of Becoming (viz. the four worlds of *Aẓilut*, *Beriʾah*, *Yeẓirah*, and *Asiyah*). For example, with regard to the *tiqun* (rectification) of the soul-parts called *Ruaḥ* and *Neshamah*, the *tikkun* of the *Ruaḥ* of *Yeẓirah* (reflecting the baroque intricacy of soul-parts as they are correspond to and are nested within each of the four different worlds) derives from the act of studying Torah כהלכתה לשמה — properly (according to legal stipulation) *and* for its own sake — the Oral Torah, including Mishnah, Talmud, and so on. Ascending higher and higher in the repair and attainment of soul-wholeness, the person achieves higher levels of soul in correspondence to his engagement with different levels of the fourfold method of PaRDeS, ultimately culminating in some of the highest levels of soul-wholeness through the study of mystical secrets. As Vital puts the matter: "The rectification of the *Neshamah* of *Beriʾah* depends upon the knowledge of the secrets and the inner mysteries of the Torah [found] in the wisdom of the *Zohar* (ותקון הנשמה דבריאה, תלוי בידיעת סודות ורזי התורה הפנימיים בחכמת הזוהר)."[26]

In the extended passage I have cited above is the assertion that a person's soul is fundamentally *lacking* or *incomplete* without the proper performance of *all* the 613 *miẓvot*. Indeed, the ontology of the soul is deemed incomplete in direct accordance with the number of specific *miẓvot* that still need to be fulfilled. This notion of what constitutes human identity in its wholeness has everything to do with the further underlying Lurianic doctrine, stated explicitly by Vital just a few passages hence in *Shaʿar ha-Gilgulim*: that the 613 *miẓvot* correlate directly to — indeed, the sparks that they carry are ontologically rooted in — the anatomy of *Adam ha-Rishon* (First Man), as I mentioned at the beginning of this section. Thus, the performance of the entirety of the 613 *miẓvot* is considered to be critical in rectifying the human soul, and consequently the original perfected body of light that was *Adam ha-Rishon* before the primordial cataclysm.[27] The attainment of this larger wholeness, as well the higher levels attained through kabbalistic Torah study, the grasp of the wisdom of the *Zohar*, as mentioned above, harkens back to the systematic statements made in this regard at the very beginning of *Shaʿar ha-Gilgulim* in the same extended passage where Vital makes clear his belief (and presumably that of his teacher, Isaac Luria) that the inner spirit, the multi-part soul of the human being, is the defining ontology of personal identity (as opposed to the *levush*, the ephemeral garment that is the physical body). There, Vital outlines the gradual, most-often many-lifetime process of attaining one's whole soul: "Know that all the *nefashot* are only from the world of *Asiyah*, all the *ruḥot* are from the world of *Yeẓirah*, and all the *neshamot* are from the world of *Beri'ah*. However, the majority of human beings do not attain [lit. "do not have"] all five parts [of the soul], which are called NR"N etc. [*nefesh*, *ruaḥ*, *neshamah*, etc.],[28] just the *nefesh* part alone, which is [drawn] from [the world of] *Asiyah*." Vital continues to further explicate that all the nuanced sub-components of each level of soul must be rectified before the person is able to proceed onward into the attainment of the next level of soul:

> Each and every person must repair all [the aspects] of *Asiyah* in its entirety. After this, he will be able to receive his *ruaḥ* from *Yeẓirah*, given that [the world of] *Yeẓirah* is greater [than] the entirety of *Asiyah*. Thus, in this way, in order to attain his *neshamah* which [derives] from [the world of] *Beri'ah*, the person must repair all the parts of his *ruaḥ* in the totality of *Yeẓirah*, and [only] afterward will he be able to receive his *neshamah* which [derives] from [the world of] *Beri'ah*.

It is precisely because of the fact that the human being (as soul) is ontologically derived from Divinity that his behaviors in the lower world are of such consequence (characterized as acts of *tiqun*). The different component parts of the human soul originate in the Being of corresponding dimensions of Divinity and divine becoming. The soul is thus an ontic extension of the divine Self, and the performance of particular *miẓvot* stimulate repair and realignment in this interconnected Great Chain of Being.

The Soul and Others: Impact and Connections

I turn now to the intriguing way in which Vital explicates the drama of romantic pairing and how it is reflected at the level of soul and soul-connectedness. In this exposition, we see an attempt, through the lens of reincarnation theory, to explain why certain couples fit together in peace and closeness and why others are destined to clash and to fight:

> Regarding the soul-mate (*bat zugo*) of a man:[29] We have already explained above as to whether the judgment of reincarnation applies to women as it does to men or not.[30] Know that our Rabbis of blessed memory said in

the first chapter of *Soṭah* (b. Soṭah, 2a), regarding the verse, "God settles the solitary into [family] homes; He releases those who are bound in imprisonment" (אלהים מושיב יחידים ביתה מוציא אסירים בכושרות),[31] that there is a first and second coupling (זווג). That which is stated (in b. Soṭah, 2a), "it is as difficult to pair them as the splitting of the Reed Sea" (קשה לזווגם כקריעת ים סוף), is referring to the second coupling. Know that the meaning of the first and second coupling is not [to be understood] according to its simple [or straightforward] sense, for many second couplings are [actually] better than the first ones, as we have seen in cases with our own eyes every day (כי כמה זווגים שניים הם טובים מן הראשונים, כמו שראינו בעי־נינו מעשים בכל יום). But the explanation of the matter may be understood through what was said by the *Sava de-Mishpatim* in the *Zohar* regarding the verse, *If he had a wife, then his wife will go out with him* (אם בעל אשה הוא ויצאה אשתו עמו) [Ex. 21:3].[32]

The [meaning of the] matter is: Know that when a man is new (כאשר האדם הוא חדש), which is to say, that it is the first time that he has entered into this world (הפעם הראשונה שבא בעוה"ז), then his soulmate is born with him, as is known (בת זווגו נולדת עמו). And when the time comes to marry her, she is brought to him in an instant [or, she happens upon him very quickly], without any difficulty [or struggle] whatsoever (וכשיגיע זמן לקיחתו אותה, מזדמנת לו ברגע, בלי שום טורח כלל ועיקר).

But if this man committed a sin, and needs to reincarnate because of it, and he is one of those about whom it is written "his wife will go out with him" — as mentioned in *Sava de-Mishpatim* — that his soul-mate is also reincarnated (שמגלגלים גם לבת זווגו), returning in reincarnation with him for his benefit (שתחזור להתגלגל עמו לטובתו) — when it comes time for this man to marry her, she will not be brought to him in an instant [that is, that their connection will not happen quickly and easily], but rather only after great difficulty [or struggle] (אינה מזדמנת לו ברגע, אלא אחר טורח גדול). For since he has reincarnated because of some sin, there are accusers against him above, and they want to obstruct [or prevent] her from him (ורוצים למנוע אותה ממנו), and [so] they insert quarrels between them (ומכניסים בהם קטטות).

[It was] about this that they said, "it is as difficult to pair them as the splitting of the Reed Sea" (קשה לזווגם כקריעת ים סוף). It is in the manner mentioned because it is called a second pairing (זווג שני), that is to say, she is his true soulmate (בת זווגו האמיתית), but she was already coupled with him a different time [in a previous life] — and now, in this reincarnation, it is called "the second coupling" (ועתה בזה הגלגול נקרא זווג שני).

For the woman herself is the original one [or "the first one"], but it is the second coupling (כי האשה היא עצמה ראשונה, אבל הזווג הוא שני). That is why it doesn't say זווג שנית, but instead זווג שני,[33] which [refers] back to the coupling and not to the woman.

Through this it will become clear to you how sometimes a man marries a woman quickly and without any struggle or fighting at all (איך לפעמים נושא אדם אשה ברגע בלי שום טורח וקטטה כלל), and sometimes he does not marry a woman except with great arguing until they are married (ולפעמים אינו נושא אשה אלא ע"י קטטות גדולות עד שישאנה). After they are married, they [achieve a state of] peace and tranquility (ואחר שנשאה הם בשלום ושלוה). This shows that it is a true [soulmate] coupling, but that this is the second coupling (וזה יורה על היות זווג גמור, אלא שהוא זווג פעם ב׳). For if she was not his soulmate (בת זוגו), there would not be peace between them after he married her (לא היה שלום ביניהם אחר שנשאה אותה).[34]

This extended passage is remarkable in several respects. The psychology of relational dynamics, of harmony and discord between couples before and after they are married, is here imbued with and explained by a kind of metaphysical-psychic determinism. The degree of fighting or tranquility between the couple is correlated directly to the interference of accusing angels above seeking to intervene in the coupling of this particular man and woman as a direct consequence of the sin or sins that the man has committed in a previous lifetime.[35] One core explanation here for why achieving the ideal of a peaceful and loving coupling is often so challenging is an earthly reverberation of the metaphysical difficulty in bringing these predestined souls back into alignment when they have gone astray; an orchestration of two soulmates who were bound together in a previous physical lifetime and who are finding their way back to one another in their new reincarnation with some degree of difficulty and impediment.

The dominant point as connected to the expression "second coupling" clearly refers to a reuniting of soulmates from a previous physical lifetime in a later one; this is how Vital builds upon the zoharic reading of Exodus 21:3, *If he had a wife, then his wife will go out with him* (אם בעל אשה הוא ויצאה אשתו עמו) — meaning, that the original true soulmate will reincarnate alongside the man to accompany him and to keep the bond intact between physical lifetimes. Nevertheless, in the first lines of the passage cited above, we do see a manifestly different usage of the term "second coupling," albeit here varied as זווגים שניים. In this use, we encounter a certain psychological attunement to the fact that in many instances a second marriage — presumably in the *same lifetime* — turns out to be better (implicitly, more peaceful or harmonious) than a first one ("for many second couplings are [actually] better than the first ones, as we have seen in cases with our own eyes every day"). This observation appears mostly to underscore the fact that often the reuniting of the man with his true soulmate first requires a period of struggle and quarreling — whether with a different first wife or with the same woman prior to marriage. In both cases, the explanation presented by Vital is that the heavenly accusers are tormenting the man and trying to obstruct his ultimate reunion with his true soulmate on account of sins committed in a previous physical lifetime.

Emotional harmony in a relationship — the manifestation of peace and tranquility — is a direct reflection of metaphysical alignment, implying that these two selves are indeed predestined soulmates. Romantic psychology is a direct function of metaphysical-ontological accord that originates from correlations beyond a specific lifetime. The phenomenon of couplings in which there is quarreling as opposed to tranquility is understood in this system to be an outer manifestation of an inherent piece of personal identity; it is a theory of psychodynamics in which a vision of character and relational compatibility is firmly rooted in a notion of innate, core selfhood — that is, whether or not these two souls are bound together in a higher cosmic sense of destiny.

LET US NOW TURN to Luria/Vital's theory about the way in which a father passes on core elements of his ontological essence to his son. On the one hand, one might argue that this parallels the physiological manner in which parents transmits their biological code in the form of DNA to their offspring, though the understanding of the soul and the ontic continuity between father and son reveals a further dimension of the anthropic rootedness in Divinity as well as the unique bond between the souls (namely. the essence of identity) of father and son. Vital then proceeds to connect this state of soul-relation and soul-transferral to that of teacher and student as well.

> [We will now discuss the matter of] the children that a man fathers (הבנים שאדם מוליד), and also the matter of students and their teacher (וגם בענין התלמידים עם הרב שלהם). Now, [first], we will discuss the matter of the children that a person fathers. Know that whether a man [marries] his soulmate (*bat zugo*) or he marries a woman who is not his soulmate, there is no difference in this matter, for he can father sons (יכול הוא להוליד בנים)

> from the sparks (*min ha-niẓoẓot*) of the souls of his root itself (*shorsho aẓmo*) or father from the souls of other roots. Also know that the father gives a portion of his soul to his sons (*ha-av hu notein ḥeleq mi-nishmato le-vanav*), and that portion becomes a garment for the soul of the son (*ve-otah ha-ḥeleq naʿasah levush el nishmat ha-ben*), and it helps and guides him [the son] on the good path. For this reason, a son is obligated to honor his father.[36]

In this passage, the act of procreation is framed primarily as a matter of conferring a portion of the father's soul onto his son — a metaphysical transferral that also carries the overt valence of ethical guidance ("Also know that the father gives a portion of his soul to his sons, and that portion becomes a garment for the soul of the son, and it helps and guides him [the son] on the good path" [ומסייעו ומדריכו בדרך הטובה]). Regardless of the mother, and whether or not she is his soulmate, Vital asserts that the man is able to "father sons from the sparks (*min ha-niẓoẓot*) of the souls of his root itself (*shorsho aẓmo*) or father from the souls of other roots."[37] He is tapped into the interconnected network of soul sparks and roots, and this giving of "a portion of his soul to his sons" thus emerges as the ultimate act of procreation and fatherhood. Indeed, as mentioned above, the son's progress in the path of goodness as constructed here is a function of this inner guiding spirit, perhaps more so than any embodied sense of ethical choice. The path toward the good according to *Shaʿar ha-Gilgulim* proceeds from the influx of that ancestry of soul roots. In Vital's portrayal, the duty to honor one's father in a physical lifetime stems directly from this guiding, advisory soul that functions as both metaphysical origin and essence.

This phenomenon is extended in *Shaʿar ha-Gilgulim* to the relationship between teacher and student, in which, like the father-to-son soul gift, there exists a similar conferral of spirit from teacher to student.[38] What is more, following dicta as early as the tannaitic period regarding the hierarchies of honor due to one's teacher versus one's father,[39] the soul-bond that results from this partial soul-transfer from teacher to student is considered to be even stronger and more enduring than the bestowal of a portion of the father's soul to the son. As Vital articulates this unending soul-bond: "For it is a stronger connection, since forever that spirit remains with the student (כי לעולם ועד נשאר ההוא רוחא עם התלמיד), established forever, and they will never separate (קיים לעולם לא יפרדו), in the secret of "*the soul of David was bonded to Jonathan*" (I Sam. 18:1). So considered, honor is tied directly in this doctrine from *Shaʿar ha-Gilgulim* to soul-indebtedness. Both father and teacher bestow portions of their soul substance onto the souls of the son/student, but just as the Mishnah argues that the hierarchy of honor favors the teacher over the father, so too Vital asserts that the soul-portion connection is stronger and more lasting in the case of the teacher-student relationship. In both cases, however, at least in the near term, there is some degree of shared soul identity between father/teacher and son/student. The inner spirit substance of the former becomes infused within/bonded to the latter.

Furthermore, with regard to the formative impact of the parent's spirit on their child, the intentionality of both the father and mother during sexual union is understood to have a decisive impact on the character of the physical child. Here we encounter not only soul-to-soul bonding and bestowal, but the parents' state of mind at the moment of physical conception also affects the ultimate personality and character traits of the child. In the deeply androcentric and misogynistic ideation of the times, the father's intentions manifest as modalities of קלות (lightness, speed, agility) in the child, and the mother's as modalities of כבדות (slowness, laziness, lethargy). In parallel to the manner in which various parts of the soul derive ontologically from different portions of Divinity or divine Becoming, the energy of the father is believed to derive from the supernal dimension known as the *Or ha-Meiqif*, whereas the energy of the mother is understood to derive from that of the *Or ha-Penimi*. These divine elements are channeled through the father and mother, respectively, into the child that is born of their sexual union. The speed and agility that derives from the divine *Or ha-Meiqif* via the father extends both to the child's engagement with the spiritual work of heaven and the study of Torah, on the one hand, and his engagement with the physical work and other aspects of the world, on the other. The inverse is true with respect to the mother and her impact on the child's character and temperament. As Vital formulates this theory:

> If the father, at the time of sexual relations, intended [that it was] for the sake of a *miẓvah* (נתכוון לשם מצוה בעת התשמיש), then the son will be quick to do the work of heaven and very great in Torah (מהיר במלאכת שמים, וגדול מאד בתורה). If the father intended for his own pleasure, then the son will be quick to do work in this world (ואם אביו נתכוון להנאת עצמו, יהיה הבן הזה מהיר במלאכת העה"ז). Likewise, the opposite: if he is slow of movement (כבד התנועה), if his mother had the intention [that it was] for the sake of a *miẓvah*, then he will be lazy (יהיה עצל) in the work of this world. If she

did not have the intention [that it was] for the sake of a *miẓvah*, the son will be lazy in the work of heaven. Through this you may understand the reason why there are little children who are sharp (חריפים) and who cannot [remain] quiet (לא יוכלו השקט), and [why] there are children who are lazy and very slow-moving (ויש ילדים עצלים כבדי התנועה מאד).[40]

As earlier, we observe here an ontic contiguity between the supernal divine dimensions (the *Or ha-Meiqif* and the *Or ha-Penimi*); the inner spiritual natures of the father and the mother, respectively; the mental intentionality of these two sexual partners in procreation; and then, finally, the way in which this chain of reverberations results in the manifestation of character, personality, and temperament in the resulting offspring of that sexual union. All is interconnected one with the other, the highest metaphysical divine dimensions ultimately resulting in the ways in which the child manifests in terms of personality and inclinations. The motivating forces of the male and the female in this theory are speed/alacrity and slowness/laziness; this reverberates in the child in both the realms of spiritual conduct (i.e., the work of heaven and Torah study) and that of the physical world. By way of example, if the father's intention at the moment of sexual congress was not lofty and God-serving, but instead lowly and pleasure seeking, then the child that results will manifest the characteristic of speed and alacrity in the realm of physical desires and pursuits as opposed to the more revered, more rarified realm of spiritual service to God and the study of Torah.

Likewise, the slowness or laziness that derives from the female force of the mother will translate into a laziness with respect to matters of this world — a characteristic that is constructed here *as a positive virtue* insofar as the child will have minor or no interest in the lowly matters of the corporeal realm and its attendant desires, thereby presumably avoiding physical sin and potentially turning his attention to matters of the spirit and the sacred. In the inverse, if the mother did not maintain the pure consciousness of intention for the sake of the *miẓvah* during sexual union, then that same laziness will be directed toward the exalted work of heaven — a decidedly negative character attribute. Thus, each in their own polarized ways, the character forces of the father and the mother shape the degree to which the child will be one who is engaged with the work of heaven or the drudgery and desire of the mundane. All in all, the character and temperament of the progeny are a matter of destiny, an innate configuration resulting from the relative purity of the parents' states of mind and intention.

Notes

1. In addition to other major works produced in recent years about the Kabbalah of sixteenth-century Tzfat — including the deep work of Lawrence Fine, *Physician of the Soul, Healer of the Cosmos: Isaac Luria and His Kabbalistic Fellowship* (Stanford: Stanford University Press, 2003), especially 150–86 and 300–58 (plus endnotes) — our study of this period in the history of Kabbalah is now certainly shaped by Jonathan Garb's impressive and erudite work *A History of Kabbalah: From the Early Modern Period to the Present Day* (Cambridge: Cambridge University Press, 2020), and perhaps even more specifically with regard to the soul, selfhood, and psychology in his book *Yearnings of the Soul: Psychological Thought in Modern Kabbalah* (Chicago: University of Chicago Press, 2015).

2. See the rich discussion of philosophical subjectivity (the idea of the self and its contours) as it manifests in the theory of reincarnation found in the writings of R. Ḥayyim Vital (a key feature in this chapter and in my larger research) in Assaf Tamari, "Niẓoẓot ha-Adam: Qavvim le-Torat ha-*Gilgul* ha-Lurianit u-le-Tefisat ha-Adam ha-Olah Mimenah/Sparks of the Person: Toward the Doctrine of Lurianic Reincarnation and the Conception of the Person That Arises From It" (MA thesis, Tel Aviv University, 2009). In particular, at least at the broader methodological and conceptual level, see 3–10 and 17–18.

3. Hayyim Vital, *Shaʿarei Kedushah* (Jerusalem: Barzani, 2005), 3:2.

4. Lit. husks, denoting demonic forces and evil within kabbalistic symbolism.

5. Vital, *Shaʿarei Kedushah*, 3:2.

6. See *Shaʿarei Kedushah,* 1:1. See also Eitan Fishbane, "A Chariot for the *Shekhinah*: Identity and the Ideal Life in Sixteenth Century Kabbalah," *Journal of Religious Ethics* 37, no. 3 (2009): 385–418, esp. 395.

7. *Shaʿar ha-Gilgulim*, 1.

8. See *Shaʿarei Kedushah,* 1:1. Also Fishbane, "A Chariot for the *Shekhinah*," 395.

9. For an extensive study of the motif of divine sonship, see Moshe Idel, *Ben: Sonship and Jewish Mysticism* (London: Continuum and The Shalom Hartman Institute, 2007). Regarding a variety of issues that emerge from this mythic and symbolic cluster, see Jonatan Benarroch, *Sabba ve-Yanuqa: Ha-El, ha-Ben, ve-ha-Mashiaḥ be-Sippurei ha-Zohar* [Sava and Yanuka: God, the Son, and the Messiah in Zoharic Narratives] (Jerusalem: Magnes Press, 2018), esp. 56–64 and 200–22. Also see Benarroch, "God and His Son: Christian Affinities in the Shaping of the Sava and Yanuka Figures in the Zohar," *Jewish Quarterly Review* 107, no. 1 (2017): 38–65. With respect to the vivid birthing imagery utilized in this passage, see the work of Ruth Kara-Ivanov Kaniel, *Ḥevlei Enosh: Ha-Leidah ba-Psychoanalizah u-va-Kabbalah* [Human Throes: Birth in Psychoanalysis and in the Kabbalah] (Jerusalem: Carmel Press, 2018) esp. 33–37, 88, 108–12, 278–85 [Hebrew].

10. See Hanoch Albeck and Julius Theodor, eds., *Midrash Bereishit Rabba* (Berlin: Akademie Verlag, 1912–1929), 1:475 (47:6). For a similar image employed earlier by Moshe Cordovero, see Fishbane, "A Chariot for the *Shekhinah*," 402–3.

11. Ḥayyim Vital, *Shaʿar ha-Gilgulim*, 17. Compare the formulation regarding the imperative of studying Torah according to the four levels of interpretation, the PaRDeS, in *Shaʿar ha-Gilgulim*, 11:

The sixth [category of positive commandments] is a specific commandment, the study of Torah [lit. engagement with Torah], which is [weighted in a] balance equivalent to all of the other commandments [combined], for the study of Torah is equivalent to all of them. And it contains four [methods of] interpretation, whose [acronym] is PaRDeS — *peshat, remez, derash,* and *sod.* One needs to strive mightily and engage with all of them to the threshold that his mind reaches; and he should request for himself a teacher who will instruct him. If [but] one of these four is missing, according to his grasp, he will reincarnate because of this (ואם חסר אחת מארבעתם כפי השגתו, יתגלגל על זה).

12. Also see Cordovero, *Pardes Rimmonim* (Koretz: TẒvi Hirsch b. Aryeh Leib & Son-in-Law, 1780), Gates 3:4 and 3:5 [Hebrew].

13. On this phenomenology, including reflections on the related term חקק and the idea of the primordial Torah in *Sefer Yeẓirah*, see Yehuda Liebes, *Torat ha-Yeẓirah shel Sefer Yeẓirah* (Jerusalem: Schocken Publishing House, 2000), 33–34. Also see Zohar, 1:15a (גליף גליפוי בטהירו עילאה).

14. See two strong precedents in *Zohar* 3:73a and Isaiah Horowitz, *Shenei Luḥot ha-Berit* (Amsterdam: 1649), Sections Toldot Adam, Introduction to Toldot Adam, 4 [Hebrew]. On the idea that the Torah emanates from a divine dimension of Being elsewhere in the writings of Vital, see *Sefer Peri Eiẓ Ḥayyim*, Shaʿar Qeriʾat Sefer Torah, 1 (נובלות חכמה של מעלה תורה, פירוש, האור שנבל ונפל מן החכמה עליונה שהוא אבא, נעשה התורה שהוא ז"א).

15. See, for example, R. Menaḥem Naḥum of Chernobyl, *Meʾor ʿEinayim*, s.v. "Bereishit be-oraita."

16. Regarding this broader correlation between 600,000 interpretations and 600,000 soul roots, see the discussion in Moshe Idel, *Absorbing Perfections: Kabbalah and Interpretation* (New Haven, CT: Yale University Press, 2002), 96–101. Also see Jonathan Garb, *Yearnings of the Soul*, 150–54.

17. Also see the discussion of this ontological continuum of divine-human identities, specifically with respect to the metaphysical overflow of God-as-Text into the human being, in Shaul Magid, *From Metaphysics to Midrash: Myth, History, and the Interpretation of Scripture in Lurianic Kabbala* (Bloomington: Indiana University Press, 2008), 206–13.

18. On this idea in earlier Kabbalah, particularly the Zohar, see Melila Hellner-Eshed, *A River Flows from Eden* (Stanford: Stanford University Press, 2009), 121–31. In Lurianic Kabbalah, sleep was also understood as rare mechanism for the bypassing of the reincarnation process through death and rebirth, allowing an individual to rectify the soul while still alive in one body. See Vital, *Shaʿar ha-Gilgulim*, 3. For a recent scholarly analysis of this belief,

including a fresh and creative consideration of this advanced phenomenon of fragmenting/splitting the soul for the sake of personal *tikkun* (rectification) and redemption within a single physical life-time, see Ẓvi Ish Shalom, *Sleep, Death, and Rebirth: Mystical Practices of Lurianic Kabbalah* (Boston: Academic Studies Press, 2021).

19. Vital, *Shaʿar ha-Gilgulim*, 17. For observations about this particular practice in the circle of Luria, see Lawrence Fine, *Physician of the Soul*, 163. For discussion of the Lurianic divinatory art of forehead reading, see Fine, *Physician of the Soul*, 153–64. This is anchored in Fine's argument about the highly embodied nature of practice and thought in the Lurianic fellowship.

20. Vital, *Shaʿar ha-Gilgulim*, 17.

21. See, for example, Backhaus, Hoeckesfeld, Born, Hohagen, and Junghanns, "Immediate as Well as Delayed Post Learning Sleep but Not Wakefulness Enhances Declarative Memory Consolidation in Children," *Neurobiology of Learning and Memory* 89, no. 1 (2008): 76–80.

22. See my discussion of this in Fishbane, *As Light Before Dawn: The Inner World of a Medieval Kabbalist* (Stanford, CA: Stanford University Press, 2009), 103–14. Cf. Elliot R. Wolfson, *A Dream Interpreted Within a Dream* (New York: Zone Books, 2011), 158–60.

23. For reflection on this primordial rootedness in *Adam ha-Rishon*, on the one hand, and the role of *gilgul* in the construction of soul identity, see Shaul Magid, *From Metaphysics to Midrash*, 53–74.

24. Though the word for soul used here by Vital is *nefesh*, I suggest that it appears to be not necessarily referring to that part of the multi-part soul according to the Lurianic theory, but rather as a reference to the entirety of the soul (made up of different parts), for attaining wholeness of soul in general requires mastery and performance of the entirety of the 613 *miẓvot*, and an imperfect performance of any of these commandments would result in the need for reincarnation.

25. Vital, *Shaʿar ha-Gilgulim*, 11.

26. Vital, *Shaʿar ha-Gilgulim*, 11.

27. For a striking post-Lurianic reverberation of this idea of the ontological connectivity between the human soul, the Torah embodied in the *miẓvot*, and their source in the divine quarry above, see Isaiah Horowitz, *Shenei Luḥot ha-Berit*, Haqdamat Toldot Adam, Beit Ḥokhmah (Tinyana), 176 and 209.

28. The highest two parts of the five-part soul, *ḥayah* and *yeḥidah*, are often elided in this manner, reflecting the belief that they are exalted dimensions of the soul that are extremely difficult to attain.

29. The English idiom "soulmate" does seem to be the best translation of the term *bat zugo* here, given the context of its usage here and in other passages, even though the Hebrew term literally only means "his pairing/partner/female part of his romantic coupling." This phrase is used in this way elsewhere in *Shaʿar ha-Gilgulim* with respect to human beings (see, for example, *Shaʿar ha-Gilgulim*, 8, 20, and 38, among other instances), and a par-

allel supernal valence with regard to the divine mythology is used in *Sefer Eẓ Ḥayyim*, 17:3 and 38:2.

30. In *Sha'ar ha-Gilgulim*, 9, Vital asserts that women do not need to reincarnate because they cleanse their sins in *Gehinnom* (the biblical and rabbinic correlate for the Christian concept of hell), whereas the fires of Gehinnom have no power over men because they fulfill the commandment of Torah study. In this respect, Vital appears to base his position on the dictum found in b. Ḥagigah, 27a. Despite the fact that this rabbinic source claims that *being a sage, talmud ḥakham*, protects against the fires of Gehenna, it does not clearly indicate protection for *all men* simply because they study Torah in a way that women putatively do not: "Rabbi Abbahu said that Rabbi Elazar said: The fire of Gehenna has no power over Torah scholars (תַּלְמִידֵי חֲכָמִים)." See Chaim Milikowsky, "Which Gehenna? Retribution and Eschatology in the Synoptic Gospels and in Early Jewish Texts," *New Testament Studies* 34, no. 2 (1988): 238–49. Also now see Dov Weiss, "Gehinnom's Punishments in Classical Rabbinic Literature," in eds. Eitan P. Fishbane and Elisha Russ-Fishbane, Jewish Culture and Creativity: Essays in Honor of Proffesor Michael Fishbane on the Occasion of His Eightieth Birthday (Boston: Academic Studies Press, 2023), 77-90.

31. This translation reflects the interpretive meaning in the Talmudic context as well as in *Sha'ar ha-Gilgulim*. The original biblical source (Ps. 68:7) meaning is somewhat different. See the rendition in *NJPS Tanakh*: "God restores the lonely to their homes, sets free the imprisoned."

32. Meaning that his wife will reincarnate with him despite the claim that men reincarnate and women do not. I have again translated the biblical verse to align with the contextual exegetical purpose; the original meaning of Ex. 21:3 may be translated as "if he had a wife, his wife shall leave with him" regarding the contextual biblical context of the acquisition of slaves and their subsequent liberation.

33. The word "second" of "second coupling" being distinguished based on its feminine or masculine Hebrew form — *sheinit* versus *sheini*.

34. *Sha'ar ha-Gilgulim*, 20.

35. Compare this and related modalities of *tikkun* and rebirth with the broad intercultural perspective developed in Gananath Obeyesekere, *Imagining Karma: Ethical Transformation in Amerindian, Buddhist, and Greek Rebirth* (Berkeley: University of California Press, 2002).

36. *Sha'ar ha-Gilgulim*, 10.

37. *Sha'ar ha-Gilgulim*, 10.

38. For parallel discussion in the context of the related matter of *ibbur*, see Moshe Idel, "The Secret of Impregnation as Metempsychosis in Kabbalah," in *Verwandlungen*, ed. Aleida Assman and Jan Assman (München: Wilhelm Fink Verlag, 2006), 341–79. See also J. H. Chajes, *Between Worlds: Dybbuks, Exorcists, and Early Modern Judaism* (Philadelphia: University of Pennsylvania Press, 2003), 14–28.

39. See M. Keritot, 6:9.

40. *Sha'ar ha-Gilgulim*, 10.

NATHANIEL BERMAN[1]

"A Seething Cauldron" of "Infinite Soul-Sparks"

9

LURIANIZING INTROJECTION/ PSYCHOANALYZING *GILGUL*

Do not make the mistake of thinking that the original soul itself repeatedly undergoes *gilgul* ... for the souls of human beings were divided infinitely...
— ḤAYYIM VITAL, *Sha'ar Ha-Gilgulim*

Introduction: An Existential Challenge, Not an Occult Curiosity

Reincarnation inescapably raises the most fundamental questions about human existence, whether one designates the latter as the "self," the "soul," the "subject," or by other analogous, though far from identical, terms. One cannot discuss reincarnation in any sense without implicitly envisioning *whose* journeys are at stake. How should one identify the being that was once "incarnated" and now is "reincarnated"? Is it a unitary or a composite being? Do its journeys from one body to another alter its identity? What are its relations with other such beings — love, antagonism, power, subordination? Is it even a "being" at all? Reflection on reincarnation thus is not merely some occult pursuit but challenges us to articulate our overall existential stance. Indeed, in my opening sentence, I put "reincarnation" in scare quotes to indicate the non-neutrality of the very word — for, in its contemporary English usage, it already implies a particular existential interpretation of terms like the kabbalistic "*gilgul*."

The notorious difficulty of translating *gilgul* is not merely some interlinguistic conundrum. "Reincarnation," the word that remains its most common English rendering, suggests that the soul is a unitary and stable substance. It once resided in one body and now has migrated to another body. Nonetheless, *Sha'ar Ha-Gilgulim*, a purported redaction by Ḥayyim Vital (1543–1620) of the teachings of Isaac Luria (1534–1572), warns us against precisely this conception: "Know that even though you will find that it has been written many times among us that So-and-So has undergone *gilgul* into So-and-So, and after that into So-and-So, etc., *do not make the mistake of thinking that the original soul itself repeatedly undergoes gilgul*. Rather, the issue is that the souls of human beings were divided infinitely — and within a single root of them there are infinite soul-sparks."[2] Each *gilgul*, in this vision, brings about a rectification, a *tikkun*, for some of these sparks, even while the others must "return" to life, "to undergo *gilgul*, and to receive *tikkun*." Moreover, as we shall see, it is far from certain that the returning sparks will all go into the same new body. The relatively autonomous destinies of these soul-sparks problematize even their affiliation with the "same" soul. When we foreground this proliferation of soul-elements, we can appreciate the value of one French translator's rendering of *gilgulim*: "the revolutions of the souls."[3] This translation has the merit of being a literal rendering of the Hebrew, as well as bearing the figurative connotation, in English as well as French, of destabilization, perhaps even violent destabilization.

In the excerpt quoted above, Vital thus recognizes two rival visions of *gilgul*: the unitary "reincarnation" of the entire soul and the variegated "revolutions" of the infinite soul-sparks. Moreover, he acknowledges that he himself has advanced both contrasting ideas ("it has been written many times among us"). Among the numerous examples of the reincarnationist idea in his work, we find his identification of Rav Sheshet (ca. fourth century CE) as a *gilgul* of Bava ben Buta (ca. first century BCE). Vital declares that the identity of the two was so close that it extended to their bodies: the blindness of Rav Sheshet was due to King Herod's blinding of Bava ben Buta centuries earlier.[4] This kind of narrative suits precisely the popular understanding of reincarnation, though it opposes Vital's own declaration that one should not understand *gilgul* in this way. Moreover, most of Vital's exposition in the *Sha'ar Ha-Gilgulim* falls between the reincarnationist and revolutionary perspectives. Vital tirelessly elaborates the baroque intricacies of the journeys of articulable, rather than infinite, multiplicities.

For example, between the unitary soul and the infinite soul-sparks we find the specific differentiation among five soul-levels: *nefesh*, *ru'aḥ*, *neshamah*, *ḥayah*, and *yeḥidah*.[5] The cycle of *gilgulim*, Vital announces, will end when each of these five soul-levels becomes perfected, "receives *tikkun*."

Nevertheless, the tension between the reincarnationist and revolutionary perspectives plays a persistent role even in such intermediate discussions — each tugging, respectively, in the direction of greater unity or proliferation. The soul-levels, for example, often serve as a defined multiplicity, a basis for forecasting an endpoint for *tikkun*. However, Vital constantly undermines this relatively manageable framework by showing how the soul-levels multiply fractally because of the layered complexity of Lurianic cosmology, with five soul-levels on each of the layers. And once we recognize that the layers themselves multiply fractally, we perceive an endless proliferation of the tasks of *tikkun*. The distinction between the defined multiplicity of the soul-levels and the infinitude of the soul-sparks becomes attenuated, and the achievement of complete *tikkun* becomes an ever-receding utopian goal.

Before turning to some of Vital's Lurianic details, I reflect on this tension through the lens of a twentieth-century "mythologist of the soul," Sigmund Freud.[6] The theme of "kabbalah and psychoanalysis" is, of course, an old one, going back at least to comments offered by Gershom Scholem.[7] In recent scholarship, this theme has become something of a subfield in itself, drawing attention from prominent writers such as Elliot Wolfson, Havivah Pedaya, Daniel Abrams, and Ruth Kara Ivanov-Kaniel, as well as many others, including myself.[8] In this brief chapter, I do not seek to make a general intervention into this subfield. Rather, I draw some specific parallels between particular texts of Freud and Vital, between specific aspects of Freud's metapsychology and Vital's metempsychosis.

Among the many tensions that marked Freud's ever-evolving oeuvre, we find one that is analogous, though by no means identical, to the opposition I have sketched in Vital: between the self as a potentially unified, self-controlled agent and the self as a superficial veneer over a plethora of disparate elements. We see this tension in acute form in the relatively late *New Introductory Lectures* (1931). On the one hand, treating the psyche as ideally the realm of a unitary ego, Freud declares that psychoanalysis seeks to "strengthen the ego, . . . to widen its field of perception and enlarge its organization, so that it can appropriate fresh portions of the id. *Where id was, there ego shall be*. It is a work of culture — not unlike the draining of the Zuider Zee."[9] On the other hand, in the very same lecture, Freud describes the ego as merely one, rather secondary, player in the psyche — seemingly rendering impossible its sovereignty, its acts of "appropriation." While the ego is "after all, merely a portion of the id,"[10] the id resists all ordering principles. It is

> the dark, inaccessible part of our personality . . . [We] call it a chaos, a *cauldron full of seething excitations*. . . . It is filled with energy reaching it from the instincts. . . . The logical laws of thought do not apply in the id . . . Contrary impulses exist side by side, without . . . diminishing each other . . . There is nothing in the id that corresponds to the idea of time . . . Wishful impulses which have never passed beyond the id, but impressions, too, which have been sunk into the id by repression, are virtually immortal.[11]

In the face of this "seething cauldron," which defies logic, morality, time, and death, one perceives the improbability of the psychic equivalent of the "draining of the Zuider Zee."[12] Yet, just as much of Vital's writing on *gilgul* falls between the extremes of reincarnation and revolution, so most of Freud's writing falls between the extremes of the unitary ego and the id's seething cauldron. Freud endlessly provides detailed analyses of the dynamic relationships within specific, rather than "seething," multiplicities.

These preliminary analogies between the deeply heterogeneous texts of Freud and Vital serve as a framework for what follows. Each writer, I contend, allows us to appreciate aspects of the other that we might otherwise marginalize. I state two of my themes at the outset here, in telegraphic form. On the one hand, Freud helps us to appreciate the significance of the fraught, sometimes sinister, power dynamics inherent in Lurianic *gilgul*, even in its "holiest" forms. On the other hand, Vital helps us to critically evaluate the residues of the unitary self in the Freudian framework. However startling, the juxtaposition of these writers yields crucial insights into the existential questions underlying both — even if the dialogue between them also, of necessity, remains interminable.

Indeed, once we relinquish an exclusive image of the soul (or the self, the ego, etc.) as a unitary substance, we begin to see that some of the key phenomena named as *gilgul* are pervasive rather than exotic. And since the image of the soul (or the self, etc.) as a unitary substance is hardly one that most contemporary philosophers and psychologists would defend, partly thanks to Freud's "Copernican revolution," a serious consideration of *gilgul* texts is in order.[13]

One obvious objection to this exercise concerns ontology. The kabbalistic writers on *gilgul*, so the objection would go, thought that metempsychosis was "really" taking place, while Freud viewed the presence of multiplicities within each person as "purely subjective." I will not resolve this ontological challenge in this short essay, largely because it poses an uncritical dichotomy between the "real" and the "subjective," as well as relying on an unexamined understanding of each term. The objection assumes simplistic views both of the meaning of "reality" to a kabbalist and the putative opposition between "subjectivity" and "objectivity" in psychoanalysis. Indeed, if the self is not a unitary substance, what does "purely subjective" mean?

Introjections

Between the unitary ego and the id's "seething cauldron" lies Freud's portrayal of introjection as key to the formation of the psyche. Freud first fully elaborated this process in *The Ego and the Id* (1923). "Introjection" consists of the "setting up" of a loved "object inside the ego."[14] Freud casts this mechanism initially as a means by which a person reconciles themselves to the loss of a loved one. Indeed, he states that this "identification" with the lost love may be "the *sole* condition under which the id can give up its objects."[15] Freud also declares that "object-cathexis" and "identification" may operate "simultaneously" — when the person both continues to love the other *and* has internalized them as part of their own ego.[16]

Introjection, however, has far broader implications. Freud proclaims that the introjection of loved others is the key determinate of an individual's being. The very "character of the ego" is the "precipitate of abandoned object-cathexes."[17] The ego thus not only "contains the history" of its object-choices":[18] it *is* the history of those choices. We have thereby moved far away from envisioning the ego as a unitary self toward a coexistence of beloved Others. Or, to put it more colloquially: "you are whom you have loved."

Introjection in *The Ego and the Id* mostly concerns lost objects of sexual desire or filial love. However, as commentators have observed (and as he himself suggests), this discussion constitutes a revision of Freud's views on mourning.[19] In the 1918 *Mourning and Melancholia*, he had portrayed healthy mourning as the "withdrawal of libido" from the dead loved one.[20] By contrast, his 1923 discussion portrays introjection as perhaps "the sole condition under which the id can give up its objects."[21] At the same time, Freud repeatedly notes that there is no guarantee that the "character" formed through introjection will be a stable or harmonious one. If the ego's "object-identifications" become "too numerous, unduly powerful and incompatible with one another," it could lead to a "disruption of the ego" — including "what is described as 'multiple personality.'"[22] Moreover, even when the disruption falls short of such a "pathological outcome," the "conflicts between the various identifications" can cause the ego to be "driven apart."[23] The introjected lost loves thus seem rather more primary than the ego who attempts to coordinate them. Moreover, they engage in power struggles both among themselves and with the introjecting ego. We will encounter an analogous inhabiting of a single body by a number of heterogeneous and often fractious others when we turn back to our discussion of *gilgul.*

Of equal significance here is Freud's emphasis on the intergenerational dimension of introjection. He discusses this dimension in relation to the super-ego, the rough Freudian equivalent of the conscience. Freud portrays the super-ego as the product of introjection: as the internalized "heir of that emotional attachment" that children have to their parents.[24] In addition, "the super-ego also takes on the influences of those who have stepped into the place of parents — educators, teachers, people chosen as ideal models."[25] Freud cautions, however, that the super-ego forms not through the introjection of these figures in their entirety, but only these figures' *own* super-egos. Moreover, the super-egos of the "ideal models" were themselves formed through the internalization of the super-egos of *their* parents and teachers. Freud sees this chain of introjections as extending indefinitely into the past, culminating in a vision of the cultural history of humanity: "[A] child's super-ego is in fact constructed on the model not of its parents but of its parents' super-ego; . . . it becomes the vehicle of tradition and of all the time-resisting judgments of value which have propagated themselves in this manner from generation to generation."[26]

After this brief overview, we have discovered a textured Freudian vision of multiplicity, alongside the alternative between unity and infinity. We perceive three complex realms, each with its own kind of multiplicity, each with its own temporality. Inhabiting, indeed, constituting, any individual's super-ego are authority figures from the recent and distant past — or rather, one aspect of these figures, their super-egos — forming a chain of cultural transmission plunging into the mists of human history. The individual's ego, on the other hand, is inhabited by, indeed constituted by, the introjected lost objects of love — the personal love history of the individual.[27] The figures introjected into the ego and super-ego, moreover, may entertain relations of power and rivalry in relation to each other. Finally, the id remains the "seething cauldron" of timeless, indeed "immortal," and often incompatible instincts.

The ontological status of Freud's three psychic agencies is indeterminate. At times, Freud portrays them as three topographical regions, at other times as distinct *personae*, at other times paints them with yet other images. And while he always refrains from taking any one description too literally, his portrayals rely on such varying imagery for their persuasiveness. What we might call the "realism" of these portrayals particularly comes to the fore when we consider the various figures, or parts of figures, whose introjection forms the ego and the super-ego.

Yet, while the internalization of other people, or rather of components of others, is a very tangible process for Freud, its precise ontological status does not seem important to him. Freud is a "mythologist of the soul." The ontological indeterminacy of his metapsychological agencies is not one that could – or indeed, should – be clarified through hermeneutical exactitude. Freud would caution us that his imagery is tropic in some sense—and do such caveats differentiate him from most kabbalistic authors?

Before I turn back to Vital on *gilgul*, I emphasize that this essay does not undertake a comparison of the "psychoanalytic idea of introjection" and the "kabbalistic idea of *gilgul*." Rather, it juxtaposes specific texts of Freud with specific texts of Vital – with the aim of reciprocally illuminating some of the strands in each author. Psychoanalysts after Freud elaborated a vast literature on introjection, but that literature is not relevant to my project here. [28]

"Soul-Pregnancies"

Just as introjection lies between the Freudian visions of the sovereign ego and the id's "seething cauldron," so does "soul-pregnancy," *ibbur*, lie between Vital's "reincarnationist" and "revolutionary" visions. In *ibbur*, a living person becomes "impregnated" with another person's soul. While Vital sometimes opposes *gilgul* to *ibbur*, he more often discusses *ibbur* as a variant of *gilgul*: "*gilgul* during life," rather than at birth.[29] I note that thirteenth-century kabbalistic texts often used *ibbur* as the general term for that which was later subsumed under *gilgul*.[30] In any case, it is with these soul-pregnancies that the Freudian vision of introjection resonates most strongly.

Ibbur comes in many varieties. At the broadest level, we may distinguish between what one might call "good" and "bad" *ibburim*. A good *ibbur* occurs when a righteous person's soul takes up residence in a living person to facilitate the latter's spiritual progress. Remarkably, Vital tells us that one living person may be impregnated with up to three righteous souls at the same time. The person's body thus becomes the dwelling place for four souls, whose interrelationships, as we shall see, may be far from stable.

This multiplicity destabilizes the unitary self, though ostensibly in an articulable, rather than "infinite," manner. A further complexity stems from the differentiation among the various soul-levels (particularly *nefesh*, *ru'aḥ*, *neshamah*). It is not the entirety of the righteous soul that becomes impregnated in the living, but a particular soul-level — in a manner analogous to Freudian introjection of particular aspects of another person, such as their super-ego. To avoid confusion here, however, I refer to "souls" rather than "soul-levels" unless directly pertinent.

Most of Vital's discussion of *ibbur* concerns the soul of a deceased righteous person impregnating a living person. However, Vital also declares that the soul of a *living* person may sometimes impregnate another living person. He also discusses the sinister version of such phenomena: when the souls of the wicked impregnate a person to lead them toward corruption.[31] When discussing this "bad *ibbur*," conventionally called "demonic possession," I often draw on the key work on the subject by J. H. Chajes.[32]

GOOD *IBBUR*

Considering "good *ibbur*" in relation to introjection, I make two preliminary observations. The figuring of the taking in of another's soul as impregnation demands reflection on gender and power dynamics. It also compels reflection on the decentering of the unitary self characteristic of what Iris Marion Young calls "pregnant subjectivity."[33] Young elaborates pregnancy's "positive disintegration of subjectivity" and its "splitting of the self into process"[34] — vivid images concerning literal pregnancy highly pertinent to Lurianic *ibbur*.

A stereotypically gendered view of pregnancy might lead one to say that Vital's "impregnated" person plays a more passive role than Freud's "introjecting" person. Vital often portrays the "impregnating" soul as having a good deal of choice about whether and how long to inhabit the impregnated person. Nevertheless, Vital also attributes agency to the impregnated person. If one performs a good deed in a particular way, one might be able to induce the soul of a specific righteous person identified with that performance to become impregnated within oneself.[35] Chajes interprets this technique as a person's "mimesis" of a desired righteous soul in order to induce it to enter their body.[36]

Freud's portrayal of introjection, moreover, also has a conjunction of passive and active elements. Freud strongly implies that introjection can only be an unconscious process, rather than deliberately willed. Nevertheless, the very term introjection suggests an action undertaken by a subject — or more precisely, for Freud, as a strategy by one of the psychic *personae* to placate another *persona* for loss: "When the ego assumes the features of the object, it is forcing itself, so to speak, upon the id as a love-object and is trying to make good the id's loss by saying: 'Look, you can love me too — I am so like the object.'"[37] We might bring together the conscious and unconscious elements in introjection with a paradoxical phrase like "unconscious agency." But we are still left wondering: if the ego is the byproduct of introjection, who or what does the introjecting? Conscious or not, this attempt to resemble the beloved recalls Chajes's "mimesis" in the context of *ibbur*.

One might, to be sure, portray *ibbur* and introjection as working in reverse directions in relation to mimesis. In *ibbur*, mimesis induces the entry of the righteous soul; in introjection, the internalization of the other *produces* the mimesis. I would not, though, overstate this difference, since the goal of *ibbur* is also an ever-greater resemblance to the impregnating guide, far beyond the original mimesis.

Strikingly, Vital offers the relationship of David and Jonathan as his key example of *ibbur* during the lifetime of the *impregnating*, as well as impregnated, soul.[38] The biblical text famously portrays this relationship as one of the most intense forms of love, whatever one thinks of recent interpretations of that love as erotic. Some have found an asymmetry in the David/Jonathan relationship. Robert Alter asserts that the text predominantly describes David as the object of Jonathan's love, rather than vice versa.[39] It is only after Jonathan's death that David calls him "my brother" and declares: "Very dear you were to me. More wondrous your love to me than the love of women" [2 Samuel 1:26, Alter]. Other verses, to be sure, might suggest that the love was reciprocal even during Jonathan's life.[40]

Vital claims that a biblical verse confirms the *ibbur* relationship between David and Jonathan: "And the *nefesh* of David cleaved to Jonathan." Vital comments: "for even though the two of them were both alive, the *nefesh* of David became impregnated in Jonathan."[41] Vital's proof-text, however, does not actually exist in the Tanakh. The verse most similar to it reads: "and the *nefesh* of Jonathan was bound to the *nefesh* of David; and he loved him as his [own] *nefesh*."[42] Vital's alteration of the verse foregrounds David's agency in coming to "cleave to Jonathan" — in contrast to the taking of initiative by Jonathan's soul in the actual verse.

Vital's surprising invocation of the David/Jonathan friendship as the model for *ibbur* during the lifetime of the impregnating soul is significant for my discussion here. One might rather have expected Vital to exemplify *ibbur* with clearer relationships of tutelage, such as teacher and student, master and servant, or parent and child. If the David/Jonathan relationship exemplifies *ibbur*, then *ibbur* resonates strongly with Freudian introjection as a way of coping with lost love — especially if we adopt Alter's view of their relationship. We thereby can see Jonathan's desire for impregnation by the soul of David as his way of coping with his anxiety about David's devotion (even leaving aside its gender and erotic implications). Indeed, the biblical text broadly hints that Jonathan is uncertain about David's constancy, portraying him as repeatedly beseeching David to swear to his love.[42] In Freudian terms, Jonathan preemptively copes with his feared abandonment by David through introjection. He offers his ego, enriched with the introjected David, to his id as worthy of its ardor in the place of his elusive friend. Jonathan's relationship to David would exemplify Freud's cases of "simultaneous" introjection and object-cathexis.

The unequal intensity of desire prevailing between impregnating souls and impregnated persons is a key, if implicit, theme in Vital's discussion of *ibbur*. Consider the example of a person who has achieved *tikkun* of the three principal soul-levels (*nefesh, ru'aḥ, neshama*). Such a person, Vital declares, can still be impregnated with a righteous soul. After death, the person will ascend to dwell together forever with the righteous person in the world-to-come.[44] *Ibbur* thus secures one's love-object for all eternity — a utopian fulfillment of Freudian introjection! In most cases, however, the asymmetry between the impregnating soul and the impregnated person entails more tenuous attachments.

The impregnating soul's participation in the impregnated person's life is both partial and conditional. When the impregnated person performs good deeds, the impregnating soul receives a reward.[45] But when the person acts wickedly, the impregnating soul receives no punishment. Even more tellingly, if the impregnated person persists in performing wicked acts, the impregnating soul simply departs: "she enters at her will and departs at her will."[46] If soul-impregnation is a form of love, it is far from the absolute variety.

The conditional and partial attachment of the impregnating soul stands in marked contrast to the way some impregnated persons (like Jonathan) *cleave* to the impregnating souls (like David). It was probably this very asymmetry that led Vital (consciously or unconsciously) to rewrite the verse about the biblical friends, inverting the directionality of the "cleaving." It is only when the impregnated person acts consistently righteously that the impregnating soul remains for the duration of the impregnated's life — and then "the two of them will ascend to the same level" in the afterlife.[47] The strictness of this condition for retaining the companionship of the impregnating soul leads the Freudian-trained eye to discern an aggressiveness reminiscent of the super-ego, to whose severity we will return.

In other passages, however, it is the impregnated person whom Vital portrays as only conditionally attached to its soul-guide. Thus, Vital declares that a person who is making spiritual progress may "merit" the replacement of the impregnating soul of one righteous person for that of a still more righteous person.[48] Vital gives an example of a person whose soul has a spiritual affinity with ("is from the same root as") ten other souls, each more righteous than the other. As the person progresses spiritually, the pregnancies succeed each other, with ever more high-quality souls replacing each other (recall that there is a limit of three at any one time).[49] This ongoing succession of pregnancies proliferates the number of souls who successively take up residence in one body, definitively destabilizing any vision of a unitary person tutored by a unitary impregnating soul.

With this dynamic of successive soul-pregnancies, we also discover *ibbur* as the kind of "vehicle of tradition" that Freud identified in introjection of authority figures into the super-ego. Vital portrays the successive replacements of the impregnating souls as reaching further and further back into time, so that one might ultimately attain the supreme privilege of being impregnated by the soul of the Patriarch Abraham.[50] The spiritual journey of a person might thus entail an unfolding connection to the entire history of the Jewish people. Such a person, of whatever biological gender, becomes something like a womb of both tradition and renewal.[51]

The vicissitudes of *ibbur*, whose complexities go far beyond my exposition here, disclose a dynamic vision of human existence as the site of the cohabitation and displacement of diverse soul-levels of both the living and the dead. This site may be that of a harmonious dialogue among a series of ever-changing impregnating spirit-guides extending back millennia. It may, on the other hand, be that of an anxious drama, beset by the constant threat of abandonment by those guides. Or both. We perceive an unstable and polyvalent terrain, akin to Freud's topography but far more turbulent.

BAD *IBBUR*

Although Vital declares that good and bad *ibburim* have analogous features, even if with reversed valences, he nevertheless differentiates them in significant ways. This differentiation stands out particularly when we consider other texts, particularly narrative texts, alongside *Sha'ar Ha-Gilgulim*. I begin with the power struggles between the righteous and wicked souls in a given body that, unsurprisingly, pervade Vital's discussion of bad *ibburim*. The relative spiritual strength of the righteous and wicked protagonists who undergo such *ibburim* ultimately determines the outcome of the drama. If the soul of a wicked person impregnates the soul of an unswervingly righteous person, the latter can prevail, bringing *tikkun* to the impregnating soul. If the soul of the wicked person impregnates itself into a mostly wicked person, however, it strengthens the wickedness of the impregnated and brings him or her to perdition. The outcomes are far less certain, however, in those cases that fall between these extremes — where the basic nature of the impregnating and impregnated are more ambiguous.

The power struggles commence at the inception of a bad *ibbur*. While a good *ibbur* occurs primarily thanks to mimesis, the souls of the wicked can enter living people in random, involuntary, and even coercive ways. In *Sha'ar Ha-Miẓvot*, for example, Vital warns of the danger posed by wicked souls who transmigrate into water. In fact, "there is no spring, pit, or water reservoir" that does not contain such wicked souls.[52] If one drinks that water, one may ingest a wicked *nefesh*, followed by a power struggle with the gravest stakes. The impregnated person can still be victorious if they can overpower the impregnating wicked spirit. But "if the person does not have the ability to rectify the *nefesh* of that wicked person, the *nefesh* will impregnate within him, and cause him to sin, and bring him down to the pit of destruction."[53]

No one, however, can be assured of victory in such struggles. Vital recounts that even Isaac Luria would exorcise water before drinking from a spring or well.[54] Since he was a supremely righteous person, Luria's dread of possession by wicked spirits implies his acknowledgment of their sheer power. Mimesis, key to the initiation of good *ibbur*, gives way to a brute power struggle, the key feature of bad *ibbur*.

The stories recounted by Vital and others, such as Luria's "water exorcisms," complexify these power dynamics. I refer particularly to a well-known exorcism story recounted by Samuel Vital (1598–1677), Ḥayyim's son and the editor of the bulk of his writings.[55] This story, which transpired in Egypt, concerned a young woman, Esther Weisser. Weisser had fallen into great mental distress — and at least some of the time, into a state of unconsciousness. When consulted by the family, Samuel at first told them to call in a non-Jewish, presumably Muslim, specialist in demons, a *palil*.[56] Upon the intervention of the *palil*, a voice from within the woman proclaimed that he was a non-Jewish spirit who had entered the woman because of his lust for her. The *palil* succeeded in ridding the woman of this *mazik* ("damager," a term often used in Jewish literature for a demon). He captured the *mazik* in a vial and buried it in the earth.

At that point, another voice spoke from within the woman. This voice declared that it was Jewish and beseeched Samuel for help in leaving the woman's body. Samuel conditioned his help on a number of oaths. The spirit had to swear neither to return to the woman's body after departing nor to harm the woman, her family, those assembled around her, or "anyone of Israel." The spirit must also leave Egypt immediately and enter *Gehinnom* for purification. (*Gehinnom* is the traditional Jewish term for the afterlife place of punishment, serving as a purgatory, rather than eternal hell, for all but the most wicked people.)

Several features of this story, whose fascinating richness I have barely touched, are directly pertinent here. First, Weisser's two *ibburim* were quite heterogeneous. The non-Jewish *mazik* was clearly evil — with the all-too-familiar ethnic stereotypes mitigated by the figure of the skillful non-Jewish *palil*. The Jewish spirit was rather more complicated, neither wholly wicked nor righteous, neither wholly malevolent toward Weisser nor wholly benevolent. Weisser herself became something like a terrain of struggle between the impregnating spirits, between those spirits and herself, and perhaps between the two moral poles of the Jewish spirit.

Freud's discussion of introjection sheds crucial light on these dynamics. We have already seen Freud's portrayal of the double-edged power relations in introjection. On the one hand, human character forms as a "precipitate" of introjected authority figures. On the other hand, these introjections initiate further power struggles within the introjecting ego. Indeed, the introjects may prove "unduly powerful and incompatible," leading to a "disruption of the ego." Moreover, resonating uncannily with Weisser's case, Freud declares that "the different identifications" may each "seize hold of consciousness in turn."[57]

The second point concerns the role of the exorcist. The story suggests that the Jewish spirit's presence in Weisser was a necessary prerequisite for entering *Gehinnom* for a more thorough purgation of sin — a two-step feature of the afterlife also explicated in the *Sha'ar Ha-Gilgulim*. If we assume that Weisser was a mostly righteous person, her relationship to the spirit might seem similar to one of the scenarios described in the *Sha'ar Ha-Gilgulim*: a righteous impregnated person helping the impregnating soul on the path of *tikkun*. However, Weisser lacked the power to do so, overcome by mental distress and even falling unconscious. The spirit only departs to *Gehinnom* when forcibly driven out by the formidable exorcist Samuel Vital.

The crucial role of exorcists during the sixteenth century, so elaborately explored by J. H. Chajes, would be unexpected for someone only familiar with the chapter of *Sha'ar Ha-Gilgulim* most devoted to bad *ibburim*.[58] That chapter does not even mention exorcists, and it is hard to see how they would fit into its framework. Exorcism introduces an additional protagonist in the power struggle between the impregnating and impregnated.

In this context, it is the role of the psychoanalyst that sheds crucial light on the kabbalistic text. The analyst is an indispensable ally to an analysand overwhelmed by powerful introjects. It is the analyst who makes it possible for the analysand to make conscious the unconscious introjects. The analysand thereby can deprive the introjects of their compulsive power and construct a more integrated ego. Like such an analysand, Weisser was helpless in the face of the heterogeneous and at least partly malevolent spirits inhabiting her. She required the intervention of the *palil* and the rabbi to expel them. It was only then that she could regain consciousness. It is telling that, when awakening, she had no memory of what had transpired during her possessed state.[59] (Of course, the parallels between the psychoanalyst and the exorcist have been drawn by many writers, beginning with Freud himself.)[60]

From our vantage point, moreover, the Weisser case brings to the fore a striking feature of the power dynamics that pervaded both much of early Freudian practice and sixteenth-century Lurianic exorcisms: gender.[61] The seemingly helpless women in both eras, subject to forces within them and yet beyond their control, ostensibly required the help of the male expert to reestablish their identities. In the eyes of the male expert, only they had the power to subjugate those internal, yet alien, forces besetting the women. In both eras, however, the power dynamics were far more complex than the images of the masterful Samuel and the unconscious Weisser, as well as of Freud and his "hysterics," suggest. Contrary to the impression given by their portrayal in Freud's texts, his female analysands were often powerful and creative women in their lives outside those texts. Indeed, some went on to play crucial collaborative roles with Freud in the very creation of psychoanalysis.[62] Ḥayyim Vital's spiritual life was also decisively shaped by a variety of spiritually powerful women, including clairvoyants, with whom he surrounded himself.[63]

Indeed, Chajes shows how "possessed" women were able to participate in, while also critiquing, authoritative discourse generally reserved for men.[64]

Finally, I turn to the light that a Freudian perspective can shed on the curiously powerful danger posed by the exorcised spirit precisely at the moment of its exit from Weisser's body — the danger that Samuel sought to obviate by compelling an oath from the spirit. Freud's theory of the instincts, as well as his portrayal of introjection, provides a crucial insight into this danger. Although his theory of the instincts evolved during his career, Freud consistently adhered to a dualistic vision. This vision eventually culminated in a grand opposition with mythical resonances: between "the sexual instincts, understood in the widest sense — Eros, if you prefer that name — and the aggressive instincts, whose aim is destruction."[65] He acknowledged that this theoretical dichotomy corresponds to the colloquial opposition between love and hate or attraction and repulsion.[66] Freud also formulated it in even more mythical terms, using the terms Love and Strife (drawing on Empedocles); some of his followers preferred the opposition between Eros and Thanatos.[67]

Freud portrays the ideal condition as "instinctual fusion," in which the two opposed forces cooperate with each other. However, the two may also become "defused" — a dangerous situation in which aggression emerges "unalloyed."[68] As an example of cooperation, Freud writes of "neutralizing" the destructive instincts by directing them away from the self and toward external threats.[69] On a more edgy note, he writes of the aggressive element in sexuality as an example of fusion. By contrast, pure sadism is a perverse example of defusion.[70] The super-ego, in particular, is a locus of the aggressive instinct. Although the super-ego forms through introjections of beloved authority figures, those introjections primarily consist of the disapproving and punishing aspect of those figures. We can see the threats of abandonment by the impregnating righteous soul in *ibbur* as an instantiation of the aggressive, even sadistic, aspect of the super-ego.

This Freudian perspective illuminates the surprising fact that it was precisely at the moment of the spirit's exit from Weisser's body that Samuel perceived the greatest danger. If introjection always has a component of eros, whether reciprocal or asymmetrical, it also has a measure of aggression, as in the threats of abandonment by the good *ibburim*. Samuel's fear of the heightened danger at the moment of the spirit's exit can be understood as a fear of instinctual defusion. Once the spirit gave up his erotic attachment to Weisser, the emergence of the aggressive instinct in its pure form posed a lethal danger, an unleashing of aggression at those present and even at "anyone of Israel." The unbounded force of Thanatos, unrestrained by Eros, demanded not only the strongest oaths as protection, but also the immediate casting of the spirit into *Gehinnom*.

Gilgul as a Field of Love and Destruction

We have seen how key features of Freudian introjection and Lurianic *gilgul* displace the unitary, stable, and sovereign subject. In its place, we found shifting configurations of multiple psychic agencies and soul-levels brought together through love and loss, emulation and aggression. These configurations lie beneath the surface veneer of those we conventionally meet as "individual human beings" in daily life. These configurations are fields of cooperation and conflict, of Love and Strife — sometimes "fused," sometimes "defused."[71] Amid all this proliferation and fragmentation, the reunification of the whole person seems like a utopian — or even eschatological — aspiration. And, indeed, it is in Vital's discussions of the resurrection of the dead at the end of days that we find his most intricate endeavors to imagine such a reunification. If the resurrected body is not the site for this reunification, then surely nothing will be. Eschatological fulfillment of this hope, however, remains far from assured — for reunification implicates some rather disturbing phenomena involving struggles over eternal life and annihilation among ostensibly loving human beings. Even at the end of days, Vital foresees the aspiration for unity often overpowered by the centrifugal forces of disintegration. I offer here three of Vital's numerous variations on this theme.

I first return to the *gilgul* of Bava ben Buta in Rav Sheshet. As I sketched in the introduction, Vital begins by portraying this *gilgul* in reincarnationist terms: a unitary soul who returned centuries later, bearing the blindness from his earlier incarnation. However, Vital then fragments that image, creating a fraught and ambivalent relationship between the two figures through a startling reading of a Talmudic story. The Talmud recounts that Rav Sheshet would exclaim in the House of Study, "Rejoice my *nefesh*, rejoice my *nefesh*, for you I have read, for you I have studied."[72] Reading this exclamation through the lens of *gilgul*, Vital inverts its plain meaning, which implies a celebration of individual happiness through study. On the contrary, Vital explains: the *nefesh* for whose benefit Rav Sheshet studied was actually that of Bava ben Buta.

For Vital, the Talmudic figure known as Rav Sheshet was actually the site of a configuration he calls "double *gilgul*": two *nefashot* in one body. This phenomenon occurs when a person has perfected one of their soul-levels and then damaged it later in life. To repair the defect, that soul-level can only return in the company of a soul-level of another person that animates the new body. This "double *gilgul*" — the presence from the beginning of life of soul-elements from disparate sources — thus differs from *ibbur*, which occurs during a person's lifetime.

The righteous Bava's *nefesh* returned in Sheshet to correct a small imperfection from its previous lifetime. Unable to return alone, but in need of no more than a small assistance from another, it returned in Sheshet's body in the company of the merest soul-spark from another's soul. The purpose of Sheshet's life was thus primarily to serve Bava's *tikkun*. Sheshet's good deeds inured to the benefit of Bava's *nefesh*. At the end of days, Vital declares, Bava's body will be resurrected with the *nefesh* perfected by Sheshet. Sheshet's body, by contrast, will be resurrected with the mere soul-spark, an impoverished spiritual state. The more powerful Bava thus will predominate, for all eternity, over the subservient Sheshet. Sheshet's seemingly joyous exclamation, "Rejoice my *nefesh*," was actually a cry of deep melancholy, "for all his labor would be taken by that other *nefesh*."[73] Sheshet seems both dedicated to his role of servitude and resentful of it, perhaps both loving and hating Bava. A later kabbalist describes this passage as "the dead inheriting the living";[74] in Freudian terms, we might describe this as the victory of Laius over Oedipus.

My second, still more unsettling, example stems from the separate, yet intertwined, fates of the different soul-levels of the "same" soul. Recall that the need for *gilgul* arises from the failure to perfect all the soul-levels in one lifetime. After the initial lifetime, one can only work on perfecting one soul-level at a time. Usually this limitation means that the body in which that soul-level attained perfection must die and the higher soul-level return in a succeeding lifetime. However, Vital tells us that it is possible that different soul-levels of the "same" soul may be present in the world at the same time, though in different human beings. Each would be working simultaneously on perfecting one of the soul-levels. Three people thus may be passing each other on the street, bearing, respectively, a *nefesh*, *ru'aḥ*, and *neshama* of the "same" soul — usually unbeknownst to them. While one might see this as an instance of a cooperative endeavor among several human beings to perfect one complete soul, Vital emphasizes the potential for rivalry among them for the ultimate claim to that soul.

Vital's example of this agonistic dimension again, surprisingly, concerns King David.[75] Vital explains that David was only able to attain a *nefesh* during his lifetime, one of the many consequences of Adam's original sin explicated at length by Vital. However, since "it was impossible for David to attain more than a *nefesh*, his *ru'aḥ* came during his lifetime into the body of another person."[76] David and this contemporary (in whose identity Vital seems uninterested) then entered into an eerie spiritual competition, in which each raced to perfect the soul-level he possessed before the other. The stakes of this competition were no less than the determination of whose body would be resurrected at the end of days. If the anonymous "possessor of the *ru'aḥ* perfected" his soul-level first, then there would be no "salvation" for David's body.[77] Only the body of the "possessor of the *ru'aḥ*" would be resurrected. This body would then possess both the *nefesh* that David had perfected and the *ru'aḥ* that he had perfected.[78] David's own body, by contrast, would be annihilated. This possibility that King David, the ancestor of the Messiah, might not arise at the final resurrection can only be astonishing to a traditionalist reader. Vital's tale of an agonistic relationship between David and an anonymous contemporary contains the seed of an entire alternative reading of the biblical narrative.

My final example concerns the sinister potential Vital discerns in certain intimate friendships between a mostly righteous and a mostly wicked person.[79] In such friendships, a variety of soul-sparks from one soul-root have arrived through *gilgul* in the two friends. One person has mostly righteous sparks, but some wicked sparks; the other has the converse. The righteous person befriends the wicked person ostensibly out of love, to induce them to repent. Vital declares, however, that, in reality, the friendship inures solely to the benefit of the righteous person. The mostly righteous person draws all the righteous sparks out of the mostly wicked person; the wicked person, in turn, receives all the wicked sparks from the mostly righteous person. The outcome is one wholly righteous person and one wholly wicked person. This relationship, like the others, seems to "fuse" love and aggressiveness, but in a sinister, ultimately fatal, manner.

Vital portrays this relationship in rather stilted syntax, perhaps a symptom of its rather shocking character. He flips between second and third person and between the descriptive and the imperative modes. I have added some bracketed words to facilitate reading this excerpt, though with the risk of mitigating its significant awkwardness:

> The righteous person pursues the wicked person [ostensibly?] to benefit him. [However,] perhaps the wicked person has sparks that were lost to you, and his wicked sparks were given to you. And through their binding together [i.e., the binding of the wicked person and righteous person] in desire and love, then the good that was in him will be removed from him and given to you. And then you will be perfected in goodness, and he will be perfected in all evil. . . . And the coals, which are the sparks of evil, that are within you, you will pour on his head.[80]

The shifting between second and third person perhaps reflects an uncertainty about the precise configuration of beneficence and malevolence in this relationship. Is Vital suggesting that the righteous person is not wholly conscious of the destructive consequences of his putatively altruistic friendship for the wicked person? Or perhaps it is Vital himself who is ambivalent about these rather ruthless power dynamics — dynamics that the unflinching Freudian gaze has helped us understand?

Intertextuality Terminable and Interminable

In the introduction, I forecast that the juxtaposition of Freud and Vital would show that reflection on *gilgul* implicates fundamental existential challenges, not merely occult curiosities. Some readers may think that I at times deviated from that demonstration, particularly in the preceding section. Disputes about whose body will claim a soul at the final resurrection, the fragmentation of a soul among a number of individual human beings, exchange of good and evil sparks between individuals: can these be anything other than occult themes or exotic objects of eccentric historiography?

I think not. I was drawn to discussing these topics in Vital precisely by reading him with Freud. Freud's theories of instinctual ambivalence and introjection provided me with keys to imaginatively embrace what initially seemed the peculiar, sinister, or absurd features of Vital's sprawling expositions. Once I had done so, though, those features often took me beyond such keys, both radicalizing Freud's vision and demanding further Freudian commentary.

If I had unlimited space for this chapter, I would turn back to psychoanalysis for reflection on the preceding section. I would, for example, introduce such notions as "the power of the dead Oedipal father," the "persistence of intergenerational trauma" — and then turn back to the kabbalistic text for further imaginative expansion, and so on indefinitely. Those analyses must await another day. But the self-limitation of this chapter to specific textual juxtapositions between Freud and Vital is not due simply to space limitations. The dialogue between psychoanalysis and kabbalah, two discourses confronting the deepest existential questions, is by its nature interminable — at least for those of us living, to borrow Chajes's phrase, "between worlds."

Notes

1. I thank my study partners, Jill Hammer, Roly Matalon and Ruby Namdar, without whom I could not have delved so deeply into the *Sha'ar Ha-Gilgulim*.

2. Ḥayyim Vital, *Sha'ar Ha-Gilgulim in Peirush Matok Midvash* (Jerusalem: Mekhon Da'at Yosef, 2006) [hereinafter SHMM], *Hakdamah* 14, I:182 (emphasis added). I provide additional explication of this passage below in Section IV. Cf. Assaf Tamari, "Human Sparks: Readings in the Lurianic Theory of Transmigration and Its Concept of the Human Subject" (MA thesis, Tel Aviv University, 2009) [Hebrew].

3. See, e.g., Ḥayyim Vital, *Sefer Ha-Gilgulim: Traité des Révolutions des Âmes*, trans. Edgard Jouet, rev. Francois Secret (Milan: Archè, 1987). Jouet drew on Knorr von Rosenroth's *De Revolutionibus Animarum, a Latin translation of Vital's Sefer Ha-Gilgulim, in Kabbala Denudata*, vol. 2 (Sulzbach: A. Lichtenthaler 1677).

4. SHMM *Hakdamah* 4, I:68.

5. I believe that the attempts to provide translations of these terms that would meaningfully differentiate them have proved futile. I leave them, therefore, in transliterated form.

6. See Scholem's comment that he knew of "dozens of better mythological concepts of the soul" than Freud's. Joseph Dan, "Foreword" to Gershom Scholem, *On the Mystical Shape of the Godhead: Basic Concepts in the Kabbalah* (New York: Schocken Books, 1991), 6.

7. See, for example, the summary in Steven M. Wasserstrom, *Religion after Religion: Gershom Scholem, Mircea Eliade, and Henry Corbin at Eranos* (Princeton: Princeton University Press, 1999), 189–90.

8. See, e.g., Daniel Abrams, *Ten Psychoanalytic Aphorisms on the Kabbalah* Los Angeles: Cherub Press, 2011); Nathaniel Berman, *Divine and Demonic in the Poetic Mythology of the Zohar: The "Other Side" of Kabbalah* (The Hague: Brill 2018); Clemence Boulouque, *On the Edge of the Abyss* (MS 2022); Ruth Kara Ivanov-Kaniel, *Birth in Kabbalah and Psychoanalysis* (Berlin: De Gruyter, 2022); Havivah Pedaya, *Kabbalah and Psychoanalysis* (Tel-Aviv: Yedi'ot aḥaronot, Sifre ḥemed, 2015) [Hebrew]; Elliot R. Wolfson, *Language, Eros, Being: Kabbalistic Hermeneutics and Poetic Imagination* (New York: Fordham University Press, 2004); Elliot R. Wolfson, *Through a Speculum that Shines: Vision and Imagination in Medieval Jewish Mysticism* (Princeton: Princeton University Press, 1994). See

also Jonathan Garb, *Yearnings of the Soul: Psychological Thought in Modern Kabbalah* (Chicago: University of Chicago Press, 2015).

9. Sigmud Freud, *New Introductory Lectures on Psychoanalysis* (1933), trans. James Strachey, in *The Standard Edition of the Complete Psychological Works of Sigmund Freud* [hereinafter SE], vol. XXII (London: Hogarth Press, 1954), 79. I note the oft-cited fact that the English translations' use of "the ego" and "the id" somewhat distort Freud's simple German "*das Ich*," "the I" and "*das Es*," "the It."

10. Freud, *New Introductory Lectures*, 75.

11. Freud, *New Introductory Lectures*, 72–73.

12. Freud, *New Introductory Lectures*, 79.

13. Freud compares his unseating of the notion that "man is sovereign in his own soul" to Copernicus's cosmological revolution. See "One of the Difficulties of Psycho-Analysis," *International Journal of Psychoanalysis* 1 (1920): 20. See also Ruth Kara Ivanov-Kaniel, *The Feminine Messiah: King David in the Image of the Shekhinah in Kabbalistic Literature* (The Hague: Brill 2021), 134–64.

14. Sigmund Freud, *The Ego and the Id* (1923), SE, vol. XIX, 29.

15. Freud, *The Ego and the Id* (emphasis added).

16. Freud, *The Ego*, 29–30.

17. Freud, *The Ego*, 29–30.

18. Freud, *The Ego*, 29–30.

19. Freud, *The Ego*, 28.

20. Freud, *Mourning and Melancholia* (1918), SE, vol. XIV, 255.

21. Freud, *The Ego*, 29.

22. Freud, *The Ego*, 30–31.

23. Freud, *The Ego*, 31.

24. Freud, *New Introductory Lectures*, 62.

25. Freud, *New Introductory Lectures*, 62.

26. Freud, *New Introductory Lectures*, 66.

27. See James A. Godley, "Introduction," in *Inheritance in Psychoanalysis*, ed. Joel Goldbach and James A. Godley (Albany: State University of New York Press, 2018), 4–5.

28. See, e.g., Nicolas Abraham and Maria Torok, *The Shell and The Kernel: Renewals of Psychoanalysis*, trans. Nicholas T. Rand (Chicago: University of Chicago Press, 1994), 99-156; Melanie Klein, *The Psychoanalysis of Children*, trans. Alix Strachey (New York: Delacorte Pres, 1975), 123-278. I am engaged in specific textual juxtapositions, not comparative disciplinary generalizations.

29. SHMM, *Hakdamah* 2, I:27. On *ibbur*, see Lawrence Fine, *Physician of the Soul, Healer of the Cosmos: Isaac Luria and his Kabbalistic Fellowship* (Stanford: Stanford University Press, 2003), 300–60; Moshe Idel, "The Secret of Impregnation as Metempsychosis," in *Verwandlungen*, ed. Aleida and Jan Assmann (Munich: Wilhelm Fink Verlag, 2006), 341–79; Shaul Magid, *From Metaphysics to Midrash: Myth, History, and the Interpretation of Scripture in Lurianic Kabbalah* (Bloomington: Indiana University Press, 2008), 111–42.

30. Gershom Scholem, *On the Mystical Shape of the Godhead* (New York: Schocken, 1991), 221–22.

31. See especially SHMM, *Hakdamah* 22, I:249–76.

32. J. H. Chajes, *Between Worlds: Dybbuks, Exorcists, and Early Modern Judaism* (Philadelphia: University of Pennsylvania Press, 2003). See also Yoram Bilu, "Dybbuk and Maggid: Two Cultural Patterns of Altered Consciousness in Judaism," *AJS Review* 21, no. 2 (1996): 341–66.

33. Iris Marion Young, "Pregnant Subjectivity and the Limits of Existential Phenomenology," in *Descriptions*, ed. C. Ihde and H. Silverman (Albany: State University of New York Press, 1985), 25–34.

34. Young, "Pregnant Subjectivity," 33.

35. SHMM, *Hakdamah* 2, I:27, 33.

36. Chajes, *Between Worlds*, 24–25.

37. Freud, *The Ego and the Id*, 30.

38. On David, kabbalah, and psychoanalysis, see Ruth Kara Ivanov-Kaniel, *Holiness and Transgression: Mothers of the Messiah in the Jewish Myth* (Boston: Academic Studies Press, 2017); *The Feminine Messiah: King David in the Image of the Shekhinah in Kabbalistic Literature* (The Hague: Brill, 2021).

39. *The Hebrew Bible, with Translation and Commentary by Robert Alter* (New York: W.W. Norton & Co., 2019), 1290.

40. See, for instance, 1 Samuel 20:17.

41. SHMM, *Hakdamah* 3, I:38.

42. 1 Samuel 18:1. I have translated this verse in a way that makes clear its relation to Vital's discussion.

43. 1 Samuel 20:14–17.

44. SHMM, *Hakdamah* 2, I:29–30.

45. SHMM, *Hakdamah* 2, I:31.

46. SHMM, *Hakdamah* 2, I:32.

47. SHMM, *Hakdamah* 2, I:32.

48. SHMM *Hakdamah* 2, I:32.

49. SHMM, *Hakdamah* 5, I:74–75.

50. SHMM, *Hakdamah* 2, I:28.

51. On other gender-shifting implications of *gilgul*, see Shaul Magid, *From Metaphysics to Midrash: Myth, History, and the Interpretation of Scripture in Lurianic Kabbala* (Bloomington: Indiana University Press, 2008), 111–42.

52. Ḥayyim Vital, *Sha'ar Ha-Miẓvot* (Jerusalem: Schoenbaum & Weiss, 1905), 43b.

53. Vital, *Sha'ar Ha-Miẓvot*, 43b.

54. Chages, *Between Worlds*, 23. See *Sha'ar Hamiẓvot*, 43b.

55. "Ma'aseh Ha-Ru'aḥ," printed in SHMM, II:561–63. See the discussion in *Between Worlds*, 85–87.

56. While the word "*palil*" usually means "judge" or "religious judge," Ḥayyim Vital often uses it to describe experts in demons and clairvoyant practices.

57. *The Ego and the Id*, 30–31.

58. SHMM, *Hakdamah* 22, I:249–76.

59. "Ma'aseh Ha-Ruah," SHMM II:563.

60. See, e.g., Sigmund Freud, "A Seventeenth-Century Demonological Neurosis" (1923), in SE IX, 67–106; Sigmund Freud, *Totem and Taboo* (1913), in SE XIII, 61; Diane Jonte-Pace, "The Psychoanalyst and Exorcist: Perspectives on Psychology and Religion," *Explore* 2 (1999): 4–11; Graeme Taylor, "Demoniacal Possession and Psychoanalytic Theory," *British Journal of Medical Psychology* (1978): 53–60.

61. For a taste of the vast literature of feminist critique of Freudian psychoanalysis, see the important essays in Charles Bernheimer and Claire Kahane, eds., *In Dora's Case: Freud — Hysteria — Feminism* (New York: Columbia University Press, 1985).

62. See, e.g., Lisa Appignanesi and John Forrester, *Freud's Women: Family, Patients, Followers* (New York: Basic Books, 1992).

63. J. H. Chajes, "Women Leading Women (and Attentive Men): Early Modern Jewish Models of Pietistic Female Authority," in *Jewish Religious Leadership: Image and Reality*, ed. Jack Wertheimer (New York: Jewish Theological Seminary Press, 2004), 237–62.

64. Chajes, *Between Worlds*, 111–13.

65. Freud, *New Introductory Lectures*, 102.

66. Freud, *New Introductory Lectures*, 102.

67. Sigmund Freud, "Analysis Terminable and Interminable," SE XXIII, 245.

68. Freud, "Analysis Terminable, SE XXIII, 245.

69. *The Ego and the Id*, 41.

70. *The Ego and the Id*, 41.

71. Cf. Arthur M. Arkin, "A Short Note on Empedocles and Freud," *American Imago* 6, no. 3 (1949): 197–203.

72. B. Pesahim, 68b.

73. SHMM, *Hakdamah* 4, I:69.

74. Yosef Ḥayyim ben Eliyahu, *Sefer Ben Yehoyada* (Jerusalem: Salomon, 1898), IV:107c [Hebrew].

75. SHMM, *Hakdamah* 7, I:110–12.

76. SHMM, *Hakdamah* 20, I:112.

77. SHMM, *Hakdamah* 20, I:112.

78. Vital cites Psalms 3:3 as a proof-text. If translated in accordance with Vital's understanding, it would read: "Many say to my *nefesh*, 'there is no salvation for it from God.'" Vital explains that the "it" in the latter part of the verse refers to David's body.

79. SHMM, *Hakdamah* 20, I:229–31.

80. SHMM, *Hakdamah* 20, I:229–31.

SHAUL MAGID

Reincarnation (*Gilgul*) as Traversing Boundaries of Identity from Lurianic Kabbalah to Joel Teitelbaum of Satmar

10

KABBALAH IS OFTEN CONCERNED, even obsessed, with boundaries and negotiating religious space between binaries and ostensibly irreconcilable entities. Largely through the realm of metaphysics and cosmology, kabbalists often suggest inversion as a path toward the reconciliation of ontological opposites where one thing becomes another as an instantiation of its own fulfilment. In this essay, I explore the notion of reincarnation (*gilgul neshamot*) first in the works of R. Hayyim Vital (1543–1620), R. Isaac Luria's erstwhile disciple, and later in the writings of Hasidic masters belonging to the Satmar dynasty. In these sources, *gilgul* is presented as a potent theosophical mechanism for transcending boundaries and affecting kabbalistic inversions, whereby differences between Jew and gentile, pure and impure, sacred and the demonic, become erased as a prelude for redemption of the soul.

Reincarnation[1] assumes a central position as a full-fledged theological doctrine in two works attributed to Hayyim Vital, *Sha'ar ha-Gilgulim* and *Sefer ha-Gilgulim* and in various later works, such as *Gilgulei Neshamot* attributed to Menachem Azaria de-Fano (1548–1620).[2] In general, in post-Zoharic literature, the three main reasons for *gilgul* are (1) to punish those whose sins remained uncleansed during one's life; (2) to rectify a particular commandment (*miẓvah*); and (3) to complete unfinished business with people, who are still alive.[3] The prevalence of discussions centered on *gilgul* in sixteenth-century works, such as *Galya Raza*, led Rachel Elior to posit that it may have been a reflection of broader social concerns, such as infant mortality, that plagued several Jewish communities at that time. The child who died, was perceived to have been a reincarnated soul, who needed to tarry only briefly in this world to make amends for previous transgressions before the soul's departure from corporeal existence.[4]

This essay will turn to another aspect of *gilgul* that has received far less attention in scholarly literature. Developed primarily in the Lurianic corpus and subsequently adopted and modified in Satmar Hasidism, *gilgul* is deployed as a theosophic trope that enables the soul to transverse what some consider the impenetrable boundaries separating Jew and gentile. The notion begins to take form in Lurianic Kabbalah around the idea of conversion which I have argued elsewhere may have informed Lurianic doctrine in the generations following the return of conversos to Judaism in the sixteenth century.[5] More generally it suggests that the convert consists of a gentile body that houses at least certain dimensions of a Jewish soul in need of return to the collective body of Israel. An extension of the notion of *gilgul* as a tool to move from the Jew to the gentile and back again may have been an inchoate Zoharic idea, developed and expanded in new ways in Lurianic Kabbalah. Using the binaries of good and evil, the Zohar complicates and even deconstructs these concepts, whereby each becomes codependent on the other in intricate ways.

The kabbalistic notion that evil needs to be included in the good, "the left contained in the right," coined by Elliot R. Wolfson in an essay by that name, appears already in the Middle Ages in the works of Joseph of Hamadan, among others, who arguably contributed to the Zoharic corpus.[6] The indwelling of the holy in the profane and the profane in the holy — and the necessity of such intermingling as part of a redemptive vision of rectification, or *tikkun*, becomes a major trope for interpreters of the Zohar, specifically among the disciples of R. Isaac Luria. Elsewhere, Wolfson puts it this way, "The ideal of piety — typified by the patriarchs and Moses — consists rather of plumbing the depths of the demonic, for only by doing so does one unite the right and the left and thereby attain gnosis of the collapse of the identity or nonidentity of opposites that bespeaks the true unity of the Godhead."[7] While this idea more generally may or may not have been inspired by issues of Christian influences on the Zohar or returning conversos in sixteenth-century Iberia and Safed, by the time we reach Hasidism in the late eighteenth and early nineteenth centuries it becomes standard doctrine and is used by some Hasidic masters in interesting and provocative ways.[8] For example, the descent of the righteous one (the *ẓaddik*) to redeem the dispersed sparks of holiness is a central tenet of Hasidic *ẓaddikism*.[9]

I further demonstrate in this chapter that *gilgul* in the Lurianic tradition extends far beyond the three functions mentioned above and becomes a cipher for the correct decoding and understanding of the Hebrew Bible and important characters therein. More importantly, *gilgul* is used as a critical mechanism to traverse the border separating Jew and gentile to redeem lost sparks embedded in the husks of evil (*kelipot*). Once the concept of *gilgul* reaches Hasidism, its mythic frame exhaustive details of soul fragmentation largely disappears but its function as a catalyst for connecting Jew and gentile, remains. For the purpose of illustrating the dynamic function of *gilgul* in the Lurianic corpus, I examine the relationship between Abraham and his idolatrous father Teraḥ, followed by Moses, Balaam, and Job, to problematize the porous boundaries between Jew and gentile. In the second part of this chapter, I examine a number of sources drawn from the Hungarian Hasidic tradition of Satmar where *gilgul* is associated with religious conversion. Finally, I conjecture that *gilgul* constitutes an integral part of the process of conversion, which both Lurianic kabbalists and Hasidic thinkers introduce as a necessary, even crucial, part of the redemptive process without which remnants of the holy would remain embedded in the dross of creation, preventing the descent of "new souls" into the world, tasked to impel it toward an intended eschatological aspiration.[10]

Entangled Souls: Abraham, Teraḥ, and Job in Hayyim Vital's *Sha'ar Ha-Pesukim*

From the rabbinic tradition onward, the notion of Abraham emerging from an idolatrous father has inspired numerous interpretations. Famous ones include the midrashic rendering that emphasize Abraham's rebellion against his father, Teraḥ's paganism by destroying his idols to prove their powerlessness against a divinity who was conceptualized as a single omnipotent ruler above all other celestial powers.[11] Abraham's complex pedigree helped inspire the notion of *Ẓaddik ben rasha*, the righteous one who emerges from evil stock, as a paradigm of Jewish heroism that we encounter in the stories of famous rabbinic figures, such as Rabbi Akiva.[12] Lurianic kabbalists are particularly interested in these kind of border crossings: between the evil and the righteous, between false religion and true worship, between wickedness and good that comes from evil. As is often the case, *gilgul* is frequently deployed as a tool to decipher the ambiguities of such a traversing and the ironies of the erasure of boundaries. In his commentary to the Book of Job in *Sha'ar Ha-Pesukim*, Hayyim Vital explores this in some detail.

Through carefully constructed exegesis, Vital connects three Biblical figures — Teraḥ, Abraham, and Job — prompting us to delve into questions of relationality among them.[13] While the categories of Jew and non-Jew as historically and religiously conditioned categories cannot yet apply to Teraḥ and Abraham at this point of the Biblical narrative, nevertheless in the rabbinic mind the former denotes false religion while the latter stands for true and correct belief discovered or acquired through prophecy. In this reading, Abraham comes to represent the quintessential embodiment of the concept of *ẓaddik ben rasha*, one who is fundamentally righteous while ostensibly having been born to a wicked parent. Vital suggests that the necessary mixing of good and evil in Abraham's soul accounts for his unique status as *ẓaddik ben rasha* and this process is ultimately connected to the concept of *gilgul*.

> You already know from *Sha'ar Ha-Gilgulim* that holy souls are given over to the *kelipot* (evil forces) by means of the sin of Adam. Thus, every time a Jew sins, that sin will continue to exist under the aegis of the *kelipot*. And when the *kelipot* see a particularly lofty soul they desire to trap it so that it is destroyed and thus cannot be rectified and will remain with them (the *kelipot*) always. Thus, they implant [this lofty soul] with the seed of an evildoer. This is the secret of a *Ẓaddik ben* [son of a] *rasha*, as it says, *who can make the pure impure? No one*. (Job 14:4). Thus, it is not at all surprising that Abraham was born from Teraḥ. Accordingly, when the goodness in Abraham's soul is empowered, it not only rectifies his soul, but also repairs all those close to it. And this is the secret of the verse according to the sages, *As for you, you shall go to your fathers in peace* (Gen. 15:15). "Your father Teraḥ will repent." Thus he [Teraḥ] had to return as Job through reincarnation (*gilgul*), as we will explain.[14]

Vital's introduction here sets the stage for the concept of *gilgul* by deriving the totality of human experience from the original sin, and the existential conditions that characterized a post-lapsarian world in which the forces of evil (here the *kelipot*) are empowered to snatch lofty souls and subjugate them to their demonic provenance in an attempt to drain holiness from them: "Thus they implant [this lofty soul] with the seed of an evildoer." This ambiguous passage seems to imply that once the lofty soul is in the provenance of the *kelipot*, the demonic forces insert a seed of an evildoer to entrap the lofty soul there, explaining the phenomenon of a *ẓaddik ben rasha*. In addition, the righteousness of the soul has the potential to overcome its evil entrapment and thereby help to eradicate evil from the world. But this requires he/she be born into it. Two dimensions of evil are alluded to here: the first, derived from the ontological context of the *kelipot*, and the second, attributed to the seed of evil implanted in the lofty soul to prevent its escape. This will later become a crucial point.

However, the demonic tactic of implantation can at times prove unsuccessful, engendering reverse outcomes. As in the case of Abraham, if the lofty soul contains enough goodness, it can actually break free of the *kelipot* and take with itself the seed of the evil soul implanted in it. The interplay between holiness, the forces of impurity and the unanticipated consequences of spiritual operations is further substantiated in the interesting proof text using the verse, *As for you, you shall go to your fathers in peace* (Genesis 15:1). God's address to Abraham includes reassurances both concerning his future progeny, who will be enslaved but subsequently released *and afterward come forth with great sustenance*, as well his own longevity to a ripe old age. Thus, the internal soul history of Abraham becomes a template for the vicissitudes of the nation of Israel, who are first entrapped in the *kelipot* of Egypt, but are subsequently freed and set on a return journey to holiness. In this sense, we might posit that the *erev rav* (mixed multitude) were placed among the Israelites to prevent any escape from the domain of evil and it is only the strong leadership and guidance of Moses that was effective enough to redeem them from the *kelipot*.[15]

At the same time, while Abraham is successful in initiating the release of Teraḥ's soul implanted in him from the power of the *kelipot*, this soul rectification is only partially complete and Teraḥ's reincarnation into the body of Job serves to finalize this process, as we will discuss below. The theosophical concept of left contained in the right or the embeddedness of the holy in the demonic and evil within the good facilitates the purification of evil, which itself gets transformed and overturned. A particularly lofty soul can completely undermine the design of the demonic and when it does, the *kelipot* not only lose the lofty soul (which is foreign to them anyway) but also a part of its ontological nature (the evil seed planted in the lofty soul). Thus, as we will see, the holy must become embedded in the demonic and the demonic must be embedded in the holy, for the process of purification to occur.

The compounded aspect of the *kelipot* in Abraham's family is accentuated in the following passage where sin is introduced into Abraham's soul not only through the actions of his father, Teraḥ, but also through the agency of his mother, Amathlai.

> Know that Teraḥ had sex with Amathlai [his wife] when she was a menstruate. And since we know that the *kelipot* are attached to [the menstruate] the *kelipot* embedded a drop [of impurity] in the soul of Abraham in order to destroy him. And this mixture would go out from them [Teraḥ and Amathlai] at their will. This is because the *kelipot* thought that [Abraham's pure soul] would be destroyed because both parents were idolaters and in addition engaged in sinning by selling idols. And more specifically, the intercourse [that produced Abraham] occurred while she was a menstruate. And this is why Abraham is called a righteous convert (*ger ẓedek*) because he began in the midst of the *kelipot*.[16]

Sex during menstruation and the sin of idolatry now become prototypes for the domain of the demonic set to ensnare Abraham's soul. Yet Abraham's loftiness defied the calculation of the *kelipot* which sought to inflict a double dose of sin on him (illicit sex and idolatry) and he was able to free himself from their grasp through the aspect of righteousness (*ẓedek*) which was a defining quality of his soul. Thus, the biblical expression *ger ẓedek* semiotically encapsulates the binary and opposing forces of left and right, the realm of evil and the holy, the convert and the inherently righteous. By moving from being external and alien to the divine, Abraham enters the inner sanctum of his essential nature, righteousness, sanctioned by God and through this transformation he simultaneously frees himself from the yoke of the *kelipot*, separating from his demonic roots, all the while unifying these opposite attributes. In a parallel fashion, as mentioned earlier, the Israelites mirror the soul journey of Abraham and were similarly extracted by God from the forty-ninth level of defilement in Egypt. Moreover, based on this reading, all Israelites, once ensnared in Egypt, are called converts (*gerim*).

In order to establish the relevance of Job to Abraham's father Teraḥ, Vital examines more closely the illicit sexual encounter between Teraḥ and Amathlai setting the narrative stage for the Biblical figure of Job as representing the final station for the transmigration of Teraḥ's soul, which is arguably the reason that this discussion appears in his reading of Job.

> And this is the secret of what is mentioned in Zohar 3.111b, "Thus he was called Teraḥ, because God boiled (*retaḥ - Teraḥ*) [Teraḥ's seed] and grafted it onto Abraham . . . "[17] But if this boiling mixture would only anger their idols, why did God mix Abraham into all of this? The intention was that

> God mixed Abraham with this [impure] drop because God was angry that Teraḥ had sex with his wife when she was a menstruate. Thus, God found a way to trick the extraneous forces (*hiẓonim*) and remove Abraham's soul from them and also graft onto that seed [of Teraḥ] itself. By this means, the *ḥiẓonim* would not complain that he [Abraham] was taken from their domain, since the seed itself was impure.[18]

This passage poignantly illustrates the interplay between two ostensibly antagonistic entities, Teraḥ and Abraham, whose embeddedness into the nature of the other instigates the process of purification and the path to perfection. The boiling of Teraḥ's seed, Vital points out, enables the intermixing and merger of two fundamentally incompatible entities, the impure and the pure. The heat acts as a chemical activator meant to break down the barrier separating these opposing qualities making malleable and porous to receive the other. The alchemical transmutation of Teraḥ's soul begins with God grafting the soul of Abraham onto his as a subterfuge to eventually extricate Teraḥ from a deep state of impurity. The secret of reincarnation, unknown to the *kelipot*, opened the possibility for Teraḥ's soul to continue its transformation and complete its purification finally in Job without alerting the *kelipot* that deemed the seed of Teraḥ so defiled that it could never be purified, even if it was not under their domain. In addition, this would result in evil descending into the world through Teraḥ. At the same time, by underscoring that Abraham's soul was itself in need of rectification because its roots in Adam came under the influence of unholiness through the worship of idols, Vital situates the concept of reincarnation as concomitant with the beginning of humankind.[19]

> God grafted many such drops from other souls onto Teraḥ, through the principle of sin and punishment (*middah kneged middah*, more lit. "getting your just desserts") because Abraham was Adam, who served idols. Thus, he was the son of Teraḥ, who was an idolatrous priest. Afterward he [Abraham] was rectified because when he went into the fiery furnace, he did not commit idolatry[20] . . . as we read in the Zohar on the verse *who can make the pure impure* (Job 14:4). *No one*, that is, it is impossible to extract a pure soul from the defiled *kelipah* without first embedding in it a drop of impurity.[21]

The idea expressed by Vital in the last sentence above leads to an intriguing theoretical speculation positing that an impure seed intermingled with a lofty soul has two theosophical functions. First, it enables the impure seed to be lifted from its impurity (at least provisionally so) through its relation to the lofty soul in which it is embedded. Second, the lofty soul embedded in the *kelipot* needs impure seed within it, to extricate itself from its impure state. This idea is furthered supported by reference to the righteous who have descended from gentiles: "With this you can understand why some *Ẓaddikim* come from gentiles or are children of evildoers or ignoramuses (*'amei ha-aretz*). I already told you in *Sha'ar Gilgulim* that Teraḥ was Abraham's father, and both were from the soul-root of Abel, but they entered the *kelipot* and Teraḥ's soul was the excess [of Abel's soul] that was mixed with the soul of Abraham. Thus, it unfolded (*nitgalgel*) and was fixed in that way.[22] Thus, Abraham also facilitated his father's repentance."[23] The necessity of the impure in the pure is that this is the only way a pure soul can do the work of rectification once inside the demonic (*kelipot*). If the lofty soul would become ensnared in the demonic and succeed in extricating itself without also containing within it a drop of impurity, no redemptive work would be accomplished. The demonic would remain unaltered. However, if a seed of evil becomes part of the lofty soul, then when it frees itself, it also liberates that drop of evil within it and the *kelipot* are weakened through that process. The notion of *ẓaddik ben rasha* then becomes a necessary part of redemptive history. But the drop of evil within him/her still awaits a final purification that is accomplished through *gilgul*. The *ẓaddik ben rasha* becomes the motif of the lofty soul that contains within itself seeds of impurity that need to be brought forth in a final redemptive act. *Gilgul* is thus introduced as the completion of this process of distillation and clarification from the state of impurity to a status of purity.

Reincarnation as a vehicle for the purification of the soul is underscored in the narrative as both the father and mother of Abraham, Teraḥ and Amathlai, are depicted as undergoing rectification as a couple in the person of Job and his wife Dinah bat Leah, respectively.[24] The hermeneutic parallel between Amathlai Teraḥ's wife, Dinah, Job's wife, and Jacob's daughter Dinah mentioned in Genesis 30:21, is further supported by other exegetical parallels among the three women. Accordingly, just as Amathlai had forced sexual intercourse with Teraḥ as a menstruate, Dinah Jacob's daughter was raped by the Hittite prince, Shekhem ben Hamor. The inappropriate sexual episode of Teraḥ and Amathlai required further rectification which unfolded through the transmigration of their souls in Job and his wife, Dina bat Leah. The intricate relationship between gendered acts of sin and their diverse forms of rectification is poignantly depicted by Vital:

There is yet another consequence to all this. The verse states, *her menstruation shall be upon him* (Lev. 15:24). That is, one who has sex with a menstruate, the defiled [substance] of the menstruation is transferred (lit. jumps) to the male. And thus, Shekhem ben Hamor carried [that impurity with him] with his sexual encounter with Dina. This, the impurity of Dina through menstruation [was charged to him] while she remained pure and untainted.

Afterward she [Dina bat Leah — a reincarnation of the Jacob's daughter Dina mentioned in Genesis] married Job, as the sages say. Therefore, Job contracted leprosy (*zara'at*) because he had sex with his wife who was a menstruate, as we see in Zohar 2.33b, "no one contracts leprosy who did not have sex with a menstruate." He was punished by leprosy, as it is known. But since Dina bat Leah had sex [in a previous incarnation as Jacob's daughter] with Shekhem ben Hamor, that punishment [of reincarnation into Job's wife] was sufficient [for her]. And as we said earlier, all the impurity [of menstruation] was inflicted on Shekhem. And she [Dina, Jacob's daughter] was pure.

I heard from my master that Teraḥ raped his wife who was a menstruate. And consequently, he was struck with leprosy. It was sufficient for her, however, because it was forced, that she would later be raped by Shekhem in order to purify her of any poison [of the first rape with Teraḥ] and thus she would not have to be stricken with boils.[25]

The above passages further complicate Vital's use of the concept of *gilgul* introducing the narrative elements of gender, rape, and the ritual impurity of menstruation. Transgression for menstrual impurity during intercourse is directly ascribed to both partners but Teraḥ is held up as the one requiring greater purification as he instigated and forced this violation on his menstruant wife. One is struck by the ostensible gender disparity in the passage that sees Teraḥ's wife being raped in consecutive incarnations, first as Amathlai and later as Dinah, Jacob's daughter. As a passive and unblemished victim of her husband's lust, the impurity he instilled in her could only be removed by the impurity of another embodied by the Biblical figure of Shekhem, an outsider to the family of Abraham. Job's leprosy serves as the final purification of Teraḥ's sin, while Job's wife Dina, a *gilgul* of Amathlai and Jacob's daughter Dinah, was not in need of further purification because the first menstruate sex-act was no longer defiling for her. For Vital then *gilgul* functions not only as a vehicle for a soul to rectify past sins but also as part of a lengthy process of liberating the pure from the impure and traversing the border between false religion (Teraḥ) and true religion (Abraham). In each case, one must be embedded in the other (impure/pure, demonic / holy) for the system to work. And *gilgul* provides the operative frame for all these processes to unfold.

Gilgul in Hungarian Hasidism: Moses of Teitelbaum, Yekutiel Yehuda Teitelbaum, and Joel Teitelbaum

Hasidism emerged in late eighteenth century Eastern Europe, in a fundamentally different historical and social context than what characterized the rise of Lurianic Kabbalah in the sixteenth-century Levant in the aftermath of the expulsion from Iberia and an influx of returning conversos. While the most defining historical movement of the seventeenth century, Sabbateanism, left an indelible mark on Hasidism, the exact nature of this influence remains a matter of scholarly debate.[26] Yet it is a matter of broad consensus that Hasidic ritual and theology were directly informed by the Lurianic tradition which by the eighteenth century had become ubiquitous, even canonical, in Eastern Europe.[27] A close examination of a series of Hasidic texts derived from the Hungarian Hasidic tradition — Moses Teitelbaum of Ujhely (1759–1841), Yekutiel Yehuda Teitelbaum (1808–1883) of Szighet, and Joel Teitelbaum of Satmar (1887–1979) — allows me to posit points of contact with, and divergence from, earlier Lurianic doctrines concerning the concept of *gilgul* as a vehicle for traversing the ostensibly opaque boundaries between holy and profane, the Jew and the gentile.

As a student of Jacob Isaac Horowitz, the Seer of Lublin (1745–1815), Moshe Teitelbaum began his rabbinic career in Przemysl in southeastern Poland and moved to Ujhely in 1808 which at that time was part of the Austria-Hungarian Empire, today Hungary, where he is often considered as one of the founders of Hungarian Hasidism. Author of many works, M. Teitelbaum's two volume *Yismaḥ Moshe,* first published in 1849, contains densely constructed homilies on the Torah and is widely considered to be his most popular work.

In general, the engagement of Hasidic masters with the details of reincarnation was less pronounced than the treatment promulgated by Lurianic kabbalists. A case in point, Hasidism did not produce texts similar in breadth or complexity to Vital's *Sha'ar Ha-Gilgulim* and *Sefer Gilgulim*, or Menahem Azariah da Fano's *Gilgulei Neshamot*. *Gilgul* was simply an accepted maxim used selectively to offer an interpretation of specific biblical or rabbinic texts.[28] M. Teitelbaum offers an intriguing reading of Deut. 26:5 in his

Yismaḥ Moshe framed by precept of "arousal from below" (*hitorerut d'le-tata*) deployed as a mechanism for awakening supernal grace to aid a person's rescue from the domain of evil and sin.[29] The operating mechanism for this reading is what M. Teitelbaum calls "*gilgul ha-kadum*" loosely rendered as a "previous *gilgul*" and called "father" in relation to subsequent *gilgulim*. Teitelbaum claims that this idea is part of Luria's understanding of *Ẓaddik ben rasha*.[30] Here Teitelbaum uses this term to link "father" to a previous *gilgul* as a way to explain the verse *My father was an Aramean*." The implication is that, the "below" in "arousal from below," refers to the previous *gilgul* of the *rasha* (Teraḥ or Aramean) that can fix the soul the *Ẓaddik*. The citation below picks up in the middle of a long discussion about sacrifices as expiation for sin.

> The principle here is that one should arouse the kindness of God even if one is still stuck in the depths of sin from head to toe. Nevertheless, the way of God is that an arousal from below is like a sewing needle that can end in goodness.[31] In addition, this arousal from below is efficacious if one hangs onto it and keeps it close such that this will alleviate the sin, as it is written, *I held him and did not let go* (Song of Songs 3:4). I said before God, "even if according to my deeds I should abandon hope, but I trust your mercy because that is your way." And this is what the verse means, *my father was an Aramean* (Deut. 26:5). It is known that the previous *gilgul* (*gilgul ha-kadum*) is called "father" juxtaposed to later *gilgulim*, as is taught by the Ari z"l regarding a *Ẓaddik ben rasha*.[32] As is known, all souls are embedded in the depths of the *kelipot* due to Adam's sin.[33] Afterwards concerning the generation of Babel [lit. the generation of division] it is known that the generation of Egypt rectified it [the generation of Babel] with *mortar and bricks* (Ex. 1:14) which mirrors [what is said about the generation of Babel], *And they said to each other, let us bake bricks and burn them hard* (Gen. 11:3). And the mortar (*hemar*) was for them like a donkey (*hamor*). In Egypt they were embedded even more deeply, as they were at the forty ninth level of impurity. And it is known there were seventy princes of impurity, thirty on the right and thirty-five on the left, and thus there were seventy languages, and you [Israel] are a holy people.[34] And *lashon ha-kodesh* cuts through [the seventy languages].[35]

The notion of *gilgul* at both the individual and the national levels (Babel and Egypt), plays an intrinsic role in repentance implying first, that *gilgul* can be a consequence of sin, thus caused and instigated by it (*gilgul ha-kadum*), and second, that *gilgul* can at the same time serve to erase and abrogate a transgression. Israel, as a nation poised to stand among seventy princes and seventy languages suggests an imbricated relationship between the powers of defilement and holiness. Thus, the trajectory of Israelite history is predicated on extricating itself from the *gilgul ha-kadum* (Adam's sin, sometimes rendered as "primordial sin" followed by *my father was an Aramean)* to be resolved later through *gilgul* in the generation of Egypt. Teitelbaum offers a carefully constructed reading of disparate Biblical themes and passages — the Israelites in Egypt with the serpent in the Garden of Eden — and later using the etymological similitude of Hebrew words, *'avrah* (Egypt), *'arum* (the naked serpent) *'erev* (*'erev rav* or the mixed multitude), that are tightly interwoven to offer an innovative interpretation of *gilgul.*

> Egypt is a *naked ('ervat) land*, totally impure from the seventy princes.[36] Therefore, the king of Egypt had to know the seventy languages. It is known that regarding the 288 sparks that fell [into the netherworld], Moses was able to elevate most (*rov*), as it is written, *And the erev rav (mixed multitude) went up with them* (Ex.12:38). This refers to the 288 fallen sparks. But the essence of the holy also fell. Moses was able to elevate the *'erev rav* himself but God had to elevate the essential nature of Israel. Understand this. And thus, it says [regarding the verse *My father was an Aramean ... he went down to Egypt ... and sojourned there with a few people* (Deut. 26:5)]. *An Aramean*, that means Satan and the evil inclination, as [Moshe] Alshekh and *Or ha-Hayyim* explain.[37] It states, *The serpent was naked* (*'arum*) (Gen. 3:1), *my father served*, referring to the primordial *gilgul*; *went down to Egypt*, there was a descent into Egypt, where they were deeply embedded in the *kelipot; and sojourned there*, this refers to the primordial *gilgul; with few people*, this refers to the people there who were embedded in the forty ninth level of defilement, under the power of the seventy princes.[38]

The connection between Egypt as "naked" (violators) and the serpent as "naked" (deceptive/demonic) suggests that both refer to illicit sexual encounters and embody the realm of impurity.[39] This then connects to the Aramean (sharing the same root ARM), which is the *gilgul ha-kadum*, that serves as the center of this section of the homily. What is added here is the 288 fallen sparks and the notion that Moses could only uplift the majority (*rov/rav*) which connects him to the *'erev rav*, (*And the 'erev rav went up with them*, Ex. 12:28).[40] At this point Teitelbaum re-reads the verse in question, *My father was an Aramean ... My father* refers to the *gilgul ha-kadum*; *Aramean* is Satan; *went down to Egypt* signifies the realm of the *kelipot*; *and sojourned there*, this refers to the necessary dwelling of the Israelites among the *kelipot*, until the time that they were finally removed — some by Moses (*'erev rav*) and the rest, by God.

The entire story of the descent and liberation from Egypt is connected to the ensnarement of the serpent (the sin of Adam, which puts all souls under the aegis of the *kelipot*), and the previous *gilgul* of the Aramean from which Israel successfully emerged. Teitelbaum's homily reinforces his initial theosophical statement that emphasizes the enduring possibility of freeing oneself from the depth of sinfulness through recourse to the theurgical principle of "arousal from below." In contrast to Lurianic texts that delve deeply into deconstructing the complex nature of the soul, Teitelbaum seems to highlight the infinite potential of human repentance, as a Jew and as the nation of Israel, that opens the path from a past of sin to a redemptive future, from impurity to purity, and lastly, from gentile to Jew. For him, Israelite history and even more so, the biblical narrative, cannot be comprehended without recourse to the concept of *gilgul* which facilitates the traversing of borders and boundaries which normally separate between binaries.

Yekutiel Yehudah Teitelbaum is known by the name of his collected works *Yetev Lev* that was originally published anonymously. He was the grandson of Moshe Teitelbaum and the grandfather of Joel Teitelbaum. Initially appointed the rabbi of the town of Stropkov in 1841, Y. Y. Teitelbaum eventually became the rabbi of Szighet in 1858 where he established his Hasidic court. He died in 1883 at the age of seventy-five. *Yetev Lev* largely follows in the footsteps of *Yismaḥ Moshe*, offering long, detailed homilies in the Hungarian *drush* tradition, focusing mostly on rabbinic/midrashic literature. While Kabbalah plays a role in these homilies they are not as mystically inflected as in many other Hasidic works. *Yetev Lev* mentions *gilgul* only a number of times, the two texts below being the most representative:

> We read in b. Shabbat 31a concerning the story of a gentile who comes to Shammai and Hillel and says, "I will convert if you can teach me the entire Torah while I stand on one foot." ... The commentators explain that the gentile is only instructed in seven [Noahide] commandments, but Israel has 613 corresponding to 248 limbs and 365 sinews [of the human body]. If so, how is it possible for each individual to fulfill all of them and thus rectify (*m'taken*) each limb and sinew? The gentile surmised that this was indeed impossible without the secret doctrine of *gilgul*, as it is written, *Look, all this God performs, two or three times with a*

> *man* (Job 33:29). And in every generation that he is reincarnated, he fulfils the deficiencies of the previous generations. But this explanation of necessary *gilgul* is not sufficient because there is a great danger in *gilgul*, as is widely known. Thus, the gentile says [to Shamai and Hillel] "Teach me the entire Torah that I will be able to fulfil it, while I stand on one foot," that is, in one incarnation (*gilgul aḥat*). Hillel responds, "that which you would not want your neighbor to do to you, do not do to him." Rashi explains, "such as theft." That is, relational laws (*mishpatim*). The context of this is that when there will be peace and unity, when a Jew fulfils a command (*miẓvah*) in the name of all of Israel, it is as if everyone fulfilled that *miẓvah*. And if you should say, what about land-dependent *miẓvot* that are impossible to fulfill in these times of exile? On this it is said "go and learn," that is, by studying in order to fulfill them, it is as if one fulfilled them, as we see with sacrifices.[41]

Y. Y. Teitelbaum offers an interesting reading of a very common Talmudic dicta regarding an aspiring convert's interaction with Hillel and Shammai. The assumption in the gentile's question as Y. Y. Teitelbaum reads it is twofold. First, if a Noahide can fulfil his/her obligation in seven miẓvot, why should a Jew take on 613 commandments, where that path of soul fulfillment would be impossible, certainly in the limited capacity of one lifetime? The solution to the convert's conundrum, namely how all the 613 commandments of the Torah can be fulfilled in a single lifetime, lies in Hillel's answer that follows Rashi: relational responsibility for one's fellow enables a person's performance of a *miẓvah* to satisfy another's obligation. That is, Hillel admits that one *gilgul* can never serve to complete one's obligation and thus the gentile's question is unanswerable without an interconnectedness that can only be operative through unity.

In another text embedded in a comment on the verse, *And should a stranger (ger) sojourn with you and do a Passover offering ... thus shall he do. One statute shall you have, for the stranger and for the native of the land* (Numbers 9:14), Y. Y. Teitelbaum adds an addition dimension worth considering. The context here begins with three answers he offers as to how one can fulfill commandments that are, for one reason or another, impossible to fulfill:

> First, by means of *gilgul*, *Look, all this God performs, two or three times with a man* (Job 33:29), one can fulfill the entire Torah; second, since all Jews are dependent on one another, if there is peace and unity, as it is written, *One nation in the land* (2 Samuel 7:23). In that case, all Israel has a portion

in what one does . . . third, by means of study for the sake of action, God unified those good thoughts with the action itself, as the Talmud teaches: [R. Ashi teaches] "one who intended (lit. thought) to perform a *miẓvah* and was unable to do so [due to circumstances beyond his control] it is as if he fulfilled it" (b. Berakhot 6a, b. Shabbat 63a, b. Kiddushin 40a). And yet the story is already known of one who was given a choice from the supernal worlds to choose either hell (*Gehenna*) or *gilgul* and he chose the hardship of *Gehenna* and did not want to be reincarnated again in this world, because *gilgul* is a dangerous choice, *who knows if he will be wise . . .* (Eccles. 2:19). And thus, the gentile asks, "Teach me the entire Torah that I will be able to fulfil it while I stand on one foot in order that I will not have to be reincarnated by force."[42]

The above passages emphasize the inherent danger in relying on *gilgul* as the preferred method for completing a soul's task, so much so that the punishment of hell (*Gehenna*) is specified as the penitence of choice over reincarnation. The key to understanding the danger inherent in reincarnation is to deconstruct the context of Ecclesiastes 2:19, the prooftext for the homily. The Biblical text expounds the vanity and futility of leaving behind a life of toil for another person to complete, who can be either wise or a fool. Thus, if one comes back a fool in a new incarnation, one can undermine everything that the person was able to accomplish in the previous *gilgul*. Understanding scripture hyperliterally, Y. Y. Teitelbaum uses this trope to discourage conversion to Judaism: one might successfully fulfil all the Noahide commandments as a non-Jew, but once converted to Judaism there is great danger that he/she might fail when the new obligation includes not 7 but 613 *miẓvot*. It is noteworthy that Y. Y. Teitelbaum, who rarely discussed the concept of *gilgul* in his written works, uses reincarnation as an exegetical tool in his homily to polemicize against conversion to Judaism.

Our final text written by Joel Teitelbaum further substantiates the adverse aspects of *gilgul* introduced earlier, exhibiting another dimension beyond *gilgul*'s ostensibly constructive purpose for perfecting the soul. While the Lurianic tradition emphasized the positive potential of *gilgul* that enabled the traversing and at times the blurring of binary categories (pure/impure, good/evil, Jew/gentile) thereby abetting final redemption, J. Teitelbaum underscored the corrosive aspect of *gilgul* that could prevent new souls from descending into the world, thereby jeopardizing the redemptive process.

Joel Teitelbaum of Satmar is perhaps the most eminent member of the Teitelbaum dynasty, at least to those outside the orbit of Hasidism. His work

Vayoel Moshe and *'Al ha-Geulah ve 'al Ha-Temurahi*, where he makes his halakhic and theological case against Zionism, has received much attention.[43] The text examined below is from a less-known work, his eight-volume collection of homilies on the Torah titled *Diveri Yoel*.[44] The context of this passage is an extended Talmudic discussion on the passage, "In messianic times, rebellion will increase" (b. Sotah 49b):

> The essence of the matter is that when a person does not complete his purpose in this world for which he was created, he has to return in another *gilgul*. In doing so, he is preventing new souls from descending to the world. And thus, he is preventing redemption. Therefore, a person who does not reveal the portion of the Torah that he received at Sinai in the world, and this portion cannot be revealed by another, he must come back to the world again through *gilgul* in order that his portion be revealed. We can thus understand the concluding words in Mishna Avot, "That your city should quickly be rebuilt and give us our portion (*helkeynu*) in your Torah." (Avot 5:2). And as we explained the words of the Tanna that in the messianic time (*ikvata d'mashikha*) "rebellion will increase in the world," thus he concludes with this prayer "It should be your will that your city should be rebuilt, and we will no longer require this trait [that is, *gilgul*]." Redemption does not come because one's portion has not yet been revealed, a portion that is specific to each individual Jew. Thus, it says give us "our portion" (*ḥelkeynu*) in your Torah in order that each one can reveal the portion specific to him. And thus, there will be no longer any need for *gilgul*, and the Temple should be rebuilt quickly.[45]
>
> It is known from the kabbalists that Moses taught the Israelites the portion of the Torah that was specific to them. That is what the midrash (*Yalkut Shimoni* # 3) implies by saying, 'in order that they will learn from you in subsequent generations in order to bring about redemption.' Moses said to Israel, if you act appropriately (*k'seder*) that is, if you reveal the portion of Torah that is specific to your soul, it will be as if you made me in my world. . . .[46] That is, by each individual revealing the portion of Torah that was meant for him, new souls will be able to enter into the world, and redemption will come near, and God will reign in all the land.[47]

The notion that each person has a specific *miẓvah* is a common trope in Hasidism although it has roots in earlier traditions. Teitelbaum uses this idea to justify *gilgul*, which deviates from earlier definitions that explained *gilgul* as a means to rectify sins and complete certain actions left unfinished in a previous life. Here it functions as a tool to offer another chance for someone who missed the opportunity to fulfil a specific *miẓvah* that is rooted in their soul, the very commandment for which the soul descended into the world. Yet this act of *gilgul* to offer the soul another opportunity, also prevents redemption because the returning souls prevent new souls from descending and it is those new souls that will inaugurate redemption.

Teitelbaum focuses on the locution in Avot, "who gives us our portion (*ḥelkeynu*) in your Torah," to suggest each person has a specific portion (*ḥelek*) that is specific to them and the lack of fulfillment of only that portion necessitates return in another life. This is nothing new. But *gilgul* now plays a central role in this idea. The rabbinic prayer in Avot is one that yearns for the obsolescence of *gilgul* since it is only the termination of the process of *gilgul* that will enable the descent of new souls at the time when redemption draws near (*ikvata d'mashikha*). Unfinished business—not any business but specific business, one's specific portion (*ḥelek*)—completes the work of redemption which can only be facilitated by new souls who never descended before and thus never sinned.

Furthermore, J. Teitelbaum expands here on a Lurianic idea that explains the ascent of a small portion of Adam's soul just before he sinned in the Garden of Eden, thereby guarding it from any form of contamination or direct contact with the world of degeneration symbolized by the *kelipot*. This aspect of Adam's soul that left before the sin, called *zihara 'ilai*, remained in the upper worlds unborn yet poised to descend in the endtime.[48] These upper sparks are equated with the "new souls."[49] Here, then, the traverse or border crossing transpires not between Jew and gentile, but through another categorical distinction, between souls of sin and new souls, between *kelipah* and ontological purity or sanctity. *Gilgul* aids the former and prevents the latter. *Gilgul* here is dangerous not because it may not work or because life on earth is full of agony, but because it stagnates covenantal completion, each *gilgul* is both an opportunity for the individual and a barrier for the collective. The cessation of *gilgul* enables the overcoming of original sin by allowing the new souls to descend, but *gilgul* cannot cease as long as individuals do not find their portion and fulfill it. This is arguably a cosmological rendering of exile.

Last, for J. Teitelbaum, *gilgul* carries religious value as a mechanism that serves the good but ultimately must be overcome. While he eschews directly contextualizing *gilgul* in the frame of conversion or boundary crossing, J. Teitelbaum accentuates the responsibility of each person to find the portion (*ḥelek*) specific to each soul that opens up in every new incarnation as means toward the perfection of the soul. Of course, we do not always know what that portion (*ḥelek*) is. *Gilgul* for J. Teitelbaum creates the conditions for that search.

Conclusion

There is little doubt that *gilgul* has become a kind of kabbalistically inflected canonical trope in both Lurianic Kabbalah and Hasidism. While the highly detailed template of *gilgul* that emerges in the Lurianic corpus, largely an innovation of Luria's circle and Moses Cordovero does not continue in Hasidism, the latter certainly inherits this idea and deploys it in interesting ways as an interpretive tool stripped of its mythical intricacies.[50] Whereas in the Lurianic materials examined above, *gilgul* functioned not only as a tool deployed to traverse the boundary separating Jew and gentile, what Hasidism seems to intuit from Lurianic teaching is the way *gilgul* operates to traverse boundaries only it can facilitate. That is, the opacity between the holy and profane, and the Jew and gentile, seems not opaque enough to prevent *gilgul* from reaching beyond seemingly categorical differences to draw one into the other in both necessary and productive ways. In Luria *gilgul* is explicit in viewing the intermingling of the souls of Teraḥ and Abraham, and then Teraḥ's *gilgul* in Job and his wife Dina bat Leah's *gilgul* of the Dina of Genesis, implying not only a story of menstruate sex but also rape, a process whereby the good not only extricates itself from evil but through *gilgul* and the implantation of the evil in good, evil is extricated from evil itself. Thus, the rectification of evil is through becoming part of the good that then redeems it, an idea that becomes a central motif in Sabbateanism.

The Hasidic texts examined here do not make such an explicit, or literal, case for traversing boundaries but curiously situate their discussion of *gilgul* in the Talmudic pericope of conversion in the exchange between the sages Hillel and Shammai and the aspiring convert. In addition, J. Teitelbaum suggests another layer whereby *gilgul* is both a necessary and negative phenomenon in that it procures soul completion yet prevents new souls from descending into the world. Thus the opaque categories between sinful soul and new souls, between a tainted aspect of the holy in the re-born soul, and what Luria calls "pure mercy" in the new soul, are navigated through the completion, and then cessation, of *gilgul*.

J. Teitelbaum suggests that the rabbinic prayer at the end of Avot is about beseeching God for the end of *gilgul* to make room for new souls to descend.

What the Hasidic texts add to Lurianic teaching is the granting of value to *gilgul* (necessary but also obstructive) that perhaps emerges once the intricacies of *gilgul*'s details are muted. Thus, *gilgul* provides another example whereby the canonicity of a Lurianic idea grants later thinkers the creative license to leave behind Lurianic detail and develop new vistas of meaning and understanding of a kabbalistic principle. In both cases (Luria and Hasidism), *gilgul* deconstructs the binary of opposites to show that boundaries of difference are never insurmountable. Quite the opposite, it is precisely by overcoming those boundaries that conditions are created for the telos of the covenantal promise. Israel is redeemed only when the very category of Israel is widened. This is not procured by the unification of the One as much as by the erasure of alienation and the intimacy of opposites.

Notes

1. Henceforth in the remainder of this chapter, I use the Hebrew term *gilgul* to refer to reincarnation.

2. Da Fano's *Gilgul Neshamot* was published in Lemberg in 1859. Yerucham Leiner of London from the famous Izbica Hasidic dynasty, reprinted Da Fano's book with annotations and corrections. An English translation of Leiner's edition under the title *Reincarnation of Souls* was published by the Ha-Ketav Institute in Jerusalem in 2001. In general, Lurianic Kabbalah does not make it to the European continent until about 1600. Thus, Da Fano likely had access to some Lurianic manuscripts but not the entire corpus.

3. See Moses Cordovero, *'Or Yakar* (Jerusalem: Achuzat Israel, 1962–1989), 21:3–5 and Giller, *Reading* the Zohar (New York: Oxford University Press, 2000), 39.

4. Rachel Elior, "The Doctrine of Transmigration in *Galya Raza*," reprinted in *Essential Papers in Kabbalah*, ed. L. Fine (New York: New York University Press, 1992), 243–69. We also see a similar interpretation concerning miscarriage in Joseph Ergas's *Shomer Emunim* mentioned below. While *gilgul* becomes prominent in the Lurianic tradition, it exists in earlier Kabbalah as well, in more muted form. See, for example, in Rami Shekalim, *Reshit Torat Ha-Nefesh ve Ha-Gilgul b'Kabbalah b'Meah 12-15* (Jerusalem: Self Published, 1994), 12–15.

5. See Shaul Magid, *From Metaphysics to Midrash: Myth, History, and the Interpretation of Scripture in Lurianic Kabbalah* (Bloomington: Indiana University Press, 2008), 75–110.

6. For the most recent study of Joseph of Hamadan, see Leore Sachs Shmueli, "*Sefer Ta'amei ha-Mizvot* on Negative Commandments of R. Joseph from Shushan," two vols. [PhD diss., Bar-Ilan University, 2019]. See also Elliot Wolfson, "The Left Contained in the Right: A Study in Zoharic Hermeneutics," *AJS Review* 11 (1986): 27–52. This notion is developed further in many of

Wolfson's subsequent work. Cf. Nathaniel Berman, *Divine and Demonic in the Poetic Mythology of the Zohar* (Leiden: Brill, 2018).

7. Wolfson, *The Duplicity of Philosophy's Shadow*, 166.

8. On the complex understanding of conversos and the notion of crossing ethnic boundaries, see Magid, "The Politics of (un) Conversion: The 'Mixed Multitude' (*erev rav*) as Conversos in Rabbi Hayyim Vital's *Eẓ Ha-Da'at Tov*,' *Jewish Quarterly Review* 95, no. 4 (2005): 625–66. On the Zohar's tacit critique of Christianity specifically related to *gilgul*, see Yonatan Bennaroch, "'The Mystery of (Re) Incarnation and the Fallen Angels': The Reincarnations of Adam, Enoch, Metatron, (Jesus), and Joseph = an Anti-Christian Polemic in the Zohar," *Journal of Medieval Religious Cultures* 44, no. 2 (2018): 117–47.

9. See Jacobs "The Lifting of Sparks in Later Jewish Mysticism," in *Jewish Spirituality II* (New York: Crossroads, 1987), 99–126 and Jacobs, "The Doctrine of *Ẓaddik* in the Thought of Elimelekh of Lizensk," The Rabbi Louis Feinberg Memorial Lecture, University of Cincinnati.

10. See the recent work, Noam Lifler, "The Death of Sabbatai Ẓevi until the Great Conversion in Solonika: The Struggle of Inheritance in the Doctrine of Occultation" [PhD diss., Jerusalem, Hebrew University, 2020]. On Sabbatean documents on conversion, see Pawel Maciejko, *Sabbatean Heresy* (Waltham: Brandeis University Press, 2017), 34–36 and 39–46. As an interesting aside, since conversion stands as a centerpiece of Sabbateanism, one would think that *gilgul* would play a central role in justifying the conversion of Sabbatai Ẓevi to Islam in 1666. In fact, that does not seem to be the case. The reasons for this are unclear. Among the moderate Sabbateans such as Nathan of Gaza or Abraham Cardozo among others, while they justified Sabbatai Ẓevi's conversion, they held it to be more a tactic than a true conversion, a ploy of the messiah to redeem the lost sparks without truly traversing any boundaries. The is not quite true for the radical Sabbateans like the Dönmeh, who converted with Sabbatai Ẓevi. In any event, surprisingly, *gilgul* does not seem to play a major role in Sabbatean doctrine where it might obviously be found.

11. Genesis Rabba 38:18 in the name of Hiyya bar Abba.

12. See for example b.Yebamot, 64a.

13. The connection between Teraḥ and Job is mentioned briefly in *Sha'ar Ha-Gilgulim*, # 36 in *Kitvei Ha-Ari* (Jerusalem: Unknown, 1988), vol. 10, 114.

14. Vital, *Sha'ar ha-Pesukim* on Job, 269, 270.

15. See Magid, *From Metaphysics to Midrash*, 75–110.

16. See b. Baba Batra 15a, and Hayyim ben Atar, *Or Ha-Hayyim* (Rahway, N.J.: Artscroll Mesorah, 2017), see his commentary to Gen. 49:9 an Num. 24:21.

17. Zohar 3.111b. This Zoharic passage begins with a quote from Job 30:26, *For I hoped for good and evil came, I expected light and darkness fell.* I assume Vital was aware of the Jobean context of this passage that then turns to Abraham and Teraḥ although he never mentions it.

18. Vital, *Sha'ar Ha-Pesukim*, 270.

19. Vital never explains what the idolatrous practices of Adam were. On

Abraham as an idolater, see Ẓvi Elimelekh of Dinov, *Igra De-Kala* (Jerusalem: Machon Benei Shileshim), vol. 1, 380 a/b [Hebrew].

20. See Rashi to Gen. 12:1 and Genesis Rabba 39:3.

21. Vital, *Sha'ar Ha-Pesukim*, 270.

22. According to my research, it does not appear that *nitgalgel* is used in the formal sense of *gilgul* here but rather "it all rolled out" that is, "this is how everything transpired."

23. Vital, *Sha'ar Ha-Pesukim*, 270.

24. According to Abba ben Kahane, Job lived in the time of Jacob and, in fact, married Jacob's daughter Dinah. See, Baba Batra 15b and Targum Yerushalmi to Job 2:9. Vital adopts a different reading here, as he regards Job's wife as a *gilgul* of Jacob's daughter Dina.

25. Vital, *Sha'ar Ha-Pesukim*, 270.

26. See Isaiah Tishby, "Between Sabbateanism and Hasidism: The Sabbateanism of the Kabbalist R. Ya'akov Koppel Lifshitz of Mezritch," in Tishby, *Netivei Emunah u Minut* (Jerusalem, Magnus Press, 1982), 204–26 [Hebrew]; and my "Early Hasidism and the Metaphysics of *Malkhut* in Yaakov (Lifhitz) Koppel's *Shaarei Gan Eden*", *Kabbalah* 27 (2012): 245–68.

27. The question of Lurianism and Hasidism is not as simple as is often thought and some scholars, such as Moshe Idel, claim that Cordoverean influence was more prominent that it seems. See Idel, *Hasidism: Between Ecstasy and Magic* (Albany: State University of New York Press, 1995), 31–146. It is certainly true that some Hasidic masters rejected Lurianic prayer *kavvanot* in favor of a more primal and simplified prayer alternative. But see Menachem Kallus, "The Relation of the Baal Shem Tov to the Practice of Lurianic *Kavannot* in Light of His Comments on the Siddur Rashkov," *Kabbalah* 2 (1997): 151–67.

28. As an example, in Teitelbaum's two volume *Yismaḥ Moshe*, aside from the text under examination, there are only ten other references to *gilgul* almost all in passing. It is interesting that Yeruham Leiner chose to reprint Da Fano's *Gilgul Neshamot* which offers a much more basic and simplified rendering of the idea than one finds in Vital's writing.

29. This notion of arousal from below as a mechanism for awakening grace is replete in the Zohar. For one study that bases itself on this principle in regard to the shofar on the New Year (Rosh ha-Shana), see Jeremy Brown, "Of Sound and Vision: The Ram's Horn in Medieval Kabbalistc Ritualogy," in *Qol Tamid*, ed. J. Freidman and J Gereboff (Claremont, CA: Claremont School of Theology Press, 2017), 83–113.

30. In fact, the term *ẓaddik ben rasha* only appears once in the Lurianic corpus in the case of Abraham and Teraḥ cited above from *Sha'ar ha-Pesukim*. Yet the phrase *gilgul ha-kadum* does not appear there and only appears in one other place aside from our text, in Joseph Ergas's (1685–1730) *Shomer Emunim* (Beit Hasmonay: Yarid ha-Sefarim, 2023). It is used by Ergas to refer to a case of explaining a miscarriage as the result of the sins of a previous *gilgul*

31. See b. Megillah 19b. "R Yohanan taught, had there been left over a crack the size of a small sewing needle in the cave where Moses and Elijah stood when God's glory was revealed to them." Teitelbaum uses this image to suggest that even if there was a chance as small as the hole of a sewing needle, an arousal from below could rectify one's sin.

32. This appears to refer to the text above in *Sha'ar Ha-Pesukim* regarding Teraḥ and Abraham as *ẓaddik ben rasha*. *For the land's nakedness ('ervat ha-aretz) you have come* (Gen. 49:9).

33. Teitelbaum suggests here that *gilgul ha-kadum* is the template of *ẓaddik ben rasha*, that is, the holy always contains within it the unholy from a past life.

34. Meaning that Israel, and *lashon ha-qodesh* are not included in the calculation of seventy but exist apart (*qodesh*) from them and *lashon ha-kodesh* is not like the other languages. On the impurity of the seventy languages and their relation to the seventy constellations, see Zohar 2.203a. On the seventy languages in relation to *lashon ha-qodesh*, see Nahman of Bratslav, *Likkutei Moharan* (Jerusalem: Pe'er Mikdoshim, 1976), I:19.3, 25d, 26a.

35. Moshe Teitelbaum, *Yismaḥ Moshe*, two vols. (Jerusalem: Dvash Temorim, 1989), vol. 2, 127d, 128a.

36. The verse reads *For the land's nakedness you have come to see* (Gen 42:12). This refers to the son of Jacob who came to Egypt to purchase food during the famine.

37. See *Or Ha-Hayyim* to Deut. 26:5, "Aramean, this is the *yezer ha-ra*, who is a great deceiver, as it says, *and the serpent was 'arum* (naked, a deceiver) (Gen 3:1).

38. Teitelbaum, *Yismaḥ Moshe*, vol. 2, 128a.

39. See for example, Robert Alter's notion on Gen. 42:9, "The idiom [nakedness] refers to that which should be hidden from an outsider's eyes, as the pudenda are all but a legitimate sexual partner." Alter, *The Hebrew Bible*, vol. 1 (New York: W.W. Norton, 2019), 164 note 10.

40. In *Eẓ ha-Da'at Tov*, Hayim Vital suggests that Moses has a special relationship and affinity with the *'erev rav*. See, for example, *Eẓ ha-Da'at Tov*, 173a where Vital calls the *'erev rav, 'am shel Moshe* (Moses's people).

41. Y.Y. Teitelbaum, *Yetev Lev*, two vols. (Brooklyn: Publisher Unidentified, 1991), vol. 1, 56a.

42. *Yetev Lev* to Numbers, vol. 2, 30d.

43. For a recent study, see Magid, "The Satmar Are Anti-Zionist. Should We Care?," *Tablet Magazine*, May 20, 2020.

44. For some important studies on Teitelbaum on the question of Zionism, see Norman Lamm, "The Ideology of Neturei Karta: According to the Satmarer Version," *Tradition* 13 (1971): 38–53; Allan Nadler, "Politics and Piety: The Satmar Rebbe," *Judaism* 31 (1982): 135–52; Aviezer Ravitzsky, "Forcing the End: Radical Anti-Zionism," in Aviezer Ravitzsky, *Messianism, Zionism, and Jewish Religious Radicalism*, trans. M. Swirsky (Chicago: University of Chicago Press,

1996), 40–78; Michael Silber, "The Emergence of Ultra-Orthodoxy: The Invention of a Tradition," in *The Uses of Tradition: Jewish Continuity since Emancipation*, ed. J. Wertheimer (New York: The Jewish Theological Seminary Press, 1992), 23–94; and Ẓvi Jonathan Kaplan, "Rabbi Yoel Teitelbaum, Zionism, and Hungarian Ultra-Orthodoxy," *Modern Judaism* (2004): 165–78. Teitelbaum's life is told in extraordinary detail in the nine volumes of Ya'akov Gelbaum's *Moshian shel Yisrael*. An abbreviated one-volume English synopsis can be found in Dovid Meisles's *The Rebbe* (New York: Israel Bookshop Publications, 2010). See also Menachem Keren-Krantz, "Rabbi Yoel Teitelbaum — The Satmar Rebbe (1887-1979)" (PhD diss., Tel Aviv University, 2013) [Hebrew], and most recently Menachem Keren-Krantz, *Ha-Kana'i: Ha-Rebb Me-Satmar R. Yoel Teitelbaum* (Jerusalem: Mercaz Zalman Shazar, 2020) [Hebrew].

45. Yoel Teitelbaum, *Divrei Yoel*, vol. 4 (Brooklyn: Ṿa'ad le-hotsa'at asefat divre Mahari Ṭav mi-Saṭmar, 2004), 356.

46. Teitelbaum quotes the midrash in a slightly different way. Instead of "It will be as if you made my world," Teitelbaum adds the word I ('*ani*) to read "I will make it as if" as opposed to "it will be as if..." making it unclear if Moses is speaking in the first person here or not.

47. Teitelbaum, *Divrei Yoel*, vol. 4, 356.

48. See *Sha'ar ha-Pesukim*, 2b–d; *Likkutei Torah* 15b, *Sha'ar ha-Gilgulim*, Intro. 32, 244 and Intro. 33, 252; and *Sefer Gilgulim*, 17 and 40. On the necessary requirements for these news souls to descend, see "Regarding light that descends to enlighten that which is below, there is a great desire for the new souls below [that contain] light that has never descended until now. This is the light of pure mercy. But if the world below is not prepared for this pure mercy these souls will not descend ... Thus this light is called "straight light" ('*or yashir*) in that it comes directly from above." In Hayyim Vital, *Eẓ Hayyim* (Jerusalem: Aharon Barazani, 2004), Gate 6, Chapter 8.

49. On the Lurianic template of "new souls," see *Sha'ar Ha-Gilgulim*, Intro. 6.

50. There are numerous verses where later authorities claim *gilgul* is alluded to, even in the Torah. For some examples, Targum to Isaiah 22:14; Targum Yonatan to Deuteronomy 33:6; and Midrash Tanhuma on Genesis, "Vayigash" # 9.

ANDREA GONDOS

The Dead Who Yearn to Die

11

SPIRIT-POSSESSION AND SOUL-HEALING IN THE ACCOUNTS OF R. HILLEL BA'AL SHEM OF EASTERN EUROPE AND R. YEHUDAH FETAYA OF BAGHDAD[1]

Look into my face. My name is Might-have-been;
I am also called No-more, Too-late, Farewell;
Unto thine ear I hold the dead-sea shell
Cast up thy Life's foam-fretted feet between;
Unto thine eyes the glass where that is seen
Which had Life's form and Love's, but by my spell
Is now a shaken shadow intolerable,
Of ultimate things unuttered the frail screen.
— **DANTE GABRIEL ROSSETTI**, ***"The Nevermore"***

Death and the Afterlife: From Dante to Safed to Baghdad

In Judaism, while death certainly seems like the concluding chapter of one's earthly life, biblical passages reveal episodes from ancient Israelite history that depict the souls traversing the seemingly impervious boundaries between the physical and immaterial realms of existence.[2] These events are often instigated by profound psychological crises and existential brokenness that demand the reforging of ordinary social and religious boundaries and push the individual toward antinomian conduct. A case in point is the adjuration of the soul of the deceased prophet Samuel by the female diviner of Ein Dor to calm and quiet the agitated soul of King Saul (1 Samuel 28:3–25). The narrative context depicts a scene where the departed soul is forcibly summoned to act as a medium for prognostication about the future and respond to a concrete question posed by the living. This setting is poignantly depicted by William Blake in his painting *Saul and the Witch of Endor*, gracing the cover of the present volume. Mental and psychological anguish concerning an impending battle with the Philistines propels King Saul to violate his own edict of outlawing necromancy and force the prophet Samuel to reappear from the grave. Set against a dark background, the scene is laid out with the white ghost of Samuel looming large at its center. The living seem agitated and visibly unsettled, while the dead prophet appears active, forceful, and indignant. We see his face, and his hands are animated and expressive, indicating engagement with the people around him and underscoring the porous borders and boundaries that separate the living from the dead. In fact, as the two cases of the present chapter demonstrate, souls frequently wander and lodge themselves in living bodies, seeking reparation for past transgressions and a release from the suffering and punishment they experience on the other side. Most importantly, they are in dire need of a therapist — a soul-doctor or exorcist — who can apply affective and relational therapy to diagnose their condition, identify the sins they committed in past lives, and prescribe the panacea that would liberate them both from the torments they cause and those they experience. While the grave and death seem proverbially silent, the dead in it are not.

Beyond the Book of Samuel, allusions to reincarnation (*gilgul*) or soul-impregnation (*ibbur*) in the Bible are scant. Additional references can be gleaned from post-biblical sources such as the opinion of the first-century historian Josephus Flavius, who claimed that demons were the souls of the wicked, and the midrashic work *Pirkei de-Rabbi Eliezer*, which contended that the generation of the flood had been transformed into evil spirits (*ruḥot* and *mazzikim*) who forsook resurrection.[3] The Talmud and rabbinic literature also display keen interest in the relationship between the natural and supernatural worlds and the role that demons play as interlocuters between these realms.[4] Yet preoccupation with the soul and the concept of reincarnation was relatively marginal to Jewish religious speculation before the Middle Ages. However, with the more robust circulation of kabbalistic texts in the thirteenth and fourteenth centuries, particularly in the Iberian Peninsula and the Mediterranean regions, the nature of the soul — its origins, structure, and vicissitude in the body, and after a person's death — became a sui generis topic intensely engaged in kabbalistic literary production in such major texts as Zoharic literature, in *Sefer ha-Temunah*, briefly in Nahmanides's oeuvre, the works of R. Joseph Shalom Ashkenazi, and the *Book Bahir*.[5]

As noted by several scholars, preoccupation with the soul and theories about reincarnation, accompanied by performative formulas and techniques, such as unifications (*yiḥudim*), had reached previously unprecedented levels of depth and creativity in sixteenth-century Safed.[6] A large number of exiled Jews arrived in the picturesque Galilean hill town in the aftermath of the expulsion of Jews from the Iberian Peninsula. They were attracted by economic opportunities due in large part to the abundance of local water reservoirs, which made textile production and the garment trade a lucrative option. Here, kabbalistic fraternities coalesced around the authoritative figures of Solomon Alkabeẓ (1500–1576),[7] Moses Cordovero (1522–1570),[8] Joseph Karo (1488–1575),[9] and R. Isaac Luria Ashkenazi, the Ari (1534–1572). Their teachings, as noted by Jonathan Garb, absorbed the biographical and psychological tendencies of medieval ecstatic kabbalah associated with the personality of Abraham Abulafia.[10]

Together these leading figures and their disciples produced works that centered on interiorization of theological concepts (*yiḥudim*), the cultivation of mindfulness by systematic incorporation of intentions or *kavvanot* into prayer, and the psychological and moral calibration of the individual through penitential acts.[11] They sought to infuse both Jewish daily life and devotional practice with greater piety and conscious focus, cultivating a form of social cohesion that lay the groundwork for a social psychology that informed later iterations of kabbalistic fellowships. The result was the emergence of mystical fraternities that spanned the disciples of R. Moses Hayyim Luzzatto (1704–1774) in Italy, various Hasidic groups in Eastern Europe, and those that coalesced in the Middle East centered on the city of Baghdad, first around R. Shalom Sharabi (1720–1777)[12] and later R. Yosef Ḥayyim (1834–1909), the Ben Ish Ḥai, and his disciples, including R. Yehudah Fetayah.[13] It should be noted that these disparate circles were unified by their hermeneutic and conceptual reliance on the Lurianic kabbalistic corpus transmitted by R. Hayyim Vital, which shaped the way they approached questions of the afterlife and particularly their espousal of the concept of soul repair or *tikkun*.[14]

In this chapter, I trace the deployment of techniques and other forms of healing rituals to treat possessions by malevolent spirits in two distinct sources. These accounts are methodologically framed within a broader discourse on shamanism and shamanic procedures within Jewish history of the early modern and the modern periods. Following Jonathan Garb's study on the shamanic dimensions of Jewish mysticism, including Hasidism, I argue that adopting this terminology is an important step in understanding and deconstructing the phenomenological aspects of Jewish mystics and healers, including *Baalei Shem* (Masters of the Name), while at the same time offering points of comparison and contact between Judaism and other religious traditions. This semantic adjustment, I posit, sheds new light on the social, cultural, and religious impact of a group of Jewish men who served as important cultural agents and whose primary function was to heal both the body and the soul, the individual along with the community.

I therefore first examine a detailed and lengthy possession account recorded in the *Book of Longing* (*Sefer ha-Ḥeshekh*), written by R. Hillel Baal Shem (c. 1690–c. 1741), to trace important, yet insufficiently explored, aspects between reincarnation and mental health in Judaism and the dynamic relationship between the living and the dead. In addition, I will investigate the treatise *Talking Souls* (*Ruḥot Mesaprot*), written by Rabbi Yehudah Fetaya of Baghdad (1859–1942), to uncover the everyday, practical, and healing dimensions of twentieth-century possession accounts.[15] It should be noted that both sources depict the soul's return to material existence as a form of negative *ibbur*, whereby the soul of a dead person inhabits the body of a living individual, frequently causing pain, discomfort, or psychological distress. As has been noted, both exorcism techniques, as well as possession narratives, have remained relatively consistent over time in the history of Judaism, and therefore an examination of these sources reveals certain commonalities while also showcasing specificities unique to the social and cultural setting of the exorcist.[16] Possession accounts, above all, are sites of contested identities with fluid borders and boundaries that frequently operate in the gray zone between religious norms and antinomian practices and, as such, open new windows on the lived, in contrast to the doctrinal and theoretical, aspects of Judaism.

The Phenomenology of Possession Accounts: Hillel Ba'al Shem and the Shamanic Tradition in Early Modern Ashkenaz

The typological category of a *Baal Shem* (Master of the Name) is defined in Judaism as a charismatic religious adept who possesses certain supernatural knowledge and whose authority and power are defined by the practical efficacy of such knowledge.[17] Reference to this group of religious experts dates back to the Middle Ages in Jewish sources, more specifically to the tenth-century responsum of Ḥai Gaon to the Jewish community of Kairouan.[18] Their healing practices can be differentiated from those of learned physicians by a more robust reliance on the integration of natural and supernatural epistemes — the knowledge and combination of angelic and demonic names, animal and plant substances, as well as artisanal methods — combined with a more holistic approach to healing. While rigorous scholarship identifying the shamanic elements in Jewish religious history is still in its infancy, and a systematic study on this topic remains an important desideratum, Jonathan Garb's defining work on the phenomenological application of shamanic trance in modern Hasidic and kabbalistic practice proffers valuable theoretical and methodological tools for future exploration of this topic. Building on an integrated model of binary typologies developed by Haviva Pedaya — the extroverted in contrast to the introverted poles of Jewish mystical-shamanic experience — Garb defines shamanism as a transformative process that begins as a movement in imaginal space, what Michel Foucault calls heterotopia, that transcends beyond "habitual frames of reference."[19] The motivation for such travel in space is a return to the individual and society — the familiar structures — with renewed spiritual energies that are potent enough to revitalize and empower. The shaman's primary objective, therefore, was to (re)galvanize both the individual and the community, whether one considers the context of Safedian Kabbalah in the sixteenth century, the activities of the Baal Shem Tov, or later groups of Hasidic masters, a path that Garb pursues in his book.

However, in this chapter I would like to foreground another typology of shamanic leadership exemplified by both R. Hillel Baal Shem and R. Yehudah Fetaya of Baghdad, which is based less on experiences of trance, or a marked tendency of interiorization,[20] and more on the role of the shaman as healer, physician of the soul, and the restorer of cosmic, individual, and communal welfare and well-being. Handwritten Jewish books of secrets and how-to books from East-Central Europe compiled from the sixteenth to the eighteenth centuries comprise new textual evidence that allows us to frame Fetaya's role as a shaman in a diachronic context. A number of these works record exorcism rituals that offer rare insight into the multiplicity of techniques available to a *Baal Shem* to commune with the souls of the dead and heal afflicted individuals by driving out malevolent spirits tormenting them. This is of crucial importance, since Fetaya's *Talking Souls* — based on its published format — contains very little "technical" information. The near-complete absence of amulets, magical formulas, and angelic and demonic names stands in marked contrast to the notebooks left behind by the Eastern European *Baalei Shem*, whose detailed accounts of the exorcisms they conducted are particularly illuminating. It is highly probable that in the editorial process of preparing the print edition, Rabbi Fetaya's original manuscript was heavily censored, which resulted in the expurgation of the magical material that may have been deemed too esoteric for broad circulation. Be that as it may, a brief assessment of an eighteenth-century exorcism script recorded in one of the most "autobiographical" manuscripts left behind by a *Baal Shem* provides useful points of contact with the narratives documented in Fetaya's *Talking Souls*, demonstrating the diffusion and impact of Lurianic kabbalah on the one hand while on the other hand underlining the pervasiveness of exorcistic traditions in Jewish communities that crossed temporal and geographical divides between East and West.[21]

The following account of an exorcism conducted by Hillel Baal Shem (c. 1690–c. 1741) and narrated in his work *Sefer ha-Ḥeshekh* (c. 1739) is extant in a manuscript housed in the Vernadsky Library in Kiev.[22] Hillel made his living as an itinerant healer in various regions of East-Central Europe, including regions of Poland, Ukraine, Lithuania, Romania, and Bukovina. This work of 411 folio pages represents a long and elaborate manuscript of Jewish magic and practical kabbalah that was found by Yohanan Petrovsky-Stern in Kiev in 1993. The work's most pervasive characteristic, which also distinguishes it from a number of other magical manuscripts, is the ubiquitous use of the first person, through which we gain a better perspective of Hillel, including his daily concerns, textual sources that were available to him, challenges he faced, and his overall attitude toward health, illness, other medical professionals, and in general the vicissitudes of his life as an itinerant miracle worker.[23]

The event unfolded in the Jewish community of Ostróg, which at this time belonged to the Polish-Lithuanian Commonwealth and was distinguished by the prominence of its rabbinic leadership in the sixteenth and seventeenth centuries, R. Shelomo Luria (Maharshal) and R. Shemu'el Eliezer Edels, respectively. A common element that connects Hillel's encounter with Yehudah Fetaya's narrative produced a century and a half later is a series of dialogues that transpire between the exorcist and the "evil soul" that prove to be transformative and contribute to the eventual success of the operation. Hillel's axiomatic statement concerning exorcism as a procedure that can be influenced by multiple factors that lie beyond the control of the *Ba'al Shem* — such as time (שעה) or space (מקום) — becomes a central pivot of the narrative. After several unsuccessful attempts to drive out the evil spirit from the body of an unnamed woman — a procedure that unfolded over the course of six days — the evil spirit, identified by name as עיעיעים or *'Y'Y'YM*, initiates a conversation with Hillel Baal Shem. Through his revelations we learn that he had taken hold of the woman at night after the Shabbat went out — a propitious time for evil spirits to restart their malicious activities — when she was pregnant with a little girl and had continued to possess her for several years. The demonic rulers appointed over him gave him permission to kill her husband, but when he wanted to proceed to slay the child as well, he was forbidden to do so; "only her husband met his end, but when I desired to kill the fetus in her womb, they withheld the permission from me."[24]

The demonic spirit plays a pivotal role in the narrative as an interlocutor between the earthly and preternatural realms disclosing hidden knowledge — concerning both matters in the heavenly realm as well as transgressive acts perpetrated by the Jewish and non-Jewish community — and specific techniques to aid and facilitate Hillel Baal Shem's therapeutic work as an exorcist. This echoes Hillel's earlier statement that sometimes a magical procedure is influenced by unseeable forces — time, or the hour of the operation — while at other times, it is impacted by a specific place, and the negative energies accumulated there. Accordingly, the demon warns him that the exorcism must be moved to a nearby village, Tutchin (possibly Tuchyn, approximately fifty-two kilometers north of Ostróg) and should not be conducted at the Ostróg synagogue — a site of unholiness where all his efforts and techniques would ultimately fail.[25] The demonic soul's confession narrating the transgressions he committed are framed by Hillel, I would contend, around a clear didactic and morally exhortative agenda against apostasy — a ubiquitous concern in East-Central Europe in the aftermath of the Sabbatean movement in the seventeenth century and its later iteration in the Frankists in the eighteenth century.[26] The religious boundary crossing the demonic spirit perpetuated in its earthly existence — conversion from Judaism to Christianity and the murder of his former co-religionists in his earthly life — is paralleled by its restless crossings from the dead to the living and back, all the while inflicting danger, pain, and death. The pregnant body of the woman he possesses mirrors his own existential state — liminal and between worlds. Expectant mothers were particularly vulnerable to the harmful activities of demons.[27] Jewish myth preserved in the Alphabet of Sira depicts Lilith as Adam's first wife, who was banished from the Garden of Eden to persist in the wastelands of the created world, from where she sends her armies to snatch and kill the fetus of pregnant women and small children after they are born. It is interesting that in this case the demonic spirit was not given permission to harm the child, only the mother.[28]

> And the soul (רוח) recounted before all the people and gave testimony of the deeds he had committed in the past. He became a heretic (may his name be obliterated), and married a non-Jewish woman, and fathered many children with her. He then murdered several Jews and when they wanted to bring him to justice, he became a priest. After many years he turned into a spirit and lay below a tree in the holy community of Ostróg, adjacent to the synagogue. During the hot days, on account of the immense heat on the holy Shabbat, the above-mentioned woman, who was pregnant, went to the tree and lay down on the ground beneath it, where the demonic spirit resided. Immediately, without delay, the spirit entered the woman through the right eye and harmed her sight (lit. covered this eye), and on the same night he hurt her husband until he died. She then delivered a baby girl, and the child was healthy and strong, and the spirit returned into the woman's body for seven consecutive years, during which he tormented her greatly and bitterly without measure, so much so, that he harmed her other eye as well, because of the intense pain she had to endure. And there was none, no expert, who knew what happened to her, what this spirit did to her. The entire incident was concealed.[29]

Surprisingly, the impetus for contracting the services of Hillel Baal Shem came from the evil spirit himself, who explained to the shamash of the community that "you should go immediately, without delay, to this man called Rabbi Hillel Baal Shem, and he will come to our community in a day or so to end my [wretched] condition by invoking adjurations of holy names at the synagogue. He might just find a cure for me."[30] From a psychological and gendered perspective, it is revealing that while the exorcism is directed at curing the woman whose body had been invaded and tormented by the male incubus, the fact that the demonic spirit is directing the procedure from the woman's body suggests that the woman lost all agency in the procedure: she is not identified by name, nor is her own voice and experience ever articulated. At the same time, from a psychological perspective, the soul desperately seeks a release and cure for his own suffering as a disembodied spirit who lacks a resting place in the afterlife.[31]

This episode also opens a window on the type of training and expertise available to a Jewish shaman and reveals the way in which exorcism, as an occult operation, fits into the modus operandi of a *Baal Shem*'s training. In this context, Hillel states that the encounter in Ostróg was the third exorcism he performed in his career, and, in contrast to the earlier attempts, it proved more complicated and required him to develop new skills. During the first procedure, he candidly admits being a dilettante who had no idea what he was doing and "how to begin, and how to use oaths (*hashba'ot*) to perform this procedure, since I only used amulets before and all the instructions and the sequence were written down in my book, into which I had copied from the books of the great light, in piety, uprightness, and knowledge concerning all the ways of the Torah, great Sage, our teacher the rabbi, Ẓevi Hirsch."[32] This brief statement reveals that Hillel's expertise progressed from book learning, based on the notebooks of his master Rabbi Ẓevi Hirsch, which was probably combined with occasional oral tutorials with him, to writing amulets, and finally using oaths or *hashba'ot*, which ostensibly represented a higher and more complex type of procedure for driving out evil spirits. Apparently, the incident in Ostróg was the first time he used "grand oaths and supplications (*hasba'ot* and *bakashot*)"[33] in addition to deploying seven Torah scrolls, blowing the ram's horn (*shofars*), as well as pronouncing a ban — all to no avail. His efforts were unsuccessful for six days during the week, and, even worse, the incubus refrained from disclosing his name.

In fact, the ultimate success of the procedure was dependent less on Hillel's own skills and prowess than on the desire of the evil spirit to find closure and an end to its own vicissitudes, which impelled him to disclose quite spontaneously "a great secret (*sod gadol*), that no [magical] procedure has any effect on me in this place, which is filled with the evil of Gentiles," on the one hand, and with the hatred of one Jew against another, on the other hand.[34] Hillel, after heeding the advice of the maggid turned dybbuk, moves the operation to Tuchyn and performs "a great adjuration (*bakashah*) with ten men, of upright conduct, and Torah scrolls, which resulted in the dybbuk's expulsion from the woman's body, through the small finger of her left foot — from under the nail of the finger — drawing a small drop of blood [as it left]. This happened on the fifth day of the week (Thursday) in the month of Elul in 5493 (1733). And she [the woman] opened [her eyes] a bit so she could see and went to the synagogue, and the cemetery, wherever she wished to go, except that in her other eye — the one through which the dybbuk entered her — she remained blind, having suffered a permanent injury."[35]

Surprisingly the relationship between the demon and Hillel did not cease with the success of the operation, and he continued to impart secrets to him long after. As we will see in Fetaya's *Talking Souls*, the liminal status of disembodied souls enabled them to become powerful interlocuters who could transcend seemingly divergent realms transposing forbidden and arcane knowledge from the preternatural to the physical world. Perhaps as a reward for their long-awaited release and repair from the punishment of trapped existence — like a genie freed from a bottle — they can metamorphose into teachers and *maggidim* aiding the work of exorcists.[36] Hillel discloses that after the conclusion of the exorcism, the demon continued to impart secrets to him, some of which may have been of a personal nature concerning wrongdoings and transgressions he had committed, while other may have been related to the nature and activities of demons.[37] He categorically refrains from revealing any of these secrets because of his great fear, distress, and anguish concerning what he heard. While admittedly both the exorcist and the possessing demon vie for control, the communicative aspect is crucial for the efficacy of the procedure because, despite the "patterned sequencing" of the ritual and the "structured behavior" of the participants, the success of the procedure seems to hinge on collaboration between the living souls of the visible physical world and the invisible realm of disembodied spirits.[38]

Rabbi Yehudah Fetaya as Soul Healer: Demonic Illness, Diagnosis, and Treatment

The kabbalistic teachings of Rabbi Yehudah Fetaya (1859–1942) of Baghdad form an integral part of the reception history of Lurianic Kabbalah mediated through the writings and theosophical system of his student Rabbi Ḥayyim Vital (1542–1620). It further represents the (Middle) Eastern, in contrast to the European, circulation and reception of this school of kabbalistic speculation as it developed its unique features in and around the Jewish communities of Baghdad.[39] He was an outstanding disciple of R. Yosef Ḥayyim, popularly known as the Ben Ish Ḥai, and an important cultural interlocutor in disseminating his teachings. He made several trips to Mandate Palestine, only to finally settle in Jerusalem in 1934, where a group of followers coalesced around his figure and established the Minhat Yehudah Seminary in his memory in 1946.[40]

Widely acclaimed both for his knowledge of theoretical kabbalah as well as for his skills as an effective amulet maker and exorcist, R. Fetaya draws on a series of fascinating accounts from the time he lived in Baghdad to write *Talking Souls*. In exploring the souls of the dead that are recycled in new host bodies, the work highlights their desperate yearning "to die" and achieve rest in the netherworld.[41] Yet, as his numerous case studies demonstrate, they cannot attain this cathartic state on their own, just as infirms are unable to heal themselves. It is the clinical gaze of the soul-doctor or shaman combined with his expert knowledge of the soul, and the isomorphic correspondences between the upper and lower worlds, that enable him to diagnose illness, prescribe the necessary treatment, and affect rectification and healing.

Like R. Hillel Baal Shem, R. Fetaya belongs to the tradition of Jewish shamanic healers, integrating diverse epistemological sources in his work — Lurianic kabbalah and myth, charismatic religious authority, as well as natural, magical, and psychological panacea. These narratives describe a world centered not on the traditional interpretation of Jewish texts and law, but on charismatic knowledge of souls, whose inability to properly die causes them spiritual anguish and produces a permanent state of restlessness. Recalling the notion of the hollow of a sling (כף הקלע),[42] these souls are depicted as moving about in the other world, catapulted like a piece of stone that flies about aimlessly into different regions of hell and purgatory. Desperation causes them to cross the boundaries that separate the living and the dead and lodge themselves in host bodies. One of the consequences of this soul-incubation is the transferal of their own existential defect to the host, who immediately becomes either physically or emotionally debilitated and unable to function in daily life. Thus, the blemish of a dead soul injures the body and soul of the living.

The world that R. Fetaya depicts is deeply concerned with the individual, its moral conduct in the world, and the consequences of human sin. Focusing on reincarnation and soul-impregnation (*ibbur*), *Talking Souls* portrays a religious world characterized by fluidity, where boundaries between body and spirit, man and woman, appear permeable and imbricated. Issues of embodiment and the complex relationship between embodied and disembodied existence are framed in the context of soul repair, a kabbalistic teaching developed most extensively in the sixteenth century by Rabbi Isaac Luria (Ari) and his student R. Ḥayyim Vital. As scholars have repeatedly noted, *tikkun* or repair occupies a central concept in Lurianic teachings and is a foundation for the theurgic potential of human action.[43] The relationship between the human being and God is predicated on an ontological stain that arose from the transgression of the first human couple, Adam and Eve.

Their sin, according to the Lurianic "meta-textual cosmic system" of interpreting the biblical text, is scattered in every subsequent generation and individual and becomes encoded in every new soul and body that descends into the material world.[44] The imbalance that sin engenders engulfs all realms of existence, against which the most potent panacea is the battle for the soul. When the soul is captured by the demonic powers in the world, it is subjugated to them, producing existential brokenness. Healing the soul, by contrast, also heals the universe, affecting each level in the great chain of being, including the ontological source of all being(s), the Creator.

Rabbi Fetaya's work, written as a personal diary or notebook, integrates the subjective voice of the narrator that is often depicted in conversation with the souls of the dead, who divulge their stories to him seeking spiritual healing and repair for their suffering in the afterlife. At the same time, the work also fits into the genre of hagiography, as the narratives are carefully framed to bolster Rabbi Fetaya's status as a powerful religious virtuoso fighting a cosmic battle. The individual case studies of the souls he encountered during his praxis in Baghdad serve to establish his religious authority, who is an equal confidant to departed souls, demons, and angelic interlocutors in the heavenly realm. In establishing his own authority, he creatively draws on earlier hagiographic accounts of the sixteenth-century kabbalist and paragon of esoteric-charismatic knowledge, R. Isaac Luria and his student R. Hayyim Vital.[45]

In his introduction, the author frames the writing of *Ruḥot Mesaprot* in the context of acquainting his readers concerning the processes (beatings of the grave), the beings (destroying spirits), the institutions (heavenly court — *beit din*), and the topography of an alternative reality — the afterlife — which, while invisible to the human eye, affects both the souls of the living and those of the dead. At the locus of R. Fetaya's literary endeavor is an emphasis on the sin-punishment paradigm, according to which every sin engenders an equal form of punishment, while at the same time foregrounding the power of repentance, which when carried out with a broken heart and with proper intention, can affectively assuage harsh judgment.

> This book explains the matter of souls that enter human beings and cause them epilepsy, which I have already described in great detail. Additionally, the beatings of the grave, and why they ask a person's name in the grave and what purpose it serves as well as what happens to a person after the beatings of the grave. It will also elucidate how they bring a person before the heavenly court (*beit din*) to give judgment

and accounting of a person's deeds. It will also highlight the loftiness of repentance and the matter of the sling shot, and the transmigration of souls.... And the reckoning of the *Gehinnom* — the order concerning what happens to a person from the time of his death until he merits to enter the Garden of Eden. Furthermore, we will describe the things that soothe the deceased soul and rescue it from affliction meted out to it by the [heavenly] court as well as what is appropriate to study at the grave of the dead, also explaining the issue of the visitation of the dead, who appear to close relatives in their dream. We will further identify the destroying spirits (*mashḥittim*) that are appointed over individuals — the image of their countenance, the shape of their body, and what they consume. We will also expound why it is not appropriate to call a newborn by the name of a deceased, unless it can be established with certainty that he [the dead person] was completely righteous (*ẓaddik tam*) and upright but at the very least one needs to perform *tikkun* to repair the soul of the dead person before the child could be called by his name. Furthermore, we will outline the mode of confession for the penitent that is apposite to the sin of the soul and, more broadly, we will recount the repair we performed for Shabbtai Ẓvi so he would merit to enter the Garden of Eden.[46]

One of the key theological concepts concerning the netherworld that R. Fetaya explicates in detail is the matter surrounding the grave, the first station on the soul's journey of rectification after death. Drawing on the two most frequently deployed intertexts — the zoharic and the Lurianic textual corpora — he posits that the "beating in the grave" is a crucial procedure in separating the husks — forces of evil — from the deceased. This is usually carried out by four angels who appear at the grave site and "who lower the bottom of the grave, making it deeper. The hollow of the grave then becomes as high as the height of the person buried there."[47] To complete the purging process, the angels need to return the soul to the body for the duration of the shaking so that entire human being could be divested of the husks that a person accrued through sin during one's lifetime. Suffering and the pursuit of righteousness in this world help to loosen these husks, while pleasure binds them. He further underlines that only two Shabbat-related activities and customs can save a person from the beating: a burial on the Shabbat day — after the fifth, that is, the beginning, of the sixth hour — as enumerated by Ḥayyim Vital in *Sha'ar ha-Kavvanot*,[48] and the fourth meal consumed at the conclusion of Shabbat.

Without delving too much into the complexities of soul roots and families — a characteristic feature of Lurianic theory and practice — R. Fetaya draws on the metaphor of a dough equally composed of fine flour and bran to illustrate the relationship between the husks and the holiness of the soul.[49] Every individual is composed of a combination of husks: "the evil urge, which enters a person the day one is born, since as a result of the sin of Adam, the evil urge and the husk become attached and rooted" in such a person.[50] Knowing the name of one's husk would reveal to a person the precise source of their husk-root, enabling him to identify the type of rectification necessary for repair and to circumvent the beating of the grave. Diagnosing the ontological root of the damage, therefore, is tantamount to healing the soul, and curiously this knowledge is rooted in language based. The remedy is concealed in the name of the husk — which in the example he cites was formed by four letters of a Psalmic verse (148:10) — and the therapeutic key lies with recovering this secret hermeneutically.

Spirit Possession and Social Criticism: Constructing Identity through Othering the Other

Bruce Lincoln's assertion that identity, social tensions, and the formation of hierarchy are often expressed through narrative discourse, finds poignant expression in R. Fetaya's account where the Muslim and Christian other frequently appear to reinforce religious values and entrench social stereotypes.[51] In reference to the man — the only person in the generation — who knew the name of his husk, this evil shell appeared during a plague episode as a Muslim warrior and revealed himself to the man in a dream: "Have no fear, for I have no intention of harming you, I want you to know that I am your husk, and I am the Scribe of the Grand Court of the Left Side. My name is טכי"י."[52] The second time he visited the man in a dream, he appeared as a common Muslim who was not antagonistic toward Jews. The third time, his distinguishing feature was a negative emotional and psychological state, morosity — frequently correlated in kabbalistic symbolism with the left, or other side, *sitra ahra* — while his religious affiliation was not immediately identifiable until he began reciting words from the Zohar. R. Fetaya's conclusion that the third, Jewish, husk might imply the sweetening of the husk of a person's soul garment can be read as religious criticism, whereby the high-ranking Muslim husk embodied the harshest, while the morose Jew husk embodied the mildest representation of evil.

In another place, Fetaya voices strong misogynistic attitudes against the education of Jewish women consonant with the patriarchic social system of Jewish communities living in Muslim-majority countries, where women were largely isolated from society and confined to their domestic role in the house. Jewish women did not receive formal education, and the opening of the first girls' school by the Alliance Israélite Universelle in Baghdad in 1893 was met with robust opposition, including that voiced by older women. Yet female enrolment in these schools grew at a steady pace, and by 1900, 132 girls studied in primary schools, and by 1910, this number tripled to 399.[53] It is around the time when the popularity of women's education becomes more widespread in upper middle-class Jewish circles that Rabbi Fetaya embeds his own criticism of this practice into an exorcism case report.

The event was triggered by the physical and emotional travails of a seventeen-year-old girl, Khatoun, who sought relief and remedy from R. Fetaya. It is revealed during the exorcism that she is possessed by a female soul called Rosa, who died as a punishment for an adulterous relationship she perpetuated for several years with her neighbor, Salman. She discloses to Fetaya that she was forcibly questioned by the heavenly court in the afterlife, who demanded her to disclose and confess all her sins to them, which she was unable to do because of the great shame that overcame her. She is rebuked by the judges, who show her the ledger that records all earthly deeds: "I was given a ledger unlike any ledgers of this world. They opened it before me and said, 'Read it.' 'I do not know how to read, I said to them.'"[54] The spirit's comment and her inability to read prompt Rabbi Fetaya to remark on the religious significance of education, including the basic ability to read a text — if you cannot read your sins, you cannot properly confess.

> (This might be what the rabbis meant when they said [b. Kiddushin 40b]: *A person is first judged for words of Torah, as it is written, Who frees fresh water is the beginning of judgment* (Proverbs 17:14). For if, when he is given the ledger to read, he says he cannot read, then they ask him why he did not study Torah. Women, however, are not obligated to study Torah, in which case we need an explanation for why people in our generation make such an effort and spend so much money teaching their daughters to read and write. After all, after their marriage, they are occupied with household chores and do not have time to study. In addition, they have the pain of pregnancy, the pain of birth, and then they are busy raising children. What, then, is the purpose of their education?

It could be, however, that the reason for teaching them to be literate is so that after their death they will have the privilege of reading in the Court ledger all the sins and abominations they have committed while they lived . . . They will not have to trouble the Court to read them their sins. Also in case, Heaven forefends, the Court makes a claim that is not written in their ledger.[55]

In other words, R. Fetaya reluctantly concludes that education is not entirely wasted on women because, while they may not reap any benefit from it during their lifetime, in their death it will provide them with a considerable advantage. As the story of Rosa demonstrates, a soul who cannot accurately enumerate the transgressions they committed receives greater and more severe punishment in the netherworld. Rosa further imparts to him technical know-how that would enable him to drive out spirits more effectively during an exorcism.

If you do not know the location where it [the dybbuk] is situated, or, if it gets away and flees from place to place, bring your mouth right up to the ear of the afflicted person so that the entire breath of the unification will fill the space inside the body. This will be even more effective than placing your hand on the limb which the spirit is inhabiting, for this causes the spirit more pain than the blows of the destroyers or the beating of the grave.[56]

The revelation regarding the psychic or metaphysical efficacy of transmitting unifications, *yiḥuddim*, into the ears of patients directly and in a hermetically sealed manner prompted Fetaya to adapt and repurpose an ordinary stethoscope. By reversing its ordinary deployment and placing "the two metal tubes into the ears of the afflicted person, and the other end, which resembles a funnel" in his own mouth, he was able to invent a new treatment mechanism that led to an improved healing outcome. The spirit's communication was essential in this process and a crucial breakthrough in R. Fetaya's development as a shaman and healer of souls.

The Rectification of Shabbtai Ẓvi and His Transformation from Dybbuk to Maggid

That the cognitive matrix of personhood, culture, and identity are in constant and fluid interaction with one another has been affirmed by cognitive theorists of religion.[57] Culture implies the embeddedness of individuals within society through reciprocal interactions and active meaning making, which allows one to make sense of the world as well as of the self in perpetual dialogue, as Jeppe Sinding Jensen aptly puts it, "considered in their cultural aspects, societies are stories."[58] Religion, she posits, "is a human project, that aims at making the world, the cosmos speak so that everything known to us may become an object of discourse through the use of narrative." Yet this activity of "making the cosmos speak" concerns not only the discursivity of the material and physical world, that has been the subject of philosophers' epistemological search ... but both physical and metaphysical worlds, such as superhuman or supernatural entities and agents."[59] Language assumes critical agency in this process of translating reality, making sense of it, and generating new "identity-forming interactions that take place between the mind, the body, and the social and physical environment they are situated in."[60]

Narrative framing in *Talking Souls* is closely intertwined with hagiography based on the meticulous construction of the charismatic personality of the Shaman-healer.[61] The story that best illustrates R. Fetaya's proficiency as a healer of souls is the dramatic retelling of the circumstances that led to rectification of the soul of Sabbatai Ẓvi, whose sins extended from the willing transgression of Jewish law and the brazen encouragement of others to follow suit, to false pretensions to be the messiah, and finally, apostasy to Islam. Arguably, the rectification of such a deeply damaged and tainted soul required the expertise of the best, and the narrative aims to couch the exorcism of Sabbatai Ẓvi's soul from the body of the Jew, named Bechor, within the context of charismatic healing rituals administered by the Ari and recorded by his disciples.[62] The techniques he uses in this operation consist of affecting unifications (*yiḥudim*),[63] whispering them into his ear, "so that the breath of the unification should enter his ear and his limbs, for the breath of the unification expels the breath of the spirit" (289). When these prove ineffective in expelling the spirit, he resorts to two other procedures: showing him sacred names, perhaps in the form of amulets (however, this is not made clear in the narrative), and blasting the ram's horn (*shofar*) into his ears. Most importantly, however, R. Fetaya begins a lengthy dialogue with the soul of Sabbatai Ẓevi, through which Sabbatai reveals that

> He died by strangulation. He did not repent and was subsequently buried in a gentile cemetery. When he was alive, the husks would appear before his eyes. The reason he became wicked was because he was not conceived in holiness. He was reincarnated in countless numbers of reincarnations ... The reason he speaks within the heart rather than through the

mouth is because the aforesaid Bechor studies Torah, by means of which he subdues the spirit within him [Sabbatai Ẓevi] and causes it pain. This is why the soul of [Sabbatai Ẓevi] interrupts his studies and relays to him foreign thoughts.[64] . . . The beginning of his downfall was when he sinned with a married woman and what I heard was true, he fornicated with a male while wearing a prayer shawl and phylacteries. He also sent a young man to be with his own wife, Sarah, and explicitly commanded him, saying, "Whatever Sarah tells you, obey her." His beating in the grave lasted twelve years. Until now he had been reincarnated in the beasts of the forest. This was his first incarnation in a person, in the aforesaid Bechor[65] . . . The Holy One, blessed be He, caused me to meet you, so that you would merit to rectify me, he said. As for you Bechor, he continued, study Zohar daily in order to elevate the soul of Sabbatai Ẓevi the son of Rebecca, at the hour of the morning watch and after mealtimes. Immerse daily, and fear no evil thoughts. If an evil thought should enter your heart, recite the verse, *My heart murmurs a good thing*, רחש לבי דבר טוב וכו (Psalms 45:2), and have in mind the Divine Name רחש as well as קרע שטן, whereby those thoughts will be gone from your heart.[66]

R. Fetaya's animated conversation with Sabbatai Ẓevi's soul exemplifies a conscious narrative strategy to construct his authority as the exorcist par excellence of his generation, surpassing even his teachers, R. Yosef Ḥayyim and R. Shimon Agassi of Baghdad. Unlike the rabbinic masters selectively mentioned in the discourse who are reticent to encounter the renegade Sabbatai's soul, they even attempt to dissuade R. Fetaya from continuing his dangerous mission. Yet, as R. Fetaya's unwavering pursuit proves to be justified, it reveals another noteworthy facet of this story. Dialogue and emphatic discourse in the spiritual realm can affect — alongside and arguably even more robustly than unifications, sacred names, and shofar sounds — a transformation and reversal in the status of a tormented soul. From an angry, resentful, and bitter disposition that hurls curses on R. Fetaya and Bechor, Sabbatai Ẓevi's soul metamorphoses into a spiritual advocate promoting and intensifying Bechor's devotional life by waking him up in the morning, urging him into the ritual bath (*mikveh*), and imploring him to study the Zohar. As for R. Fetaya, instead of denouncing, he entreated him to accelerate his exorcistic rituals so he could finally leave the body of Bechor and merit to enter Hell. Reflecting Yoram Bilu's conceptualization concerning the two basic typologies of altered states of conscious, Sabbatai Ẓevi's soul is transformed from a corrosive dybbuk to the positive maggid type. Aiding the souls of the dead, R. Fetaya as an exorcist benefited the living by rechanneling the positive psychological energies into the present.[67]

Conclusion

The analysis of textual sources of possession accounts from geographically disparate regions — Eastern Europe and Baghdad — that are further separated by a temporal span of several hundred years has revealed that possession is a contested site in Judaism, where social, religious, and therapeutic dimensions intersect with and shape one another. Shared affinities between Hillel Ba'al Shem's exorcism account and those recorded in the notebook of Yehudah Fetaya include both common technical apparatuses — various linguistic adjurations of magical names and the use of sacred objects, like Torah scrolls and the ram's horn (*shofar*), alongside robust oral communication and dialogue between the exorcist and possessing spirit.[68] In addition, *yiḥudim* — ritual formulas based on Lurianic exemplars that were verbal and usually communicated into the ear of the possessed person to produce unification with the possessing soul — formed an essential practice in R. Fetaya's technical repertoire as an exorcist. It is important to underline that, in contrast to earlier inferences that emphasized the meditative aspects of *yiḥudim*, in R. Fetaya's narrative they are clearly verbal, incantational, and extremely powerful, shaking the evil spirit out of its comfort, causing it agitation, and consequently loosening its grip on the host,[69] making the spirit weak. In both accounts, exorcism becomes a point of departure for relationality between the exorcist and the evil spirit, leading to a fundamental transformation in their relationship, whereby the dominating invasive spirit that originally entered the host body as a dybbuk metamorphoses into a maggid — a positive mentor-angel — who bestows additional secrets, esoteric techniques, and practical knowledge on the exorcist to facilitate the success of the operation.

From the narrative and literary points of view, both works were written in the first-person with highly detailed autobiographical information, which provide the reader with a psychologically more nuanced presentation of these events. Exorcism procedures are depicted as highly dramatized complex rituals, where all involved walked a tightrope between life and death, heaven and hell, sanity and madness. They were spiritual-physical operations fraught with danger — not unlike the removal and cutting of a malignant growth — that were fundamentally therapeutic and results-oriented in nature, aimed at the restoration of balance for the individual, the community, and the cosmos at large. Perhaps in the end we may conclude that possession accounts above all provide "polyphony" in the words of Mikhail Bakhtin, a narrative world that grants validity to all voices[70] — those of the dead and those of the living — revealing with equal nuance the subtle murmurings of the unconscious and the exigencies of an oft-painful reality, and finally confirming gender biases and the promulgation of socially ingrained power structures, the active-subjugating male possessing spirit and the passive-subdued female body. Death itself, in the final count, is polyphonic and is far from being monologic — it merely opens paths for repair and restoration either on the other side or by catapulting souls back into new bodies through reincarnation or into host bodies through soul-impregnation (*ibbur*). All souls long for a resting place, a place of peace and repose — even the dead may yearn to die.

Notes

1. I would like to acknowledge and thank Dr. Agata Paluch, head of the Emmy Noether Research Group, "Patterns of Knowledge Circulation: The Transmission and Reception of Jewish Esoteric Knowledge in Manuscript and Print in Early Modern East-Central Europe," as well as the DFG (German Research Council), project number 401023278, for their support that enabled my research for this article.

2. On death in early modern kabbalistic literature, see Avriel Bar-Levav, "Ritualization of Death and Life: The Ethical Will of Rabbi Naphtali ha-Kohen Katz," in *Judaism in Practice: From the Middle Ages through the Early Modern Period*, ed. Lawrence Fine (Princeton: Princeton University Press, 2001), 155–67; Avriel Bar-Levav, "Rabbi Aaron Berakhiah of Modena and Rabbi Naftali Hakohen Katz: Founding Fathers of Books for the Sick," *Asufot* 9 (1995): 189–233 [Hebrew]; Avriel Bar-Levav, "Books of the Sick and the Dying in Jewish Conduct Literature," *Jerusalem Studies in Jewish Thought* 14 (1998): 342–91 [Hebrew].

3. J. H. Chajes, *Between Worlds: Dybbuks, Exorcists, and Early Modern Judaism* (Philadelphia: University of Pennsylvania Press, 2003), 11.

4. See the recently published monograph by Sara Ronis, *Demons in the Details: Demonic Discourse and Rabbinic Culture in Late Antique Babylonia* (Oakland: University of California Press, 2022).

5. For a brilliant overview of reincarnation in Italy during the Renaissance, see Brian Ogren, *Renaissance and Rebirth: Reincarnation in Early Modern Italian Kabbalah* (Leiden, Brill, 2009). Ogren draws attention to the fact that intense engagement with debates centered on the fate of the soul were reflective of a deeper preoccupation with identity and the self, see 71–101.

6. On the prevalent practice of *yiḥudim* among the kabbalists of Safed, see Lawrence Fine, "The Contemplative Practice of Yihudim in Lurianic Kabbalah," in *Jewish Spirituality: From the Sixteenth-Century Revival to the Present*, ed. Arthur Green (New York: Crossroads, 1987), 64–98.

7. See Bracha Sack, *Solomon Had a Vineyard: God, the Torah, and Israel in R. Shlomo Halevi Alkabetz's Writings* (Beer Sheva: Ben Gurion University of the Negev Press, 2018) [Hebrew]; Bracha Sack, *The Secret Teaching of R. Shlomo Halevi Alkabetz* (PhD diss., Brandeis University, 1977).

8. Two comprehensive studies on Moses Cordovero offer an excellent scholarly treatment of his kabbalistic ideas; Bracha Sack, "Some Remarks on Rabbi Moses Cordovero's *Shemua be-'Inyan ha-Gilgul*," in *Perspectives on Jewish Thought and Mysticism*, ed. Alfred L. Ivry, Elliot R. Wolfson, and Allan Arkush (London: Routledge, 2016), 277–88; Bracha Sack, *Through the Gates of Rabbi Moses Cordovero's Kabbalah* (Beer Sheva: Ben-Gurion University of the Negev Press, 1995) [Hebrew]; Bracha Sack, *From the Fountains of Sefer Elimah by R. Moses Cordovero and Studies in his Kabbalah* (Beer Sheva: Ben-Gurion University of the Negev Press, 2013) [Hebrew]. For a more recent engagement with Moses Cordovero's kabbalah, especially concerning angels, see Yoed Kadari, *Cordovero's Angels: Between Theoretical and Practical Kabbalah* (Los Angeles: Cherub Press, 2022) [Hebrew].

9. Karo himself was both a halakhic decisor and a kabbalist; see Solomon Schechter, "Safed in the Sixteenth Century: A City of Legists and Mystics," in *Studies in Judaism* (Piscataway, NJ: Gorgias Press, 2003), 202–88. See also Rachel Elior, "Joseph Karo and Israel Ba'al Shem Tov: Mystical Metamorphosis, Kabbalistic Inspiration, Spiritual Internalization," *Tarbiẓ* 65 (1996): 671–710 [Hebrew].

10. Jonathan Garb, "The Psychological Turn in Sixteenth Century Kabbalah," in *Les Mystiques Juives Chretiennes rt Musulmanes dans l'Egypte Medievale*, ed. Giuseppe Cecere, Mireille Loubet, and Samuela Pagani (Cairo: Institut Français d'Archéologie Orientale du Caire, 2013), 109–26, especially 111.

11. The rudimentary work on Luria and his mystical practice remains; Lawrence Fine, *Physician of the Soul, Healer of the Cosmos: Isaac Luria and His Kabbalistic Fellowship* (Stanford: Stanford University Press, 2004).

12. For an excellent and comprehensive survey of the Sharabi school and its pietistic practices, see Pinchas Giller, *Shalom Sha'rabi and the Kabbalists of Beit El* (Oxford: Oxford University Press, 2008).

13. Giller, *Shalom Sha'rabi*, 112.

14. On the concept of *tikkun*, see Assaf Nabarro, "Tikkun: From Lurianic Kabbalah to Popular Culture" (PhD diss., Ben-Gurion University of the Negev, 2006) [Hebrew]. On the gendered aspects of *tikkun*, see Elliot R. Wolfson, "*Tikkun ha-Shekhinah*: Redemption and the Overcoming of Gender Dimorphism in the Messianic Kabbalah of Moses Hayyim Luzzatto," *History of Religions* 36, no. 4 (1997): 289–332.

15. For an excellent collection of essays devoted to an interdisciplinary survey of possession in Judaism from the Middle Ages until contemporary times, see Matt Goldish, ed., *Spirit Possession in Judaism: Cases and Studies from the Middle Ages to the Present* (Detroit: Wayne University Press, 2003).

16. See Chajes, *Between Worlds*, 3.

17. Nimrod Zinger, *The Ba'al Shem and the Doctor*, 98.

18. Ḥai Gaon alludes to two typical activities associated with *ba'alei shem*: the first consists of a combination of angelic and divine names as well as natural substances for protection on the road against robbers and the natural elements, such as a stormy sea. The second refers to road-hopping and traveling large distances in a short period of time. See Nimrod Zinger, *The Ba'al Shem and the Doctor*, 99.

19. See Jonathan Garb, *Shamanic Trance in Modern Kabbalah* (Chicago: University of Chicago Press, 2011), 24–31. Moshe Rosman was one of the first scholars to designate the Ba'al Shem Tov as a shaman, drawing primarily on the work of Mircea Eliade, and to discuss his religious role in this capacity; see Moshe Rosman, *Founder of Hasidism: The Quest for the Historical Ba'al Shem Tov* (Berkeley: University of California Press, 1996), 13–16, 108, 111. Surprisingly, Immanuel Etkes, in his book on the Ba'al Shem Tov, makes only a minimal attempt to contextualize the activities of the Besht within a broader discourse on shamanism; see the only reference to shamanism in the context of the preparations the Besht undertook to become a *Ba'al Shem*; Immanuel Etkes, *The Besht: Magician, Mystic, Leader* (Waltham: Brandeis University Press, 2005), 56. For Haviva Pedaya's analysis of shamanism, see Haviva Pedaya, "Two Types of Ecstatic Experience in Hasidism," *Da'at* 55 (2005): 73–108 [Hebrew]; H. Pedaya, "Review of Immanuel Etkes: The Besht," *Zion* 70 (2005): 248–65; Etkes, "Review of Moshe Rosman: The Founder of Hasidism," *Zion* 69 (2004): 515–24; Etkes, "The Ba'al Shem Tov, R. Jacob Joseph of Polonnoye, and the Maggid of Mezirech: Outlines for a Religious Typology," *Da'at* 45 (2000): 25–73 [Hebrew]. For one of the first comprehensive treatments on Hasidism and shamanism, see Moshe Idel, *Ascensions on High in Jewish Mysticism: Pillars, Lines, Ladders* (Budapest: Central European University, 2005), 1–13.

20. See Ron Margolin, *The Human Temple: Religious Interiorization and the Structuring of Inner Life in Early Hasidism* (Jerusalem: Magnes Press, 2005) [Hebrew].

21. For an excellent study on early modern possession accounts in Ashkenazi manuscripts of magic, see Sara Zfatman, *Leave, Impure One: Jewish Exorcism in Early Modern Ashkenaz* (Jerusalem: Magnes Press, 2015) [Hebrew]. Zfatman adroitly notes the terminological shift from the Safedian usage of the term evil soul (*ruaḥ ra'ah*) to the eighteenth-century expression dybbuk (that which is attached), which placed greater emphasis on the mode — attachment — by which the malignant spirit operated. See Zfatman, *Leave Impure One*, XIV, fn. 7.

For an extensive analysis of the origins and iteration of the term dybbuk, see Morris M. Faierstein, "The Dybbuk: The Origins and History of a Concept," in *This World and the World to Come in Jewish Belief and Practice*, ed. Leonard J. Greenspoon (West Lafayette: Purdue University Press, 2017), 135–50.

22. On Hillel Ba'al Shem in general, see the defining article by Yohanan Petrovsky-Shtern, "The Master of an Evil Name: Hillel Baal Shem and His '*Sefer ha-Ḥeshekh*,'" *AJS Review* 28, no. 2 (2004): 217–48. For a recent study of Hillel Baal Shem's *Sefer ha-Ḥeshekh*, see the master's thesis of Sofia Korn, "The Manuscript of *Sefer ha-Ḥeshekh* and Its Medical Advice" [Ukranian] (M.A. thesis, National University of Kiev, Mohyla Academy, Department of History, 2020).

23. Petrovsky-Shtern has an insightful discussion of this exorcism case in his article "The Master of an Evil Name," 226–31. My intention here is less to connect the incident to the social ramifications of Hillel's position within the Jewish community, the direction that Petrovsky-Shtern takes, than to deconstruct Hillel's expertise as a *ba'al shem*, including his unique training, techniques, and experience as a healer of the soul. I am especially interested in the dialogical character of this exorcism and what it reveals about the reciprocal relationship between exorcist and the disembodied soul. The translation of primary passages is my own.

24. Vernadsky National Library of Ukraine, Orientalia Department, Judaica Manuscript Collection, *Sefer ha-Ḥeshekh*, MS OR. 178, 125a–b.

25. For a social-historical reading of the context of this exorcism, see Petrovsky-Shtern, "The Master of an Evil Name," 230, where he highlights the various points of tension among the participants who appear in this story: Hillel, the communal authority in Ostróg, ordinary Jews who live in the town, the Christians, and the Church officials, as well as the demon.

26. See Pawel Maciejko, *The Mixed Multitude: Jacob Frank and the Frankist Movement, 1755–1816* (Philadelphia: University of Pennsylvania Press, 2011). For additional reading on apostasy and Jewish-Christian relations in the Eastern European context, see Edward Fram and Magda Teter, "Apostasy, Fraud, and the Beginning of Hebrew Printing in Cracow," *AJS Review* 30, no. 1 (2006): 31–66; Magda Teter, *Jews and Heretics in Catholic Poland: A Beleaguered Church in the Post-Reformation Era* (New York: Cambridge University Press, 2005); Magda Teter, "The Legend of Ger Zedek of Wilno as Polemic and Reassurance," *AJS Review* 29, no. 2 (2005): 237–64; Magda Teter, "Jewish Conversions to Catholicism in the Polish-Lithuanian Commonwealth of the Seventeenth and Eighteenth Centuries," *Jewish History* 17, no. 3 (2003): 257–83.

27. See Gedalya Nigal, *Dybbuk Tales*, 26–28.

28. *Alphabet of Ben Sira*, https://www.sefaria.org/Otzar_Midrashim%2C_The_Aleph_Bet_of_ben_Sira%2C_The_Alphabet_of_ben_Sira%2C_(alternative_version).33?lang=bi.

29. *Sefer ha-Ḥeshekh*, MS OR. 178, 125b–126a. An incident connected to magical activities and possibly caused by demons is recounted by R. Hayyim Vital in *Book of Visions* (*Sefer ha-Heznoyot*). This event leaves him with a loss of his

eyesight for which he seeks remedy from an Arab sorcerer and magician, Sheik Ibn Ayyub. See Morris M. Faierstein, *Jewish Mystical Autobiographies: Book of Visions and Book of Secrets* (New York: Paulist Press, 1999), 50–51.

30. *Sefer ha-Ḥeshekh* MS OR. 178, 126a–b.

31. On the gendered aspects of spirit possession, see J. H. Chajes, "He Said She Said: Hearing the Voices of Pneumatic Early Modern Jewish Women," *Nashim* 10 (2005): 99–125.

32. *Sefer ha-Ḥeshekh* MS OR. 178, 126b. Hillel's mentor was Rabbi Ẓevi Hirsch (d. 1724) from Mezerich. He was from a prominent rabbinic family — his grandfather, R. Ẓevi Hirsch, was the head of the rabbinic court and appears in seventeenth-century responsa literature. He himself served as the head of the rabbinic court and also was the author of a responsa collection, *Torat Ḥayyim* (Lublin 1708, 1724). It is clear, however, that in addition to his rabbinic erudition, Ẓevi Hirsch was erudite in both theoretical and practical Kabbalah and had a substantial library of relevant works that Hillel was invited to consult and copy from. See Petrovsky-Shtern, "The Master of an Evil Name," 225, and fn. 44–46 on the same page. For additional reference on Ẓevi Hirsch, see Meir Edelboym, *Di yidn-shtot Mezrich* (Buenos-Aires: Mezricher-lanslayt- farayn in Argentina, 1957), 294–97.

33. *Sefer ha-Ḥeshekh* MS OR. 178, 126b.

34. *Sefer ha-Ḥeshekh* MS OR. 178, 126b–127a.

35. *Sefer ha-Ḥeshekh* MS OR. 178, 127a.

36. Yoram Bilu, "*Dybbuk* and *Maggid*: Two Cultural Patterns of Altered Consciousness in Judaism," *AJS Review* 21, no. 2 (1996): 341–66. See also J. H. Chajes, "Judgments Sweetened: Possession and Exorcism in Early Modern Jewish Culture," *Journal of Early Modern History* 1, no. 2 (1997): 124–69. On salient examples of the benevolent type of possession accounts (through a maggid), see J. Z. Werblowsky, *Joseph Karo: Lawyer and Mystic* (Philadelphia: Jewish Publication Society, 1977); Lawrence Fine, "Maggidic Revelation in the Teachings of Isaac Luria," in *Mystics, Philosophers, and Politicians: Essays in Jewish Intellectual History in Honor of Alexander Altmann*, ed. J. Reinharz, D. Swetschinski, and K. Bland (Durham: Duke University Press, 1982), 141–57.

> 37. And the evil spirit would soon reveal to me terrible secrets and no more should be mentioned about it in this book, on account of my worry, anxiety, and distress! The One, who said to His world, "Enough!" should also proclaim concerning my suffering, "Enough!" May I merit to repair all the defect I caused — having sinned, done wrong, and transgressed (Mishnah Yoma 3:8), both in my youth and more recently. For there is no person on earth who does good, but does not also sin; a fortiori, a person who uses holy names in this bitter exile, alas, I have done it all, for the sake of saving Jewish souls so they would acknowledge that there is a God in heaven who judges, blessed is He and blessed in His name, who gave from his wisdom to those who fear Him so they

could carry out [magical] operations, with God's help. (*Sefer ha-Ḥeshekh* MS OR. 178, 127a–b)

38. See Yoram Bilu, "The Moroccan Demon in Israel: The Case of 'Evil Spirit Disease,'" *Ethos* 8, no. 1 (1980): 24–38; for this expression, see 27.

39. Concerning a historical contextualization of Yehudah Fetaya among the sages and scholars of Babylonian- Iraqi Jewry, see Avraham Ben-Ya'akov, *The Jews of Babylonia: From the End of the Geonic Era until Today* (Jerusalem: Sivan Press Ltd., 1979), 200–3 [Hebrew]. For a defining compilation of the history of possession accounts including those that appear in Fetaya's *Minhat Yehudah*, see Gedalya Nigal, *Dybbuk Tales in Jewish Literature/Sippurei Dybbuk be-Sifrut Yisrael* (Jerusalem: Reuven Mass, 1983) [Hebrew].

40. Jonathan Meir, *Kabbalistic Circles in Jerusalem: 1896–1948*, trans. Avi Aronsky (Leiden: Brill, 2016), 60, fn. 126.

41. See Meir, *Kabbalistic Circles in Jerusalem*, 61. On Fetaya's life, see Yehoshuah Moshe, *Sefer Kets ha-Yamin* (Jerusalem: Bakal, 1967), 47–50 [Hebrew]; Yishai Shaul Dvir, *Ish mi-Beit Lehem Yehudah* (Bnei Brak: Dvir, 2012) [Hebrew]. On R. Fetaya's proficiency as a shaman-exorcist, see Aescoly, "The Rectifier of Sabbatai Ẓvi's Soul," 214, 238, 243; Ya'ari, *Ta'alumat Sefer*, 13, 150–53; Nigal, *Dybbuk Tales*, 198–227. As Meir points out, Fetaya's mentor, R. Shimon Agassi, also deployed dreams and exorcism as a shaman-healer, see his "Visions and Revelations of Elijah," in *The Book on the Teachings Concerning Reincarnation/Sefer Torat ha-Gilgul* (Jerusalem: Ahavat Shalom, 2014) [Hebrew]; see J. Meir, *Kabbalistic Circles*, 61.

42. The notion that the soul of a wicked person is punished in the afterlife by being deprived of a resting place and instead slung around like a stone in a slingshot originates from the Bible, 1 Samuel 25:28. In this context, this expression is articulated by Abigail, the wicked Nabal's wife, in her speech to King David, where she depicts two contradictory fates of the human soul: accordingly, the righteous soul is bound up, becomes attached to, and is incorporated into a bundle of life, an assemblage of similar spiritual entities. This state is contrasted by Abigail with the solitary, atomized, and disconnected state of the souls of sinners, who wander aimlessly devoid of peace and rest in the afterlife. The Zohar expands this idea further and uses the trope of the slingshot to describe the punishment of wicked souls (see Zohar 1: 107a; 1:217b; 2:59b; 2:99b; 2:142b; 3:24b; 3:25a; 3:186a: 3:213b).

43. Fine, *Physician of the Soul*, 150–87; Shaul Magid, "Conjugal Union, Mourning, and Talmud Torah in R. Isaac Luria's *Tikkun Haẓot*," *Da'at* 36 (1996): 17–45; Assaf Tamari, "Medicalizing Magic and Ethics: Rereading Lurianic Practice," *Jewish Quarterly Review* 112, no. 3 (2022): 434–67, 434.

44. See Shaul Magid, "From Theosophy to Midrash: Lurianic Exegesis and the Garden of Eden," *AJS Review* 22, no. 1 (1997): 37–75; concerning this formulation, see 58.

45. See A. Z. Aescoly, *Book of Visions Sefer Hezyonot* (Jerusalem: Mosad Harav Kook, 1954); a second critical edition was published by Morris M. Faierstein,

Sefer Hezyonot: Yomano shel R. Hayyim Vital (Jerusalem: Machon Ben Ẓvi, 2005) [Hebrew]; Morris M Faierstein, *Jewish Mystical Autobiographies*. Concerning Lurianic hagiographic literature in the seventeenth century, see Meir Benayahu, *Toldot ha-Ari* (Jerusalem: Machon Ben Ẓvi, 1967) [Hebrew].

46. Yehudah Fetaya, *Sefer Ruḥot Mesaprot* (Jerusalem: A. H. Bronstein, 1954), 2 [Hebrew]. The quote is in my translation. The printers explain that *Ruḥot Mesaprot* originally comprised a section of a larger work titled *Minḥat Yehudah*, written by Fetaya and published in Baghdad in 1933; nevertheless, they felt it constituted a free-standing thematic unit that deserved to be printed and studied on its own.

47. Yehudah Fetaya, *The Offering of Judah* (*Minḥat Yehudah*), trans. Avraham Leader (Jerusalem: Mechon HaKtav, 2010), 280. For ease of reference, I use the English translation of the work by Avraham Leader, with some exceptions.

48. Hayyim Vital, *Sha'ar ha-Kavvanot* (Jerusalem: Mekhor Hayyim, 1962/63), 62a.

49. Vital, *Sha'ar ha-Kavvanot*, 282. For an essential study on the Lurianic concept of evil, see Isaiah Tishby, *The Doctrine of Evil and the Shell in Lurianic Kabbalah* (Jerusalem: Schocken, 1984). By comparison, for the Zoharic interpretation of evil, see Nathaniel Berman, *Divine and Demonic in the Poetic Mythology of the Zohar* (Leiden: Brill, 2018).

50. Fetaya, *The Offering*, 281.

51. Bruce Lincoln, *Discourse and the Construction of Society: Comparative Studies of Myth, Ritual, and Classification* (New York: Oxford University Press, 1989), 3.

52. Fetaya, *The Offering*, 284.

53. Shaul Sehayik, "Changes in the Status of Urban Jewish Women in Iraq at the End of the Nineteenth Century," *Pe'amim* 36 (1988): 64–88 [Hebrew]; Naomi Gale, "Iraqi Jewish Women," Shalvi Encyclopedia of Jewish Women, Jewish Women's Archive, https://jwa.org/encyclopedia/article/iraqi-jewish-women.

54. Fetaya, *The Offering*, 320.

55. Fetaya, *The Offering*, 321.

56. Fetaya, *The Offering*, 333.

57. Jeppe Sinding Jensen, "Framing Religious Narrative, Cognition and Culture Theoretically," in *Religious Narrative, Cognition and Culture: Image and Word in the Mind of Narrative*, ed. Armin W. Geertz and Jeppe Sinding Jensen (Sheffield: Equinox Publishing, 2011), 35. See the excellent application of the cognitive approach to Christian and Jewish exorcism and demonological accounts in Ildiko Glaser-Hille, "The Demonic Book Club: Demonology, Social Discourses, and the Creation of Identity in German Demonic Ritual Magic, 1350-1580" (PhD diss., Concordia University, 2019).

58. Jensen, "Framing," 36.

59. Jensen, "Framing," 38.

60. Glaser-Hille, "The Demonic," 74.

61. Ann Taves, "Non-Ordinary Powers: Charisma, Special Affordances, and

the Study of Religion," in *Mental Culture: Classical Social Theory and the Cognitive Science of Religion*, ed. Dimitris Xygalatas and William W. McCorkle Jr. (Durham: Acumen Publishing Limited, 2013), 81.

62. Lawrence Fine, *Physician of the Soul, Healer of the Cosmos* (Stanford: Stanford University Press, 2003).

63. On the technique of *yiḥudim* and its prevalent deployment in Lurianic healing rituals, see Lawrence Fine, "The Contemplative Practice of Yihudim in Lurianic Kabbalah," in *Jewish Spirituality: From the Sixteenth-Century Revival to the Present*, ed. Arthur Green (New York: Crossroads, 1987), 64–98.

64. Fetaya, *The Offering*, 299.

65. Fetaya, *The Offering*, 301.

66. Fetaya, *The Offering*, 302.

67. Yoram Bilu, "Dybbuk and Maggid: Two Cultural Patterns of Altered Consciousness in Judaism," *AJS Review* 21, no. 2 (1996): 341–66.

68. In fact, Eli Yassif notes that "technical procedures of exorcism hardly changed during the hundreds of years of their recording." See Eli Yassif, "*Between Worlds: Dybbuks, Exorcists, and Early Modern Judaism* by J. H. Chajes," *History of Religions* 46, no. 2 (2006): 179–84.

69. See Chajes, *Between Worlds*, 21.

70. Caryl Emerson, "Mikhail Bakhtin," Filosofia: An Encyclopedia of Russian Thought, https://filosofia.dickinson.edu/encyclopedia/bakhtin-mikhail/.

SECTION IV

HASIDIC TEACHINGS ON REINCARNATION

BETWEEN THE INDIVIDUAL AND THE COMMUNITY

ARIEL EVAN MAYSE

Devotion Reborn

12

GILGUL AND THE LIFE OF PRAXIS IN HASIDISM

THE THEOLOGY OF HASIDISM builds on the armature of medieval and early modern Kabbalah.[1] While Hasidic sermons draw from a very wide panorama of Jewish mystical sources and may appear to melt away into a multitude of footnotes,[2] their creativity is often visible precisely in the creative synthesis and reinterpretation of earlier traditions. This is equally true of the countless Hasidic homilies, letters, hagiographical tales, and even Talmudic commentaries[3] in which the concept of *gilgul* ("transmigration," "reincarnation" or "rebirth") operates as a central theme.[4] Hasidism, a movement of pietistic religious renewal that emerged in the eighteenth century and swept across eastern Europe, is saturated by a folk culture in which the presence of spiritual rebirth was taken for granted. These teachings do not substantively add to the intricate Lurianic theories of *gilgul*,[5] yet they subtly but unmistakably transform the concept of rebirth as a "gift," which is understood as an expression of divine compassion and love. Hasidic teachings, moreover, invoke the concept of *gilgul* to underscore the vital importance of this-worldly spiritual action.[6]

The present chapter examines Hasidic teachings that connect transmigration to the life of religious praxis. A small number of Hasidic teachings use *gilgul* to probe struggles with theodicy, unexplained suffering, and impermanence, but the vast majority link rebirth to issues of ritual.[7] Some refer to *gilgul* as necessitated by transgression or because the worshipper failed to fulfill some commandment; others describe rebirth as necessitated by failure to serve God through sanctifying ordinary actions. I examine the role of the Hasidic leader *ẓaddik* as a healer of souls who descends into the physical world to help others break free from the cycles of *gilgul*. The chapter concludes with striking reinterpretations of the concept of rebirth in the literatures of twentieth-century Hasidism, a phenomenon that must be contextualized within larger religious, cultural, and intellectual trends. These texts emphasize the spiritual opportunities afforded by *gilgul*, yet they underscore that awareness of the possibility of rebirth should shape religious praxis during one's current lifetime. The soul's work ought to be completed through the *miẓvot*, raising up those fallen fragments of sacred light that are also aspects of the worshipper's own soul.

The concept of a cycle of death, transmigration, and rebirth (*saṃsāra* or *punarjanma*) is a well-known feature of both Buddhism and Hinduism. In many cases, Hasidic and Buddhist or Indic teachings evince a similar tension between the ubiquity of rebirth and the specific focus on this-worldly "action" (*karma*). Many Buddhist and Hindu thinkers viewed *saṃsāra* as part of an automatic and ever-unfolding "flow of life-powers" that includes "successive states of birth, death and rebirth";[8] these same traditions have developed a robust ritual world for averting karmic consequences.[9] The twinned concepts of *saṃsāra* and *karma* thus place "responsibility for the present upon each individual's past," suggests Austin B. Creel, but "at the same time, the future is dependent upon present behavior."[10] For Tibetan Buddhists, one's ultimate aim must be to break free from the "wheel of rebirth"[11] through taking refuge in the Dharma and through various kinds of virtuous action.[12] A careful conversation with these sophisticated religious traditions will, in my estimation, offer us an opportunity to think more deeply about Hasidic teachings on *gilgul* and the intertwined themes of fate, destiny, and the meaning of religious this-worldly religious practice.

The Body, Commandments, and the Self

Hasidic sources assume that one's present circumstances in this world reflect actions in previous lives. Though presented as a unique spiritual opportunity, rebirth is not held up as the permanent ideal; Hasidic literature is filled with exhortations to perform the *miẓvot* correctly so as to avoid the need for transmigration.[13] Such teachings often invoke the Lurianic tradition that one must perform each of the 613 commandments correctly to pass beyond the cycles of rebirth,[14] generally presenting this claim without extensively discussing its intricate metaphysical and cosmological underpinnings: "One who lacks that garment for the World to Come [woven] by the commandments," claims Ya'akov Yosef of Pollonye (d. 1783), "must return and undergo rebirth naked (*'arum*) in this world, until fulfilling all 613 commandments with purity, as is explained in *Sefer ha-Gilgulim*."[15] The *miẓvot* create a "cloak" (*ḥaluka*) or "garment" (*levush*) worn by the soul after death, and one must be reborn into this world if the sublime mantle has not been finished.[16] Each *miẓvah* represents a discrete ritual act, and together these threads of inspiration are stitched into a garment that delivers the soul from the process of rebirth.

This Lurianic tradition was also favored by Shneur Zalman of Liady (1745–1812), who emphatically underscored: "A Jew must be reborn many times until all 613 commandments of the Torah have been fulfilled in thought, speech and action, completing the garments of his soul and repairing them, so that no garment is missing."[17] The *miẓvot* must be correctly executed in the domains of action, language, and intellection or contemplation, thus uniting mind and body and weaving a holistic garment for the soul. For the intellectually inclined Shneur Zalman, a noted rabbinic scholar as well as a mystical theologian of remarkable depth,[18] escaping the cycle of rebirth is not just a matter of *doing* the *miẓvot* correctly; rather for him, *knowing* and mental or intellectual grasp of the Torah is of primary import: "One who can understand quite a bit but is lazy and grasps only a little, must be reincarnated until one grasps and understands all that is possible for his soul to grasp in knowledge of Torah."[19]

The triad of "thought, speech, and action" (*maḥashavah*, *dibbur*, and *ma'aseh*) came directly to Shneur Zalman from the works of medieval Kabbalah, and the writings of Moshe Cordovero in particular,[20] but this mode of organization has a fascinating conceptual parallel in Vajrayana Buddhism. The Buddha is said to have referred to domains of "body" (*kāya*), "speech" (*vāk*), and "mind" (*citta*), described as the "three doors" or "gates" (*trid-vāra*), avenues through which human beings act in the world and ought to seek enlightenment. In tantric practice, these three domains serve to guide visualization practices and organize forms of ritual empowerment that transform the practitioners' heart-mind, body, and modes of speech.[21]

The "alien" or "distracting thoughts" that accost one in worship are often said to originate within the self as the direct result of actions in previous lives.[22] The topic of *gilgul* also surfaces in Hasidic meditations on how the body is itself constructed through the *miẓvot*, for properly performing these rituals heals the physical body and leaves an imprint on it.[23] Levi Yitshak of Barditchev (1740–1809) writes:

We know that the Kabbalists and the investigators of God [i.e., the philosophers] disagreed regarding the body in which a person, who has been reborn several times, will be resurrected.[24] The Kabbalists claim that it will be the first body, whereas the philosophers maintain that it is the most recent body.

I believe there is a middle path. We know that the 248 positive commandments correspond to the 248 limbs, and the 365 negative commandments to the sinews... [25] One who fulfills the entire Torah repairs and completes the construction of his body, with its 248 limbs and 365 sinews. If one is deficient in a *miẓvah*, the corresponding limb is damaged and will be missing ... One must be reborn many times until all the *miẓvot* are repaired, and, through this, all of the limbs are healed.[26]

The worshipper's body and soul must be perfected through the ritual craft of the *miẓvot*, and, if this connective work is not accomplished during a single lifetime, one must undergo rebirth until the task is done. This, claims Levi Yitshak, is key for answering the question regarding the identity of the resurrected body. One's future corpus — a perfected body filled with a completed spirit — is a constellation of limbs assembled from this spiritual work accomplished across many different lifetimes.[27] The resurrected human self is assembled from multiple dimensions that are all brought together into a single bodily instrument of illumination that carries one into the World to Come and the end of the cycles of rebirth.[28]

A deep philosophical question emerges from successive states of reincarnation: "Why are we here?"[29] There is some debate in Hasidic sources about whether or not an individual is, or ought to be, aware of actions in previous lives. Discovering such knowledge is sometimes said to be very difficult, requiring strong powers of internal discernment and speculation.[30] Sometimes it is the teacher's task to reveal past lives to their disciples,[31] although many teachings suggest that one who pays constant attention to the movements of their religious life can attain knowledge of why they have been reborn.[32] Given that *gilgul* comes about for a specific purpose, many Hasidic sources often describe awareness of rebirth part of understanding one's unique connection to the *miẓvot* in this world:

Each individual can understand and know why one has been reborn. When one sees that his heart is drawn more to this *miẓvah* than to all the others, he knows that he has been reborn because of this. He was lacking that particular *miẓvah*. And if one sees that he is drawn to a particular transgression above all others, such that his heart verily burns for it, he may thus know that he sinned in a pervious *gilgul* in this matter and must repair it.[33]

One is forced to undergo rebirth because of unfinished spiritual work, suggests Menahem Nahum of Chernobil (c. 1730–1797), and this specific knowledge may be gleaned from one's intuitive yearning for particular modes of praxis in this life. Each person has a particular *mizṿah* to which they are more connected, a foundational realm of practice in which one must expend additional physical, emotional, and contemplative effort.[34] *Gilgul* is also necessitated if one undertakes a new mode of worship but cannot finish the practice, whether a *mizṿah* or some other kind of devotional project. Naftali of Ropshits (1760–1827) explains: "One who begins to conduct himself in some new way in the service of God . . . and has not completed it . . . must be reincarnated several times to complete that which he began."[35] Transmigration, therefore, is linked not only to compliance with the 613 commandments, but to individual modes of praxis connected to a worshipper's unique, personal spiritual journey. Even the legally minded Shnuer Zalman notes that one must be reincarnated to fulfill all of the commandments, but we are reborn for the purpose of paying mind to a specific *mizṿah* in each lifetime.[36]

The looming specter of *gilgul*, a consequence merited "even if one lacks one of the rabbinic *mizṿot*," surely functioned to shore up religious authority and ensure compliance with the *mizṿot*.[37] While irreligiosity among the youth was by no means unknown even in the small cities of Eastern Europe in the 1700s, Hasidism shifted its teachings on religious practice in the decades before and immediately after the Congress of Vienna. With the appearance of Haskalah and the threat of breakdown of *halakhic* norms on the horizon, Hasidic leaders no longer referred to rote worship (called *mizṿat anashim melumadah*) as the chief enemy of spiritual life. They sought to defend the *mizṿot* and *halakhah* against a growing enemy.[38] Significant dimensions of Hasidic discourse on the commandments — and, hence, *gilgul* — are part of an attempt to produce a compelling religious doctrine against those who sought to modify Jewish observance or reform it.

This line of thinking appears in the teachings of Ẓvi Elimelekh Shapira of Dinov (1785–1841), an important Hasidic leader and legal authority in Galicia and Hungary who twinned fierce anti-modern rhetoric with mystical reflections on ritual life.[39] His fascinating book *Derekh Pekudeikha*, a work that interprets many important commandments through prisms of thought, speech, and action, justifies key elements of his project through reference to *gilgul*:

> The soul is hewn from below the Throne of Glory. It is a full spiritual structure, composed of 248 spiritual limbs and 365 spiritual sinews. Why does it come to this world? Each limb and sinew must be illuminated through action in this world, the realm of action, through performing the 248 positive commandments that correspond to the 248 soul-limbs and the 365 negative precepts that correspond to its sinews . . . Through fulfilling all of them, the spiritual body is created, the garment called the "cloak of the rabbis," worn by the soul in the Garden of Eden.[40]

The soul, as we have seen, descends from its supernal origin to construct a garment. Much as the worshipper's body needs to be transformed through praxis, the soul's spiritual structure must be illuminated through performing the *miẓvot*. The consequences of failing to do so, claims Ẓvi Elimelekh Shapira, are dire: "If an individual fails to fulfill even one of the commandments, he must be reincarnated [*le-hitgalgel*] or implanted [*le-hit'aber*]. . . . If one is too lazy to perform a commandment within his power, then he must truly be reincarnated."[41] Shapira's opening presents a distillation of Lurianic teaching, emphasizing the importance of fulfilling the commandments, but his innovation lies in his creative deployment of this framing throughout this important treatise that often goes overlooked in academic scholarship on Hasidism.

The communal dimension of this project, moreover, ought to be underscored, since it is the collective process of *gilgul* that all souls come back to rest in the Divine. "I have heard that a person accrues sins from previous or earlier births," claims Moshe Efrayim Hayyim, "But when one prays for sinners, then his own transgressions are repairs as well."[42] Highlighting the network of human interconnectivity, Ẓvi Elimelekh Shapira writes:

> I have also received [this tradition] about one who has been prevented from performing some commandment. If he sees a friend about to fulfill this commandment, he should help him perform it both physically and monetarily. All Israel are a single body, and all souls share a single root. This is particularly true when one's friend intends to do it in the name of all Israel, as in the formula customarily said [before a commandment]: "For the sake of uniting the blessed Holy One and *Shekhinah* in the name of all Israel."[43]

The Jewish people share a common origin in the Divine.[44] Despite the multiplicity of human phenomena that results from *gilgul*, the people of Israel remain connected and may therefore assist one another in seeking to transcend the cycles of rebirth.

Hasidic sources, as is well-known, extend the life of ritual beyond the traditional actions of the *miẓvot*. Many Hasidic homilies argue that even ordinary deeds like eating, drinking, business dealings, or sexual intercourse may be sanctified and imbued with theurgic power if they are performed with attunement, attention, and presence.[45] Scholem noted that Hasidism thus brought together the once-distinct concepts of attachment (*devekut*) and the notion that cosmic restoration (*tikkun*) is accomplished as the individual restores the fallen sacred sparks that originated within him.[46] These sparks, dispersed and reborn as souls in search of repair, fill the material world and call on worshippers to return them to their origin in the Divine.[47] The fragments of divinity encountered in such moments of ordinary illumination are far from random; they are intimately connected to the worshipper:[48] "All of one's food, dwelling and business, his generation and his spouse," claims Ya'akov Yosef of Pollonye, "everything comes to the person as progeny (*toledot*) of his sparks."[49] "One raises up the spark that is within the food," claims Levi Yitshak, "If one does not do so, the spark in that food must be reborn again until one eats it with the intention to uplift it."[50] One who eats to sate their appetite, rather than to perform this sacred work, must undergo rebirth as well.[51] The worshipper's quest to unite and redeem the sparks is an expression of love for God and, one might argue, also for other people: "The blessed Holy One is a compassionate father. No stray [soul] remains outcast,[52] and must be reborn several times, returning to this world over and over again."[53] Rather than referring to *gilgul* as a punishment in which the soul is cast back into the messy, unhappy physical world by a capricious God, Hasidic sources highlight the opportunity of rebirth as an act of compassion and divine love that serves to infuse religious practice with a new spectrum of meaning and intention.[54]

Lives of the *Ẓaddikim*

As astutely noted by Jonathan Garb, despite advancing little doctrinal innovation regarding the notion of *gilgul*, Hasidism nonetheless offered "a substantial hagiographical discourse on the various incarnations of the Hasidic master" that aimed to establish their authority. This statement can be traced in the various accounts of exceptional birth or identity associated with *Ẓaddikim*, some of which were autobiographical. The concept of reincarnation also was crucial for the famed Maiden of Ludmir, a storied figure and purported female Hasidic leader who was not related by blood to a male *Ẓaddik*: "In the absence of a biological link," writes Nathaniel Deutsch, "the doctrine of reincarnation established a spiritual connection between the Maiden of Ludmir and a male *Ẓaddik*." In addition, the *Ẓaddik*'s current exalted status may well reflect something that transpired in earlier births. The *Ẓaddik* earns rest and respite in the World to Come, but any repose and security enjoyed in this present life is the direct result of merit accrued through having been a *Ẓaddik* in previous incarnations.[55]

The practice of raising up souls compelled to undergo rebirth is often left to spiritually talented individuals, figures who take responsibility for the cosmic well-being of their community, for the entire generation, and even for long-dead individuals in need of repair. Claims to authority by Hasidic leaders were often justified through appeal to their status in previous incarnations, their material circumstances, and spiritual power depicted as the direct result of merit accrued in earlier incarnations.[56] In some cases, this enduring virtue arises less from the correct performance of the *miẓvot* and more from spiritual power that was a result of the *devekut* or mindfulness with which they completed a particular commandment of the Torah.[57]

The conceptual link between the *Ẓaddik* and reincarnation, however, involves more than a quest for spiritual lineage and authority. The idea of *gilgul* held an array of implications for the *Ẓaddik*'s religious praxis as well: "There are holy sparks connected to the root of each and every *Ẓaddik*'s soul. He must repair them and raise them up. This is even true of his servants, beasts, and belongings. All have sacred sparks that must be repaired and lifted up to their source."[58] The *Ẓaddik* must be alert to the fallen aspects of divinity, understanding that each of these reborn souls or sparks must be healed and restored to their divine root.

These fragments are related to the root of the leader's own soul and his previous incarnations, but many Hasidic teachings underscore that *Ẓaddikim* undergo the process of rebirth to help others and assist them in breaking free from this cycle. Countless hagiographical tales refer to souls being forced to transmigrate because they were not zealous in keeping certain commandments, and Hasidic leaders are charged with helping to free them from this temporal prison.[59] These teachers, as noted, are also tasked with revealing their disciples' past lives,[60] charting their various rebirths, and communicating how to overcome this cycle.[61] Sometimes righteous souls return as a burst of vital energy (called *'ibbur*) that "impregnates" a worshipper to complete some ritual or meritorious deed with greater intensity,[62] but in many other sources, full rebirth for the sake of others is described as the raison d'être of the *Ẓaddik*:

> One will become reborn to uplift the rungs of people who are his sparks, and his branches., so that they are all repaired. But when he descends in order to repair others, he does not wish to, because he is afraid that that he will not return and will come to sin, until being promised that he will not come to sin. It seems to say this in *Sefer ha-Gilgulim*.[63] Perhaps this is the meaning of the Mishnah: "One who brings merit to the many will not come to sin (m. Avot 5:18)."[64]

Raising up these individuals is not necessarily an easy task, and sometimes the Ẓaddik's job demands the fierce eye of rebuke.[65] But, much as in Buddhism, where certain kinds of religious specialists are responsible for such rituals for breaking the cycle of rebirth, the *Ẓaddik* is bound by duty and metaphysics to assist others.[66] There is sometimes a distinction made in the Buddhist literature between rebirth — the uncontrolled continuity through states of existence in *saṃsāra* characterized by suffering — and reincarnation, or the willful and controlled rebirth by dint of spiritual mastery, as in the Tibetan lama system.[67] Many branches of Buddhism further recognize the concept bodhisattvas, enlightened individuals who defer their escape from *saṃsāra* to help others. Likewise, the *Ẓaddik*, a figure of tremendous spirit and power, is delivered back to this world and reborn to help other people[68] — even their enemies.[69]

The experience of rebirth is complicated and fraught, to be sure, and many Hasidic sources describe the fear of those poised to reenter the world. One poignant homily refers to the soul of the *Ẓaddik*, sensing the trepidation of those other souls poised at the entrance to paradise, sweeping them down into the physical world and assuring them that they will never be lost.[70] It is worth noting, however, that the Hasidic sources connect such communal concerns to the *Ẓaddik*'s own spiritual peregrinations even within this lifetime. The vacillations of his religious life, including his descent from a state of spiritual attainment, are necessary because so many other souls have fallen and become trapped in this world:

> Why is it that one has to fall from one's rung? There are fallen souls; some have been fallen since the six days of Creation, while others fall in each generation and are reincarnated. Those souls wander, not having the means to come to God. Within their lifetimes they were involved in

> worldly frivolities and accomplished nothing. When the *Ẓaddik* falls from his rung and afterwards rises up, as in "Seven times the *Ẓaddik* falls and stands up" (Prov. 24:16), he goes up to God and uplifts those souls with him. He can only uplift those souls that are of his root. That is why every person has to fall from his rung, to uplift those souls that belong to his root. Understand this.[71]

The *Ẓaddik* must rectify these fallen souls, but doing so requires him to undergo a similar moment of religious descent. The careful reader, of course, will see that Menahem Nahum of Chernobil has subtly expanded this dynamic to include all spiritual seekers. While the *Ẓaddik* may rest at the center of this dynamic, offering a model as to how to lift up the wandering souls, all individuals must descend — and subsequently ascend — to accomplish some type of critical spiritual work.

Often the *Ẓaddikim* are said to be sent back to the lowest, most complicated situations.[72] But what if the soul of a *Ẓaddik* does not wish to undertake the burden of returning to this world? This question arises in the teachings of Nahman of Bratslav, for whom soul-repair is a recurrent theme. One of his famous sermons includes a parable about a gardener embodied by the *Ẓaddik* who heals "wandering" or "naked souls" (*neshamot 'arumot*),[73] terms generally invoked in discussions of *gilgul*, but the novelty in Nahman's teaching is the power of the *Ẓaddik* to heal souls *without* their need to undergo *gilgul*.[74]

Another fascinating story discloses Nahman's unique teachings concerning *gilgul*. Set against the narrative backdrop of a funeral procession, Nahman and his disciple, Nathan Shternhartz, dialogue on the nature of life and death: "The dead person is probably laughing at their tears for him," claims Nahman, "since crying about someone who passes from this world is like saying, 'better for you to extend your days in this world and suffer more afflictions and bitterness.'"[75] Nathan suggests that this person will continue to suffer in the grave, but Nahman replies that posthumous discomfort does not endure for long: "I asked him again," writes Nathan, "but surely there are rebirths, and perhaps he will need to be born yet again into this world. If so, what use was his departing from this world's suffering now."[76] One can, claims Nahman in a moment of staggering audacity, simply refuse to be reborn. Nathan is understandably astonished, but Nahman assures him that stubborn protestation postmortem in the heavenly world can prevent one from undergoing transmigration. Electrified, and perhaps still puzzled,

Nathan shares the following with the reader: "I took this [advice] to heart, binding it to my mind in order to remember it very well. Perhaps I will merit to remember it in the World to Come, putting this claim before the supernal court so that I can refuse to be reincarnated."[77]

Kabbalistic and Hasidic tradition, however, held that cycles of transmigration ultimately depended on human action reflecting a nearly automatic system of cause and effect. Likewise, in many classical works of Hindu philosophy, "the system of rebirth is a mechanical one, the acts one does inevitably determining what happens in the future."[78] A somewhat different position emerges from the devotionally oriented works of the pietistic *bhakti* movement, in which "one's efforts are made not to escape from rebirth, but rather to attain God."[79] Emphasizing the values of loyalty, devotion, and loving obeisance, in *bhakti* writings, "*saṃsāra* itself is conceived not as an intricate mechanism for the recompense of one's acts, but rather as a nightmarish condition from which the only release is God."[80] Hasidic sources share many of these values, including the powerful yearning to take refuge in the Divine, though they generally do not describe this-worldly existence in such draconian and pessimistic terms. Nahman of Bratslav, drawing upon the rabbinic tradition of arguing with the God,[81] goes one step further: the cycles of rebirth may be broken by one who is willing to stand up to the Divine.

Twentieth-Century Transformations: "The Merit of Women"

The concept of *gilgul* was a controversial doctrine long before it was incorporated into the fabric of Hasidism. Mentioned, and dismissed, already in the ninth century in the debates between Saadia Gaon and the Karaites, the mythos of rebirth became an important doctrine in the writings of medieval kabbalists — especially in sixteenth-century Lurianic Kabbalah. Nevertheless, *gilgul* remained a largely esoteric concept even as beliefs and practices reflecting a commitment to rebirth spread as part of the ritualized culture that emerged from the Safed renaissance of the late sixteenth century. In the twentieth century, as part of the general push away from esotericism that characterized twentieth-century Kabbalah more generally,[82] Hasidic sources were willing to speak at great length about the question of rebirth. Yeruham Meir Leiner, the brother of a Hasidic master, reflected on the centrality of *gilgul* in Kabbalah in the introduction to the Lublin 1907 edition of Menahem Azariah de Fano's *Gilgulei Neshamot*:

> In this short book, small in length but great in substance, the author illuminates our eyes by giving us a firm foundation in our faith, establishing belief in reincarnation as an unmovable support for the Jewish people. Many philosophized about this belief, not wishing to give it any foundation or standing in our holy Torah, but the portion of Jacob is not with any of them! We believe in everything in which our holy teachers had faith.... We are believers, the children of believers, and do not follow investigations of the mind ... They [i.e., our teachers] founded a strong and unmoving foundation in the God's Torah of this faith, the faith in reincarnation, which is also one of the foundations of [our] religion upon which all the house of Israel rely upon.[83]

The Kabbalists had advocated strenuously for belief in *gilgul* as a central pillar of religious faith and commitment, but Yeruham Meir Leiner understood that this doctrine remained largely out of the limelight and was not well-known beyond elite circles. Because it could not be properly understood through philosophical reasoning and was subject to terrible misunderstanding, reflection on *gilgul* had been preserved — often purposefully — as the purview of the elect who were immersed in kabbalistic wisdom. But Leiner considered the need for a shift in approach, seeing in early twentieth-century Hasidism an exoteric push that could overturn previous fears:

> The study of this wisdom was hidden in the hearts of the Sages, and was passed on only to their choicest disciples, those known to them as true God-fearers. It is not so in our own day, praise the Lord, for the books of the Zohar and Lurianic Kabbalah are accessible to all. Many are those who contemplate them; they study these works with fear and holiness according to the explanations of our teacher, the Ba'al Shem Tov. Now there is no fear or trepidation in revealing belief in the reincarnation of souls to the masses. "It has turned to the contrary" (Est. 9:1): it further strengthens the foundations of faith in the hearts of the people, and from this fear will come to all flesh. This was also the intention of our great teacher Rabbi Menahem Azaria de Fano in [writing] this book.[84]

This impetus to foreground the topic of *gilgul* surely reflects a kind of exoteric thrust within Hasidism, and within twentieth-century Hasidism in particular. It may also reflect a possible contact point between European Kabbalah and the traditions of Indic and Buddhist religion. As Moshe Idel has suggested, acquaintance with Tibetan religion is evident in a Hebrew text published in 1814 in the very same printing house where the hagiographical tales of the Ba'al Shem Tov first appeared.[85] Swami Vivekananda visited both Europe and the United States in the 1890s, where his particular recasting of *advaita vedānta* was met with tremendous acclaim, and over the next decades, various kinds of Hindu philosophy, Buddhist thinking, and Yogic reflection reached the Jews of both Western and Eastern Europe.[86] The famed Avraham Yitshak ha-Cohen Kook, for example, was deeply intrigued by Buddhism in the early twentieth century,[87] and by the time Leiner published this kabbalistic book in 1907, the possibility of contacts with other religious thinking on the nature of rebirth is not impossible to imagine.

As the concept of *gilgul* has been interpreted and reinterpreted in Israel and the United States in the twentieth and early twenty-first centuries, it has often been brought together with ideas from these so-called Eastern traditions.[88] Some figures, like Norman Lamm (1927–2020), a noted Orthodox rabbi and president of Yeshiva University from 1976 to 2003, sought to disambiguate Judaism from Hinduism by underscoring that Jews *do not* (and ought not to) believe in reincarnation.[89] By contrast, Zalman Schachter-Shalomi (1924–2014), a highly creative teacher and leader deeply shaped by the ethos and cultures of Hasidism, underscored belief in rebirth and reincarnation as an important theological connection between Tibetan Buddhism and Judaism.[90] Shachter-Shalomi, moreover, developed his own type of religious syncretism that opened new possibilities for learning from other faith traditions:[91] "The purity of the intention has to be there," claimed Shachter-Shalomi in an oral address on concepts of *gilgul*. "You can mix religions, I do believe that you can, and that nobody is free from mixing. There is influence that comes through in all sorts of ways. The people who have said that you can't mix have basically been the managers of religious institutions. . . . I don't know whether you can create any borders for the mind as to what reality is all about."[92] His interpretations generally reflect a preeminent turn toward the individual that is so endemic to New Age movements,[93] but he also sought to use the concept of *gilgul* to grapple with the devastation of the Holocaust.[94]

A remarkable constellation of twentieth-century teachings on *gilgul* comes from the works of Menahem Mendel Schneerson of Lubavitch (1902–1994), a sophisticated theologian and an important figure in American Judaism who served as the Seventh Rebbe of Chabad. While not party to Schachter-Shalomi's overt blending of religious ideologies, Schneerson — like the Hasidic teachers and masters before him — never operated in a vacuum but was influenced, albeit sometimes implicitly and in an unacknowledged way, by larger religious and intellectual systems around him. Schneerson's teachings on *gilgul* are largely continuous with earlier Hasidism in their emphasis on this-worldly concerns, but at the same time they represent a novel development on several key points that may have been particularly appealing to his American audience. Schneerson's attempt to exoterize *gilgul* in the twentieth century, moreover, and use it as a tool to diffuse some of the teachings of Chabad seems to coalesce with a number of twentieth-century spiritual and intellectual ideas and movements.[95]

Schneerson invokes the notion of transmigration to highlight the layered spiritual identity of each person. Because most souls of "our generations" have been reborn at least once, claims Schneerson, they possess a unique potential; "one must know that the goodness from previous rebirths may be revealed to him; this can aid one in his service. Not only in terms of mind and character traits — interior powers — but also in thought, speech, and deed — external matters ... and in ordinarily life."[96] The legacy of rebirth is not a hinderance or a burden, but a reservoir of spiritual potential to be tapped while serving God in this world. In fact, Schneerson makes the striking claim — one with little precedent in Hasidic thought on *gilgul* — that one's previous sins do not accumulate in the same way. Positive actions stand forever, since "when a Jew does a *miẓvah*, it stands for all eternity,"[97] whereas wickedness or transgression lacks true power and "is nothing more than hiddenness and concealment."[98] Through repentance, misdeeds are transformed into goodness, becoming metabolized into the positive dimensions of the spirit.[99] In a sense, then, this generation — teaches Schneerson — is the culmination of the work of all the previous generations, and that is why the messiah can arrive imminently.[100]

This does not, of course, mean that one should look only to the past, since the potential of past lives can only be fully realized in the present. The day of one's death is a particularly auspicious time for this surge of religious empowerment:

> Regarding the idea of departure [from this world], it says [in the teachings of Shneur Zalman of Liady][101] that the day of one's death draws together all the service (*'avodah*) and hard work (*horevanya*) that one has toiled throughout his entire life. The time of one's departure is the completion of the soul's work that it needed to accomplish with the body. Even if it must be reborn another time, this is the completion of the work that it needs to do in *this* body.[102]

The day of death is the moment of reckoning, and, even if rebirth might be necessary, the experience of passing from this world is the culmination of the soul's spiritual labor. One must be mindful and aware of this fact, claims Schneerson, as the moment of departure draws nigh.

The dramatic scene of Shim'on bar Yohai's death in the Zohar, the subject of Shneur Zalman's homily, offers a remarkable description of empowerment and revelation at the time of one's passing from the world. It is striking, then, that Hasidic literature includes very few such descriptions and none tying the moment of death to questions of reincarnation. It is noteworthy that the *Book of Departure* (*Sefer ha-Histalkut*, 1930), a compendium about the deaths of Hasidic masters, makes no mention of rebirth.[103] In fact, Hasidism — following much of earlier Kabbalah — focuses on the parents' intentions at the moment of conception as governing one's rebirth.[104] Schneerson's point returns us to the worlds of Buddhism. "What is said to be crucial in the process of rebirth is one's state of mind at the time of death," claims Rupert Gethin. "It is understood that at death significant acts performed during one's life tend to present themselves to one's mind."[105] Schneerson's text has highlighted for us that the existential confrontation with death is key to the entire notion of *gilgul*: "The sadness of death and the inability to accept it as final," suggests Wendy Doniger O'Flaherty, should be seen as "sentiments which must lie very near the heart of the spirit that created the karma doctrine."[106] From this there emerges a serious philosophical question: "whether a person can expect to reap the full harvest of his deeds, good and evil, in this world or whether the moral outcome of certain deeds will be actualized only at the moment of death or in a realm beyond this one."[107] Schneerson suggests that "the full harvest" of one's actions does reach its zenith at the time of death, but the arc of impact stretches back into the past and far into the future.

Another key idea emerges from a fascinating letter sent by Schneerson as a reply to a query by David Stukhammer (d. 1963), one of the first Chabad Hasidim to come to the United States from Poland (he arrived in 1920) and a founder of the *Tomchei Temimim* yeshivah in New York. In 1943, he asked Schneerson about the seeming contradictions in Jewish teachings about the possibility that a wicked individual, sunken in impurity, may subsequently become united with and connected to the light of divinity.[108] Schneerson marshals an impressive number of different arguments as to why this is indeed possible, drawing upon Hasidic traditions as well as rabbinic sources. He highlights the tremendous power of repentance, even if only private, and underscores that such individuals may be healed simply through prayer and other kinds of merit-building rituals. All Jews, claims Schneerson, are connected to God at the very deepest and most essential levels, though this work may not be accomplished in this life.

It says in the *Shulḥan 'Arukh* of the *Admor ha-Zaken* [i.e., Shneur Zalman of Liady] in the laws of Torah Study (Ch. 4:3) that "a wicked person will repent, either in this lifetime or in another, as it says, *No stray [soul] remains outcast* (2 Sam 14:14).[109] In the *Tanya* (end of ch. 39) it says: "*surely* one will repent in the end, either in this life or another," for "no stray remains outcast."[110]

> Even if one's body has become corrupted, explains Schneerson, the soul will be reborn because it is pure, perfect, and essential and cannot be sundered by the fallacies of the body.[111] This new bodily form will hold all the parts of the soul, as *gilgul* purifies in ways that even purgatory cannot.[112]

Schneerson closes this letter to the learned recipient with a repercussive passage from the early modern kabbalistic text, *Emeq ha-Melekh*:

> Blessed is Y-H-V-H, the God of Abraham, the person of love, who never stopped his love and truth from his people Israel, so that no stray remains outcast, for his compassion for all creation is never ending, as it says, "and his compassion on all his works." Therefore, all Israel has a portion in the world to Come, as it says, "and your people are all righteous; they shall inherit the land forever; the branch of My planting, the work of My hands, wherein I glory." (Isaiah 60:21)[113]

Doctrinally there is little new in Schneerson's presentation, yet he is clearly cognizant of the plight of non-religious Jews in a new American context. Rather than pushing them away, Schneerson opted for the position of his father-in-law, Yosef Yitzchok Schneersohn, in finding ways to bring these Jews into the orbit of religion through this-worldly engagement. It is fascinating to see Schneerson reflecting on such matters some eight years before he even began to serve as leader of the Chabad community.

Finally, Schneerson draws upon *gilgul* in linking past to future in his messianic vision. While notions of rebirth and transmigration can and have been used to bolster rabbinic power and combat the inroads of modernization or religious reform, the idea may also justify profound sociological and theological innovation. Following his father-in-law once more yet adding substantively to his case, Schneerson sought to rethink the place of women in twentieth-century Chabad Hasidism, using the concept of transmigration to argue that the status of women in the present ought to preemptively reflect that of the generation of redemption.

> One of the innovations of my saintly father-in-law, the Rebbe and leader of our generation ... was his engagement and dedication to work with and attend to Jewish women and girls as well, in matters of Judaism, Torah, and commandments (including, and especially, the teachings of Hasidism [*torat ha-hasidut*] ... The source for this ... is the fact that women came before men in many foundational matters of the Jewish people.[114] Moreover, and now this is the essential point — they have a unique connection to redemption. The Sages taught that "the Israelites were redeemed from Egypt because of the righteous women in that generation."[115] This is true also of the future redemption ... the reward of the righteous women in that generation, as the Sage said, "The generations are redeemed because of the righteous women in that generation."[116] In particular, the Lurianic writings explain that the generation of the future redemption will be a reincarnation of the generation that left Egypt. For this reason, the righteous women of our generation, by virtue of whom we are redeemed, are the very same righteous women that left Egypt.[117]

Flexing time against the grain, Schneerson argued that the future redemption will take place because of the merit of women, reincarnations of their present-day forms, and therefore women in the contemporary Hasidic community ought to be treated with a measure of equality.

> Ours is the final generation of exile and the first of redemption. My saintly father-in-law the Rebbe said that all matters of worship have been finished and stand waiting to greet the face of our righteous Messiah. Therefore, he tried to work with and attend to the women even more, to hasten and spur on the redemption by the merit of those righteous women. In addition, the virtue of the women of Israel is emphasized (not only in *bringing* the redemption, but also and especially) *in the redemption itself*.[118]

Without fully eclipsing the distinctions between men and women, unimaginable in his traditional and highly gender-segregated society, Schneerson's theological radicalism[119] is all the more striking because it reflects a changing social situation in which women have become integral parts of the outreach machine that defines postwar Chabad Hasidism.[120] It is through such hermeneutical feats that profound, even radical, intellectual transformations happen within the conservative worlds of modern Hasidism, as concepts are deftly reborn and subtly reinterpreted to address the broader discourse on gender, socioreligious continuity, and cohesion in a dazzlingly new cultural and historical context.

Notes

1. On Hasidism, see David Biale et al., *Hasidism: A New History* (Princeton: Princeton University Press, 2019).

2. See Moshe Idel, "Martin Buber and Gershom Scholem on Hasidism: A Critical Appraisal," in *Hasidism Reappraised*, ed. A. Rapoport-Albert (Liverpool: Littman Library of Jewish Civilization in association with Liverpool University Press, 1998), 176–202.

3. See Pinhas Horowitz, *Sefer Hafla'ah* (New York, 1944), fol. 65a (commenting on b. Kettubot 68a). See also *Panim Yafot — Mahadurah Tinyana, be-hukkotai*, 245.

4. Kabbalistic works of particular importance for Hasidic thinking on *gilgul* include Hayyim Vital, *Sefer ha-Gilgulim* (1684); Shmuel Vital; *Sha'ar ha-Gilgulim* (1875); Menahem Azariah de Fano, *Gilgulei Neshamot* (1907); and *Emeq ha-Melekh* (Amsterdam, 1648) [Hebrew].

5. Jonathan Garb, *Shamanic Trance in Modern Kabbalah* (Chicago: University of Chicago Press, 2011), 100.

6. Arthur Green, ed., *The Light of the Eyes* (Stanford: Stanford University Press, 2021), 583 n. 8. See, more broadly, Seth Brody, "'Open to Me the Gates of Righteousness': The Pursuit of Holiness and Non-Duality in Early Hasidic Teaching," *Jewish Quarterly Review* 89 (1998): 3–44; and Tsippi Kauffman, *In all Your Ways Know Him: The Concept of God and* Avodah be-Gashmiyut *in the Early Stages of Hasidism* (Ramat-Gan: Bar-Ilan University Press, 2009) [Hebrew].

7. See, for example, R. Dov Baer Friedman of Mezritsh, *Toledot Ya'akov Yosef* (Jerusalem: 2011), *Re'eh*, 3:1208; Yaakov Yosef of Ostrow, *Rav Yevi* (Slavita: Mem Shapira, 1892), *Hiddushei Tehilim*, 2:517; and Yisra'el Moshe Bromberg, *Toledot ha-Nifla'ot* (Warsaw: n.p., 1899), 4–6; Ariel Evan Mayse and Sam Berrin Shonkoff, trans., *Hasidism: Writings on Devotion, Community and Life in the Modern World* (Waltham: Brandeis University Press, 2020), 95.

8. J. Bruce Long, "'The Concepts of Human Action and Rebirth in the Mahābhārata," in *Karma and Rebirth in Classical Indian Traditions*, ed. Wendy Doniger O'Flaherty (Berkeley: University of California Press, 1980), 57–58.

9. Geoffrey Samuel, *Introducing Tibetan Buddhism* (Abingdon: Routledge: 2012), 165–85; Rupert Gethin, *The Foundations of Buddhism* (Oxford: Oxford University Press, 2002), 216–18.

10. Austin B. Creel, "Contemporary Philosophical Treatments of Karma and Rebirth," in *Karma and Rebirth: Post Classical Developments*, ed. R. W. Neufeldt (Albany: State University of New York Press, 1986), 3.

11. Samuel, *Introducing Tibetan Buddhism*, 115.

12. Samuel, *Introducing Tibetan Buddhism*, 92.

13. R. Levi Isaac of Barditshev, *Kedushat Levi* (New York: 1995), *va-Ethanan*, 1:383–84. See also *Me'or 'Einayim, be-midbar*, 1:252; Green, trans., *Light of the Eyes*, 583.

14. Isaac Luria, *The Writings of the Ari, Sha'ar ha-Miẓvot* (Jerusalem: Unknown, 2019), Introduction (*Hakdamah*), 1: "Know that all the soul-sparks of

each and every soul are obligated to fulfill all 613 commandments, except for those that are impossible to perform." See also *'Aravei Nahal, hayyei sarah, derush* no. 3; ibid., *'ekev, derush* no. 6; ibid., *shoftim, derush* no. 4 [Hebrew].

15. R. Yaakov Yoseph of Pollonye, *Toledot Ya'akov Yosef, va-Yishlah* 1:191, interpreting *Sefer ha-Gilgulim*, ch. 4.

16. Gershom Scholem, "The Paradisic Garb of Souls and the Origin of the Concept of *Haluka de-Rabbanan*," *Tarbiẓ* 24 (1954): 290–306 [Hebrew].

17. R. Shne'ur Zalman of Liady, *Likkutei Amarim — Tanya* (New York: Kehot Publication Society, 2009), *Iggeret ha-Kodesh*, ch. 19, fol. 128b [Hebrew].

18. R. Shne'ur Zalman of Liady, *Hilkhot Talmud Torah* (New York: Kehot, 2000), ch. 1:4 [Hebrew].

19. For a contemporary reflection on studying Jewish law *halakhah* to escape rebirth, see Avraham Israel Moshe Salmon, *Netivot Kodesh: Mo'adim u-Zemanim — Hag ha-Pesah* (Jerusalem: Mechon Hadas, 2002), ch. 6, 98 [Hebrew].

20. Bracha Sack, "The Concept of Thought, Speech, and Action," *Da'at* 50–52 (2003): 221–41 [Hebrew].

21. See Robert Beer, *The Handbook of Tibetan Buddhist Symbols* (Boulder: Shambhala Publications, 2003), 186.

22. Moshe Shoham, *Divrei Moshe* (Benei Berak: Machon Nahalat Ẓvi, 2019), *Lekh Lekha*, 25. See also *Likkutei Moharan* 2:121 [Hebrew].

23. Yaakov Yosef of Ostrow, *Rav Yevi* (Slavita: Mem Shapira, 1892), vol. 2, *hiddushei tehilim*, 517. See also Moses Cordovero, *Pardes Rimmonim* (Koretz: TẒvi Hirsch b. Aryeh Leib, 1780), 1:4; Shabetai Sheftel ben Akiva Horowitz, *Shefa' Tal* (Bilzorka: Mordekhai, 1807), fol. 7c in gloss [Hebrew].

24. Zohar 1:131b, 2:100a, and 3:308a; *Tikkunei Zohar*, no. 40, fol. 82a; Abraham ben Mordechai Azulay, *Hesed le-Avraham* 5:19; Hayyim Vital, *Sefer ha-Gilgulim*, ch. 10–12; Immanuel Hai Ricchi, *Mishnat Hasidim* (Amsterdam: n.p., 1740), chapter on the resurrection of the dead (*Tehiyat ha-Metim*) [Hebrew].

25. On this parallel and its importance in early Hasidism, see Ariel Evan Mayse, *Laws of the Spirit: Ritual, Mysticism, and the Commandments in Early Hasidism* (Stanford: Stanford University Press, 2024).

26. R. Levi Isaac of Barditshev, *Kedushat Levi, va-Ethanan*, 1:384 [Hebrew].

27. R. Levi Isaac of Barditshev, *Kedushat Levi*, vol. 1, *va-Ethanan*, 384 [Hebrew].

28. See also R. Elimelekh of Lizhensk, *No'am Elimelekh* (Jerusalem: n.p., 1996), *Mishpatim*, 87 [Hebrew].

29. See Arvind Sharma and Ray Bharati, *Classical Hindu Thought: An Introduction* (Oxford: Oxford University Press, 2000), 9–10.

30. See Reuven Horowitz, *Duda'im ba- Sadeh* (Tel Aviv: n.p., 1964), on the portion, *be-Har*. Cited in Be-Reish Galei (New York: Yeshivah Machon Zera Avraham, 2019) [henceforth, RG], no. 19. RG19 and Moses Teitelbaum, *Yismah Moshe* (Brooklyn: n.p., 2019), portion on *Noah*, RG67 [Hebrew].

31. On the kabbalistic background, see Lawrence Fine, *Physician of the Soul, Healer of the Cosmos; Isaac Luria and his Kabbalistic Fellowship* (Stanford: Stanford University Press, 2003).

32. See Shneur Zalman, *Sha'arei ha-Yihud ve-ha-Emunah* (Shklow: n.p., 1820), Introduction (*Petah u-mevo she'arim*), RG35 [Hebrew].

33. R. Menahem Nahum Twersky of Chernobyl, *Me'or 'Einayim*, 2 vols. (Jerusalem: n.p., 2012), *Yisamah Lev — Pesahim*, 1:545 [Hebrew].

34. R. Meir b. Samuel ha-Levi Rottenburg, *Or la-Shamayim* (Lublin: M. M. Schneid Mester, 1909), portion on *Pinhas*, RG134 [Hebrew].

35. Rabbi Naftali TẒvi Horowitz, *Zera' Kodesh* (Jerusalem: n.p., 2016), *Shoftim*, 1:319 [Hebrew].

36. Shneur Zalman of Liady, *Likkutei Amarim — Tanya, Iggeret ha-kodesh*, ch. 7 [Hebrew].

37. R. Elimelekh of Lizhensk, *Ma'or va-Shemesh* (Jerusalem: n.p., 1992), vol. 1, *Aharei mot*, 354 [Hebrew].

38. See Shmuel Feiner, *The Origins of Jewish Secularization in Eighteenth-Century Europe* (Philadelphia: University of Pennsylvania Press, 2011), esp. 20–21. 99, 206–9, 252, 254–55l and the critique of Sorotzkin, *Orthodoxy and Modern Disciplination: The Production of the Jewish Tradition in Europe in Modern Times* (Tel Aviv: Kibbutz ha-Meuhad, 2011) [Hebrew].

39. See Raphael Mahler, *Hasidism and the Jewish Enlightenment: Their Confrontation in Galicia and Poland in the First Half of the Nineteenth Century*, trans. Eugene Orenstein, Aaron Klein, and Jenny Machlowitz Klein (Philadelphia: Jewish Publication Society of America, 1985).

40. Ẓvi Elimelekh Shapira of Dinov, *Derekh Pekudeikha* (Benei Berak: n.p., 2014), Introduction, no. 2, 24. On this garment or cloak, see above.

41. Ẓvi Elimelekh Shapira of Dinov, *Derekh Pekudeikha, hakdamah* no. 3, 27–28. See also Zohar *Hai, Pinhas* 213a.

42. R. Moses Hayyim Efrayim of Sudilkov, *Degel Mahaneh Efrayim* (Jerusalem: n.p., 2013), *Likkutim*, 609.

43. Ẓvi Elimelekh Shapira of Dinov, *Derekh Pekudeikha*, Introduction (*Hakdamah*), no. 4. [Hebrew].

44. See also the source translated in Arthur Green, *Speaking Torah: Spiritual Teachings from Around the Maggid's Table*, with Ebn Leader, Ariel Evan Mayse, and Or N. Rose (Nashville: Jewish Lights, 2013), 1:296.

45. See T. Kauffman, *In All Your Ways*.

46. Gershom Scholem, "*Gilgul:* The Transmigration of Souls," in *On the Mystical Shape of the Godhead* (New York: Schocken Books, 1991), 243–45. See also Louis Jacobs, "The Uplifting of Sparks in Later Jewish Mysticism," in *Jewish Spirituality II: From the Sixteenth-Century Revival to the Present*, ed. Arthur Green (New York: Crossroad, 1987), 99–126.

47. R. Ẓvi Elimelekh of Dinow, *Benei Yissakhar* (Zolkiev: S. D. Meir Haffer, 1850), vol. 2, sections on *Ma'amarei Hodesh Sivan* 5:18, 67. See also vol. 1, *Ma'amarei ha-Shabbatot* 10:4, 126; and *Sha'ar ha-Misvsot*, *'Ekev*.

48. See Kalonymus Kalman Epstein, *Ma'or va-Shemesh*, *Rimzei Kohelet* (Warsaw: Brothers Argel Brand, 1877), on untoward or excessive desire for money as a cause for rebirth, RG122 [Hebrew].

49. Ya'akov Yosef of Pollonye, *Toledot Ya'akov Yosef, Kedoshim*, 2:637.

50. R. Levi Isaac of Barditshev, *Kedushat Levi, Likkutim*, 2:435.

51. R. Elimelekh of Lizhensk, *No'am Elimelekh, Mi-Kets*, 48. See also *Rav Yevi, Hiddushei Torah*, 2:26, and H. Vital, *Sefer ha-Gilgulim*, 58.

52. See 2 Sam. 14:14.

53. Ya'akov Yosef of Pollonye, *Toledot Ya'akov Yosef, Re'eh*, 3:1209 [Hebrew].

54. *Rav Yevi, Hiddushei Tehilim*, 2:505 [Hebrew].

55. See Garb, *Shamanic Trance*, 100; Nathaniel Deutsch, *The Maiden of Ludmir: A Jewish Holy Woman and Her World* (Berkeley: University of California Press, 2003), 123; and the materials by Yitshak Isaac Safrin of Komarno in Morris M. Faierstein, *Jewish Mystical Autobiographies: Book of Visions and Book of Secrets* (New York: Paulist Press, 1999).

56. R. Yaacov Yosef of Pollonye, *Toledot Ya'akov Yosef, Re'eh*, 3:1211; *Or Yitshak, Likkutei Or Yitshak* RG53; *Be'er Mayim Hayim, Bo* RG87; and *No'am Elimelekh, Mishpatim*, RG20 [Hebrew].

57. *Yismah Moshe*, section *Tetsvaveh*, RG125 [Hebrew].

58. R. Moses Hayyim Efrayim of Sudilkov, *Degel Mahaneh Efrayim, Lekh Lekha*, 32. See also Scholem, "*Gilgul*," 246; and Moshe Idel, "The *Ẓaddik* and His Soul's Sparks: From Kabbalah to Hasidism," *Jewish Quarterly Review* 103, no. 2 (2013): 196–240.

59. See Ben-Amos, Dan and Jerome Mintz, *In Praise of the Baal Shem Tov [Shivhei ha-BeSHT] The First Collection of Legends About the Founder of Hasidism* (Bloomington: Indiana University Press, 1970), esp. nos. 12, 108, 215, 250.

60. R. Aharon Rata, *Shomer Emunim* (Jerusalem: Anonymous, 1942), Introduction (*Mevo ha-Sha'ar*), ch. 12–13, fol. 30a–32a [Hebrew]; and Yizhak of Radziwill, *Or Yitshak* (Brooklyn: Machon Or Yizhak, 2005), *Likkutei Or Yitshak Shonot*, RG53 [Hebrew].

61. See *Kedushat Levi, likkutim*, 2:449; *She'erit Yis'rael, sha'ar ha-hitkashrut likkutim*, 12b; *Tif'eret* Shlomo, *hayei sarah*. RG5; and ibid., *va-yera*. RG28

62. *Yismah Moshe*, Part 3, *Likkutim Avakat Rokhel*. RG30; *Or la-Shamayim, shemot* RG29; *Berit Avram*, section *'Ekev* RG23; and *Tif'eret Shlomo, va-Yehi*. RG61 [Hebrew].

63. Hayyim Vital, *Sefer ha-Gilgulim*, ch. 5 [Hebrew].

64. R. Yaakov Yosef of Polnoy, *Toledot Ya'akov Yosef* (Koretz: Ẓvi Hirsch Baer, 1780), *Hayyei Sarah*, 1:125. See also Hanoch Meyer of Alesk, *Siddur Lev Same'ah* (Lemberg: Dov Luria, 1862), *Derekh ha-Tefillah*, 13 [Hebrew].

65. *Kedushat Levi, Noah*, 1:13 [Hebrew].

66. See Samuel, *Introducing Tibetan Buddhism*, 129–64.

67. See Samuel, *Introducing Tibetan Buddhism*, 145.

68. See Ẓvi Elimelekh Shapira of Dinow, *Agra de-Kalla* (Jerusalem: n.p., 1964), section *Hayyei Sarah*.

69. R. Jacob Joseph of Pollnoye, *Ben Porat Yosef* (Jerusalem: n.p., 2011), *Noah*, 1:121; *Lev Same'ah*, Section *Lekh lekha*. RG38 [Hebrew].

70. See in *Siddur Lev Same'ah*, Section *Derekh ha-tefillah* 13. RG136.

71. See R. Menahem Nahum Twersky of Chernobyl, *Me'or Einayim, Yitro*, 1:173; translated in Green, *Light of the Eyes: Homilies on the Torah* (Stanford: Stanford University Press, 2021).

72. *Or la-Shamayim*, section on *Hukkat*. RG44; *Kav ve-Naki, likkutei nakh*, 53b.

73. R. Nahman of Bratslav, *Likkutei Moharan* (Bratslav: R. Nathan's Publishing House, 1821), I:65 [Hebrew].

74. See Yakov Travis, "Adorning the Souls of the Dead: Rabbi Nahman of Bratslav and *Tikkun ha-Neshamot*," in *God's Voice from the Void*, ed. Shaul Magid (Albany: State University of New York Press, 2002), 155–92.

75. Nahman of Bratslav, *Hayyei Moharan* (Lemberg: Abraham Drücker, 1874), no. 446 [Hebrew].

76. Nahman of Bratslav, *Hayyei Moharan*, no. 446.

77. Nahman of Bratslav, *Hayyei Moharan*, no. 446.

78. George L. Hart 3rd, "Theory of Reincarnation Among the Tamils," 131.

79. Hart, "Theory of Reincarnation," 132.

80. Hart, "Theory of Reincarnation," 133.

81. See Dov Weiss, *Pious Irreverence: Confronting God in Rabbinic Judaism* (Philadelphia: University of Pennsylvania Press, 2017).

82. See Jonathan Garb, *The Chosen Will Become Herds: Studies in Twentieth Century Kabbalah*, trans. Yaffah Berkovits-Murciano (New Haven: Yale University Press, 2009), esp. 21–36, 100–22.

83. Menahem Azariah de Fano, *Gilgulei Neshamot*, ed. Yeruham Meir Leiner (Lublin: n.p., 1907), 3 [Hebrew].

84. Azariah de Fano, *Gilgulei Neshamot*, 5.

85. See Moshe Idel, *Golem, an Augmented Edition* (New York: Ktav Publishing House, forthcoming), 407–12; Moshe Idel, *Ben: Sonship and Jewish Mysticism* (London: Continuum, 2007), 575–76 n. 69.

86. See Sebastian Musch, *Jewish Encounters with Buddhism in German Culture: Between Moses and Buddha, 1890-1940* (Cham, Switzerland: Palgrave Macmillan, 2019); and Moshe Idel, "The Rebbe of Piaseczno: Between Two Trends in Hasidism," in *Hasidism, Suffering, and Renewal: The Prewar and Holocaust Legacy of Kalonymus Kalman Shapira*, ed. Don Seeman, Daniel Reiser, Ariel Evan Mayse (Albany: State University of New York, 2021), 60.

87. See Amir Mashiach, "Rabbi Kook and Buddhism," *Da'at*, 70 (2011): 81–96 [Hebrew].

88. See Emily Sigalow, *American JewBu: Jews, Buddhists, and Religious Change* (Princeton: Princeton University Press, 2022), esp. 24–29, 69, 110, 161, 170.

89. See Alan Brill, *Rabbi on the Ganges: A Jewish-Hindu Encounter* (Lanham: Lexington Books, 2020), 122–23.

90. See the account in Rodger Kamanetz, *The Jew in the Lotus: A Poet's Rediscovery of Jewish Identity in Buddhist India* (San Francisco: Harper, 1994), 72–90; and the work by his student Yonasson Gershom, *Jewish Tales of Reincarnation* (Lanham: Jason Aronson, 2000).

91. See Or N. Rose, "Envisioning a Jewish Monastic Community: Zalman Schachter-Shalomi, Catholicism, and the B'nai Or Fellowship," *Studies in Christian-Jewish Relations* (forthcoming); and Ariel Evan Mayse, "Renewal and Redemption: Spirituality, Law, and Religious Praxis in the Writings of Rabbi Zalman Schachter-Shalomi," *Journal of Religion* 101 (2021): 455–504.

92. "Kabbalah in the Modern Age, part 3 of 3," Zalman M. Schachter-Shalomi Collection, University of Colorado, Boulder.

93. See Boaz Huss, "The New Age of Kabbalah: Contemporary Kabbalah, the New Age and Postmodern Spirituality," *Journal of Modern Jewish Studies* 6, no. 2 (2007): 107–25.

94. See Zalman Schachter-Shalomi, "Thoughts on the Shoah: Two Jewish Holocaust Reincarnation Cases," *Tikkun Magazine* 2 (1987): 1; and Yonassan Gershom, *Beyond the Ashes: Cases of Reincarnation from the Holocaust* (Virginia Beach: ARE Press, 1992).

95. See the idiosyncratic Dov Ber Pinson, *Reincarnation in Judaism: The Journey of the Soul* (Lanham: Jason Aronson, 1999). A vast array of teachings about reincarnation, including translations of Hasidic and kabbalistic sources, are available on the website Chabad.org.

96. Menachem Mendel Schneerson, *Likkutei Sihot* (Brooklyn: Kehot, 2006), 1:247. See also Hayyim Vital, *Sha'ar ha-Gilgulim*, *hakdamah* 3 and 4.

97. Menachem Mendel Schneerson, *Likkutei Sihot*, 1:247.

98. Menachem Mendel Schneerson, *Likkutei Sihot*, 1:247.

99. See b. Yoma 86a–b.

100. On the paradoxical virtues of the present "lower" generations, see Yehoshua Heschel of Apta, *Ohev Yisra'el* (Zhitomir: Grandsons of the Rebbe, 1863), *Likkutim hadashim 'Ekev*, RG99 [Hebrew].

101. See Shneur Zalman of Liady, *Siddur Admor ha-Zaken* (Shklow: Yisrael Jaffe, 1803), *Derushei LaG ba-Omer*, and *Likkutei Amarim — Tanya, iggeret ha-kodesh* (Slavita: Moshe Shapira, 1796), no. 27.

102. *Likkutei Sihot*, vol. 1, 286.

103. See the translation of this work, Joel H. Baron and Sara Paasche-Orlow, trans. *Deathbed Wisdom of the Hasidic Masters: The Book of Departure and Caring for People at the End of Life* (Nashville: Jewish Lights, 2016).

104. See Zohar *Hai*, *Balak* 197; and *Derekh Pekudeikha*, *miẓvah* no. 1, *mahashavah* 4.

105. Gethin, *Foundations of Buddhism*, 217; Margaret Gouin, *Tibetan Rituals of Death Buddhist Funerary Practices*, 12–15.

106. Wendy Doniger O'Flaherty, "Karma and Rebirth in the Vedas and Puranas," 15.

107. J. Bruce Long, "Human Action and Rebirth in the Mahabharata," 51.

108. See R. Menahem Mendel Schneerson, *Iggerot Kodesh* (New York: Kehot, 1997), vol. 1, no. 85, 141 [Hebrew].

109. Shneur Zalman of Liady, *Shulḥan 'Arukh ha-Rav* (Kapust: n.p., 1794), section *Hilkhot Talmud Torah* 4:3 [Hebrew], *Hilchos Talmud Torah: The Laws of*

Torah Study from the Shulchan Aruch of Rabbi Shneur Zalman of Liadi, trans. Eliyahu Touger and Uri Kaploun (Brooklyn: Kehot, 2004) (bilingual edition).

110. Menahem Mendel Schneerson, *Iggerot Kodesh*, vol. 1, no. 85. 147.

111. See Hayyim Vital, *Sha'ar ha-Gilgulim*, *hakdamah* no. 11; *Sefer ha-Gilgulim*, ch. 5.

112. Elijah de Vidas, *Reshit Ḥokhmah* (Venice: Di Gara, 1579), "The Gate of Fear (*Sha'ar ha-Yirah*)," ch. 13 [Hebrew].

113. Nafthali H. Bachrach, *Emeq ha-Melekh* (Jerusalem: Yerid ha-Sefarim, 2003), vol. 2, 16:45, 917–18 [Hebrew].

114. Schneerson offers revelation, the construction of the Tabernacle, and the sin of the golden calf as examples in which Jewish traditions describes the merit of women outshining that of men.

115. b. Sotah 11b.

116. See *Yalkut Ruth*, no. 606.

117. *Torat Menahem* 5752 [1991/1992] (Brooklyn: Kehot Publication Society, 1993), 2: 183–84; trans. Mayse and Shonkoff, *Hasidism*, 266–67.

118. *Torat Menahem* 5752 [1991/1992], 183–84; Mayse and Shonkoff, *Hasidism*, 267.

119. See Elliot R. Wolfson, *Open Secret: Postmessianic Messianism and the Mystical Revision of Menahem Mendel Schneerson* (New York: Columbia University Press, 2009), esp. 200–23.

120. See Ada Rapaport-Albert, "The Emergence of a Female Constituency in Twentieth-Century Habad Hasidism," in *Hasidic Studies: Essays in History and Gender* (Liverpool: Littman Library of Jewish Civilization, 2018), 368–426; Ada Rapaport-Albert, "From Woman as Hasid to Woman as '*Ẓaddik*' in the Teachings of the Last Two Lubavitcher Rebbes," in *Hasidic Studies: Essays in History and Gender* (Liverpool: Littman Library of Jewish Civilization, 2018), 427–70; Naftali Loewenthal, "From Ladies Auxiliary to Shluchos Network: Women's Activism in Twentieth-Century Habad," *Hasidism Beyond Modernity: Essays in Habad Thought and History* (Liverpool: Littman Library of Jewish Civilization, 2021), 305–22.

ROEE Y. GOLDSCHMIDT

Reincarnation in Hasidic Literature

13

HAGIOGRAPHY, SOCIAL JUSTICE, AND HALAKHAH

Reincarnation and Hagiography

One of the most fanciful stories in *Shivḥei haBesht*[1] depicts how Rabbi Israel ben Eliezer (the Besht), the eighteenth-century Jewish kabbalist and healer and putative founder of Hasidism,[2] miraculously traveled to a desert, where he encountered an enormous frog.[3] This frog, so the reader discovers, is none other than the reincarnated soul of a Jewish sage who did not meticulously observe the commandment of ritual hand washing. As a result, he gradually threw off the yoke of the Torah and other commandments until eventually "he transgressed almost the entire Torah."[4] The punishment decreed was proportional to his sin. His reincarnation into a frog, an animal that resides in water, reflected the commandment he transgressed. Being exiled to a far-flung place that was never visited by Jews, he was cut off from a redeemer who could have "raised up" and repaired his soul. The frog further informs the Besht that his sentence had already lasted 500 years, and even Rabbi Isaac Luria of Safed (1534–1572), who was known for his ability to identify and restore souls,[5] could not help him because he did not know of his existence.[6] The story is deployed as a literary device to establish the authority of the Besht as a charismatic master whose prowess to raise up and repair the reincarnated souls of sinners created a direct link with Isaac Luria. The Hasidic hagiographic literature frequently used motifs drawn from the Lurianic hagiographic writings, including extensive use of such topics as reincarnation, exorcism, and dybbuks (malignant possessing spirits or ghosts), and in the process deployed both direct and implicit comparisons with the sages of Safed.[7] Indeed, soul repair of previously reincarnated individuals constituted a recurring leitmotif in narrative accounts that aimed to glorify Hasidic leaders who succeeded in repairing their students' souls and exorcising dybbuks.[8]

In crafting an idealized image of the *ẓadik*, Hasidic hagiographic literature frequently used reincarnation as a tool to establish a connection between biblical figures of the ancient Israelite past and Hasidic leaders. Re-creating the vicious battle for political and spiritual leadership of the Jewish people that ensued between Kings David and Saul, Hasidic stories depicted the Besht as the reincarnation of the soul of King David, while Rabbi Nachman of Kossov (d. 1756) was identified as the reincarnation of King Saul.[9] For this reason, according to the author of *Shivḥei ha-Besht*, Rabbi Nachman of Kossov persecuted the Besht during the latter's early days, mirroring how Saul persecuted David.[10] Elsewhere, the Besht is mentioned as a reincarnation of Rabbi Saadia Gaon.[11] Such depictions appear also in later periods. Thus, for example, Rabbi Iṣḥaq Ayziq Yehuda Yeḥiel Safrin of Komarno (1806–1874) frames his redemptive-messianic mission by providing a fascinating account of the many reincarnations his soul underwent, originating from the soul-root of Jeroboam ben Nabat, the first king of the northern Israelite Kingdom after the reign of King Solomon.[12] The narrative establishes Jeroboam ben Nabat as a failed redeemer whose many transgressions prevented him from repairing his own exulted soul and consequently bringing upon Rabbi Iṣḥaq Ayziq "twisted reincarnations, that had he repaired my soul I would not have had to come to this world and there would have been redemption for all of Israel."[13] In establishing his own authority, Rabbi Ayziq builds on elements borrowed from Lurianic teachings that emphasize the redemptive aspects of reincarnation through which soul-sparks — trapped in all manifestations of the created world — could be restored to their antediluvian source in *Adam Kadmon*, in whom the divine light was unified before the primordial sin.[14] Similarly to Rabbi Iṣḥaq Ayziq, many Hasidic *Ẓaddikim* tended to explain their personal connection to the souls of important people in Jewish history via reincarnation.[15]

Furthermore, divergent conceptualizations of reincarnation played a vital role in distinguishing among various Hasidic courts, rebbes, and followers. Drawing a complex portrait concerning why a Hasid decides to follow a particular rebbe and not another, R. Elimelekh of Leżajsk evoked the relationship between Isaac Luria and his student Rabbi Hayyim Vital to demonstrate the enduring link that exists between two souls whose roots are originally bound together.[16] Using the Levitical passage that delineates the laws of the Sabbatical year (*Shemittahh*) as his base text, R. Elimelekh presents the *ẓadik* as one who can assist and act on behalf of a Hasid because of their kinship based on a common ontological root in the Garden of Eden: "*Then shall his kinsman that is next unto him come, and shall redeem that which his brother hath sold* (Lev. 25:25), and he is the *ẓadik* close to him in the Garden of Eden, in the binding up of his soul from one root; 'and shall redeem that which his brother hath sold,' that they will aid him and will help him leave this inferior world and cleave to upper worlds."[17] It should be noted that this passage establishes a parallel between the impoverished Israelite, who, in spite of the biblical injunction against profiting from the produce of the land in the seventh year (*Shemittahh*), sells his crops, necessitating the recovery of the merchandise by his next of kin, and the Hasid, who is equally dependent on the *ẓadik* to intercede on his behalf in the heavenly realm to effect the redemption of his soul.

Later, at the end of the nineteenth century, Rabbi Mordechai Backerman reformulates this idea, denoting a polemical shift against the need for competition among Hasidic courts and emphasizing instead that the choice to follow a particular *Ẓaddik* arises from the likeness and complementarity between the master and his disciple based on primordial connectedness of their soul roots: "it is known that every soul is attracted to its root, which leads to the *Ẓaddik* who was together with it in the upper world."[18] Unsurprisingly, reincarnation became a central motif in Hasidic hagiographic literature, and it gained a very central place in the kabbalistic homiletical and ethical (musar) literature produced by the Hasidim. The idea of reincarnation also became embedded in Jewish culture in Central and Eastern Europe via various, widely disseminated kabbalistic works,[19] such as Rabbi Menachem Recanati's *Commentary on the Torah*,[20] *Sefer Hatemunah*, *ha-Peliah*, and *ha-Kanah*; *Sefer Shushan Sodot* by Rabbi Moshe of Kiev; the Zohar; the Lurianic *Sefer Ha-Gilgulim*;[21] *Sefer Gilgulei Ha-Neshamot* by Rabbi Menachem Azaria of Fano;[22] and others. Moreover, the kabbalistic *musar* literature that was widespread in Eastern and Central Europe in the period prior to Hasidism broadly discussed reincarnation of the soul and its moral implications.[23] This literature deeply influenced Hasidic literature, and as a result we find the idea of the reincarnation in a wide range of literary genres employed by Hasidic writers.

Reincarnation in Hasidic Thought and Its Roots in Homiletical and Ethical Texts

While scholars have discussed the motif of reincarnation in hagiographic literature, they have largely neglected its role in homiletical and ethical writings (musar) despite the significant role it plays therein. One of the main reasons for this oversight can be attributed to Gershom Scholem's approach to Hasidism, which he saw as a movement that sought to "neutralize" the "messianic idea" prevalent in the teachings of Isaac Luria. Scholem, who regarded Hasidism as the "last stage" of Jewish mysticism, depicted it as a turning point in the development of kabbalistic ideas. He explained that Lurianic speculation concerning communal and universal redemption was transformed by the followers of the Besht into a religious matter privately cultivated by the individual through pietistic practices such as *devekut*, intense forms of attachment to the divine and "communion with God."[24] Scholem sought to emphasize the parts of Hasidic homiletical literature that in his opinion transformed the elevation of the divine sparks into a personal and mystical issue highlighting man's closeness to God, thus neutralizing the Sabbatean messianic elements. According to Gershom Scholem, the great messianic expectation for redemption that took place in the seventeenth century with the appearance of the false messiah Shabbtai Ẓvi and the attendant disillusionment and rupture following his conversion to Islam in 1666 demanded a change concerning the messianic idea. This transformation, Scholem maintained, came about through Hasidism and its teachings, which responded to the spiritual needs of Jews living in Eastern Europe and thus contributed to the pervasive acceptance of Hasidic ideas in the first half of the eighteenth century. However, Scholem's historiosophical approach came under harsh criticism by his student Isaiah Tishby.[25] In contrast to Scholem's, Tishby's work, based on a wide-ranging survey of homiletical literature, demonstrated that "the messianic foundation" of Lurianic kabbalah was not necessarily a traumatic factor in the eighteenth century that demanded the neutralization of messianism.[26]

Scholem posited that the main principle of Lurianic *tikkun* (restoration) differs fundamentally from what was expounded by the Besht: the latter shifted the center of gravity from repairing the *Shekhinah* (divine presence) to repairing the "sparks of individual souls."[27] He further argued that the messianic basis of Lurianic kabbalah aimed to restore the world and bring about the general "redemption" of the *Shekhinah*, while, by contrast, in

Hasidism, this *tikkun* (repair), advanced on a "personal" level and in a person's "immediate" environment, relies on the principle of *devekut*.[28] Scholem believed that the words attributed to Rabbi Ya'aqov Yosef of Polnoy — one of the most prominent students of the Besht, who imparted to most of his rabbis teachings known to us today — reflect an original approach to the issue of reincarnation, arguing that "there is no such phrasing of the idea anywhere else in earlier kabbalistic works."[29] Yet, despite Scholem's belief that Rabbi Ya'aqov Yosef's interpretation of the Lurianic teachings concerning reincarnation and the raising up of holy sparks is unique to Hasidism, at the beginning of the section that Scholem quotes, Rabbi Ya'aqov Yosef himself noted the Lurianic source of his innovation. There he refers the reader to the Lurianic work of intentions (*kavvanot*), *Peri Eẓ Ḥayyim* (citing a specific page number in the manuscript in his possession),[30] which Rabbi Ya'aqov Yosef quotes almost word for word. This quote depicts a man's journeys during his lifetime to all the geographical places in which he will find the sparks connected to the root of his soul, to raise them up:

> And when the first man sinned he caused a defect in all the worlds, and afterwards it was necessary that the sparks of holiness should fall from him and they mixed with all four winds of the world and all seventy nations, each one took its part, and those same sparks, they do not have the power to leave, [they can do so] only by means of Israel following the commandments and praying, and through their prayers, can they raise them up . . . Therefore, Israel needs to go into exile with the *Shekhinah* in all seventy tongues to collect the sparks of holiness. And in this you will understand how the sin of the first man caused all the exiles until the messianic age. And behold, here too is the reason, you will understand why Israel needed to go into exile in Babylon and Persia and Greece, etc., and you will also understand why there were four exiles and also why in these four exiles all of Israel was exiled, but to the rest of the seventy nations even one [member of the nation] of Israel was exiled there, it is as though all Israel was exiled there . . . and when the souls were exiled, the main part of all the sparks of the souls went there . . . and therefore all of Israel needed to be exiled to these four. Because every man will be able to take out of there these holy sparks that relate to the root of his soul and raise them up.[31]

Thus, the personal aspect of raising up the sparks is evident in the writings of Rabbi *Ḥayyim* Vital, and these sparks, as the passage highlights, are further connected in an individual manner to the root of each person's soul. Consequently, each human being is obligated to raise them up as part of the general *tikkun* of the *Shekhinah*.

In the next section, we will see how the students of the Besht expanded this principle of soul connections in a way that expressed the association between the sparks of the soul and practical aspects of daily life by focusing attention on prayer, the redirection of "foreign thoughts" through raising them up, and the importance of social justice. In addition, we will see how this idea affected the Hasidic literature that sought to expose the reasons for the commandments.

Reincarnation and Raising Up of Foreign Thoughts [*Maḥshavot Zarot*]

While Hasidim followed the teachings of Isaac Luria and accepted the Lurianic emphasis on reincarnation as central to the process of divine restoration (*tiqun*), nevertheless they did not shy away from adding their own unique interpretations and commentaries. We find one such example in the writings of Rabbi Moses Shoham of Dolina (1730–1820), a Lurianic kabbalist and author of the book of Lurianic devotions (*kavvanot*) called *Saraf Peri Eẓ Ḥayyim*.[32] Rabbi Moses explains the idea of "raising up foreign thoughts" during prayer: this is part of the raising up of man's personal sparks and the repairing of parts of his soul.[33] Ḥaym Vital's assertion, as found in his book *Eẓ Ḥayyim*, that the sparks of holiness can be raised up via prayer, becomes more relevant and assumes a practical application to reincarnation in the words of Rabbi Moses of Dolina:

> Indeed, behold it is explained in new books in the name of the holy rabbi, the Besht, of blessed memory ... and the root of the matter is that the foreign thoughts that come to a person during prayer or while one is busy with Torah, these are those same sparks of holiness that fell via that same man into the husks, either in this reincarnation or in a previous one, or via the sin of the first man, which all the souls of Israel were included in it. And therefore, every one of the nations of Israel must play his part in repairing the sparks. And, therefore, when a man stands at prayer and wants to devote himself to holiness, then they come to him, those same sparks, in order that he may repair them ... and I myself heard from the mouth of his holiness, of blessed memory, in these exact words, that one needs to be very inventive regarding the matter of foreign thoughts

> that come to a man when he stands at prayer, because they are truly his powers, coming to him so that he may repair them.[34]

Rabbi Moshe expresses an interesting, psychologically nuanced way of understanding negative states of consciousness. According to him, attention deficit during prayer or the wandering of thoughts to unholy topics does not constitute a behavioral anomaly that prevents a person from reaching higher levels of holiness and therefore requires correction. Rather, he encourages his readers, in the name of the Besht, to see such cognitive interferences as vestiges of sinful acts from previous reincarnations that emerge for this person with the invitation to be repaired. For Rabbi Moshe, therefore, these foreign thoughts represent the Lurianic idea of raising up the sparks, as they contain the same essence that a person damaged, in this reincarnation or in another, or they were allotted to him as part of the general repair of the primordial sin. For this reason, distraction during prayer is both a necessary and an inherent part of prayer that demands the devout to create certain "fences" or "limitations" to overcome these defects and repair them:

> And behold, to understand the words of his holiness, of blessed memory, regarding the meaning of this "being inventive." However, the matter is that the coming of these thoughts is a revealed example that is made evident to man via dreams, that the revelation of the matter does not come explicitly, only when he comes dressed and disappears in a certain vision. As is explained in *Eẓ Ḥayyim* . . . and therefore it is necessary to be inventive and to understand a matter within a matter, the matter of the defect, to understand it and to repair it via setting personal bounds in this regard, and he will begin to pray with more fervor and devotion, and then, by doing so, he raises up these sparks, returning them to holiness[35]

Based on the words of Rabbi Moses of Dolina, the processes of raising up the sparks and repairing the defects are also connected to previous incarnations or to the primordial sin. His formulation for dealing with foreign thoughts during prayer is not merely theoretical but relies also on practical instructions. His source for this idea, which he attributes to the Besht, already appears in various editions of the homilies of Rabbi Ḥayyim Vital, in his book *Eẓ Ḥayyim*, and in *Peri Eẓ Ḥayyim*. However, Rabbi Moses of Dolina develops these ideas further, endowing them with existential and practical meaning.

Reincarnation and Social Justice

From another perspective, Rabbi Ya'aqov Yosef of Polnoy (1719–1783), the author of the first published book of Hasidism,[36] was also instrumental in developing the social aspect of reincarnation. He applied this concept to explain and justify disparities between socioeconomic levels within Jewish society. In so doing, he drew on a range of opinions expressed in the homiletical literature composed by the sages of Poland in the generations preceding the followers of the Besht in the sixteenth and seventeenth centuries. Many Eastern European thinkers and preachers in these generations discussed why the rich merited most of the plenty in this world, offering different explanations for this. Thus, for example, Rabbi Avraham Horowitz, in his book *Yesh Noḥalin*, composed at the end of the sixteenth century, justifies the deference associated with the social status of the wealthy as decreed from above and as a means leading to the sustenance of the community: "Because they have respect before the Holy One, blessed be He, we too respect them. Because without the grace and truth that they perform, their wealth would be stopped up. And therefore, it is advisable to respect them."[37]

The idea that the wealthy deserve their riches because of their good deeds and because they give charity depicts their wealth as a reward for generous hearts and fairness in business.[38] Yet in many other places, preachers suggested other reasons based on the words of the Talmudic precept that "Length of life, children, and sustenance do not depend on one's merit, but rather they depend upon fate (*mazal*),"[39] suggesting that personal wealth is decreed from above and is not directly conditioned by reward and punishment.[40] This approach was also adopted by Rabbi Moshe Isserles, who explained:

> And occasionally concerning livelihood, plenty of sustenance is at times a reason to reject God, as it is said: "Riches hoarded by their owner for his misfortune" (Ecclesiastes 5,12) and this sustenance does not depend on merit to be granted and as a matter of fact his merits [would not] yield sustenance. Rather, everything depends on fortune which is determined at the moment a person is born (*mazal*), according to the wisdom [*da'at*] by which he was born, or created, which is the preparation of his nature in this world[41] [see b. Niddah 16b, *Tanhuma Pekudei* 3]. If the blessed Holy One knows that his nature would make him sin being rich, would his merits prevent him from using his wealth for sin? Still, it is impossible to gain wealth by merits, unless God would make him a different nature

> and change his fortune, which is impossible because of the freedom of choice granted to man in his predetermined fortune.[42]

Other thinkers in Eastern Europe from the same period have expressed similar ideas, including Rabbi David Darshan of Cracow,[43] Rabbi Isaiah Ha-Levi Horowitz — the holy Shelah[44] — and others.[45]

Rabbi Ya'aqov Yosef of Polnoy, who was influenced by the homiletical literature of previous generations, suggested a similar explanation that combines these two approaches:

> And behold it is written in the writings of Rabbi Isaac Luria, may his memory live in the next world ... the reason for the commandment never to return to Egypt is that they had already found all the sparks [there] ... and the reason for all the exiles is to find the sparks, and here in Egypt it is not necessary, etc.... and because the entire purpose of a person is to find the sparks, it is necessary to understand therefore why the poor man will find few sparks in little merchandise, and the rich will find them via a lot of merchandise and will find an abundance of sparks. Why do these [the rich and the poor] differ from one another? And it is necessary to say that it is known ... *for the Lord is a God of knowledge* (1 Samuel 2:3). He knows how many sparks a man needs to find and thus gives him the length of his life [necessary for this]. The poor man has already found his sparks in the previous reincarnation, and he only needs to find a few, while the rich man is the opposite.[46]

Rabbi Ya'aqov Yosef embeds his justification for socioeconomic disparities prevalent in Jewish society of his time within the theosophical system of Lurianic Kabbalah deploying the concept of reincarnation. In contrast to earlier formulations articulated by preachers and authors of *musar* (ethical) works in the sixteenth and seventeenth centuries, he posits that wealth is not determined by righteousness, charitable behavior, or fate, but rather based on planetary constellations at the time of birth. Rather, just as in the previous section foreign thoughts during prayer signaled a need for more intense engagement with past sins through *tikkun*, wealth in an inverted way invites its owner to be more actively involved in the process of raising up holy sparks, which they neglected to in previous reincarnations. By contrast, the poor have already completed and fulfilled this divine task in previous incarnations and therefore enjoy a more elevated status than the wealthy based on the unique spiritual perspective adopted by Rabbi Ya'aqov Yosef.[47]

Hasidic Rationalization of the Commandments: The Halakhic Dimensions of Reincarnation

Rabbi Ya'aqov Yosef of Polnoy, at the very heart of his long and casuistry-filled introduction to his work *Toldot Ya'aqov Yosef*, describes his motivation for composing this work and its organizing principle, "My heart was filled to explicate, with the help of God, these 613 commandments, how they are relevant at all times and in all periods, and they are in every man, and how there is a place in it to cleave to Him, blessed be He, in every one of the 613 commandments."[48] Published late in the life of Rabbi Ya'aqov Yosef as the first book of homilies printed by followers of the Besht,[49] it includes a wide range of sermons, some of which he delivered at specific events, while others he composed as novellae for his own use.[50]

The commandments for Rabbi Ya'aqov Yosef were at the heart of Jewish life, and a person's spiritual perfection, *devekut*, depended on their proper fulfillment when the physical action was conjoined and infused with proper mental and emotional concentration.[51] He further elaborates on this idea in his introduction:

> And the food of the spiritual limbs comes from fulfilling the entire Torah that is made up of 613 commandments, likened to the 613 limbs of the body, and each one of the 248 limbs is fed from the individual commandment that is linked to that same limb ... and know and understand ... that this is a great principle for the entire Torah and divine service, to reach the level of *But you, that did cleave unto the Lord* (Deut. 4:4) and the positive commandment, *to Him shall you cleave* (Deut. 10:20).[52]

Subsequently, he refines this statement by highlighting the importance of fulfilling the commandments in two dimensions: assuming exactitude in the corporeal performance of the act — by means of the limbs and parts of the body — as well as adopting the proper spiritual comportment through awareness, clarity of intention, and focused thought while performing a divinely ordained decree. Performing the commandments without intention, without connection between the act and the thought and the reason for the commandment, is likely to lead to destructive results:

> According to that which I received, the main thing is that he cleaves to the commandment in doing it, meaning that he will see that he will not be divided and separated from the worlds wherein the root of the commandment lies, and he will link his thought there, then from the act of

> those below [humans], the heavenly ones are woken, and there will be unification via the commandment that he performs here ... And know and understand and be careful regarding this ... and so he will be careful regarding Torah and prayer.[53]

A motif that appears repeatedly and extensively in this work is the need to perform all the commandments perfectly in terms of act and intention to complete man's role in this world. Each and every commandment constitutes part of the "garment," known as *ḥaluqa derabanan* (the supernal garment worn in the world to come), a concept to which the kabbalistic literature attributes multiple meanings.[54] This garment of the soul is woven from man's good deeds and the study of Torah and is elucidated in several places in *Sefer Ha-Zohar*.[55] When a person dedicates one's life to the commandments in body and soul, such an individual is able to fully realize one's role in the world without necessitating further reincarnations. This idea is developed already in Lurianic literature and provides the theoretical basis for Rabbi Ya'aqov Yosef's conceptualization: "Because it is necessary that he perform the commandments without any negative thoughts; if he garbs them in materialism, they remain in this world and will not go with him to the world to come. He will return to this world naked, reincarnated, until he will merit to perform all 613 commandments in purity as is outlined in *Sefer Ha-Gilgulim*."[56] The demand for the perfect performance of the commandments recurs frequently in *Sefer Toldot Ya'aqov Yosef*.[57] This garment is "woven" around the spiritual limbs of a person through the performance of the 613 commandments, which reflect the structure of the body.[58] The 365 positive commandments are parallel to the limbs, and the 248 negative commandments are parallel to the ligaments that bind the limbs to one another. According to this perception, which also draws on Lurianic teachings, reincarnation is necessary to carry out the commandments of the Torah with complete perfection after the repair of all defects and sins. If a person fails to repair all the defects, his *ḥaluqa derabanan* will not be completed. Thus, he will have to return in further reincarnations, entailing pain and much suffering.

Another Hasidic work that delineates the rationales for the commandments is *Sefer Derekh Piqudekha* by Rabbi Ṣevi Elimelekh Shapira of Dinov, which was written in the first half of the nineteenth century.[59] The main motivation for writing this book, as in the case of *Sefer Toldot Ya'aqov Yosef*, was to enable readers to perform the commandments perfectly, thus facilitating a person's spiritual repair and the completion of his *ḥaluqa derabanan*, ensuring that he will not require further reincarnations. However, while *Sefer Toldot Ya'aqov Yosef* was from the outset edited from a range of homilies given by Rabbi Ya'aqov Yosef of Polnoy during his own lifetime, Rabbi Ṣevi Elimelekh of Dinov composed *Sefer Derekh Piqudekha* with the explicit aim of explaining the hidden reasons for the commandments. The structure of his work reflects an idea found in *Sefer Ha-Gilgulim* that the commandments should be fulfilled on three levels: in practice, in speech, and in thought.[60] The "practical" part relates to the performative dimensions of the commandment, including a description, usually quite extensive, of all the details concerning the *halakhah* in question. Under "speech," Rabbi Ṣevi Elimelekh seeks to impart to the reader novellae, sections of halakhic casuistry, and some of his kabbalistic innovations, and he even notes that every person is obligated to derive innovations about all the commandments as part of the commandment to study Torah. Apart from this, there are many reasons for every commandment, and man is obligated to discover the reasons connected to the root of his soul.

In the section concerning "thought," Rabbi Ṣevi Elimelekh seeks to illuminate the reasons for every commandment via allusions (*remez*) and kabbalistic interpretations (*sod*), integrating both kabbalistic and non-kabbalistic ideas. In certain places, he stretches the boundaries of each commandment, thus enabling the performance of all the commandments and the completion of the *ḥaluqa derabanan* allotting each person a share in the process of messianic repair. Yet Rabbi Ṣevi Elimelekh disagreed, often on technical grounds, with the Lurianic precept that every soul must be reincarnated in the future to fulfil those commandments he was unable to perform in this lifetime. He underlined that a person is no longer able to perform certain laws, for instance, that were connected to the Jerusalem Temple, which no longer stands. Instead, Rabbi Ṣevi Elimelekh offered various forms of substitution for the performance of such precepts, by using thought and speech for instance in place of the actual physical act. In this way it is possible to perform all the commandments, even if only partially.

Torah study functioned as another substitute in Rabbi Elimelekh's system, which he applied both to the laws connected to the sacrificial offerings as well as to the commandment of *be fruitful and multiply* (Genesis 1:28). Thus, for example, he suggests repairing the sparks connected to bringing sacrifices through prayer, confession, or words of praise (*hallel*) and thanksgiving, basing himself on widely used interpretations of the verse *So will we render for bullocks the offering of our lips* (Hosea 14:3).[61] He also praises the moral and spiritual benefit arising from intellectual pursuits, such as learning or simple reading, that aim to understand the laws of the sacrifices connected to the Temple.[62] Casuistry enables us to "understand a thing from within a thing,"[63] and in this way one can extricate a foundational principle and reason connected to a commandment that cannot be performed in the current time. His theory states that a commandment can be fulfilled through another commandment that is connected to the same principle. According to his theory, the commandments can also assume a practical character by means of the moral customs or conduct connected to "the reason" of a commandment.[64] Rabbi Ṣevi Elimelekh clarifies in various ways how the reasons for the commandments, even completely allegorical ones, enable the fulfillment of all 613 commandments, thus allowing every man to achieve his *tikkun*. For example, he questions how the commandment to be fruitful and multiply can be possible to perform by studying Torah for someone who is unable to marry and have children (for various reasons), similarly to Ben Azai, who did not marry because his soul desired only the Torah.[65] Through a far-reaching interpretation, which he calls *remez* (allusion), he lists ten points of similarity between Torah study and married life, suggesting that whoever cannot have children or live a married life can complete his *tikkun* via these allusions.[66]

In another place, he explains that Torah study is like having sex in a number of ways. According to him, the duty of the man to talk to his wife before having intercourse and to arouse her sexual desire through speech are similar to a rabbi who teaches his students by starting each lesson with humor, which will in turn arouse the hearts of the students for receiving the teachings of the Torah. He closes by adding that just as a man is required to respect his wife, similarly the rabbi is also obligated to respect his students. Overall, *Sefer Derekh Piqudekha* emphasized the opportunity that each person must repair all the commandments of the Torah during one's own lifetime and complete one's personal *tikkuns* without the need for reincarnation. This is achieved by "stretching" the boundaries of every commandment and by studying the various rationales for them.

Conclusion

As this chapter has demonstrated, reincarnation constituted a recurring motif in Eastern European Jewish culture in the eighteenth and nineteenth centuries and was represented in diverse Hasidic literary genres. Building on Lurianic concepts, reincarnation plays a central role in hagiographic literature that emphasized divine service through prayer, *devekut*, and social responsibility. The eighteenth century fundamentally transformed the structure of Eastern European Jewish communities, and with the rise of Hasidism, the image of the *ẓaddik* became the central pivot of religious life. The idea of reincarnation was further deployed by Hasidic writers to justify community organization and hierarchy by using the Lurianic concept of soul roots to explain the natural affinity between a particular *Ẓaddik* and his followers. Furthermore, the definition of social classes in the newly reconfigured Hasidic communal structure also reflected kabbalistic ideas. The greatness of the *ẓaddik* was determined, among other things, by his ability to see and correct incarnations of souls, or by the fact that the soul of the *Ẓaddik* was itself comprised of incarnation of the soul of an important figure in Jewish history.

At the transition from the early modern to the modern period in Eastern Europe, Lurianic traditions, in conjunction with other kabbalistic teachings and a unique method of Talmud study in traditional rabbinic study halls (*batei midrash*), have further shaped Hasidic culture and practice. The Lurianic idea of reincarnation receives an existential and practical interpretation in the works of R. Moshe Shoham of Dolina, who reconceptualized the raising of soul-sparks as an everyday human phenomenon. Similarly, the reflections of a person's heart during prayer direct his attention to moments where he failed during his life or in another incarnation, which he must then rectify. Finally, this chapter showed how the encounter between Lurianic literature and other kabbalistic traditions, combined with the scholarly-Talmudic style of learning in Eastern European study halls, led to innovative work in the field of understanding the kabbalistic meaning of the commandments as explicated in the writings of R. Ẓevi Elimelekh.

Notes

1. Avraham Rubinstein, ed., *In Praise of the Ba'al Shem Tov* (Jerusalem: Rubin Mass Press, 1995) [Hebrew] (1st ed., Kopost: Israel Yofe, 1816).

2. Moshe Rosman, *Founder of Hasidism: A Quest for the Historical Ba'al Shem Tov* (Berkeley: University of California Press, 1996).

3. Rubinstein, *In Praise of the Besht*, 52–53. And *In Praise of the Besht*, 329 in a slightly different version according to the Lubavitch manuscript. On this manuscript and its facsimile edition, see Yehoshua Mondshine, ed., *Shivhei Ha-Baal Shem Tov: A Facsimile of a Unique Manuscript, Variant Versions & Appendices* (Jerusalem: Ha-Naḥal, 1982) [Hebrew].

4. Rubinstein, *In Praise of the Besht*, 53.

5. On Luria as a healer of the soul, see Lawrence Fine, *Physician of the Soul,*

Healer of the Cosmos: Isaac Luria and his Kabbalistic Fellowship (Stanford: Stanford University Press, 2003), 150–86; Ronit Meroz, "'Zelem' (Image) and Medicine in the Lurianic Teaching (according to the writing of R. Hayim Vital)," *Koroth* 8, nos. 5–6 (1982): 170–77; Assaf Tamari, "The Body Discourse of Lurianic Kabbalah" (PhD diss., Ben-Gurion University of the Negev, 2016).

6. For another example of this, see Rubinstein, *In Praise of the Besht*, 178–80, 210–12; Josef Dan, *The Hasidic Story — Its History and Development* (Jerusalem: Keter, 1975), 68–74 [Hebrew].

7. Morris M. Faierstein, "The Dibbuk in the Mayse Book," *Shofar* 30, no. 1 (2011): 94–103.

8. There are many examples of this motif discussed by Gedalyah Nigal concerning reincarnation and the dybbuk in Hasidic literature. See Gedalyah Nigal, *The Hasidic Tale: Its History and Topics* (Jerusalem: Hasidic Literature Research Institute, 1981), 185–201 [Hebrew].

9. On Rabbi Nachman as a part of the Besht's circle, see Abraham J. Heschel, *The Circle of the Baal Shem Tov: Studies in Hasidism*, ed. Samuel H. Dresner (Chicago: University of Chicago Press, 1985), 113–51.

10. Rubinstein, *In Praise of the Besht*, 291.

11. Rubinstein, *In Praise of the Besht*, 154.

12. Nabal's sin consisted of having made two calves of gold and built two temples during his lifetime, one in Beth-el and a second in Dan: *For the sins of Jeroboam which he sinned, and wherewith he made Israel to sin; because of his provocation wherewith he provoked the Lord, the God of Israel* (1 Kings 15:30).

13. Iṣḥaq Ayziq Yehuda Yeḥiel Safrin of Komarno, *Megilat Starim*, ed. Naftali Ben Menaḥem (Jerusalem: Ha-Rav Quq Institute, 1940), 7–8 [Hebrew]; cf. Jonathan Meir, *Imagined Hasidism: The Anti-Hasidic Writing of Joseph Perl* (Jerusalem: Bialik Institute, 2013), 142–44 [Hebrew].

14. On this, see at length Isaiah Tishby, *The Doctrine of Evil and Kelipah in Lurianic Kabbalah* (Jerusalem: Magnes, 1984), 103–5 [Hebrew]; Gershom Scholem, *Elements of the Kabbalah and Its Symbolism*, trans. Josef Ben-Shlomo (Jerusalem: Bialik Institute, 1980), 308–9 [Hebrew]; Ronit Meroz, "Redemption in Lurianic Teaching" (PhD diss., Hebrew University, 1988), 277–87 [Hebrew]; Assaf Tamari, "Human Sparks: Readings in the Lurianic Theory of Transmigration and Its Concept of the Human Subject" (MA thesis, Tel Aviv University, 2009), 18–33 [Hebrew].

15. Nigal, *The Hasidic Tale*, 185–86.

16. Hayyim Vital, *Sha'ar Ha-Gilgulim* (Jerusalem, 1988), 110, 125–26, 133, 135–36.

17. R. Elimelekh of Leżajsk, *No'am Elimelekh* (Lvov: Shlomo Rapaport, 1787), 68b. biblical translations are from the JPS Tanakh (Philadelphia: Jewish Publication Society of America, 1917).

18. Mordechai Bruckman, *Migdal David* (Peitrikow, 1930), 50. See at length Ada Rapoport-Albert, "The Hasidic Movement after 1772: Continuity and Change," *Zion* 55, no. 2 (1990): 232–37 [Hebrew].

19. For the popularization of kabbalistic ideas in print using study guides, see Andrea Gondos, *Kabbalah in Print: The Study and Popularization of Jewish Mysticism in Early Modernity* (New York: State University of New York Press, 2020); Andrea Gondos, "New Kabbalistic Genres and Their Readers in Early Modern Europe," in *Connecting Histories: Jews and Their Others in Early Modern Europe*, ed. Francesca Bregoli and David Ruderman (Philadelphia: University of Pennsylvania Press, 2019), 67–85.

20. Printed in Lublin in 1585 together with the explanation of the commentary by Menahem Recanati that was written by Rabbi Mordechai Yoffe, *Levush Or Yeqarot*.

21. Printed in Frankfurt in 1784. A relatively short section dealing with reincarnation of souls was printed as part of the edition of the Lurianic sermons given by Moshe Trinqi, *Sefer Ha-Kavvanot* (Venice: Pietro and Lorenzo Bragadin, 1620).

22. R. Menaḥem Azarya of Fano, *Sefer Gilgulei Neshamot* (Frankfurt an der Oder: n.p., 1711). Ordered alphabetically, it links the reincarnation of various personalities from the Bible, Mishnah, and Talmud.

23. See for instance, R. Ẓevi Hirsh Qaydanover, *Qav Ha-Yashar* (Frankfurt am Main: Johannes Wust, 1706), 11b, 80a–81b, 92a–94a, 126a–b.

24. Gershom Scholem, *The Latest Phase: Essays on Hasidism by Gershom Scholem*, ed. David Assaf and Esther Liebes (Jerusalem: Magnes Press, 2008), 9–11; G. Scholem, *Devarim Be-Go: Pirqe Moreshet Ve-Tḥiya* (Tel Aviv: Ofaqim, 1975), 357–58 [Hebrew]; Moshe Idel, *Kabbalah: New Perspectives* (New Haven: Yale University Press, 1990), 161–68 [Hebrew]; Moshe Idel, *Hasidism: Between Ecstasy and Magic* (Jerusalem: Schocken, 2000), 407–24, 407 n. 3 [Hebrew].

25. Isaiah Tishby, "The Messianic Idea and Messianic Trends in the Growth of Hasidism," *Zion* 32 (1967): 1–45.

26. See Tishby, "The Messianic Idea"; Idel, *Hasidism*, 88–90. See also on messianism, Rachel Elior, "Breaking the Boundaries of Times and Space," in *Apocalyptic Time*, ed. Albert I. Baumgarten (Leiden: Brill, 2000), 187–97.

27. "The Neutralization of the Messianic Element in Early Hasidism," *Journal of Jewish Studies* 20 (1969): 41.

28. Scholem, *The Latest Phase*, 237–58; Scholem, "The Neutralization of the Messianic element," 25–55.

29. Scholem, "The Neutralization of the Messianic Element," 41.

30. Ya'aqov Yosef of Polnoy, *Ketonet Passim*, ed. Iṣḥaq Eikhen (Jerusalem: n.p., 2011), 271.

31. Hayyim Vital, *Peri Eẓ Ḥayyim* (Jerusalem: n.p., 1980), 15–16.

32. Roee Goldschmidt, "The Study of Lurianic Kabbalah in the Circle of the Baal Shem Tov — R. Moshe Shoham of Dolina's Saraf *Peri Eẓ* Hayyim," *Kabbalah: Journal for the Study of Jewish Mystical Texts* 29 (2013): 209–86 [Hebrew].

33. The raising up of foreign thoughts is a topic that concerned a great deal of Hasidim; see Joseph Weiss, "Beginnings of Hasidim," *Zion* 16 (1951): 88–103; Moshe Idel, "Tefila, Eqstaza Ve-Maḥshavot Zarot," in *Yashan Me-Penei Ḥadash*,

ed. David Assaf and Ada Rapoport-Albert (Jerusalem: Shazar Institute, 2009), 57–118.

34. Moses Shoham of Dolina, *Divrei Moshe* (Polnoy, 1801), 9a.

35. *Divrei Moshe*, 9a.

36. See https://yivoencyclopedia.org/article.aspx/Yaakov_Yosef_of_Pollonye.

37. Avraham Horowitz, *Yesh Noḥalin* (Amsterdam: n.p., 1701), 34a.

38. This idea appears for example also in Shmuel Ha-Levi Eidelles (MARSHA), *Ḥidushe Agadot* (Lublin: Ẓvi ben Avraham Jaffe, 1627), section *Eruvin* 86a.

39. See b. Moed Katan, 28a.

40. Translation from the William Davidson Talmud, www.sefaria.org.il/Moed_Katan.2a?lang=bi.

41. See b. Niddah 16b, *Tanhuma, Pequdei* 3.

42. Moses Isserles, *Torat Ha-Olah*, vol. 3 (Prague: n.p., 1570), 117a–b.

43. See at length the long homily by David Darshan, *Ktav Hitnaẓlut Le-Darshamin* (Lublin: n.p., 1568), 4b–9a.

44. Isaiah Horowitz, *Two Tablets of the Covenant* [*Shne Luḥot Ha-Brit*] (Amsterdam: Emmanuel Benbenisti, 1649), 114 b.

45. On this topic and other sources, see Ḥayyim Hillel Ben Sasson, *Hagut Ve-Hanhaga: Hashqafotehem Ha-Ḥevratiot Be-Shalhei Yemei Ha-Benayim* (Jerusalem: Bialik Institute, 1959), 75–110 [Hebrew].

46. Ya'akov Yosef of Polnoy, *Toldot Ya'aqov Yosef*, ed. Iṣḥaq Eichen (Jerusalem: n.p., 2011), 291.

47. It is important to note that the motif of reincarnation of the soul as an explanation for divine justice appears in many places in Hasidic hagiographic literature. On this, see Gedalyah Nigal, "*Gilgul* Ne`shamot Ke-'Emṣai Le-Tiqun Avel Kaspi," *Sinai* 106 (1990): 63–71; Jonathan Goral, "Dmuto Shel Ha-Besht Be-Sipurei 'Am Shel Yehude Gruzya," *Yeda' 'Am* 65–66 (2005): 86–96 [Hebrew].

48. *Toldot Ya'aqov Yosef*, 14. See also Roee Goldschmidt, *Homiletic Literature in Eastern Europe: Rhetoric,Talmudic Erudition and Social Stature* (Jerusalem: Magnes Press, 2022) 88–9; Leore Sachs-Shmueli and Roee Goldschmidt , "Kabbalistic Literature Concerning Rationales for the Commandments: Hasidism and Kabbalah in Their Cultural Context", *JQR* 114 (2024): 45–49; Chaim Elly Moseson, "From Spoken Word to the Discourse of the Acavdemy: Reading the Sources for the Teaching of the Besht," (PhD diss., Boston University, 2017), 162–63; Gedalyah Nigal, *Manhig Ve-'Eda* (Jerusalem: Yehuda Publishers, 1962), 19–21; Samuel H. Dresner, *The Ẓaddik* (London: Schocken, 1960), 247–49.

49. *Toldot Ya'aqov Yosef* was first printed in Koretz, 1780.

50. See at length Goldschmidt, *Homiletuc Literature*, 83-130.

51. See Ron Margolin, *Human Temple: Religious Interiorization and the Structuring of Inner Life in Early Hasidism* (Jerusalem: Magnes Press, 2005), 288–91, 323–27 [Hebrew].

52. *Toldot Ya'aqov Yosef*, 1–2, 951, 980, 981.

53. *Toldot Ya'aqov Yosef*, 16. The importance of focusing the thought when performing a commandment is mentioned again at the end of the printed introduction in another section that was apparently added from the handwritten notes of Rabbi Ya'aqov Yosef to the introduction that were included in the printed text. Ibid., 39. Rabbi Ya'aqov Yosef notes the idea in a section with the addition "because we mentioned in the introduction," meaning that this is not part of the original introduction. Sefer *Toldot* Ya'*aqov Yosef* was edited a number of times, and many sections were apparently added from the notes of Rabbi Ya'aqov Yosef or other writings that the printers selected. On its editing and for more examples of this, see Goldschmidt, "Editing Methods of Homiletical Literature," 210–18; Zeev Gries, *The Book in Early Hasidim* (Tel Aviv: Hakibutz Hameuchad, 1992), 54–56 [Hebrew]; Mendel Piekarz, *The Beginning of Hasidim* (Jerusalem: Bialik Institute, 1998), 15–18. Concerning the lack of consistency in the writings of Rabbi Ya'aqov Yosef with regard to 'Avodah Be-Gashmiyut, see Tsippi Kauffman, *In All Your Ways Know Him: The Concept of God and Avodah Be-Gashmiyut in the Early Stages of Hasidism* (Ramat Gan: Bar-Ilan University Press, 2009), 370–71.

54. On this concept, see Gershom Scholem, "The Paradisic Garb of Souls and the Origin of the Concept of 'Haluka de-Rabbanan,'" *Tarbiẓ* 24 (1955): 290–306; reprinted in Scholem, *Devils, Demons and Souls*, ed. Esther Liebes (Jerusalem: Yad Ben Ẓvi, 2004), 215–45 [Hebrew]. On a similar idea in Muslim literature, see David H. Beneth, "Haluqa de-Rabbanan, Hibbur Yafeh min ha-Yeshu'ah and a Mohammedan Tradition," *Tarbiẓ* 25 (1956): 331–36 and compare to Scholem's comments in the article noted above, published in *Devils, Demons and Souls*, 235, note 1 and 236, note 4.

55. Zohar 2, 71. For further discussion of *Sefer Ha-Zohar*, see Dorith Cohen-Aloro, "Magic and Sorcery in the Zohar" (PhD diss., Hebrew University of Jerusalem, 1989), 126–27, cf. 105–40. Elliot R. Wolfson noted the disparity between the secret of the clothing in the teachings of Nahmanides and Rabbi Moses de Leon; see Elliot R. Wolfson, "The Secret of the Garment in Naḥmanides," *Da'at* 24 (1990): XXV–XLIX. And see also ibid., XXVII-XXVI, note 9. The term *ḥaluka derabanan* appears in the Zohar, 1, 71, but, as Scholem demonstrated, this phrase did not appear in the manuscripts and early print versions of the Zohar and was included in printed editions only from the eighteenth century; see Scholem, "The Paradisic Garb of Souls," 225–26.

56. *Toldot Ya'aqov Yosef*, 191.

57. Ibid., 65, 77, 112, 455–59, 531, 560, 722, 810–11, 1299, 1311–12.

58. The comparison between the 613 limbs and the 613 commandments in the Torah is based on midrash; see, for example, *Midrash Tanḥuma*, ed. Shlomo Buber (Vilnius: Rom, 1903), Deut. Khi-Teṣe, 33–34.

59. Rabbi Ṣevi Elimelekh of Dinov is known mainly for his widely circulating book *Benei Issachar* but also for his sharp stance against the maskilim, on the one hand, and his educational approach that emphasized his independent thought, on the other. See Mendel Piekarz, *The Hasidic Leadership: Authority*

and Faith in Zadicim as Reflected in the Hasidic Literature (Jerusalem: Bialik Institute, 1999), 336–62; Raya Haran, "Freedom of Thought in a World of Belief: The Teachings of the Zhidachov-Komarno Dynasty," *Jerusalem Studies in Jewish Thought* 20 (2007): 305–52; Roee Goldschmidt, "Talmudic Study Methods and Kabbalistic Literary Creativity in Eastern-European Kabbalah," *Kabbalah* 45 (2019): 245–74; Benjamin Brown, "Haḥmarah, Ḥamisha Tipusim Min Ha-'Et Ha-Ḥadasha," *Dine Israel* 20–21 (2001–2002): 182–84, notes 223, 226. On his biography, see Yqutiel Qamelhor, *Dor-De'a: 'Arba' Tequfot Be-Reshit Ha-Ḥasidut*, new ed. (Jerusalem: Yerid Ha-Ḥasidut, 2016), 424–32; Uri Tal (Taubes), "Rabbi Ṣevi Elimelekh Me-Dinov Ve-Milḥamto Ba-Haskalah" (MA thesis, Hebrew University, 1957), appendix III, 2–4.

60. *Sefer Ha-Gilgulim* (Amsterdam, 1684), 4b.

61. See, for example, b. Yoma 86a; *Bamidbar Raba*, Qoraḥ, 6; *Midrash Agadah*, ed. Shlomo Buber, vol. 2 (Vienna: Panata Press, 1894), 40; and more. In the words of Rabbi Menachem Azariah of Fano, "prayer atones like the sacrifices," Menaḥem Azarya of Fano, *Asara Ma'amarot*, Ma'amar Em Kol Ḥay (Venice: De-Gara, 1597), 64b.

62. See for example his remarks on bringing the Passover sacrifice; Rabbi Ṣevi Elimelekh of Dynów, *Derekh Piqudekha* (Lemberg: Klinghofer and Babad, 1914), 42a.

63. Rabbi Ṣevi Elimelekh of Dynów, *Derekh Piqudekha*, 8a.

64. Rabbi Ṣevi Elimelekh of Dynów, *Derekh Piqudekha*, 8a.

65. See b. Sotah, 4b; b. Ketubot 63a, and Tosafot, note "Barteyh."

66. *Derekh Piqudekha*, 27a.

LEORE SACHS-SHMUELI

The Bratslav Hasidic Approach to Reincarnation into Animals

14

MORALITY, SOCIETY, AND ECONOMIC CONCERNS

Introduction to Ritual Slaughter in Bratslav Hasidism

Traditions regarding the reincarnation of human souls in animals, which can be traced to thirteenth-century Spanish Kabbalah, directly influenced practical dimensions of Jewish life first among sixteenth- and seventeenth-century kabbalists and later in wider Hasidic circles stimulating greater concern for the proper observance of kosher slaughter in an effort to minimize the suffering of animals. This belief, combined with social and economic interests, encouraged Hasidic leaders to appoint their own ritual slaughterers, a trend that aroused controversies in various Jewish communities. This chapter addresses the role played by kabbalistic teachings regarding reincarnation in this regard, enumerating the textual sources that informed early Bratslav writings and their social significance for the development of this group. It further argues that R. Nahman of Bratslav and his student, R. Nathan of Nemerov, adapted this belief differently, reflecting diverse stages in the social formation of Bratslav Hasidism. The discussion herein enables us to identify how Hasidic leaders adapted the earlier belief in reincarnation to exploit its didactic-moral power and develop a political-social tool, part of their efforts to establish socially independent Hasidic societies that wielded economic power.

Chone Shmeruk's article regarding Hasidic ritual slaughter discusses the social-economic power that the Hasidic ritual slaughterers possessed and the reasons that this matter sparked disagreements.[1] Moreover, it sheds light on how ostensibly halakhic arguments were rooted in economic circumstances — the kosher meat taxes (*krafki*) constituted a central portion of the community's income; therefore, the community created mechanisms to supervise the slaughterers. The rabbinic hegemony controlled the granting of "licenses" to slaughterers, issuing them only to a select few. Considering this economic-social situation and the kabbalistic tradition on which Hasidism relied, Hasidic communities had a twofold interest in appointing their own slaughterers: the openly stated motivation following kabbalistic theories that demanded the use of a highly polished knife when conducting ritual slaughter, and a second goal, to gain economic power over the meat taxes. This historical context, together with additional historical facts spotlighted by scholars of Bratslav Hasidism,[2] is applied here to a textual analysis of the kabbalistic reasons for kosher slaughter provided by early Bratslav literature.

Combining these two issues, my chapter sheds further light on the social-political motivation behind Rabbi Nathan's homiletical project and his decision to pen his book as a work offering rationales for the commandments. Indeed, this was a direct continuation of the medieval genre of rationales for the commandments while at the same time reflecting the new challenges that the Hasidic halakhic authorities faced, issues not discussed in this medieval literature, for example the sectarianism of the Hasidim as an organizational-social unit distinct from the wider community and the disagreements with their opponents (the *mitnagdim*). Many view Rabbi Nathan's tendency to pragmatism — reducing the complexity of the source on which his homilies drew in *Likutei Moharan* — as a consequence of his desire to consolidate a "mass" Hasidic community and part of his efforts to give the Hasidim tools to confront internal and external disagreements.[3] Focusing on the topic of ritual slaughter exposes an additional aspect of the role that reincarnation played in Rabbi Nathan's political efforts to shape and build the Bratslav Hasidic community.[4]

The Historical Context

An announcement published in Brody in 1772 placed a ban on Hasidic ritual slaughter, more specifically disallowing the use of highly polished knives.[5] In fact, in the late eighteenth century, rabbis and communal authorities issued various bans and pamphlets against the Hasidim, condemning their separate Hasidic prayer quorums, failure to study Torah and the disparagement of Torah scholars, changes in dress, strange behavior, greed, celebration the anniversaries of saintly rabbis' deaths and other feasts, and suspicions of Sabbateanism. [6] Likewise, they prohibited the consumption of meat prepared by Hasidic ritual slaughterers.[7] Although the Vilna Gaon never recorded in writing a condemnation of ritual slaughter, he is said to have done so orally.[8] This fact, together with the fact that various bans (Brody 1772, Minsk, 1797) were published by the community and not by rabbis, suggests that the main concern was not halakhic but rather economic.[9]

We find several stories connected to Hasidic ritual slaughter in stories concerning the founder of Hasidism, the Besht in the hagiographic collection, *Shivḥei ha-Besht*, which was printed in Kopys in 1815 (and with which Rabbi Nathan was certainly familiar). These narratives describe the punctiliousness of the Besht and his followers regarding knives for ritual slaughter, testifying to the religious importance they attributed to this matter.[10] In a letter written in 1811, Rabbi Shneur Zalman of Liadi argued that the use of polished knives was not a Hasidic innovation but rather that Hasidim had helped to spread this concept.[11] In the Bratslav context, David Assaf emphasizes that the central problem communal leaders voiced concerning Bratslav ritual slaughterers was connected to the development of modern Orthodoxy and the fact that the Bratslav Hasidim did not obey the local halakhic authority, which was responsible for generating unity and ensuring the observance of a single halakhic norm.[12] Because of their central role in collecting taxes, the ritual slaughterers apparently had a high status in Jewish society, leading them to feel a sense of "pride." Indeed, we find indications of this in the book *Ḥayei Moharan*, written by Nathan Sternhartz[13] One account incidentally reveals that in 1778 a ritual slaughterer gave Rabbi Nachman a special chair,[14] indicating that he was a man of substantial financial means and that he sought to prove his loyalty to the *ẓadik*.

The appointment of Hasidic ritual slaughterers contributed to constructing the Hasidic community in several ways. First, the slaughterers' role in collecting taxes for the community enabled the transfer of money to the new Hasidic society (and affected the financial situation of communities that harassed and opposed the Hasidim). Second, insisting that the meat be slaughtered by a certain slaughterer encouraged Hasidim to share meals with one another and avoid eating with those who were not members of their community or were not punctilious in this regard (similarly to the establishment of Hasidic prayer quorums using a specific liturgical rite). A third aspect that has not been discussed concerns the emotional-didactic role of the belief in reincarnation as a punishment for sinners. The idea that when a person eats an animal, he may be eating one of his relatives who was reincarnated as that animal, thus facilitating the latter's spiritual repair, is a shocking concept that originated in the Middle Ages and appears in both folk tales and Hasidic homilies. For example, a tale in *Shivḥei ha-Besht* describes how Reb Yudl, who refused to eat meat slaughtered with a damaged knife, consequently ate his father, the preacher, who was reincarnated as a fish.[15] A similar tale in *Shivḥei ha-Besht* concerns Reb Yehiel Mikhel of Zolochev: he also ate a fish that was in fact his father.[16] On the one hand, these stories and Hasidic homilies offered the opportunity for spiritual repair and the raising up of the souls through ritual slaughter and consumption by the *ẓadik* in a state of purity;[17] however, on the other hand, such tales emphasize the threat of reincarnation as a punishment for sinners. Indeed, they employ the emotion of fear to intensify the obligation to ethos, norms, and halakha.

The fact that reincarnation was considered a terrifying punishment, and not only a positive opportunity to repair sins, is evident from the words of Rabbi Nachman, as quoted in *Ḥayei Moharan*:

> Once we stood before him, and they were carrying a corpse past the windows of his house, and there were people walking after the body, crying and lamenting ... He answered and said: "The dead can laugh. The deceased is probably laughing inside at the fact that they are crying about him, because they are crying that he is no longer in this world, as though saying to him, Were it not good if you would lengthen more days in this world and suffer many more sorrows in this world and have more bitterness in this world, if you would blacken yourself more in this world." I asked him, "Will he not also have no rest from sorrows there ... ?" He replied, "At any rate now, it is the end and the completion of sufferings ... and afterwards he will merit according to what he did ..." I asked him again, "Is there a possibility of reincarnating, and if so, what good is it that he is now rid of the sorrows of this world?" He replied, "If he wants, he can insist and argue that he does not want to be reincarnated and return to this world again." I asked him, "And will it help that he does not want to be reincarnated?" He answered, "Certainly, it will help, if he will insist and argue, 'Do with me what you will here [...], only I will not return to this world again, God forbid.' (And he said it

in these words: 'Finish with me here.') Certainly, he will be able to do it." And I asked him, of blessed memory, again and again if this will help, and he said that certainly it will help if he will be persistent in his position.[18]

This passage depicts death as a redemption from suffering and the sorrows of the world. By comparison, reincarnation is presented as a more severe form of punishment, forcing the soul to return to the world of suffering. Thus, while death signals the end of this-worldly sorrows, reincarnation is a continuation of the bitterness, more severe than the sufferings of hell, *Gehinom*, which purifies the sinner's soul.[19] Accordingly, the notion of reincarnation serves as a powerful deterrent against engaging in sinful actions. It underscores the crucial role played by a kosher ritual slaughterer and the consumption of food in a state of purity. These practices are seen as instrumental in freeing the soul from the unending cycle of suffering.

A Collection of Laws—*Likutei Halakhot* by Rabbi Nathan of Nemerov

Likutei Halakhot (*A Collection of Laws*) by Rabbi Nathan of Nemerov (1780–1845) is an extensive work, written intermittently over a period of forty years and completed a few days before the author's death in 1845.[20] Its primary goal is to offer rationales for the halakhot detailed in the four parts of the popular Jewish law code, the *Shulḥan 'Arukh* (*Prepared Table*), written by the sixteenth-century legist and kabbalist Joseph Karo, incorporating the teachings of Rabbi Nahman of Bratslav. Rabbi Nathan, as the student and faithful scribe of Rabbi Nahman, adapted the latter's "teachings," his Hasidic homilies, while also stamping them with his own personal mark, thus creating a commentary on various passages of the *Shulḥan 'Arukh*. Rabbi Nathan assumed the leadership and organization of Bratslav Hasidism after the death of his teacher, although he encountered some opposition from some of Rabbi Nahman's veteran followers, who objected to his leadership style.[21] There can be no doubt regarding the centrality of *Likutei halakhot* to Bratslav Hasidim, alongside *Likutei Moharan*, and likewise it is a treasure trove for the development of the Bratslav branch of Hasidism.

Mendel Piekarz saw *Likutei Halakhot* as a response and reaction to the many persecutions that Rabbi Nathan suffered, first and foremost at the hands of Rabbi Moshe Ẓvi of Savran, and he analyzes the traces of this dispute in the text.[22] In addition to the internal Hasidic disputes, as Ron Margolin demonstrates, the work must also be read in the context of Rabbi

Nathan's struggle with the Galician maskilim.[23] Roee Horen, following Piekarz, widened the understanding of how the role of the *ẓadik* is constructed in this text as an organizing principle of Bratslav Hasidism after the death of Rabbi Nahman.[24] Following this line, Jonatan Meir proposed that Rabbi Nathan refrained from printing the work because of the disputes surrounding him, in particular because of his extremely clear statements regarding the status of Rabbi Nahman as the *ẓadik* of the generation who lives even after his death, statements that he moderated in other works because of the criticism they aroused.[25] As Meir claims, the composition of these works and their printing helped to shape the theology of Bratslav Hasidism and its organization as a Hasidic stream that lives and is defined around the Bratslav library without a *ẓadik*, ensuring that Rabbi Nahman continues *to live* among his followers even after his death.[26] Rabbi Nathan made efforts to publish this work only as the internal disputes faded, and the various volumes of the book were printed with the support of Rabbi Nahman of Tolchyn.[27] Furthermore, Meir emphasizes the ritualization of Rabbi Nathan's thought through the creation of a series of rituals designed to consolidate the Hasidic group in the complex and humiliating reality that they faced following the death of their leader.[28] In a recent study, Daniel Hundert emphasized the nomistic foundations of Rabbi Nahman's teachings and their implementation in the exegetical endeavors of Rabbi Natan in *Likutei halakhot* and the revitalizing and creative cultural role of the halakha and its rationales in Rabbi Nathan's complex engagement with the Haskalah.[29]

In addition to these studies, I argue that providing a comprehensive and uniquely Bratslav interpretation of the *Shulḥan 'arukh* was intended to strengthen the foundations of obligation to halakhic practice and its meaning as another layer of the battle with the maskilim. This idea is supported by the words of Rabbi Nathan in his introduction to the work: "And the main goal is that through this [code] he will come to act, to be aroused in this way to carry out the words of our rabbi, of blessed memory, in simplicity." Accordingly, the lengthy homilies were intended to strengthen loyalty to the teachings of the (departed) rabbi, arousing greater enthusiasm for observing the commandments in his followers. Furthermore, Rabbi Natan stated in his introduction:

> Know that all the things that our rabbi, of blessed memory, revealed are totally new introductions … and all of them are guidance and wonderful ways through which one can come closer to God, blessed be He, each

> and every person, wherever one is. And the main thing is to carry them out in simplicity according to what came forth from his mouth in innocence and simplicity. However, due to the materiality of our body and the murkiness of our minds, it is very hard and difficult to enter into the heart of man the innocence and simplicity of these things, because the mind of every person tends after the wisdoms of the world, most of which distort the heart from the point of actual truth.[30]

These statements indicate the educational-social aim of the work: beyond the discursive aspects of the homilies, it sought to mold an emotional obligation to halakhic practice that will connect man with his creator via the *ẓadik*. The political-social goal of *Likutei halakhot* is in fact similar to the aim of Rabbi Nathan's other works: it seeks to create a ritual system that will consolidate the new group of Hasidim after the death of the *ẓadik*. As we will see, the discussion on reincarnation and ritual slaughter is an additional facet of this system.

Reincarnation in Animals in *Likutei Moharan* and Kosher Slaughter

To understand how Rabbi Nahman shaped the rationale for ritual slaughter and reinforced the position of kosher slaughterers, it is instrumental to consult his words in *Likutei Moharan* as well as the kabbalistic sources on which he drew. Comparing the words of Rabbi Nahman and Rabbi Nathan, together with an examination of the diachronic context and the sources that Rabbi Nahman employed, will shed light on Rabbi Nahman's innovation and originality in his interpretation of reincarnation of the soul. Likewise, it will demonstrate how Rabbi Nathan abandoned this innovative approach only to return to classic kabbalistic traditions.

When relating to this topic, Rabbi Nathan combined two different teachings from *Likutei Moharan*.[31] In teaching 31, Rabbi Nahman expropriated the belief in the reincarnation of the soul from its accepted meaning — the dualistic belief that the human soul represents an essence beyond the material and is liable to be reincarnated in another creature after death — and gave it a new meaning. Thus, he depicted a process that occurs in a person's lifetime, with a clearly monistic aspect:

> And know, it is not enough for a person to just long in [his] heart. He has to express his yearnings orally ... For the soul comes forth primarily from speech and this is the meaning of the verse, *There is hevel (a vanity)*

> *done upon the earth* (Eccl. 8:14). This is the concept of the reincarnation of souls. When a person longs for something and afterwards expresses his longing with the *hevel* (breath) of his mouth, then the soul is created. This soul, the "speaking spirit," travels in the air and reaches another person. It arouses longing in this other person.[32]

According to Rabbi Nahman, the soul is like desire, both sharing an air-like material aspect that can pass from one being to another. It follows from his words that for him reincarnation of the soul is not limited to a postmortem process. Rather, it is the transferal of the soul, which he identifies with desire, and is realized via a physical essence — a person's breath. Thus, reincarnation refers to the movement of the soul-breath physically in the air, transferring the desire from one person to another. In the second edition of *Likutei Moharan,* which Rabbi Nathan edited and printed in his home, he added a long section expanding on this matter:

> Through the articulation of the letters in the air, the speech [is made], from which the souls go forth. This is because the air is the life-force of all things, and without air it is impossible to live. This corresponds to the soul, and the souls come forth and are reincarnated. In sum: The yearnings and longings for a holy thing are very precious. Through them a soul comes into being. It is then completed by means of speech, as explained, and comes forth and is reincarnated.... The reverse is also true. How much evil is caused by the yearning for an evil thing, God forbid. For the soul that comes into being as a result of evil yearnings is occasionally reincarnated within the *ẓadik* and can cause him to sin, God forbid. This corresponds to, *There is hevel (a vanity) done upon the earth* (Eccl. 8:14). *Hevel* alludes to the *hevel* (breath) of the mouth from which the souls come forth.[33]

Here the soul is not an entity that precedes life but rather a product of human speech. Human speech that expresses a yearning and desire creates the soul, which has physical substance, "breath of the mouth," with moral responsibilities. Indeed, when the desire is in accordance with divine service it is good, and when it leads to sin, it can further perpetuate evil in the world. When such a soul is created, it has independent existence, separate from the person who pronounced it, and it also facilitates "reincarnation of the soul," passing between different people, and has the power to draw good or bad deeds. This influence is exerted even in opposition to the will of the person receiving it. Consequently, it can cause the *ẓadik* to desire evil and even to sin. This is an original adaptation and fusion of the idea of reincarnation with the concept of strange thoughts (as articulated by Rabbi Yaakov Yosef of Pollonye, apparently drawing on the Besht), which derive from sinners and enter the soul of the *ẓadik*. However, while Yaakov Yosef, in his *Toldot Ya'akov Yosef*, emphasized the opportunity for the repair of a foreign thought as it becomes sweetened and holy when it enters the soul of the *ẓadik*, here the text concentrates on the danger that this transfer represents for the *ẓadik*. Moreover, Rabbi Nahman added to this a concrete, physical aspect, fusing it with the teachings about reincarnation of soul — a process that occurs following a person's death and not in one's lifetime. He also dismantled the perception of the soul as one entity found in a person throughout his entire lifetime, disassembling the person into many souls, which are dynamic, blurring the boundary between the I and the other, and even questioning the existence of the self as an identifiable and defined entity. Although we find a precedent for this in the Lurianic work *Sha'ar ha-Gilgulim* by Hayyim Vital, here it is possible to identify an additional step of dismantlement and metamorphosis of the belief in reincarnation.

Despite Rabbi Nahman's originality, as highlighted in connection with teaching 31, when discussing this belief in the context of the role of kosher slaughter, he did not highlight the monistic aspects of identifying the soul with desire and a person's breath but rather employed classical kabbalistic traditions available to him. Availing himself of diverse literary means, he arouses the emotion of fear, emphasizing the central role of the ritual slaughterer and of kosher slaughter, highlighting their theological and, surprisingly, economic significance:

> For the blood is the soul, which is involved in reincarnation and the ritual slaughterer must have in mind to elevate the soul that comes in reincarnation, and the ritual slaughterer must have in mind to elevate the soul that is in the blood. Also, for the most part, lack of livelihood — which has diminished in recent generations — is on account of unworthy ritual slaughterers. . . . For the worthy ritual slaughterer feeds and sustains the Jewish people. This is because the worthy ritual slaughterer clothes the soul in the level of animal within the level of human — namely, within the spoken word of the blessing he recites. This spoken word is an aspect of the *Shekhinah* . . . This is the meaning of the verse, *God's sword is filled with blood* (Isa. 34:6) of the souls that ascend into her as an aspect of *mayin nukvin* (female waters) . . . This is also the explanation of *We get our bread at the peril of our souls, because of the sword of the wilderness* (Lam. 5:9). In

> other words, this is when the ritual slaughterer is unworthy and does not elevate the soul as an aspect of *mayin nukvin* — so that when he stands ready with his knife to slaughter the animal, he resembles a murderer of souls. Then his knife is *the sword of the MiDBaR (wilderness)* and not *God's sword*, which is the sword of the *MeDaBeR* (speaker). And this causes suffering to the animal's soul, which cries out bitterly ... and now it has *no place to rest its feet* (Gen. 8:9). Woe to that ritual slaughterer! Woe to the soul! For he murdered the soul and put it in the hand of its enemies. Thus, the Divine Presence does not have the *mayin nukvin* (female waters) with which to draw food for its household. Because of this, *We get our bread at the peril of our souls* (Lam. 5:9) with great strain and struggle.[34]

Here the ritual slaughterer is responsible for the process of repairing the soul that was reincarnated in an animal while, at the same time, the livelihood of the Jewish people also depends on him. The slaughterer kills not only the animal but also an animal housing a human soul. Thus, if he is unworthy, Rabbi Nahman condemns him as no less than a "murderer of souls." This heavy responsibility is intensified by the emotional depiction of the sorrow felt by the soul, which consequently loses an opportunity for repair: "And this causes suffering to the animal's soul, which cries out bitterly [...] and now it has *no place to rest its feet*." The rhetorical use of the word "woe" is intended to rouse the slaughterer to ensure that the slaughter is carried out without any defect and to motivate consumers of the meat to purchase meat only from a kosher slaughter. The financial context of Rabbi Nahman's discussion is rooted in the economic role of the ritual slaughterers in his period. Likewise, the need to reinforce and motivate the Hasidim to perform ritual slaughter is also expressed in Rabbi Nahman's promise that kosher slaughter ensures a good livelihood for the Jewish people.[35] Thus, while consumers must pay a high price for the kosher meat, they will be rewarded for so doing and will benefit from this financial expense, receiving in return a plentiful livelihood.

Kabbalistic Sources

Which sources did Rabbi Nahman draw upon when connecting the knife used for kosher slaughter with reincarnation? There are multiple theories regarding the origin of this belief in the Jewish tradition,[36] but early references to the doctrine of reincarnation into animals appear in thirteenth-century kabbalistic works.[37] Rabbi Nahman does not specify his exact source; indeed, in the eighteenth and nineteenth centuries this medieval idea[38] was widespread because of works such as *Sefer hakana;*[39] *Sefer hamiẓvot* by Rabbi Chaim Vital, edited by Meir Popers; *Ḥesed le'Avraham*; *Shevet musar*; and *Shenei luḥot habrit.*[40] To understand the development of this idea and its adaptation by Hasidism, I trace here a number of sources that were instrumental in molding the connection between the belief in reincarnation and kosher slaughter.[41] It seems that the first medieval source linking reincarnation of the soul in animals with the halakhic demand for ritual slaughter using an unblemished knife occurs in the writings of Rabbi Joseph of Hamadan:

> "Lo, all these things doth God work, twice, yea thrice, with a man," (Job 33:29).[42] If he is innocent, this is good, and if not, he is brought into a beast. As it is said, "An offering unto the LORD, ye shall bring your offering of the cattle" (Leviticus 1:2), meaning he was of you and now he is a beast. And accordingly, we do not slaughter with a blemish in order to avoid causing sorrow to the human race, and accordingly it is written "then thou shalt kill of thy herd and of thy flock . . . and thou shalt eat" (Deuteronomy 12:21). And man shall not slaughter the herd and flock of others. Rather always, as the Torah said, you shall know that even though that this beast was a man, your friend or your enemy, you shall slaughter it.[43]

In fact, the sorrow that arouses the kabbalist's pity concerns the human soul reincarnated in an animal rather than sorrow for the animal's soul: "And accordingly we do not slaughter with a blemish in order to avoid causing sorrow to the human race."[44] Causing suffering to animals is the reason for the prohibition against slaughtering with a defective knife. Furthermore, this source explains in a kabbalistic manner that the reincarnation of the soul in an animal is the esoteric reason for the prohibition against using a blemished knife.[45] According to Rabbi Joseph of Hamadan, causing suffering to animals entails an aspect of the commandment *Love your neighbor as yourself* (Leviticus 19: 18) because animals are in fact reincarnations of evil members of the nation of Israel.[46]

This idea was absorbed into the Lurianic kabbalah and from there passed on to Hasidism. Indeed, the connection between the belief in reincarnation and the imperative to exercise caution regarding slaughter with a blemished knife was adopted by Rabbi Hayyim Vital in his work *Sha'ar ha-Miẓvot*:

> Furthermore we will explain there the second aspect, and this is the matter of the souls that are reincarnated into the bodies of beasts, and

animals, and birds, and therefore it is necessary for the slaughterer to have in mind these two intentions: the first is to sweeten the judgments and the stringent strengths (*gevurot*) through the slaughter and the second is that using this intention, which we will elucidate, the punishment of that reincarnated person will be completed and he will be repaired and be worthy to come afterwards into the body of a man at the time of his birth, like the rest of the upright souls of human beings.[47]

Under his influence, the kabbalistic work by Naftali Bachrach, *Emeq ha-Melekh* (Amsterdam 1648), which circulated in Eastern Europe, developed a similar idea:

> And if he slaughtered with a knife that was defective, behold he caused a defect in God (denoted by the Hebrew letters *Yud-Heh*), and he is cut off from the community. The [Hebrew word for] community (*kahal*) in numerical value (*gematriya*) is equal to defect (*pegima*). And his sentence is the plague, and he is reincarnated as a dog that eats carrion, or as a kosher beast, but will not merit worthy slaughter, as punishment *quid pro quo*, only he will be given over to the hand of the slaughtered and will come out carrion from under his hand, *quid pro quo*. As it is said, *Whoever sheds human blood, by human [hands] his blood be shed* (Genesis 9:6), implying himself, that *his blood will be shed.*[48]

Naftali Bachrach threatens a slaughterer who fails to perform kosher slaughter with reincarnation as an animal that will not merit kosher slaughter — punishment quid pro quo, one of the main principles in suiting the punishment of reincarnation to each sin in the writings of Rabbi Joseph Shushan,[49] which was copied by Rabbi Menachem Recanati.[50] Furthermore, Ya'akov Ẓemaḥ, in his kabbalistic halakhic book concerning the laws of kosher slaughter, *Zevaḥ Shlemim*, integrated the kabbalistic considerations of reincarnation and ritual slaughter as a possibility for their repair.[51]

Another kabbalistic work dating from the beginning of the modern period that influenced the development of the kabbalistic *musar* literature in Europe, *Shevet Musar* by Rabbi Elijah of Izmir, discusses extensively the reason for kabbalistic ritual slaughter, centering on the belief in reincarnation. In chapter 36, Rabbi Elijah considers the kabbalistic rationale for ritual slaughter, and it is evident that the belief in reincarnation serves here as a threatening didactic tool, *Ye shall not make yourselves detestable* (Leviticus 11:43) with beasts and birds ... and see and understand to what extent man's power is beautiful in fulfilling the commandments and to what extent his power becomes evil in committing a sin."[52] This hints at the fate of the sinner — he makes his soul detestable, and consequently he will be reincarnated after his death in an animal.[53] Indeed, this connection is faithful to the source of this belief in *Sefer Ta'amei ha-Miẓvot* (*The Book of the Reasons for the Commandments*) by the fourteenth-century kabbalist Rabbi Joseph Hamadan. Elijah of Izmir continued, adding that only *ẓadikim* are worthy of eating meat because the first man was permitted to eat meat before his sin, whereas afterward it was forbidden: "And after he sinned, behold he seemed like a beast, as it is said, *But man abideth not in honour; he is like the beasts that perish* (Psalm 49:13) because once he and the beast are one and equal why would he kill his own species, *The voice of thy brother's blood cries unto Me* (Genesis 4:10), and spills his blood unjustly because he is not worthy of this, therefore he was told not to eat meat after his sin, lest he add crime to his sin."[54]

The question of why he would kill a member of one's own species is taken from Rabbi Yosef's homily: the slaughtered beast is "of the human species," indeed a human soul is reincarnated in it; and vice versa, whoever is ignorant and sins "like the beasts" is considered a beast, since only by fulfilling the divinely ordained commandments can a Jewish person attain and be worthy of humanity (therefore, the ignorant as well as non-Jews are not considered human). The status of the masses as beasts was also adopted by Rabbi Nathan in *Likutei Halakhot*.[55] To this unsettling homily Rabbi Elijah further added another graphic notion applying the verse regarding the murder of Abel, *your brother's blood cries*, to a sinner killing an animal in which a human soul has been reincarnated.

When comparing these sources to the Bratslav tradition, it seems that both Rabbi Nahman and Rabbi Nathan adopted the medieval idea connecting the belief in reincarnation to the need for meticulous kosher slaughter. However, rather than emphasizing the pain caused to the soul, they instead concentrate on the responsibility for repairing the reincarnated soul, which is liable to miss the opportunity for repair if the slaughter is not carried out by a kosher slaughterer. Thus, the Bratslav teachings do not focus on the suffering of the animals but on the suffering of the soul that has been reincarnated and the possibility that it will continue to be reincarnated unless the animal is slaughtered using an unblemished knife. The focus is the repair that the slaughterer can facilitate, and accordingly the slaughterer must conduct himself uprightly in terms of character, practice, and intention.

The Rationale for Kosher Slaughter in *Likutei Halakhot*

As was noted, the dispute with the Rabbi of Savran constituted a central episode in the life of Rabbi Natan. For the Rabbi of Savran, Bratslav Hasidim constituted internal Hasidic opposition.[56] In an announcement published in *Hamelitz* in 1864, thirty years after the events occurred, the Rabbi of Savran declared various steps to be taken against this Hasidic stream, including disqualifying their slaughter.[57] As Assaf also notes, the disqualification of teachers, prayer leaders, and slaughterers was clearly intended to lead to the economic and social collapse of the post-Nahman Bratslav Hasidism. Thus, we can understand the need to empower the Bratslav slaughterers and to provide spiritual propaganda that would withstand external social pressures. In the Laws of Artisans (*Ḥoshen Mishpat, Hilkhot Omanim*, 4), Rabbi Nathan combines Rabbi Nahman's two teachings on this matter, teaching 31 and teaching 36:

> Take now, I pray thee, your weapons, as the Sages said, "check your knife and slaughter well" (Genesis Rabbah 65:13), so that you will not feed me carrion. The slaughter is for the raising up of souls from living to speaking, as is known, because there are some souls that are reincarnated in animals and beasts, as is known, that it is necessary to raise them up and sift them via the commandment of ritual slaughter. And all the reincarnation of souls are caused by, *There is a breath/ frustration that is done upon the earth* (Ecclesiastes 8:14), as is explained in that teaching,[58] via the evil yearnings from which evil and reincarnated souls are made. And when they have no repentance, then they are forced to be reincarnated in animals and beasts, according to the defect of the yearnings and the souls, and they need to be sifted and repaired by slaughter . . . and this is [the meaning of] "check your knife and slaughter well" (Genesis Rabbah 65:13), in order to raise up the soul, it is necessary that the knife of the slaughterer will be absolutely perfect.[59]

This leads to several important conclusions regarding the rationale for slaughter, both vis-à-vis the continuity of the moral-didactic use of reincarnation and the adaptation and adjustment of this belief in the modern period.

Indeed, in a direct continuation of its medieval and early modern kabbalistic usage, the belief in reincarnation is employed here to deter sin and to arouse repentance: whoever sins and does not repent creates a defect in his soul, leading to reincarnation in animals and beasts. Likewise, this passage adopts the kabbalistic tradition of Rabbi Joseph of Hamadan, who explained the importance of slaughter with an unblemished knife. However, here the sin can be psychological-mental, dependent on "evil yearnings," and not only the result of practical acts.[60] While the medieval kabbalists closely connected reincarnation with practical sins, in the modern period, sinful thought became a central arena requiring repair. As Hayyim Vital noted in *Sha'ar hagilgulim*: "You must know that man needs to carry out all 613 commandments, in act and also in speech ... and in thought, if he does not carry out all of them on all three levels, he will be reincarnated, until he will carry out all 613 commandments on all three levels."[61] For Rabbi Nahman, thought was of particular importance, and therefore he demanded caution and constant deep internal analysis in managing internal desires and yearnings.[62]

The topic of reincarnation arises on several occasions in *Likutei Halakhot*, albeit extensively in the Laws of Artisans, contextualizing the question of kosher slaughter within laws concerning financial matters. Considering Shmeruk's social-economic analysis, endowing Hasidic slaughter with a kabbalistic meaning served to transfer the political-financial power from the slaughterers operating on behalf of the community to the Hasidic slaughterers. Beyond constituting a source of tension between Hasidim and their opponents, the kabbalistic discussion placed kosher slaughter in a new financial context. Here we find not only the rationale for punctiliousness regarding the laws of slaughter but also a political-economic inclination to instate new tax collectors, reorganizing the Jewish economy. Thus, Rabbi Nahman, and, as we will see below, following him Rabbi Nathan, emphasized the great economic benefits to be reaped by turning to Hasidic slaughterers (alluding to the fact that Hasidic slaughterers demanded a higher price and that these kabbalistic homilies sought to compensate the Hasidim with an assurance of future benefit). Here we see that by applying a kabbalistic interpretation to commandments concerning damages and financial matters, Rabbi Nathan responded to changing social needs and offered new legal solutions.[63]

Fear, Ritual Slaughter, and Reincarnation

A further discussion of the laws of slaughter is found in Rabbi Nathan's *Likutei Halakhot*, (section *Yoreh De'ah* on "Laws of Slaughter"), emphasizing how fear constitutes an essential component of this commandment:

> This is regarding ritual slaughter, because the main principle of ritual slaughter alludes to fear, which alludes to the knife ... therefore it is necessary that the knife be whole and without any defect, that it have no lack or defect whatsoever (*Yoreh De'ah* 18, paragraph 2), because ... as it is said, *for there is no want for them that fear Him* (Psalm 34:10). And, therefore, it is necessary that the knife be perfect, without any defect, so that it will allude to fear. This alludes to perfection without any defect. Because there is no want to them that fear him, as above, because the ritual slaughter makes the meat kosher, to be eaten by the Jewish people, and the eating of the Jewish people is instead of the sacrifice.[64]

The sharp sword of the ritual slaughter symbolizes fear, both in terms of the central religious emotion in worship and the theosophic power of the laws. The religious demand for perfect fear leads to the obligation to use the unblemished, polished knife as a symbol of it. Kosher slaughter endows eating with a theurgic and ritual dimension because it replaces the sacrifices. This fear is aroused even more forcefully when combined with the belief in reincarnation, a matter that is explicated immediately after this paragraph: "Because the main principle of ritual slaughter is to raise up the souls that have been reincarnated in beasts ... And through the ritual slaughterer, they are raised up."[65] The knowledge that human souls whose repair depends on kosher slaughter exist in the slaughtered beasts and birds further heightens the fear. This fear is connected to the fact that ritual slaughter involves a kind of human sacrifice; the slaughterer must see the animals before him as semi-human creatures. In addition, the prohibition against any defect in the knife echoes the determination that the defects of sin lead to reincarnation; to avoid finding himself reincarnated and under the slaughterer's knife, the slaughterer must avoid any kind of defect as he carries out his role. The different aspects arouse fear, leading to an operative-political demand, and immediately after discussing the punishment of reincarnation, Rabbi Nathan warns that it is necessary to ensure the appointment of a kosher slaughterer, according to the standards of the Hasidic community:

> And, therefore, the ritual slaughterer must have a share in the Torah, and one must be very punctilious with regard to a slaughterer who is kosher and pious [...] the main principle of ritual slaughter, that is raising up souls from the fate of exile is via the Torah, as was said above. [...] in order that he will have the power to sift and raise up the souls, which alludes to raising up the honor to its root, behold, to fear, which alludes

> to the knife, which alludes to perfect fear, etc., as above. And this is what they must do, [they must] check the knife also after the slaughter (*Yoreh De'ah* 18, paragraph 12) because during the slaughter the knife must be more perfect, because then they make the souls that are parts of the Glory (*kavod*), which makes the fear perfect, alluding to the knife. But these are the fallen and reincarnated souls [. . .] because they face many obstacles and it is necessary to suffer many exertions before they rise up to holiness, because the filthy garments in which they were clothed prevent them and drive a wedge between them and the holiness, etc. see there. And for this reason we are very stringent regarding ritual slaughter, and if there is any doubt regarding the slaughter, it is not kosher, because great exertions are necessary to raise up the souls that were reincarnated in beasts, alluding to the filthy garments in which they are clothed, and it is necessary to remove the filthy garments from them, that is to raise them up and to sift them from the bodies of the beasts, and this entails great exertions. Because they face many obstacles, as was said above.[66]

The demand for kosher slaughter is accompanied by statements emphasizing the great effort demanded (great exertions) on the part of the slaughterer to enable the reincarnated souls to divest themselves of the filthy clothing — the animal body — and to don new garments in the form of a purified body (whether in a new reincarnation as a human being or even the clothing of a new soul). Rabbi Nathan's demands demonstrate a direct continuation of medieval kabbalistic discourse concerning belief in the reincarnation of the soul as punishment and the opportunity to repair the defect of sin via kosher slaughter. He emphasizes the responsibility of the ritual slaughterer to use a knife without any defect, in accordance with the traditions of Rabbi Joseph of Hamadan. Yet these kabbalistic materials are also endowed with a new meaning, used to support the appointment of slaughterers who were aware of their decisive role in the repair that the slaughter facilitated, in turn enabling the consumption of kosher food, which takes the place of the ritual of the sacrifices.

Conclusion

A comparison of Rabbi Nahman of Bratslav's treatment of reincarnation as a rationale for ritual slaughter in *Likutei Moharan* with his student Rabbi Nathan's discussion of the topic reveals a direct transmission of ideas from master to student. At the same time, while Rabbi Nahman endowed the idea of reincarnation with a new, original, and somewhat metaphorical interpretation, Rabbi Nathan delved deeper into its more medieval kabbalistic meaning. To reach new readers, including the less learned segments of Jewish society, R. Nathan used the concept of reincarnation, didactically focusing on its concrete and realistic deployment of transmigration in daily life. This also demonstrates the renewed use, in the modern period, of the didactic power of reincarnation as found in its kabbalistic sources and its social-cultural role "beyond the elite" for the wider community of believers. Similarly, R. Nathan's reconceptualization of the doctrine offers a vivid example of Rabbi Nathan's leadership, which aimed to strengthen Bratslav halakhic authority. This accords with the words of Avraham Hazan, the son of Rabbi Nachman of Toltsyn, Rabbi Nathan's student, in the introduction to his book *Kokhavei or*: "It is necessary to occupy oneself more with the Nathan of Nemerov's literature than the works of the Admor (R. Nachman), may the memory of the saintly man be a blessing . . . because the Admor . . . was able to draw down terrible things and to arouse and to strengthen also clumsy people and those lying in the depths of *Sheol* (the Netherworld), like us."[67] To attain his didactic objectives and reach out to the "clumsy" people — those subject to desires and strongly connected to corporality — R. Nathan appealed to the concrete emotion of fear in his writings. Beyond this didactic aim, Rabbi Nathan's political interests are also evident here: he sought to build a mass following and to recruit new members without the guiding presence of a living Admor. Finally, the reality of the meat taxes, the central role played by the ritual slaughterers in collecting the taxes and passing them on to the community or state treasury, the economic-political context, and the battle between Hasidim and their opponents over these profits all made it necessary to endow Hasidic ritual slaughter with particular theological significance by foregrounding reincarnation as a central doctrine to Bratslav.

Notes

1. Chone Shmeruk, "The Social Implications of Hasidic Slaughter," *Zion* 20 (1955): 47–72 [Hebrew].

2. These are mentioned below according to the matter at hand.

3. On the pragmatism of this work, see Roee Horen, "Judaism as Viewed through the Prism of Faith in the Righteous — A Study of the Works of R. Nathan of Nemirov," *Kabbalah* 24 (2011): 263–304 [Hebrew].

4. Regarding the social-political aim of the work *Likutei Tefilot*, see Jonatan Meir, "R. Nathan Sternhartz's *Liqqutei tefilot* and the Formation of Bratslav Hasidism," *Journal of Jewish Thought and Philosophy* 24 (2016): 60–94.

5. Shmeruk, "The Social Implications," 47.

6. For example, see the introduction to the critical edition by Mordecai Wilensky, *Hasidim and Mitnaggedim: A Study of the Controversy between Them in the Years 1772–1815* (Jerusalem: Bialik Institute, 1990), 27 [Hebrew].

7. Wilensky, *Hasidim and Mitnaggedim*, 28–29.

8. Wilensky, *Hasidim and Mitnaggedim*, 18; Shmeruk, "The Social Implications," 66.

9. For the social context that served as a platform for the topic of ritual slaughter among the followers of the Besht under the influence of Yeshayahu ben Avraham Ha-Levi Horowitz (HaShelah), see Mendel Piekarz, *The Beginning of Hasidism: Ideological Trends in Derush and Musar Literature* (Jerusalem: Bialik Institute, 1978), 383–87 [Hebrew].

10. See, for example, the stories in *In Praise of the Baal Shem Tov: The Earliest Collection of Legends about the Founder of Hasidism*, trans. and ed. Dan Ben Amos and Jerome R. Mintz (Lanham: Rowman and Littlefield Publishers, 1993), 40, 42, 43, 45, 55, 125, 166, 192, 207, 209, 254.

11. See Shaul Stampfer, "The Dispute over Polished Knives and Hasidic Shechita," *Jerusalem Studies in Jewish Thought* 15 (1999): 201–2 [Hebrew].

12. David Assaf, *Untold Stories of the Hasidim: Crisis and Discontent in the History of Hasidim*, trans. Dena Ordan (Waltham: Brandeis University Press, 2010), 144.

13. Nathan Sternhartz, *Siḥot Moharan*, in *Ḥayei Moharan*, vol. 2 (Lemberg: Avraham Y. Heschel Draker, 1874), section "Avodat Hashem," 22, column 4: "One asked him whether to be a teacher of small children. He replied in the negative (because he, of blessed memory, said that three things are not important in his eyes: a slaughterer, a teacher of young children, and a Hasid in a small town, because it is easy to stumble over pride, God forbid). The status of the ritual slaughterers gave them a reason to be proud and patronizing."

14. See Sternhartz, *Ḥayei Moharan*, vol. 1, 14, column 4: "And at the same time the ritual slaughterer from Teplik brought him a wonderful chair."

15. *In Praise of the Baal Shem Tov*, 133–34. This story contains further aspects about repairing souls — the son repairs the sin of his father by crying when he sees a drowning dog, which was in fact the reincarnation of a man whom his father harassed. Indeed, after telling the Besht about this, he determined that Yudl was in fact a reincarnation of the prophet Samuel.

16. *In Praise of the Baal Shem Tov*, 258–59.

17. This topic is very broad. See, for example, the story about Rabbi Menachem Nachum who, while eating, raised up the soul of a sinner that was reincarnated in a bird, as related by Rabbi Shlomo Gavriel Rozental, *Hitgalut haẒaddikim*, ed. Gedaliah Negal (Jerusalem: Carmel, 1996), 85. There is also a discussion in Tsippi Kaufman, *In All Your Ways Know Him: The Concept of God and Avodah Begashmiyut in the Early Stages of Hasidism* (Ramat Gan: Bar Ilan Uni-

versity Press, 2009), 317 [Hebrew]. Regarding raising up of sparks in plants, animals, and man, see *Magid Devarav leYa'akov*, ed. Rivka Schatz-Uffenheimer (Jerusalem: Magnes Press, 1976), homily 68 (and its parallel in *Or ha'emet* by Rabbi Dov of Meziritsch [Zhitomir, 1899], 41a and 22a). For a discussion of this matter in the teaching of the Magid see Kaufman, *In All Your Ways Know Him*, 303–4. Rabbi Natan broadened the discussion of raising up the sparks of the soul that fell into food; see for example *Likutei Halakhot*, *Oraḥ ḥayim*, hilkhot betsi'at ha-pat, 5, 2, 154: "For the main thing in eating is to sift the holy sparks that are in everything, and these sparks are the sparks of holy souls that fell down and became mixed with the place where they fell."And see the further discussion there.

18. *Ḥayei Moharan*, 646.

19. Compare a later version of this idea in Rabbi Aharele Roth, *Sefer Taharat Kodesh*, vol. 2 (Jerusalem: n.p., 1954), 21: "The holy rabbi from Rizin, may his merits protect us, described one man who came to the upper world and he had no sins, only he was not able to come to his place, because in his youth, while a child of seven years old, he once ate a beigel without washing his hands. And they gave him a choice: either he would go down and be reincarnated or he would eat a beigel of fire. And he chose to eat the beigel of fire because he refused to be reincarnated. And he began to eat the beigel and he ate half of it for three years and the sorrow came upon him until he felt regret and chose to be reincarnated and told the story to inform people about the punishments for sins, until here his words."

20. Yitshak Yudlov, "Mahadurah rishonah shel 'Likutei halakhot,' ḥelek oraḥ ḥayim, me'et R. Natan Shternharts," *Kiriyat Sefer* 62 (1988): 933–35 [Hebrew].

21. On the opposition and the internal disagreement regarding Rabbi Natan, see Meir, "R. Nathan Sternhartz's *Liqqutei tefilot*," 77–79.

22. Mendel Piekarz, "The Lessons of the Composition 'Liqutei Halakhot,'" *Zion 69* (2004): 203–40 [Hebrew]; Mendel Piekarz, *Studies in Braslav Hasidism* (Jerusalem, 1972), 265–67 [Hebrew]. For additional studies regarding the sociohistorical context of Nathan of Nemerov's activity and the persecutions he suffered, see Ẓvi Mark, "Why did Moses Ẓvi of Savran Persecute R. Nathan of Nemirov and Bratslav Hasidim," *Zion* 69 (2004): 487–500 [Hebrew]; David Assaf, *Untold Stories*, 120–22, 148–49. For further sources, see Meir, "R. Nathan Strenhartz's *Liqqutei tefilot*," 84, n. 77.

23. Ron Margolin, "Religion and Its Denial in Braslav Hasidic Thought According to the Book 'Likutei Halakhot' by Rabbi Nathan Sternherz" (MA diss., Haifa University, 1992) [Hebrew]. The entire dissertation discusses how Rabbi Nathan tackled the maskilim; see in particular 10–73.

24. Horen, "Judaism as Viewed," 263–304.

25. Meir, "R. Nathan Sternhartz's *Liqqutei tefilot*," 71–19, 85–86.

26. Meir, "R. Nathan Sternhartz's *Liqqutei tefilot*." And see especially the statement quoted in Rabbi Nathan's letter written before his death, ibid., 91;

“One must draw near the rebbe [Rabbi Nahman]. But if there is no Rebbe, one connects to the pen.” For a clarification of this issue and the metaphorical understanding that Rabbi Nahman lives through the dissemination of his teachings, see Ẓvi Mark, *Scroll of Secrets: The Hidden Messianic Vision of R. Nahman of Breslav*, trans. Naftali Moses (Brighton: Academic Studies Press, 2010), 187–204.

27. Ẓvi Mark, *Scroll of Secrets*, 90, note 101; Assaf, *Untold Stories*, 142–49. The centrality of disputes in the life of Rabbi Nathan, and the methods via which he responded to them in his writing, led Ariel Burger to devote an interdisciplinary study to analyzing the strategies for conflict revolution that he developed, characterizing them as nonviolent politics. See Ariel Burger, “Hasidic Nonviolence: R. Noson of Bratzlav’s Hermeneutics of Conflict Transformation” (PhD diss., Boston University, 2008).

28. Meir, “R. Nathan Sternhartz’s *Liqqutei tefilot*,” 55. On the ritual of the pilgrimage to Rabbi Nahman’s grave and its role, see Ẓvi Mark, “A Righteous Man Caught in the Jaws of the Sitra Ahkra, the Holy Man, and the Profane Site: The Pilgrimage to the Grave of Rabbi Naḥman of Bratslav in Uman on Rosh Hashanah,” *Reshit* 2 (2010): 112–46 [Hebrew]; Jonatan Meir, “Goral ha-T*Ẓaddikim*: A Forgotten Satire against Bratslav Hasidism and the Pilgrimage to Uman,” *Dehak: Journal of Hebrew Literature* 4 (2014): 283–313]Hebrew].

29. Daniel Hundert, “Believing in Oneself: An Analysis of the Views of R. Noson Sternharts of Nemirov on the Enlightenment” (PhD diss., Concordia University, 2020), 47–54.

30. Sternhartz, *Likutei Halakhot* (Yas: n.p., 1843), 2a.

31. Specifically, *Likutei Moharan*, 141 teachings 31 and 37.

32. *Likutei Moharan*, 141, teaching 35, 8. This can be found on 44b of the Jerusalem 1975 edition (and 52b of the first edition printed in Ostrog). The translation here is adapted from https://www.sefaria.org.il/Likutei_Moharan.

33. *Likutei Moharan*, 45c.

34. Hayyim Vital, *Sha’ar Miẓvot*, parashat *Re’eh* (Jerusalem: n.p., 1972), 61a–b, where a hint at the connection between charity and ritual slaughter is evident in the discussion concerning ritual slaughter, providing the rationale for reincarnation and the care to be taken with the knife. This is adjacent to the commandment to give charity, which is discussed immediately afterward. However, this association is not explicitly addressed by Vital.

35. *Likutei Moharan* (Ostrog, 1808), 60b–61a.

36. Scholars disagree regarding the concept of the soul and the teaching of reincarnation in general, and in animals in particular, in rabbinic literature, and to what extent this was influenced by the Pythagorean and Platonic Greek concepts. For a discussion of this topic, see Dina Ripsman-Elyon, *Reincarnation in Jewish Mysticism and Gnositicism* (New York: Edwin Mellen Press, 2003), 67–73.

37. On this, see Leore Sachs-Shmueli, “The Rationale of the Negative Commandments by R. Joseph Hamadan: A Critical Edition and Study of Taboo

at the Time of the Composition of the Zohar" (PhD diss., Bar-Ilan University), vol. 1, 184–216, see on 9 [Hebrew]; Leore Sachs-Shmueli, "Human-Animal Reincarnation and Animal Grief in Kabbalah," *Journal of Jewish Thought and Philosophy* 31 (2023): 30–56.

38. And see also, for example, Meir Ibn Gabbai's *Sefer 'Avodat ha-Kodesh*, vol. 2 (Warsaw: Brothers Levin Epstein, 1883), 34, which, under the influence of Rabbi Yosef, and apparently with the mediation of the medieval kabbalist Menahem Recanati, connected the punishment of reincarnation for forbidden sexual acts and the demand for an unblemished knife, which will prevent the causing of any sorrow to the reincarnated soul:

And this is what he said regarding forbidden sexual encounters, that soul is cut off from his people and it is no longer known within its people, only in the beast, therefore, *and ye shall slay the beast* (Leviticus 20:9), *for all His ways are justice* (Deuteronomy 32:4). And moreover, they said regarding the punishment that comes upon the beast, he will end up becoming a bat (*atalef*), because he was wrapped (*nitatef*) in sin, and precisely because he did not repent. And they said, moreover, the five things that disqualify the slaughter, they are halakhah from Moses that was given on Sinai, and all the precisions of the slaughter that came in the words of our rabbis, of blessed memory, and checking the knife to ensure that it will not be defective for the benefit of the souls reincarnated in beasts and fowl, so that the slaughter will not be disqualified, and they will delayed more and suffer.

39. The discussion of reincarnation in beasts in *Sefer ha-Kanah* was influenced by Rabbi Joseph of Hamadan with the mediation of Menahem Recanati, as discussed by Michal Oron. On this, see Michal Kushnir-Oron, "*The Sefer ha-Peli'ah* and *Sefer ha-Kanah*: Their Kabbalistic Principles, Social and Religious Criticism and Literary Composition" (PhD diss., Hebrew University, 1980), 82, 303, 307, n. 15–16 [Hebrew].

40. On this, see Ronit Meroz, "Selection from Ephraim Penzieri: Luria's Sermon in Jerusalem and the Kabbalah of Taking Food," *Jerusalem Studies of Jewish Thought* 10 (1992): 211–57 [Hebrew]. For example, for the homiletical and ideological foundations regarding the concept of reincarnation in animals, which draw on Rabbi Joseph of Hamadan and passed on to later kabbalists, see *Shevet musar* by Rabbi Elijah ben Avraham Hacohen of Izmir (Salzburg: n.p., 1761), chapter 36. He includes Rabbi Joseph's homily on Leviticus 1:2 as indicating that the souls of sinners are reincarnated in the sacrificed beasts, and to this he added a prayer for the ritual slaughterer that he may have worthy intentions during the slaughter. See *Shevet musar* 70, column c–71 column a. The occupation with reincarnation in animals as a rationale for the sacrifice is also cited in his book *Midrash tefilot*, *Anaf gilgulim*, "regarding the matter of reincarnation and the sacrifice" (Warsaw, 1875), 125 column a–125 column b. For a discussion of these sources in the context of the social meaning of Hasidic slaughter and its kabbalistic sources, see Shmeruk, "The Social

Implications," 47–72. There he notes Avraham Azulai's *Sefer ḥesed le'Avraham* (Amsterdam: Emanuel Atias, 1785) as the source used by the Eliyahu of Izmir's *Shevet Mussar* (Dyhrenfurth: Rachel and her sons, Michal and Shimon, 1796), and he also suggested that the books *Sefer ha-Kanah* and *Sefer ha-Peli'ah* were the sources used by the author of *Sefer hesed le'Avraham*. However, he was not aware of the words of Rabbi Joseph. For the discussions of Avraham Azulay, which bear the stamp of Rabbi Joseph, see Azulay, *Ḥesed le'Avraham* (section, *Nahar* 24: *Besod hagilgul ufratav*), 36 column 2–37 column a. Regarding the punctiliousness of the author Isaiah Horowitz in *Shnei Luḥot ha-Berit (Two Tablets of the Covenant)* (Amsterdam: Emanuel Atias, 1698), *Sha'ar ha-Otiot*, 64b with respect to blemishes in the knife (albeit without the kabbalistic rationale). *Ḥesed le'Avraham* discusses matters of ritual slaughter and reincarnation on several occasions (but they are not the source for Rabbi Nahman's statements, because indeed they are not developed).

41. For more on the kabbalistic context of the belief in reincarnation of the soul into beasts and the laws of kosher food at the end of the thirteenth century and beginning of the fourteenth century, see Moshe Idel, "'Ta'amei ha'ofot hateme'im' le R. David ben Yehuda haḥasid umashma'utam," *'Alei Shefer: Meḥkarim besifrut hahagut hayehudit — mugashim likhvod harav Dr. Aleksander Shafran*, ed. Moshe Halamish (Ramat Gan: Bar Ilan University Press, 1990), 11–27. On Rabbi Joseph Ashkenazi's belief in reincarnation, see chapter 6, in this volume.

42. On this verse as indicating a limitation on the number of incarnations, compare the Zohar, part 3, 217; Moshe Idel, "Commentaries on the "Secret of 'Ibbur" in 13th Century Kabbalah and Their Significance for the Understanding of the Kabbalah at Its Inception and Its Development," *Da'at* 73 (2012): 6 [Hebrew]. All biblical quotations are from *Tanakh* (Philadelphia: JPS, 1917).

43. Sachs-Shmueli, "The Rationale of the Negative Commandments," vol. 2, commandment 57, 218–19.

44. Sachs-Shmueli, "The Rationale of the Negative Commandments," vol. 2, commandment 57, on 220; and commandment 63, on 308.

45. Sachs-Shmueli, "The Rationale of the Negative Commandments," vol. 2, commandments, 56, 57, 65, 67.

46. Sachs-Shmueli, "The Rationale of the Negative Commandments," vol. 2, commandment 65.

47. Hayyim Vital, *Shar ha-Miẓvot, Re'eh* (Jerusalem, 1902), 46b.

48. *Emek hamelekh* by Naftali Hertz Bachrach, *Sha'ar Tikkunei Teshuva* (Amsterdam, 1648), chapter 12, fol. 20c–d. An additional adaption of the section is found in Rabbi Menahem Azaria of Fano, *Ma'amar* tikunei *teshuva*, chapter 19. And see Meroz, "Selection from Ephraim Penzieri," 226. Vital's influence regarding this issue is also evident in a Hasidic book from the beginning of the twentieth century, *Shem mi-Shemuel*, Vayikra, 1511: "In . . . the words of Rabbi Hayyim Vital, because if the man sins as an animal, he goes down and is re-

incarnated as an animal, because he sinned like it, and the reincarnated soul finds repair in bringing the beast as a sacrifice, and via its slaughter and its burning it is repaired and goes up in a pleasing smell."

49. On the principle of quid pro quo in relation to the punishment of reincarnation in the writings of Rabbi Joseph, see Sachs-Shmueli, "The Rationale of the Negative Commandments," vol. 1, 204–5.

50. For a list of the reincarnations according to sins quid pro quo summarized by Recanati and based on Rabbi Joseph, as well as its influence on later kabbalistic works such as *Sefer hakana* and others, see Sachs-Shmueli, "The Rationale of the Negative Commandments," vol. 1, 208–12.

51. For an autograph manuscript of the work, see Jerusalem manuscript, MS. The National Library of Israel, 1935=28.

52. Eliyah ha-Cohen of Izmir, *Shevet Musar* (Sulzbach: Itzhak ben R. Leib, 1761), 70b.

53. On fear as a means of deterring sin and motivating repentance in this work, see Ilaria Briata, "Repentance through Fear: Cosmic and Body Horror in Shevet Musar," *European Journal of Jewish Studies* 14 (2020): 264–84.

54. *Shevet Musar*, 70 column c.

55. Nathan Sternhartz, *Likutei halakhot* (Jerusalem, 1995), *Ḥoshen Mishpat* b, laws of damages, 5, 415: "And therefore *he made booths for his cattle* (Genesis 33:17). Cattle alludes to the masses of the people still far from his holy place, who are like beasts because everyone who has no knowledge is not a member of civilization (*Yishuv*) and he is a beast in the form of a man."

56. See above note 22.

57. Piekarz, *Studies in Braslav Hasidism*, 266.

58. *Likutei Moharan*, 141, teaching 31.

59. Sternhartz, *Likutei Halakhot*, section *Ḥoshen Mishpat*, laws of artisans, 4. The phrasing of the Jerusalem manuscript:

Because the ritual slaughter is for the raising up of souls from living to speaking, as is known, because there are a few reincarnated souls via the commandment of ritual slaughter and all the reincarnations of the souls are drawn in terms of 'there is *hevel*,' because due to the evil desires from which souls are made bad and are reincarnated etc. until they can cause [others] to sin, God forbid. And if they do not repent, then they must be reincarnated in animals and beasts according to the defect of the desires and the souls and they need to be sifted and repaired by ritual slaughter [. . .] and this is [the meaning of] "check your knife and slaughter well."

60. For an additional use of reincarnation in animals by Rabbi Nathan as a didactic moral tool to inspire fear among sinners who sin because of "a lack of seriousness and sense," and pity toward animals as a rationale for the commandment *You shall not muzzle the ox when he treadeth out the corn* (Deut. 25:4), see *Likutei halakhot*, Ḥoshen mishpat, 2, laws of hiring workers, 2, 522–23:

And this alludes to *You shall not muzzle the ox when he treadeth out the corn* (Deut. 25:4), because the Torah has mercy even on beasts, because there are reincarnations of souls in beasts and animals, as it is known, as the Baal Shem Tov, of blessed memory, said, we eat people and drink people, and we ride on people, etc. Because everywhere there are sparks of souls of people and the extent of the mercy on the soul reincarnated in a beast or a bird cannot be imagined [. . .] because due to the sins of this person, God forbid, he fell and was reincarnated in a beast, etc., and because the beast etc., it alludes to the sins resulting from a lack of sense and seriousness, which alludes to bestial behavior, because all the sins are the acts of beasts, lack of sense.

61. Ḥayyim Vital, *Sha'ar ha-Gilgulim* (Jerusalem, 1988), introduction 11, 40, column a. And see also the reception of these matters by Rabbi Shneur Zalman of Liadi, *Igeret ha-Kodesh*, Tanya 4, 29: "It is known from the Ari, of blessed memory, that every person of Israel needs to be reincarnated in many reincarnations until he will carry out all 613 commandments of the Torah in thought, in speech, and in act, to complete the clothing of his soul and to repair it so that there will be no lack in his clothing."

62. On Rabbi Nahman's concept of yearning and desire and in particular sexual desire in *Likutei Moharan*, see Ẓvi Mark, *The Religious Thought of Rabbi Nachman of Bratslav* (New York: Continuum, 2009), 47–55; Shaul Magid, "Through the Void: The Absence of God in R. Naḥman of Bratzlav's 'Likkutei MoHaRan,'" *Harvard Theological Review* 88, no. 4 (1995): 500–7.

63. This is despite the halakhic limitations that Englard emphasized in his article. On this, see Izhak Englard, "Mysticism and Law: Reflections on 'Liqute Halakhot' from the School of Rabbi Nahman of Bratslav," *Annual of the Institute for Research of Jewish Law* 6/7 (1979–1980): 29–43. Alon Goshen-Gottstein has tackled these fundamental questions at great length; see Alon Goshen-Gottstein, "Halakhah and the Spiritual Life: An Introduction to 'Likkutei Halakhot,' by R. Nathan Sternhartz of Nemirov," in *The Quest for Halakhah*, ed. Amihai Berholz (Tel Aviv: Yediot Aharonot, 2003), 260–67 [Hebrew].

64. Sternhartz, *Likutei Halakhot, Yoreh De'ah*, 1, "Laws of Ritual Slaughter," Halakhah 3, sign 1.

65. Sternhartz, *Likutei Halakhot, Yoreh De'ah*, 1, "Laws of Ritual Slaughter," Halakhah 3, sign 2.

66. *Likutei Halakhot, Yoreh De'ah*, 1, "Laws of Ritual Slaughter," Halakhah 3, sign 2.

67. Nathan of Nemerov, *Kokhavei Or*, Introduction (Jerusalem, 1972), 5, note 7; see further H. Horen, "Judaism as Viewed," 272.

CONTRIBUTORS

JAMES A. Diamond is the Joseph and Wolf Lebovic Chair of Jewish Studies at the University of Waterloo. His principal areas of study include biblical exegesis and hermeneutics, medieval Jewish thought and philosophy, Maimonides, rabbinics, and Holocaust theology. He has published widely on all areas of Jewish thought. He firmly believes he is original and not reincarnated.

EITAN P. FISHBANE is professor of Jewish thought at JTS, where he teaches courses in the literature and history of Jewish mysticism, from medieval Kabbalah to modern Hasidism. He is the author or editor of six books, the latest of which was published by Oxford University Press, *The Art of Mystical Narrative: A Poetics of the Zohar* (2018). His previous publication is *As Light Before Dawn: The Inner World of a Medieval Kabbalist* (Stanford University Press, 2009).

PINCHAS GILLER was brought up in Cocoa Beach, Florida. He was ordained at Yeshiva University and received his doctorate at the Graduate Theological Union, Berkeley. He has written four books, *The Enlightened Will Shine: Symbolism and Theurgy in the Later Strata of the Zohar* (Albany: State University of New York Press, 1993), *Reading the Zohar* (Oxford: Oxford University Press, 1993), *Shalom Shar'abi and the Kabbalists of Beit El* (Oxford: Oxford University Press; 2000), and *Kabbalah: A Guide for the Perplexed* (Continuum Press; 2011). He has also edited *Be'er Moshe al ha-Torah* by Moshe ha-Kohen Reicherson. Rabbi Giller is professor of Jewish thought at the American Jewish University, Los Angeles.

ROEE Y. GOLDSCHMIDT is a lecturer in the Department of History, Philosophy and Judaic Studies, The Open University, Raanana. He is the author of *Homiletic Literature in Eastern Europe: Rhetoric, Talmudic and Social* Stature [Hebrew], published by Magnes Press in 2022.

ANDREA GONDOS is a visiting assistant professor in the Department of Religion and Classics at the University of Rochester. She is the author of *Kabbalah in Print: The Study and Popularization of Jewish Mysticism in Early Modernity* (Albany: State University of New York Press, 2020). She has authored several journal articles, and her forthcoming essay, "The Female Body and the Male Gaze: Magic, Kabbalah, and Medicine in Early Modern East-Central Europe," to be published in *Jewish Quarterly Review,* is based on her most recent research on Jewish magic and the agency of Jewish magic healers, *Ba'alei Shem* (Masters of the Name). She is currently working on her second monograph, titled *Chaining Lilith, Gendering the Body: Women, Medicine, and Practical Kabbalah in Early Modern Judaism*.

ELLEN D. HASKELL is the Herman & Zelda Bernard Distinguished Professor of Jewish Studies, professor of religious studies, and director of Jewish studies at the University of North Carolina Greensboro. Educated at the University of Chicago Divinity School and the University of Michigan, she is the author of two books: *Suckling at My Mother's Breasts: The Image of a Nursing God in Jewish Mysticism* (Albany: State University of New York Press, 2012) and *Mystical Resistance: Uncovering the Zohar's Conversations with Christianity* (Oxford: Oxford University Press, 2016).

MOSHE IDEL is the Max Cooper Professor of Jewish Thought Emeritus at the Hebrew University of Jerusalem, senior researcher at the Shalom Hartman Institute, and a member of the Israeli Academy for Sciences and Humanities. He has authored scores of books and academic articles and is a world-renowned scholar of Jewish mystical and philosophical traditions.

RUTH KARA-IVANOV KANIEL is a senior lecturer in the department of Jewish History and Thought at the University of Haifa and Research Fellow at the Tel Aviv Institute for Contemporary Psychoanalysis and at the Shalom Hartman Institute (Jerusalem). Her publications include *Holiness and Transgression: Mothers of the Messiah in Jewish Myth* (ASP, 2017); *The Feminine Messiah: King David in the Image of the Shekhina in Kabbalistic Literature* (Brill, 2021) and, recently, *Birth in Kabbalah and Psychoanalysis* (De Gruyter, 2022). She has also published two books of poetry: *The World Has No Silence* and *The Soul is Moved.*

HARTLEY LACHTER is associate professor of religion studies at Lehigh University, where he holds the Philip and Muriel Berman Chair in Jewish Studies. His scholarship focuses on medieval Kabbalah, with a particular emphasis on the relationship between Jewish historical experiences and the development of kabbalistic discourses. He is the author of the monograph *Kabbalistic Revolution: Reimagining Judaism in Medieval Spain*, published by Rutgers University Press in 2014, and *Kabbalah and Catastrophe: Historical Memory in Premodern Jewish Mysticism*, forthcoming with Stanford University Press.

SHAUL MAGID is professor of Jewish studies at Dartmouth College, Kogod Senior Research Fellow at the Shalom Hartman Institute of North America, senior fellow at the Center for the Study of World Religions at Harvard University, and rabbi of the Fire Island Synagogue. Author of numerous books, one of his most recent works is *Meir Kahane: The Public Life and Political Thought of an American Jewish Radical* (Princeton: Princeton University Press, 2021).

ARIEL EVAN MAYSE is an assistant professor of religious studies at Stanford University, rabbi-in-residence at Atiq: Jewish Maker Institute, and the senior scholar-in-residence at the Institute for Jewish Spirituality and Society. He holds a PhD in Jewish studies from Harvard University and rabbinic ordination from Beit Midrash Har'el in Israel, and is the author of *Speaking Infinities: God and Language in the Teachings of Rabbi Dov Ber of Mezritsh* (Philadelphia: University of Pennsylvania Press, 2020), the two-volume *A New Hasidism: Roots* and *A New Hasidism: Branches*, with Arthur Green (Philadelphia: Jewish Publication Society and University of Nebraska Press, 2019), and the forthcoming *Laws of the Spirit: Ritual, Mysticism, and the Commandments in Early Hasidism* (Stanford University Press).

LEORE SACHS-SHMUELI is a member of the senior faculty in the Department of Jewish Philosophy at Bar Ilan University. Her expertise lies in the fields of Kabbalah and Hasidism, with a particular emphasis on topics related to ethics and morality, the rationale of commandments, the history of emotions, sexuality, and gender studies. She is an author of the forthcoming books: *Taboo and Prohibitions in Castilian Kabbalah* (Schocken-JTS Press, Hebrew); *Sefer Toldot Adam by R. Joseph of Hamadan: A Critical Annotated Edition* (Ben Ẓvi Institute, Hebrew); and *The Rationales of the Negative Commandments by Joseph of Hamdan: A Critical Edition and Study* (The World Union of Jewish Studies Press).

JONNIE SCHNYTZER holds a PhD from Bar Ilan University's Department of Jewish Philosophy, where he wrote about the oeuvre of thirteenth-century kabbalist Rabbi Joseph ben Shalom Ashkenazi and prepared a critical edition of his commentary on *Sefer Yetsirah*, forthcoming with Cherub Press. Currently a postdoctoral fellow at Ben Gurion University, he is working on a project, "Beyond the Anthropocentric: Ecological Perceptions of Being in Medieval Kabbalah."

INDEX

Abel (biblical person), 12, 39, 78, 86, 100, 103, 104, 256, 359
Abraham (biblical person), 12, 86, 235, 251, 252, 256–258, 266, 268n17, 269, 270n32, 318
Abrams, Daniel, 44n26, 44n32, 46n45, 65n2, 68n16, 70n35, 89n1, 89n9, 92n47, 92n50, 117n11, 118n19, 144n7, 227, 244n8
Abulafia, Abraham, 143n4, 275
Abulafia, Toderus, 6, 21, 37, 43n22, 45n38, 65n1
Adam (biblical person), 38, 39, 78, 86, 115, 118n30, 121n66, 136, 137, 141, 142, 147n55, 255, 268n8, 268n19, 283; and Lilith (first wife), 279; *Kadmon*, 13, 85, 328: *pnei Adam*, 156–158; primordial, 83; ha-Rishon (First Man), 210, 212; (original) sin of, 252, 259-261, 286; soul of, 12, 265
Aderet, Solomon ibn, 34, 44n27, 100
Afterman, Adam, 29, 43n10, 198n45
Agassi, R. Shimon, 290, 297n41
Albo, Joseph, 4, 17, 178, 191–193
Alkabeẓ, R. Shlomo, 275, 293n7
amulet, 277, 281, 289; maker, 282
angel(ic), 111, 130, 152, 160, 161, 170n90, 179–180, 191–192, 204–205, 277, 285, 291, 293n8, 294n18; accusing, 215; demiurgic, 77; demonic, 84; destroying, 117n11; fallen, 89, 268n8; interlocutors, 284; Metatron, 86; ministering, 133; of God, 155, 157; sphere of, 167; supernal, 130, 138
Angelet, Joseph, 97–100, 102–109, 112–115, 118n32; 119n33, 119n36, 119n38, 120n50, 121n53, 121n57-58, 121n63, 122n70; "Twenty- Four Secrets," 97–98, 105, 110, 116n2, 116n4, 117n9-11, 118n19, 118n23-28; *Sefer Qupat ha-Rokhelin* (*The Book of a Peddler's Basket*), 104; "The Secret of the Calendrical *Ibbur*," 114, 121n54
animals, 1, 7, 11, 17, 137–138, 154–155, 160–161, 167, 192, 277, 327, 348, 350, 355, 357, 359, 362–363, 366n17, 367n36, 369n48, 370; beastly, 10; clean, 1; head of, 158; impure, 129, 157; kingdom, 158, 163; Nebuchadnezzar into, 174n57; pipe of, 158; pity towards, 370n60; reincarnation into, 7, 9, 20, 28, 30, 84, 148n62, 162, 174n61, 174n62, 200n73, 347, 353, 356, 358-360, 368n40, 370n59, 370n60, 371n60; sacrifices, 196; slaughter of, 157, 160, 356, 359; soul, 84, 353–57; suffering of, 8, 14, 347, 357, 359, 368n37
Ashkenazi, Isaac Luria (Ari), 17, 167, 275 (see also Lurianic Kabbalah)

Ashkenazi, Joseph ben Shalom 5, 10, 16–17, 43n16, 104–107, 112, 118n32, 119n34, 120n40, 144n12, 148n62, 148n63, 151–175, 275, 369n41
atonement, 16, 61, 103, 107–108, 110, 112, 181, 183; Day of, 112
arousal, from below, 259, 261, 269n29, 270n31; Jewish captor's, 13
Assaf, David, 349, 360, 365n12, 366n22, 367n27
Azriel of Gerona 6, 29, 33, 34, 41n4, 43n18, 99, 117n12
Azulay, Abraham, 1, 13, 23n30, 369n40; *Ba'alei Berit*, 23n30; *Hesed le-Avraham*, 1, 321n24, 369n40

Babel, generation of, 259
Babylonia, 292n4, 297n39; Babylonian Talmud, 71n45; 114, 130–131, 163
Bachrach, Naftali Hertz, *Emek ha-Melekh*, 326n113, 358, 369n48
Baghdad, 18–19, 153, 273, 275–277, 282, 283–284, 287, 290–291, 298n46
Bahir, Book (*Sefer ha-Bahir*), 2–5, 16, 21n4, 28–30, 35, 39–40, 41n4, 42n10, 44n32, 50, 62, 65n2, 66n9, 72n62, 73–75, 88, 89n1, 89, 92n47, 99, 100–102, 118n19, 118n21–22, 130, 275
Ba'al Shem, 18, 19, 278, 291, 294n17, 295n23
Ba'al Shem Tov, Israel (Besht), 293n9, 295, 314, 315, 340n1
Balaam (biblical person), 12, 251
Bar-Asher, Avishai, 68n16, 89n2, 92n41, 172n26
Bar-Levav, Avriel, 292n2
beating, heart, 80, of the grave, 284–286, 288, 290
Bedersi, Yedayah, 187–188, 193
Bennaroch, Jonathan, 268n8, 94n97
Ben Shammai, Haggai, 21n2, 47n53, 170n8, 196n27
Berman, Nathaniel, 117n11, 244n8, 268n6, 298n49,
Bilu, Yoram, 245n31, 290, 296n36, 297n38, 299n67
Binah (sefirah), 38, 98, 103, 105–108, 110–115, 117, 119, 121–122, 127–128, 137, 141, 144n10, 165
birth, 2, 5, 8, 30, 44n30, 52–53, 108–109, 112, 114–115, 120, 140, 156, 158, 220n9, 231, 244n8, 308–310, 335, 358; birthing, 5, 10, 107, 220; cycle of, 10, 14, 79, 80–81, 83; cosmic system of, 89; giving, 34, 36, 208; pain of, 287; rebirth 1, 14, 20, 22n19, 23n25, 49, 52–53, 57, 60–61, 63, 66n9, 80, 90n14, 94n106, 145n19, 169n3, 186, 199n60, 200n74, 203–204, 221n18, 223n35; 292n5, 303, 304, 306–307, 309–313, 315–318, 320n8, 320n10, 321n19, 322n48, 325n48, 325n106
blessing(s), 34, 36, 103, 105, 113, 355, 364
body, 1, 4–5, 9, 16, 20, 28, 35, 38, 50, 53, 55, 56, 58–60, 64, 66n3, 69n30, 74–75, 80–83, 85, 103, 107–109, 118n24, 119n34, 126–127, 130–131, 132, 133, 139, 154–156, 160, 162, 167, 178, 179–182, 184, 186, 190–191, 221, 225–226, 231–232, 235–243, 247n77, 274, 276, 283–285, 288–291, 305–306, 308, 316, 318, 336, 341n5, 350, 353, 358; animal, 363, 370n53; and commandments, 304, 337; divine, 85; Edomite, 140; exile of, 129, 133, 142; female, 45n34, 70n35, 117n11, 292; foreign, 82; gentile, 138, 140, 250, 253; human, 27, 30, 35, 49, 50, 85, 131, 152, 161, 191–192,195n18, 195n21, 196n26, 197n43, 199n65, 206, 208, 209, 211, 261; impure, 84; Jesus's, 51; Jewish, 66n4; 66n6–7; new, 53; non-procreative, 57; people of the, 72n66; perfected, 212; performing, 66n4, 70n34; physical, 85, 154, 156–158, 162, 165–166, 178, 211, 213, 305; pleasures

of, 185; pregnant, 279; reincarnated, 56; resurrected, 240–243, 306; sociopolitical, 52; spiritual, 308; surface of, 62; woman's, 236, 280–281; worshipper's, 308
bondswoman, 81
Brethren of Purity (*Ikhwān al- ṣafā'*), 153, 170n9, 171n21; *Epistles of* (*Rasā'il Ikhwān al- ṣafā'*), 17, 171n21
Brown, Benjamin, 345n59
Brown, Jeremy, 121n59, 269n29
Bruckman, Mordechai, 341n18
Buddhism, 2, 14–15, 23n34, 80, 88, 304–305, 311, 315, 317, 320n9, 320n11-12, 323n65-67, 324n86, 325n105

Cain (biblical person), 12, 38–39, 86, 93n80
canon(ical), 15, 181, 258, 266; Jewish, 189; Zoharic, 77
Chajes, Y. H., 232–233, 237–238, 243, 246n32, 246n36; *Between Worlds*, 66n10, 69n26, 70n38, 69n26, 70n38-39, 223n38, 245n31, 245n35, 292n3, 294n16, 296n31, 299n68-69
Christian(s), 51, 64, 66, 67n15, 295n25; bodies, 51
commandments (*miẓvah/ miẓvot*), 2, 22n12, 28, 30, 32, 40, 43n18, 58, 64, 95n109, 148n60, 160, 171n20, 173n38, 173n46, 179, 186, 189, 210-211, 218-219, 222n24, 249-250, 262- 265, 267, 304–308, 310, 316, 319, 321n24, 325n104, 327, 331–332, 336–339, 340, 344n58, 348, 352, 358–359, 361, 367n37, 369n43-46, 370n49-50, 371n61; 613 commandments, 85, 262, 304–305, 307; biblical, 166–167, 169n5, 183; narrative and, 4; Noahide, 261, 263; negative 95n109; performance of, 18, 20, 59, 125, 146n28; procreation 53-54, 57; positive, 211, 221n11, 306, 308; rationalizing, 20; secrets of, 6
community, 12, 14, 20, 53, 59,114, 276–277, 310, 320n7, 325n91, 334, 340, 348–349; Bratslav, 348; Chabad, 318; Hasidic, 319, 348–349, 358, 361–362, 364; holy, 280; income of, 348; Jewish, 9, 50–51, 22n15, 277–279, 295n23, 61, 64; of Israel, 87; philosophical, 88; Provencal, 52; Spanish, 52
Cordovero, Moses, 13, 46n52, 76, 84, 321n23, 126, 143n5, 144n5, 221n10, 266, 275, 293n8, 305; *Or Yakar*, 46n52, 267n3; *Pardes Rimonim*, 91n20; 221n12, 321n23; *Shemua be-'Inyan ha- Gilgul*, 46n52, 293n8
cosmic cycles (*shemittot*), 57, 126, 129, 141, 143n4; *Book of Cosmic Cycles* (*Sefer ha-Temunah*), 17
covenant, 60, 68n16, 125, 131, 141–142, 221n14, 265, 267
Crescas, Hasdai, 4, 17, 178, 188–193

Dan, Joseph, 121n65, 244n6, 21n4, 90n10
dark(ness), 31, 76, 83–84, 88, 105–106, 114, 117n11, 134, 166, 228, 268n17, 274; land of, 166
David (biblical King), 138, 233–234, 242
David Darshan of Cracow, 335, 343n43, 244n13, 245n37, 297n42, 328
de Leon, Moses, 113, 1222n68, 126, 145n18, 148n61, 149n73, 344n55, 65n2
death, 39, 49–50, 52, 55, 57–58, 61, 76, 79, 81, 83, 89, 98–100, 105–107, 110–112, 114–115, 119n34, 131, 136–137, 148n58, 156, 164–166, 179, 184, 187, 193n1, 197n45, 199n65, 221n18, 222n18, 228, 234, 268n10, 273–274, 279, 285, 288, 291–292, 305, 312; and rebirth, 304; by kiss, 185; husband's, 59; Jonathan's, 233; shadow of, 166; taste of, 61; wheel of, 81
defect, 109, 120, 186, 240, 283, 296, 331, 333, 337, 356–358, 360, 362–363, 368, 370

Derekh Piqudekha, 337–339, 345n62-66
devekut, 20, 206, 309, 310, 330–331, 336, 339–340
Dinah (biblical person), 256–257, 269n24
divine, 6, 7, 9–11, 73, 98, 102–103, 106–107, 111–113, 115, 117n11, 130–131, 140–141, 152, 205, 244, 254, 298n49, 308, 313, 330; attribute, 17, 128–129, 141, 164; becoming, 213, 218; behavior, 27; being, 11, 109, 205, 208, 210; body, 85; child, 206; commandment, 63; compassion, 303; countenance, 77, 88; creation, 208; dimensions, 219, 221n14; emanation, 77, 88, 181, 204; family, 83, 109; feminine, 70n35, 78; forces, 133; grace, 30, 50, 61, 131; hypostases of, 101; image, 43n10; immanence, 77, 88; intervention, 190; justice, 14, 17, 22n21-22, 140, 152, 164, 177, 182–183, 343n47; judgment, 10, 129, 159, 166; law, 125; light, 13, 134, 207, 210, 328; love, 129, 309; mercy, 136; mind, 79; mother's womb, 110; name, 42n5, 42n10, 121n57, 145n18, 165, 290, 294n18; origin in, 309; plan, 135, 152, 164, 167; potencies, 6; presence, 31, 33–34, 78, 356; protection, 125; providence, 139, 142, 159–160; punishment, 50, 147n50; realm, 6, 98, 137, 158, 167, 212; reproduction, 108; repentance, 114; restoration, 332; self, 206–208, 213; service, 336, 339, 354; sonship, 220n9; soul, 78; source, 204; sparks, 330; structure, 82; thought, 85; throne, 69n29; union, 33; unity, 45n35; voice, 35; wisdom, 191–192; world, 36, 108, 156
diviner, of Ein Dor, 274
Douglas, Mary, 50, 65n3, 66n11, 69n25, 72n65
dybbuk (see also possession) 66n10, 223n38, 245n32, 281, 288, 290, 291, 292, 294, 295n21, 295n24, 296n36, 297n39, 297n41, 299n67-68, 328, 341n8

earth(ly), 7, 49, 57, 59, 61, 71, 83, 98–99, 106, 108, 112, 114, 127, 134, 142, 157, 159, 166, 186, 193, 206, 215, 237, 265, 273, 279, 287, 296, 354, 360
eating, 66n5, 70n38, 130, 309, 349, 350, 362, 365n17, 366n17, 160–161, 173n42, 173n49, 184; from Tree of Knowledge, 136, meat, 359
Egypt(ian), 10, 120n42, 163, 236–237, 253–254, 259, 260–261, 270n36, 293n10, 319, 335
Eilberg-Schwartz, Howard, 64, 65n3, 69n30, 72n66
Elimelekh of Leżajsk, 328, 341n17
Elior, Rachel, 23n26, 47n52, 70n38, 95n109, 143n3, 147n47, 148n60, 168n3, 250, 267n4, 293n9, 342n26
Elqayam, Avraham, 45n35
embodiment, 16, 49, 50–51, 53–56, 60, 62–64, 67n13, 77, 112, 173n49, 186, 205, 252, 260, 283
emotion, 198n45, 362; emotional, 11, 13, 77, 216, 230, 286–287, 307, 336, 350, 353, 356; emotionally, 54, 283; of fear, 350, 355, 364
Etkes, Immanuel, 294n19
Eve (biblical person), 38, 86, 115, 121n66, 136, 142, 283
exegesis, 6, 102, 104, 130, 179, 188, 203, 252; biblical, 194n9; kabbalistic, 181; Lurianic, 198n47, 297n44; philosophical, 181; radical, 104; textual, 191
exile, 17, 79, 84, 86, 98, 113, 116n6, 119n39, 121n58, 128–129, 131–132, 134, 137–138, 142, 143n3, 262, 265, 331, 335, 362; bitter, 296; current, 131, 132; end of, 141; exiled, 74, 84, 327; existential, 98; final, 132, 319; go into, 331; harshness of, 127; Jews in, 139; lengthy, 129; national, 132;

of the body, 133, 134, 142; of the soul, 133, 134
exorcism, 236–239, 278–282, 287–289, 291, 294n21, 295n23, 295n25, 296n36, 297n41, 298n57, 299n68, 328; Lurianic, 238; techniques, 276; rituals, 277
exorcist, 66n10, 223n38, 237–238, 246n32, 247n60, 274, 276, 278–279, 282, 290–292, 295n23, 297n41, 299n68

Faierstein, Morris, 295n21, 296n29, 297n45, 323n55, 341n7
Fano, Menachem Azariah da, 249, 258, 267n2, 269, 313, 314, 230n4, 324n83-n84, 329, 342n22, 369n48
family, 2, 7, 15–16, 39, 52–55, 57–58, 69n33, 81, 108, 120n47, 122n71, 214, 236, 247n62; Abraham's, 253, 257; divine, 83, 109; life, 184; Jewish, 7; rabbinic, 296n32
Felix, Iris, 115n1, 116n2, 118n32, 120n42, 121n64
Fetaya, Yehudah, 18–19, 273, 275–278, 283–291, 297, 297n39, n41; *Minḥat Yehudah*, 297n39, 297n41, 298n47, 298n50, n52, n54-56, 299n64, n66; *Ruḥot Mesaprot* (*Talking Souls*), 277–278, 282, 298n46
Fine, Lawrence, 69n26, 70n38, 72n60, 94n97, 116n6, 121n66, 147n47, 220n1, 222n19, 245n29, 267n4, 292n2, 293n6, 293n11, 296n36, 297n43, 299n62, 321n31, 340n5
Fishbane, Eitan, 23n31, 65n2, 72n64, 220n6, 220n8, 221n10, 222n22
Fishbane, Michael, 65n2, 92n50, 186, 197n45
food, 95n109, 160–161, 170n13, 270n36, 309, 336, 351, 356, 366n17, 368n40; kosher, 363, 369n41
Freud, Sigmund, 18, 108, 120n47, 227–235, 237–239, 241, 243, 244n6-9, 245n17-26, 245n36, 247n60-n62
Garb, Jonathan, 19, 172n33, 220n1, 221n16, 244n8, 275–277, 293n10, 294n19, 309, 320n5, 323n55, 324n82
garment, 58, 72n62, 74, 108, 186, 206, 211, 217, 275, 305, 308, 322n40, 337, 344n55, 363; ephemeral, 213; filthy, 363; human, 205; soul, 286; worn, 62
gender(ed), 7, 15–16, 20, 22n10, 35, 38, 45n35, 49, 68n16, 69n26, 70n35, 84, 101, 232, 234, 235, 238, 256, 257, 280, 284, 292, 293n14, 296n31, 319, 326n120; engendering, 6, 51, 53, 253
Gentile(s), 2, 7, 11–12, 18, 135, 249–251, 256, 258, 261–263, 265–266, 281, 289; bodies, 138–140; nations, 135, 138; oppression, 139
Gevurah (sefirah) 33, 77, 105, 111, 122n70, 127, 163-164
Gikatilla, Joseph 113, 116n2, 120n39, 126, 145n18, 147n49, 160, 172n33, 173n45
gilgul (reincarnation), 1, 5, 16, 18–19, 28, 29, 40, 41n3, 45n33, 46n52, 54, 55, 61–63, 65n1, 66n10, 70n42, 73–88, 91n30, 97–98, 103, 105–106, 109, 111–112, 114–115, 116n3, 117n7-8, 128, 130–132, 138, 142, 152, 154, 160, 174n56, 222n23; 226, 228, 230–231, 240–243, 246n50, 250, 252, 293n8, 297n41, 303–310, 312–318; Angelet and, 112, 119n33; as birth, 108; 109, as fixing (*tiqqun*), 84; as replacement (*hitḥalfut*), 120n40; as traversing boundaries, 249; Ashkenazi, Shalom and, 119n34; Bahir and, 89n2, 102; cycles of, 99, 303, 320n4, 322n46, 323n58, 343n47; halakhah and, 194n5, 210; in Lurianic tradition, 228, 239, 251; in the Zohar, 54, 89n2; levirate marriage and, 116n5; of aquatic species, 162; of souls, 155, 171n20,n21;

gilgul (cont'd)
of physical bodies, 161; psychoanalysis and, 225; secret of, 87, 107, 110, 112, 115, 159; theory of, 203
Giller, Pinchas, 7, 16, 21n10, 22n11, 65n1, 66n8-9, 69n26, 70, 71n46, 71n52, 90n12, 90n16, 92n35, 92n49-50, 93, 95n107, 148n65, 169n5, 267n3, 293n12-13
Goldish, Matt, 21n6, 294n15
Goldreich, Amos, 94n98, 95n107, 118n17, 146n33-34, 90n10, 90n16, 94n98, 95n107, 118n17, 146n33
Gondos, Andrea, 22n18, 45n35, 198n45, 342n19
Gottlieb, Ephraim, 44n24, 45n35, 90n11, 91n16, 92n48, 92n50
grave, 194n5, 274, 284–285, 288, 290, 312, 367n28, beating of the, 285–286
Green, Arthur, 65n2, 91n23, 195n20, 293n6, 299n63, 320n6, 320n13, 322n44, 324n71
Gries, Zeev, 344n53

hagiographic literature, 14, 298n45, 327–330, 339, 343n47
ḥalitzah (ritual of the sandal), 32, 51, 52, 69n22
halakha (Jewish Law) 2–3, 6–8, 12, 20, 39, 79, 111, 120n42, 179, 194n5, 200n75, 293n9, 307, 321n19, 336-339, 348-371
Hallamish, Moshe, 119n32, 145n22, 148n65, 168n3, 171n15, 171n18, 172–177, 195n22
Ham (biblical person), 86
Hamadan, Joseph R., 95n109, 116n4, 137, 146n28, 148n65, 160, 167, 169n5, 171n20, 173n46, 250, 267n6, 357, 359, 361, 367n37, 368n39
Hamnuna Sabba, 87, 94n97
Hasidism, 2, 14, 23n31, 47n52, 47n54, 70n38, 119n34, 143n4, 195n21, 251, 258, 263–264, 266–267, 269n26-27, 276, 294n19, 303, 304, 307–309, 313–317, 320n1, 320n2, 320n6, 320n7, 321n25, 322n39, 323n58, 324n86, 326n117, 329–331, 334, 341n9, 341n13, 342n24, 343n51, 344n53, 348, 357; Bratslav, 20, 347–348, 351–352, 360, 365n4, 365n9, 366n22, 367n28, 370n57; Chabad, 318–319, 326n120; early, 207, 269n26; founder of, 327, 349; Hasidic masters, 2; 7, 15, 153, 249, 251, 258, 269n27, 277, 309, 313, 317, 325n103; history of, 15, Hungarian, 258; reincarnation in, 14; rise of, 340; Satmar, 250–251; shamanic dimension, 19
Haskell, Ellen, 16, 49, 66n12, 67n15, 68n16, 68n17, 70n35, 72n61
he-Hasid, David ben Yehuda, 119n32, 127, 128, 144n12, 145n22, 148n62, 148n64, 169n3, 170n9, 170n15
Hecker, Joel, 50, 66n5, 66n7, 72n64, 173n49, 173n50
heaven, 28, 53, 69n29, 87, 108, 112, 118n24, 133, 140, 152, 186, 203, 218–219, 291, 296, 337; and earth, 99, 114; heavenly accusers, 216; heavenly chariot, 32, 157; heavenly constellation, 98; heavenly court, 284–285, 287; heavenly creatures, 62; heavenly governors, 135, heavenly learning, 209; heavenly realm, 208, 279, 284, 329; heavenly Torah, 208; heavenly world, 31, 163, 181, 312
hell (Gehenna), 28, 53, 127, 156, 164, 166, 167, 169n7, 223, 237, 263, 283, 290, 291, 351,
Hellner-Eshed, Melila, 91n17, 92n41, 94n97, 117n11, 148n62, 221n18,
hermeneutics, 65n2, 68n17, 91n18, 92n50, 118n18, 168n3, 175n64, 194n10, 195n20, 208, 244n8, 267n6, 367n27
Ḥesed (sefirah), 33, 77, 105, 110–111, 127, 129
hysterics, 238; hysteria, 247n61

Hillel Baal Shem, 18, 19, 273, 276, 277–280, 283, 295n22; *Sefer ha-Ḥesekh*, 19, 276, 295n22, 295n24, 295n29, 296n30, 296n32-35, 297n37
Hinduism, 2, 15, 88, 304, 315
Hod (sefirah), 34
Ḥokhmah (sefirah), 31, 35, 38, 86, 103, 105, 222n27
Holy Letter (Iggeret ha-kodesh), 51, 160, 173n43, 321n17
Horowitz, Avraham, 334, 343n37
Horowitz, Isaiah Ha-Levi (Shelah), 221n14, 222n27, 335, 343n44, 365n9, 369n40
Horowitz, Jacob Isaac (Seer of Lublin), 258
Horowitz, Pinchas, 320n3
Horowitz, Reuven, 321
Huss, Boaz, 22n19, 47n52, 65n2, 94n98-99, 325n93

ibbur, see impregnation
Ibn Gabbai, Meir, 40, 148n65, 368n38
Idel, Moshe, 5–6, 15, 21n8-9, 22n14, 23n29, 23n30, 41n1-4, 42n9, 45n37, 46n51--52, 50, 53, 66n7, 68n19-20, 70n34, 90n11, 269n27, 294n19, 314, 320n2, 323n58, 324n85-86, 342n24, 342n33, 369n41-42
identity/ self, 4, 18, 23n31, 28, 54, 64, 66n3-7, 78, 82, 84, 90n10, 105, 116, 172n21, 177–178, 184–185, 190, 199n65, 203, 205–206, 208–209, 211–213, 216, 218, 220n6, 222n23, 225–226, 238, 242, 249–250, 286, 288–289, 292n5, 306, 309, 316, 324n90
idolatry, 129, 180, 254–255
imperfection, human, 181, 192, 240
impregnation, *ibbur*, 5–6, 27, 29, 44n24, 97–99, 104, 106–110, 114–115, 116n3-4, 119n34, 120n45, 122n71, 144n11, 152, 171n21, 173n37, 223n38, 231–241, 245n29, 274, 276, 283, 292, 310, 369n42; bad, 232, 235–236; calendrical, 111–112, 114, 121n54-56; good, 232, 236; secret of, 31, 33, 39, 97, 102, 103, 107, 156;
incarnation, 1, 84, 183, 240, 257, 290, 309, 310; demonic line of, 86; divine, 205; final, 79; negative, 81; new, 263, 265; of Abraham, 86; of the *Shekhinah*, 82, 83; of the soul, 340; one, 262; physical, 81, 190; previous, 333, 335; *ẓaddik*'s, 78
incest, incestuous, 101
indigenous traditions, 53
intentions (*kavvanah/kavvanot*), 70n38, 170n13, 269n27, 275, 332
Iṣḥaq Ayziq Yehuda Yeḥiel Safrin of Komarno, 323n55, 328, 341n13
Israel ben Eliezer (see under Baal Shem Tov)
Isserles, Moses, 334, 343n42

Jensen, Jeppe Sinding, 289, 298n59
Jewish history, 3, 125–126, 130–132, 134–135, 138, 140–142, 143n1, 276, 328, 340
Jeroboam ben Nabat (biblical person), 328, 341n12
judgment, 77, 100, 127, 129, 135–136, 139, 155, 157, 162, 165, 213, 287; divine, 10, 129, 152, 159, 166; final, 9; ethical, 102; harsh, 127, 128, 284; of transmigration, 161, 213; Prince of, 111; sefirah of, 163 (see also under *Gevurah*); sweeten, 358
justice, 2, 3, 126–127, 134–135, 154, 182, 280, 368n38; attribute of, 44; divine, 14, 17, 22n22, 140, 152, 164, 177, 182–183, 190, 343n47; social, 20, 332, 334; true, 151, 161
Kara-Ivanov Kaniel, Ruth, 116n2, 120n43-44, 220n9
Karaite, 163–164, 180, 195n15, 313,
Karma, 20, 23n32, 66n9, 74n33, 76, 81, 88, 90n14, 94n106, 223n35, 304, 317, 320n8, 320n10, 325n106
Karo, Joseph 35, 45n34, 146n35, 275, 293n9, 296n36, 351

Katz, Ya'aqov Yosef of Polnoy, 330–331, 334–338, 342n30, 343–344
Kauffman, Tsippi, 320n6, 322n45, 344n53
Keter (Crown) sefirah, *Elyon* (supernal), 157–158
Keter Shem Tov, 99, 118n29
kelipot/ qelipot (husks), 12, 37, 204, 251–256, 259–261, 265
Koren, Sharon, 121n67, 148n61
kosher, 14, 347–348, 351, 353, slaughter, 355–363, 369
Kreisel, Howard, 117n11, 122n68, 199n63

Lachter, Hartley, 67n12, 68n16
Leiner, Yeruham Meir 267n2, 269n28, 313-315, 324n83
Leon, Moses de, 65n2, 68n16, 113, 122n68, 126, 145n18, 148n61, 149n73, 344n55
leprosy, 257
Levi Yitshak of Barditchev, 305–306, 309
levirate marriage (*yibbum*), 6–8, 31–32, 38, 40, 43n16, 51–53, 55, 57, 59–60, 62, 64, 69n21, 69n24, 69n32, 70n33, 71n56, 84, 108, 116n5, 200n75, 211
Liebes, Yehudah, 46n41, 65n2, 68n16; 72n67, 90n11, 91n17, 92n41, 93n62, 94n97, 115n1, 117n11, 118n17, 120n40, 120n46, 120n49-50, 121n66, 168n3, 170n13-14, 221n13
Likkutei Halakhot, 371n63
Likkutei Moharan, 270n34, 321n22, 324n73, 371n62
lineage, Jewish, 50, 53, 57, 63, 85–87; family, 58; of the Messiah, 116n5; soul, 86
Livnat ha-Sapir, 116n2, 121n54, 122n70
Lurianic Kabbalah, 11, 13, 21n6, 39, 45n34, 46n45, 70n38, 85, 94n97, 116n6, 121n66, 153, 170n13, 198n47, 201, 221n18, 222n18, 245n29, 249, 250, 258, 267n2, 283; 293n14, 293n49, 299n63, 313, 330, 335, 341n5, 342n32, 357; and Hasidism, 266; history of, 282; impact of, 278; Zohar and, 314
Luzzatto, Moses Hayyim, 275, 293n14

Ma'arekhet ha-Elohut, 36–38, 40, 45n35-n38, 46n39-50, 119n34, 128, 144n12-n13, 147n49, 147n55
Maciejko, Pawel, 295n26, 268n10
madness, 291
magic magical, 277–279, 281, 283, 291, 294n21, 295n29, 297n43; 298n57; 344n55; operation, 297n37
Magid, Shaul, 23n28, 198n47, 221, 222n23, 245n29, 246n51, 267n5, 268n8, 268n15, 270n43, 297n43-44, 324n74, 366n17, 371n62
maidservant, 81–83
Maimonides, Moses, 4, 28, 68n20, 121n60, 153, 173n51, 178, 180, 183–189, 191
Malkhut (sefirah, Kingship, see also *Shekhinah*), 32–35, 37, 43n16, 45n38, 76, 78, 88, 102– 103, 106, 108, 110–115, 128, 148n58, 156
Margaliot, Reuven Moshe, 66n9, 69n27, 72n59, 89n1, 92n47
Margolin, Ron, 23n31, 294n20, 343n51, 351, 366n23
Mark, Zvi, 366n22, 367n27-28, 371n62
Matt, Daniel C., 68n16, 69n27, 71, 72n59, 144n12
matter, concealed, 139; physical, 5, 132, 139, 152, 154, 159–162, 173n42, 174n59; spiritual, 154, 160–161
Meir, Jonathan, 297n40-41, 341n13, 352, 365n4, 367n28
Menahem Mendel Schneerson of Lubavitch, 315-319, 325-326
Menahem Nahum of Chernobil, 221n15, 307, 312, 322n33, 324n71
menstruation 257, 148n61, 254-257, 266
Meroz, Ronit, 65n2, 70n38, 89, 90n10-11, 91n16, 94n97-99, 95n107, 115n1,

116n6, 117n11, 118n17, 170n13, 341n5, 341n14, 368n40, 369n48
Messiah, 12, 72n58, 75, 90n13, 102–104, 116n5, 118n30, 121n59, 130, 132, 134, 169n5, 173n42, 220n9, 242, 245n13, 245n38, 268n10, 289, 316; false, 330; feminine, 244n13; son of David, 102; son of Joseph, 131; righteous, 319
messianic idea, 116n7, 330, 342n25-26
messianic redemption, 16, 125, 128, 133, 135
Messianism, 168n3, 171n21, 270n44, 326n119, 330, 342n26
Metatron, 12, 77–78, 82, 86, 91n17, 91n18, 93n76, 94n97, 268n8
metempsychosis, 1–4, 6, 8–12, 15, 18, 21n8, 22n21, 23n16, 28, 41n1, 117n13, 119n34, 120n40, 148n63, 149n78, 152, 154–155, 159–160, 162–163, 165, 167, 168n2, 169n3, 171n20, 174n56, 175n67, 188, 195n15, 223n38, 227–228, 245n28, ; doctrine of, 109, 180, 195n17; in Islam, 170n10; secret of, 172n23
Moon, 36, 38, 46n41, 98–99, 109, 111–112, 159; defect of, 120n50; diminution, 37, 99, 119n32, 168n3; *ibbur* of, 36– 37, 110, new, 36, 40, 112, 114, sefirah *Malkuth*/ Shekhinah and, 45n37, 106
Mopsik, Charles, 45n34
Moses, (biblical person), 11–12, 78, 86–87, 94n98, 100, 103, 113–114, 127, 185, 187, 250, 251, 253, 260, 261, 264, 269n31, 270n40, 271n46, 324n86,368n3; soul of, 13
Moses Shoham of Dolina, 20, 332-333, 340, 342n32, 343n34
Moses Efrayim Hayyim of Sudlikuv, *Degel Mahane Efrayim* 308, 322n42, 323n58

Nachman of Kossov, 328
Nahman of Bratslav, 14, 270n34, 312–313, 324n73-77, 347, 351, 363, 367n28, 371n63
Nahmanides, 15–16, 29, 30–31, 35–40, 42n9-10, 43n13, 44n31, 45n33, 45n37, 46n42, 46n47, 52, 99–100, 105–106, 118n29, 120n52, 121n52, 126, 130, 143n4, 144n6, 144-13, 146n32, 146n34, 147n55, 148n61, 149n73, 197n44, 275, 344n55
nefesh (spirit), 27, 42, 54, 65n1, 76, 80, 83, 119, 155–159, 165, 172n35, 213, 222n24, 227, 231,234, 236, 240–241, 247n77, of David, 233; of Jonathan, 233; wicked, 236
neshamah (higher soul), 54, 65n1, 76–85, 87, 156–159, 165, 172n35, 212–213, 227, 232, 234, 241
Nigal, Gedalyah, 70n38, 295n27, 297n39, 297n41, 341n8, 341n15, 343n47-48,

oath(s) (*hashbaot*), 236, 239, 281
Ogren, Brian, 1, 22n19-20, 22n23, 23n25, 143n4, 145n19, 169n3, 170n11, 199n60, 200n74, 292n5
Oron, Michal, 21n9, 41n3, 42n7, 45n38, 65n1, 66n10, 69n21, 92n50, 118n17, 144n8, 146n31, 147, 148n64, 368n39
owl, 165

Paluch, Agata, 91n18, 292n1
Paradise/ Gan Eden, 58, 127, 136, 142, 172n26, 265, 279, 285, 297n44, 311; heavenly, 208; serpent in, 260; soul in, 308; spiritual, 129; 329
Pedaya, Haviva, 29, 41n4, 42n5, 42n7, 42n10, 119n32, 119n39, 121n52, 143n4, 144n6, 144n13, 146n32, 149n73, 168n3, 227, 244n8, 277, 294n19
Petrovsky-Shtern, Yohanan, 295–296
Philo of Alexandria, 179–180, 194n8, 194n9
physiognomy, 62, 67n15, 72n60, 72n61
Piekerz, Mendel, 344n53, 345n59, 351, 365n9, 366n22
plague, 117n11, 129, 286, 358

possession/ possessing (*dybbuk*) by spirit 18-19, 21n6, 83 65-166, 232, 236, 238–239, 242, 246n60, 275-276, 279, 282, 286-287, 291-292, 294n15, 294n21, 291n31, 291n36, 297n39
poverty, 105–106, 110, 115n1, 119n39
procreation, 6, 11, 51–55, 58–59, 63–64, 114, 206, 219, 219,
psychoanalysis, 227, 229, 238, 243–244, 244n8-9, 245n13, 245n27–28, 246n38, 247n61
punishment, 4, 7, 28, 53, 57–58, 63–64, 70n41, 73, 84, 97, 104–105, 111, 114, 122n71, 127, 130, 132–133, 137–138, 164, 167, 177, 182, 234, 237, 257, 284, 287, 309, 327, 351, 358, 364, 366n19, 368n38, 370n49, ; divine, 50, 147n50; of death, 61; of hell, 263, of trapped existence, 282; of wicked souls, 297n42; reincarnation as, 11, 20, 350, 358, 362, 363; reward and, 183–185, 187–188, 192, 334; severe, 288; sin and, 255; suffering and, 274
purification, 112, 119n34, 133, 162, 237, 253, 255–257; of Adam's soul, 12, 138; of evil, 253; of the divine world, 108; of Terah's sin, 257; of the soul, 74–75, 102, 159, 256

Rachel and Leah (the Matriarchs), 11, 16, 99, 111–113, 115, 121n57, 121n66-67
radiance, 181, hypostatic, 181; of the Shekhinah, 184
Rapaport-Albert, Ada, 326n120
Recanati, Menachem, 40, 43, 137, 148n60, 368n38, 368n39, *Commentary on the Torah*, 44n33, 148n60; *Commentary on the Commandments*, 43n18, 148n60
Regev, Shaul, 200n75,
repentance (see *teshuvah*)
reproduction, 16, 50-57, 63-64, 108
resurrection 16, 52, 54–58, 63–64, 70n40-n41, 70n43, 71n49, 71n51, 76, 185, 187, 190, 197n38, 199n65, 240-243, 274, 306, 321n24
retribution 182, 223n30
Rispsman–Elyon, Dana, 367n36
ritual 3, 6-8, 14, 18-19, 31, 49-51, 59, 66n6, 92n51, 115, 164-165, 167, 168n3, 196n29, 258, 269n29, 282, 298n51, 298n57, 303-313, 318, 321n25, 325n105, 327, 352-353, 367n28; of exorcism 277, 290–291; of *halitzah*, 32, 51, 52, 69n22; of healing 275, 289-290, 299n63; of menstruation, 257; of *yiḥudim*, 291; slaughter, 347–349, 351, 353, 355–356
ritual bath (mikveh), 290
Roi, Biti, 89, 90n11, 91n16, 91n26, 93n53,115n1, 118n17
Rosman, Moshe, 294n19, 340n2
ruaḥ (soul), 54, 65, 76, 80, 83–84, 156–158, 212–213; evil, 296
Ruderman, David, 9, 22n21-22, 23n24, 342n19
Ruth (biblical person), 113; and Boaz, 11, soul of, 138

Sa'adia Gaon, 182, 313, 328
Saba de-Mishpatim (zoharic unit), see Zohar
Sabbatean 258, 266, 268n10, 269n26, 279, 330, 349
Sabbatical year (*shemitah)*, 216, 329,
Sack, Brakha, 46n52; 115n1, 143n5, 293n7-8, 321n20
Sachs-Shmueli, Leore, 22n12, 95n109, 116n2, 121n64, 137, 146n28, 148n60-61, 169n5, 171n20, 173n38, 367n37, 369n43-47, 370n49-50
sadistic, 239
sadness, of death, 317
Samael, 11, 110–112; 121n65
Samuel (biblical prophet), 273–274, 365n15
Saraf Pri Eẓ Ḥaym, 332, 342n32
Schnytzer, Jonnie, 119n34, 120n40, 148n63, 173n40, 42, 175n74, 369n41
Scholem, Gershom, xi, 3–5, 21n1, 21n3-5, 28–29, 41n3-9, 43m22, 44–46,

65n1-2, 66n8-10, 69n26, 69n29, 70n39, 70n42, 71n47, 73, 79, 83, 89n2, 90n10, 91n30-31, 93, 98, 101, 116n6-7, 117n11, 118n19-20, 121n65,141, 143n4-5, 144n5, 144n15, 145n20-21, 146n27, 146n44, 148, 149, 158, 167, 168n3, 170n15, 172n34, 173n43, 174n62-63, 227, 244n6-7, 246n30, 309, 320n2, 321n16, 322n46, 323n58, 330–331, 341n14, 342n24, 342n28-29, 344n54
seed, 31, 39, 100, 102, 242; bad, 86; impure, 255–256; mixed, 100, 102; new, 100; of Israel, 139; of an evildoer, 252–253; old, 100, 101, Teraḥ's, 254–255

Sefer ha-Kanah, 126, 136, 138, 144n8, 146n35, 147n49, 147n50, 147n56-57, 148n64, 368n39, 369n40
Sefer ha-Peli'ah, 126, 136, 144n8, 146n35, 147n49-50, 147n56-57, 148n59, 148n64, 368n39, 369n40
Sefer ha-Temunah (*Book of Cosmic Cycles*), 17, 28–29, 40, 126–129, 131–133, 136–137, 140–141, 143n4, 144n12, 144n15, 145n18, 145n23-24, 146–149, 190n9, 275
Sefer Shushan Sodot 44n33, 329
Sefer Yeẓira, 105, 207, 221n13
Sefer Yeẓira, Commentary on (by Joseph Ashkenazi, pseudo Raavad) 104–106, 119n35, 119n37, 102n41, 154–155, 162-164, 168n1-n3, 172n23; commentary by Nahmanides 44n30; Commentary by Isaac the Blind 42n5
Segol, Marla, 66n6-7, 70n35, 89n1
self(hood), 2, 13, 17–20, 88, 122n72, 199n65, 203, 208, 216, 220n1-2, 225, 227–229; divine, 206–208, 213, 239, 289, 292, 304–306, 355, ; censorship, 8; extinction of, 115; human, 203–205; image, 87; improvement, 28; perfection, 3, 188; reflection, 51, 63; transformation of, 10; understanding, 100; unitary, 229, 231–232
Shekalim, Rami, *Torat ha- Nefesh ve-haGilgul be- Reishit ha- Kabbalah*, 144n16, 147n53
Shekhem ben Hamor (biblical person), 256–257
Shelah, see Horowitz, Isaiah
Shem Tov ibn Gaon, 5, 40, 99–100, 102– 106, 112, 117n14, 117n15, 130n29
Shem Tov ibn Shem Tov, 5, 134, 139
sefirot(ic), 77–78, 80, 98–99, 105, 108–109, 113–115 152, 158, 161, 164, 166; emanation, 82, 204; Godhead, 158, 164, 167; hierarchy, 82, 84; lower, 127–128; of nothingness, 119n35; paradigms, 87; schema, 105; structure, 15, 103, 111; system, 107, 155; ten, 6, 15, 37, 101, 104, 134, 162, 205–206; tree, 82–83; upper, 31, 106; world of, 34–35
sermon, 9, 312, 336; Hasidic, 303; Lurianic, 95n109, 170n13, 200n76, 342n21, 368n40
serpent, 84, 86, 261, 270n37; fiery, 129; filth of, 12; in the Garden of Eden, 260; naked, 260
sexual(ity), 22n10, 51, 66n6, 68n20, 70n35, 77, 89n1, 92n50, 101, 147n45, 173n44, 239, 254, 309, 339; desire, 78, 229, 239, 371n62; family and, 15; forbidden, 368n38; forced, illicit, 254–255, 260; immorality, 129; instincts, 239–240; marital, 68n16; meaning, 101; partners, 219, 270n39; union, 218–219; with menstruant, 257, 266
Shabbatai Zvi, 285, 288, 330,
shaman(ic)/ shamanism, 19, 276, 277, 281, 283, 288, 289, 294n19, 297n41, 320n5, 323n55,
shame, 72n64, 113, 287
Shapira, Ṣevi Elimelekh of Dinov 308, 322, 328n68, 337-339

Shekhinah (see also *Malkhut*), 16, 23n31, 31-37, 45n37, 46n40, 76, 78-83, 85, 87-95, 97-115, 117n8, 117n11, 119n39, 121n59, 128, 141, 220n6, 220n8, 245n13, 245n37, 293n14, 308, 330-332, 335
Shela, *Shnei Luhot ha-berit*, see Horowitz
shemittot (cosmic cycles), 17, 126–127, 132, 141–142, 144n5, 149n71, 329
Shivḥei haBesht, 327
Shkalim, Rami, 21n7
Shneur Zalman of Liady, 305, 316-318, 322n32, 322n36, 325n101, 325n109, 349, 371n61
Shulḥan 'Arukh, 351-352
sin, 4, 11, 16, 45n35, 53–54, 61–62, 74, 75, 84–86, 102–104, 111, 114, 127, 129–133, 135, 142, 164, 181-184, 200n76, 211, 214–215, 236–237, 249, 252–255, 259, 264–266, 269n30, 270n31, 274, 287–288, 296n36, 297n42, 307–308, 311, 316, 331–333, 370n59, 370n60; 371n60, 390n48; Adam's, 78, 136, 252, 259–261, 286, 331–335, 337; bodily, 53; Edenic, 210; erasure of, 107; Eve's, 136, 142; fear of, 167; gendered acts of, 256; in Gehinnom, 223n30; human, 9, 50, 283–285, 350–351, 354–355, 358– 363 365n15, 365n17, 366n19, 368n38, 368n40; Nabal's, 341n12; of idolatry, 254; of Joseph's brothers, 30; of Shabbatai Zvi, 289; of the golden calf, 326n114; 327; original, 147n55, 241, 265; physical, 219; primordial, 260, 328,333; punishment for, 28, 105; reincarnation according to, 370n50; repair of, 30; Teraḥ's, 257
Sinai, 264
sinew(s), 261, 306, 308
sitra aḥra (the other side), 11, 112, 286
slavegirl, 81–82
slaughter, ritual, 347–349, 351, 353, 355–356
social, 2, 12, 14, 19, 276; 291, 292, 295, 334, 353, 361, 364, 365n9, 368n40; anxiety, 55; boundaries, 64, 273; classes, 340; cohesion, 275; collapse, 360; consequences, 50; concerns, 50, 250; context, 258; criticism, 286; environment, 289; impact, 2; institutions, 53; interest, 347–348; justice, 327, 332, 334, ; margins, 51; networks, 54; pollution, 50; psychology, 275; responsibility, 20, 339; restrictions, 125; setting, 276; situation, 319; status, 84, 334; stereotypes, 286; structure, 49–50; system, 287; tension, 286
soul, 27; 54, 65, 76, 80, 83, 119, 155–159, 165, 172n35, 186–188, 190–191, 193, 194n2, 194n5, 195n21, 197n38, 199n65, 200n70, 200n76, 203–204, 207–213, 222n24, 227, 236, 240–241; bliss, 186; composite, 187, 198n47; divine, 206; human, 192, 206; of a man, 189; of David, 233; of Jonathan, 234; quarry of, 205; roots, 207, 217
soulmate, 214–216
spark(s), xi, 13, 79–80, 85, 181, 210, 212, 217, 265, 309, 310-311, 332–333, 335, 371n60; dispersed, 251; divine, 330; evil, 243; fallen, 260; holy, 309, 331, 335, 338; lost, 11, 251, 268; sacred, 309, 310; raising up, 366n17; righteous, 242; soul, 13, 18, 30, 107, 195n21, 217, 225–227, 242–243,320n14; 328, 340; wicked, 242
spirit, 5–6, 11, 57–60, 63, 71n51; 71n54; 72n62; 84, 129, 132, 134, 137, 152, 156–162, 165– 166, 172n35, 174n57-59, 180, 211, 213, 217–218, 235–240, 280, 287–291, 293n6, 293n9, 306, 316, 328; body and, 283, 317; breath of, 289; cutting off, 164; demonic, 280; destroying, 284–285; disembodied, 282; evil, 236, 238,

274, 275, 279, 281, 291, 294n21, 296n37, 297n38; holy, 43; Jewish, 237; naked, 59, 71n54; non-Jewish, 2361–237; of Ruben, 180; possession, 286, 291–292, 294n15, 296n31
spiritual(ity), 2, 3, 5, 10, 14–16, 18, 60, 23n31, 27, 55–56, 152, 154, 155–162, 197n38, 205, 219, 231, 235–236, 238, 284, 299n63, 308, 310, 325n91, 325n93, 328; ; advocate, 290; affinity, 234; benefit, 338; burden, 72n63; competition, 241; conduct, 219; contraries, 164; countenance, 62; development, 28, 209; energies, 277; entities, 166, 297n42; excision, 105, 122n70-71; exile, 132; existence, 62; faculties, 28; ideas, 316; identity, 316; impregnation, 97, 103; journey, 235, 307; labor, 317; leadership, 328; letters, 62; life, 307, 371n63; limbs, 308, 336–337; location, 78; operation, 253; opportunities, 304; paradises, 129; peregrinations, 311; perfection, 336; perspective, 335; position, 86; potential, 316; power, 310; propaganda, 360; realm, 138, 290; rebirth, 303; refinement, 131; repair, 63, 337, 350; seekers, 312; sinews, 308; state, 241; status, 61–62; structure, 156; strength, 236; substance, 156, 191; tool, 112; work, 218, 306–307, 312

Tamari, Assaf, 23n32, 220n2, 244n2, 297n43, 341n5, 341n14
Teitelbaum, Joel (Yoel), 249, 258, 263, 265–266, 269n28, 270n31, 270n38, 270n41, 270n44, 271n44, 290n33
Teitelbaum, Yehudah Yekutiel, 261–263
Teitelbaum, Moses, 258–261, 270n35, 321n30
temporal, ix, 1–3, 9, 19, 30, 126–127, 129, 182, 230, 278, 291, 310
teshuva (repentance, sefirah *Binah*) 34, 98, 112, 119n39; *tikkunei*, 339; theurgy/ theurgical 2, 13, 66n4, 66n7, 70n34, 90n12, 114, 172n33, 261, 283, 309, 362
Tiferet (sefirah), 33–34, 36, 44n29, 77, 82, 137; 148n58, 156, as the Sun, 106; *shemittah* of, 136
Tishby, Isaiah, 42n9, 65n1, 330, 342n25-26; *Wisdom of the Zohar* (*Mishnat ha-Zohar*), 42n9, 66n8, 90n15, 117n8, 121n59, 172n26; *Paths of Faiths and Heresy* (*Netivei Emunah uMinut*), 269n26; *The Doctrine of Evil and the Shell in Lurianic Kabbalah*, 298n49, 341n14
tikkun (correction, restoration, repair, rectification) 16, 18, 30, 102, 106, 200n76, 212, *T* 222n18, 223n35, 226–227, 234–237, 250, 275, 283, 285, 293n14, 309, 324n74,
Toldot Ya'aqov Yosef see Ya'aqov Yosef Katz of Polnoy

unifications, 267, 337

Vital, Hayyim, 11–13, 18, 23n33, 23n28, 75, 153, 202–223, 225–249
'Eẓ Ha Da'at Tov, 268n8, 271n48
'Eẓ Ḥayyim, 223n29, 270n40
Peri Eẓ Ḥayyim, 221n14, 331-333, 342n31-n32
Sefer ha-Gilgulim (Book of Reincarnations), 23n33, 244n3, 249, 305, 311, 320n4, 321n15, 323n51, 323n63, 326n111, 329, 337–338, 345n60
Sefer ha-Hezyonot (*Book of Visions*), 11
Sefer Gilgulei Ha-Neshamot, 329
Sha'ar ha-Kavvanot (*Gate of Intentions*), 285, 295n48-n49
Sha'ar ha-Mizvot (*Gate of the Commandments*), 236, 246n52–54, 320n14, 357
Sha'ar ha-Pesukim, 251, 252, 268n14, 268n18, 269, 270n32, 271n48

Sha'arei Kedushah (*Gates of Holiness*), 203–205

water, 56, 80–81, 137, 198n45, 236, 287, 327, exorcism, 236; female, 355–356; reservoirs, 275; waterwheel, 80
Weiss, Dov, 324n81
Weiss, Joseph, 342n33
Weiss, Tzahi, 43n23, 46n40, 92n50, 145n18
Weisser, Esther, 236–240
Werblowsky, Zvi, 41n4, 146n35, 195n17, 296n36
Wolfson, Elliot R., 21n4, 46n52, 65n2, 68n16, 69n26, 70n35, 91n18, 92n50, 117n11, 118n18, 146n45, 168n3, 175n64, 195n20, 197n44, 222n22, 227, 244n8, 250, 267n6-7, 293n8, 293n14, 326n119, 344n55
woman, 32, 34–35, 44, 59, 69n22, 110, 113, 120n42, 136, 156, 211, 215–216, 236, 279, 281, 283, 326n120; evil, 117n11; 35; married, 290; non-Jewish, 13, 280; pregnant, 36, 44, 44n24, 109; widowed, 211, womb of, 7

Yassif, Eli, 53, 69n30-31, 299n68
Yesod (sefirah, Foundation), 34, 44n29, 77-78, 87, 101
Yesh Noḥalin by Avraham Horowitz 334, 343n37
yeshiva, 315, 317
yiḥudim (ritual unification), 275, 288–291
Yisraeli, Oded, 21n10, 71n46, 88, 90n13, 94n105, 122n68, 147n55

ẓadik, *ẓaddikim*, as a saint in Hasidism, 12-14, 20, 46n52, 47n54, 91n63, 195n21, 251, 259, 304, 310–312, 323n58, 326n120, 328–329, 340, 343n48, 349–355, 364n3, 365n17, 367n28; in kabbalah, 78, 87; *ẓaddik* ben rasha (a righteous son of a wicked) 251–253, 259, 269n30, 270n32-n33; perfect (*tam*), 285; *ve-ra lo* (the suffering of the righteous), 84
Zinger, Nimrod, 294n17-18
Zohar (*Sefer ha-Zohar*), 15–16, 49, 50–56, 59–64, 65n1, 69n27, 73–74, 76–77, 80–83, 87– 89, 89n2, 92n50, 99, 102, 104, 111, 113, 121n66, 122n68, 126, 159, 181, 212, 214, 221n14, 221n18, 250, 254–255, 257, 268n8, 268n17, 270n34, 286, 297, 321n24, 322n41, 325n104, 329, 337, 344n55, 369n42; as a book, 75; books of, 314; canonical 15; death in, 317; editions of, 2; interpretation of evil in, 298n49; language of, 107; literature, 74–75, 107–108, 117n8, 121n59, 158, 167, 169, 172n26, 249, 275; on levirate marriage, 70n33, 116n5; nature of, 89n9; physiognomy in, 62; sections of, 6, 76, 81, 83, 191; Shekhinah in, 119n39; study of, 290; teachings on reincarnation in, 52, 63, 70n35; women in, 71n56; *Yanuka* narrative in, 71n58
Guf ha-Zohar, 16, 49-50, 71n60
Saba de-Mishpatim, 6, 21n10, 55, 57, 60, 69n21,69n32, 70n36, 71n46, 76n52, 76, 81–82, 88, 90n13, 92n50, 116n14, 148n65, 159, 169n5, 173n37, 214, 321n28
Tikkunei ha-Zohar, 16, 43n44, 50, 73–95, 100, 116n4, 118n17, 321n24, 331–335, 339
Tikkunei Zohar Hadash, 91n21
Zohar Ḥadash, 82, 90n12, 91n18, 145n18; Metatron in, 91n18
Zohar ha- Raki'a, 95n109
Zoharic, author, 173n37; canon, 77; commandments, 22n12; corpus, 250; gender, 45n33; idea, 250; reading of Exodus, 215; sexuality 21n10; themes, 88; textual tradition, 14, 285

www.ingramcontent.com/pod-product-compliance
Lightning Source LLC
Chambersburg PA
CBHW031210100825
30784CB00038B/1
9798855800050